Handbook of Research on Advances in Health Informatics and Electronic Healthcare Applications:
Global Adoption and Impact of Information Communication Technologies

Khalil Khoumbati
University of Sindh, Pakistan

Yogesh K. Dwivedi
Swansea University, UK

Aradhana Srivastava
Participatory Research in Asia (PRIA), India

Banita Lal
Nottingham Trent University, UK

Medical Information Science REFERENCE

MEDICAL INFORMATION SCIENCE REFERENCE

Hershey · New York

Director of Editorial Content: Kristin Klinger
Senior Managing Editor: Jamie Snavely
Assistant Managing Editor: Michael Brehm
Publishing Assistant: Sean Woznicki
Typesetter: Michael Brehm
Cover Design: Lisa Tosheff
Printed at: Yurchak Printing Inc.

Published in the United States of America by
Medical Information Science Reference (an imprint of IGI Global)
701 E. Chocolate Avenue
Hershey PA 17033
Tel: 717-533-8845
Fax: 717-533-8661
E-mail: cust@igi-global.com
Web site: http://www.igi-global.com/reference

Library of Congress Cataloging-in-Publication Data

Handbook of research on advances in health informatics and electronic healthcare applications : global adoption and impact of information communication technologies / Khalil Khoumbati ... [et al.], editors.
p. ; cm.
Includes bibliographical references and index.
Summary: "This book presents a comprehensive resource elucidating the adoption and usage of health informatics"--Provided by publisher.
ISBN 978-1-60566-030-1 (h/c)
1. Medical informatics--Handbooks, manuals, etc. I. Khoumbati, Khalil, 1965-
[DNLM: 1. Medical Informatics--trends. W 26.5 H2353 2010]
R858.H322 2010
651.5'04261--dc22
2009001900

British Cataloguing in Publication Data
A Cataloguing in Publication record for this book is available from the British Library.

All work contributed to this book is new, previously-unpublished material. The views expressed in this book are those of the authors, but not necessarily of the publisher.

Dedicated

To Mehboob, Abdullaha, Raheela, Rawal, Rameela, Rahmeen and Rabia

—**Khalil Khoumbati**

To Kamlesh Bhaya, Sarita Bhabhi, Atul and Vipul

—**Yogesh K. Dwivedi**

To my parents, for being there for me always

—**Aradhana Srivastava**

To Meena, Angela, Ravi, Bobby

—**Banita Lal**

Editorial Advisory Board

List of Reviewers

Dim Pet, *University of Athens, Greece*
Raj Gururajan, *University of Southern Queensland–Toowoomba, Australia*
Inger Dybdahl Sorby, *Norwegian University of Science and Technology, Norway*
Navonil Mustafee, *University of Warwick, UK*
James G. Anderson, *Purdue University, USA*
Sevgi Ozkan, *Brunel University UK*
Vasiliki Mantzana, *University of Athens, Greece*
Herbert Daly, *Brunel University UK*
Tillal Eldabi, *Brunel University UK*
Schmitz Dominik, *Fraunhofer FIT, Schloss Birlinghoven, Augustin, Germany*
Geoffrey Jalleh, *Curtin University of Technology, Perth, Western Australia*
Bernd Carsten Stahl, *Computing Sciences and Engineering, Ireland*
Dominik Schmitz, *Fraunhofer FIT, Schloss Birlinghoven, Augustin, Germany*
Joseph Weill *Medical College of Cornell University, USA*
Maryati Mohd, *University Kebangsaan Malaysia*
Dr Yu-An Huang, *National Chengchi University, Taiwan*
Hamid Alalwany, *Brunel University UK*
Nesaar Banderker, *Information Systems Consultant, PBT Group, South Africa*
Imran Tasadduq, *National University of Emerging Sciences , Pakistan*
Shahid Hussain Larik, *University of Sindh, Pakistan*
Syed Misbahuddin, *UoH, Saudi Arabia*
Luisa Piris , *Brunel University UK*
Sigurd Eskeland, *University of Agder, Norway*
Geoffrey Jalleh, *Curtin University of Technology, Perth, Western Australia*
David Sier, *Mathematical and Information Sciences, Clayton MDC, Clayton, Australia*
Kethers, Stefanie, *CSIRO ICT Centre, Australia*
Simon J.E. Taylor, *Brunel University UK*
Lampros K. Stergioulas, *Brunel University UK*
Nisar A Memon, *Sindh University, Pakistan*
Khalil Khoumbati, *University of Sindh, Pakistan*
Yogesh K. Dwivedi, *Swansea University, Swansea, UK*
Banita Lal, *Swansea University, UK*
Asadullaha Shah, *ISRA University, Hyderabad Pakistan*
Ghullam Sarwar Shah, *Brunel University UK*
Shazad Ahmed Memon, *Brunel University UK*

List of Contributors

Ammenwerth, Elske / *University for Health Sciences, Medical Informatics & Technology, Austria* 477
Anderson, James G. / *Purdue University, USA* 144, 385
Archer, Norm / *McMaster University, Canada* 446
Balas, Andrew / *Old Dominion University, USA* 385
Bandara, Wasana / *Queensland University of Technology, Australia* 289
Banderker, Nesaar / *University of Cape Town, South Africa* 368
Baykal, Nazife / *Informatics Institute Metu, Turkey* 74
Brailsford, Sally / *University of Southampton, UK* 255
Bürkle, Thomas / *University of Erlangen, Germany* 477
Chahal, Kirandeep / *Brunel University, UK* 190
Dahl, Yngve / *Telenor Research & Innovation, Norway* 52
Daly, Herbert / *Brunel University, UK* 190
Dorj, Phurb / *Jigme Dorji Wangchuck National Referral Hospital, Bhutan* 410
Eldabi, Tillal / *Brunel University, UK* 190
Eskeland, Sigurd / *University of Agder, Norway* 274
Faxvaag, Arild / *Norwegian University of Science and Technology, Norway* 52
Gans, Günter / *RWTH Aachen University, Germany* 205
Gräber, Stefan / *University Hospital of Saarland, Germany* 477
Gullà, Vincenzo / *Advanced Digital Technologies (ADITECH SRL), Italy* 91
Gururajan, Raj / *University of Southern Queensland, Australia* 109
Hamid, Alalwany / *Brunel University, UK* 1
Harrison, Michael I. / *Agency for Healthcare Research and Quality, USA* 33
Hasan, Sharique / *Carnegie Mellon University, USA* 234
Huang, Yu-An / *National Chi Nan University, Taiwan* 221
Iller, Carola / *University of Heidelberg, Germany* 477
Johnson, Michael P. / *The University of Massachusetts Boston, USA* 234
Josefsson, Ulrika / *University of Gothenburg, Sweden* 353
Katsaliaki, Korina / *Middlesex University, UK* 255
Kethers, Stefanie / *Monash University, Australia* 205
Klepack, William / *Dryden Family Medicine, USA* 423
Koppel, Ross / *University of Pennsylvania, USA* 33
Kyhlbäck, Hans / *Blekinge Institute of Technology, Sweden* 319

Table of Contents

Section 3
Health Informatics and E-Health Applications

Section 4
Health Informatics and E-Health Impact

Section 5
Further Reading

Detailed Table of Contents

clinicians in their patient-centered activities. The chapter summarizes four sub studies performed during the project. Each study presents different approaches to user-centered design of PoCCS. Findings from these studies confirm the need for mobile information and communication technology (ICT) in hospitals. Furthermore, the studies demonstrate how more user involvement and complementary approaches to traditional requirements engineering (RE) and system development methods can be useful when developing mobile information and communication systems for clinicians.

This chapter supports the idea that the effectiveness of IT systems is not an exact measure and a more systematic approach needs to be taken when evaluating success of an IT system. In this study, authors have evaluated an assessment method, process based information systems effectiveness (PRISE), which is based on a novel model of information systems effectiveness in the healthcare domain. The results of the case series provide specific implications concerning the applicability of a general "information systems assessment" approach, in the medical context.

The aim of this chapter is to focus on some of the most significant results, carried out by researchers and healthcare organisations in Italy and Europe, and attempt to draw a suitable model, which taking advantage of the wide broadband deployment and cost effective approach, can be of help to identify solutions addressing sustainable telemedicine service networks. The study gives the reader some highlights on the enormous growth and development that have characterized the telecommunication industry in this last decade (1990-2000), which has seen the domination of Internet, the IP protocols, along with the new and much more economic broad band approach, allowing end users to access advanced network services in a much easier, faster, and economic way, than some years ago these events open new frontiers of interactive applications, related to data transmission, video, and IP voice, originating new services, which one can find useful and comfortable for itself, but in a more general contest are essential tools to improve social benefits and communities quality of life

Section 2
Health Informatics and E-Health Tools and Technologies

Section 2 includes five chapters dedicated to understanding the tools and technologies for health informatics and e-health. The first chapter (Chapter 7) presents an Indian case study to illustrate drivers of wireless technology in healthcare. This is followed by Chapter 8, which discusses health grids in health informatics. The third chapter (Chapter 9) within this section attempts to examine use of information technology for improving patient safety. Then, the fourth chapter (Chapter 10) presents a multimethod modelling approach in healthcare. Finally, Chapter 11 presents an emergency medical data transmission systems and technologies.

Traditional technology adoption models identified 'ease of use' and 'usefulness' as the dominating factors for technology adoption. However, recent studies in healthcare have established that these two factors are not always reliable on their own and other factors may influence technology adoption. To establish the identity of these factors, a mixed method approach was used and data were collected through interviews and a survey. The survey instrument was specifically developed for this study so that it is relevant to the Indian healthcare setting. Authors identified clinical management and technological barriers as the dominant factors influencing the wireless handheld technology adoption in the Indian healthcare environment. The results of this study showed that new technology models will benefit by considering the clinical influences of wireless handheld technology, in addition to known factors. The scope of this study is restricted to wireless handheld devices such as PDAs, smart telephones, and handheld PCs.

Healthcare is a vast domain encapsulating not only multiple sub-domains or sub-sectors but also many diverse operations and logistics within each sub-sector. This diversity needs to be handled in a systematic and well-characterized manner in order to maintain consistency of various healthcare tasks. Integration of health information systems within each healthcare sub-sectors is crucial for ubiquitous access and sharing of information. The emerging technology of HealthGrids holds the promise to successfully integrate health information systems and various healthcare entities onto a common, globally shared and easily accessible platform. Many different types of HealthGrids exist but there lacks a taxonomy to classify them into a hierarchical order. This chapter presents a well-characterized taxonomy of different types of HealthGrid and classifies them into four major types, namely BioGrid, MediGrid, PharmaGrid and CareGrid. Each of these HealthGrids possesses dedicated features and functionalities. The proposed taxonomy serves to better understand the realtionship among various HealthGrid types and would lay a basis for future research.

quality of service parameters available in UMTS. This could help the physicians in monitoring several patients who are either in transit or at a triage unit on a disaster site. Results of the application of data reduction algorithm over CAN packets and feasibility studies in transfer of data over UMTS are presented and discussed.

Section 3
Health Informatics and E-Health Applications

Section 3 includes six chapters dedicated to understanding health informatics and e-health applications. The first chapter presents a multi-method approach for modelling organizational issues in health care. The second chapter attempted to the trust relationships in a healthcare network. Chapter 14 examines resource alignment of ICT in Taiwanese small dialysis centers. Chapter 15 presents guideline representation ontologies for evidence-based medicine practice. The fifth chapter investigates the distributed simulation of a healthcare supply chain. Finally, Chapter 17 discusses security and privacy aspects for medical application scenario.

Healthcare organisations increasingly use simulation and modelling techniques to analyse their procedures and policies. Modelling activities attempt to help meet the challenges, constraints and requirements for efficiency encountered in the modern healthcare environment. A variety of techniques are used, often applied in different roles and by different functions in the organization. Even as these approaches are becoming established in healthcare, modelling methodology continues to develop. Recent research has investigated the benefits of considering multiple approaches in the analysis of problems. This chapter reports on the use of simulation and modelling in healthcare and examines the factors driving the increasingly widespread use of these techniques. The developing practice of multi method modelling and some of the benefits it may provide are discussed in detail. Focusing specifically on healthcare, examples of how these ideas may be used in healthcare modelling are presented. Finally the challenges to implementing this new approach effectively in a healthcare environment are discussed.

David Sier, CSIRO Mathematical and Information Sciences, Australia Public hospitals currently face an ever increasing demand on their resources, and there are many attempts at streamlining processes and patient flows. However, in many cases, optimizing processes is not enough, as 'soft' factors such as the relationships between hospital wards influence how efficiently the resources needed to treat patients are utilized. These factors are often ignored when attempting to improve patient flows. This chapter describes a case study investigating the relationships between an acute stroke ward and a specialist stroke rehabilitation ward of a large metropolitan health service. The motivation for this study was the hospital management's interest in improving communication and collaboration across wards as a means to optimize hospital processes, and thus, patient care. To assess the relationships between the two wards, authors examined the patient handover process that links the wards' activities and applied the Trust-Confidence-Distrust (TCD) framework, which was developed to model trust relationships in social networks, to examine the trust relationships between the wards.

The literature on cooperative alliances has been criticized for its relatively narrow concentration on large firms and for ignoring small and medium-sized enterprises (SME) alliances where large firms do not operate in similar ways. Due to their size SMEs are more likely to seek external expertise. For small dialysis centers, they often form alliances to obtain these scarce resources. Unlike large firms which own a lot of slack resources to be able to form alliances with many partners, these small dialysis centers tend to form alliances with only a small number of partners and therefore, their dependence on these partners is higher than large firms. Hence, authors conducted case study to investigate the use of complementary and supplementary information communication technology (ICT) resources among several small healthcare centers in Taiwan and evaluated how different types of resource alignment affect the performances of alliances. One contribution of the chapter is that the contribution of dissimilar ICT resources by both the focal and partner firms has a significant positive impact on alliance sustainable commitment. The results also reveal that there is a positive relationship between the contribution of dissimilar ICT resources by the partner firms and alliance performance. However, the contribution of dissimilar ICT resources alone by the focal dialysis centers has no significant impact on alliance performance.

The first part of this chapter presents the evolution of ontology research in guideline representation. Several representative ontologies are reviewed and discussed, with in-depth analyses of two popular models: GLIF (Guideline Interchange Format) and PROforma. The second part of the chapter analyzes seven key elements constituting a guideline representation. It also discusses the criteria for evaluating competing ontologies and some known limitations in the existing models. At the end of this chapter, four key steps are outlined that converts a guideline into computerized representation, which can be then used in Clinical Decision Support Systems (CDSSs).

Discrete-Event Simulation (DES) is a decision support technique that allows stakeholders to conduct experiments with models that represent real-world systems of interest. Its use in healthcare is comparatively new. Healthcare needs have grown and healthcare organisations become larger, more complex and more costly. There has never been a greater need for carefully informed decisions and policy. DES is valuable as it can provide evidence of how to cope with these complex health problems. However, the size of a healthcare system can lead to large models that can take an extremely long time to simulate. This chapter investigates how a technique called *distributed simulation* allows using multiple computers to speed up this simulation. Based on a case study of the UK National Blood Service we demonstrate the effectiveness of this technique and argue that it is a vital technique in healthcare informatics with respect to supporting decision making in large healthcare systems.

This chapter discusses security and privacy aspects for medical application scenario. Chapter analyze what kind security and privacy enforcements would be needed and how it can be achieved by technological means. Authors reviewed cryptographic mechanisms and solutions that can be useful in this context.

Section 4
Health Informatics and E-Health Impact

Section 4 includes five chapters dedicated to understanding the adoption, use and impact of health informatics and e-health. The first chapter (Chapter 18) presents a process architecture approach to manage health process reforms. This is followed by Chapter 19 discusses how to replace an old functioning information system with a new one. The third chapter (Chapter 20) presents a quality assurance approach to healthcare. Then fourth chapter (Chapter 21) explores the multifaceted E-patient context, in an effort to contribute to an increased patient-centeredness of this form of technology development. Finally, Chapter 22 reports on an investigation into the factors influencing the adoption of mobile devices by doctors in the public healthcare sector in the Western Cape, South Africa.

Process modeling is an embedded component of most BPM initiatives, yet a resource intensive task. How process models can be derived efficiently (i.e. with less resources and time) and effectively (at a high quality to meet the specific needs) is an integral element of interest to most organisations, however, this area of research is still in its infancy. This paper aims to address this gap by proposing a 'process-pattern' based approach to process modeling where models are created within a 'process architecture'. The overall study design consists of an action research approach, depicting how the proposed 'process patterns within a process architecture' concept has been derived and evaluated within an Australian based public health institution. The contributions from this work are twofold. From the perspective of practice, it offers a validated high level example of a process pattern for an Integrated Risk Management Program for health. From an academic perspective: it presents a validated Risk Management process pattern for delivering health services which can be used as best practice or a benchmark in further research. The action research method applied within can also be re-applied to design and validate further process patterns within different contexts.

This chapter addresses a problem that is often experienced when ICT systems are being implemented in a work practice. Posed as a question, it might be formulated like this: What does it take to replace an old functioning information system with a new one? Findings are grounded on a long-term case study at a community elder care. Chapter used the Development Work Research (DWR) approach that is an interventionist methodology comprising ethnography as well as design experiment. During the case study, a new digital case book for the community wound care was developed. However, as it turned out, the nurses´ established practice favored the old-fashioned mobile information system. First conclusion of this chapter is that an old-fashioned information system within health care work will not successfully be replaced by a new one, unless the new is better "as a whole", that is, better supports work practices of a range of occupational and professional workers. Second conclusion is that when designing information system for the public sector, system designers will almost always face dilemmas based on a contradiction between central, high level interest and local level work-practice perspectives. The third conclusion is that in order to succeed in the design of new information and communication system, the distinctive features of the work activities in question have to be delineated by ethnographic studies, and taken into consideration in the design process.

W Edwards Deming argues that quality is not an entity but derives from using feedback, iteratively to seek improvement to processes, in order to increase productivity and to make better use of resources. This chapter proposes that supporting this form of quality assurance (QA) using information systems (IS) has the potential to deliver a return on investment. An object-oriented analysis, where healthcare is viewed as the delivery of interdependent processes to which Deming's form of QA is applied, results in a class model of data types that has some useful characteristics. It is able to store data about medical and non-medical events; to save descriptions of procedures and to represent the QA process itself. With software based on the model, organisations will have a memory of previous attempts at making improvements as well as data about feedback from patients and staff to drive future change.

The area of E-health development for patient-healthcare interaction has lately received significant attention by the health informatics community. Increasingly healthcare and information technology (IT) developers are proposed to take seriously the needs and preferences of the patients. This chapter explores the multifaceted E-patient context, in an effort to contribute to an increased patient-centeredness of this form of technology development. Patient-centeredness is captured in terms of personalization as an attempt to depart from patients' specific context to contribute to technology design and use. Using a qualitative approach, the chapter reports from 25 in-depth interviews performed with Swedish patients and representatives of patient associations. Six themes of the E-patient context derive from the findings (diagnosis, demographics, access, preferences, coping, and patient role). The results present a fine-grained picture of the E-patient context adding to previous approaches of personalization. The introductory discussion reflects on the themes in relation to their tentative implications for the development of patient-centered personalized E-health for patient-healthcare interaction.

Doctors working in the South African public healthcare sector are faced with the unique resource constraints prevalent in a developing country. Mobile information and communication technologies (ICTs) hold the promise of improving the quality of healthcare, but this potential can only be unlocked if individuals decide to adopt the new technologies. Understanding the factors that influence the doctor's adoption of a technology is therefore vital. This chapter reports on an investigation into the factors influencing the adoption of mobile devices by doctors in the public healthcare sector in the Western Cape, South Africa. The research methodology was shaped by qualitative enquiry and described through thematic analysis. Chapter confirmed the key adoption factors identified in prior research: job relevance, usefulness, perceived user resources and device characteristics. However, some additional adoption factors were uncovered in this research, namely patient influence, support structures from national government and hospital administration, and unease in respect of malpractice legal suits.

Section 5
Further Reading

The section 5 includes eight chapters dedicated to further reading for better understanding on computerization of primary care, open source software and mobile health. The first chapter (Chapter 23) is about the computerization of primary care in the United States. The second chapter (Chapter 24) presents open source software a key component of E-Health in developing nations. This is followed by Chapter 25 discusses physician characteristics associated with early adoption of electronic medical records in smaller group practices. The forth chapter (Chapter 26) explains about an e-healthcare mobile application: A stakeholders' analysis experience of reading. The fifth chapter (Chapter 27) explores the mobile e-health: Making the case. Further Chapter 28 discusses on the Internet, health information, and managing health: An examination of boomers and seniors. In the (Chapter 29) an evaluation of health information systems: Challenges and approaches is presented. Finally, Chapter 30 reports on mobile information systems in a hospital organization setting.

In this chapter the authors have attempt to assess the current level of information technology used by primary care physicians in the U.S. Primary care physicians listed by the American Medical Association were contacted by e-mail and asked to complete a Web-based questionnaire. A total of 2,145 physicians responded. Overall, between 20% and 25% of primary care physicians reported using electronic medical records, e-prescribing, point-of-care decision support tools, and electronic communication with patients. This indicates a slow rate of adoption since 2000. Differences in adoption rates suggest that future surveys need to differentiate primary care and office-based physicians by specialty. An important finding is that one-third of the physicians surveyed expressed no interest in the four IT applications.

This chapter describes some aspects of open source e-health software that are particularly relevant to developing nations, issues and problems that may arise and suggests some future areas for research and action. Suggestions for critical success factors are included. In this much of the discussion is related to a case study of a training and e-health project, currently running in the Himalayan kingdom of Bhutan.

specific information from the database. Furthermore, the information retrieved from the database can be acted upon by the client. In doing so, the database is updated by the client. This is demonstrated via the retrieval and updating of patient records by doctors.

Foreword

Information Technology (IT) is being widely used at the different levels in healthcare organizations. IT now encompasses new tools and healthcare services that are delivered or enhanced through the Internet and other advanced networking technologies and speech recognition tools. All the technological developments in the field of health informatics have been made in providing well functioning systems to healthcare organizations to improve healthcare services. Since last several years, a lot of attention has been focused on the tools, techniques and methods towards the development of health informatics and electronics healthcare systems. In my opinion this book is another attempt to fill the gap that still exists. This book is divided in five major sections with having total 30 chapters. These chapters discuss the range of topics covering Evaluation, Tools and Technologies, Applications and Impact on health informatics and electronics healthcare systems. This book is the combination of academic and practitioners of the authors, to assist the healthcare organizations to get advance benefits from both perspectives. The academics have tried to provide the evaluation, impact and application of health informatics. On other hand the practitioners have attempt to provide the insight of new tools and technologies that are being used for the provision of better healthcare services. Therefore, this book provides an advance understanding of health informatics in the global perspective. It will help to understand the process for the adoption and usage of health informatics to the decision makers while taking the decision for the adoption of health informatics in their countries.

Angappa Gunasekaran
University of Massachusetts, USA

Angappa Gunasekaran *is a professor of management in the Charlton College of Business at the University of Massachusetts (North Dartmouth, USA). Previously, he has held academic positions in Canada, India, Finland, Australia, and Great Britain. He has a BE and ME from the University of Madras and a PhD from the Indian Institute of Technology. He teaches and conducts research in operations management and information systems. He serves on the editorial board of 20 journals and edits a journal. He has published about 160 articles in journals, 60 articles in conference proceedings, and two edited books. In addition, he has organized several conferences in the emerging areas of operations management and information systems. He has extensive editorial experience that includes serving as guest editor of many high profile journals. He has received outstanding paper and excellence in teaching awards. His current areas of research include supply chain management, enterprise resource planning, e-commerce, and benchmarking.*

Preface

The adoption of health informatics within healthcare organisations is characterised by a series of phases since the 1960s. Initially, health informatics adoption began in financial systems in the 1960s, which provided support to the organisations' billing, payroll, accounting and reporting systems. During this phase, health informatics adoption was clear and straightforward (e.g. elimination of clerical positions). Clinical departments took a major initiative during the 1970s that supported their internal activities such as radiology, laboratory and pharmacy. Financial systems once again became prominent in the 1980s with major investments in cost accounting and materials management systems[1]. During the 1990s, attention turned towards enterprise-wide clinical systems, including clinical data repositories and visions of a fully computerised electronic patient medical record. All the technological developments in the field of health informatics have been made in providing well functioning systems to healthcare organisations in order to improve healthcare services. Computerised Patient Record (CPR) systems; the adoption of the Internet along with Intranet and Extranet; Asynchronous Transfer Mode (ATM) networks along with local area networks; wide area networks; enterprise systems; integration approaches and remote diagnostics via telemedicine have experienced significant growth in recent years[2].

The adoption of the Internet in healthcare has significant impacts on the delivery of healthcare services and has bridged the gap between healthcare providers, patients, suppliers and other stakeholders. In addition, the Internet is used by healthcare organisations to support operational management including employment announcement and staff recruitment. The adoption of the Internet has led to the concept of intranets and extranets and a number of medical intranets and extranets have been developed and implemented for different purposes, such as for internal and external sharing of medical information and patients' insurance eligibility, which have been greatly facilitated by broadband Internet. The need for most patients to take on more responsibility for their healthcare is made easier by an increasing availability of medical information on the Internet. Thus, the number of specialised or health-related web portals is increasing. Such developments in this area suggest that health informatics has the potential to facilitate the innovation of health care delivery and that innovation is truly needed[3].

The above clearly suggests that accessibility, adoption and use of health informatics tools are likely to transform and affect almost every aspect of better healthcare services. Therefore, it is important to understand the development in the domain of health informatics within the context of both developed and developing countries. Most countries with highly developed health systems are investing heavily in computer hardware and software in the expectation of higher quality for lower costs. Recent systematic reviews show that health informatics is providing a range of benefits, particularly in the areas of prevention and care to the patients. However, there remains a relative lack of published evaluations of informatics tools and methods. The uncritical adoption of new systems, based on the pressures of technological push, continue to discredit policy makers who have had to commit significant resources despite inadequate information on what can be realistically expected from a proposed system. In the context of developing countries, this becomes all the more significant since the resources are not abundant, and hence warrant extremely judicious use. Thus, studies from the developing countries' perspective become invaluable in guiding the adoption of new technologies and tools, and technologies related with health informatics within this context.

In line with the above, the overall mission of "**The Handbook of Research on Advances in Health Informatics and Electronic Healthcare Applications: Global Adoption and Impact of Information Communication Technologies**" is to provide an understanding of the global adoption and impact of Information and Communication Technologies (ICTs) within the area of Health Informatics. Corresponding to the mission, the 30 chapters comprising this Handbook have discussed a range of topics covering Evaluation, Tools and Technologies, Applications and Impact on health informatics and electronic healthcare systems. The book highlights the major areas of adoption of health informatics in both developed and developing countries, and further examines the constraints, experiences and outcomes, as well as identifying policy concerns and planning implications. In effect, this Handbook provides an advanced understanding of health informatics from a global perspective. This Handbook contributes towards theory, practice and policy. Theoretically, it exerts efforts towards expanding the knowledge within the area by synthesising and evaluating the appropriate literature in order to enhance the understanding of health informatics adoption, usage and impact from the perspectives of both developed and developing countries. The Handbook will form an aid for gaining an improved appreciation of the factors such as costs, benefits and barriers associated with its adoption. Therefore, the Handbook can potentially help healthcare organisations, development functionaries as well as policy makers to understand the impact of health informatics on health care administration and health outcomes for providing better healthcare services and reducing medical errors.

The Handbook is organised into 30 chapters, co-authored by 55 contributors from 34 different institutions/organisations located in more than 30 countries (such as Australia, Italy, India, Norway, the United Kingdom, and the United States of America). Such geographical and institutional variety indicates that the Handbook has drawn on a collection of wide and diverse outlooks. The 30 chapters have been organised into five sections: Health Informatics and E-Health Evaluation (six Chapters); Health Informatics and E-Health Tools and Technologies (five Chapters); Health Informatics and E-Health Applications (six Chapters); Health Informatics and E-Health Impact (five Chapters) and further reading (eight Chapters).

Considering the richness and depth of the content, we firmly believe that this handbook will be an excellent resource for readers/audiences who wish to learn more on how to encourage the successful adoption of emerging information and telecommunication technologies in healthcare, both in the context of developed and developing countries. The chapters included in this Handbook are also useful for readers who are interested in learning about how various research approaches and methods fit with different theories. The target audience for the Handbook includes Healthcare Service Providers, Policy Makers, Academics/Researchers, Students of IS and IT Management.

We sincerely hope that this Handbook will provide a positive contribution to the area of information systems in general and health informatics specifically. In order to make further research progress and improvement in the understanding of this area, we would like to welcome feedback and comments about this Handbook from readers. Comments and constructive suggestions can be sent to the Editors of IGI Global at the address provided at the beginning of the Handbook.

Sincerely,

Khalil Khoumbati, Jamshoro, Sindh, Pakistan
Yogesh K. Dwivedi, Swansea, UK
Aradhana Srivastava, New Delhi, India
Banita Lal, Nottingham, UK
December 2008

ENDNOTES

[1] Grimson, J. (2001). Delivering the Electronic Healthcare Record for the 21st Century. *International Journal of Medical Informatics, 64*(2-3), 111-127.

[2] Kim, K. & Michelman, J. (1990). An Examination of Factors for the Strategic Use of Information Systems in the Healthcare Industry. *MIS Quarterly, 14*(2), 201-215

[3] Khoumbati, K., Themistocleous, M. & Irani, Z. (2006). Evaluating the Adoption of Enterprise Application Integration in Healthcare Organizations. *Journal of Management Information System, 22*(4), 69-108.

Section 1
Health Informatics and E-Health Evaluation

Chapter 1
Towards an Evaluation Framework for E-Health Services:
Evaluating Criteria from Users Perspective

Alalwany Hamid
Brunel University, UK

Alshawi Sarmad
Brunel University, UK

ABSTRACT

The purpose of this study is to explore the user's perspective in evaluating e-health services, and to present evaluation criteria that influence user's utilization and satisfaction of e-health services. The evaluation criteria are based on two lines of studies relating to the behaviour of users of new products or services and on broad examining and critical analysis of the existing evaluations initiatives in e health context. The evaluation criteria can serve as part of an e-health evaluation framework, and also to provide useful tools to allow the development of successful e-health initiatives by assisting the healthcare organisation to address areas that require further attention.

BACKGROUND

Globally, the healthcare services are considered to be the biggest service industry, and they are taking top priority, receiving enormous investments, and are growing at a rapid pace in most developed countries (Mitchell, 2000; Pan American Health Organization, 1999)

E-health, which are basically enabled and driven by the use of information and communication technologies in healthcare have the potential to change the healthcare industry worldwide in terms of their infrastructures, and the costs and quality of services (Wickramasinghe and Misra, 2004; Wickramasinghe and Goldberg, 2004).

E-health is a very broad term encompassing various activities in an evolving field. As such, for practical reasons, in this paper the used definition is the one that has been adopted by the World Health Organization. According to the Organisation, E-health can be defined as 'being the leveraging of the information and communication technology (ICT) to connect

DOI: 10.4018/978-1-60566-030-1.ch001

provider and patients and governments; to educate and inform healthcare professionals, managers and consumers; to stimulate innovation in care delivery and health system management; and, to improve our healthcare system' (Hans Oh et al. 2005).

E-health evaluation may be carried out during planning, development, or operation of an e-health system (Brender, 2006). The purposes of e-health evaluation are also varying from one case to another. For example, the purpose could be to encourage the use of information systems in healthcare through assessing the risks and benefits for both users and government institutions (Friedman and Wyatt, 2000), or the purpose could be to provide the basis for the decisions about an e-health system under investigation or its implementation context (Brender, 2006).

E-Health evaluation involved many stakeholders, users being the most important (Gustafson & Wyatt, 2004). Therefore, assessing e-health from users' perspective should address all the key factors that influence the users' acceptance to the new adopted technologies including the risks and benefits associated with the design and implementation of the e-health initiative in specific contexts.

The research in the area of information systems evaluation in general and e-health evaluation in particular is a complicated and difficult subject (Friedman and Wyatt, 2000; Serafeimidis and Smithson, 2000; Peffers and Saarinen, 2002). The complexity and difficulty lies in the challenges faced at the intersection of three areas, each well-known for its complexity; healthcare services, information systems, and evaluation methodologies.

Healthcare services are well-known to be a complex domain. This is related to the fact that healthcare is a safety-critical area, dictated by complex regulations especially those that apply to manage directly patients information, medical knowledge itself and methods of healthcare delivery which are changing rapidly (Friedman and Wyatt, 2000)

Information systems and their evaluation is also another complex domain, especially when considering both the social and technical context of their use. This is due in great part to the opinion that information systems research and e-health systems as a part of it, is a social science as much as an information systems science (Mingers, and Stowell, 1997). The case of e-health is even more complicated, as its social aspects have greater impact on the system success or failure than any other information system.

The final and more important challenges are the complexity and difficulty of establishing evaluation methodologies, while the evaluation domain is suffering from the limited experience of using methods, the unfamiliarity with evaluation techniques and the difficulty in interpreting results (Ballantine et al. 1999; Farbey et al. 1999; Powell, 1999).

The main aim of this study is to explore the users' perspective in evaluating e-health services and to present evaluation criteria that influence users' utilization and satisfaction of e-health services. The evaluation criteria can serve as part of e-health evaluation framework, and also to provide useful and necessary tools to allow the development of successful e-health initiatives by assisting the healthcare organisation to identify and thus address areas that require further attention. The selection process of the evaluation criteria will take into account the challenges faced at the intersection of the three areas, healthcare services, information systems, and evaluation methodologies.

THE RESEARCH APPROACH

To explore the users' perspective in evaluating e-health services and to present the evaluation criteria that influence users' utilization and satisfaction of e-health services, it is imperative to select a relevant research approach that takes into account the general aims of the research study.

The process of selecting and deploying appropriate research approach for this study, is an important and critical issue, and should only be decided on after considering a number of factors including;

- The research question and its context (how to identify the key factors that influence users' utilization and satisfaction of e-health services?)
- The multi-dimensional aspects of e-health, as it has different roots and complex relationships associated with using information communications technologies, management as well as health regulations, and governments policies.
- The large number of stakeholders involve in e-health evaluation, each with their own particular needs, values and objectives.

As this study forms a part of a research project which will progress through a number of phases, the research will be based on a sequential multi-method approach (Creswell, 2003). Adopting the sequential multi-method approach paves the way to the use of the appropriate method for each research phase and creates the opportunity for multiple analyses about the same collected data.

This study represents phase one of the research project, and will be based mainly on two lines of studies relating to the behaviour of users of new products or services. These studies are: diffusion of innovations (Rogers, 1995) and technology acceptance (Davis, 1989). The aim of using both studies is to build theoretical framework that aids in the selection process of the evaluation criteria influencing users' utilization and satisfaction of e-health services. Broad examining and critical analysis of the existing evaluations initiatives specifically those who were based on e-health services case studies was also used to overcome the limitation of the theoretical framework.

In the next phase of the research project the authors will carry out an empirical validation and examination of the proposed evaluation criteria, the validation will be performed through case study methodology (Yin, 2003). This process is very important; it will address potential improvements, and verify the adaptability of the proposed criteria to various e-health contexts.

TOWARDS AN EVALUATION FRAMEWORK FOR E-HEALTH SERVICES

Though the development of a comprehensive evaluation framework for e-health services is beyond the remit of this study, it is vital to examine the current evaluation frameworks in order to choose the appropriate evaluation approach and select the suitable framework that can accommodate the proposed evaluation criteria. We have selected for our analysis a number of evaluation approaches that we believe are more suitable for the evaluation in the healthcare context.

The evaluation of government e-services in general, and e-health services in particular as many researchers agree, is both an under developed and under managed area in theory and practice (Brender, 2006; Friedman and Wyatt 2000; Lofstedt, 2005). Nevertheless, the research field in this area has been the focus of a number of studies which take different approaches.

One of these studies is focused mainly on the evaluation criteria, which can be called criteria-based evaluation approach. What is typical for this approach is that the information systems interface and the interaction between users and the systems work as a basis for the evaluation together with a set of predefined criteria. The chosen criteria rule the evaluation process and its results (Cronholm and Goldkuhl, 2003). In the same direction and based on what drives the evaluation, Cronholm and Goldkuhl (2003) identified another two approaches named goal-based and goal-free evaluations. The goal-based evaluations use goals from the organisational context to assess the information system. Goal-free evaluation is based on gathering data about a broad range of actual effects of the system and evaluating the importance of these effects in meeting demonstrated needs (Patton, 1990). Among the three previous approaches, the criteria based one is the most appropriate for e-health services evaluations. The appropriateness stems from the fact that e-health applications are principally complex in nature, hence they require an approach that can be derived from a multitude of perspectives and theories such as TAM or DOI.

Another group of evaluation studied were introduced to address one or more of the perspectives of the system stakeholders. Freeman (1984) was among the first, who introduced the stakeholders' concept. Since then, several researchers have adopted the stakeholders approach in their research of information systems evaluation. However, there is only limited literature that recognizes healthcare stakeholders and their changing role in the evaluation of e-health services.

Moreover, even in the limited literature available on healthcare stakeholders, the description and identification of these stakeholders seems to be generally ignored (Mantzana and Themistocleous, 2006).

For practical reasons this study will only focus on the e-health users' perspective. We believe that the acceptance and satisfaction of e-health services are dependent primarily on users' motivation to adopt and utilize these services, user utilization being important for the success of e-health services. However, only few studies have investigated the key factors that influence user' adoption of e-services (Lofstedt, 2005).

The stakeholder's evaluation approach is part of the school which suggested five levels of evaluation approaches for healthcare information systems, which are macro, sector, firm, application, and stakeholder. This suggests that different criteria would inevitably apply to each of these approaches (Connell, and Young, 2007).

There is also another group of evaluation studies which is defined by the basis on which the evaluation is performed. In this direction Grover et al. (1996) categorize three approaches: Comparative, normative and improvement. In the comparative approach, the evaluation is based on comparing a particular system with other similar systems. The normative approach compares the system against a theoretical ideal system or, in essence, against best practice. The improvement approach is intended to assess how much the system has improved over time. In this study we intend to use only the comparative and normative approaches because the main aim is toward proposing evaluation criteria for proposed implementations rather than historical ones.

Furthermore, another group of evaluation studies classified evaluations is based on when the assessment is performed (Brender, 2006; Cronholm & Goldkuhl, 2003; Grover et al, 1996). According to these studies the evaluation can be carried out during the analysis and planning phase, or during the development and the adaptation phases, or after the development has completed and the system is in use. An example of this kind of evaluation is process evaluation approach which is intended to evaluate the efficient use of resources, and is normally performed during the analysis and planning phase. There is also the response evaluation approach which assesses the users reaction to the system, usually performed during the final stage of implementation, or while the system is in use. The equity implementation model presented by Lauer et al (2000) is an example of the response evaluation approach. The model was based on the equity theory (Adams, 1965), a well-established theory in the social sciences and was adopted in e-health assessments to examine and understand user reaction to the implementation of a system. Lauer et al, (2000) stated that the focus of this approach is on the effect of the changes that such a system brings about on the system users.

The last example in this group is the impact evaluation approach, which is intended to assess the overall social and technical impact of the system on users and organisations, and is normally performed while the system is in use. According to Grover et al. (1996), because the impact evaluation is the most comprehensive, it is the most difficult approach to undertake. The impact evaluation approach can be quite beneficial in evaluating e-health services because it would comprehensively recognize users and organisations needs, by measuring the acceptability as well as the risks and benefits of e-health services (Gustafson and Wyatt, 2004). In this study, the focus will only be on the criteria that influence the user's reaction to the e-health services and the social, economical and technical effects of these services.

To conclude, we suggest that the appropriate evaluation framework for e-health services which can accommodate the proposed evaluation criteria would have the following characteristics:

- The framework is criteria-based. The criteria can be grounded in, and derived from, one or more specific perspectives or theories.
- The framework only considers one stakeholder or a group of stallholders with a common perspective in an evaluation process (In this study it is users' perspective)
- The framework combines both comparative and normative approaches toward proposing evaluation criteria for e-health services.
- The framework only considers the criteria that influence the user's reaction to e-health services, and the impact of these services on the users.

USERS' BEHAVIOUR TOWARDS NEW PRODUCTS OR SERVICES

There are many studies on the behaviour of consumers of new products and services, these studies were adopted in research to predict user's acceptance of innovations including e-health services. Towards aiding the selection process of the evaluation criteria those influencing users' utilization and satisfaction of e-health services, this study will make use of two lines of these studies

The first one is Diffusion of Innovations Theory (DOI). DOI is one of the popular theories which were introduced by Rogers (1995) to explain how a new idea or innovation propagates in a social system. The theory is based on 50 years of research, and was adopted by many researchers in different research fields including the e-government research. For example, the theory was used by Carter, and Belanger, (2004) to assess the citizen adoption of e-government initiatives. Since being introduced, the diffusion of innovations theory was adopted in different ways in many studies including the use of the important part of the theory and the well-known S-shaped curve of adoption and the categorization of adopters.

In applying diffusion theory to e-health services evaluation, the most relevant points to recognize are the innovation perceived attributes identified by Rogers' study and their applicability to e-health services: Rogers (1995) describes the characteristics of an innovation in terms of its perceived attributes, and these attributes are responsible in controlling the rates of diffusion of the innovation. Rogers (1995) identified three primary perceived attributes, which are relative advantage, compatibility, and complexity. He added two other innovation attributes, which are trialability and observability.

From the five factors of DOI theory, we will only include in this study the primary ones, which are relative advantage, compatibility, and complexity. We believe that the other two, trialability and observability, are not pertinent for e-health services. Rogers (1995) considers trialability and observability as less important than the other three. Tornatzky and Klein (1982) have the same view, and they conclude that relative advantage, compatibility, and complexity are the most relevant factors to adoption research.

The second line of studies relating to the behaviour of users to new products or services is

Technology Acceptance Model (TAM) (Davis, 1989). TAM is widely used to study user acceptance of technology. It was designed to examine the mediating role of perceived ease of use and perceived usefulness in their relation between systems characteristics as external variables and the probability of system use as an indicator of system success. However, as noted by several researchers (Hufnagel & Conca, 1994; Melone, 1990; Paul *et al.* 2003), TAM suffers from the absence of significant factors, including considering both human and social change processes and their affects on the adoption and utilization of new information systems. Paul *et al.* (2003) added that although technology acceptance model is useful, using TAM specifically in empirical research may give inconsistent results.

The technological acceptance model was used in the evaluation of e-services in the public sector by many research studies (Al-adawi et al. 2005;Carter, and Belanger, 2004). The model was also applied to healthcare by Lapointe et al (2002). In applying technology acceptance model to e-health services evaluation in this study, we will consider the mediating role of both perceived ease of use and perceived usefulness and their influence in the users' utilization and satisfaction of e-health services

PROPOSED E-HEALTH EVALUATION CRITERIA

E-government services evaluation and e-health services evaluation in particular are unable to reveal the full value of e-government projects without considering the perspectives of all the e-government services stakeholders and the e-government value measures presented by evaluation criteria consisted of all the key issues perceived by each of the stakeholders.

As mentioned earlier healthcare services are known to be a complex domain. This is related to the fact that healthcare is a safety critical area, dictated by a complex regulations. These regulations should be carefully considered in the selection process of the evaluation criteria, and in the description of the criteria used for a specific e-health service.

Hence, the proposed criteria are derived from two sources. The first source is two lines of studies relating to the behaviour of users of new products or services. The second source is a broad examination of the existing evaluations initiatives specifically those who were based on e-health services case studies. The first source represented by DOI and TAM which are popular and widely used theories, but still have their own merits and limitations. One of the main limitations of both theories is that they are not conclusive models and they suffer from the absence of significant factors. To adapt both theories for e-health context and overcome their limitations, critical analysis of e-health services case studies were used.

Considering the technical perspective, the economic perspective, and the social perspective in selecting and grouping the proposed evaluation criteria for this study, the criteria will be grouped in three sets of criteria, which are usability, direct costs and benefits, and trust. This classification should serve the deployment of the evaluation framework.

The Usability Criteria

The first set of evaluation criteria is the usability criteria. Usability in the proposed criteria may represent perceived ease of use and perceived usefulness as depicted by Davis (1989) technology acceptance model (TAM), or complexity as defined by Rogers (1995) diffusion of innovation.

Davis (1989) defines perceived usefulness as "the degree to which a person believes that using a particular system would enhance his or her job performance". He also defines perceived ease of use as "the degree to which a person believes that using a particular system would be free of effort". Rogers (1995) defines complexity as the "degree to which an innovation is perceived as difficult to understand and use"

We believe that perceived ease of use is predicted to influence perceived usefulness, since the easier a system is to use, the more useful it can be. We also believe that complexity and perceived ease of use are measures for the same issue. Therefore we are considering the three issues belonging to the same set and they will be represented by the usability criteria.

Usability has different interpretations and meanings depending on the context of use. Bevan and Macleod (1993) define usability as the quality of interaction within a particular context. Another description of usability which considers user's perspective is proposed by Nielson (1993), according to him, usability relates to how well users can use the functionality of a system or service in terms of what it can do. Researchers have provided broad dimensions and introduced long lists of aspects by which the usability can be assessed. These include accessibility (Steinfeld & Danford, 1999), functionality (Melander-Wikman et al. 2005; Nielson, 1993; Steinfeld & Danford, 1999), compatibility (Bevan et al. 2007; Chau and Hu (2001), user' satisfaction, easy to learn and use (Melander-Wikman et al. 2005; Nielson, 1993), and user interface (Melander-Wikman et al. 2005).

Accessibility is an important subset of usability. According to Terry Ma, and Zaphiris (2003), accessibility means an effective and efficient user interface which is inclusive of more people in more situations and can achieve user satisfaction. Those people are different in their accessibily requirments and needs. A high percentage of them particularly those who suffer from disabilities or cronic illness are more likely in need than others for accessible and effective e-health services. Mont (2007) reported that an estimated 20 percent of American and Australian populations and 12.2 percent of British population have disabilities. Another research by Lenhart et al. (2003), shows a high percentage of about 38 percent of Americans with disabilities are using the Internet. The same research also shows that users with disabilities are more likely than the general population to use e-health services and have access to these services only from home.

Accessibility requirements for e-health services should generally accommodate all people, but particularly remove or reduce all the barriers that can hamper disabled people from fully benefiting from e-health services. One of the efforts for determining accessibility is the guidelines developed by the "Web Accessibility Initiative", a working group of the World Wide Web Consortium (Caldwell et al. 2007)

Despite the importance of accessibly in influencing the users' perspective of e-services in public sector and e-health services in particular, studies show that governments either ignored or did not pay enough attention to the accessibility importance. According to the Global e-government Survey conducted by World Market Research Centre and Brown University (2001), only 2% of government websites worldwide have some form of disability access and only 7% of the e-government websites were accessible. Another study by West (2000) show that only 15 percent of American government websites offer some form of disability access, such as TTY (Text Telephone) or TDD (Telephone Device for the Deaf) or are approved by disability organizations. The study also revealed that only 4 percent of American government websites offer foreign language translation features on their websites. Another example for ignoring accessibly in healthcare services is a cross-sectional study by Zeng and Parmento (2004). The study was aiming to evaluate the accessibility of consumer health information of 108 Web sites, and reported that no Web site met all the accessibly criteria in their assessing framework.

Compatibility is another important criterion to be included in the usability criteria. According to Rogers (1995), compatibility is measured by the degree to which an innovation is perceived as being consistent with the existing values, past experiences, and needs of potential users. Chau and Hu (2001) argued that compatibility is positively affecting user's attitude toward accepting new technologies in healthcare environments. They based their argument on the assumption that users would be more likely to consider technology useful if they perceived it to be compatible with their existing practices. In addition, users would consider technology easy to use if they did not need to change their practices significantly in an environment that can not cope with radical change.

Functionality is a broad criterion of the usability criteria which supposes to cover the user's requirements from a system to perform specific tasks in a specific situation; this includes accuracy, validity, robustly, speed and availability (Melander-Wikman et al. 2005).

User satisfaction is generally regarded as one of the most important measures of system or service success and should be included in the proposed usability criteria. The user satisfaction criterion can be measured by various dimensions including utility, reliability, efficiency, customization and flexibility (Horan et al. 2006).

Table 1 summarizes the proposed usability criteria, list of measuring aspects by which the criteria can be assessed and suggestions for measuring descriptions. The aim of proposing the measuring descriptions is to provide general guide for assessing these aspects. The applicability of the descriptions for specific context is out of the scope of this study.

The Direct Costs and Benefits Criteria

The second set contains the direct costs and benefits criteria. The criteria in this set are primarily based on Rogers's relative advantage. According to Rogers (1995), relative advantage is "the degree to which an innovation is seen as being superior to its predecessor". It is essentially a cost–benefit analysis of how useful a given innovation when compared with what is already available. Relative advantage represents mostly the economic return involved in the adoption of an innovation, but could also include the immediacy of reward, social prestige, or savings in time and effort (Rogers, 1995). The direct costs and benefits criteria have traditionally dominated the traditional information system evaluation process, and they were criticized by many authors (Farbey et al. 1995; Serafeimidis and Smithson, 2000) for their limited relevance to the role of information systems. This limitation is in their definition of stakeholders, targeting only direct tangible costs and benefits and being only based on accounting and financial instruments. On the other hand, many authors (Eng, 2002; Glasgow, 2007; Gustafson & Wyatt, 2004; Smaglik et al. 1998) argue that direct costs and benefits are important and should be considered in evaluating e-health services. Despite the above mentioned opinions regarding the limitations of using the economic issues in the evaluation; we tend to support the opinion of including them as part of the evaluation criteria because healthcare services have a high economic impact on governments and citizens comparing to any other services (Bower, 2005; Friedman and Wyatt, 2000; Gustafson, 2001).

One of the efforts in assessing the direct financial cost and benefits of e-health is the e-health impact project which was commissioned by the European Commission (DG Information Society and Media) (Stroetmann et al. 2006). The main aim of the project was to evaluate the economic and productivity impact of e-health services. The research project developed a generic economic assessment and evaluation framework for e-health applications, and was mainly focused on citizens' perspective in assessing ten e-health application cases. The ten cases were selected from across the European Union for their proven, sustainable e-health application. The result of the assessment, which was carried over a period of 15 years, indicates a positive, sustainable economic impact of these e-health services.

Table 1. The usability criteria and suggestions for measuring descriptions

Evaluation Criteria	Measuring Aspects	Suggestions for Measuring Descriptions
Easy to learn and use	Easy to learn	Measured by the time needed to learn to work with a service.
	Easy to use	Assessed by the simplicity of the service and how easy it is to understand and comprehend its functions
Accessibility	Content Accessibility	Measured by the degree of compliance with the Web Content Accessibility Guidelines
	User interface	Judged by the available options of user interfaces (e.g. Graphical interface, Multi-screen interface, Attentive User Interface).
	Disability access & translation	Is the system offering some form of disability access and foreign language translation features?
Compatibility	Compatibility	Assessed by how quickly and easily the e-service can fit into the whole healthcare system.
Functionality	Accuracy	Measured by the degree to which information provided by the service is free of errors.
	Validity	Measured by the clarity and regularity of information updating.
	Robustly	Judged by the technical functionality of the service.
	Speed	Judged by the system response time; web page load time; download time.
	Availability	Assessed by the availability of the service 24hrs/7days per week and the existing of alternative choices.
User satisfaction	Utility	Assessed by the completeness and usefulness of the service content (Loiacono et al., 2002)
	Reliability	Judged by the appropriately of the service functions in terms of the technology as well as the accuracy of the content (Zeithaml et al. 2000).
	Efficiency	Judged by the time spent to complete the information task, quality of the information found, appropriateness of information found, and satisfaction with the outcome (Wang et al., 2005).
	Customization	Measured by the degree of service tailrarity to meet the needs of individual user (Burgess, 2004).
	Flexibility	Assessed by whether a system or a service provides choice of ways to state a need and delivers dynamic information (Zeithaml et al. 2000).

Table 2 summarizes the proposed direct costs and benefits criteria and suggestions for measuring descriptions for e-health services evaluation. Adopting the proposed evaluation criteria and their descriptions for a specific e-health service should take into account the relevancy of each of the evaluation criterion to the prevailing situation. This mainly depends on the maturity of the e-health initiative, and could lead to partial use of the evaluation criteria.

The Trust Criteria

The third set of the proposed evaluation criteria is the trust criteria. Trust has been acknowledged as a crucial property of information systems that provide e-services in a variety of contexts, because failing to address the trust aspects correctly may have a profound impact on the e-services (Fruhling, and Lee, 2004;Presti et al. 2006). The aspects of trust must be tackled properly during

Table 2. The direct costs and benefits criteria and suggestions for measuring descriptions

Evaluation Criteria	Measuring Aspects	Suggestions for Measuring Descriptions
Costs	Money Saving	How much money the citizens are saving by using the e-health service.
	Time Saving	How much time the citizens are saving by using the e-health service.
Benefits	Effort Saving	Measured by the degree of convenience in using a particular e-health service.
	Quality	Assessed by the added value to the Citizens information and knowledge about their conditions, diagnoses, treatment options and healthcare facilities, as well as the appropriate timing of the service
	Access	Judged by access level comparing to the same quality of services through alternative channel.

the development and use of e-services. Trust can be defined as "the willingness of a party to be vulnerable to the actions of another party based on the expectation that the other will perform a particular action important to the trustor, irrespective of the ability to monitor or control that other party" (Mayer et al. 1995). Trust in e-health services is associated with data security and privacy of personal health data (Rodrigues, 2003). Given the sensitive nature of healthcare information, trust requires maintaining security in handling of patients' information, protecting their privacy, and assuring them that their personal information will be treated confidentially. Without this assurance, it will be difficult to promote the use of e-health services.

Enhancing trust involves enhancing security measures. This requires a large variety of measures and principles. Slaymaker et al. (2004) identified several aspects for security to be considered in any e-health project. These aspects include: user authentication, encrypted data movement, data integrity, security breach detection, physical security, audit trails, client and server authentication, and availability.

Trust in e-health services is also associated with the privacy of personal health data. According to Davis et al. (1999) "Privacy is the state of being free from intrusion, and in the context of health care, it concerns the responsibility of a care provider to protect a patient from any disclosure (i.e., discovery by others), even unintentional, of personal health data by providing security to the patient and the patient's records".

Moor (1997), stated that the main consideration in developing policies for protecting privacy is to make sure that the right people, and only the right people, have access to relevant information at the right time. Moor (1997) also proposed a controlled and restricted access technique for managing privacy. The technique is based on setting up zones of privacy and provides the opportunity for different people to be authorized for different levels of access to different kind of information at different times.

In practice, studies show that governments and health organizations have different levels of consideration for trust, security and privacy in their initiatives. An example is the study of Jarvinen (2005) which concludes that governments and health organizations have low levels of consideration for privacy. The study which covers 39 American health organizations reveals numerous examples of practices that make the customer vulnerable can be found in the analysed healthcare privacy policies. These practices include the absence of an adequate privacy notice, not give the users reasonable control over their information and the use of technical and confusing language in the privacy policies that make it difficult for the user to fully understand them. Another study by West (2000) also confirms

Table 3. The trust criteria and suggestions for measuring descriptions

Evaluation Criteria	Measuring Aspects	Suggestions for Measuring Descriptions
Security	User authentication	Measured by how strong the user authentication is and if its key capabilities are sufficient for e-Health services
	Encrypted data movement	Assessed by the suitability of the technology used to protect the transfer of data.
	Data integrity	Determined by if the information is complete, whole, valid and digitally signed when required
	Security breach detection	Judged by the ability of the system to monitor and look for suspicious activity on the network.
	Physical security	Assessed by how secure is the area that holding the database equipments and if it is located in an area with limited and controlled access.
	Audit trails	Judged by the ability of the system to record the modification of data, to keep the most up to date version of data and to retrieve old versions of data.
Privacy	Responsibility	Measured by the degree of protection supplied by the healthcare organization for patient information from any disclosure.
	Access Control	Assessed by the degree of control on different level of access to different kind of information at different time.
	Confidentiality	Measured by the degree of compliance with the UK Data Protection Act (1998)

similar finding. The study shows that there is very low consideration to the security and privacy in the American e-government websites. The study reveals that only 7 percent of American government websites have a privacy policy, and another 5 percent show some form of security policy. On the other hand, there are positive examples for the consideration of security and privacy such as the privacy provisions in Canada or quality seals for e-government services which was introduced in Austria (Aichholzer, (2003).

Table 3 summarizes the proposed trust criteria and suggestions for measuring the aspects of the criteria. Although the table provides clear and useful set of criteria, the criteria are general and it may be necessary to modify them to suite specific e-health initiative. The aim of proposing the measuring descriptions is to provide general guide for assessing the criteria aspects. The applicability of the description for specific context is out of the scope of this study.

CONCLUSION

This study argues that e-health services evaluation framework should be criteria based, while the criteria can be grounded in, and derived from, one or more specific perspectives or theories, and cannot be entirely framed within the bounds of a single theory or perspective. Understanding the multi-disciplinary nature of e-health services evaluation and the challenges that it faces is the first requisite towards dealing effectively with the complexities, and overcoming the barriers of e-health services evaluation.

This chapter provides a set of clear and useful e-health evaluation criteria that can be used to help achieve better citizen services utilization, to serve as part of e-health evaluation framework, and to address areas that require further attention in the development of future e-health initiatives.

The proposed criteria were mainly derived from two sources. The first source was two lines of studies relating to the behaviour of users of new products or services. The second source was a broad examining of the existing evaluations initiatives, specifically those who were based on e-health services case studies. Hence, general evaluation criteria were proposed that cover the technical, economic and social aspects affecting citizen utilization of e-government services. The proposed evaluation criteria can also be adapted to a specific e-health service by analysing the criteria that apply in that situation.

The limitation of this study lies in the absence of empirical validation and examination of the proposed evaluation criteria that has not yet been applied in the fieldwork. Hence, the proposed factors require an empirical validation which will be performed by the authors in the next stage of this research using multiple case study strategy and will form the basis for further research.

REFERENCES

Adams, J. S. (1965). Inequity in social exchange. In L. Berkowitz (Ed.), *Advances in experimental social psychology*. New York: Academic Press.

Aichholzer, G. (2003). Scenarios of e-government in 2010 and implications for strategy design. *Electronic Journal of E-government*. Retrieved from http://www.ejeg.com

Al-adawi, Z., Yousafzai, S., & Pallister, J. (2005). Conceptual model of citizen adoption of e-government. *The Second International Conference on Innovations in Information Technology, IIT'05*.

Ballantine, J. A., Galliers, R. D., & Stray, S. J. (1999). Information systems technology evaluation practices: Evidence from UK organizations. In L. P. Willcocks & S. Lester (Eds.), *Beyond the IT productivity paradox* (pp. 123-149). Chichester, UK: John Wiley & Sons.

Bevan, N., & Macleod, M. (1993). Usability assessment and measurement. In M. Kelly (Ed.), *The management and measurement of software quality*. Ashgate Technical/Gower Press.

Bevan, N., Petrie, H., & Claridge, N. (2007). Strategies for providing guidance on usability and accessibility. In *Proceedings HCI International 2007*. Springer.

Bower, A. (2005). *The diffusion and value of healthcare information technology*. RAND Corporation, Library of Congress Cataloging-in-Publication Data.

Brender, J. (2006). *Handbook of evaluation methods for health informatics*. USA: Elsevier Academic Press Publications.

Burgess, L. (2004, October 13-15). A conceptual framework for understanding and measuring perceived service quality in net-based customer support systems. *CollECTeR LatAm Conference*, Santiago, Chile.

Caldwell, B., Cooper, M., Reid, L., & Vanderheiden, G. (2007, December 11). *Web content accessibility guidelines 2.0, W3C working draft*.

Carter, L., & Belanger, F. (2004). Citizen adoption of electronic government initiatives. IN *Proceedings of 37th Annual Hawaii International Conference on System Sciences*, Big Island, Hawaii.

Chau, P., & Hu, P. (2001). Information technology acceptance by individual professionals: A model comparison approach. *Decision Sciences, 32*(4). doi:10.1111/j.1540-5915.2001.tb00978.x

Connell, N., & Young, T. (2007). Evaluating healthcare information systems through an "enterprise" perspective. *Information & Management, 44*(4), 433–440. doi:10.1016/j.im.2007.04.002

Creswell, J. W. (2003). *Research design. Qualitative, quantitative, and mixed methods approaches*. Thousand Oaks, CA: SAGE Publications.

Cronholm, S., & Goldkuhl, G. (2003, September 25-26). Six generic types of information systems evaluation. *The 10th European Conference on Information Technology Evaluation (ECITE-2003)*, Madrid.

Davis, F. (1989). Perceived usefulness, perceived ease of use, and user acceptance of information technology. *MIS Quarterly, 13*(3), 319–340. doi:10.2307/249008

Davis, L., Domm, J., Konikoff, M., & Miller, R. (1999). Attitudes of first-year medical students toward the confidentiality of computerized patient records. *Journal of the American Medical Informatics Association, 6*(1).

Eng, T. R. (2002). E-Health research and evaluation: Challenges and opportunities. *Journal of Health Communication, 7*(4), 267–272. doi:10.1080/10810730290001747

Farbey, B., Land, F., & Targett, D. (1995). A taxonomy of information systems applications: The benefits evaluation ladder. *European Journal of Information Systems, 4*, 41–50. doi:10.1057/ejis.1995.5

Farbey, B., Land, F., & Targett, D. (1999). Evaluating investments in IT: Findings and a framework. In L. P. Willcocks & S. Lester (Eds.), *Beyond the IT productivity paradox* (pp. 183-215). Chichester, UK: John Wiley & Sons.

Freeman, R. E. (1984). *Strategic management: A stakeholder approach.* Cambridge, MA: Ballinger Publishing Co.

Friedman, C., & Wyatt, J. (2000). Evaluation methods in medical informatics. New York: Springer-Verlag.

Fruhling, A., & Lee, S. (2004, September). Designing trustworthy e-health services for rural consumers. [*American Medical Informatics Association Proceedings.*]. *Medinfo*, ▪▪▪, 2004.

Glasgow, R. E. (2007). E-Health evaluation and dissemination research. *American Journal of Preventive Medicine, 32*(5Suppl), S119–S126. doi:10.1016/j.amepre.2007.01.023

Grover, V., Jeong, S. R., & Segars, A. H. (1996). Information systems effectiveness: The construct space and patterns of applications. *Information & Management, 31*(4). doi:10.1016/S0378-7206(96)01079-8

Gustafson, D., Hawkins, R., Pingree, S., McTavish, F., Arora, N., & Salner, J. (2001). Effect of computer support on younger women with breast cancer. *Journal of General Internal Medicine, 16*, 435–445. doi:10.1046/j.1525-1497.2001.016007435.x

Gustafson, D., & Wyatt, J. (2004). Evaluation of e-health systems and services. *British Medical Journal, 328*, 1150. doi:10.1136/bmj.328.7449.1150

Hans, O., Rizo, C., Enkin, M., & Jadad, A. (2005, February 24). What is e-health? A systematic review of published definitions. *Journal of Medical Internet Research.*

Horan, T., Abhichandani, T., & Rayalu, R. (2006). Assessing user satisfaction of e-government services: Development and testing of quality-in-use satisfaction with advanced traveler information systems (ATIS). *In Proceedings of the 39th Hawaii International Conference on System Sciences.*

Hufnagel, E. M., & Conca, C. (1994). Use response data: The potential for errors and biases. *Information Systems Research, 5*, 48–73. doi:10.1287/isre.5.1.48

Jarvinen, O. (2005). *Privacy management of e-health. Content analysis of 39 U.S. health providers' privacy policies.* Turku School of Economics and Business Administration, Series A.

Lapointe, L., Lamothe, L., & Fortin, J. P. (2002). The dynamics of IT adoption in a major change process in healthcare delivery. In *Proceedings of the 35th HICSS Conference,* Big Island, Hawaii.

Lauer, T., Joshi, K., & Browdy, T. (2000). Use of the equity implementation model to review clinical system implementation efforts. *Journal of the American Medical Informatics Association, 7*(1).

Lenhart, A., Horrigan, J., Rainie, L., Allen, K., Boyce, A., Madden, M., et al. (2003). *The ever-shifting Internet population. A new look at Internet access and the digital divide.* Washington, D.C.: Pew Internet & American Life Project.

Lofstedt, U. (2005). E-Government–assessment of current research and some proposals for future directions. *International Journal of Public Information Systems, 2005*(1).

Loiacono, E. T., Watson, R. T., & Goodhue, D. L. (2002, Winter). Webqual: A Web site quality instrument. In *Proceedings of the AMA Winter Marketing Educators' Conference*, Austin, TX.

Mantzana, V., & Themistocleous, M. (2006). A method for the identification of actors involved in the adoption of innovations in healthcare organizations. In *Proceedings of the 39th Hawaii International Conference on System Sciences.*

Mayer, R. C., Davis, J. H., & Schoorman, F. D. (1995). An integrative model of organizational trust. *Academy of Management Review, 20*(3), 709–734. doi:10.2307/258792

Melander-Wikman, A., Jansson, M., & Gard, G. (2005). The mobihealth usability evaluation questionnaire. *E-health International Journal.*

Melone, N. P. (1990). A theoretical assessment of the user satisfaction construct in information systems research. *Management Science, 36*, 76–91. doi:10.1287/mnsc.36.1.76

Mingers, J., & Stowell, F. (1997). *Information systems: An emerging discipline? Information systems series* (pp. 239-266). London: McGraw-Hill.

Mitchell, J. (2000). Increasing the cost-effectiveness of telemedicine by embracing e-health. *Journal of Telemedicine and Telecare, 6*(Suppl 1), 16–19. doi:10.1258/1357633001934500

Mont, D. (2007). *Measuring disability prevalence* (SP Discussion Paper No. 0706). Retrieved from http://siteresources.worldbank.org/DISABILITY/Resources/Data/MontPrevalence.pdf

Moor, J. H. (1997). Towards a theory of privacy in the information age. *Computers & Society, 27*(3), 27–32. doi:10.1145/270858.270866

Nielsen, J. (1993). Usability engineering (interactive technologies). New York: Academic Press, Orlando.

Pan American Health Organization. (1999). *Setting up healthcare services information systems: A guide for requirement analysis, application specification, and procurement.* Washington, D.C.: Essential Drugs and Technology Program, Division of Health Systems and Services Development, PAHO/WHO.

Patton, M. Q. (1990). *Qualitative evaluation and research methods, second ed.* London: Sage Publications.

Paul, L., John, I., & Pierre, C. (2003, January). Why do people use information technology? A critical review of the technology acceptance model. *Association for Information Systems, 40*(3), 191.

Peffers, K., & Saarinen, T. (2002). Measuring the business value of IT investments: Inferences from a study of senior bank executives. *Journal of Organizational Computing and Electronic Commerce, 12*(1), 17–38. doi:10.1207/S15327744JOCE1201_03

Powell, P. L. (1999). Evaluation of information technology investments: Business as usual. In L. P. Willcocks & S. Lester (Eds.), *Beyond the IT productivity paradox* (pp. 151-182). Chichester, UK: John Wiley & Sonspp.

Presti, S., Butler, M., Leuschel, M., & Booth, C. (2006). Holistic trust design of e-services. In R. Song, L. Korba & G. Yee (Eds.), *Trust in e-services: Technologies, practices, and challenges* (pp. 113-139). Hershey, PA: Idea Group Publishing.

Rodrigues, R. (2003). Deploying e-health solutions in Latin America and the Caribbean: Development and policy issues. *Forum PL11: Workshop on Telemedicine,* Geneva.

Rogers, E. M. (1995). *Diffusion of innovations, fourth ed.* New York: The Free Press.

Serafeimidis, V., & Smithson, S. (2000). Information systems evaluation in practice: A case study of organizational change. *Journal of Information Technology, 15*(2), 93–105. doi:10.1080/026839600344294

Slaymaker, M., Politou, E., Power, D., & Lloyd, S. (2004). E-Health security issues: The eDiaMoND perspective. In *Proceedings of the 2004 UK e-Science All Hands Meeting.*

Smaglik, P., Hawkins, R., Pingree, S., & Gustafson, D. (1998). The quality of interactive computer use among HIV infected individuals. *Journal of Health Communication, 3,* 53–68. doi:10.1080/108107398127508

Steinfeld, E., & Danford, G. S. (1999). *Enabling environments. Measuring the impact of environment on disability and rehabilitation.* New York: Kluwer Academic.

Stroetmann, K., Jones, T., & Dobrev, A. (2006, May 10-12). Evaluating the economic impact of e-health applications approach and method. *E-Health Conference 2006*, Malaga, Spain.

Terry Ma, H., & Zaphiris, P. (2003). The usability and content accessibility of the e-government in the UK. London: Centre for Human-Computer Interaction Design, City University. Retrieved from http://www.soi.city.ac.uk/~zaphiri/Papers/HCII2003/HCII2003-Accessibility.pdf

Tornatzky, L., & Klein, K. (1982). Innovation characteristics and innovation adoption-implementation: A meta-analysis of findings. *IEEE Transactions on Engineering Management, 29*(1), 28–45.

Wang, L., Bretschneider, S., & Gant, J. (2005). Evaluating Web-based e-government services with a citizen-centric approach. In *Proceedings of 38th Annual Hawaii International Conference on Systems Sciences*, Big Island, Hawaii.

West, D. (2000). *Assessing e-government: The Internet, democracy, and service delivery by state and federal governments.* Brown University. Retrieved from www.insidepolitics.org/policyreports.html

Wickramasinghe, N., & Goldberg, S. (2004). How M=EC2 in healthcare. *International Journal of Mobile Commerce.*

Wickramasinghe, N., & Misra, S. (2004). A wireless trust model for healthcare. *International Journal e-Health.*

World Markets Research Centre & Brown University. (2001). *Global e-government survey 2001.* Retrieved from http://www.worldmarketsanalysis.com/pdf/e-govreport.pdf

Yin, R. K. (2003). *Case study research: Design and methods, third ed.* Thousand Oaks, CA: Sage Publications.

Zeithaml, V. A., Parasuraman, A., & Malhotra, A. (2000). A conceptual framework for understanding e-service quality: Implications for future research and managerial practice. *Marketing Sciences Institute: Working Paper Series, 00*(115), 2000.

Zeng, X., & Parmanto, B. (2004). Web content accessibility of consumer health information. Web sites for people with disabilities: A cross sectional evaluation. *Journal of Medical Internet Research*, *6*(2), e19. doi:10.2196/jmir.6.2.e19

KEY TERMS AND DEFINITIONS

Direct Costs and Benefits Criteria: Refers to the tangible set of criteria that normally dominates traditional information system evaluation.

Evaluation Framework: Refers to a model by which the evaluation process will be guided through a number of phases including; determine the evaluation goals, choose the evaluation approach and methods, identify the practical issues, decide how to deal with the ethical issues, and determine how to interpret and present the evaluation outcomes.

Trust Criteria: Refers to the set of criteria that covers data security and privacy of personal data.

Usability Criteria: Refers to the set of criteria which represents how well users can use a system or service in terms of what it can do. This may include; accessibility, functionality, compatibility, user' satisfaction, easy to learn and use, and user interface.

User's Perspective: Refers to the perception of actors in the demand side which are affected by and/or affected in a specific service or system.

Chapter 2
Evaluating Healthcare IT and Understanding the Work of Healthcare are Entangled Processes

Joseph Schulman
New York Presbyterian Hospital, USA

ABSTRACT

Parallel to the monumental problem of replacing paper- and pen-based patient information management systems with electronic ones is the problem of evaluating the extent to which the change represents an improvement. Meaningful and useful evaluation rests upon: a) explicitly conceptualizing the goals and tasks of the daily clinical work; b) thinking of electronic information management technology as a cognitive tool; c) explicitly representing in the tool the pertinent information elements; d) selecting among possibilities for representing a problem formulation so as to facilitate the solution; and e) appreciating the dynamic interaction between the work and the tool–that changing a tool necessarily changes the work. Anchored in the story of how one hospital committee learned to think about the purpose and impact of a patient information management system, this chapter gives practical insight to these evaluative considerations.

INTRODUCTION

This chapter grew out of a story about how a committee of clinicians and information technology (IT) professionals learned to think more clearly about healthcare IT; to think about it in a somewhat deductive manner. Since healthcare IT is a tool to aid the work of healthcare, the group ultimately determined that critical reflection entails identifying what may be considered first principles that justify and inform the work itself. At the outset, the committee's task of characterizing IT success versus failure seemed perfectly clear. But only so until they began to understand the crucial distinction between healthcare system tasks and goals, and that activity without clarity of purpose may be activity without value. From these insights emerged an interrogative framework anchored in clear notions of purpose and designed to yield operational understanding. Over time, the essential idea became

DOI: 10.4018/978-1-60566-030-1.ch002

evident: clinical work and tools are calibrated to each other. The committee came to appreciate that a tool achieving quick user acceptance may be one that makes little use of its technological potential; and that workers may be unaware that their early opinions about new tools reflect their imposing the specifics of the previous work/tool interaction on the present one. The story of how this group learned to think about evaluating healthcare IT was originally published in the Journal of the American Medical Informatics Association and is reprinted here with permission: "Discovering how to think about a hospital patient information system by struggling to evaluate it: a committee's journal."(J. Schulman, G.J. Kuperman, A. Kharbanda, & R. Kaushal, 2007)

Of equal importance to understanding first principles that underpin the work of healthcare is an understanding of first principles for designing IT to aid that work. One such principle is the notion of a problem space – discussed in the committee's journal, later in this chapter. This chapter begins by examining additional foundational principles of IT design. These include the notion of a cognitive tool; exactly which information elements one ought to pay attention to; considerations for selecting among representational options so as to facilitate solving an information management problem; the vital importance of explicitly conceptualizing the bulk of the daily work in order to deftly manage it via database technology; and the idea that our tools generally determine how we think and work.

COGNITIVE TOOLS

IT is a cognitive tool. A cognitive tool is an artifact to represent and express what one knows; it may even help one to discover new knowledge. It is intended to aid human cognitive processing,(Jonassen) to extend and facilitate what one could otherwise achieve unaided. The point of such a tool is not to relieve health care providers of the actual task of cognitive processing, but to *extend* providers' cognitive abilities. Users should be able to process more information than if they had no tool. Note that whether or not such a tool is available, providers must think deeply about the information at hand. The tool should promote deeper, more critical reflection and help the user discover relevant ideas that might have been missed without the tool. Rather than solely make the current task array easier, cognitive tools should enable the user to perform additional tasks that were always pertinent to the work but otherwise unfeasible.(Jonassen) Moreover, since the truly intelligent system is the user – not the tool, the tool ought to be largely controlled by the user. In contrast, all too commonly current technology imposes constraints on exactly how the user may formulate and think about a problem.

WHICH ELEMENTS OF THE DAILY WORK SHALL WE ATTEND TO?

One way to think about IT as a tool to facilitate the daily clinical work – which largely entails formulating and solving problems – is to decompose the work into its component processes:(Robertson, Elliot, & Washington, 2007)

1. Seeking information
2. Presenting information
3. Organizing knowledge

Thus, IT affects cognition and ultimately action because it frames the way its users think. How does this happen? From a user perspective, a particular database software implementation is essentially a template of blanks to be filled in or to be viewed. Each template directs attention to particular aspects of work (formulating and solving problems) and to particular data elements – and discounts or ignores others. Templates underpin not only healthcare database software but also similarly intended word processor or spreadsheet applications; and to some extent, templates also underpin the mental models of providers who manage their patient information with pen and paper. In any case, rather than reflecting the real importance of the selected data elements, the framing and focus of such templates may derive from what is readily measured or represented or from what decision makers determine based on legacy and/or accepted belief. For some IT implementations, the framing and focus may be apropos for specific types of patients or pathophysiological conditions, but it may be uniformly applied to an inappropriately wide range of patients and conditions.

DOES HOW WE REPRESENT WHAT WE PAY ATTENTION TO, MATTER?

Whatever the framing and focus of an IT implementation, it amounts to a specific representational system; a map of the reality over which it is hoped the tool will provide greater mastery. Such a system includes:(Norman, 1993)

1. That which is to be represented
2. That which does the representing; symbols

This map – whether represented in consciousness or in a cognitive tool such as a database software application – must itself exist as a representation: a metarepresentation.(Norman, 1993) It is the meta-representation – the mental model of reality – that one tends to reflect upon.(Norman, 1993) Very importantly, often more than one way exists to represent the selected aspect of reality. So it is central to evaluative thinking to ask: How does one choose among the possibilities?

The answer entails evaluating the suitability of each representation for solving the associated problem. In the words of popular wisdom, "there's more than one way to skin a cat." It turns out that a problem's difficulty and its very nature are related to its representational or meta-representational specifics. This abstract idea becomes concrete and much clearer after considering two games: one called "15," and the second, the well-known "tic tac toe."(Guerlain, Hayes, Pritchett, & Smith, 2001; Norman, 1993)

The game of "15": Two players may select, without replacement, any of the nine digits – 1, 2, 3, 4, 5, 6, 7, 8, 9. A player may take one digit in turn. The aim is to be the first player to get any three digits that add up to 15.

Consider this game scenario:(Norman, 1993) Player A selects 8. Player B selects 2. On the second round, A selects 4 and B selects 3. On round three, A selects 5; now, what digit should B select next? Please pause and try to answer the question.

Most people find this a difficult problem to solve. It produces cognitive overload. Tasks include mentally keeping track of game rules; which player selected which digit; which digits remain; and which remaining combination is preferred: both players' numbers must be added in various combinations of three digits and then one must decide either to block the opponent or advance toward winning.

Now consider a second game.

The game of "tic tac toe": Most readers know this game from childhood. Played on a 3 X 3 matrix, the aim is to be the first player to position three identical symbols – either X's or O's – in a straight line.

Consider this game scenario: Player A uses X symbols and Player B uses O symbols. Figure 1 shows the game at round number 3; now, where should Player B place an O next? Again, please pause to answer the question.

Most readers (and children) find this problem easy to solve. They quickly determine that Player B should place an O in the lower right cell (Table 1).

Why does "15" seem difficult and "tic tac toe" easy? It is because the way the information about the "tic tac toe" game is represented enables one

Table 1. Game scenario (Norman, 1993)

X	O	X
	X	
O		

to see the solution "at a glance." No memory and little additional reflection are needed. In contrast, "15" as represented above provides no memory or other information processing aids.

But "15" need not be so difficult a game. As mentioned earlier, often more than one way exists to represent an aspect of reality; and that a task's difficulty and its very nature are related to its representation or meta-representation. The game "15" may be represented differently, graphically, as if it were "tic tac toe." Imagine that player A and Player B played "15" such that they arranged the available digits as though they were X's and O's in "tic tac toe." The upper portion of Table 2 illustrates one possible configuration reflecting the earlier game scenario:(Norman, 1993)

After referring to the matrix in the upper portion of Table 2 and the game in play in the lower right, it's readily apparent that the digit Player B should select on round three is 6, in the lower right cell. The lower left portion of Table 2 highlights the parallel with "tic tac toe."

PROBLEM ISOMORPHS

The games of "15" and "tic tac toe" illustrate a key first principle for healthcare IT design, the notion of problem isomorphs.(Norman, 1993; Simon, 1996) In each game, the problem, the essential question to be answered, is actually the same. The tasks involved in answering the essential question, and the attendant difficulty, differ greatly because of how the relevant aspect of reality was represented. For either "tic tac toe" or "15," graphically representing the information as the matrix illustrated in Figure 2 aids the player by providing some "external memory."(Guerlain et al., 2001) Note, however, that for a given problem the preferred representational choice may depend on whether a person or a computer is doing the data processing. Although it is easier for a person to solve "15" when graphically represented, it is easier for a computer to do so when it is arithmetically represented.(Norman, 1993) It is easier for a person to solve "tic tac toe" when spatially represented. However, many people would find it much more complicated and unintuitive to write a computer program for solving "tic tac toe."(Norman, 1993) Thus, optimal representation

Table 2. Player A's selections are bold; Player B's selections are in Italics

4	3	8
9	5	1
2	7	6

X	*O*	**X**
	X	
O		

4	*3*	**8**
	5	
2		

depends on the available knowledge that may be brought to bear, the problem-solving algorithm applied, and the performance characteristics of the computational system.

The great variation in healthcare and the way it is documented, often with little association to outcomes (Blumenthal, 1994; The Center for the Evaluative Clinical Sciences, 1998), suggests that the notion of problem isomorphs could be beneficial to usefully conceptualizing healthcare and evaluating healthcare IT. Eddy observed that "When different physicians are recommending different things for essentially the same patients, it is impossible to claim that they are all doing the right thing."(Eddy, 2005) Here is one elementary illustration of the relevance of problem isomorphs to healthcare IT evaluation. To answer a question or solve a problem, an IT user often must navigate among several windows on a computer monitor. This forces the user to rely on human memory and cancels some of the machine potential for leveraging recall. (Think again about the experience of playing the arithmetically represented game of "15.") In some software applications, once a particular view has opened the user can't go back to check another with related information without losing information already entered on the current screen view. Imagine how helpful it would be for clinicians if a specific array of data elements particularly pertinent to a patient's problem profile was available on a single screen view – something like the graphically represented game of "15."

In summary:

1. Try to discriminate bad representations that produce a cognitive quagmire from good representations that can point to the answer
2. Recognize that the very concept of the problem to be solved may change when workers have cognitive tools that expand their perceptual capability, their memory, and their computational skills

When the only tool you have is a hammer, everything looks like a nail ~Abraham Maslow

CAN WE RECOGNIZE IT SUCCESS WHEN WE LOOK AT IT?

Success vs. Failure: Is the Glass Half Empty or Half Full? (Reprinted from Schulman, 2006. Used with permission)

Van Der Meijden et al reviewed publications between 1991 and 2001 that evaluated inpatient information systems requiring data entry and retrieval by health care professionals.(Van Der Meijden, Tange, Troost, & Hasman, 2003) They found a plethora of studies extensively describing system failures but could find no study that explicitly defined system success. Indeed, health information systems are rather prone to failing. (Littlejohns, Wyatt, & Garvician, 2003) One fundamental for learning from an information system failure is to disentangle user resistance to change(Rogers, 1995) from suboptimal technical solutions. Those who protest the changes occurring in patient information technology must come to see that the real choice does not include the status quo.(Department of Health, 2002; Dick, Steen, Detmer, & eds., 1997) (Thompson & Brailer, 2004) Bearing in mind that user acceptance need not imply a problem successfully solved, see Lorenzi and Riley(Lorenzi & Riley, 2000) for a review of individual and organizational factors that influence people to accept new information technology.

Success/Failure Permutations

It is probably clear by now that "How to recognize IT success?" begs other questions: How well have the representations been matched to the tasks? Are the correct tasks being performed – how does one know? A variety of possibilities are possible:

1. A well-conceived and/or implemented software application of an adequately conceptualized work reality
2. A well-conceived and/or implemented software application of an inadequately conceptualized work reality
3. A poorly-conceived and/or implemented software application of an adequately conceptualized work reality
4. A poorly-conceived and/or implemented software application of an inadequately conceptualized work reality

A substantial portion of healthcare IT shortcomings may derive from the current work reality and how it is conceptualized.(C. Nemeth & Cook, 2005; C. P. Nemeth, Cook, & Woods, 2004) The daily work of healthcare may appear to unfold smoothly, but only because clinicians are doing many thing to make it appear so. Closer examination reveals an exceedingly complicated, vague, variable, inconsistent, and fast-paced reality.(C. Nemeth & Cook, 2005) Experienced clinicians know that clinical processes may be implicit or even ad hoc – and vary with each patient.(Joseph Schulman, 2004) These realities of under-conceptualization and procedural anarchy are "hiding in plain sight."(C. Nemeth & Cook, 2005) Those who cannot recognize what is actually unfolding before them cannot understand the work as it truly is and therefore cannot create appropriately supportive cognitive tools.(C. Nemeth & Cook, 2005) What is needed to move beyond this difficulty is to apply to healthcare IT cognitive engineering methods and meticulous observation of the clinical work as it actually is – in distinction to what workers would like to imagine it is.

A perhaps contrasting view is expressed in an intriguingly titled article, "Designs are hypotheses about how artifacts shape cognition and collaboration."(Woods, 1998) The author appears to assume that software designers begin with an adequately conceptualized work reality (possibilities #1 and #3 in the above list). He makes two points. First, our tools determine how we think and work – and how we do these things with our co-workers. Secondly, an implemented design's actual performance in aiding cognition and collaboration must be explicitly tested. Of course, testing the design hypothesis requires data describing appropriate outcome variables and predictor variables. This, in turn, requires a conceptual framework for that which we wish the tool to help us with.

Are we trapped in a conundrum of determining whether the chicken or the egg comes first? Here is how one group saw their way out.

DISCOVERING HOW TO THINK ABOUT A HOSPITAL PATIENT INFORMATION SYSTEM BY STRUGGLING TO EVALUATE IT: A COMMITTEE'S JOURNAL (REPRINTED FROM SCHULMAN, KUPERMAN, KHARBANDA, & KAUSHAL, 2007. USED WITH PERMISSION)

Alice came to a fork in the road. "Which road do I take?" she asked. "Where do you want to go?" responded the Cheshire cat. "I don't know," Alice answered. "Then," said the cat, "it doesn't matter." ~Lewis Carroll, Alice in Wonderland

As organizations transition from paper to electronic media for storing and managing patient information, front-line clinicians experience disquieting feelings that may range between vague distress and profound disruption of their world. These clinicians face "dilemmas of transformation in the age of the smart machine."(Zuboff, 1988) We think it is crucial that all involved in this transformation strive for clarity in understanding how technology restructures the work situation, how a computer-based patient information system can "abstract thought from action"(Zuboff,

1988) – not only automate but also *informate* (Zuboff, 1988) – reveal activities, events, entities, ideas, and information to some degree previously opaque; and how work tasks, work flow, and tools dynamically interact.

Hospital information technology (IT) committees represent a part of an organization's strategy for crossing the chasm separating the culture of paper media and the culture of electronic media. (Healthcare Information and Management Systems Society, 2006; Shortliffe, 2005; Wyatt, 1995) These committees commonly include front-line clinicians. These individuals may have little experience with either the potential or the pitfalls of the technology over which they adjudicate, and little experience in how to critically think about the issues. To draw attention to this aspect of the unfolding transformation and contribute to the conversation about how to make sense of it, we summarize our committee's early experience.

In the Beginning, the Task Seemed So Clear

We work at a large academic hospital. Our committee is comprised of administrators, clinicians including physicians, nurses and pharmacists, and IT specialists. Our charge is to improve our inpatient clinical IT systems by determining: desirable features for our electronic patient information management system; how to minimize work disruption during system implementation; and how to evaluate the consequences of replacing the previous technology. In particular, we were asked to suggest exactly what to measure in order to determine whether the IT system is successful. At the outset, this seemed rather straightforward to many members. So at the first meeting the group quickly crafted a list of "short term goals." These included assembling an inventory of resources from which we could obtain evaluation data, planning to assess the medical error reporting system for IT related events, and conducting an IT user survey.

Stepping Back

Then one of us spoke up. "These aren't goals. They're tasks. Before deciding what to do (task), shouldn't we say exactly what we want to achieve (goal)? For example, depending on our goal, we might prefer to track trigger events (sentinel metrics (Resar, Rozich, & Classen, 2003)) instead of analyzing data from the medical error reporting system."

Several of the clinicians, understandably, conceptualized the committee work as they do their clinical work. After a patient's history, physical exam, and ancillary data are presented on rounds, they often immediately rattle off the next lab studies and images to obtain. If pressed on this issue, they say they're so accustomed to their work that in the blink of an eye they (implicitly) determine the goals those labs and images are intended to promote. However, test this assertion by asking: "If the laboratory tests and images you need – for instance, a CBC, CRP, and a chest X-ray – provide the answers you seek, then precisely what is the question these answers inform?" Some workers simply respond with a puzzled look, some will articulate a reply; but the replies tend to vary among respondents – and infrequently are they framed as questions. Rarely, someone will articulate the question the studies, the "answers," indeed inform: "What is the estimated probability my patient has condition *x*, given the results of these studies?" Activity without clarity of purpose may be activity without value. If the estimated probability that a patient has condition *x*, given confirmatory study results, does not exceed a threshold value justifying the benefits/risks of treatment, the studies, the "answers," are unnecessary. Similarly, evaluation data should only be collected if they help to answer a specific question designed to explicitly probe goal achievement.

Identification of Purpose

At our next meeting, we tried again to articulate what we wanted to accomplish over the short-term: 1) We want to identify existing data sources that can inform evaluation of our work and to understand the sources' strengths and weaknesses. 2) As a foundation for evaluation, we want to enumerate the intended consequences of the current IT implementations and discover some of the unintended consequences. Although in hindsight #1 was still quite vague and #2 essentially stated that the goal was to create a list of goals, we pressed on.

"What are we trying to achieve in the long term?" 1) We want to be able to describe the effects of our clinical interventions, including otherwise unapparent effects we would not know of without analyzing aggregated patient data. 2) We want to use the potential of IT to improve the care we provide.

This sounded pretty good. Even so, we acknowledged the imprecision by following with the question embedded in our committee's charge: "How do we define success – how will we know when we have achieved these goals?" We did not appreciate at the time, that the idea we began to grapple with might be more usefully conceived as a continuous variable, a spectrum of "doing a good job," rather than binary, success/failure. (Aarts, Doorewaard, & Berg, 2004) Nor did we appreciate the need to operationally define "doing a good job"; or that crafting this definition was at the core of our measurement task; nor the need to consider the multiple evaluative perspectives from which achievement might be framed, for example, the committee's, the clinical staff's, the IT department, the organization. We did appreciate that answering the question entailed developing evaluative criteria for our information management tool, along with evaluative criteria for our clinical performance.

We were starting to get it: identifying what we measure comes *after* developing a clear, explicitly articulated idea of what we're trying to achieve. This idea of what we're trying to achieve must do more than sound lofty and laudable. It must describe what the system is to be about at the core. Without such clarity, we'd ultimately just collect lots of data without gaining knowledge. By this formulation we recognized too, that our work was enmeshed with that of another committee charged with developing clinical performance metrics. Although we actually were back where we started, we sensed that we could now make a more informed choice about the path to take.

Broad Goals

In discussing candidate goals, members indicated that IT was important because it represented a means for reducing errors. So we scrutinized a widely accepted definition of error:

"... all those occasions in which a planned sequence of mental or physical activities fails to achieve its intended outcome, and when these failures cannot be attributed to the intervention of some chance agency."(Reason, 1990)

Clearly, we needed to achieve much more conceptual clarity and specify our ideas in greater detail. The notion of error makes no sense until we precisely identify the intended outcome, i.e. the goal of the activity.

Our deliberations also led us to Norman's (Norman, 1993) and Zuboff's (Zuboff, 1988) notion of IT as a cognitive tool – something that should make us smarter than we are without it. Therefore, taking account of the various users at our hospital, we pondered how to think about the main features this cognitive tool should offer.

Herbert Simon helped point the way:

"Solving a problem simply means representing it so as to make the solution transparent ... a problem space in which the search for the solution can take place ... Focus of attention is the key to success – focusing on the particular features of the situation

that are relevant to the problem, then building a problem space containing these features but omitting the irrelevant ones." (Simon, 1996)

A new candidate goal and associated evaluative criteria were revealed. Now we asked, "To what extent does our tool aid in creating a productive problem space?"

By now, most of us had completely forgotten that we initially thought the committee's charge could be straightforwardly dispatched. We understood that it was so complex we must break it up into more manageable chunks. We identified broad categories within which to articulate hospital IT goals and problems

- Business, i.e. billing and collections
- Regulatory compliance
- Reporting
- Patient documentation
- Electronic prescribing
- Decision support and other cognitive enhancements
- Referrals
- Clinical performance evaluation and quality improvement
    - Exposure-outcome relationships
- Patient registries
- Workflow and efficiency

Criteria for Measures

We were beginning to share the view that collecting data is merely the tip of the iceberg that is IT measurement. Data collection is buoyed by a body of explicit performance questions whose answers have potential to advance our purpose. Proposed measures must plausibly inform those answers by withstanding rigorous and uniform scrutiny:

- What dimension of IT use or patient care does this measure inform us about?
    - With what overarching aim does this dimension resonate? That is, if a list of explicit aims and a fine-grained process map of our entire enterprise were spread before us, precisely which aim and process component(s) does this measure enable us to associate?
        - Such measurement activity should both derive from, and test hypotheses about causal sequences
- What results do we expect, i.e. what is our hypothesis?
- How would we interpret results that might be displayed? (This entails working with fabricated, "dummy data," during planning.)
- What might we do differently once we know this thing?
- What target performance range do we seek to achieve for this measurement variable?

This interrogative framework depends on clear notions of purpose, intended outcomes. However, systems may produce surprises: unintended, undesired outcomes. How might the committee learn about unintended consequences of IT? We discovered another daunting challenge. Sometimes, we wouldn't know in advance what to look for; even worse, we might not recognize what we were looking at after it occurred. As a first step, we would measure unintended IT consequences via some type of user survey. Practical considerations required that we draw a sample from all users. Therefore, we would have to determine how to sample. Our thoughts increasingly reflected our experience: "First, we should discuss detailed, explicit aims of the survey. That way, we'll have a clearer idea of what to do. For example, if one aim is to gain insight to whether responses might be biased by user's experience with antecedent technology, we might consider including complementary "fly-on-wall" observers' reports."

Learning from Others

We considered the wide range of IT already implemented – for which corresponding goals often appeared to be implicit at best. And we considered the practical reality that committee members could devote only a small fraction of their total work time to this effort. It seemed sensible to develop ever-more fine-grained goals in conjunction with accumulating insights via learning from what others have done in these areas. That is, we would start with others' evaluative frameworks, reflect on the goals they (at least implicitly) seek to establish, and over time, refine our own concept of our goals and how we determine that we achieve them.

We drew heavily from the excellent overview of Ash, Berg, and Coiera (Ash, Berg, & Coiera, 2004) to draft an extensive conceptual framework for probing clinicians' experience using our institution's patient information management system (Box 1). The work/tool interaction section of Box 1 merits additional discussion. The content and flow of the daily work – the tasks constituting the means of achieving the (hopefully explicit) aims – reflect what is possible and practical at the time. The tools are designed to facilitate the work, and similarly reflect what is possible and practical at the time. Thus the notion of what constitutes the daily work, operationally framed, varies over time. Note that the aims of the daily work tend to be more stable than the tasks selected to achieve the aims. To illustrate, in the days of paper-based patient records, clinicians would never dream of instantly computing a patient's post-test probability of a particular disease as soon as a test result is reported. Today, this is indeed possible. Although such Bayesian computation was always consistent with the aims of clinical work, it may become part of the daily work when it is possible and practical.

Our Revelation

The essential point is that clinical work and tools are calibrated to each other. If a tool is changed, the work flow and/or fine structure it is intended to support must necessarily change. (Aarts et al., 2004) Thus, stakeholders must consider as an aspect of progress the need to recalibrate work flow and/or fine structure to new tools' capabilities; ever mindful of the aims that motivate the work. A tool achieving quick user acceptance may be one that makes little use of its technological potential and correspondingly less likely to advance the goals or justify the investment. The "aha moment" arrives with the understanding that preserving existing problem solving approaches that suppress evident potential for more effectively and/or efficiently advancing the goals is antithetical to progress. A problem space with which workers are comfortable may, when new tasks are enabled, be rendered suboptimal. Therefore, in the context of the goals of the enterprise, we define user acceptance as a result of judging not a new tool in isolation, but a new work/tool dyad. A short "test drive" yields an answer to the wrong question.

Workers long accustomed to a particular way of working may have difficulty imagining new ways made possible by tools that enable things they never dreamed of. Indeed, workers may be unaware that their early opinions about new tools reflect their imposing the specifics of the previous work/tool interaction on the present one. To further illustrate this important idea of dynamically calibrating work and tools to each other, we invited members to consider this question: "If all you had to do was ask for it, what do you wish your patient information management tool could do?"

- Serve me new and relevant information without my having to open a specific patient's record – the information system should "find me" when necessary

- Support Bayesian decision making (compute post-test disease probability)
- Enable me to access it remotely (from home)
- Configure multiple windows into one coherent display, as I deem necessary
- Optimize the problem space in relation to the nature of the problem, rather than the same configuration for every patient
- Facilitate communication among consultants
- Improve communication efficiency; minimize interactions and interruptions
    - Communicate with other involved providers from within a patient record
        - Document communication and results
    - Prevent duplication of efforts, prevent memory lapse
- Promote an explicit list of patient-specific goals for the day, articulated as part of daily patient rounds
- Support a shared to-do list among all care providers

The point of this invitation was to illuminate the way one's conceptualization of work is molded by one's notion of what is possible. The aim was to highlight contrasts: the difference between the items enumerated on a current task list and a potential ideal task list; the gap between the way tasks are done and potentially more efficient/effective alternatives enabled by technological advancement. Pondering such contrasts promotes creativity in formulating a problem space and solution. (Simon, 1996) Although the invitation was not intended to encourage user expectations with which tool builders could not keep up, some low level of discord appears desirable for stoking the flame of continual improvement.

Lessons We Learned

In conclusion, although evaluating a clinical IT implementation is a daunting challenge, it is central to managing the organization. IT evaluation should be founded upon explicit understanding of the goals of the enterprise – *necessarily the first step in the process*, appreciating the incessant work/tool interaction, and expecting that these change over time. This view thus calls for:

- Persuading the user community that their choices do not include the status quo
- Discriminating user resistance to change from suboptimal technical solutions(Rogers, 1995; J. Schulman, 2006)
- Appreciating that user acceptance need not imply a problem successfully solved(Lorenzi & Riley, 2000; J. Schulman, 2006)
- Setting realistic expectations; understanding that early iterations of a solution may produce only tolerable or promising results, i.e. it is impossible to anticipate every issue that will arise after implementation.(J. Schulman, 2006)
- Appreciating that the appropriate evaluative study design may be a matter of controversy. Randomized controlled trials, though a gold-standard for discriminating an intervention effect, are typically infeasible. Some outcomes may not even be quantifiable; however, they may be analyzed using widely accepted qualitative methods.(Stoop, Heathfield, de Mul, & Berg, 2004)
- Periodically re-thinking the boundaries and elements of the problem space

Daunting as IT evaluation may be, it is unavoidable because, as our story illustrates, it is central

Box 1. Conceptual framework for probing clinicians' experience using a patient information management system

Dimension of IT tool use: Work Flow

- Data entry
  - Do we impose perceived additional work tasks?
  - Is information displayed in a visual format that facilitates the task?
    - Fonts
    - Background color
    - Content structure
- Data retrieval
  - Individual patients
  - Aggregates of patients
  - How soon after creation is a record available?
- Interruptions: when distracted by a competing task, do users lose track of thoughts and where they were in the record by the time they return to it or does the tool remember for them?
- System response time; down time
- Ease of system access
- Feature navigation: ease, and possibility to toggle between features
- Juxtaposition error: is a data element so close to something else on the screen that the wrong option may easily be clicked or an item read in error?
- Have users devised workarounds? That is, have users devised strategies and tactics enabling them to live with the system despite demands they deem unrealistic, inefficient, or harmful?
- To what extent does this tool promote entering information only once, but enable presenting it in varied contexts?

Dimension of IT tool use: Cognitive enhancement/impedance

- Does this tool overwhelm users (cause cognitive overload) by overemphasizing
  - structured and ''complete'' information entry
  - alerts and reminders
  - If so, please provide detailed explanation
- Does this tool cleave information that belongs together, forcing users to switch between different screens, so that users feel deprived of the overview desired?
  - If so, please provide detailed explanation
- Standard phrases
  - Are readability and information value of reports diminished by over-use of standard phrases?
    - Does the availability of these standard phrases discourage users' composing thoughts and crafting meaning?
    - As users read a narrative, is understanding sometimes confounded by uncertainty whether a sentence or clause represents thoughtful word use – a spot-on description; or merely a conveniently available selection – a more or less apropos description?
- Have others over-used cut and paste or copy and paste text manipulation?
  - Redundant information
  - Inaccurate information
- Are data provided as abstract cues, or do they contain sufficient context to establish their referential function?(Zuboff, 1988)
- Do users feel they function more as data entry workers or as knowledge workers?
  - Do users feel their identity as a professional has changed by using this tool?
    - If so, how?
- To what extent does this tool draw out users' intellect in working with the data and aid their creating meaning from it?(Zuboff, 1988)

Dimension of IT tool use: Communication

- To what extent do users think that another professional reviewing their entry will grasp the essence of what they intended to communicate?
  - Do users think that "entering" their contribution to the patient record replaces their previous means of initiating and communicating their plans?
  - Have users noticed a change in the amount of direct interaction among physicians, nurses, and pharmacy?
    - If so, in what direction?
      - Is this perceived to be in their patient's and their interests?
  - Has overall reliance on the computer system as a source of answers to clinical questions increased, decreased, or stayed the same?

Box 1. Continued

Dimension of IT tool use: Work/tool interaction
Does the tool seem to
- Speed or slow the daily work?
- Make users feel smarter or dumber?
- Force users to change the way they think?
  - About the patient
  - About the work
  - If so, is the change good or bad?
- What do users need that they're not getting?
- What are users getting that they don't need?
- For each of the above, exactly how has the user determined this?

to healthcare. Fortunately, as we engage with the challenge we become increasingly energized. We urge others to serve on committees such as ours because the rewards of this arduous, often frustrating, endeavor are nothing less than greater clarity about the essence of our work in healthcare, greater mastery in achieving its purpose, and a greater sense of meaning in our daily tasks.

CONCLUSION

Evaluating healthcare IT and understanding the work of healthcare are entangled processes because clinical work and associated information management tools are calibrated to each other. The point of such tools is to extend providers' cognitive abilities: promote deeper, more critical reflection, and help the user discover relevant ideas that might have been missed without the tool; all the while speeding the flow of the component tasks constituting the daily work. However, healthcare IT can aid providers in their work only to the extent that providers and IT designers understand *exactly* what the work is to achieve and by what means. Lofty and laudable-sounding goals generally are uninformative for IT design. Explicit, operationally defined goals; work tasks designed to efficiently and effectively achieve the goals; and clear ideas of what is meant by "efficiently" and "effectively"; these are the prerequisites for evaluative thinking.

Since one's concept of work is molded by one's notion of what is possible, the work of healthcare and IT tools to facilitate it exist in a dynamic, changeable relationship. This relationship resembles the evolutionary dynamic between biological organisms and their complex and ever-changing environment. The concept of a successful organism is meaningless without a specified environmental context. As that environment changes – and indeed it continually changes – so does the evaluative framework for determining what constitutes success.

REFERENCES

Aarts, J., Doorewaard, H., & Berg, M. (2004). Understanding Implementation: The case of a computerized physician order entry system in a large Dutch university medical center. *Journal of the American Medical Informatics Association, 11*(3), 207–216. doi:10.1197/jamia.M1372

Ash, J. S., Berg, M., & Coiera, E. (2004). Some unintended consequences of information technology in healthcare: The nature of patient care information system-related errors. *Journal of the American Medical Informatics Association, 11*(2), 104–112. doi:10.1197/jamia.M1471

Blumenthal, D. (1994). The variation phenomenon in 1994. *The New England Journal of Medicine, 331*(15), 1017–1018. doi:10.1056/NEJM199410133311511

Department of Health. (2002). *Delivering 21st century IT support for the NHS: National specification for integrated care records service*. Retrieved on July 26, 2004, from http://www.dh.gov.uk/assetRoot/04/07/16/76/04071676.pdf

Dick, R. S., Steen, E. B., & Detmer, D. E. (Eds.). (1997). *The computer-based patient record: An essential technology for healthcare* (revised ed.). National Academy Press.

Eddy, D. M. (2005). Evidence-based medicine: A unified approach. *Health Affairs, 24*(1), 9–17. doi:10.1377/hlthaff.24.1.9

Guerlain, S., Hayes, C., Pritchett, A., & Smith, P. (2001). Exercises/techniques for teaching cognitive systems engineering. In *Proceedings of the Human Factors and Ergonomics Society 45th Annual Meeting*.

Healthcare Information and Management Systems Society. (2006). *A desire for change: Strong leadership required in the EMR-EHR Revolution*. Retrieved on May 23, 2007, from http://www.himss.org/content/files/davies/Davies_WP_Leadership.pdf

Jonassen, D. H. *Technology as cognitive tools: Learners as designers*. Retrieved in 2007, from http://itech1.coe.uga.edu/itforum/paper1/paper1.html

Littlejohns, P., Wyatt, J. C., & Garvician, L. (2003). Evaluating computerised health information systems: Hard lessons still to be learnt. *British Medical Journal, 326*, 860–863. doi:10.1136/bmj.326.7394.860

Lorenzi, N. M., & Riley, R. T. (2000). Managing change: An overview. *Journal of the American Medical Informatics Association, 7*(2), 116–124.

Nemeth, C., & Cook, R. (2005). Hiding in plain sight: What Koppel et al. tell us about healthcare IT. *Journal of Biomedical Informatics, 38*, 262-263. doi:10.1016/j.jbi.2005.05.010

Nemeth, C. P., Cook, R. I., & Woods, D. D. (2004). The messy details: Insights from the study of technical work in healthcare. *IEEE Transactions on Systems, Man, and Cybernetics, 34*, 689–692. doi:10.1109/TSMCA.2004.836802

Norman, D. A. (1993). *Things that make us smart*. Cambridge, MA: Perseus Books.

Reason, J. (1990). *Human error*. Cambridge, UK: Cambridge University Press.

Resar, R., Rozich, J., & Classen, D. (2003). Methodology and rationale for the measurement of harm with trigger tools. *Quality & Safety in Health Care, 12*(6), 39–45.

Robertson, B., Elliot, L., & Washington, D. (2007, October 3). Cognitive tools. *Emerging perspectives on learning, teaching, and technology.* Retrieved on December 3, 2007, from http://projects.coe.uga.edu/epltt/index.php?title=Cognitive_Tools

Rogers, E. M. (1995). *Diffusion of innovations, fourth ed.* New York: The Free Press.

Schulman, J. (2004). *Evaluating the processes of neonatal intensive care*. London: BMJ Books.

Schulman, J. (2006). *Managing your patients' data in the neonatal and pediatric ICU: An introduction to databases and statistical analysis*. Oxford, UK: Blackwell.

Schulman, J., Kuperman, G. J., Kharbanda, A., & Kaushal, R. (2007). Discovering how to think about a hospital patient information system by struggling to evaluate it: A committee's journal. *Journal of the American Medical Informatics Association, 14*(5), 537–541. doi:10.1197/jamia.M2436

Schulman, J., Kuperman, G. J., Kharbanda, A., & Kaushal, R. (2007). Discovering how to think about a hospital patient information system by struggling to evaluate it: A committee's journal. *Journal of the American Medical Informatics Association, 14*(5), 537–541. doi:10.1197/jamia.M2436

Shortliffe, E. H. (2005). Strategic action in health information technology: Why the obvious has taken so long. *Health Affairs, 24*(5), 1222–1233. doi:10.1377/hlthaff.24.5.1222

Simon, H. A. (1996). *The sciences of the artificial.* Cambridge, MA: The MIT Press.

Stoop, A., Heathfield, H., de Mul, M., & Berg, M. (2004). Evaluation of patient care information systems: theory and practice. In M. Berg, E. Coiera, H. Heathfield, et al. (Eds.), *Health information management* (pp. 206-229). London: Routledge.

The Center for the Evaluative Clinical Sciences. D. M. S. (1998). *The Dartmouth atlas of healthcare 1998.* Chicago: American Hospital Publishing.

Thompson, T. G., & Brailer, D. J. (2004). *The decade of health information technology: Delivering consumer-centric and information-rich healthcare.* Retrieved on July 23, 2004, from http://www.hhs.gov/onchit/framework/hitframework.pdf

Van Der Meijden, M. J., Tange, H. J., Troost, J., & Hasman, A. (2003). Determinents of success of inpatient clinical information systems: A literature review. *Journal of the American Medical Informatics Association, 10*(3), 235–243. doi:10.1197/jamia.M1094

Woods, D. D. (1998). Designs are hypotheses about how artifacts shape cognition and collaboration. *Ergonomics, 41*(2), 168–173. doi:10.1080/001401398187215

Wyatt, J. C. (1995). Hospital information management: the need for clinical leadership. *BMJ (Clinical Research Ed.), 311*, 175–178.

Zuboff, S. (1988). *In the age of the smart machine: The future of work and power.* New York: Basic Books.

KEY TERMS AND DEFINITIONS

Cognitive Tool: an artifact to represent and express what one knows; intended to aid human cognitive processing, to extend and facilitate what one could otherwise achieve unaided.

Electronic Information Management Technology (IT): typically, a database software application (less sophisticated implementations occur in word-processing or spreadsheet software) running on some configuration of computer hardware

Goal, Aim, Purpose: That which one seeks to achieve via a particular work operation; a desired result.

IT Evaluation: the process of determining the degree to which an IT implementation facilitates the work of an individual or organization

Meta-Representation: the representation of the representational system – the explicit map of the portion of reality of interest. Reflection on the chosen map of reality actually tends to occur upon the meta-representation – the mental model of reality.

Patient Information Management System: a data management system that facilitates processing of patient information

Problem Isomorph: a single problem can be stated in various ways, and often therefore can be variously represented. The particular representation, or problem isomorph, can influence the difficulty of solving the problem.

Problem Space: the collection of possible information configurations and actions that may transform them, in order to advance toward a goal; i.e. the circumstances within which the search for the solution to a problem can take place.

Problem Solving: the process of moving from a starting point in the problem space to the goal.

Representational System: a map of the reality over which it is hoped the associated cognitive tool will provide greater mastery. Such a system includes both that which is to be represented and that which does the representing – symbols.

Task: one of a set of actions – specific steps in a process – contributing to achieving a goal.

Chapter 3
Interactive Sociotechnical Analysis:
Identifying and Coping with Unintended Consequences of IT Implementation

Michael I. Harrison
Agency for Healthcare Research and Quality, USA

Ross Koppel
University of Pennsylvania, USA

ABSTRACT

Many unintended and undesired consequences of healthcare information technologies (HIT) are generated by interactions between newly introduced HIT and the existing healthcare organization's sociotechnical system--its workflows, culture, social interactions, physical environment, and technologies. This chapter presents and illustrates a model of these interactions that we call interactive sociotechnical analysis (ISTA). ISTA places special emphasis on recursive processes (i.e., feedback loops that alter the uses of the newly introduced HIT) promote second-level changes in the social system, and sometimes lead to changes in the new HIT systems themselves. We discuss ISTA's implications for improving HIT implementation practices and suggest how clinicians, IT specialists, and managers can better anticipate likely consequences of introducing HIT; more effectively diagnose unforeseeable consequences which emerge during implementation; and better respond to these emerging consequences.

INTRODUCTION

Electronic Health Records (EMR), Computerized Physician Order Entry (CPOE), and Decision Support Systems (DSS) promise to contribute substantially to the quality of care (Bates, 2005; Chaudhry et al., 2006; Shamliyan, 2007). Nonetheless, implementation of these types of Health Information Technology (HIT) in the United States has fallen far short of this promise and has often produced disappointing results (Blumenthal & Glaser, 2007; Crosson et al., 2007; Fitzhenry et al., 2007; Grossman, Gerland, Reed, & Fahlman, 2007; Linder, Ma, Bates, Middleton, & Stafford, 2007; Chaudhry et al., 2006; Sidorov, 2006). Some HIT projects have been scaled back or abandoned altogether (Conn, 2007).

DOI: 10.4018/978-1-60566-030-1.ch003

Many of these disappointments reflect undesired and unanticipated consequences that emerge during the HIT's implementation (Ash, Sittig, Poon et al., 2007). In an earlier paper we traced common, unanticipated consequences to five types of sociotechnical interactions among new HIT and the provider organization's existing social and technical systems -- including workflows, culture, social interactions, physical infrastructure, and technologies (Harrison, Koppel, & Bar-Lev, 2007). In that paper we presented the main types of interactions in a conceptual framework (or model) we call Interactive Sociotechnical Analysis (ISTA),

This chapter starts with a review of ISTA's background and its main features. Then, drawing on published studies and on our and others' observations, we provide an array of illustrations of unintended consequences that arose from the processes depicted in the ISTA model. There follows a discussion of ISTA's implications for improving HIT implementation practices. In particular we suggest ways in which clinicians (i.e., physicians and nurses), IT specialists, and managers can better anticipate the likely consequences of HIT implementation; more effectively diagnose unforeseeable consequences which emerge during implementation; and better respond to these emerging consequences.

BACKGROUND

Studies of Unintended Consequences

A growing body of research and user reports reveals many unanticipated and undesired consequences of implementation (Aarts, Ash, & Berg, 2007; Ash, Berg, & Coiera, 2004; Campbell, Sittig, Ash, Guappone, & Dykstra, 2006; Han et al., 2005; Koppel et al., 2005; Rosenbloom et al., 2006; Schneider & Schneider, 2006; Silverstein, 2006; Wachter, 2004, 2006; Wears & Berg, 2005). Unanticipated and undesirable consequences, which are usually just called unintended consequences (Ash, Sittig, Dykstra et al., 2007), often undermine patient safety practices and occasionally harm patients (Weiner, Kfuri, Chan, & Fowles, 2007; Campbell, Sittig, Ash, Guappone, & Dykstra, 2007; McAlearney, Vrontos, Schneider, Christine R. Curran, & Pedersen, 2007). Unintended consequences also lead to cost escalations, resistance to implementation, and sometimes to failures of HIT projects (Silverstein, 2006).

The literature on HIT's unintended consequences documents these interactions and contains several typologies and conceptual frameworks that help guide research and practice (Ash, et al., 2004; Ash, Sittig, Dykstra et al., 2007; Campbell et al., 2006). Our previous paper (Harrison, Koppel, & Bar-Lev, 2007) provides a detailed comparison of the ISTA model to the best-known typologies (Ash, et al., 2004; Campbell et al., 2006). One of the most important differences concerns the typologies' usability. Conceptual frameworks are usually more helpful when they represent important empirical variations through just a few distinctive types.

To enhance ISTA's usability we sought to encompass the diverse sociotechnical sources of unintended consequences within just five types, and we characterized these types in terms of a very limited set of concepts. Moreover, we placed greater emphasis than previous studies did on consequences resulting from emergent interactions and containing recursive feedback loops among elements of the sociotechnical system – for example, effects of HIT on clinical practices and relations, which in turn shape the way that HIT is used.

Research Foundations

ISTA draws on five distinct bodies of research. First, traditional sociotechnical systems (STS) research documents dynamic, mutual influences among the social subsystem (people, tasks, relationships), the technical subsystem (technologies, techniques, task performance methods, work settings), and their social and organizational environments (Fox, 1995). Early STS work focused on attaining an optimum balance between the social system -- including the needs of the workers -- and the technologies used in manufacturing and extraction industries. Later STS research in healthcare showed how sociotechnical forces shape work processes, which impact employee motivation and patient outcomes (Chisholm & Ziegenfuss, 1986; Systems Engineering Initiative for Patient Safety, 2003).

Sociotechnical studies of office automation indicate that early designers of management information systems adopted a "rational/static" approach that focused mainly on enhancing information processing efficiency and managerial control (Mumford & Banks, 1967; Bostrom & Heinen, 1977a). This narrow, mechanistic approach overlooks effects of new information systems on employees and their organization and fails to grasp the dynamic and interconnected nature of organizations as systems. In contrast, sociotechnical analysts advocate applying the STS principles of participative design and autonomous work groups to the introduction of new computer systems.(Bostrom & Heinen, 1977b; Mumford, 1983).

Second, the closely-related field of ergonomics examines effects of work technologies and physical environments on individuals (International Ergonomics Association, 2006; Carayon & Smith, 2000). Ergonomics points to crucial interactions among work organization, patient, provider, and organizational factors (Karsh, Holden, Alper, & Or, 2006). Macro ergonomics examines how features of work organization -- including physical settings, tasks, technology, and organizational arrangements -- affect individual stress and performance (Carayon, 2006; Carayon & Smith, 2000). Ergonomic practitioners design physical, cognitive, and organizational work features that fit peoples' needs, abilities, and limitations.

Traditional sociotechnical and ergonomic analyses stress the benefits of appropriate design of technologies, but they tend to treat designed configurations as stable over time and consistent across contexts. Hence, traditional STS and ergonomic research examines how technological features affect people and social systems but does not explore the other side of that relationship: how social systems shape technology and its uses (Kling, 2000). In contrast, several other research streams recognize that technology and the social world are intertwined and influence one another.

The third body of research includes social construction of technology studies, along with the broader negotiated-order and interpretive traditions on which social construction draws (Giddens, 1984; Maines & Charlton, 1985; Weick, 1979). Researchers in these fields show how interactions among technology users -- including managers, clinicians, and other healthcare staff -- help select, reinterpret, modify, and even create technologies. (Aarts, Doorewaard, & Berg, 2004; Cornford, 2003; Orlikowski, 2000; Pinch & Biker, 1987; Weick, 1979, 1990). From this vantage point, as people adopt and use technologies, they alter them and transform relations among the technologies and their organizational contexts.

Fourth, technology-in-practice, shows that technologies such as EMR and CPOE are not just shaped by practitioners; they also mediate practice (Berg, 1997; Weick, 1979). Healthcare emerges through collaborative work and tight interconnections among people, tools, machines, documents, and organizational routines (Bar Lev & Harrison, 2006; Berg, 1999; Timmermans & Berg, 2003).

Social informatics, the fifth research field on which ISTA builds, applies insights from the research just reviewed. Following social construction and technology-in-practice, social informatics explicitly acknowledges the embeddedness of information technologies within organizations and broader social contexts (Kling, 2000). Thus nearly identical information technologies can be applied and used very differently because of the many, complex interactions among people, between people and equipment, and even between sets of equipment (Kling, McKim, & King, 2003).

Methodology

To clarify the aims and limitations of this chapter, we will briefly explain the logic we used to develop the ISTA types. Then we will describe our procedure for selecting examples of each type and the methods behind each example.

The main goals of this chapter are analytic, rather than empirical. We seek to model the main *types* of interactions that lead to unintended consequences, but do not attempt to estimate the frequency or distribution of these types. Nor do we seek to develop and test hypotheses about the causes or consequences of each interaction type. Rather than reporting systematically gathered data on the ISTA types, we provide illustrations of each type of these interactions.

We used a combination of deductive and inductive reasoning to develop ISTA. Using deduction we moved from findings and insights from the five bodies of research summarized above to generalizations about possible sources of unintended consequences. For example, both theoretic and empirical findings led us to generalize that users' reactions to new HIT and their local adaptations of it may diverge so dramatically from the original HIT design that managers and IT designers are forced to reconfigure some HIT features. This hypothesis led us to create one of the interaction types presented in our ISTA typology.

Once we had developed the typology, we sought a broad mix of illustrations of how each type works. We combed published studies, observations from our own studies, reports of problems with HIT literature appearing on the web (e.g., Silverstein, 2006). In addition we solicited illustrations from clinicians interested in HIT and working with it. We selected for this chapter the examples that most clearly illustrated each type and that did not require lengthy explanation.

Fourteen of the seventeen examples provided below were drawn from published studies of HIT implementation in acute care hospitals. These studies used a wide range of data gathering and analytic techniques, including observations of HIT use, interviews with users, and examination of documents relating to HIT implementation. Details on these methods are available in the original sources.

ISTA FRAMEWORK

From the research foundations reviewed above, we draw four key features of ISTA, which are sometimes neglected in discussions of the consequences of implementing HIT:

- The importance of examining actual uses of HIT ("HIT-in-use"), rather than uses that were planned or envisioned by designers or managers
- The impact on HIT use of technical and physical settings of work
- Users' renegotiation and reinterpretation of HIT features
- Interaction and interdependence among social and technical systems and recursive relations (i.e., feedback loops) among sociotechnical subcomponents.

The ISTA framework thus encourages us to stop viewing HIT innovations as things and instead treat them as elements within unfolding processes of sociotechnical interaction. From the viewpoint of ISTA, the results of HIT innovation can never be fully determined by the technology. Sociotechnical interactions are dynamic, emergent, hard to understand, and often surprising -- conditions characterizing complex adaptive systems (Plsek, 2001). ISTA rejects popular mechanistic assumptions that HIT implementation problems can be solved with more or better HIT and that proper HIT implementation depends primarily on training and technical support. ISTA thus diverges from the prevailing IT engineering approach, which models existing administrative and clinical practices in new HIT solutions, fine tunes them, and freezes these solutions and required user behaviors (Cornford, 2003; Davidson & Heineke, 2007).

Figure 1 provides a graphic portrayal of the ISTA framework. It shows interactions among subcomponents of the sociotechnical system that act as major sources of unintended consequences. Other interaction types could be derived logically, but these do not appear to affect unintended consequences as strongly as the ones shown. The five interaction types are:

1. **New HIT changes existing social system.**
2. **Technical & physical infrastructures mediate HIT use:** Interaction of new HIT with existing technical and physical conditions affects HIT-in-use.
3. **Social system mediates HIT use:** Interaction of new HIT with the social system affects HIT-in-use.
4. **HIT-in-use changes social system:** Interaction of new HIT with the social system affects HIT-in-use, which then further changes the social system.
5. **HIT-social system interactions engender HIT redesign:** Interaction of new HIT with the social system affects HIT-in-use, which then leads to changes in HIT properties.

Arrows in Figure 1 show the impact of one STS subcomponent on another and correspond to the five interaction types. Arrow 1 shows effects of newly implemented HIT on the Social System subcomponent within the adopting organization. Arrows that pass through a subcomponent show sociotechnical interactions. For example, Arrow 2 depicts interac-

Figure 1. Interactive sociotechnical systems

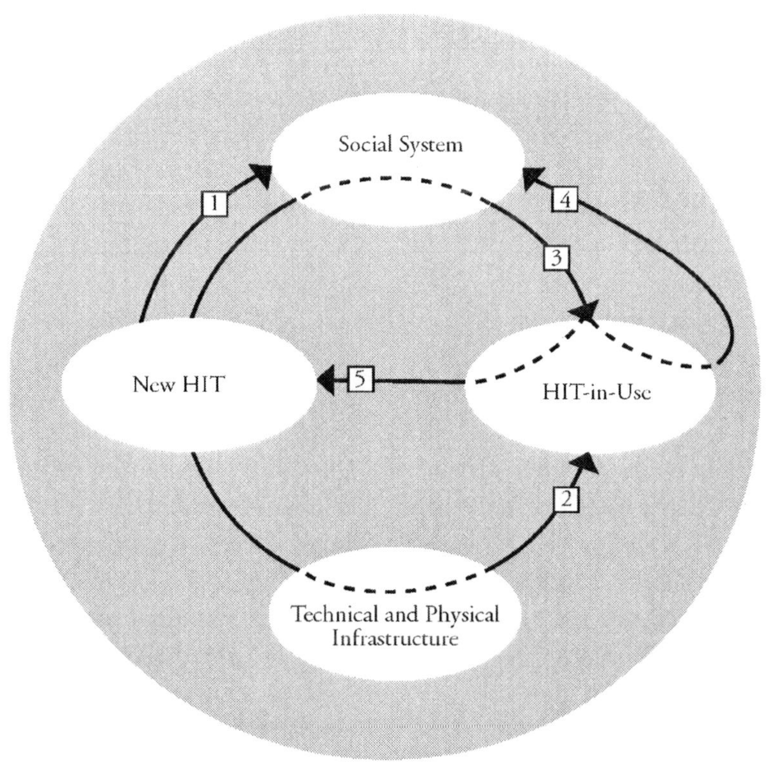

tion between New HIT and the existing Technical and Physical Infrastructures. This interaction in turn shapes HIT-in-Use. Arrow 3 shows the effects on HIT-in-Use of interactions between new HIT and the organization's Social System. Arrows 4 and 5 indicate that, once shaped by the interactions shown by Arrow 3, HIT-in-Use can produce further changes in the Social System (Arrow 4) or in New HIT's formal properties (Arrow 5).

The ISTA typology contains both continuities and departures from previous models of unintended consequences and from other previous studies of HIT outcomes. The first two ISTA types are widely discussed in STS and ergonomics. Type 3 is prominent in the literature on unintended consequences but has received less attention from other researchers in information technology and healthcare. Types 4 and 5 are less fully developed in most discussions of unintended consequences and virtually absent from the broader literature on HIT.

CONSEQUENCES OF SOCIOTECHNICAL INTERACTIONS

Let us now illustrate how each ISTA type can lead to unintended consequences.

Type 1: New HIT Changes Existing Social System

This type captures processes through which HIT interventions in healthcare organizations alter prior patterns of work, communication, or relationships among clinicians. HIT designers often seek to alter work practices but are too often surprised by interactions with HIT that engender undesirable changes.

Many of these changes involve disruptions of communication routines. Consider, for example, the following observations (Koppel, Davidson, Wears, & Sinsky, in press):

A teen-age woman met with her doctor for a routine physical examination. She sat to the physician's right, slightly behind his desk. The physician, in turn sat at the desk facing the computer screen. This arrangement meant that the physician's body and face were turned away from the patient. The physician, who was not a particularly good typist, was nonetheless intent on simultaneously questioning his patient and recording her remarks in the computer. Unable to type while looking at her, his eyes were assiduously glued to the screen. He asked a series of questions which were physically addressed to the computer screen rather than the patient. The observer noted several things that the doctor missed as he typed the information into the EMR: 1) the patient provided facial and body-language cues suggesting that she was occasionally being facetious. 2) Her facial behavior and a pause indicated doubt in response to one question. 3) A hand movement suggested that she was holding something back, as she provided a vague response to a sensitive question about her sexual activity.

Miscommunications or failures to perceive subtle verbal and physical cues like these could produce serious misunderstandings by the physician or lead to additional, unnecessary probing by the physician that would further weaken the already fragile physician-patient relationship. We do not mean to suggest by this example that when physicians wrote their notes by hand they always attended to the patient's nuanced communications and correctly interpreted them. But at least prior to the EMR, the computer screen and keyboard did not pose additional barriers between doctor and patient. EMRs require a lot of the physician's attention. Despite their advantages, the large number of EMR screens, subroutines, and templates draw the physician's attention away from the patient. Some argue that physician distraction results mainly from poor typing ability; as their typing gets better the distraction of entering information into the EMR will diminish. Certainly poor typing skills don't help. But the real question remains: Can one pay careful attention to subtle patient clues while focusing on a complex computer screen full of questions and check-off boxes?

Sometimes HIT's disruption of the ongoing social system has far more serious consequences. A well-known study on CPOE provides two examples (Han et al., 2005):

First, introduction of CPOE into a tertiary children's hospital reduced bedside nurse-physician interaction about critically ill infants. Nurses had fewer opportunities to provide feedback that sometimes led to beneficial medication changes. Second, CPOE procedures altered communication between transport teams and the emergency room (ER). Prior to introduction of CPOE, transport teams radioed the ER, so ER staff could order medications and complete admission forms before the patient's arrival. When CPOE was launched, transport staff had to provide patient information in the ER, and treatment was delayed until after ER staff entered the data. Resulting delays and reduced clinician interaction may have contributed to higher mortality rates after introduction of CPOE.

Studies of this sort (also Campbell et al., 2006; Patterson, Cook, & Render, 2002) show how HIT implementation can alter or disrupt oral communication among clinicians, even when talk is faster, more clinically accurate, and safer than transmitting information through HIT. The challenge when introducing HIT is to improve problematic and dangerous forms of communication, such as illegible prescriptions, without undermining vital communication flows among clinicians and with patients.

Type 2: Technical and Physical Infrastructures Mediate HIT Use

Poor fit between new HIT and existing technical and physical infrastructures is a common source of unintended consequences. Most noticeable to HIT specialists are problems of interface between new and existing IT. These problems are a frequent source of technical failure for new HIT and can lead to poor decisions, delays, data loss, errors, and unnecessary testing (Aspden et al., 2006; Koppel et al., 2005; Davidson & Heineke, 2007).

The following example shows how interface issues may affect implementation of remote ICU monitoring (e-ICU):

Many hospitals are implementing e-ICUs --where a clinical team in a remote center observes patients in scores of ICUs across dozens of hospitals using cameras, microphones, body and medication monitors. The e-ICU enables hospitals to reduce ICU staffs during off-hours. However, many of the hospitals implementing the e-ICU lack electronically integrated progress notes or nursing notes. Instead, these notes must be faxed to clinicians in the remote monitoring center (F. Sites, RN, Operations Director, Penn E-lert eICU, Univ. of Pennsylvania Health System, Personal Communication, Oct. 2, 2006). Busy nurses cannot always collect and fax these documents in a timely manner, and off-site clinicians often must rely on monitors without progress and nursing notes. These clinicians report that the lack of paper-based information is troubling and occasionally causes serious problems. The delayed or missing information obliges them to make decisions with partial information. In addition, they find it cumbersome to combine on-line and paper-based information.

"Paper persistence" is another common consequence of inadequate integration of new HIT and existing information systems (Campbell et al., 2006). Use of paper was widespread in the five institutions studied by Campbell and her colleagues. In some cases, staff had to print out CPOE orders and then manually reenter them into the local department's clinical information system.

Poor interfaces between HIT and the physical settings in which it is deployed may also lead to workarounds and other unanticipated HIT uses; these deviations from the planned uses of HIT sometimes harm safety, quality, or efficiency. IT designers lacking awareness of ergonomics may overlook simple, yet fateful environmental features, such as the physical ease with which computers can be accessed or moved. Here is a particularly vivid illustration of the consequences of such oversight:

Many hospitals use personal computers affixed to carts to provide bedside access. Unfortunately, in one hospital, the utility of these computers on wheels ("COWs") was limited by their being too "fat" to fit readily into patient rooms (N. Rodenhausen, RN, CNO and Sr. V.P. Patient Care Services, N.Y. Downtown Hospital, Personal Communication, May 12, 2006). As a result, nurses using COWS tethered in the hallway during barcode scanning may not hear or see alarms for wrong patients or medication errors.

Other features of work layout -- including noise, overcrowding, and distracting illumination -- affect work healthcare performance and safety (Alvarado, 2007) and may have unanticipated, negative effects on HIT use. Inappropriate physical layouts can extend data-entry time, reduce face-to-face communication, and increase distractions (Koppel et al., 2005a). For example, as staff walk across a busy floor to terminals, encounters with several patients and staff may lead them to forget or garble information obtained at the bedside.

Type 3: Social System Mediates HIT Use

Reinterpretations and negotiations about new HIT often lead to different HIT uses from those intended by HIT's designers. Yet technical experts sometimes discount the potential impact on HIT-in-use of negotiation and reinterpretation. For instance, many electronic systems call for real-time documentation of medication administration. However, when nurses under heavy work loads encounter cumbersome software for medication administration, the nurses often delay medication charting until the end of their shifts (Bar Lev & Harrison, 2006; Koppel et al., 2005a). This unsanctioned practice can generate inaccurate recording of medication times and quantities, inappropriate duplication of prescriptions, less efficient communication between physicians and nurses, and reduced efficacy of software safety checks

To take another example, consider how nurses sometimes learn to work around unwieldy barcoding procedures:

In hospitals with Barcode Medication Administration Systems (patient and medication barcoding), nurses are frequently frustrated and delayed by torn or missing barcode-wristbands (Patterson, Cook, & Render, 2002). They sometimes cope with these difficulties and speed the process of scanning patients' wristbands by printing additional patient barcodes and affixing them to supply cabinets, doors jams, scanning equipment, nurses' key rings, and nursing stations (Koppel, Wetternick, Telles, & Karsh, in press). Although these workarounds help nurses perform their work and seem efficient, they undermine medication barcode safety features by allowing scanning and recording of medications away from the patient. Thus scanned medications for several different patients might be put on the same tray or in the same pocket. Because the scanning data reflect apparently flawless administrations, the errors may go unnoticed.

An important reason that HIT-in-use so often diverges from designed HIT is that the original designs fail to take reflect ongoing features of the work system and of social relations among practitioners, including collaborative and interactive work patterns (Ash, et al., 2004; Patterson, Cook, & Render, 2002). Here is a vivid illustration of the effects of ignoring work flow when implementing HIT. It comes from an observational study of the introduction of system-wide CPOE into an ICU (Cheng, 2003):

Before introduction of CPOE, nurses were used to alerting physicians about changes in patients' conditions. Physicians often gave oral orders to nurses and only signed orders after the nurses had transcribed and administered them. The CPOE required physicians to initiate orders, pharmacists to check them, and clerks to deliver them to nurses for administration. Imposition of this linear workflow led to delays in delivery of orders, left nurses in doubt whether physicians had initiated orders, and sometimes produced divergent printed orders: the physician's original and the pharmacist's modification. In response, nurses continued to initiate orders by making suggestions to physicians. Nurses also frequently interrupted physicians to ensure that orders had been entered into the CPOE system. Moreover, nurses assumed responsibility for deciding what to do when the CPOE system presented them with conflicting medication orders.

Workarounds like these may help preserve important forms of collaboration that are not supported by an HIT design. But such workarounds may also make care less efficient and compromise safety and quality.

Type 4: HIT-in-Use Changes Social System

This type shows how HIT implementation can lead to recursive interaction involving an undesirable feedback loop between HIT-in-use and prevailing work patterns and relationships. In this type of interaction, use of new HIT is altered by the care organization' social system (as in Type 3), but then the HIT-in-use leads to new and additional changes in the social system. Consider the following example (LaRosa & Koppel, 2007):

New HIT (i.e., CPOE and EMRs) allows Infectious Disease (ID) fellows to access information on patients for whom housestaff wish to prescribe newer, expensive antibiotics. The ID fellows seek to limit use of expensive, broad-spectrum antibiotics, Housestaff, however, are often eager to try new antimicrobials and to avoid the ID approval process. Housestaff developed "stealth dosing," waiting until the ID fellows go off-duty at 10 PM to order the restricted antimicrobials. The next morning, ID fellows review the previous night's orders and sometimes demand medication changes. But changing antibiotic regimes can be problematic, so ID fellows let many such orders stand even if they are not ideal. Because ID fellows often take no remedial actions and housestaff can game the system, stealth dosing constrains the ID-fellows' authority and weakens the antimicrobial oversight process.

The beginning of this example sounds like the ICU example (Type 3). Housestaff workarounds lead to unanticipated HIT uses (stealth dosing). But the continuation of the stealth dosing example shows that the HIT-in-use (i.e., stealth dosing) also feeds back to adversely affect authority relations.

Recently we observed another instance in which HIT-in-use ultimately led to a change for the worse in clinical practice and in relations between a clinical specialty and the hospital management:

One hospital system responded to changes in regulatory requirements regarding suicide assessment by rolling out a "Self-Harm Assessment" and building this tool into its CPOE templates. In one of the system's member hospitals, management only consulted with a single psychiatrist when it decided to automate the suicide assessment. No other clinicians were notified prior to implementation of this change in HIT implementation. These decisions produced a surge of inappropriate psychiatric referrals. For instance, an 84 year old man sustained an acute CVA [bad stroke] with hemiparesis [weakness on one side of the body]. In the process of being admitted to the hospital, he was asked a routine nursing intake question: "Have you ever felt life was not worth living?" When he responded in the affirmative, the DSS automatically ordered a psychiatric consultation to assess for suicidality. Neither the admitting physician, primary physician, nursing staff, family, nor the patient were asked or informed about the consultation. The psychiatrist deemed the patient not actively suicidal. Although psychiatrists and other clinicians complained about the DSS procedure several months ago, it has thus far not been changed. Delays in DSS re-programming, the hospital corporation's concern for regulatory compliance, and bureaucratic processes have all been blamed for the inability to change the automated referral structure. Currently the psychiatrists are overwhelmed by many unnecessary consultations generated through DSS, rather than through the exercise of clinical judgment. As a result, the psychiatrists have less time to treat patients who legitimately require psychiatric attention. Further, because patients who need medication and medication titration are not as carefully monitored as before, they are more often disruptive to the hospitals' other patients, staff, and activities. These disruptions also strain relations with other colleagues and hospital staff.

This case clearly shows how the social system (regulatory concerns and lack of consultation with clinicians on HIT innovations) affects HIT-in-use (automatic, unjustified psychiatric referrals), which then further alters the social system (psychiatry becomes overloaded, patients needing attention disturb others, and staff interactions are strained).

Here is yet another illustration of recursive, sociotechnical feedback captured in our fourth interaction type. In this instance the result is an unanticipated and undesirable change in the clinical routine:

Several CPOE systems use "forced fields," which require that certain information be inserted before physicians can continue ordering medications.. Physicians sometimes regard the forced fields as a nuisance. For instance, an internist who wants to enter Tylenol for an adult must enter the patient's weight, even though Tylenol is not especially dose-specific to an adult's weight. This doctor has seen the patient a few times and estimates her weight at about 150 lbs (when, in fact, she is 30 pounds heavier). Although the internist is somewhat uncertain about the weight, the physician is not overly concerned since precise weight is not critical for the dosage. Unfortunately, that estimated information then enters into the required data field and becomes embedded in the patient's electronic record. The next physician to access the record is a nephrologist, for whom patient weight may be critically important. That nephrologist has no idea that 150 lbs was a guess, and makes a delicate calculation of dosage and schedule based on the weight provided by the record.

Like the stealth dosing episode, this illustration starts with a process that fits Type 3: New HIT (the EMR template requiring entry of patient's weight) interacts with the social system (physician's assumption that the template is simply a barrier to rapid ordering of the required medication – rather than a source of data for subsequent treatments) to produce unintended HIT-in-use (entry of presumed, imprecise value for weight). The HIT-in-use then leads to further changes in the social system when the next physician who sees the patient forgoes checking the data in the patient admissions record or in other nursing documentation files and instead relies on the conjectural weight recorded in the EMR.

Type 5: HIT-Social System Interactions Engender HIT Redesign

This type involves an even more dramatic effect of recursive feedback from the social system to HIT than that described in Type 4. Here users' reactions to new HIT and their local adaptations of it diverge so dramatically from the original HIT design that managers and IT designers are forced to reconfigure some HIT features. In one major medical center with a homegrown EMR, this type of process undermined a primary design feature of the EMR (Bar Lev & Harrison, 2006):

Shortly after the EMR was introduced, physicians objected to forced-choices in diagnostic templates. Accustomed to submitting handwritten notes, physicians viewed template options as masking diagnostic ambiguities and even requiring premature conclusions about etiology. For example, pediatricians often admitted children for observation upon presentation of serious symptoms; in some of these admissions the physicians had not yet determined a clear-cut diagnosis. In response to pressure from the physicians, the IT team redesigned the software to allow free-text entries of diagnoses.

In the vascular surgery department of the same institution, there were also dramatic consequences of clinician reactions to HIT (Bar Lev & Harrison, 2005):

When the EMR software was first introduced to the ward, it required free-text entry by nurses. In practice, the nurses condensed their entries to the minimum. This tendency reflected the nurses' typing difficulties, their already heavy work load, and their unwillingness to extend their work day to complete EMR entries. In response to the problem, the department's management, which had some autonomy in the EMR design, had a series of templates created containing descriptive statements that could simply be clicked when they were appropriate. The hope was that ease of data entry would keep nurses from leaving out details from their notes. The unexpected result, according to the head nurse, was that the nurses began "to fit the patient to the template format, rather than the other way around." Patients' records became so similar as to be indistinguishable. Nurses used the "click-on" option rather unselectively and seemed to stop reporting on their patients as individuals. Management soon abandoned its experiment in providing precoded options and returned free-text entry of nursing notes.

Sometimes, the impact of user reactions and of HIT-in-use only shows up over a longer period of time. Take, for example, recent developments in DSS:

When ordering medications via the computer, some systems incorporate off-the-shelf DSS. These generate warnings about doses or interactions, which quickly become overwhelming, and are ignored as "alarm fatigue" sets in (Ash, et al., 2004; Aspden et al., 2006). Physician annoyance and ignored warnings lead managers to deactivate the alarms. Subsequently IT designers seek to reintroduce selected warnings that have been approved by in-house clinicians. Another managerial response involves "tiered" alarms, where warning levels mirror possible harm levels: physicians may ignore low-harm alarms, must acknowledge more serious alarms, and must explain overrides of the most serious alarms (van der Sijs, Aarts, Vulto, & Berg, 2006).

In this case, HIT innovations trigger responses by individuals (ignoring warnings), by managers (removing, then introducing new warnings), and by technology designers (tiered alarms).

IMPLICATIONS

ISTA leads us to expect emergent and unintended developments, as HIT interacts with existing systems. Thus ISTA emphasizes the complexity and the inherently surprising nature of HIT implementation.

Recognition of emergent, unintended consequences and appropriate response to them require learning during implementation (Ash, et al., 2004). To facilitate learning, IT designers and users need to adopt a flexible and experimental approach: This approach treats unintended consequences as opportunities for understanding the sociotechnical system and promoting alignment between the sociotechnical system and the IT (Argyris & Schon, 1996; Harrison and Shirom, 1999).

To promote this type of learning, we developed the following diagnostic questions which IT designers and users can pose about sociotechnical interactions and their unintended consequences:

1. How does new HIT influence the healthcare organization's current social system, and, particularly, practitioner behavior and relations?
2. How do existing technologies and physical environments influence actual uses of HIT (HIT-in-use)?
3. How does the healthcare organization's social system affect HIT-in-use?
4. How does HIT-in-use then affect the social system?
5. In turn, how do these changes in the social system lead to reconfigurations of IT's formal properties?

We also identified practices that can support learning throughout implementation.

Box 1 lists the recommended practices. Use of teams and representation of end users (physicians, nurses, managers) and IT staff (vendors and in-house) during planning and throughout implementation promotes learning by surfacing problems and solutions (Knox & Simpson, 2004). Team representativeness fosters recognition of variations in needs and perceptions among different practitioners, units, and organizations (Carayon, 2006).

Some potential implementation developments can be anticipated or discovered through pilots, dry runs, and use of outside experts; but many ST interactions only become evident during actual use. Learning about implementation requires frequent feedback to implementation teams via active questioning, on-site observation, and surveys of diverse groups of users (Ash., et al., 2003; Harrison & Shirom, 1999; Koppel et al., 2005). Hence HIT implementation should be closely followed during initial installation and adjustments made as needed in implementation tactics. After the initial go-live period, monitoring is critical. Direct and frequent contact with

Box 1. Recommendations for HIT implementation projects

1. Create multidisciplinary implementation teams, including managers, nurses, physicians, vendors, internal IT staff, outside experts not connected to the vendor or any single department, and quality improvement personnel.
2. Identify gaps and weaknesses in current practices and then design improvements in delivery processes and clinical practice into HIT; preserve constructive work patterns, norms, and structures.
3. Use dry runs and pilots to uncover critical sociotechnical interactions.
4. Actively observe and investigate how people work, what they think about their work, and how they use HIT.
5. Periodically assess implementation progress and examine effects of HIT on workflows and the social system. Obtain frequent feedback from users on their reactions to HIT and practice changes following implementation.
6. Modify implementation to cope with emerging and unanticipated developments, improve sociotechnical fit, and enhance outcomes.
7. Work with vendors, internal IT personnel, and clinicians to retool HIT as needed.
8. *Expect surprises and learn from them.*

users and gathering of granular data about user experiences are essential. Observations and interviews including open-ended questions reveal critical assumptions about how work should be done – recall the tendency of nurses to postpone medication entry and to work around barcoding procedures, as described above.

Granular information also helps implementers discover work practices not reflected in HIT-mediated information, including interactions among practitioners, timing of data entry, and contextual information (e.g., Bar Lev & Harrison, 2006; Koppel et al., 2005). For example, when physicians and nurses discuss a case, they routinely weigh the experience and status of people offering information, their certainty, and sense of urgency – contextual factors that may be missing from electronic records.

ISTA can help move HIT beyond the automation of current work practices toward the redesign of work processes – identifying and redesigning inefficient, dangerous, or suboptimal practices (Harrison & Shirom, 1999; Institute of Medicine, 2001). Redesign can also focus on supporting neglected but constructive practices, such as face-to-face practitioner consultations (Ash, et al., 2004). This type of IT-supported redesign requires early assessment of gaps between current and ideal practice, along with cooperation and constructive confrontation among managers and clinicians.

Ongoing re-examination and retooling of HIT interfaces and functions allows meaningful responses to experiences and emerging needs -- including changes in support, training, design, workflow, and the pace of HIT introduction. Implementation teams should work with vendors or internal designers to remove bugs, improve functionalities, and address HIT's sociotechnical consequences. Those who have successfully installed sophisticated HIT products typically report close and long-term work with vendors, consultants, or internal designers (Bates, 2005; Chaudhry et al., 2006). They made adjustments which went well beyond fine tuning and included major revisions. HIT implementers, however, must weigh the advantages of meeting user expectations and mirroring local practices against the benefits of standardization and of sustaining systems interoperability.

DISCUSSION

Growing awareness of HIT implementation's mixed results contributes to its surprisingly shallow market penetration in the United States (Ash & Bates, 2005; Blumenthal & Glaser, 2007; California Healthcare Foundation, 2008; Jha et al., 2006). While some vendors and lobbyists still proclaim HIT as a panacea for an ailing healthcare system, users already know that HIT produces many unanticipated and undesired consequences. They also know that unintended consequences can sometimes undermine quality and safety and can lead to implementation failure.

The ISTA model may make it easier for researchers and practitioners to identify and respond to unanticipated consequences. ISTA may be particularly useful because of its distinctive focus on recursive processes (Types 4 and 5) -- where system interactions produce unanticipated, second-level effects. Further research, including observational studies of actual HIT use, should assess the generalizability of our typology and further refine it. Particular attention is needed to recursive and emergent processes in HIT implementation.

While not absolving new technology developers from their responsibilities to offer responsive, safe, and useful products, ISTA places analysis of the dynamics of healthcare organizing (Weick, 1979) at the center of HIT implementation. Many of the most important consequences of sociotechnical interactions emerge as new HIT becomes intertwined with the ongoing sociotechnical system. These developments cannot be fully anticipated during HIT design and implementation planning.

To spot such unfolding consequences of sociotechnical interactions, managers, designers, clinicians, and researchers need to carefully track HIT-in-use throughout implementation and provide feedback on emerging consequences.

In the long run, some of HIT's unintended consequences may play a role in helping HIT designers and healthcare professionals learn to deploy HIT more effectively. Of course, practitioners of HIT and medicine cannot tolerate developments that harm patients; HIT implementation therefore must proceed with caution. Familiarity with the ISTA model can help clinicians, managers, and designers become more aware of critical, unfolding processes in HIT implementation. This awareness will, in turn, help these practitioners realize HIT's potential for improving healthcare safety, quality, and efficiency.

ACKNOWLEDGMENT

The following individuals reported incidents that are incorporated into this manuscript or informed our thinking about unintended consequences: Nancy Rodenhausen MS, RN, N.Y. Downtown Hospital (NY); Christine A. Sinsky, MD, Medical Associates, P.C. (Dubuque, Iowa); Frank Sites, RN, Penn E-lert eICU, Univ. of Pennsylvania Health System; Joel L. Telles, PhD, Main Line Health (Bryn Mawr, PA.). Prof. Michel Vilette, Argo Paritech (Paris, France). The following individuals provided invaluable technical assistance in preparing the manuscript: Sandra Cummings and Mary Rolston of AHRQ's Public Affairs Division and Caryn Mc Manus of AHRQ's Information Resources Center. Ross Koppel was supported in part by a grant from the Agency for Healthcare Research and Quality (P01 HS11530).

DISCLAIMER

The views expressed in this paper are the authors' and do not reflect those of the United States, Department of Health and Human Services or the University of Pennsylvania.

IRB: IRB approval was not requested.

REFERENCES

Aarts, J., Ash, J., & Berg, M. (2007). Extending the understanding of computerized physician order entry: Implications for professional collaboration, workflow, and quality of care. *International Journal of Medical Informatics*, *76*(Suppl 1), 4–13. doi:10.1016/j.ijmedinf.2006.05.009

Aarts, J., Doorewaard, H., & Berg, M. (2004). Understanding implementation: The case of a computerized physician order entry system in a large Dutch university medical center. *Journal of the American Medical Informatics Association*, *11*(3), 207–216. doi:10.1197/jamia.M1372

Alvarado, C. (2007). The physical environment in healthcare. In P. Carayon (Ed.), *Handbook of human factors and ergonomics in health care and patient safety* (pp. 287-307). Mahwah, NJ: Erlbaum.

Argyris, C., & Schon, D. (1996). *Organizational learning II: Theory, method, and practice*. Reading, MA: Addison-Wesley.

Ash, J. S., & Bates, D. W. (2005). Factors and forces affecting EHR system adoption: Report of a 2004 ACMI discussion. *Journal of the American Medical Informatics Association*, *12*(1), 8–12. doi:10.1197/jamia.M1684

Ash, J. S., Berg, M., & Coiera, E. (2004). Some unintended consequences of information technology in healthcare: The nature of patient care information system-related errors. *Journal of the American Medical Informatics Association, 11*(2), 104–112. doi:10.1197/jamia.M1471

Ash, J. S., Gorman, P. N., Lavelle, M., Payne, T. H., Massaro, T. A., Frantz, G. L., & Lyman, J. A. (2003). A cross-site qualitative study of physician order entry. *Journal of the American Medical Informatics Association, 10*(2), 188–200. doi:10.1197/jamia.M770

Ash, J. S., Sittig, D. F., Dykstra, R. H., Guappone, K., Carpenter, J. D., & Seshadri, V. (2007). Categorizing the unintended sociotechnical consequences of computerized provider order entry. *International Journal of Medical Informatics, 76*(Suppl 1), 21–27. doi:10.1016/j.ijmedinf.2006.05.017

Ash, J. S., Sittig, D. F., Poon, E. G., Guappone, K., Campbell, E., & Dykstra, R. H. (2007). The extent and importance of unintended consequences related to computerized provider order entry. *Journal of the American Medical Informatics Association, 14*(4), 415–423. doi:10.1197/jamia.M2373

Aspden, P., Julie, W., Bootman, J. L., & Cronenwett, L. R. (Eds.). (2006). *Preventing medication errors*. Washington, D.C.: National Academies Press.

Bar Lev, S., & Harrison, M. (2005). Localization of health IT: How users "repair" electronic medical record systems. *Best Paper Proceedings of the 2005 Academy of Management Meeting*, Honolulu, Hawaii.

Bar Lev, S., & Harrison, M. I. (2006). Negotiating time scripts during implementation of an electronic medical record. *Health Care Management Review, 31*(1), 11–17.

Bates, D. (2005). Computerized physician order entry and medication errors: Finding a balance. *Journal of Biomedical Informatics, 38*(4), 259–261. doi:10.1016/j.jbi.2005.05.003

Berg, M. (1997). *Rationalizing medical work: Decision support techniques and medical practices*. Cambridge, MA: MIT Press.

Berg, M. (1999). Patient care information systems and healthcare work: A sociotechnical approach. *International Journal of Medical Informatics, 55*(2), 87–101. doi:10.1016/S1386-5056(99)00011-8

Blumenthal, D., & Glaser, J. (2007). Information technology comes to medicine. *The New England Journal of Medicine, 356*(24), 2527–2534. doi:10.1056/NEJMhpr066212

Bostrom, R. P., & Heinen, J. S. (1977a). MIS problems and failures: A sociotechnical perspective part I: The causes. *MIS Quarterly, 1*(3), 17–32. doi:10.2307/248710

Bostrom, R. P., & Heinen, J. S. (1977b). MIS problems and failures: A sociotechnical perspective part II: The application of sociotechnical theory. *MIS Quarterly, 1*(December), 11–28. doi:10.2307/249019

California Healthcare Foundation. (2008). *Snapshot: The state of healthcare information technology in California*. Retrieved on January 24, 2008, from http://www.chcf.org/documents/chronicdisease/HITSnapshot08.pdf

Campbell, E., Sittig, D., Ash, J., Guappone, K., & Dykstra, R. (2006). Types of unintended consequences related to computerized provider order entry. *Journal of the American Medical Informatics Association, 13*(5), 547–556. doi:10.1197/jamia.M2042

Campbell, E., Sittig, D., Ash, J., Guappone, K., & Dykstra, R. (2007). In reply to "e-Iatrogenisis: the most critical consequence of CPOE and other HIT." *Journal of the American Medical Informatics Association, 14*(3), 389–390. doi:10.1197/jamia.M2385

Carayon, P. (2006). Human factors and ergonomics in healthcare and patient safety. In P. Carayon (Ed.), *Handbook of human factors and ergonomics in healthcare and patient safety*. Mahwah, NJ: Lawrence Erlbaum Associates.

Carayon, P., & Smith, M. (2000). Work organization and ergonomics. *Applied Ergonomics, 31*, 649–662. doi:10.1016/S0003-6870(00)00040-5

Chaudhry, B., Wang, W., Wu, S., Maglione, M., Mojica, W., & Roth, E. (2006). Systematic review: Impact of health information technology on quality, efficiency, and costs of medical care. *Annals of Internal Medicine, 144*(10), 742–752.

Cheng, C. G. M. K., Geller, E., & Levitt, R. E. (2003). The effects of CPOE on ICU workflow: An observational study. In *Proceedings of the Medical Informatics Symposium,* Palo Alto, CA.

Chisholm, R. F., & Ziegenfuss, J. T. (1986). A review of applications of the sociotechnical systems approach to healthcare organizations. *The Journal of Applied Behavioral Science, 22*(3), 315–327. doi:10.1177/002188638602200310

Conn, J. C. (2007, October 30). Failure, deinstallation of EHRs abound: Study. *Modern Healthcare*. Retrieved on November 2, 2007, from http://www.modernhealthcare.com/apps/pbcs.dll/article?AID=/20071030/FREE/310300002/0/FRONTPAGE

Cornford, T. (2003). Information systems and new technologies: Taking shape in use. In C. Avgerou & R. La Rovere (Eds.), *Information systems and the economics of innovation* (pp. 1-16). London: Edward Elgar.

Crosson, J. C., Ohman-Strickland, P. A., Hahn, K. A., DiCicco-Bloom, B., Shaw, E., & Orzano, A. J. (2007). Electronic medical records and diabetes quality of care: Results from a sample of family medicine practices. *Annals of Family Medicine, 5*(3), 209–215. doi:10.1370/afm.696

Davidson, S., & Heineke, J. (2007). Toward an effective strategy for the diffusion and use of clinical information systems. *Journal of the American Medical Informatics Association, 14*(3), 361–367. doi:10.1197/jamia.M2254

Fitzhenry, F., Peterson, J. F., Arrieta, M., Waitman, L. R., Schildcrout, J. S., & Miller, R. A. (2007). Medication administration discrepancies persist despite electronic ordering. *Journal of the American Medical Informatics Association, 14*(6), 756–764. doi:10.1197/jamia.M2359

Fox, W. (1995). Sociotechnical system principles and guidelines: Past and present. *The Journal of Applied Behavioral Science, 31*(1), 91–105. doi:10.1177/0021886395311009

Giddens, A. (1984). *The constitutions of society: Outline of the theory of structuration*. Berkeley University of California Press.

Han, Y. Y., Carcillo, J. A., Venkataraman, S. T., Robert, S. B., Clark, R., & Watson, S. (2005). Unexpected increased mortality after implementation of a commercially sold computerized physician order entry system. *Pediatrics, 116*(6), 1506–1512. doi:10.1542/peds.2005-1287

Harrison, M., Koppel, R., & Bar-Lev, S. (2007). Reducing unintended consequences of health information technology through interactive sociotechnical analysis. *Journal of the American Medical Informatics Association, 14*(5), 542–549. doi:10.1197/jamia.M2384

Harrison, M. I., & Shirom, A. (1999). *Organizational diagnosis and assessment: Bridging theory and practice*. Thousand Oaks, CA: Sage.

Institute of Medicine. (2001). *Crossing the quality chasm: A new health system for the 21st century*. Washington, D.C.: National Academy Press.

International Ergonomics Association. (2006). *The discipline of ergonomics*. Retrieved on August 8, 2006, from http://www.iea.cc/ergonomics/

Jha, A. K., Ferris, T. G., Donelan, K., DesRoches, C., Shields, A., & Rosenbaum, S. (2006). How common are electronic health records in the United States? A summary of the evidence. *Health Affairs*, *25*, w496–w507. doi:10.1377/hlthaff.25.w496

Karsh, B.-T., Holden, R. J., Alper, S. J., & Or, C. K. L. (2006). A human factors engineering paradigm for patient safety: Designing to support the performance of the healthcare professional. *Quality and safety in health care, 15*(suppl_1), i59-i65.

Kling, R. (2000). Learning about information technologies and social change: The contribution of social informatics. *The Information Society*, *16*(3), 217–232. doi:10.1080/01972240050133661

Kling, R., McKim, G., & King, A. (2003). A bit more to it: Scholarly communication forums as sociotechnical interaction networks. *Journal of the American Society for Information Science and Technology*, *54*(1), 47–67. doi:10.1002/asi.10154

Knox, G. E., & Simpson, K. R. (2004). Teamwork: The fundamental building block of high reliability organizations and patient safety. In B. Youngberg & J. Hatlie (Eds.), *The patient safety handbook* (pp. 379-414). Boston: Jones and Bartleett.

Koppel, R., Davidson, S. M., Wears, R. L., & Sinsky, C. (in press). Healthcare information technology to the rescue: Panacea, golden calf, and fat cows. In R. F. J. Waring & E. Rowley, (Eds.), *Patient safety: Critical perspectives*. Ithaca, NY: ILR Press Cornell University Press.

Koppel, R., Metlay, J. P., Cohen, A., Abaluck, B., Localio, A. R., & Kimmel, S. E. (2005). Role of computerized physician order entry systems in facilitating medication errors. *Journal of the American Medical Association*, *293*(10), 1197–1203. doi:10.1001/jama.293.10.1197

Koppel, R., Wetternick, T., Telles, J. L., & Karsh, B.-T. (in press). Workarounds to barcode medication administration systems: Their occurrences, causes, and threats to patient safety. *Journal of the American Medical Informatics Association*, *15*(4), 408-423.

LaRosa, & Koppel, R. (2007). Evaluation of antimicrobal therapy. *Infection Control and Hospital Epidemiology*, *28*(5), 551–556. doi:10.1086/513535

Linder, J. A., Ma, J., Bates, D. W., Middleton, B., & Stafford, R. S. (2007). Electronic health record use and the quality of ambulatory care in the United States. *Archives of Internal Medicine*, *167*(13), 1400–1405. doi:10.1001/archinte.167.13.1400

Maines, D., & Charlton, J. (1985). The negotiated order approach to the analysis of social organization. In H. Farberman & R. Perinbanayagam (Eds.), *Studies in symbolic interaction (foundations of interpretive sociology: original essays in symbolic interaction)* (Vol. Suppl. 1, pp. 263-270). Greenwich, CT: JAI.

McAlearney, A. S., Vrontos, J., Schneider, P. J., Curran, C. R., Czerwinski, B. S., & Pedersen, C. A. (2007). Strategic work-arounds to accommodate new technology: The case of smart pumps in hospital care. *Journal of Patient Safety*, *3*(2), 75–81. doi:10.1097/01.jps.0000242987.93789.63

Mumford, E. (1983). *Designing human systems for new technology: The ETHICS method.* Retrieved on May 7, 2007, from http://www.enid.u-net.com/C1book1.htm

Mumford, E., & Banks, O. (1967). *The computer and the clerk.* London: Routledge & Kegan Paul.

Orlikowski, W. (2000). Using technology and constituting structures: A practice lens for studying technology in organizations. *Organization Science*, *11*(4), 404–428. doi:10.1287/orsc.11.4.404.14600

Patterson, E., Cook, R., & Render, M. (2002). Improving patient safety by identifying side effects from introducing bar coding in medication administration. *Journal of the American Medical Informatics Association*, *9*(5), 540–553. doi:10.1197/jamia.M1061

Pinch, T., & Biker, W. (1987). The social construction of facts and artifacts: Or how the sociology of science and the sociology of technology might benefit each other. In W. E. Biker, T. Hughes & T. Pinch (Eds.), *The social construction of technology systems: New directions in the sociology and history of technology*. Cambridge, MA: MIT Press.

Plsek, P. (2001). Redesigning healthcare with insights from the science of complex adaptive systems. In Institute of Medicine, *Crossing the quality chasm: A new health system for the 21st century* (pp. 309-322). Washington, D.C.: National Academy of Sciences.

Rosenbloom, S. T., Harrell, F., Lehman, C., Schneider, J., Spooner, S., & Johnson, K. (2006). Perceived increase in mortality after process and policy changes implemented with computerized physician order entry [letter]. *Pediatrics*, *117*(4), 1452–1455. doi:10.1542/peds.2005-3163

Schneider, J. E., & Schneider, K. H. (2006). *Report on electronic health record-associated errors and near miss reporting systems*. Rockville, MD: Agency for Healthcare Research and Quality.

Shamliyan, T., & Kane, R. (2007, June 26). Just what the doctor ordered. Review of the evidence of the impact of computerized physician order entry system on medication errors. *Health Services Research, Online Early Articles.*

Sidorov, J. (2006). It ain't necessarily so: The electronic health record and the unlikely prospect of reducing healthcare costs. *Health Affairs*, *25*(4), 1079–1085. doi:10.1377/hlthaff.25.4.1079

Silverstein, S. (2006). Sociotechnologic issues in clinical computing: Common examples of healthcare IT failure. Retrieved on April 21, 2006, from http://www.ischool.drexel.edu.faculty/ssilverstein/failurecases/

Systems Engineering Initiative for Patient Safety. (2003). *SEIPS model*. Retrieved on May 12, 2006, from http://www2.fpm.wisc.edu/seips/SEIPS

Timmermans, S., & Berg, M. (2003). The practice of medical technology. *Sociology of Health & Illness*, *25*(3), 97–114.

van der Sijs, H., Aarts, J., Vulto, A., & Berg, M. (2006). Overriding of drug safety alerts in computerized physician order entry. *Journal of the American Medical Informatics Association*, *13*(2), 138–147. doi:10.1197/jamia.M1809

Wachter, R. (2004). The end of the beginning: Patient safety five years after 'to err is human'. *Health Affairs*, *23*(Suppl. 2), W4-534–W545.

Wachter, R. (2006). Expected and unanticipated consequences of the quality and information technology revolutions. *Journal of the American Medical Association*, *295*(23), 2780–2783. doi:10.1001/jama.295.23.2780

Wears, R., & Berg, M. (2005). Computer technology and clinical work: Still waiting for Godot. *Journal of the American Medical Association*, *293*(10), 1261–1263. doi:10.1001/jama.293.10.1261

Weick, K. (1979). *The social psychology of organizing, second ed.* New York: McGraw-Hill.

Weick, K. (1990). Technology as equivoque: Sensemaking in new technologies. In P. Goodman & L. Sproull (Eds.), *Technology and organizations* (pp. 1-44). San Francisco: Jossey Bass.

Weiner, J., Kfuri, T., Chan, K., & Fowles, J. (2007). "e-Iatrogensis": The most critical unintended consequence of CPOE and HIT. *Journal of the American Medical Informatics Association, 14*(3), 387–388. doi:10.1197/jamia.M2338

KEY TERMS AND DEFINITIONS

Emergent Processes: social and organizational processes, such as an altered forms of communication or work flow among clinicians, that gradually develop and become apparent during implementation of HIT -- rather than being present and apparent before implementation.

Ergonomics: also known as human factors, ergonomics is the development and application of knowledge of human capacities to the design of systems, organizations, jobs, technologies, and products. The aim is to enhance safety, efficiency, and usability.

HIT-in-Use: refers to actual uses of Health Information Technology, in contrast to those that were intended by HIT designers or managers.

Sociotechnical Systems: an approach to organizational research and development that treats organizational behavior and performance as emerging through interactions and alignments among the technical subsystem, social subsystem, and the organization's social and organizational context.

Sociotechnical Interaction: mutual influence among the technical and social subsystems and among their components (e.g., interaction of technologies and physical setting of work – both of which are part of the technical subsystem).

Recursive Interaction: refers to system feedback loops that alter the uses of the newly introduced HIT, promote second-level changes in the social system, and sometimes lead to changes in HIT configurations

Unintended Consequences: unanticipated side effects of interventions into organizations.

Chapter 4
The MOBEL Project: Experiences from Applying User-Centered Methods for Designing Mobile ICT for Hospitals

Inger Dybdahl Sørby
Norwegian University of Science and Technology, Norway

Line Melby
Norwegian University of Science and Technology, Norway

Yngve Dahl
Telenor Research & Innovation, Norway

Gry Seland
Norwegian University of Science and Technology, Norway

Pieter Toussaint
Norwegian University of Science and Technology, Norway

Øystein Nytrø
Norwegian University of Science and Technology, Norway

Arild Faxvaag
Norwegian University of Science and Technology, Norway

ABSTRACT

This chapter presents results and experiences from the MOBEL (MOBile ELectronic patient record) project at the Norwegian University of Science and Technology (NTNU) in Trondheim, Norway. MOBEL was a multidisciplinary research project established in 2000. The problem area of the project was communication and information needs in hospital wards, and the aim of the project was to develop and explore methods and prototypes for point of care clinical information systems (PoCCS) that support clinicians in their patient-centered activities. The chapter summarizes four sub studies performed during the project. Each study presents different approaches to user-centered design of PoCCS. Findings from these studies confirm the need for mobile information and communication technology (ICT) in

DOI: 10.4018/978-1-60566-030-1.ch004

hospitals. Furthermore, the studies demonstrate how more user involvement and complementary approaches to traditional requirements engineering (RE) and system development methods can be useful when developing mobile information and communication systems for clinicians.

INTRODUCTION

The Information and communication systems that are employed in today's health organizations are still to a high extent designed according to what can be called the desktop computer interaction model. The underlying assumption of this model is that support must be given to an individual user at a stable location. This model works well in most office environments, where users interact with information systems at their office desk, performing mostly isolated and well-demarcated tasks. However, as will be argued in this chapter, the model does not readily apply to clinical work. Clinical work is inherently different from office work in a number of important aspects. This implies that different types of systems are needed to support clinical work and moreover that different approaches and methods are used for designing these systems. This insight motivated the MOBEL (MOBile ELectronic patient record) project that will be presented in this chapter.

The MOBEL project consisted of four separate studies (denoted here as *Study A* to *D*). They have each pursued a set of different research questions, but seen together they form a continuum of *user-centered* design approaches. The main research focus of *Study A* was to obtain in-depth understanding of information- and communication practices amongst physicians in a mobile clinical setting. *Study B* aimed at developing a method for performing structured observation and analysis of clinical work as a basis for empirical based requirements engineering. In *Study C*, the focus was on involving users more actively in the system design process, by including health personnel in role playing workshops. And finally, the main focus of *Study D* was to investigate evaluation criteria for sensor-based interaction techniques providing mobile health care personnel point of care access to medical information.

This chapter summarizes the objectives, research approaches and findings of the MOBEL studies. The objective of the chapter is to contribute to the body of knowledge that is relevant for designing mobile ICT for hospitals. Findings from the project confirm the aforementioned characteristics of clinical work, and stress the need for mobile ICT in hospitals. Furthermore, the studies demonstrate how more user involvement and complementary approaches to traditional requirements engineering (RE) and system development methods can be useful when developing mobile information and communication systems for clinicians.

The next section of the chapter briefly presents the problem area and an overview of the project. In the following sections *studies A* to *D* are described in more detail, and finally, a summary and some concluding remarks are given.

THE MOBEL PROJECT

The MOBEL project was established in 2000 as an interdisciplinary research project under the strategic area of medical technology at the Norwegian University of Science and Technology (NTNU).[1] The basic insight motivating the project was that clinical work has some specific characteristics that distinguish it from what can be referred to as 'office work'. The most prominent of these characteristics are:

- **It is inherently *mobile*:** Clinicians have to move between patients who are physically distributed and interact with colleagues at different locations. There is not one, stable workplace.
- **It is information intensive:** Doing clinical work requires a lot of information. This involves information about the nature and stages of the patient's disease(s), his clinical condition, the actions taken and the actions planned. Furthermore, a lot of information is produced as a result of clinical work.
- **It is highly *collaborative*:** Clinicians work in teams. Their work involves shared responsibilities, collective planning, team decision making, multidisciplinary work, and continuous negotiation of responsibilities for actions.
- **It is inherently *multi-tasking*:** A clinician is normally involved in providing care for more than one patient at a time. Often they are interrupted in their work and have to change their attention to another patient or clinical task.

Information and communication systems that support clinical work must take into account these characteristics. This does not only require different systems than the ones currently in place, but it also requires different approaches to designing these systems. The focus in the design process must not so much be on isolated clinical tasks performed by individual clinicians, but more on the communication and coordination that take place in point of care situations.

The main objective of the MOBEL project was to develop and explore methods and prototypes for point of care clinical information systems (PoCCS) that support clinicians in their patient-centered activities. Three research issues were central to the project:

1. How to gain insight at work practices at the point of care?
2. How to derive requirements for PoCCS?
3. How to evaluate prototypes of PoCCS in a controlled and feasible way?

The four MOBEL-studies presented in this chapter have each addressed different aspects relevant for understanding and designing systems for mobile clinical work. They are methodologically related, in the sense that they address the different phases of what literature refers to as *user-centered design.*

User-centered design is a philosophy and a collection of methods where knowledge about users and their involvement in the design process is central. The extent to which users are involved varies with different methods. In some cases users are consulted at specific times during the design process. Other methods imply a more continuous involvement of users, by adopting them as partners throughout the entire design process. Approaches in which users have deep impact on the design process are often referred to as participatory design (Ehn, 1988; Greenbaum & Kyng, 1991), or the Scandinavian approach (Kyng, 1994).

User-centered design was first applied as a large-scale software design methodology to get feedback on the usability of the graphical interfaces designed for the Xerox "Star" workstation in late 1970s. Norman and Draper (1986) popularized the term through their book *User-Centered System Design: New Perspectives on Human-Computer Interaction*. Norman (1988) drew further on the concept in *The Psychology of Everyday Things (POET)*.

Figure 1 shows how the different approaches of the studies presented in this chapter are related. Although the project was based on user-centered approaches, the different studies involved users in different ways and in different stages. *Studies A* and *B* are based on field studies; observing real

Figure 1. Research approaches and connections between the MOBEL studies

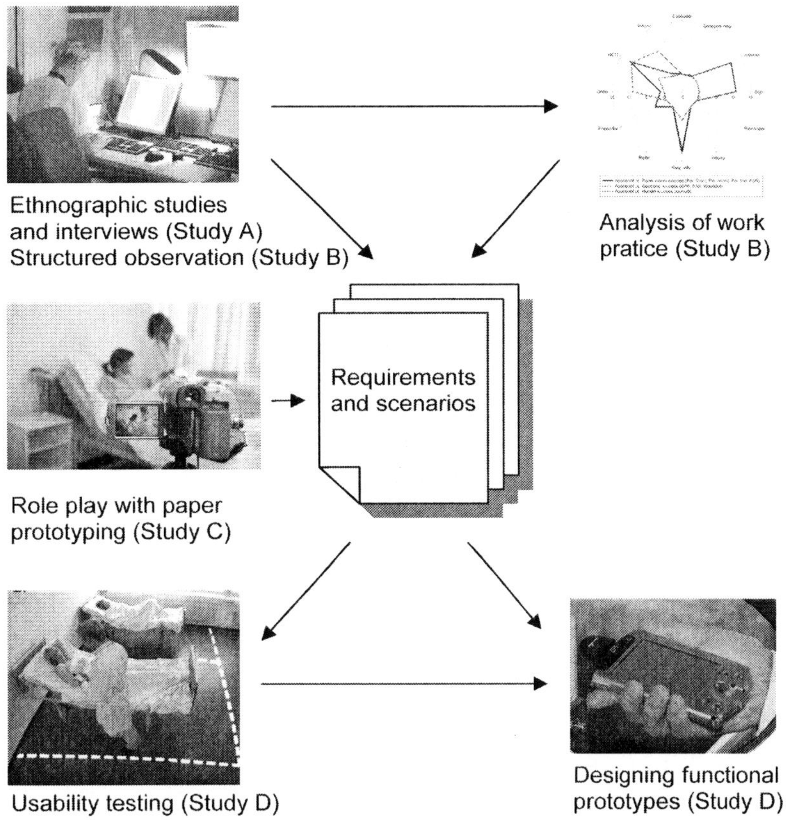

users (i.e. physicians and nurses) in real clinical settings. Hence, they were mostly involved with research issue 1 and 2 identified above. *Study C* moved the users out of the hospital wards and actively involved them in role play, developing new situations and solutions of problems that they found relevant. This study was involved with research issues 2 and 3 mostly. This also holds true for *Study D* in which prototypes of messaging systems were developed and evaluated with real users in a usability laboratory configured as a small hospital ward.

The following sections provide a more detailed presentation of the objectives, research approaches and findings of *Study A* to *D*.

STUDY A: UNDERSTANDING CLINICAL INFORMATION AND COMMUNICATION PRACTICES IN MOBILE WORK: AN ETHNOGRAPHIC APPROACH

The motivation behind *Study A* was that computer systems in Norwegian hospitals predominantly have been stationary, meaning that clinicians receive little computer support at the point of care. This led to a desire of investigating clinical work in hospital wards in more detail, particularly focusing on how clinicians communicate and work with information. The study had an explicit focus on *mobile* work (Melby, 2007).

Objectives: Study A

The main objective of *Study A* was to obtain in-depth understanding of information and communication practices amongst physicians in a mobile clinical setting, by conducting participant observation in a hospital ward. More specifically, the following research questions were pursued: How do clinicians collect, transfer and store information? What are their information needs and how are these needs solved? How do clinicians communicate, e.g. what mediums are used? Due to the focus on mobile work situations, the study domain was limited to the investigation of clinical work performed outside physicians' offices.

Research Approach: Ethnographic Study

The theoretical approach in *Study A* was a combination of concepts from medical sociology and Science and Technology Studies (STS), or what we may call a socio-technical approach. Such an approach makes it pertinent to understand how the organization works; how work practices are carried out, how routines are established and sustained, and how actors organize and reorganize their work in a constantly changing environment. The research has drawn on concepts like articulation work (Strauss, Fagerhaug, Suczek, & Wiener, 1997), coordination (Berg, 1999), standardization (Timmermans & Berg, 2003) and boundary objects (Star & Griesemer, 1989). Using an STS perspective implies applying a broad definition of technology. Investigating health personnel's use of technologies for mediation of information and knowledge thus includes studying the use of mundane technologies, like a piece of paper, to the use of sophisticated technologies, like advanced clinical information systems (Timmermans & Berg, 2003). Since the technologies are embedded in relations to other tools, people, and working practices, it is not possible to study the technology in itself, it must be studied *in practice*. In *Study A*, it was thus studied how a number of technologies play a part in the mediation of information and knowledge, and how the social and material artifacts mutually constitute each other in a hospital ward. Furthermore, the study focused on physicians' expressed information needs, the use of procedures and guidelines in clinical mobile settings, and finally on how certain objects may function as communicative devices or 'boundary objects' between the different groups of health personnel.

Methodologically, the study has been drawing on ethnographic data collected from one hospital department during two periods of fieldwork. Ethnography or participant observation denotes a research method where the researcher takes part in peoples' everyday life and everyday activities over a period of time. The aim is to obtain first-hand knowledge about social processes in a real life setting (Dingwall, 1997; Silverman, 2001). Participant observation is a method that may be useful in different kinds of research projects, including projects that aim at providing input to design. First of all, participant observation provides knowledge about what people actually do, and not what they say they are doing. By using participant observation we avoid problems of people not remembering what they have done, or people not telling the truth, or becoming normative. Secondly, it is a useful method for investigating how people are interacting with their environment. The interplay between social and material actors is often an important focus in observational studies, and it was a core theme in *Study A*.

The first period of fieldwork took place in 2001 and lasted for one month, while the second period took place during a four-month period in 2002. In addition to participant observation, informal interviews with health personnel were conducted. The observational data was documented through field notes. In addition, health personnel's presentation of patient histories, discussions of test- and laboratory results and discussions of ward patients were recorded and subsequently transcribed and

Figure 2. Discussion of ward patients' test and laboratory result

analyzed. In total, 30 different meetings were recorded.

Ethnography has been criticized for taking too long time and to only offer snapshots of current practice. Ethnographic data may, however, be analyzed and used in different ways and may thus be tailored to provide input to requirements (Randall, Harper, & Rouncefield, 2007). In *Study A* the main objective was to obtain knowledge of current practice. However, in collaboration with *Study B*, there was also an objective to investigate ways of utilizing observational data as basis for design.

Findings: Study A

Study A had a broad and mainly explorative objective, but was confined to the study of clinical mobile work, especially looking into the information and communication practices taking place in the ward. The clinicians were not actively involved in the study, except for being observed while conducting their daily work, e.g. they were not explicitly providing input to requirements or design. Only on a few occasions during the interviews, clinicians directly expressed needs for specific kinds of computer support. One example of this was the request for a screen on the wall, where clinicians jointly could see patient information, e.g. from the patient record, while discussing a particular patient.

The main findings of *Study A* underline how coordination and mediation of knowledge and information are core tasks for health personnel. The study also shows that medical knowledge is a product of negotiations between the personnel, meaning that medical work is very much collaborative work.

Furthermore, the study shows that clinical work to a great extent is characterized by flexible and improvised practices, even though standards and guidelines do exist. The flexible character of clinical work – and the need to keep clinical work flexible – implies that applying standard procedures are challenging and that such standards must be subject to discussions and tinkering. The study also emphasizes the need for mobile systems in hospitals that support collaborative and flexible work.

Study A also showed that there are no seamless information and communication technology in the ward. On the contrary, health personnel are using a number of different and complementary technologies in a skilful way. The content in these different information and communication technologies overlap and provide information redundancy. This redundancy could be seen as an *advantage* since important information could be found in different sources, but it could also be a *disadvantage* if the information sources are not updated simultaneously.

The analyses of the observations show that sources of information have to be easily accessible to be used. At the same time health personnel assess the credibility of the sources, and credibility seems to be put higher than easy access. Furthermore, the study shows that hospital physicians demand several types of information. In the study the need for seven different information types were assessed, and the information types most in demand were patient data and medical knowledge. This kind of information is by far also the easiest to integrate into computer systems. The information parallels the information found in the patient record or in medical reference works.

Even though there exist a myriad of information sources at the hospital, physicians quite frequently still experience a lack of information. This may in turn affect how they perform their work. The study shows that paper-based mediums still are important, and documentation, collection and planning happened primarily through paper mediums. The electronic patient record was seldom used. The study shows that there is a great need for common spaces where health personnel may negotiate, discuss and coordinate clinical information. The great challenge is to design good places or spaces where health personnel can meet. Such a place or space may take a virtual form, or it may take the form of a mobile computer system brought into the different clinical situations.

STUDY B: REQUIREMENTS ENGINEERING FOR MOBILE HEALTH INFORMATION SYSTEMS

As described in the previous section, the main objective of *Study A* was to obtain knowledge of current practice by using participant observation, but also to investigate ways of utilizing observational data as basis for design. *Study B* was also based on understanding current clinical practice, but the focus of the research performed in *Study B* was to explore *how* observation and analysis of clinicians' information and communication behavior could be used as an approach to requirements engineering (RE) for mobile health information systems (Sørby, 2007).

Objectives: Study B

The main objective of *Study B* was to investigate how knowledge about clinical information and communication practice can be transformed into specific requirements for PoCCS. The study focused on exploring a method for identifying and recording knowledge about actors, roles, situations, procedures, information, communicative acts, and other rich context information in real hospital ward situations. The ultimate goal of the research was to elicit and produce requirements to context-aware user interfaces for clinicians (i.e. physicians, nurses, and other allied healthcare professionals working with hospital patients) (Coiera, 2003).

Research Approach

Characterizing Cooperation in the Ward

In order to get a general understanding of the domain and a view of how the current information sources were used in the hospital wards, an initial observational study was conducted in collaboration with *Study A*. Five days of observations in two hospital wards were supplemented with informal interviews with the health personnel, in addition to insights from the more extensive participative observational study performed in a third ward (described in *StudyA*). During the study, the observers followed physicians and nurses in their daily patient-centered work, taking free-text notes. Based on the notes and supplementary information, 11 example scenarios were extracted. The scenarios included meetings, ward rounds, medication administering and other important ward situations. Subsequently, the scenarios were characterized by means of a previously developed framework, consisting of attributes with corresponding predefined values. The attributes were grouped in three main sections: *process attributes*, *input attributes*, and *outcomes*, see (Sørby, Melby, & Nytrø, 2006) and (Sørby, Melby, & Seland, 2005) for details. The main attributes were related to the produced or exchanged information; e.g. information type, amount, medium, information flow, and time perspective. Other important attributes concerned contextual information such as participants/actors, and planning, delegation, and decision-making issues. Table 1 shows an example scenario abstracted from the observations with corresponding characterization.

Structured Observations

The initial study outlined above revealed a need for more extensive and detailed observations of clinicians' information and communication behavior. This led to the development of a method for structured, focused observation of clinicians' communication and information behavior. Structured observation can be defined as the planned watching and recording of behavior and/or events as they occur within a well-known/predefined environment. The method was developed iteratively through several observational studies consisting of a total of more than 400 hours of observation. It is based on manual observation of clinicians in hospital wards in their daily, patient-centered work such as pre rounds meetings, ward rounds, and patient discharge. The field data is recorded by means of note-taking forms, which can be adapted according to current focus of interest. The observation forms include fields consisting of predefined codes with primary emphasis on information sources and information types, but the forms also include free-text fields, which enables recording of context information such as situation or event trigger, reason for admission, illness history, the purpose of the act being performed, and the outcome of the act. This rich context data allows for further investigation of findings in the initial analyses. Figure 3 shows an example form and extract from observational data recorded at the Department of Cardiology during summer 2005 (translated from Norwegian).

Analysis of Communicative Behaviour

In order to analyze data obtained through the structured observations a goal has been to develop a technique for transforming observational field data to visualizations of profiles of the communicative behavior of individual physicians or nurses, roles, or other groups of healthcare personnel. Visualization of communicative behavior provides the opportunity to elucidate variations among *individual* clinicians, as well as between different clinical roles and activities in various hospital wards. We have used the narratives in the observations, background knowledge, and the codified information to classify communicative activities according to a limited set of predefined communicative acts (e.g. 'inform', 'prescribe' and 'navigate into common understanding (NCU)'). The approach is described in detail in (Sørby & Nytrø, 2007). Figure 4 shows examples of communicative acts profiles for two residents working in different wards; Department of Cardiology (Resident9) and Division of Gastroenterology (Resident1). Figure 4a shows the profile of Resident9 during 22 pre rounds situations (total number of comm. acts: 192), while Figure 4b shows the corresponding profile for Resident1 during 37

Table 1. Example scenario (S3) and characterization

S3: Medication - per patient *One of the nurses in the patient care team uses information from the patient chart to put today's medications for the ward patients onto a medicine tray. Later, the nurse in charge inspects the medicine tray to ensure that the medicines correspond to the recorded information on the patient chart*

Facet	Attribute	Value(s) S3
Process	Number of participants	2-4
	Number of roles	Two
	Number of role levels	Two
	Composition	Predetermined
	Decomposition	Yes
	Scenario nature	Formal
	Regularity	Daily
	Scheduling	On the spot
	Variance of required info.	Somewhat
	Location(s)	Predetermined, fixed
	Spatiality	One place
	Temporality	Asynchronous
	Information exchange	One-to-many
	Initiation	On demand, Precondition
	Delay tolerance of scenario start	None
Information input	Novelty	To some
	Recorded	Patient record
	Longevity	Short term
	Medium/mode	Text
	Scope	All
	Delay tolerance of input info.	None
Output/ Produced outcome	Explicit	Yes
	Shared	Yes
	Novelty	To some
	Recorded	Patient record
	Longevity	Long term
	Type of produced Information	Cooperative Constructive
	Medium/mode	Text
	Scope	Patient care team members
	Delegation of responsibility	Predefined
	Delegation of tasks	Predefined
	Delay tolerance	None
	Outcome type known in adv.	Yes

Figure 3. Example form and excerpt from observational data – Dept. of Cardiology (translated from Norwegian). Main actor: Resident 9 (R9). Information sources are Patient list (PATLIST), Nurse (NUR), the Electronic Patient Record (EPR), the Patient Chart (PC), and Patient (PAT). 'I/O' indicates the direction of the information exchange (In (I)/ Out (O)), and the main information types are Changes (NEW), Findings and examination results (FINDEX), and Medications (MED).

Activity	Rule/trigger	Location	Main actor	Role	Co-actor(s)	Role(s)	Patient-ID	Reason for admission (RfA)	Time	Informaiton Source	Direction I/O	Information	Purpose	Patient category
Pre-rounds	Continue after interruption	OFF4	R9	PR	Nur9	GR	P57	Admitted due to unstable angina. Must be carefully watched when considering further treatment.	10:50	PATLIST	I	NAME	Name of the patient	New patient for the pysician. Under investigation
										NUR	I	NEW	Changes since admission	
										EPR	I	ALL	Overview of patient	
										NUR	O	FINDEX	Info. about examination	
										PC	I	MED	Review med.	
									11:05	PC	O	MED	Sign	
Examin.	The physician is under specialization and is obliged to perform a certain number of US examinations. Will receive a pager call if such an examin. is to be performed	OFF4	R9	PR	CP13 on phone (Nur9GR)	Ex	P67		11:10				The physician is paged from the ultrasound lab. Both the patient and the ultrasound machine are ready	
		LAB2	R9	PR	CP13	Ex	P67		11:45				Perform US examination	
Suppl. work	Quest. arose after pre-rounds. Asks before ward round in order to be able to give the answer to the patient during round	LAB3	R9	PR	CP12	Ex	P55	As previously described	11:50				Discuss with colleague if the patient can delay aniography until tomorrow or if the pat. should start on K-vit. and wait for INR level to decrease until tomorrow.	New patient for the physician. Particular examination
Rounds	After pre-rounds	PR10	R9	PR	Nur9	GR	P41	Like Day 12	12:02	PATLIST	I	NAMEROOM	Overview of name of patient and where patient is placed	Under investigation
										PAT	O	MED	Inform about cease of med	
										PAT	O	FINDEX	Info about result of examination	
									12:08	PAT	I	NEW	Changes since yesterday	

pre rounds situations (total number of comm. acts: 225). The figure shows the percentage distribution of the different communicative acts for the two residents. The unbroken lines show the communicative acts performed by means of paper-based sources (e.g. the patient chart and personal notes); the dotted lines show the use of electronic sources (e.g. the EPR) and the stippled lines show

Figure 4. Example of comm. acts profiles for two residents in different wards during pre rounds situations. a: Resident9 (Dept. of Cardiology), # Comm. Acts: 192 (22 pre rounds situations), b: Resident1 (Div. of Gastroenterology), # Comm. Acts: 225 (37 pre rounds situations)

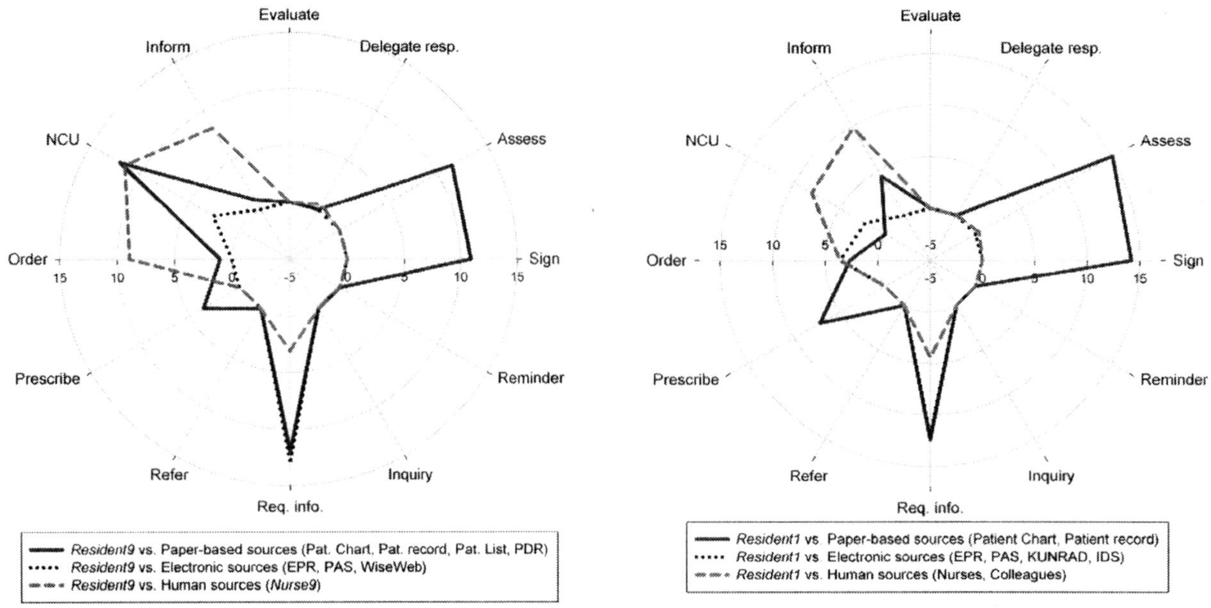

the use of human sources (e.g. colleagues and nurses). The figure reflects the variations in the communicative patterns of the two residents and indicates how new information and communication systems must be flexible and adaptive to the different users' needs.

Findings: Study B

The research performed in this part of the MOBEL project has mainly concentrated on the development of an approach to structured, focused observation and analysis of clinicians' communication and information behavior. The main strength of such an approach is that it enables efficient field data recording at appropriate abstraction levels, and the recorded data requires a minimum of transcription before further analysis. The technique combines structured, predefined coding of field data with free-text fields, which enables both quantitative and qualitative analysis of the data. This is useful for understanding the context of the communication and information behavior of the clinicians being observed, and leads to valuable insight into clinical work which is necessary when designing new information systems. The approach can also be used after the implementation of a new system in order to compare information and communication behavior before and after a new system has been introduced.

Medical students were found to be particularly suited for performing observations in the hospital wards. Both clinicians and patients are used to being followed by medical students, and they are found less intrusive than system developers and computer science students. Due to their domain knowledge and their role as apprentices and future users of the information systems they can also function as mediators between the end users and the system developers, both during the data collection and the analysis phases of the studies.

Combining the structured observation approach with knowledge and insights from in-depth observational studies as described in *Study A* provides a strong foundation for creating empirically grounded use cases and scenarios. These use cases and scenarios can then be used as a basis for further requirements engineering and development of new clinical information systems.

STUDY C: USER INVOLVEMENT WITH ROLE PLAY AND LOW-FIDELITY PROTOTYPING

While *Study A* and *Study B* were based on field studies and observations of health care workers' current information and communication practice, *Study C* 'Creative system development through dramatization of use scenarios' had a different approach. In this study we wanted to investigate whether users (health care workers) are able to envision mobile, ergonomic and contextual aspects of clinical systems that do not yet exist, i.e. is it possible to involve users more actively in the design of future clinical information systems? The overall goal of *Study C* was to explore and develop role play as a method to involve users in the process of developing and understanding requirements for mobile clinical systems in hospitals. Based on current practice scenarios identified in *Studies A* and *B*, health care workers were invited to participate in workshops aiming at improving and developing the scenarios into future solutions.

Objectives: Study C

Role play with low fidelity prototyping was chosen as the method in focus in this study for several reasons. First of all, role playing brings users and developers 'out of the chair' and into the physical, social, and embodied reality of mobile computing (Svanæs & Seland, 2004). This is important for development of clinical IT systems to support health care personnel's mobile or nomadic work (Bardram & Bossen, 2005). Secondly, role play is a promising method for exploring current and future work practices and to understand hospital work without disturbing patients and clinicians. Thirdly, acting out everyday work situations and drawing screen sketches on paper require no technical skills. The role play and the prototyping enable users and system developers to achieve a common understanding about work processes, IT-systems and possible solutions and thus become a tool for communication. And finally, even though role play has been used by several designers during the last decade, little empirical data is gathered on role play as a design method. Role play is not yet fully understood as a system development method, nor has it been methodically applied (Kuutti, Iacucci, & Iacucci, 2002).

The research on role play with low fidelity prototyping in this study has mainly focused on understanding 1) how role play workshops can be organized and facilitated to enhance user involvement, and 2) strengths, weaknesses and when to use the method in a system development process.

Research Approach

The empirical material for this study was gathered through eight role play workshops, where five were directly related to mobile devices in hospitals (Seland, 2006; Svanæs & Seland, 2004). The participants in the health related workshops were nurses and physicians from the local hospital. These workshops were held in a 1:1 architectural model of a future hospital ward, containing several patient rooms, meeting rooms, laboratory, and reception area. For each workshop we added and evaluated a new element, such as "involving a theatre instructor", "involving real users", "involving system developers" and "starting the day with field data", and in this way the workshop format was gradually refined.

After our first attempts to systematize role play as a method, we ended up with a general two-step format focusing on current and future work practice. In each workshop the participants were

Figure 5. Workshop description

Four nurses and one physician from the University Hospital in Trondheim are participating in a workshop in order to develop ideas about future mobile Electronic Patient Record (EPR) systems. They have identified some everyday scenarios based on their current work practice, and have created a short role play from one of the scenarios. Two of the nurses and the physician play themselves, while one nurse takes the role of a patient.

Next, the workshop facilitator introduces some simple models created of foam and paper, and tells the workshop participants that these are models of future technology, which may soon be available. He asks the workshop participants to replay their scene, but to stop acting and 'freeze' if they see an opportunity for introducing new technology.

The nurses and the physician continue acting. At some point in the scene the physician asks the nurse for a paper form for ordering blood tests. Then the physician interrupts herself and says: *"Freeze, you do not have to go and find the form for me, I can have it here in my computer"*. She grabs one of the foam models of the size of a personal digital assistant (PDA), and attaches a sticky note to it. On the sticky note she sketches what she would want to see on the PDA: *"Order blood test"*.

The workshop participants continue playing and improvising until they are satisfied with the solution. The result from the workshop is a current practice scenario, and a future practice scenario with accompanying low-fidelity prototypes.

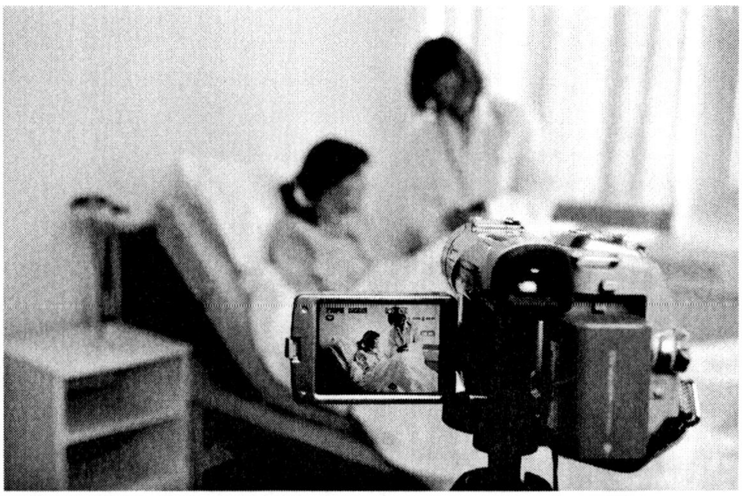

divided into two groups, and each group started brainstorming on current work practice. Some of the ideas from the brainstorming session were elaborated into a typical work scenario, where the participants either had to search for or register some information. As workshop organizers we encouraged the participants to focus on situations that were slightly complicated and that preferably involved several people. After the initial agreement on the scenario, the participants rehearsed their scenario, and showed their performance for the other group. In the second step of the workshop, the groups transformed their current practice scenario into a future practice scenario. The change from current to future practice was done by a process called 'design-in-action', where the participants improvised how they would use new information technology, services and mobile devices while acting. Each time a participant or an observer found a need for some information, the role play was stopped and the participants discussed whether they needed it or not. If the answer was 'yes' the idea was sketched down and the role play continued. A typical course of a workshop is presented in Figure 5.

Each workshop day was closed by a discussion among the participants about ideas they had developed and their view on the applicability of role play as a system development method. In addition there was an evaluation session with seven health informatics developers, who discussed limitations and advantages of role play with low fidelity prototyping as a system development method, and in which phases of the system development process such methods could be useful. These discussions were video taped and transcribed, and the main results from these evaluations are presented in the next section.

Findings: Study C

The main outcomes from the series of workshops were related to the organization and the format of such activities (for more detail see (Seland, 2006)). The system developers evaluating the workshops perceived the method as valuable for involving nurses and physicians in actively sharing information needs and developing requirements for new solutions. For example, being able to 'freeze' a play and ask "What type of information do you need now?" was considered useful since it was possible to get immediate feedback on suggested solutions.

We as role play organizers observed that role playing was very natural for the health care professionals when they acted themselves. They required very little theatre warm up exercises. In fact, some nurses even started to improvise as if they were in their roles when they were asked to brainstorm a typical everyday scenario. One nurse asked another: "How long have you been ill?" etc. and a second nurse responded as if she were a patient. From this we concluded that role play is a natural means for health care professionals to describe their stories, and share their system requirements.

When improvising with low-fidelity prototypes, the nurses and the physicians had many useful ideas. Some ideas appeared because the role play and the context of the play acted as cues, while other suggestions had been thought through in advance. In the second case, the concreteness of the role play situations and the possibility of sketching user interfaces on paper made it easy for the participants to present and to share their ideas with the other workshop participants.

Role play with low-fidelity prototyping was perceived as useful for fast exploration of new ideas and for establishing a common ground for the system developers and end users. The approach has also proven beneficial when system developers have little or no knowledge of the domain and when it is inconvenient to perform field studies. We believe that role play is a useful complementary technique to other system development methods to enhance user participation in early phases of the system development process. However, role play is not perceived as sufficient to create an overall understanding of a system and must be supplemented with other methods (such as those presented in *Studies A* and *B*) when designing mobile systems for hospitals.

STUDY D: CONDUCTING LABORATORY-BASED USABILITY EVALUATIONS OF MOBILE ICT IN SIMULATED CLINICAL ENVIRONMENTS

The introduction of mobile and context-aware ICT into clinical work has raised new challenges related to how we evaluate this type of technology. While the human-computer interaction community has contributed to develop a well-established understanding of how to evaluate desktop computer systems, less is known about how to conduct usability evaluations of mobile ICT. In clinical settings, in particular, mobile ICT is likely to be used in rapidly changing use situations with different physical and social characteristics. In order to produce valid results, the research settings in which usability evaluations are conducted need to reflect these dynamic aspects of use.

Objectives: Study D

This part of the MOBEL project aimed to provide empirically grounded guidelines for how to conduct formative usability evaluations of mobile ICT supporting clinical work at the point of care (Dahl, 2007).

Research Approach

Evaluating mobile ICT for hospitals is challenging. In particular, conducting evaluations in realistic environments can raise difficulties. Because of patient safety and information confidentiality it is often not feasible to conduct such evaluations in the field (i.e. in actual hospital wards). In the field it can also be challenging to achieve a sufficient degree of control over the research setting, which is often required to conduct systematic evaluations of IT solutions. Likewise, conducting evaluations of mobile designs for clinical care in conventional usability laboratories is generally not an appropriate option. Standard usability laboratories are intended for evaluation of desktop applications, and generally not suited for recreating aspects like mobility and interaction in physical space (Kjeldskov & Skov, 2007).

To assess the user-perceived usability of the different candidate solutions (see below) supporting mobility, we invited nurses and physicians to test prototypes as part of simulated point of care scenarios acted out in the same full-scale ward model that was used in *Study C*.

Supporting Point of Care Access to Medical Information with Ubiquitous Computing

Much of the current part of the MOBEL project has been inspired by, and builds on principles, associated with context-aware and ubiquitous computing (UbiComp). A central notion in the ubiquitous computing paradigm is to integrate computers into the physical environment, thereby allowing places and objects that surround us to become *physical interfaces* through which we can interact with computers (Weiser, 1991). By enabling computers embedded into the physical environment to automatically sense and adapt to their use context, ubiquitous computing seeks to seamlessly integrate computer technology with activities taking place in the real world.

Ubiquitous computing builds on the premise of changing use situations. Mobility and interruptions are often the cause of such change. This has made hospitals attractive candidates for ubiquitous computing solutions (Bardram, 2004).

Supporting Point of Care Access to Medical Information with Ubiquitous Computing: Prototypes

Earlier work on interaction in digitally augmented space suggests that different configurations of the elements that form the physical interface of ubiquitous computing solutions might have an impact on how such solutions are experienced by users in situ (Svanæs, 2001). To further explore the dynamic relationship between physical entities and the role they play in interaction with point of care systems, we designed four candidate solutions. Each solution combined implicit or explicit (location or token-based) sensor input provided by users, with mobile or fixed (PDA-based or bedside terminal) output.

Figures 6-9 show the evaluated design solutions. In Figure 6, information from a patient's medical record is automatically retrieved and presented on the hospital worker's handheld device as he comes within a predefined range (indicated by the white dashed line) of a given patient. In Figure 7, patient information retrieval is also based on the physical location of the hospital worker, but in contrast to the previous solution the information is automatically presented on a fixed bedside terminal.

Figure 8 and Figure 9 show interaction design solutions in which user input is provided explicitly via physical tokens (i.e. barcode cards). In Figure 8, the hospital worker uses a mobile device with a token reader to scan a patient's ID tag attached to her bed. Scanning the patient's ID tag causes the corresponding medical information to be presented on the hospital worker's device. Lastly, in Figure 9, the tokens and the computer device have changed roles. In this setup the hospital worker carries the tokens identifying each patient with him. Medical information concerning a specific patient is presented on fixed bedside terminals when his or her corresponding token is scanned.

As the current study focused on what constitutes the physical interface of UbiComp solutions for point of care access to medical information, only simplified graphical user interface representations of medical records were used as terminal output.

Findings: Study D

The test design and results are described in detail in Dahl and Svanæs (2008). The main contribution of the laboratory evaluations and the major methodological implications of the study are summarized below.

Usability Criteria for Mobile ICT for Hospitals

Based on observations of how the prototypes were used during the evaluation and feedback from the participants, we found that the usability of the evaluated prototypes were to a large extent determined by factors related to the immediate physical and social use situation. This included ergonomic aspects such as the ability to have both hands free for physical interaction with patients (e.g., examinations, assistance). It also included aspects relevant for the communication between the caregiver and the patient at the point of care. Examples of the latter included the extent to which a particular configuration of I/O devices had an interruptive effect on the conversation, and to which degree the configuration facilitated caregiver-patient communication (e.g., the possibility of using the terminal as a shared visual display during consultations).

Figure 6. The hospital worker's position in physical space is used to automatically retrieve medical information concerning a patient who is physically close. The information is presented on a portable device

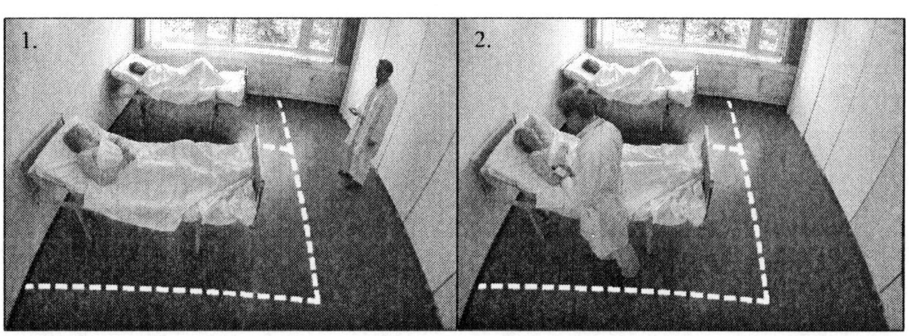

Figure 7. Fixed bedside terminals replace the mobile device used in the interaction design solution shown in Figure 6

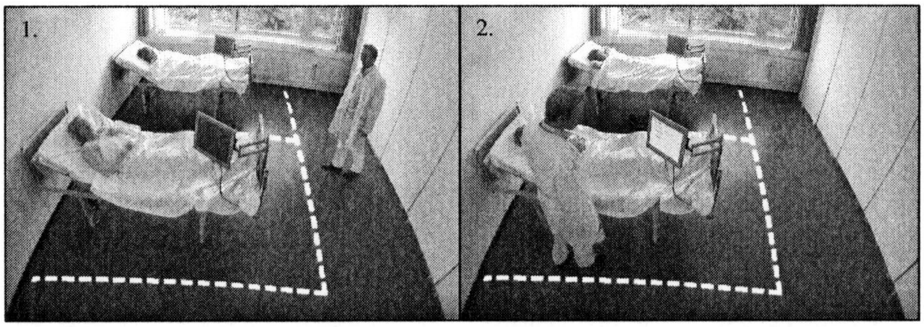

Figure 8. The location-aware zones surrounding each patient bed in Figures 6 and 7 are replaced by physical tokens (cards) containing bar codes. The tokens act as physical links to the patients' medical record. Scanning the barcode on a token with a mobile device retrieves the corresponding information

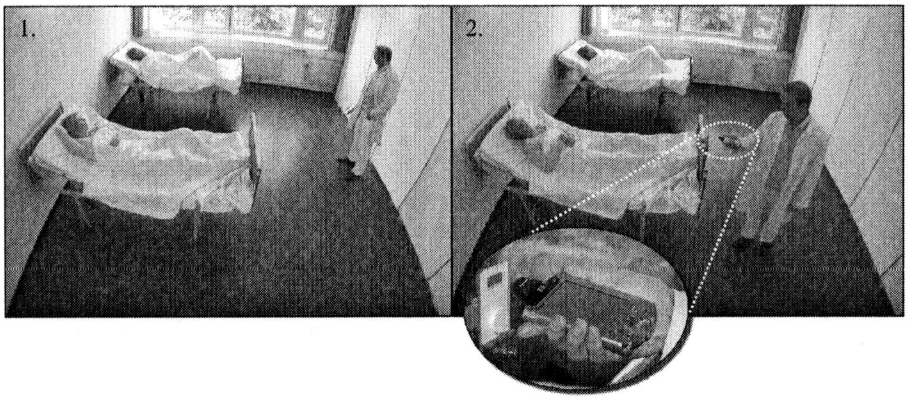

Figure 9. Tokens and devices switch roles vis-à-vis Figure 8

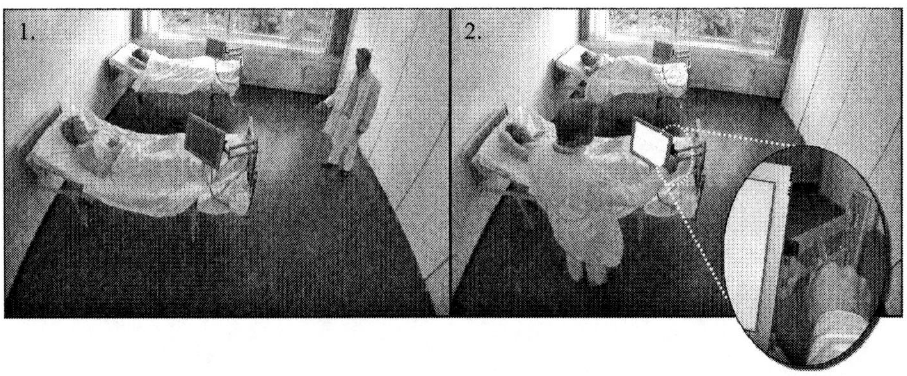

Methodological Implications

Based on the findings above we will briefly discuss the methodological implications that usability evaluations of mobile ICT for hospitals raise.

Realistic Test Environments can Help Detect Subtle Design Flaws and Qualities

Feedback from the hospital workers participating in the evaluation suggested that the perceived usability of the different techniques was subject to factors beyond the terminal interface and the technical design as such. Often, this was related to subtle qualities of the designs, such as the possibility to share screen content with patients, or hide it from casual bystanders, and the ability to keep face-to-face contact with the patient. Generally, these are examples of aspects that are not captured with summative evaluations performed in conventional usability laboratories. In essence, this highlights the need for conducting usability evaluations of mobile ICT for clinical work in the physical environments and care scenarios that closely simulate actual work situations.

Simple Prototypes Tested in Realistic Settings can Promote Reflections Among End Users

From our experiences from the laboratory evaluations we also found that practical usability experiments, with simplified candidate solutions and end users performing simulated tasks in realistic settings, encourage participants to relate the testing to their own work experiences, and comment on the usability of the prototypes as if the testing was conducted in their actual work environment. We found that during experiments, simple prototypes can act as vehicles for reflection for participants. Such qualitative feedback from end users is often highly valuable in early phases of design, when functionalities and features to implement are not yet set in stone.

The Contextual Nature of the Usability of Mobile ICT Raises the Need for Evaluating Multiple Design Solutions

The current approach has contributed to identify subtle contextual factors that can affect the usability of the mobile designs. It has also highlighted that for mobile ICT and UbiComp the total user experience does not separate physical aspects of a system (ergonomic flexibility) from software aspects. Lastly, the current study has shown that approximating at design time the contextual factors that affect the usability in an immediate situation is difficult. This can be viewed as an incentive for designers of mobile ICT and point of care systems to consider a number of complementary solutions, and then implement the set of solutions found most suitable.

SUMMARY AND CONCLUDING REMARKS

Of the different phases traditionally distinguished in requirements engineering, the elicitation phase has proved to be more problematic. The name of this phase suggests that requirements are out there, waiting to be elicited or discovered. It is clear that this is an oversimplification. Work practices, actors, communicative behavior and the like, are out there to be observed and analyzed. Requirements for information systems that support and are embedded in these work practices must be derived from these observations and analyses. Exactly how this derivation takes place is still very much an unresolved issue, and can be seen as one of the major challenges faced by systems development and requirements engineering.

In health informatics this issue is very prominent. Successful applications that support real clinical work are few. An important reason for this could be that we still lack the knowledge as to which aspects of health care work should be taken into account in order to inform design. And, furthermore, it is unclear how the obtained insights into health care work actually do inform design.

The studies presented in this chapter focus on this issue, or, in other words, on the transition from knowledge about the clinical workplace to specified requirements for supporting information systems. The transition is achieved as follows (see Figure 10): Extensive workplace studies result in empirically grounded scenarios. These scenarios can be played out in role playing workshops that result in functional specifications of supporting technologies. These functional specifications are turned into prototypes that will be assessed in experimental clinical settings in a laboratory environment.

It is clear that the presented studies are in-depth investigations into important aspects of the transition from work practice to system requirements. Linking the results into an integrated method for requirements elicitation and specification is the next step. The concept of 'clinical scenario' is pivotal in this. It bridges the workplace study to the role playing workshops and the prototype development. The exact specification of a scenario is, however, still an open question. It is clear that the Unified Modeling Language (UML) approach that restricts use case scenarios to man-machine interaction sequences is much too restrictive. Purely narrative fragments, relating sequences of events, are probably too unrestrictive. There has not yet been any substantial theory proposed about the exact information that must be contained in these scenarios and the format in which this information should be framed.

Future research will focus on the role of the clinical scenario in bridging work practices and requirements. Major questions that will be addressed are:

- How are workplace observations accounted for in clinical scenarios?
- How are clinical scenarios specified?
- How do clinical scenarios inform system requirements?

Figure 10. from clinical knowledge to specified requirements

ACKNOWLEDGMENT

The research presented in this chapter was financed by the NTNU Innovation Fund for Business and Industry (Næringslivets Idéfond for NTNU), Allforsk Research, and Telenor Research and Innovation (R&I).

REFERENCES

Bardram, J. E. (2004). Applications of context-aware computing in hospital work: Examples and design principles. In *Proceedings of the 2004 ACM Symposium on Applied Computing* (pp. 1574-1579). Nicosia, Cyprus: ACM.

Bardram, J. E., & Bossen, C. (2005). Mobility work: The spatial dimension of collaboration at a hospital. [CSCW]. *Computer Supported Cooperative Work*, *14*(2), 131–160. doi:10.1007/s10606-005-0989-y

Berg, M. (1999). Patient care information systems and healthcare work: A sociotechnical approach. *International Journal of Medical Informatics*, *55*(2), 87–101. doi:10.1016/S1386-5056(99)00011-8

Coiera, E. (2003). *Guide to health informatics, second ed.* London: Hodder Arnold.

Dahl, Y. (2007). *Ubiquitous computing at point of care in hospitals: A user-centered approach.* Doctoral Thesis. Norwegian University of Science and Technology 2007:147.

Dahl, Y., & Svanæs, D. (2008). A comparison of location and token-based interaction techniques for point-of-care access to medical information. *Personal and Ubiquitous Computing*, *12*(6), 459–478. doi:10.1007/s00779-007-0141-8

Dingwall, R. (1997). Accounts, interviews, and observations. In G. Miller & R. Dingwall (Eds.), *Context and method in qualitative research*. London: Sage Publications.

Ehn, P. (1988). Work oriented design of computer artifacts. *Arbetslivscentrum (Swedish Center for Working Life)*.

Greenbaum, J., & Kyng, M. E. (1991). *Design at work: Cooperative design of computer systems*. Hillsdale, NJ: Lawrence Erlbaum.

Kjeldskov, J., & Skov, M. B. (2007). Studying usability in sitro: Simulating real world phenomena in controlled environments. *International Journal of Human-Computer Interaction*, *22*(1-2), 7–37. doi:10.1207/s15327590ijhc2201-02_2

Kuutti, K., Iacucci, G., & Iacucci, C. (2002). *Acting to know: Improving creativity in the design of mobile services by using performances.* Paper presented at The Fourth Conference on Creativity & Cognition, Loughborough, UK.

Kyng, M. (1994). Scandinavian design: Users in product development. In *Proceedings of the SIGCHI conference on Human Factors in Computing Systems: Celebrating interdependence* (pp. 3-9). New York & Boston: ACM Press.

Melby, L. (2007). *Talk, pen, and paper: A sociological analysis of the use of medical information and communication practices among hospital physicians (in Norwegian).* Doctoral Thesis. Norwegian University of Science and Technology, 2007:80.

Norman, D. (1988). *The psychology of everyday things*. New York: Basic Books.

Norman, D., & Draper, S. W. (1986). *User centered system design: New perspectives on human-computer interaction*. Lawrence Erlbaum Associates Inc.

Randall, D., Harper, R., & Rouncefield, M. (2007). *Fieldwork for design. Theory and practice*. London: Springer.

Seland, G. (2006). System designer assessments of role play as a design method: A qualitative study. In *Proceedings of the 4th Nordic Conference on Human-Computer Interaction: Changing roles* (pp. 222-231). New York: ACM Press.

Silverman, D. (2001). *Interpreting qualitative data*. London: Sage Publications.

Sørby, I. D. (2007). *Observing and analyzing clinicians' information and communication behaviour: An approach to requirements engineering for mobile health information systems.* Doctoral Thesis. Norwegian University of Science and Technology, 2007:220.

Sørby, I. D., Melby, L., & Nytrø, Ø. (2006). Characterizing cooperation in the ward: Framework for producing requirements to mobile electronic healthcare records. *International Journal of Healthcare Technology and Management, 7*(6), 506–521.

Sørby, I. D., Melby, L., & Seland, G. (2005). Using scenarios and drama improvisation for identifying and analysing requirements for mobile electronic patient records. In J. L. Maté & A. Silva (Eds.), *Requirements engineering for sociotechnical systems* (pp. 266-283). Hershey, PA: Information Science Publishing.

Sørby, I. D., & Nytrø, Ø. (2007). Analysis of communicative behaviour: Profiling roles and activities. *Studies in Health Technology and Informatics, 130*, 111–120.

Star, S. L., & Griesemer, J. R. (1989). Institutional ecology, translations, and boundary objects: Amateurs and professionals in Berkley's Museum of Vertebrate Zoology 1907-39. *Social Studies of Science, 19*, 387–420. doi:10.1177/030631289019003001

Strauss, A. L., Fagerhaug, S., Suczek, B., & Wiener, C. (1997). *Social organization of medical work*. New Brunswick: Transaction Publishers.

Svanæs, D. (2001). Context-aware technology: A phenomenological perspective. *Human-Computer Interaction, 16*(2), 379–400. doi:10.1207/S15327051HCI16234_17

Svanæs, D., & Seland, G. (2004). Putting the users center stage: Role playing and low-fi prototyping enable end users to design mobile systems. In *Proceedings of the SIGCHI Conference on Human Factors in Computing Systems (CHI 2004)* (pp. 479-486). New York: ACM Press.

Timmermans, S., & Berg, M. (2003). *The gold standard. The challenge of evidence-based medicine and standardization in healthcare*. Philadelphia: Temple University Press.

Weiser, M. (1991). The computer for the 21st century. *Scientific American, 265*(3), 66–75.

Westbrook, J. I., & Gosling, A. S. (2002). *The impact of point of care clinical systems on healthcare: A review of the evidence and a framework for evaluation*. Sydney, Australia: Centre for Health Informatics, University of New South Wales.

KEY TERMS & DEFINITIONS

Low-fidelity prototype: A prototype that is sketchy and simple and often is created with foam models and drawings on paper. It has some characteristics of the target product, but may differ in interaction style, visual appearance or level of detail. Low-fidelity prototypes are often developed to visualize or test early design ideas.

Point of care clinical systems (PoCCS): Information systems that support clinicians by allowing easy input and retrieval of information as close as possible to where care takes place (Westbrook & Gosling, 2002).

Role play: In this chapter, role play is defined as the acting of relevant and representative scenarios from everyday work situations by prospective end users. The users either play their usual role or a role they know very well. As soon as the role play participants have agreed on setting, main actors, and most important plot, a scenario is improvised.

Socio-technical approach: An approach that recognizes the interrelatedness of social and technical aspects of an organization. Socio-technical insights may be used to inform the design of computer systems.

Structured observation: The planned watching and recording of behavior and events as they occur within a well-known or predefined environment

Ubiquitous computing: A human-computer interaction model introduced by Mark Weiser (Weiser 1991), where computer technology to a high degree allows itself to reside silently into the background of the users' attention. A central notion in the ubiquitous computing paradigm is to integrate computers seamlessly into our everyday activities and physical environments. By enabling these embedded computers to automatically sense and adapt to their use context, ubiquitous computing seeks to render the computer "invisible" in use.

Usability: The extent to which a product can be used by specific users to achieve specified goals with effectiveness, efficiency and satisfaction in a specified context of use (ISO 9241).

User-centered design approach: A collection of methods where knowledge about users and their involvement in the design process is central.

ENDNOTES

1 The MOBEL project included participants from Department of Sociology and Political Science, Department of Linguistics, Department of Electronics and Telecommunication, Department of Computer and Information Science, and Faculty of Medicine at The Norwegian University of Science and Technology (NTNU).

Chapter 5
Process-Based Evaluation of Hospital Information Systems:
Application of an Information Systems Success Model (PRISE) in the Healthcare Domain

Sevgi Ozkan
Brunel University Business School, UK

Nazife Baykal
Informatics Institute Metu, Turkey

Murat Sincan
Informatics Institute Metu, Turkey

ABSTRACT

Although there is limited research and evidence base, it is reasonable to expect that high quality information technology is an integral factor in the success of today's healthcare sector. However, the healthcare sector is considered to be low level investor in information technology (IT) when compared to other sectors. There are studies that look at the sums spent on health IT as a basis for determining how effective the IT systems are. We support the idea that the effectiveness of IT systems is not an exact measure and a more systematic approach needs to be taken when evaluating success of an IT system. In this study, we have evaluated an assessment method, process based information systems effectiveness (PRISE), which is based on a novel model of information systems effectiveness in the healthcare domain. The results of our case series provide specific implications concerning the applicability of a general "information systems assessment" approach, in the medical context.

INTRODUCTION

Health care organizations and patients can benefit greatly from the appropriate and effective use of information systems (hereafter IS) (Kaushal, Barker and Bates, 2001). Effective implementation of IT in health care has the potential to save billions of dollars while reducing morbidity and mortality (Chaudhry, Wang, Wu, Maglione, Mojica, Roth, Morton, and

DOI: 10.4018/978-1-60566-030-1.ch005

Shekelle, 2006). As Burke and Menachemi (2004) stated in the paper, in the recent years, health care investment in IT has experienced a significant increase, which in parallel results with an increase in IT capabilities. Empirical research has shown that effective information systems in healthcare organizations are associated with reduced costs and with better care and organizational performance (Chang and King, 2005; Li and Ye, 1999), which suggests a connection between IS process improvement and organizational effectiveness. However the impact of IS implementations are hard to measure and identify (Jayasuriya, 1997). Researchers also suggest that the impact of IS is usually accidental rather than planned (Borum and Christiansen, 2006).

While the effectiveness of information systems is recognized as an important issue, the definition of IS effectiveness in the information systems literature is not yet mature and consistent (Ozkan, Hackney and Bilgen, 2007). Various models such as Capability Maturity Model (CMM/CMMI) (SEI, 2007), Control Objectives for Information Technology (COBIT) (ISACA, 2007) and Information Technology Infrastructure Library (ITIL) (OGC, 2007), have been proposed and used by the IT industry (Ozkan et al, 2007). IS management and evaluation frameworks are not limited to the above mentioned and the list includes approaches that range from the generic ISO 9001 (Braa and Ogrim, 1995), Six Sigma (Schroeder, 2007), and EFQM (EFQM, 2006; Donahue and Vanostenberg, 2000) models through IT specific models such as SPICE (SEI, 2007), ISO 9126, ISO 20000 (ISO,2007), to healthcare-IT specific models such as Q-Rec (Q-Rec,2007), Joint Commission International Information Management Standard (Donahue and Vanostenberg, 2000) and HIS-Monitor (Ammenwerth et al, 2007). Each of these approaches has a distinct focus, and its own strengths and weaknesses.

In their seminal review paper, DeLone and McLean defined IS success in terms of success in six categories. These categories were system quality, information quality, user and user satisfaction, individual impact and organizational impact (DeLone and McLean, 2003). In 2003, they revised their model to include service quality as another quality category and they united individual and organizational impact into one "net benefits" category (DeLone and McLean, 2003).

Proper evaluation and assessment is essential for the ongoing improvement of information systems. Yet, a great number of studies that evaluate the organizational aspects of hospital information systems (hereafter HIS) are based on exploratory methods (i.e. do not test a pre-defined hypothesis) (Ammenwerth and Keizer, 2005). Objective and explanatory measurement methods are needed to better evaluate organizational aspects of IS, both in general IS and in HIS context. Another deficiency of the IS evaluation studies is that the evaluated system usually has a limited focus (Ammenwerth and Keizer, 2005), either in functionality or localization (i.e. departmental systems). Among the explanatory studies that utilize formal assessment and/or measurement data rather than user feedback or satisfaction, there are very few studies that have a wider focus and evaluate enterprise-wide systems (Ammenwerth and Keizer, 2005)

It is logical to think that there must be a strong relationship between "improvement in managing IS" and "overall performance of the organization" as measured by effectiveness. Systematic measurements are needed to test this hypothesis. The first step in attracting attention to this area is to review the current level and status of information systems management practices. As Eccles (1991) says, "What gets measured gets attention". To improve the current status we need to measure IS management and IS effectiveness, although effectiveness is extremely hard to measure (Borum and Christiansen, 2006) because of the highly complex "sociotechnical systems" that make up an information system.

DeLone and McLean emphasize the need for a validated measuring instrument which could provide a standardized evaluation of information systems effectiveness; this would permit comparisons across departments, systems, users and organizations (DeLone and McLean, 2003). Such a measurement would help to build a cumulative research tradition which could clarify effectiveness measures.

IS evaluation is an active and organization-dependent undertaking. Organizations need a comprehensive framework for assessment to help and guide them, in developing an IS evaluation methodology.

This study takes a method used previously in non-medical settings and applies it to the health care domain. We also aim to show how organizational factors are related to the management of IS processes.

RATIONALE FOR THE STUDY

Several studies have looked at the effects of information systems on health care organizations (Jayasuriya, 1997). Electronic health records is the single most important type of system evaluated, followed by clinical physician order entry (CPOE), clinical decision support systems (CDSS), telemedicine, radiology information systems (RIS) and picture archiving and communication systems (PACS) (Keizer and Ammenwerth, 2005). Numerous health care-specific information systems are used in a modern health care facility; their effect on both organizational performance and health care quality is important. The combined effect is also more than the sum of their individual impacts on the organization.

Before we delve more into information systems evaluation, we need to clarify the difference between IT and IS. Information Systems is a wider concept than information technology and is closely related to organizational functions and information requirements (Wilcocks and Lester, 1993; Ozkan, 2004, 2005; Ozkan and Bilgen 2003). IS are both affected by organizational practices and in return have an effect on the organization. Methods are needed to make these relationships between organizational factors (i.e. size, effectiveness, human resources, and financial health) and information systems, visible and measurable. IS projects are more likely to fail than succeed but a correlation between organizational factors and IS success, could guide decision makers in planning and implementing systems.

OBJECTIVES OF THE STUDY

Our objective is to use the PRISE evaluation tool to measure the level of process maturity of hospital information systems. Although the acronym HIS is generally used for "hospital information systems" and "health information systems" interchangeably, our focus in this study is limited to "hospital information systems" and does not include other information systems used in health care settings. We use the following definition for a Hospital Information System: "Computer system designed to support the comprehensive information requirements of hospitals and medical centers, including patient, clinical, ancillary and financial management" (Shortcliffe and Cimino, 2006).

Information systems are composed of elements; some are easier to measure than others. An assessment framework that only focuses on discrete "easy to measure" elements cannot show the whole picture or provide an exclusive assessment of the success of a system (Perera et al, 2007). Central processor unit utilization time and network load are easily measured, but the usability of a new graphical user interface or the usefulness of a decision support advice might be harder to measure.

The goal of an HIS evaluation framework is to provide a set of measures and performance indicators that can be used to predict the quality of processes that ultimately result in better outcomes at either a user/patient or cost saving level(Perera et al, 2007). Development of a universal set of indicators and measures require best practice data and established validity pertaining to the individual indicators (Perera et al, 2007). This scope of evidence is only possible through many studies that provide this kind of scientific proof from numerous different systems and implementation settings. One of our goals is to provide methodology and data that contributes to this body of knowledge.

PRISE is a novel, comprehensive and innovative approach to assessing the effectiveness of IS processes; it was developed by one of the authors of this paper as part of a PhD thesis (Ozkan et al, 2007) and to help organizations evaluate their IS management with a strong process focus. The PRISE questions can be asked by an external assessor or reviewed internally for self evaluation. PRISE has 10 process areas, all of which are all related to IS. Each area includes more detailed questions which are scored on a scale that has six levels. Each score level from 0 to 5 represents a different level of maturity in IS processes.

PRISE has successfully evaluated IS process maturity in non-health care technology organizations as applied in the original PhD thesis (Ozkan, 2006; Ozkan et al, 2007). Since there is a lack of specific health IS assessment frameworks, we believe that the application of general IS assessment frameworks such as PRISE might suggest how health IS assessment methods should be developed and applied.

We hypothesize that there are correlations between PRISE scores and organizational factors within a health care organization. Identifying these correlations will guide future research in determining causal relationships between these organizational factors and IS success. Our research question is: "*Is there a relationship between certain organizational factors and PRISE scores?*"

RESEARCH METHODOLOGY

Organizational Setting

The assessment was carried out in Turkish health care provider organizations with inpatient capabilities: state hospitals, private hospitals and academic medical centers (university hospitals). The Hospital Information Systems (HIS) were assessed using the information systems success assessment tool: PRISE (Process Research for Information Systems Evaluation). All of the hospitals used commercial software systems with little or no internal development of support or maintenance. The research did not involve any general and administrative systems (i.e. accounting information systems) nor any departmental information system confined to that department.

Study Design

819 hospitals were initially contacted via e-mail. A total of 4 e-mail reminders were sent to all the target hospitals. Total number of institutions which agreed to participate in our study is 17. Each health care organization was sent an e-mail message with an attached copy of the assessment tool (see appendix) and instructions on how to use it. The institutions were asked to assign a senior IS officer to complete the self-assessment process.

Prise Evaluation Tool

The Hospital Information Systems (HIS) were assessed using the information systems success assessment tool: PRISE (Process Research for Information Systems Evaluation). PRISE (Ozkan, 2006; Ozkan, Hackney and Bilgen, 2007) was

Table 1. PRISE process areas

	Process code	Process Definition
People	P1	Definition of the IS organization and relationships
	P2	Education and training of users
	P3	Provision of assistance and advice to IS users
Resources	P4	IS interactions
	P5	Configuration management
	P6	Performance and capacity management
	P7	Operations management
Services and Benefits	P8	Continuous service
	P9	Change management
	P10	Monitoring services

developed to provide a comprehensive and integrative information systems assessment framework. Jayasuriya et al, note that most other approaches to evaluate IS effectiveness lack an integrated approach; they may yield convenient solutions within their specific contexts, but they do not comply with all of the guidelines in the literature (Borum and Christiansen, 2006). PRISE aims to provide an integrated approach to IS evaluation by complying with the guidelines.

The PRISE model consists of three main components: People, Resources, Services and Benefits, with a total of 10 process areas within those components (Table 1). The model consists of 92 questions in 10 process groups, which are assesses on a 6 level scale as shown in Table 2.

Participants

10 of the participants were State hospitals, owned by the government and run by the Ministry of Health. Some of these state hospitals are third level research hospitals but most are secondary level care hospitals. The University hospitals that participated in our study are also owned by the government. Only 2 of the participating hospitals were privately owned. Table 3 shows a detailed distribution of the participants.

We had participants from thirteen different provinces of a total of 81 provinces in Turkey. 13 health care providers were from provincial centers and 4 of them were from smaller towns. The number of beds ranged from 19 to 1200 with a mean of 411. The number of physicians ranged between 10 and 1390 with a mean of 276. 13 of

Table 2. PRISE scale

Level	Explanation
0	Non existent
1	Initial /Ad Hoc
2	Repeatable but intuitive
3	Defined process
4	Managed and measurable
5	Optimized

Table 3. Hospital type

Hospital Type	Number
State hospital	10
University Hospital	4
Private Hospital	1
Medical Center	1
Mouth and dental health center	1
Total	17

the institutions had an internal IT or IS department independent of an outsource company. Not surprisingly, the hospitals that were located in provincial centers (urban centers) had IT/IS departments and the hospitals in small towns (rural centers) did not; 12 of the hospitals had 2 or fewer people employed in the IT/IS departments. One institution employed 31 people in IT/IS services. This large variation in the number of IT/IS services personnel (standard deviation SD=7.9) reflects organizational differences in the approach to IT/IS management.

Our participants had a mean of 4.2 years of experience (SD=3.1) with their enterprise-wide information systems and they had been using their most recent installation for a mean of 3 years (SD=2.9). We found that 10 hospitals had not changed vendors and used only the information system currently in use. The average number of different IS used was 1.6 (SD=0.8). We found that 13 hospitals used only one enterprise-wide information system for their information processing needs.

None of the participating institutions had a model of its enterprise workflow and business processes prior to the last installation. Nor did they have any previous experience with a formal IT/IS assessment or evaluation framework such as COBIT (ISACA, 2007), CMMI (SEI,2007) or ITIL (OGC,2007).

All of our participants utilized an outside company to provide IT services although some health care providers in Turkey use software developed in-house.

Application of the Tool and the Conduct of the Study

Each self assessor was asked to report according to the above scale. The assessment form that was e-mailed to hospitals included instructions about PRISE and information about the logistics of the study; there was a link to a web site that had textual and video training about PRISE and additional questions regarding organizational factors. The respondents had to give a numerical value for each item on the scale based on the level definitions according to a pre-defined scale. Each participant was asked to fill in the assessment forms and return the results to the researchers. There are two main reasons for choosing the self assessment method. First, PRISE is neither a legal nor an industry standard, but rather a publicly available free guideline. For a framework that is not formally endorsed the only viable dissemination method is adoption and self assessment .Second, although self assessment of IS processes is a major undertaking requiring a lot of preparation and effort, we believe this self assessment model can help organizations become aware of weaknesses in their IS processes and practices as they get some practice in IS evaluation. Since there is currently no economic or legal incentive for PRISE adoption, we believe that self assessment and improving the assessment methodology to better support this approach, is the most viable approach at the present time.

FINDINGS

In order to examine the data, statistical and qualitative analysis methods have been used. Descriptive statistics were run to analyze the collected data. The responses to the questionnaire were analyzed using the SPSS (Statistical Package for the Social Sciences) 15.0 Windows software program. Charts and tables were created from the data using SPSS features.

Table 4 shows that PRISE scores ranged between 0.4 – 3.54 (SD=0.86). The mean for all cases was 2.18 and the median was 2.11. The scores for individual process areas varied; the minimum scores for each process area ranged from 0.0-0.7 and the maximums ranged from 3.33-4.7.

13 health care providers (76.5%) received scores of 3 or lower. Level 3 signifies a documented process and a standard way of carrying

Table 4. PRISE scores

PRISEProcess	P1	P2	P3	P4	P5	P6	P7	P8	P9	P10	Total
Mean	2.47	2.31	2.28	1.53	2.21	2.19	2.35	2.56	1.87	2.02	2.18
Median	2.22	2.44	2.00	1.40	2.09	2.00	2.42	2.56	1.80	2.00	2.11
Std. Deviation	0.97	1.06	1.07	1.20	1.03	1.00	0.76	1.11	0.88	1.10	0.86
Minimum	0.67	0.22	0.70	0.00	0.55	0.33	0.58	0.44	0.18	0.10	0.40
Maximum	4.11	3.75	3.80	3.80	4.09	3.50	3.33	4.78	4.00	4.10	3.54

The process areas, P4 – IS interactions, and P9 – Change management received the lowest mean scores. Process areas, P1- Definition of the IS organization and relationships, and P8 – Continuous service received the highest mean scores.

out IS related management activities. We checked whether there were any statistically significant relationships between process scores and such organizational factors as location (being in a provincial center rather than a smaller town) or size of the target population. Mann-Whitney U tests showed significant differences in P5-Configuration management and in P8-Continuous service process areas for health care institutions with different target populations. We used Spearman's bivariate correlation analysis to see if there were any significant correlations in these differences. Our data shows a strong positive correlation between the target population of the institution and P5-Configuration management scores with a correlation coefficient of 0.573 ($P = 0.02$).

We also explored whether the providers' own size (number of beds and/or number of physicians) were associated with any difference in the PRISE scores. We analyzed the results with Mann-Whitney U test and found that none of the process areas showed any significant differences.

We expected to find a correlation between the number of IT staff and certain process area scores. We found that the higher the number of IT personnel, the higher an institution scored on P8-Continuous service process area; organizations which give importance to maintaining a continuous level of service must have sufficient resources to perform such tasks. The number of IT personnel was also positively correlated with the overall PRISE score (see Table 5). The overall PRISE Score was calculated by taking the mean of all 92 PRISE questions.

Table 5. Correlation between the number of IT personnel and certain PRISE scores

			P8	PRISE Score	IT personnel
Spearman's rho	P8	Correlation Coefficient	1.000	0.896(**)	0.632(**)
		Sig. (2-tailed)	.	0.000	0.006
	PRISE Score	Correlation Coefficient	0.896(**)	1.000	0.534(*)
		Sig. (2-tailed)	0.000	.	0.027
	IT personnel	Correlation Coefficient	**0.632(**)**	**0.534(*)**	1.000
		Sig. (2-tailed)	**0.006**	**0.027**	.

** Correlation is significant at the 0.01 level (2-tailed).
* Correlation is significant at the 0.05 level (2-tailed).
-- N=17

DISCUSSION AND LESSONS LEARNED

It is imperative to provide quality care while reducing soaring health care costs. To accomplish, we must know if the models we apply in other industries will also result in efficiency and effectiveness in health care information systems. The only way we can achieve this is through evidence-based health care informatics.

More research should identify factors that result in effective health care information systems. We also need to prove that IT actually reduces costs instead of being a cost center for the enterprise. Information systems assessment and health informatics evaluation are aspects of evidence-based health informatics that can provide answers to these important questions. We believe our study is a contribution and a step forward in showing that health care information systems can benefit from the IS assessment models used in other industries.

PRISE contained some questions that were not really suited to a hospital setting. Despite their many differences, all our participant hospitals had consistently higher or lower scores on certain process areas, indicating that regardless of size, location, ownership model or focus, they shared certain characteristics.

This situation is illustrated by the "P5-Configuration management process" area which contains 11 questions, some of which did not apply closely in health care settings. Although there is a certain amount of software development activity, none of our health care institutions primarily developed software; they all bought or outsourced their IT services. In this situation, contract management and service management activities become more important than management of development activities. Yet, our data showed a strong positive correlation between the target population of the institution and P5-Configuration Management area scores. We believe this is due to the fact that software development, hence configuration-management related activities were only carried out in larger hospitals that were generally located in large urban areas. Our analysis also reflect a similar relationship between IT personnel number and P5- Configuration management process area; these hospitals could afford tailored software (developed either by their own personnel or by contractors) to increase the functionality of their systems, and they reported higher level management practices in the area of configuration-management process. This result suggests that small rural hospitals should be supported in terms of IT personnel and software development since every institution has specific information needs that can be satisfied with appropriate development.

All of the participating institutions had some form of management support and initiatives to implement better IS/IT management practices. Some hospitals were required to plan and document IS management activities for external reasons such as quality improvement and accreditation (i.e. ISO 9001 and/or JCI Accreditation); others had people at the top management level with IT/IS know-how. Both of these resulted in relatively higher scores in P1- Definition of the IS organization and relationships. We believe that these relatively higher scores did not translate into higher scores in other process areas, because of a lack of organizational culture and effective communication in terms of IT/IS management.

We found that despite their differences, all organizations share common strong and weak process areas. It is not surprising that process area "1-Definition of the IS organization and relationships" and process area "8-Continuous services" have higher scores than other process areas. All organizations were aware that good IS management and the provision of continuous service is crucial to the continuity of their business operations and a failure to maintain business continuity could result not just in catastrophic financial losses but even in the loss of patient lives.

Organizations received generally lower scores for the process areas "4-IS interactions" and

"9-Change management"; given the current nature of medical services in Turkey, this result is quite normal. Hospitals operate within their own defined domains; they are not concerned about data sharing and interoperability. Process area "9-Change management and monitoring services" is another weak side of these organizations. These results may be partially due to a lack of understanding of general change management and monitoring services, which in turn, affects IS as well. Organizations did not have a clear understanding of either of these concepts; we found that most if not all the items in this section, were implemented only at a very basic level.

Probably our most important finding was the correlation between the Total PRISE score and number of IT personnel in a hospital. IT personnel number was the only organizational factor correlated with total PRISE scores; other factors were found to be correlated with scores for sub process areas. This finding indicates that the human factor is very important in IS processes' success and that appropriate staffing of IT departments is closely related to the quality of information systems.

Although the PRISE model, is very thorough in assessing the IS processes of a general organization, we believe it can be more effectively applied in health care domain if it is modified for the specific needs and attributes of health care organizations.

Some things were not evaluated thoroughly by PRISE. These included the outsourcing model (which was very common in the IS sourcing of our participating organizations) and some other very important health-IS related issues such as privacy and confidentiality, workflow management issues and outcomes management, PRISE covers the breadth of IS assessment, but lacks specific questions or the depth necessary to effectively evaluate issues regarding clinical aspects of hospital information systems. A new model that can address such issues must be developed to improve assessment in the health care IS domain. Such a model can be a promising future research topic.

It is important to note that the findings from this research study are useful for the following IS stakeholders: (1) IS managers, (2) IS users, (3) IS developers. The evaluation of IS processes of an IS organization, i.e. in this study "hospitals", by means of using PRISE model are primarily valuable for the managers of hospitals.

LIMITATIONS

Our study assumed that every health care organization had a functional organization-wide HIS and was capable of using a questionnaire-based self assessment tool to evaluate its own effectiveness in managing IS. We observed that both the motivation and the capability to conduct such a self assessment were less than expected resulting in a low participation rate in our study. More participation could have allowed us to generalize the results of our case study country-wide. A future project that receives financial support may be able to reach more hospitals and perform a more thorough analysis of IS management.

Application of PRISE may yield different results, if a trained assessor carries out the assessment. An increase in the number of hospitals participating in our study would produce a better statistical analysis and might show different relationships between PRISE scores and organizational characteristics. We believe that organizational effectiveness should also be measured and compared with the results of PRISE measurements. It would be very important for future research to study whether higher PRISE scores, meaning a better information system, are related to better financial and medical outcomes. We believe our study is an important attempt to objectively measure management practices related to the information systems in the health care environment. Hopefully our findings will pave the way for improvement in health care information systems, perhaps leading to better health care.

ACKNOWLEDGMENT

We would like to thank Prof. Elske Ammenwerth and Dr. Aysu Betin-Can for their valuable comments on the drafts of our manuscript. This paper is supported by an JMIR Institutional Membership grant form Birim Bilgi Islem Teknolojileri AS . This grant had no support or any requirements that might have had any affect on the scientific quality or content of this research paper. The sponsor had no role in the conduct of our study, in the reporting of our findings or in reviewing our paper.

CONFLICT OF INTEREST

PRISE is a freely available tool. One of the authors is a faculty member at the university that governs one of the participating hospitals; however this fact had no affect on the conduct of our study, nor did it affect our reporting in any way. The authors did not receive any financial support.

REFERENCES

Ammenwerth, E., & de Keizer, N. (2005). An inventory of evaluation studies of information technology in healthcare-trends in evaluation research 1982-2002. *Methods of Information in Medicine*, *44*(1), 44–56.

Ammenwerth, E., Ehlers, F., Hirsch, B., & Gratl, G. (2007). HIS-Monitor: An approach to assess the quality of information processing in hospitals. *International Journal of Medical Informatics*, *76*(2-3), 216–225. doi:10.1016/j.ijmedinf.2006.05.004

Borum, F., & Christiansen, J. K. (2006). Actors and structure in IS projects: What makes implementation happen? *Scandinavian Journal of Management*, *22*(3), 213–237. doi:10.1016/j.scaman.2006.10.006

Braa, K., & Ogrim, L. (1995). Critical view of the application of the Iso standard for quality assurance. *Information Systems Journal*, *5*(4), 253–269. doi:10.1111/j.1365-2575.1995.tb00098.x

Burke, D. E., & Menachemi, N. (2004). Opening the black box: Measuring hospital information technology capability. *Health Care Management Review*, *29*(3), 207–217.

Chang, J. C. J., & King, W. R. (2005). Measuring the performance of information systems: A functional scorecard. *Journal of Management Information Systems*, *22*(1), 85–115.

Chaudhry, B., Wang, J., Wu, S., Maglione, M., Mojica, W., & Roth, E. (2006). Systematic review: Impact of health information technology on quality, efficiency, and costs of medical care. *Annals of Internal Medicine*, *144*(10), 742–752.

de Keizer, N., & Ammenwerth, E. (2005). Trends in evaluation research 1982-2002: A study on how the quality of IT evaluation studies develop. *Studies in Health Technology and Informatics*, *116*, 581–586.

DeLone, W. H., & McLean, E. R. (2003). The DeLone and McLean model of information systems success: A ten-year update. *Journal of Management Information Systems*, *19*(4), 9–30.

Donahue, K. T., & Vanostenberg, P. (2000). Joint commission international accreditation: Relationship to four models of evaluation. *International Journal for Quality in Health Care*, *12*(3), 243–246. doi:10.1093/intqhc/12.3.243

Eccles, R. G. (1991). The performance-measurement manifesto. *Harvard Business Review*, *69*(1), 131–137.

EFQM. (2006). *The EFQM excellence award.* Retrieved on October 10, 2007, from http://www.efqm.org/2006

ISACA. (2007). *COBIT: Control objectives for information and related technology*. Retrieved on November 11, 2007, from www.isaca.org/cobit/

ISO-20000. (2007). *ISO 20000*. Retrieved on August 13, 2007, from http://en.wikipedia.org/wiki/ISO/IEC_20000

ISO-9126. (2007). *The ISO 9126 standard*. Retrieved on August 13, 2007, from http://en.wikipedia.org/wiki/ISO_9126

Jayasuriya, R. (1997). Evaluating health information systems: An assessment of frameworks. *Australian Health Review*, *20*(3), 68–85.

Kaushal, R., Barker, K. N., & Bates, D. W. (2001). How can information technology improve patient safety and reduce medication errors in children's healthcare? *Archives of Pediatrics & Adolescent Medicine*, *155*(9), 1002–1007.

Li, M. F., & Ye, L. R. (1999). Information technology and firm performance: Linking with environmental, strategic, and managerial contexts. *Information & Management*, *35*(1), 43–51. doi:10.1016/S0378-7206(98)00075-5

Office of Government Commerce. (2007). *IT infrastructure library (ITIL), Office of government commerce*. Retrieved on August 13, 2007, from http://www.ogc.gov.uk/guidance_itil_4672.asp

Ozkan, S. (2004) Information systems quality vs. software quality: A process based assessment model within the context of organisation. In *Proceedings of the 9th Association of Information Management Conference, AIM2004*, Paris, France.

Ozkan, S. (2005). All together now: Merging information technology quality and other business performance management frameworks. *Cutter IT Journal The Journal of Information Technology Management*, *18*(3), 16–20.

Ozkan, S. (2006) *PB-ISAM: A process-based framework for information systems effectiveness assessment in organisational contexts*. Unpublished doctoral dissertation, Middle East Technical University, Turkey.

Ozkan, S., & Bilgen, S. (2003). Notes towards IS assessment: A comparison of two models within the context of the Internet. In *Proceedings of the IADIS International Conference WWW/Internet 2003* (Vol. 2, pp.1215-1219), Faro, Portugal.

Ozkan, S., Hackney, R., & Bilgen, S. (2007). Process based information systems for international business evaluation. *Journal of Enterprise Information Management*, *20*(6), 700–725. doi:10.1108/17410390710830736

Perera, R., Dowell, T., Crampton, P., & Kearns, R. (2007). Panning for gold: An evidence-based tool for assessment of performance indicators in primary healthcare. *Health Policy (Amsterdam)*, *80*(2), 314–327. doi:10.1016/j.healthpol.2006.03.011

Q-rec European Quality Labelling and Certification of Electronic Health Record Systems (EHRs). Retrieved on August 13, 2007, from: http://www.eurorec.org/projects/qrec.cfm

Schroeder, R. G., Linderman, K., Liedtke, C., & Choo, A. S. (2007). Six sigma: Definition and underlying theory. *Journal of Operations Management*.

Shortliffe, E. H., & Cimino, J. J. (Eds.). (2006). *Biomedical informatics computer applications in healthcare and biomedicine*. Springer-Verlag.

Software Engineering Institute. *CMMI: Capability maturity model integrated*. Retrieved on November 1, 2007, from www.sei.cmu.edu/cmmi/

Software Quality Institute GU. *SPICE software process improvement and capability determination*. Retrieved on August 13, 2007, from: http://www.sqi.gu.edu.au/spice/

Willcocks, L., & Lester, S. (1993, May 17-19). How do organizations evaluate and control information-systems investments-recent UK survey evidence. In D. Avison, et al. (Eds.), *Human, organizational, and social dimensions of IS development. Proceedings of the IFIPWG8.2 Working Group Conference,* Noordwijkerhout, Netherlands. Amsterdam: Elsevier North Holland.

KEY TERMS AND DEFINITIONS

Information systems effectiveness: Refers to the systematic approach needs to be taken when evaluating success of an information system.

Information systems evaluation: It is the process that contains several criteria through which key areas of the proposed information systems will be evaluated.

Information systems resources: The resources of the information systems refer to people hardware software and data.

Information technology management: According to Michael K. Badawy Information Technology Management is concerned with exploring and understanding **IT** as a corporate resource that determines both the strategic and operational capabilities of the firm in designing and developing products and services for maximum customer satisfaction, corporate productivity, profitability and competitiveness

APPENDIX

Process: P1 Definition of the IS organisation and relationships

Component of PRISE: People

Questions:

1. Does the IS organisation communicate its goals and results at all levels?
2. Is the IS organised to be involved in all decision processes, respond to key organisation initiatives and focus on all corporate automation needs?
3. Is the IS organisational model aligned with the organisation functions and does is adapt rapidly to changes in the organisation environment?
4. Through encouraging and promoting the taking of responsibility, does the IS organisation develop and grow individuals and heightens collaboration?
5. Are there clear command and control processes, with segregation where needed, specialisation where required and empowerment where beneficial?
6. Does the IS organisation properly position security, internal control and quality functions, and adequately balances supervision and empowerment?
7. Is the IS organisation flexible to adapt to risk and crisis situations and moves from a hierarchical model, when all is well, to a team-based model when pressure mounts, empowering individuals in times of crisis?
8. Can a strong management control be established over the outsourcing of IS services, with a clear policy, and awareness of the total cost of outsourcing?
9. Are essential IS functions explicitly identified in the organisation model, with clearly specified roles and responsibilities?

Process: P2 Education and training of users

Component of PRISE: People

Questions:

1. Is there a comprehensive education and training program, focused on individual and corporate needs in place?
2. Are these education and training programs supported by budgets, resources, facilities and trainers?
3. Are training and education critical components of the employee career paths?
4. Do employees and managers identify and document training needs?
5. Is the needed training provided in a timely manner?
6. Is there senior management support to ensure that employees perform their duties in an ethical and secure manner?

7. Do employees receive system security practices training in protecting against harm from failures affecting availability, confidentiality and integrity?
8. Does the corporate policy require that all employees receive a basic training program covering ethical conducts, system security practices and permitted use of IS resources?
9. Is there management acceptance that training costs are investments in lowering the total costs of technology ownership?

Process: P3 Provision of assistance and advice to IS users

Component of PRISE: People

Questions:

1. Are there up-to-date and easily accessible Frequently Asked Questions (FAQs) and their answers available?
2. Do knowledgeable and customer-oriented support staff resolve problems in close co-operation with the problem management staff?
3. Are all user inquiries consistently and thoroughly registered by the help desk?
4. Are the user inquiries that cannot be resolved in a timely manner appropriately escalated?
5. Is the clearance of user inquiries monitored?
6. Are user questions resolved in a timely manner?
7. Are those user inquiries that cannot be resolved in a timely manner investigated and acted upon?
8. Does the management monitor trends to identify root causes in a proactive manner and follow up with analysis and the development of sustainable solutions?
9. Are there corporate policies and programs defined for training users in technology use and security practices?
10. Is there management awareness of the cost of support services and user downtime and of the need to take action on root-cause issues?
11. Are support costs charged back to the business using simple tools and clear policies?

Process: P4 IS Interactions

Component of PRISE: Resources

Questions:

1. Are communication with the customers done via the Internet medium ?
2. Is there an extensive use of the other information systems web pages?
3. Is there an extensive interaction with the customer via the Internet?
4. Is the use of other information systems documented?
5. Is there an extensive use of similar information systems for improvement?

Process: P5 Configuration Management

Component of PRISE: Resources

Questions:

1. Are there owners established for all configuration elements who responsible for maintaining the inventory and controlling change?
2. Is the configuration information maintained and accessible, based on up-to-date inventories and a comprehensive naming convention?
3. Is there an appropriate software library structure in place, addressing the needs of development, testing and production environments?
4. Is there a release management policy and a system to enforce it?
5. Are record keeping and physical custody duties kept segregated?
6. Is there an integration with procurement and change management processes?
7. Are vendor catalogues and configuration aligned?
8. Do configuration baselines exist, identifying the minimum standard components and integration requirements, consistency and integration criteria?
9. Is there an automatic configuration detection and checking mechanism available?
10. Is there an automatic distribution and upgrade process implemented?
11. Is there zero tolerance for illegal software?

Process: P6 Performance and capacity management

Component of PRISE: Resources

Questions:

1. Are the performance and capacity implications of IS service requirements for all critical business processes clearly understood?
2. Are the performance requirements included in all IS development and maintenance projects?
3. Are the capacity and performance issues dealt with at all appropriate stages in the system acquisition and deployment methodology?
4. Is the technology infrastructure regularly reviewed to take advantage of cost/performance ratios and enable the acquisition of resources providing maximum performance capability at the lowest price?
5. Are skills and tools available to analyse current and forecasted capacity?
6. Is the current and projected capacity and usage information made available to users and management in an understandable and usable form?

Process: P7 Operations management

Component of PRISE: Resources

Questions:

1. Are operations instructions well defined, according to standards, and with provision of clear cut-off and restart points?
2. Is there a high degree of standardisation of operations?
3. Is there close co-ordination with related processes, including problem and change management functions, and availability and continuity management?
4. Is there a high degree of automation of operations tasks?
5. Are operational processes re-engineered to work effectively with automated tools?
6. Is rationalisation and standardisation of systems management tools implemented?
7. Is the input and output handling, as much as possible, confined to the users?
8. Are changes to job schedules strictly controlled?
9. Are there strict acceptance procedures for new job schedules, including documentation delivered?
10. Are there preventive maintenance schemes in place?
11. Are the service support agreements with vendors defined and enforced?
12. Are there clear and concise detection, inspection and escalation procedures established?

Process: P8 Continuous Service

Component of PRISE: Services and Benefits

Questions:

1. Is there a no-break power system installed and regularly tested?
2. Are potential availability risks proactively detected and addressed?
3. Are the critical infrastructure components identified and continuously monitored?
4. Is the continuous service provision a continuum of advance capacity planning, acquisition of high-availability components, needed redundancy, existence of tested contingency plans and the removal of single points of failure?
5. Is there a procedural action taken on the lessons learned from actual downtime incidents and test executions of contingency plans?
6. Is the availability requirements analysis performed regularly?
7. Are the agreements used to raise awareness and increase cooperation with suppliers for continuity needs?
8. Is the escalation process clearly understood and based on a classification of availability incidents?
9. Are the costs of interrupted service specified and quantified where possible, providing the motivation to develop appropriate plans and arrange for contingency facilities?

Process: P9 Change Management

Component of PRISE: Services and Benefits

Questions:

1. Are change policies clear and known and are they rigorously and systematically implemented?
2. Is the change management strongly integrated with release management and is it an integral part of configuration management?
3. Is there a rapid and efficient planning, approval and initiation process covering identification, categorisation, impact assessment and prioritisation of changes?
4. Are there automated process tools available to support workflow definition, pro-forma workplans, approval templates, testing, configuration and distribution?
5. Are there expedient and comprehensive acceptance test procedures applied prior to making the change?
6. Is there a system for tracking and following individual changes, as well as change process parameters, in place?
7. Is there a formal process for hand-over from development to operations defined?
8. Do the changes take the impact on capacity and performance requirements into account?
9. Is there a complete and up-to-date application and configuration documentation available?
10. Is there a process in place to manage co-ordination between changes, recognising interdependencies?
11. Is there an independent process for verification of the success or failure of change implemented?
12. Is there segregation of duties between development and production?

Process: P10 Monitoring services

Component of PRISE: Services and Benefits

Questions:

1. Are there useful, accurate and timely management reports available?
2. Have the processes been defined and understood what the targets are and how to achieve them?
3. Do the measurements of IS performance include financial, operational, customer and organisational learning criteria that ensure alignment with organisation-wide goals?
4. Are there clearly understood and communicated process objectives?
5. Is there a framework established for defining and implementing IS management reporting requirements?
6. Is there a knowledge base of historical performance established?
7. Is there a consistent application of the right limited number of performance indicators?
8. Is there an increased number of process improvement opportunities detected and acted upon?
9. Is the management satisfied with performance reporting?
10. Is there reduced number of outstanding process deficiencies observed?

Chapter 6
How does Telemedicine Benefit from Broadband Technologies?

Vincenzo Gullà
Advanced Digital Technologies (ADITECH SRL), Italy

ABSTRACT

The present chapter focuses on some aspects of the state of the art of telemedicine systems and their use over broadband. It starts with a brief summary of the most popular telecommunication technologies to give the reader an overview of today's broadband technology and methods. Some important deployment data are included showing the global growth and use in many countries. Results of very significant **pilot projects** *using videocommunication implemented in Italy and in Europe are taken into consideration, demonstrating the benefits of the patient's psychological status in conjunction with health care assistance. The chapter proposition is to show a business model, based on an Italian reality exploiting the Marche region population development and healthcare statistics. The simulation example is the adaptation of telemedicine solution for* **early hospital discharge** *applied to a public healthcare structure, typically a hospital. The model takes into account the possible adaptation of an "early discharge solution" implemented with portable telemonitoring light videocommunication terminals, which, thanks to broadband availability, may be installed at the patient's home for a predefined period (typically 7 to 10 days). The simulation aims to highlight and dimension cost reduction or, in a more appropriate view, give the percentage of resource that can be relocated to provide a better service and how a national healthcare service may take advantage of these scenarios.*

INTRODUCTION

Telemedicine has been a matter of research and convulsive generation of pilot networks and trials in all the world, all aiming to find the most appropriate solution and draw the economic model that could be of reference to define directives and guidelines which may help to provide remote medical cares.

The aim of this paper is to focus on some of the most significant results, carried out by researchers

DOI: 10.4018/978-1-60566-030-1.ch006

and healthcare organisations, in Italy and Europe and attempt to draw a suitable model, which taking advantage of the wide broadband deployment and cost effective approach, can be of help to identify solutions addressing sustainable telemedicine service networks.

The study gives the reader some highlights on the enormous growth and development that have characterized the telecommunication industry in this last decade (1990-2000), which has seen the domination of Internet, the IP protocols along with the new and much more economic broad band approach, allowing end users to access advanced network services in a much easer, faster and economic way, than some years ago these events open new frontiers of interactive applications, related to data transmission, video and IP voice, originating new services, which one can find useful and comfortable for itself, but in a more general contest are essential tools to improve social benefits and communities quality of life Gulla (2006), Tao (2005), (2004) Kevin (2003).

The study hereby exploited, wants to make the point on how these consolidated technologies, properly assembled and merged with more medical needs, have been successfully employed in pilot networks and trials, in many countries and have proven to be a suitable aid to provide better cares to elderly and weak persons, as well as a compelling support to healthcare and telemedicine applications and services.

But technology suitability and availability in not the only issue to permit that a feasible solution may be replicable and widely deployed in sustainable manner. Successfulness is still cost related and a more critical factor is the identification on the most appropriate telemedicine business model. As a matter of fact telemedicine applications addressed a few years ago would have cost impact higher than 30-40% or even more compared to today's solutions and broadband cost benefits (Pelissero and Velo, 2004), Gulla (2005), Gulla (2006).

This paper shares the authors experience in this field as an aid to those who seriously intend to design, implement and run local telemedicine networks, given that the final objective is to improve the quality of health care assistance and benefit from innovative technology cost saving methods and lesson learned experiences. Bearing in mind that any model cannot be successfully replicable if not designed in accordance with the local available resources, service requirements and constrains and local health policies.

METHODOLOGY

The study starts with a brief introduction to the most popular telecommunication technologies, gives an overview of today's broadband technology and **last mile** methods implemented by most of the telecommunication carriers, to reach end users with a suitable and useful bandwidth Gulla (2007). Broadband deployments data are included to give a measurement of how fast this technology is being used in all the world, providing the most recent available deployment data, thus proven the availability of broadband technology in many countries.

Results of very significant **pilot projects** carried out by carriers, service providers, universities and research centres in Italy and in Europe making use of **videocommunication** and vital parameters data gathering medical devices are taken into consideration, for showing that this technology not only allows the doctor to have a more complete view of the patient in understanding the patients psychological status to give more appropriate guidance and make more accurate analysis, but also to assure the patient that he is being visited by someone providing the necessary moral support Cleland (2006), Parati (2006), Klapan (2005).

The paper will then illustrate a business model, based on an Italian reality exploiting the Marche region population development and health care statistics. The simulation example is the adaptation of telemedicine solution for **early hospital discharge** applied to a public health care structure, typically a hospital. The model takes into account the possible adaptation of an "early discharge solution" implemented with portable telemonitoring light videocommunication terminals, which, thanks to broadband availability, may be installed at the patients' home for a predefined period (typically 7 to 10 days). The simulation aims to highlight and dimension cost reduction or, in a more appropriate view, give the percentage of resource that can be relocated to provide a better service .and how may a national health care services take advantage of these scenarios

A LOOK TO BROADBAND BACKGROUND

As stated by many regulatory bodies and as the majority of telecommunication market have agreed on, broadband was in somehow defined as a communication link having a transmission speed ranging form 144Kbps (kilobits per second) to several Megabits. Other technologies, that today we may define "older" but are still on the market place, such as ISDN[1] (can reach 128Kbps over twisted pair, so even if it could not be anymore considered in the field of Broadband technology, ISDN is really the precursor of today's broadband digital links. In Figure 1, a summary of the last 20 years technology evolution in terms of bandwidth growth Gulla (2006) is illustrated in a graphic to give the reader an overall picture.

SHDSL Single-Pair high-speed digital subscriber line is a symmetric technology that grants the same transmission and receiving speed on a twisted pair telephone line Combination of the twisted pair (2+2) may improve the available bandwidth for a better exploitation of the transmission mean (theoretically up to 10 Mbps). The asymmetric family ADSL (asymmetric digital subscriber lines) has a theoretical speed of 1Mb upstream and 6-8 downstream. Other flavors such as ADSL2 or 2+ have improved the data transmission speed to 20Mbps. VDSL (very high speed DSL) may reach in some cases a theoretical speed of 100Mbps (VDSL2). All these technologies suffer severe distance attenuation, that is to say a loss of bandwidth depending of the distance between the Central Office and the end user.

Today the most developed and wide spread Broadband technologies are: xDSL, Cable, Fibber and Wireless such as Wifi, WiMax and last but not least 3G mobile technologies .

xDSL: The most deployed broadband flavour in the world resulting to be DSL (Digital Subscriber Line) taking advantage of it's physical layer: **twisted pair**- the backbone of analogue telephone

Figure 1. shows the differentiation between symmetric and asymmetric technologies

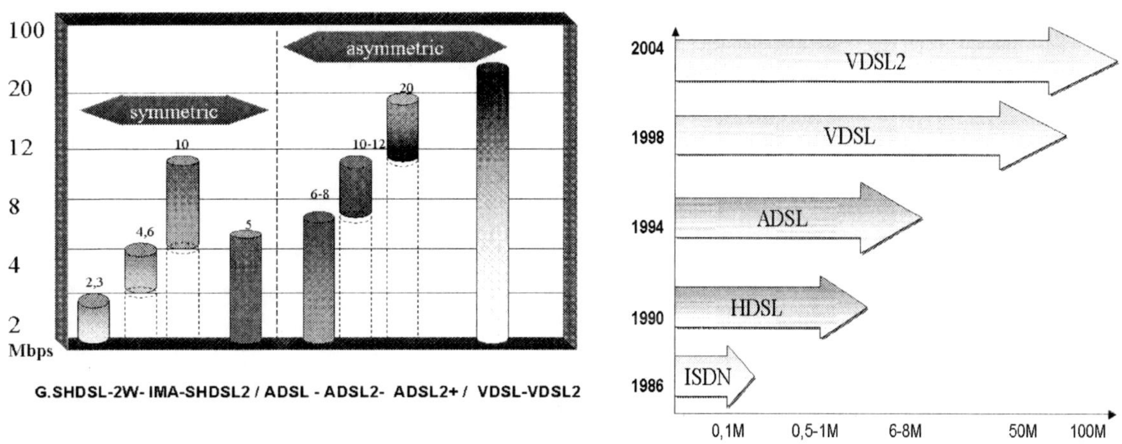

Figure 2.

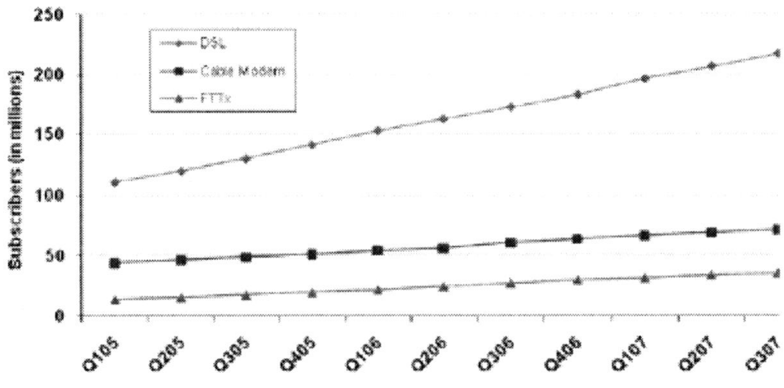

lines, which have the highest penetration ratio compared to any other technology deployed in the last 50 years. Therefore telcos investors address xDSL taking advantage of the lower deployment cost compared to any other communication technology. Figure 2Varley, (2007).

Digital Subscriber Lines (DSL) is divided in different flavours in relation to the provided bandwidth as shown hereafter Gulla (2006). (see Figure 3)

Cable: Second to DSL is cable technology, which had a great development in many countries thanks to the Cable TV channel delivery service and latter is some countries taking advantage of IP technology, grooming together voice and data and allowing TV companies to enter the telecommunication market sector. Some countries policies' have originated networks characterized by long **twisted pair** trunks, which now penalise broadband transaction over the last mile and local loops.

Cable technology is a shared technology among users, it has sometimes bandwidth limitations for individual use, especially on the uplink or return channel and in rush hours

Fibber is with no doubt the highest available bandwidth delivery technology, but today suffers from higher deployment costs compared to DSL and Cables. Many analyst agree that the next future will be characterized by hybrid networks deployments, with fibber getting more and more closer to buildings and in some cases, when architectonic barriers or cost/benefits analysis drivers allow, FTTH (Fibber to the home) directly to homes, in other, maybe involving mostly old towns, will be combined together with new xDSL technologies such as VDSL2 in the last mile (or even shorter loops) to deliver something near its theoretically potential 100Mbps bandwidth capability.

Wireless In addition other interesting scenarios are raising with Wireless technologies where Wifi (802.11) plays the prime actor . Most countries regulatory bodies have shown some reluctant to allow radio outdoor frequency spectrum sharing for commercial services, and grant Wifi services only to limited public areas better known as "Wifi hotspots" that are commonly available in airports, train stations, hotel, schools campus, etc.

Indeed Wifi gives great advantages allowing to access networks and interned from wherever one can be, providing a shared bandwidth .

WiMAX (802.16) is nowadays being deployed in many areas, addressing MAN (Metro Area Networks) applications. The technology is being considered of great interest and may show, in the very next future, more powerful perspectives and better economic opportunities, characterized by a larger bandwidth (theoretically 75Mhz) and a

Figure 3. Source: DSLForum [15] the graphics gives an idea of how the bandwidth decreases with distance increase . Distance is measured for the nearest Central Office to the end users home

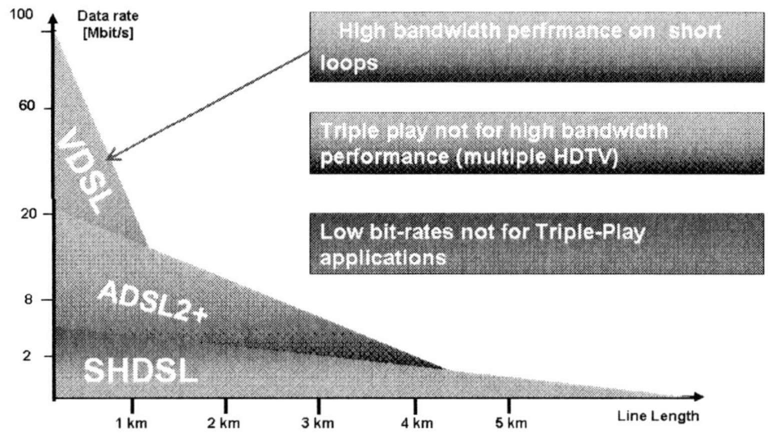

wider reach, industries believe it will be heavily used to bring broadband in rural and remote areas (mountains, country towns and small villages) and probably it will take over wifi hotspot business as well. Roaming is the critical aspect but it will not be a major barrier to wide deployment.

3G UMTS is the raising mobile technology, famous for its mobile video-telephony applications having allocated an individual bandwidth of 128 to 2Mb, depending of environmental and network configuration constrains, it is a powerful candidate for mobile broadband applications that improves info-mobile services as well as fixed ones. Limitations to intensive use may come from economic aspects and cost evaluations. At the end most of the technologies will be addressed as complimentary and probably different broad band technologies will be adopted together to allow everyone from any place to access broadband links Tao (2005).

THE MARKET HIGHLIGHTS

The **IP broadband** era has put Telecom companies under tremendous pressure. The new operators entering the IP market, eroding the incumbents analogue voice margins with an increasingly fierce competition, has forced the operators to invest heavily in broadband infrastructures and introduce more value added data services, addressing business customers, to recover the continuous loss . In many cases telecoms had to redesign their business model with a much faster and dynamic market approach addressing innovation.

This is a heavy task for most but the broadband market today has shown that there are no survivors without innovation. The market is also showing signs of saturation, convergence is increasing fast and residential lines are decreasing as well, for instance in the United States lines have already decreased to 140 million and is expected to fall to 120 million by 2010. Pech (2004). The lesson learned is that to keep the market leaderships one must look very deep and understand the needs that become drivers and therefore business. We don't want to go in telecommunication business models details here, but highlight that broadband opens to many and more innovative opportunities and in this research attentions needs to be addressed to important raising requirements, sometimes left beside by aggressive market plans, but could represent a very promising market such as for instance **social drivers**.

Symmetric or asymmetric connections delivered by broadband links offers wide amount of data interactivity as a basic feature and this makes the difference with other entertainment or communications media. Once the end user get used to this functionality he will asks for more, understanding the usefulness and potentials of receiving and transmitting huge amount of data. The Internet experience has given large proof of this statement and young generations are the biggest players in the digital gamming, file downloading and entertainment market.

Up to now, this has been the predominant key factor pushing the demand for wider deployment of broadband worldwide. Multimedia applications such as download of music, films, pictures have raised the demand for more bandwidth availability and specially for Peer to Peer services, as well as leading the industries to invest in more entertainment media equipment and services (gamming set top boxes, IPTV, etc). But other than entertainment, TV or business applications broadband is a mean that has the power to improve men's quality of life. There are many fields of social applications not really addressed by the big economic players because of market immaturity: numbers don't show a fast return of investments and the business models are not yet so profitable. Probably this is due to the fact the broadband economic playground should include players such as social stakeholders, more motivated to longer mid term view. The benefits that a wide band interactive data transmission pipeline can generate in terms of social services is enormous and sometimes essential, not only to improve the quality of service delivery but also to allow a wider cost effective social services to end users.

Figure 4.

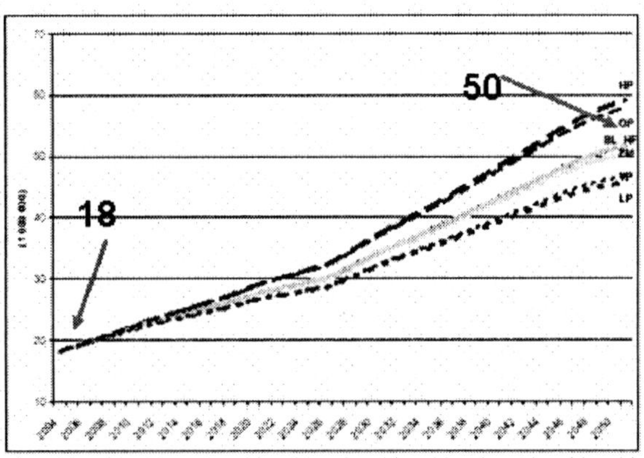

Projected total population aged 80 years and over, Trend scenario variants, EU-25, 2004-2051. Source: Eurostat, EUROPOP2004

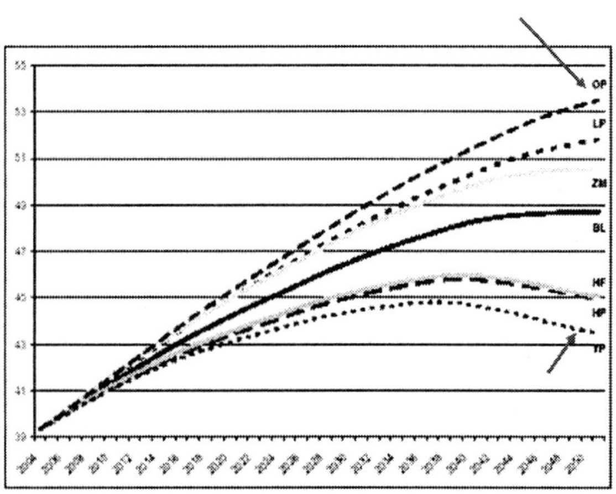

: Projected median age. Trend scenario variants. EU-25, 2004-2051. Source: Eurostat, EUROPOP2004

POPULATION GROWTH

One serious and very dramatic factor being a concern for many governments in the western and eastern world is the fast growth of elderly people, in US called **Baby Booming**. The overage aging is growing fast as well as life expectation . In the last 30 years in Europe the over 60's have raised more than 50%. European statistics show a further increasing trend in elderly dependence as well. (see Figure 4)

Today there is one elderly inactive person for every 4, In Europe the number is expected to raise at a ratio of 1 elderly over 2 active persons. (see Figure 5)

This impressive growing factors are main critical ones effecting the health care assistance system, leading to estimate impressive increase of assistance and care request for the next decade. This will be and in some cases is already the new social assistance and welfare scenario, furthermore being the population ageing an irreversible factor there are no doubts at all, that the growth in numbers could not effected or influenced by any market or business factor. The question here is how to face this event with satisfactory solutions for:the health care stakeholders, the end users and the governments, bearing in mind the two most important topics: economy of investments and quality of life improvement.

BROADBAND AND SOCIAL BENEFITS

E-Health Highlights

Today's live environment is a fast changing and ageing society, requiring new and more challenging needs. Most elderly in the western world live by their own or with family relatives, they sometimes are subject to age diseases, have difficulties to move, are unable to take care of themselves, or just feel lonely.

It would be desirable to have some sort of technological assistance that can keep an "eye" on them, keep their health under control, remote monitor vital parameters, advice relatives of any raising need or alarming event, or allow to talk to a doctor when ever this is needed for physiological or medical support. In other words enables these people to be independent in their own homes, improving their quality of life. Nevertheless such solutions can give a very positive contribution to prevent unnecessary hospital admission or early de-hospitalization providing additional cost effective savings. Many trials and pilot projects deployed over the Eastern world have demonstrated unquestionable cost savings

Broadband will play a crucial role in this irreversible social scenario. Broadband is not a technology that can just create an alternative way

Figure 5.

Figure 6.

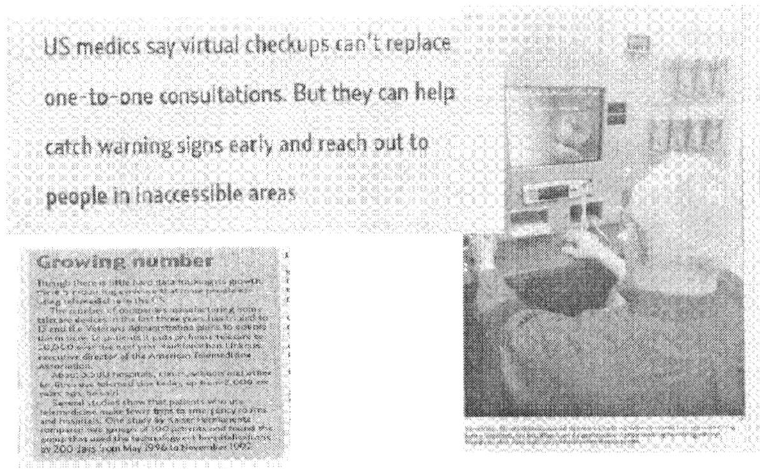

to inform or deliver TV and entertainment programs, it has a more concrete role of excellence, supporting live quality improvement and services for the benefit of all Gulla (2007).

Triple play makes possible to live monitor vital parameters, make a remote medical visit, assist a patients using technology which provides data, video and voice. The solutions does not necessary require inventing new sophisticated IT end user technologies or go so far to new and innovative special developed computers. (see Figure 6)

As all the applications that succeeded the approach must be kept simple and easy to use. Thinking about the most common media equipment available in homes one will certainly drop his eyes on two home devices: TV sets and telephones that are the very best candidates to become carriers of welfare and social health care services. (see Figure 7)

TELEMEDICINE EXPERIENCES IN EU

Studies carried out in many European countries have shown the benefits of telemedicine solutions in both home care and home assistance. The projects have initially used telephone based solutions for vital parameters monitoring for different health pathologies and for elderly remote assistance and telecare.

UK, Germany and the Netherlands conducted recently the TEN-HMS project (TRANS EUROPE NETWORK HOME CARE MANAGEMENT SYSTEM) . Scope of the trial was to compare the effects of managing hearth failures with conventional nurse support and home telemonitoring, based on telephony vital parameters monitoring Cleland (2006). (see Figure 8)

Results have shown the advantages in terms or staff improvement efficiency, patient quality of life and health . Telemonitoring was demon-

Figure 7.

Figure 8.

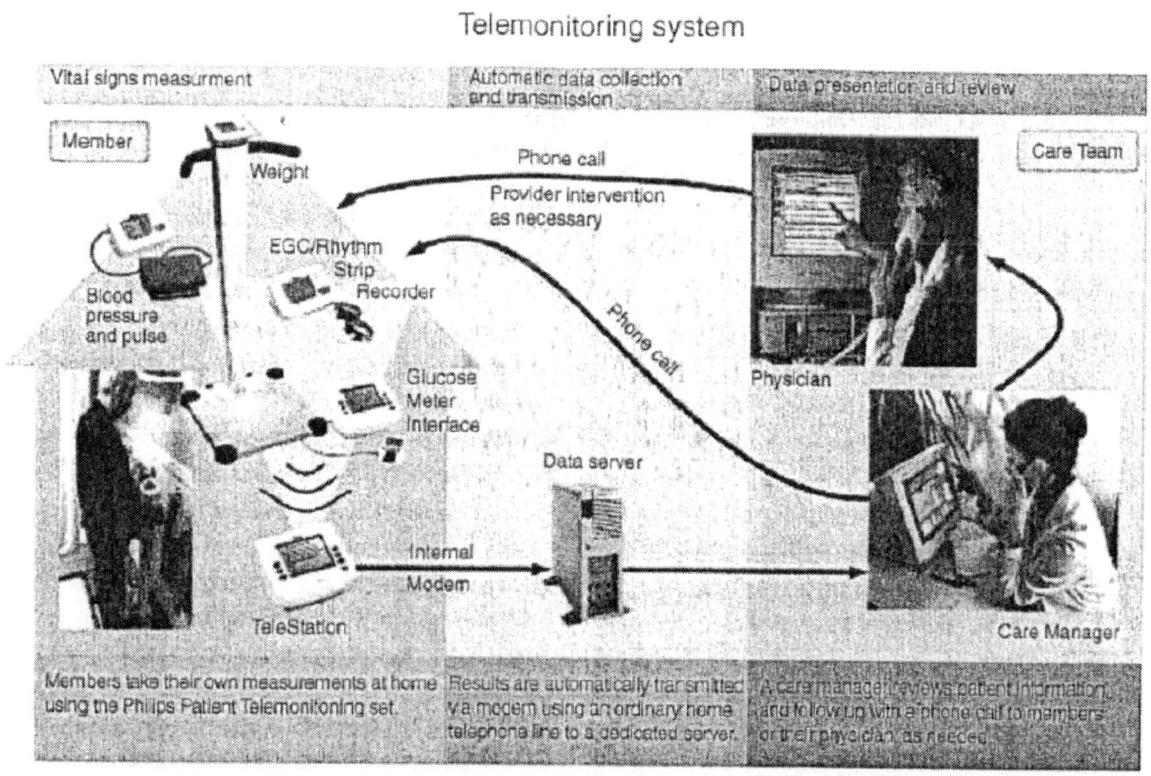

strated to be suitable for heart failure monitoring showing substantial reduction in mortality of patients under continuous remote control . Other experiences such as for instance the one conducted in Italy by the INRCA: National Institute for Elderly Heart Care, was focused to the integration of data with videocommunication to simulate a remote specialist doctor visiting a patient in its own home. The trial conducted in the year 2000-2001 included rest houses and private homes. The service provided was to the patients was **post hospitalization**, monitoring for patients suffering of heart failures and moral support, involved 89 sites. (see Figure 9)

The results achieved are impressive. A very high number of incoming calls, that otherwise would have required hospital admission, were solved directly with the doctors' remote visit and vital parameters (such as blood pressure, heart rate, heart and ling auscultation, etc) detection and control Cleland (2006). More that the 65% of emergency calls were solved without moving the patients resulting and a further improvement in ones life quality. (see Figure 10)

Furthermore, in this trial homes were linked to the care givers by means of ISDN 128Kbps lines, to allow two way videocommunication and data transmission.128 Kbps was the minimum bandwidth to support a good quality videocommunication (recommended by H263 compression protocols). The doctors site was equipped with a vital parameter measurement software acting also

Figure 9.

as a database to store the patients history and visit results. Cost issues were in any how very high due to the type of equipment used, only professional videoconference systems were available and ISDN lines traffic was very expensive and not deployable on large scale. The cost for line installation and the data transmission traffic over an ISDN line could not justify, on a long term, home care services compared to a hospital long stay.

In anyhow the trial demonstrate that remote care delivery was achievable with excellent results . Other experiences conducted in the Netherlands and Austria, all focusing videocommunication as a mean to assist elderly and provide home care services have highlighted the importance of such technology in home care. The trials were managed by two companies specialized in home care assistance Thoma (2006).

1. Volkshilfe Styria, an Austrian care-provider active in the state of Styria with about 1700 employees.
2. Sensire, a Dutch care-provider with about 15.000 employees.

The Austrian care provider Volkshilfe project was co-financed by the EU during July 2004 to July 2005. The project was based on POTS (analogue telephone lines with only 33.6kbps). In Q2 2006 Volkshilfe will enter the next phase of the project using specially designed equipment on broadband IP networks (up to 384kbps). Telekom Austria, the largest telecom provider in Austria, provided assistance with the project.

In 2003, the Dutch care provider Sensire, began to implement video communication over ISDN (128kbps). In 2006, Sensire's video network includes 700 installations mainly via broadband IP networks (up to 384kbps). The network services are provided by KPN, the largest telecom provider in the Netherlands.

Findings resulting from the trials:

- Patients show a higher level of accuracy and

Figure 10.

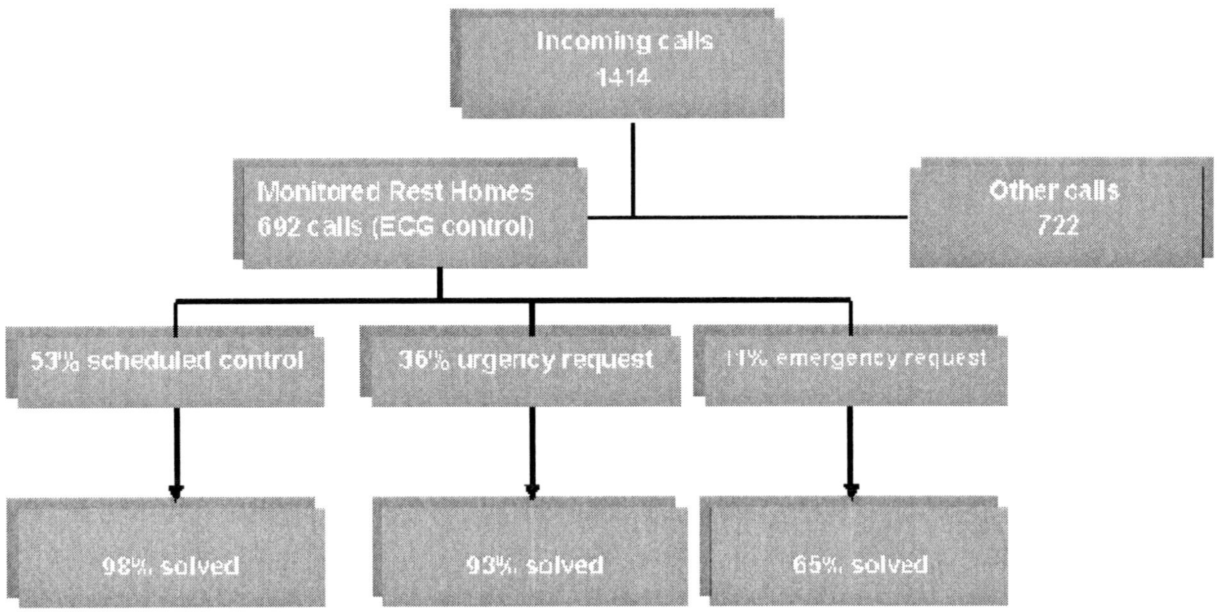

improved assessment that lead to more efficiency during the caregiver's on-site visit.

- technology appears to be a problem for the elderly at first sight, but after a brief training they become familiar with the system and use it accordingly.
- Patients encourage the caregiver to call them to see how they are and are much happier to check their current condition.
- Patients prefer more frequent video visits compared to less frequent face-to-face visits.
- Nurses agree that video is appropriate to replace home visits and is useful as an additional service.
- Ease of handling, good picture and audio quality, suitable design for the elderly (font size, symbols, readability…), compactness, and support are basic requirements for such a system.

The network configuration for delivery of IP home care services addressed by the two companies is shown hereafter. The patients home are equipped with either a TV set top box or a video telephone, both with data interfaces for electrometrical device monitoring .

Tilting cameras with enhanced features such as zooming and remote control make the call centre operations more simple and efficient. The experience resulting in a quality of life improvement for elderly they could keep there usual life stile feeling more safe and under control for the remote presents of expert care givers. (see Figure 11)

Early De-Hospitalization Cost Benefits

Among the addressable Broadband health care applications showing potentials of return of investments for heath care stakeholders, carriers and service providers is the early **de-hospitalization** or early hospital demission.

On of the major cost factors why healthcare is expensive other than staff is because hospitals provide a 24 h hotel service including access to monitoring by nursing and medical staff. Most patients choose for hospitalization because

Figure 11.

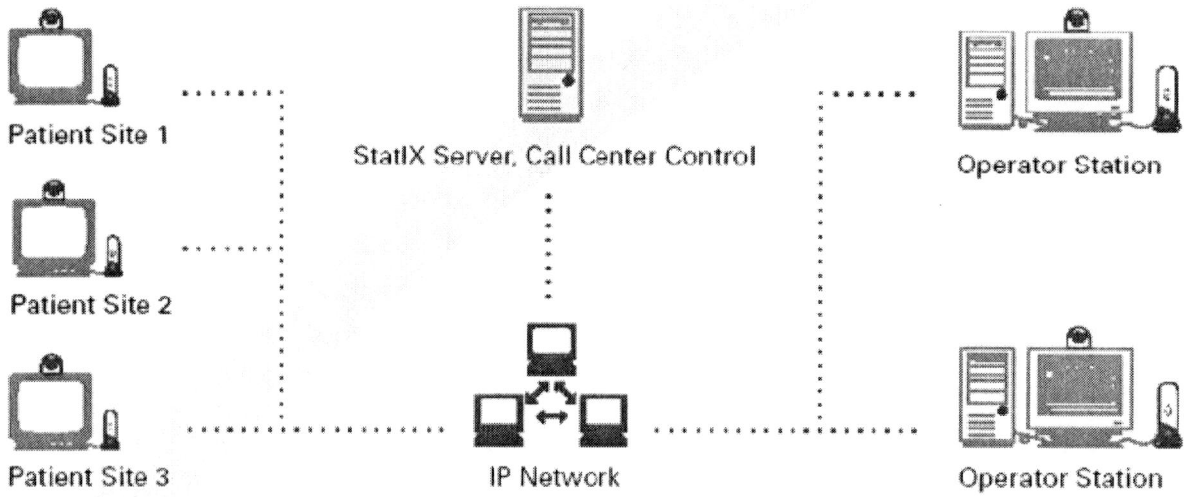

monitored by expert staff, but once a patient has been hospitalized he often remains there for long periods, due both to the critical phase management and secondly care assessment, causing unavoidable cost increments for the social structures.

It is unlikely that sending patients home to soon may result in early readmission unless the patients is in somehow kept under control even after discharged by the hospital . The solution to this critical issues I to keep monitoring the patient in his own home environment using tele-medicine sysetms. Such solutions experienced in many trials have shown their potentials to decrease both unwanted early readmission and hospital costs.

In the previous chapters we have exploited trials experienced in many countries and different health care delivery environments, all showing the medical, moral and quality of life validity of telemedicine solutions. In the following we want to show how these solutions can give a great contributions to make healthcare more cost efficient applied to early de-hospitalization.

The simulation basically shows that it is possible to reduce the number of hospital days stay, monitoring the patient for part of the required care time, in his own home. The parameters used to make this simulation are taking from the yearly health care statistics of the Italian Region Marche, for a medium town hospital and can be easily applied to any other local model. Data were combined together with the national health care statistics (ISTAT)

This business model shows the benefits that a medical health care structure can achieve, allowing cost saving and contemporary better use of health care infrastructures, as well as the quality of patients life being controlled in his own environment surrounded by his relatives. The reference solution configuration is similar to those used in the Netherlands or Austria. A network of special TV set to boxes or video telephones in the patients home, connected to a video call center managed by the hospital department and care givers able to interface electro medical devises such as: SpO2, ECG, Weight scale, blood pressure, Vital parameters, etc. Equipped with special emergency and patients retrieval functionalities that allow the call center operator to have a continuous control. Bidirectional broadband links of at least 384Kpbs are sufficient to provide a very good image quality together with data and voice. The remote visit takes place on the home TV set and the patients is no longer forced to stay in the hospital or to face traffic jam or long waiting queue for medical visits or routing vital parameters control. (see Figure 12)

Basic Hypothesis

The simulation was based on the following inputs:

over 65 aged population trend statistics for the 2005-2010 time window (data provided by ISTAT)

- Percentage of hospital admission for over 65, observed during the 2000-2001 time window: 29% (data detected from a experimental project conducted by INRCA)
- Average yearly hospital admission growth:10%
- Early de-hospitalization potential patients 14% (+1%yearly increment)
- 36 health care structures (hospitals and clinics existing in the observed Italian region) (see Figure 13 and Figure 14)

Project Data

- Average hospital admission: 9 days
- Average daily admission cost € 500 (DRG)
- 5 days hospital stay +4 days hospital home care assistance
- The Tele-video-monitoring system is installed at the patients home for the 4-7 days after hospital discharge)

Figure 12

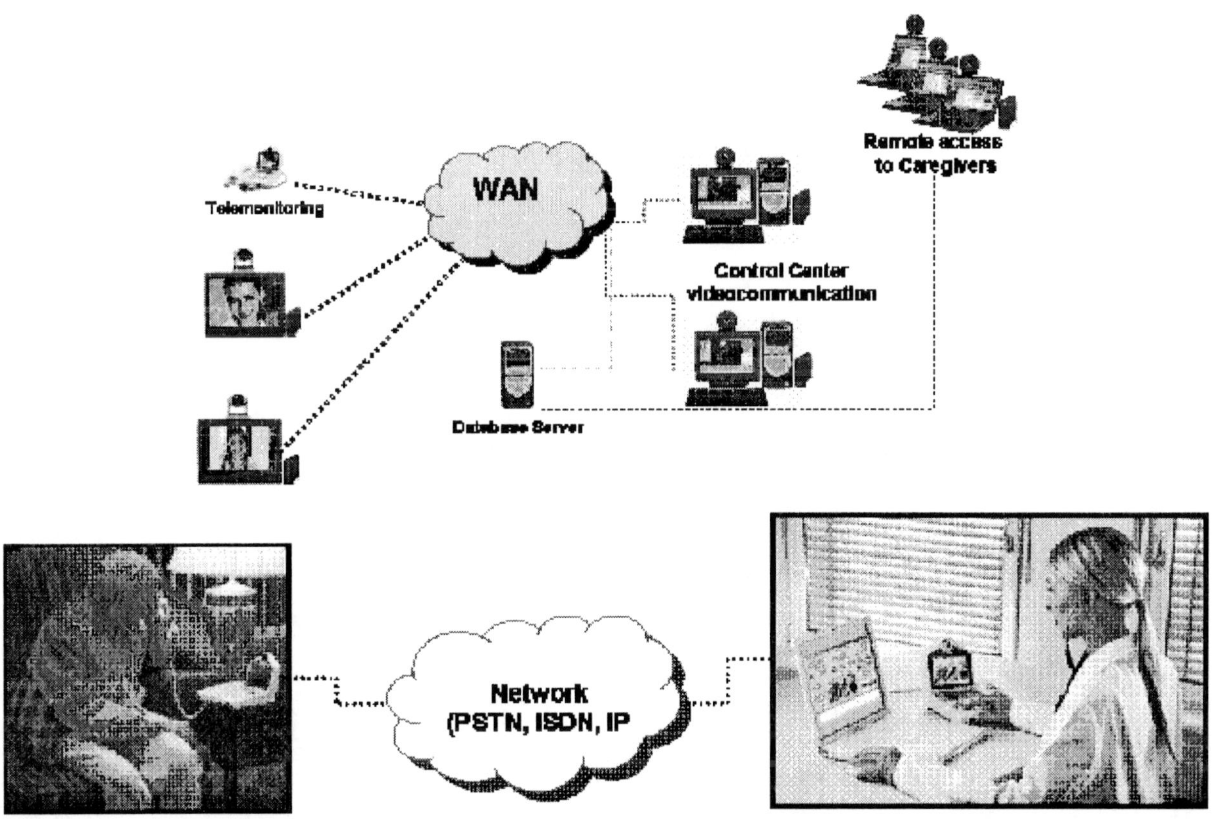

Figure 13.

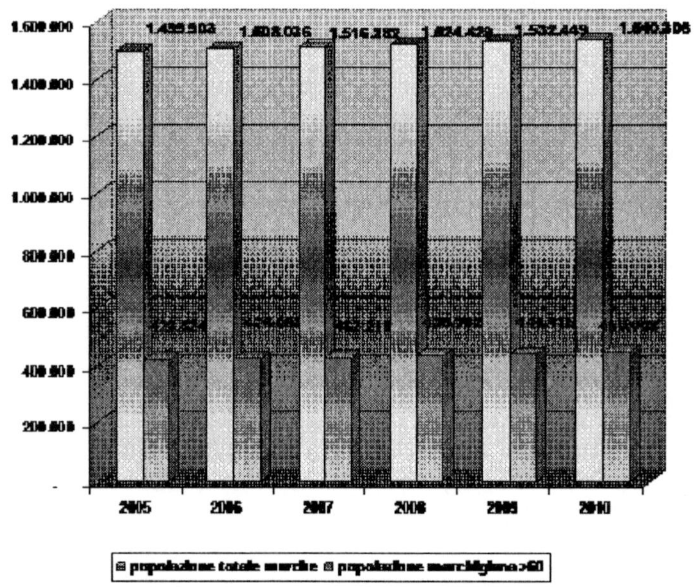

- Overall population growth results in a overall increment of 2,6%
- Over 60 aged population growth is 5,9% (ISTAT), double compared to the overall development.

Figure 14

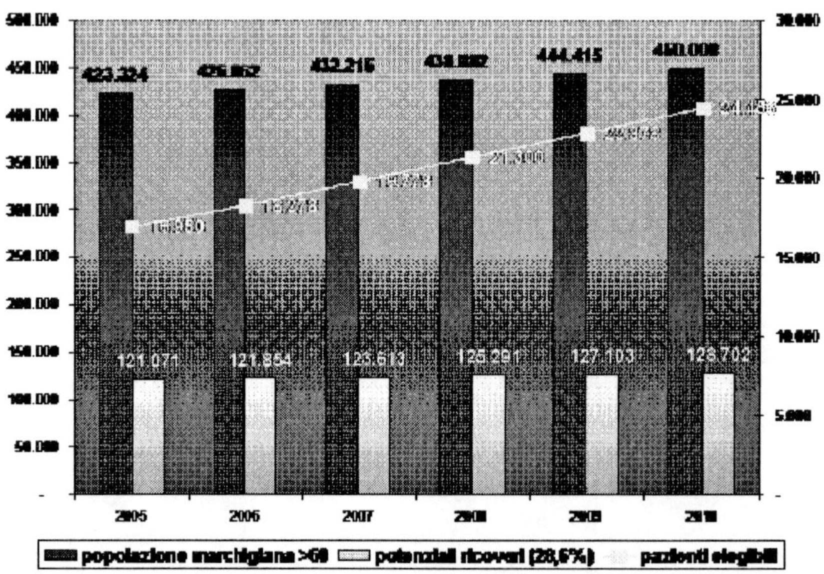

- Over 60 aged population growth in 5 years time window increase of nearly 30.000 units
- 6% potential hospitalizations demand increase
- 16.960 patients representing the 14% of hospitalized units can benefit of early discharge .This number can increase to 24.000 in 5 years representing the 18% of the total demand

- Home care assistance is provided by the hospital on a 24 hour basis
- Equipment finance amortization is assumed to last 3 years with 10% loan bank interest
- Installation, training and equipment maintenance is all included in the economic computation (see Figure 15)

The model main basic is that the service is provided directly by the hospital to early discharged patients in their own homes. The previous mentioned trials have demonstrated that the "you se me I see you approach" guarantees continues link between care givers and patients, specially when he is in its own home, this indeed results in a better life quality improvement.

The patient has a more friendly approach and feels to be under safe control and receives assistance directly at home.

- Video is an aid to train and assists end user's family and relatives
- Patient is more confident with its own doctor and nurse
- Interactive video allows the remote operator to have complete knowledge and control of any event that could compromise end user's health or safe conditions

The economic benefits deriving from this computation are projected in the following graphics and one can notice that the cost saving trend is around 30% in the first year. (see Figure 16)

CONCLUSION

This study shows that it is possible to provide very high quality and cost effective remote monitoring for home care applications with today's IP broadband technology . Broadband deployment has a chance to make this application even more feasible and cost attractive. No doubts on the quality of life improvement perception for patients and elderly people neither on the cost benefits achievable by care givers. It is essential in the very near future to find means, tools and solutions to provide more efficient and cost effective health care . The only way to achieve this objective is to allow medical and social assistant staff to be more efficient and provide support to a wider number of people

Figure 15

Project data summary	2005	2006	2007	2008	2009	2010
• Home care terminals per year	15	20	20	25	25	25
• Video Call center post per hospital	2					
• Patients hospital per month under early discharge	39	42	46	49	53	57
• Patients per year	471	508	550	592	636	679
• Health care assistants (nurse)	4	4	4	4	4	4

Figure 16.

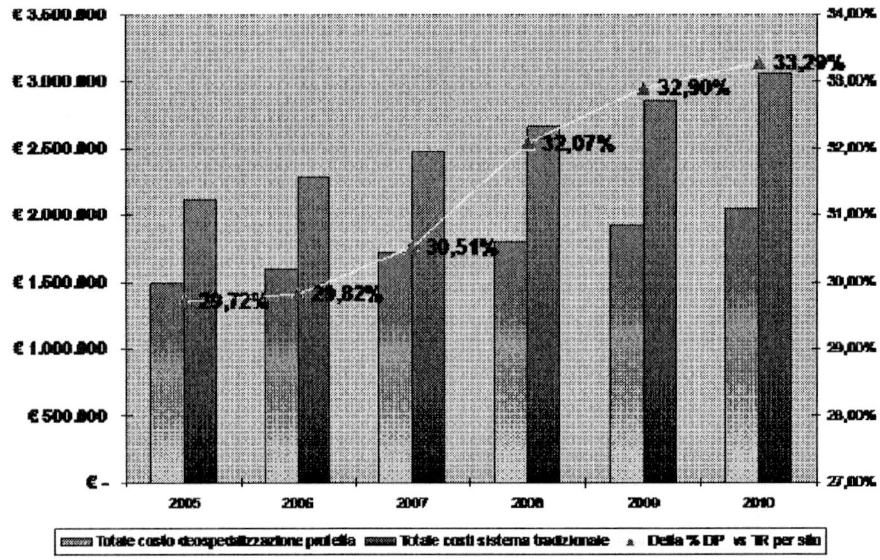

without increasing costs, and the study provided is showing how this is possible. It is indeed an opportunity that broadband stakeholders need to address in there research for new and more attractive applications .Broadband telemedicine today shows very interesting and promising return of investments to service providers, care givers and end users.

REFERENCES

Cleland, J. (2006). An investigation of the effect of telemedicine on outcomes in Europe: The trans-European network–home care management system study. *Dis Manage Health Outcomes.*

Gulla, V. (2005). *Telemedicine potential business models*. Retrieved from http://www.aditechsrl.com/doc/WP_Telemedicine_potential_Business.pdf

Gulla, V. (2005, November 19-21). *The telemedicine market a fast growing technology.* Paper presented at the E-Merging/E-Learning conference, Dubai.

Gulla, V. (2006). *Broadband in Europe markets and trends*. Paper presented at the *WCIT 2004, Information Technology Conference,* Athens, May 19-21, 2004.

Gulla, V. (2006, November). *Understanding DSL developments*. DSL Forum Market Committee Chairman–Carriers World CEE Conference Acts, Budapest.

Gulla, V. (2007, June). *Telemedicine is a driver for quality of life improving broadband application.* Paper presented at the 3rd Croatian & International Congress on Telemedicine and e-Health. Retrieved from http://www.aditechsrl.com/doc/WP_Absstract_proposal_handbook%20.pdf

Kevin. (2003). *Dean essays from innovators.* Edited by Connected Health.

Klapan, I. (2005). *Telemedicine*. Telemedicine Association Zagreb.

Parati., G. (2006). *Roberto Antonicelli "manuale di telemedicina."* Pavia: EDVIES.

Pech, E. (2004). *Making innovation happen* (Tech. Rep.). Detecon, Inc.

Pelissero, G., & Velo, D. (2004). *Competition in health systems*. European Union, AIOP.

Tao, W. (2005). *IP broadband access network construction–network marketing department* (Tech. Rep.). Huawei Technologies Co., Ltd.

Thoma, P., Elisabeth, H., Bart, V., Rolf, S., & Andre, H. (2006). *Telecare-practical experience with video communication in home care*. Published for the Med-e-Tel conference.

Vanier, F. (2008). *World broadband statistics Q1*. Point Topic Ltd.

Varley, P. (2007). *World broadband statistics Q2*. Point Topic Ltd.

KEY TERMS AND DEFINITIONS

Early hospital discharge: It is applied to a public health care structure, typically a hospital.

IP broadband: The network configuration for delivery of IP home care services.

Last mile: The method implemented by most of the telecommunication carriers, to reach end users with a suitable and useful bandwidth.

Social drivers: The driver related to understand the needs of business.

Video communication: Form of telecommunication through which live image communication being performed.

ENDNOTE

1 Integrated Service Digital Network (ISDN) technology widely deployed in Europe for data transmission- typically starting from 64Kbps to 128 and combined up to 384Kbps. This technology was very popular for videocommunication applications.

Section 2

Health Informatics and E-Health Tools and Technologies

Chapter 7
Organisational Factors and Technological Barriers as Determinants for the Intention to Use Wireless Handheld Technology in Healthcare Environment:
An Indian Case Study

Raj Gururajan
University of Southern Queensland, Australia

ABSTRACT

Traditional technology adoption models identified 'ease of use' and 'usefulness' as the dominating factors for technology adoption. However, recent studies in healthcare have established that these two factors are not always reliable on their own and other factors may influence technology adoption. To establish the identity of these factors, a mixed method approach was used and data were collected through interviews and a survey. The survey instrument was specifically developed for this study so that it is relevant to the Indian healthcare setting. Authors identified clinical management and technological barriers as the dominant factors influencing the wireless handheld technology adoption in the Indian healthcare environment. The results of this study showed that new technology models will benefit by considering the clinical influences of wireless handheld technology, in addition to known factors. The scope of this study is restricted to wireless handheld devices such as PDAs, smart telephones, and handheld PCs.

INTRODUCTION

In the last few years, high expectations, technological developments, and effective and efficient services have been shown to be prerequisites for improvements in the healthcare domain (Rogoski, 2005). Latest trends in the healthcare sector include the design of more flexible and efficient service provider frameworks aimed at providing health

DOI: 10.4018/978-1-60566-030-1.ch007

services to all stakeholders. In order to implement such frameworks, wireless technology is increasingly being used in the healthcare sector (e.g. data management automation). A decrease in the cost of wireless devices and improved awareness of the benefits that ensue by using related wireless applications are two of the contributing factors towards the increased use of wireless technology in this sector (Gururajan, Quaddus, et al., 2005). Even though the future of this technology and its usability is promising, its adoption is still in its infancy, which is attributed to the complex and critical nature of the healthcare environment. In the current competitive and complex business environment, technology developments have played a critical role in delivering high quality of care (Reinecke, 2004). However, there is limited knowledge and empirical research on the effectiveness and adoption of wireless technology in general, and in the Indian healthcare system in particular.

Recent research has established that investment in emerging Information Technology (IT), including Information Systems (IS), can lead to productivity gains only if they are accepted and effectively used by respective stakeholders. Consequently, acceptance and utilization of IT/IS in the healthcare environment have been central themes in the information systems literature. Therefore, the fundamental focus of this research is to investigate and examine the influence of internal and external determinants on the usefulness of wireless technology. Further, this research also assesses how its acceptance contributes to the adoption of wireless technology. I believe that this research is the first of its kind attempted in the Indian healthcare domain and it employs empirical evidence to explore the impact of wireless technology and its usefulness in the Indian healthcare system. The Indian healthcare domain is at the forefront in adopting the latest medical technologies and applications, as evidenced by media reports and, as such, it constitutes an excellent context for validating existing adoption theories and extending them.

The main contribution of this research includes the identification of a set of drivers and barriers to using wireless technology in a given Indian healthcare setting. In addition to this, for the first time, a set of clinical factors influencing the adoption of wireless technology has been identified and validated using a second order regression model.

BACKGROUND

The concept of wireless technology in healthcare is discussed in many studies (Dyer, 2003; Hu et al., 2002; Sausser, 2003; Simpson, 2003; Wisnicki, 2002). For example, Wisnicki (2002) provides details of how broadband technology, an essential component of wireless technology, can be used in healthcare. While prior studies agree that wireless applications have the potential to address the endemic problems of healthcare, very limited information can be found about the determinants of such applications (Gururajan et al., 2005; Gururajan et al., 2004). In general, the majority of the works reviewed are descriptive about the benefits of wireless handheld devices in healthcare in general, and medicine in particular. There is only a small number of studies that provide evidence-based information concerning these devices in healthcare (Fischer et al. 2003; Sax et al. 2005). Furthermore, five major studies in the area of healthcare (evaluated by (Spil & Schuring, 2006) testing the Technology Acceptance Model (TAM) produced findings which were inconsistent with the body of knowledge in non-healthcare settings. With 'Perceived Ease of Use' and 'Perceived Usefulness' as the major TAM attributes, these studies found that in the health environment, 'Perceived Usefulness' is an important attribute in technology adoption, while 'Perceived Ease of Use' was found to have no effect (Spil & Schuring, 2006). This is different to findings reported in non-health IS studies, where both attributes were found to be reliable technology adoption predictors. Therefore, further empirical investigation is required to explain the reasons why this variation exists in healthcare.

TAM in Healthcare Context

In healthcare literature, the discussion on wireless technology falls into three periods. For example, studies prior to and including 2000 discussed the status of wireless technology and the possible role the technology can play in healthcare. Studies between 2000 and 2003 discussed how wireless technology can be deployed in healthcare and the potential benefits the technology can bring to healthcare. It should be noted that these studies were only 'discussion' type studies. The majority of these studies did not provide any empirical evidence as to the use or acceptance of wireless technology in healthcare domains. Studies from 2004 to the current date have collected data to establish the usefulness of wireless technology in healthcare. These studies, to some extent, have focussed on the PDAs as these devices have been found to be useful in the nursing domain for clinical data management.

The studies between 2000 and 2003 discussed various capabilities of wireless technology in clinical domains. For example, how broadband technology can be used in healthcare was discussed by (Wisnicki, 2002); the ability to address the prevailing healthcare staff crisis by adopting intelligent solutions using agent and wireless technology that can identify the need and match the need with available resources in a timely and efficient manner was outlined by Davis (2002); better compliance with the rigorous regulatory framework was highlighted by Wisnicki (2002); reduction in medication errors and hence the benefits that can be realised was discussed by Turisco (2000); provision for greater flexibility and mobility of healthcare workers in performing their work was portrayed by Athey & Stern (2002); and effective management of the increasingly complex information challenges and improved access to information from anywhere at anytime was discussed by Stuart & Bawany (2001). Our review clearly identified that all these studies were only implying the potential of wireless technology and did not provide any empirical evidence.

While prior studies agreed that wireless applications have the potential to address the endemic problems of healthcare, very limited information can be found about the determinants of such wireless applications in order to establish the adoption of technology in a given healthcare context (Gururajan et al., 2005; Gururajan et al., 2004). During the period of 2004–2006, studies emerged in the area of technology acceptance, specifically focussing on the acceptance of wireless technology in healthcare domains. These studies were empirical in nature and were testing the available models of technology acceptance or a variation in order to ascertain whether previous models hold good for a new technology in a specific domain. These studies were reported in a book titled *E-Health Systems Diffusion and Use,* published by Idea Group Publishing in 2006 (Spil & Schuring, 2006). In addition, there is a need to explore whether further attributes exist which may influence the adoption of wireless applications in the healthcare environment.

In essence, the recent studies appear to suggest that the current models of technology acceptance or its derivatives are not suitable to predict the adoption factors of wireless technology in a healthcare environment. Strong support can also be derived from three specific studies that have tested TAM models in healthcare. The first study, conducted by Jayasuriya (1998), established that ease of use was not significant in a clinical domain. The second study by Chau & Hin (2002) echoed similar sentiments. The third study by Hu et al. (1999) also found similar findings. Further, recent studies conducted by Howard et a. (2006) also established that ease of use was not significant in determining factors of adoption in a clinical domain in regard to wireless technology. Further, Ivers & Gururajan (2006) also found that there are other factors beyond the TAM models influencing the acceptance of technology.

Interviews conducted by Gururajan and Moloney et al. (2005) with 30 Queensland nursing staff members revealed that clinical usefulness of wireless technology is far more significant than ease of use factor as established in TAM. Another focus group discussions between Gururajan and Quaddus et al. (2005) and Western Australian senior health managers by also indicated that aspects of clinical usefulness such as integration of clinical data may be a more significant factor than the ease of use factor. Howard et al. (2006) also identified clinical usefulness is far more influencing than the ease of use factor while determining factors of adoption of wireless technology in the Indian healthcare domain.

However, the recent findings that the ease of use factor is not strongly significant in the healthcare domain when determining wireless technology adoption warrants explanation—as this is different to many other reported studies in the generic IS domain where both attributes (ease of use and perceived usefulness) were reported to be reliable predictors.

This variation requires further empirical investigation in order to explain the reason behind this variation specific to healthcare. Therefore, there is a need to identify attributes that assist in the adoption of wireless applications in the healthcare environment. We argue that the initial validity of TAM was predominantly established by testing the model with students as surrogates in a generic software application domain. This environment is very different to the healthcare environment, where skills are at different levels. Further, the healthcare environment is complex, sensitive and time critical. These could be some of the reasons why TAM did not perform as expected in healthcare settings.

Therefore, there appears to be a basis to identify factors that contribute to the adoption of technologies in healthcare settings. Given that wireless technologies have started making inroads in healthcare, the overarching purpose of the research is to identify the factors that influence the adoption of wireless technology in the Indian healthcare system. The rationale of the purpose is justified by the fact that India is a leader in software technologies, especially medical applications. Further, India is emerging as a 'health tourism' nation, due to the advancement in medical technology and reduction in cost in offering high quality health services—as highlighted by various print media. However, our initial review of available literature indicated that this area is under-researched. Collectively, these aspects led to the following research question:

- What are the determinants for the adoption of wireless technology by physicians in the Indian healthcare system?

The first stage of this study is focused on answering the research question qualitatively and the second stage on answering the research question quantitatively. Details as to how the research question was answered are provided in the research methodology section below.

METHODOLOGY

The research question dictates the need for quantitative research methods, while the behavioural component of the same investigation dictates qualitative research methods. The rationale for this approach is based on the notion that behavioural components require a thorough understanding of how users apply wireless technology in a given setting in order to understand behavioural issues. To extract 'tacit' aspects, this is best accomplished by applying a qualitative approach. A quantitative instrument can then be developed to extract the quantitative aspects, such as the opinion scores.

Health professionals view the term 'wireless technology' in different ways, either as a product or a process. The combined domain of wireless technology and healthcare is relatively new in the Indian IS domain. While IS studies have discussed the impact of Information & Communication Technology (ICT) tools and associated behavioural intentions on healthcare users, limited information can be found as to how the combination of wireless technology and healthcare settings would influence users who are already conversant with novel and advanced medical technologies (Spil & Schuring, 2006). The workplace or organizational factors that influence such combinations are yet to be explored in detail. Such an exploration has close association with the choice of research method, as these methods pave the way for proper inquiry into the factors that determine technology acceptance in a given setting. On this basis, the suitability of one research method over another has to be carefully weighed. Consequently, this study identified an exploratory approach to be suitable for the initial investigation. This approach is particularly favourable in confirming the direction of the study, variables chosen for the study, and in helping refine the literature. The exploratory study can also possibly eliminate some variables, while providing opportunities for including emerging variables.

Qualitative Data Collection

As argued, for the first stage of this research the investigators used a qualitative approach to collect initial sets of themes for the adoption of wireless technology in the Indian healthcare system. For this purpose, 30 physicians operating in Indian healthcare were identified randomly. These physicians were aware of wireless technology, or were using some form of wireless technology in their workplace. They were derived from both public and private hospitals. I included certain administrative type physicians in order to identify aspects pertaining to the use of wireless technology in administration. Demographic details were not recorded to guarantee anonymity. These physicians were interviewed over a period of six months by an independent member (external to the team) who identified the attributes for the adoption of wireless technology by physicians in the Indian healthcare system. This approach was deliberate to address criticisms of 'bias' in the interview process. Further, due to linguistic issues, I required a person with proficiency in both the Indian language and English. The interview questions were derived from existing literature and our experience of conducting similar studies in Australia. The interviews were conducted over a 45-60 minute period and recorded using a digital recorder. Once they were recorded, the interviews were transcribed.

Quantitative Data Collection

This study developed a survey instrument from the interview data. The main reason for this digressed attitude was that previously tested instruments in the technology domain were not relevant to a healthcare setting and were found to be inadequate in answering the research question. The data from the interviews were used to develop specific ranges of questions to gather a more detailed view from the wider population. This survey instrument was pilot tested to capture the information reflecting the perceptions and practice of those adopting wireless technology in the Indian healthcare system. Particularly, it focussed on what internal and external environmental factors affect the adoption of wireless technology and the extent of this influence. The survey was then distributed to over 300 physicians randomly chosen from the telephone book, and a total of 200 responses were received. The survey responses were then entered into a spreadsheet file. A Visual Basic interface was written to generate numerical codes for various elements of the survey for data analysis using SPSS. The coded spreadsheet file was then copied onto a SPSS file format.

Table 1. The factors driving and inhibiting wireless technology adoption in healthcare

Drivers	Barriers
• Save-time	• Legal barriers
• Improve-clinical-workflow	• Administrative purpose
• Efficiency-in-communication	• Communication with physicians
• Delivery-of-high-qual-info	• Patient education
• Better-quality-of-service	• Communication with colleagues
• Save-effort	• Obtain lab results
• Improve-clinical-performance	• Note taking
• More-contact-time-with-patients	• Electronic medical records
• Improved-delivery-of-information	• Device usage barrier
• Reduce-overall-cost	• Benefit evaluation barrier
• Positive-impact-on-patient-safety	• Resource barrier
• Reduce-inaccuracies	• Electronic prescribing
• Improve-public-image	
• Reduce-medical-errors	
• Easy-access-to-data	
• Attract-more-practitioners	
• Reduce-workload	

DATA ANALYSIS

Qualitative data was analysed using the NVivo (version 7) application, which helped identify the initial themes from the interviews. Quantitative data were analysed using SPSS, which helped identify the factors and their correlation for the adoption of wireless technology in the Indian healthcare setting.

Qualitative Data Analysis

Prior to coding schemes on the qualitative data, reliability was assured through saturation of themes during interviews. Qualitative data was manually coded to extract themes that had an impact on wireless technology acceptance as stated by the physicians. In total, 63 themes were extracted from the interviews. The initial themes include awareness, cost factors, advantages and disadvantages, medical errors, information sharing, current state of technology, usefulness and role of wireless technology, and technology awareness. On the basis of the interviews and the literature review, the themes were classified into drivers and barriers as shown in the following table. Drivers were themes that exhibited positive tone, and barriers were themes with negative tone. The classification of drivers and barriers was subjective. I did not conduct in-depth discourse analysis on the data as this stage was expected to provide only the scope for the quantitative study. This purpose of developing the list of drivers and inhibitors was to provide a direction for the development of the survey instrument for the collection of quantitative data in order to capture the wider community views and to generalize the outcome of the research. This grouping is presented in Table 1.

It is to be noted that the content of the Table 1 is consistent with findings of previous studies conducted by Gururajan et al. (2004; 2005). This prompted conducting a quantitative study in order to establish causality among dependent and independent variables, as well as external validity and generalisability.

Quantitative Data Analyses

In order to ensure statistical reliability, suitable tests were run on the entire instrument, as well as selected group of variables. For example, the reliability test returned a Cronbach alpha value of 0.965 for the instrument, indicating high reliability (Zikmund, 1994). I ran this test because the instrument was generated from the interview data and, hence, it was necessary to establish statistical

Table 2. The factors driving and inhibiting wireless technology adoption in healthcare from data analysis of survey result

Drivers	Loading values	Barriers	Loading values
improve-clinical-workflow	.798	poor technology barrier	.605
tech-support	.764	time for training barrier	.572
delivery-of-high-qual-info	.760	tech expertise barrier	.554
save-time	.757	benefit evaluation barrier	.503
better-quality-of-service	.749	legal barriers	.465
save-effort	.743	solutions barrier	.444
improved-delivery-of-information	.732	system migration barrier	.442
efficiency-in-communication	.730	technical support barrier	.436
more-contact-time-with-patients	.725	lack of support barrier	.352
improve-clinical-performance	.702	device access barrier	.316
more-training	.699	device comfort barrier	.248
improve-public-image	.695	funding barrier	-.225
easy-access-to-data	.692	security as barrier	.224
positive-impact-on-patient-safety	.679	device usage barrier	.208
reduce-inaccuracies	.659		
reduce-workload	.657		
reduce-medical-errors	.650		
reduce-overall-cost	.634		
attract-more-practitioners	.600		
Org-culture	.464		

reliability. In addition, reliability tests were also run for three factor groupings, namely, drivers, inhibitors of adoption, and other technology factors. The reliability tests returned values of 0.941, 0.447 and 0.536, respectively, indicating that the data were suitable for factor analysis testing.

I did not run any demographic analysis as the main aim of the research was to identify the determinants for the adoption of wireless technology. Therefore, it was decided that a correlation matrix would be suitable followed by a factor analysis. The correlation matrix was conducted on the questionnaire items and found to be acceptable. The matrix is not reported in this study because factor analysis provides the correlation implicitly.

As a second step, survey data were analysed for factor analysis using SPSS. I used the exploratory factor analysis techniques for this purpose. For the purpose of the study, a principal component analysis (PCA) was conducted using a Varimax rotation with a factor loading of 0.5. I ran the factor analysis with 2 factor components in order to verify the driver and barrier themes extracted from the interview qualitative data. It is evident from Table 2 that the two factor component matrix identified drivers and the barriers for the adoption of wireless technology in the Indian healthcare setting. This finding is consistent and aligned with the findings of the qualitative data collection stage (i.e. first stage) of this research.

Table 3. The factors driving wireless technology adoption in healthcare from data analysis of survey result

	Organizational	Management	Clinical
save-effort	.716		
reduce-overall-cost	.708		
reduce-inaccuracies	.703		
save-time	.667		
easy-access-to-data	.659		
attract-more-practitioners		.769	
improve-public-image		.680	
tech-support		.680	
reduce-workload			.817
improve-clinical-performance			.797

Subsequent to the two component factor analysis, I ran another analysis on the driver factors alone to identify factor groups emerging from the data. This resulted in three major groups emerging within the drivers as indicated in Table 3.

I titled these three groups of factors as 'organisational', 'management' and 'clinical'. It should be noted that these titles are subjective and based on the questionnaire items. For example, saving effort, reducing cost, etc. are organisations issues and, hence, the title 'organisational'. Thus, the organisational components include wireless technology drivers that can generate specific benefits for organisations. The management components represent the benefits that healthcare managers can realise using wireless technology. The clinical components encompass clinical drivers of using wireless technology.

A similar factor model was generated for the inhibitors. The model resulted in Table 4:

Similar to the drivers, the inhibitors also resulted in three specific categories. The 'technology' category includes technology factors that inhibit wireless adoption in Indian healthcare.

Table 4. The factors inhibiting wireless technology adoption in healthcare from data analysis of survey result

	Technology	Resource	Usage
poor technology barrier	.625		
time for training barrier	.582		
solutions barrier	.575		
benefit evaluation barrier	.528		
tech expertise barrier	.527		
system migration barrier	.511		
funding barrier		-.749	
resource barrier		-.690	
technical support barrier			.542
device usage barrier			.519

Table 5. The factors 'clinical usefulness' of wireless technology adoption in healthcare from data analysis of survey result

	General Communication	Clinical Communication	Records Management
Obtain lab results	.837		
Administrative purpose	.770		
Electronic prescribing	.670		
Medical database referral	.632		
Patient education		.727	
Communication with colleagues		.707	
Communication with patients		.676	
Drug administration		.596	
Communication with physicians		.548	
Electronic Medical Records			.764
Generating exception list			.738
Note taking			.617
Disease state management			.563

The 'resource' category encompasses resource barriers that are currently being encountered in the healthcare setting. Finally the 'usage' category is comprised of inhibiting factors, which are associated with usage issues.

In addition to the two factor groups, namely drivers and inhibitors, I also identified a third, and named this 'clinical usefulness'; its components are shown in Table 5.

This factor group yielded three components. The first component deals with the general communication aspects facilitated by wireless technology in healthcare settings. The second component refers to clinical communication using wireless technology. The third component is specific to records management. In summary, the data analyses yielded three specific categories of factors which can affect the adoption of wireless technologies in the healthcare setting. These comprise adoption drivers, inhibitors, and clinical usefulness.

The factor analysis provided me with initial answers to the research questions: the factors that determine the adoption of wireless technology.

Hypotheses Formulation and Testing

Based on the evidence collected, the three sets of factors, namely, drivers, barriers and clinical usefulness, contribute to the adoption of wireless technology in healthcare. I hypothesise that the drivers positively impact clinical usefulness, whereas the barriers have a negative impact on it. While the drivers and barriers include factors beyond the technology aspects, their respective influences are restricted to the clinical domain as this is where the usefulness of wireless technology can be experienced. Therefore, the following two hypotheses were generated for testing:

H1: Drivers of wireless technology positively impact clinical usefulness.
H2. Barriers to wireless technology negatively impact clinical usefulness.

I digressed away from the traditional regression modeling because I felt that the data may be insufficient to run a traditional regression model.

Further, the intention of the study is NOT to develop a cause and effect model, but to determine the factors identified. Therefore, a Partial Least Square (PLS) model was developed in order to test the hypotheses. The rationale for using PLS includes: PLS is used for confirmatory factor analysis (CFA); the pattern of loadings of items on the latent constructs is explicit; PLS provides strong convergent and discriminant validity; p-value of t-value is significant (over 0.50 level) for constructs; and measurement items load highly on theoretically assigned factors and not highly on other factors.

PLS MODEL DEVELOPMENT

In order to develop the PLS model, a PLS Graph prototype was used. Initially, the individual drivers, barriers and clinical usefulness were tested for CFA scores and these were found to be reliable. When the CFA was found to be satisfactory, a model was built with clinical infuences as dependent variable on drivers and barriers. The factors of these three constructs were linked using PLS Graph software and the model was run. The final outcome is shown in Figure 1 below.

Figure 1 shows that the factor loading (the number on the path: for example, for the construct

Figure 1. PLS model of adoption of wireless technologies in Indian healthcare

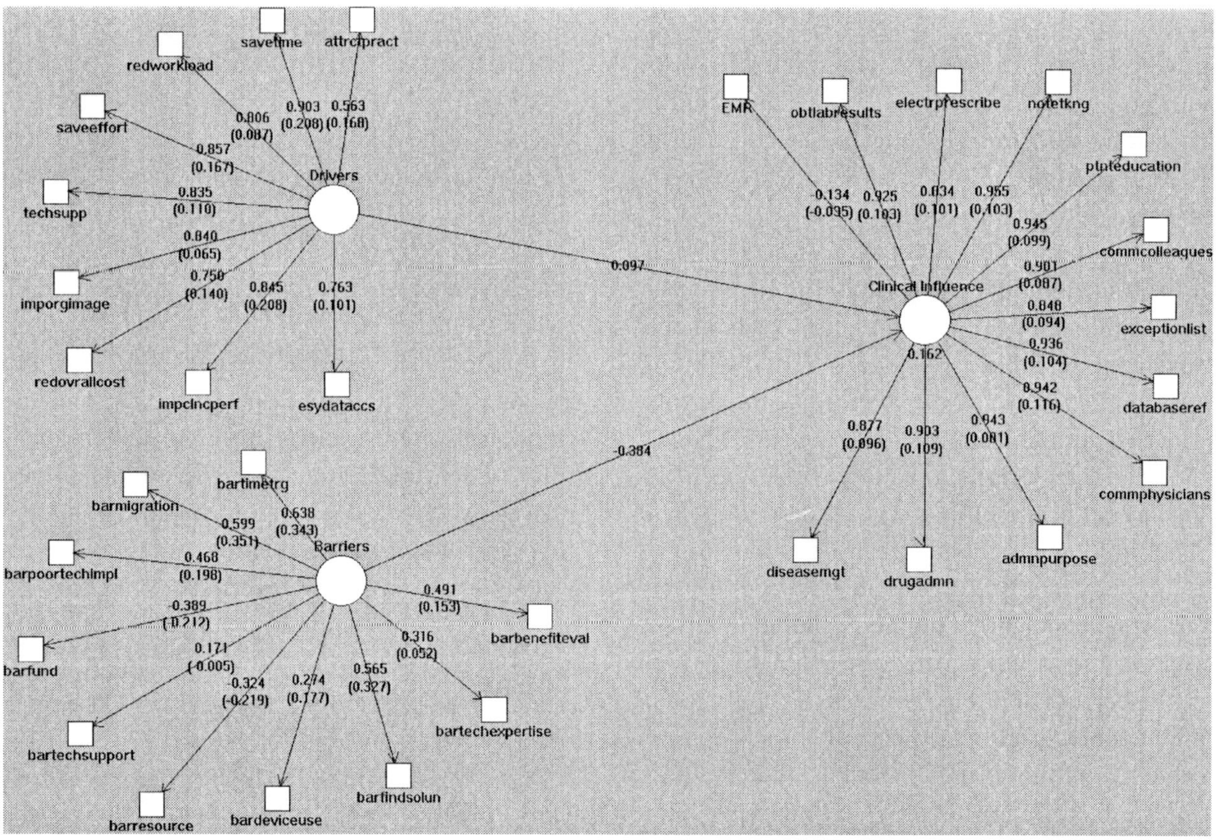

Drivers, the 'esydataccs' has 0.763) and the factor weight (the number in the parantheses: for example, 0.101) for almost all factors are reliable. The drivers and clinical usefulness load very highly (over 0.8 for most of the items), indicating a high reliability. Further, all variables have a t-value of over 1.96 to indicate high convergent validity.

Upon construct validation, a simple PLS (consolidated) model was developed to test the hypotheses. The model consists of clinical usefulness as the dependent variable, and drivers and barriers as independent variables. The model was run with PLS Graph program and the screenshot shown in Figure 2 displays the values along the link from Drivers to Clinical Usefulness, and Bariers to Clinical Usefulness. As hypothesised, drivers exhibited a positive loading (0.097) and the barriers exhibited a negative loading (-0.384). The number below the circle Clinical Usefulness is the construct R^2, which is calculated and displayed for each dependent variable. The lower the R^2, the minimum the error in the model. In the model the R2 values for the dependent variable 'Clinical Usefulness' is 0.167. This is not high and, hence, the error is minimal. This is shown in Figure 2.

IMPLICATIONS

Clearly, wireless technology can be used to facilitate access to clinical information and communications between clinicians, maximise clinician time, increase patient safety, and accomplish the strategic and business goals of health organisations. Taken together, these factors have a direct impact on clinical usefulness and its effectiveness. However, achieving clinical usefulness with wire-

Figure 2. Result of model testing

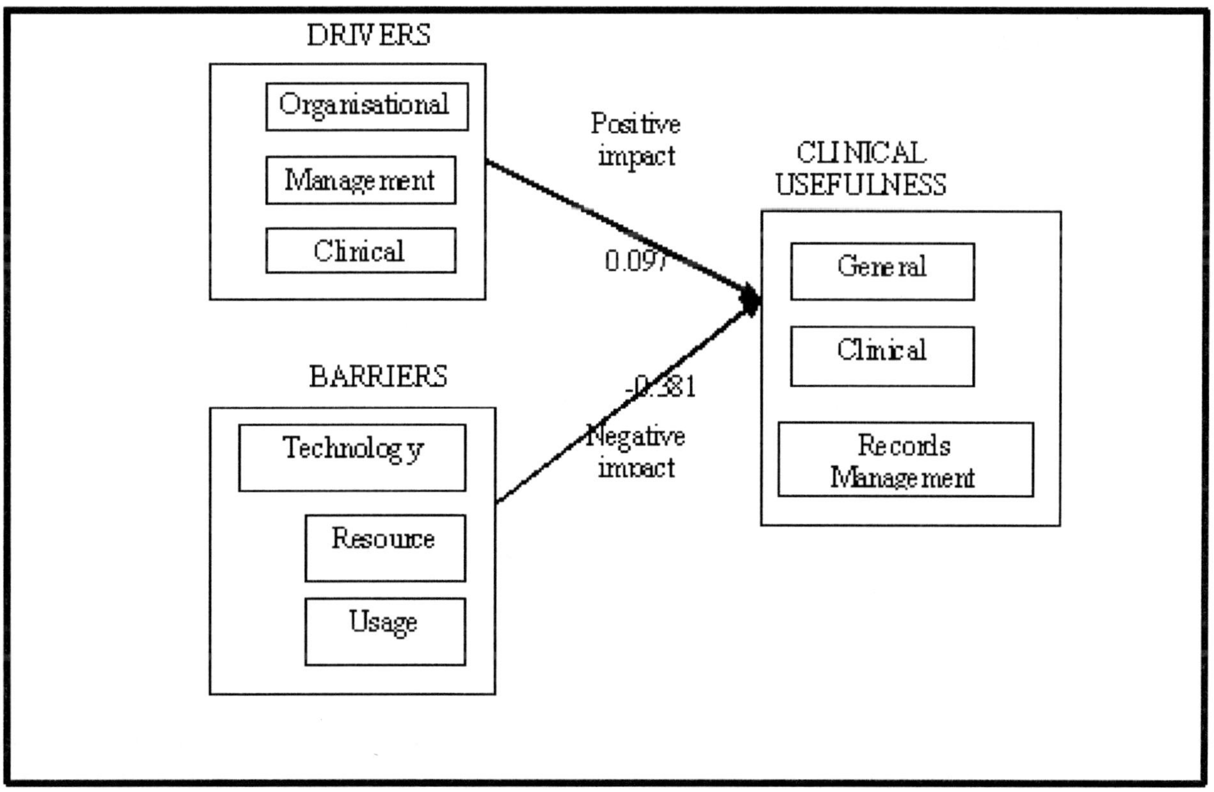

less handheld devices can be a challenge and has several implications.

Firstly, the highest security standards must be achieved. This includes direct end-to-end data encryption, authentication, authorisation, maintenance of audit logs and session management (Chen et al. 2004). While high security standards are essential, their implementation is likely to affect usability. For example, the download and encryption of patient information from the server where it is stored into a wireless handheld device may not be prompt. Sax et al. (2005) argue that clinicians may experience increasingly longer time lags when they carry out increasingly more complex procedures. This is likely to adversely affect clinical usefulness and, hence, decrease user acceptance.

Closely associated with security is also the issue of patient confidentiality, which is of significant importance and concern. Although wireless handheld devices have locking security features and password protection functions which activate during periods of inactivity, the frequent use of these functions during the clinicians' busy daily schedules may have an impact on clinical usefulness. (see Figure 1 and Figure 2)

Secondly, the design of an effective human-computer interface, while challenging, constitutes a key factor for the acceptance of the technology and its routine use by healthcare workers (Chen et al. 2004). This is an important development consideration as the relevant information should be easy to navigate and read, and has to be presented in an organised fashion when required within the resource limitations (e.g. screen size and bandwidth) of a wireless handheld environment. Usability factors are not only likely to constitute an acceptance barrier, but can also be the cause of medical errors. Bates et al. (2001) argue, 'While it may be easy and common to blame operators for accidents [or errors], investigation often indicates that an operator "erred" because the system was poorly designed' (p. 301). Therefore, medical errors can also occur due to poor usability. Taken together, these factors would contribute to reduce medical errors. By implication, it is important to involve users in the design of the wireless applications, thereby maximising their clinical usefulness.

Thirdly, simply acquiring and implementing wireless technology alone would be insufficient to accomplish clinical usefulness and, subsequently, drive adoption and diffusion. Wireless technology should be integrated with process improvement and organisational change. Process improvement requires the optimisation of clinical processes and should be supported by technology, rather than driven by it (Smith 2004). Ultimately, this is likely to generate significant patient outcomes and financial improvements with health organisations.

Fourthly, as suggested by the empirical evidence collected in this study, cost constitutes an important factor which will affect the integration and, subsequently, the success of wireless handheld devices in the healthcare setting (Sax et al. 2003). Typically costs include the software, the server, upgrades of healthcare organisations' existing networks and legacy systems, the costs of the handheld units themselves, as well as maintenance and support. While existing research in this area argues that such technology has the potential to decrease charting time and medical errors and enhance patient care quality, there is no evidence that comparisons of costs before and after the implementation of wireless technology have been made. This suggests that further research is required, but also, most importantly, it shows that, indirectly, costs have the potential to affect clinical usefulness and threaten widespread adoption.

FUTURE RESEARCH

This research is an exploratory study to identify clinical influences of wireless technology applicable to the Indian healthcare system. While data were obtained on perceived opinions, actual measurement of usefulness of wireless technology in a clinical setting was not conducted. Currently, another project is being conducted that would enable measurement of clinical influences of using wireless technology in an objective manner. This new project will provide some insights into the efficiency gains of using wireless technology and the challenges people encounter in using this technology.

This study is confined to the Indian healthcare setting, which limits the generalisability of its findings. However, this study is also the first of its nature and, as a result, it has prepared the groundwork for further research which can confirm (or refute) whether the findings reported in this study are applicable to other settings. Data are collected using the same instruments in Australia, Taiwan and India. It is anticipated the data collection to be completed by in 2009.. This exercise, it is hoped, will enable to extend the notion to broader populations.

REFERENCES

Athey, S., & Stern, S. (2002). The impact of information technology on emergency health care outcomes. *The Rand Journal of Economics*, *33*(3), 399–388. doi:10.2307/3087465

Bates, D. W., Cohen, M., Leape, L. L., Overhage, M., Shabot, M. M., & Sheridan, T. (2001). Reducing the frequency of errors in medicine using information technology. *Journal of the American Medical Informatics Association*, *8*(4), 299–308.

Chau, P. Y. K., & Hu, P. J.-H. (2002). Investigating healthcare professionals' decision to accept telemedicine technology: An empirical test of competing theories. *Information & Management*, *39*, 297–311. doi:10.1016/S0378-7206(01)00098-2

Chen, E., Mendoca, E. A., McKnight, L. K., Stetson, P. D., Lei, J., & Cimino, J. J. (2003). PalmCIS: A Wireless Handheld Application for Satisfying Clinician Information Needs. *Journal of the American Medical Informatics Association*, *11*(1), 19–28. doi:10.1197/jamia.M1387

Chismar, W. R., & Wiley-Patton, S. (2006). Predicting Internet Use: Applying the Extended Technology Acceptance Model to the Healthcare Environment. In T.A.M. Spil & R.W. Schuring (Eds.), *E-Health Systems Diffusion and Use: The Innovation, the User and the USE IT Model*. Hershey, PA: Idea Group Publishing.

Davies, F. D., Bagozzi, R. P., & Warshaw, P. R. (1989). User acceptance of computer technology: A comparison of two theoretical models. *Communications of the ACM*, *35*(8), 982–1003.

Davis, R. (2002). Pursue front end solutions to revenue problems. *Healthcare Financial Management*, *56*(8), 30–36.

Davis, S., & Bostrom, R. (1993). Training end users: An experimental investigation of the roles of the computer interface and training methods. *MIS Quarterly*, (1): 61–85. doi:10.2307/249510

Dyer, O. (2003). Patients will be reminded of appointments by text messages. *British Medical Journal*, *326*(402), 281.

Fischer, S., Stewart, T. E., Mehta, S., Wax, R., & Lapinsky, R. (2003). Handheld Computing in Medicine. *Journal of the American Medical Informatics Association*, *10*(2), 139–149. doi:10.1197/jamia.M1180

Gururajan, R., et al. (2005). *Drivers and Barriers to adoption of wireless handheld system in WA healthcare: Selected views*. Paper presented at the HIC 2005, Melbourne, Australia.

Gururajan, R., Moloney, C., & Kerr, D. (2005). *Drivers for wireless handheld technology: views from Queensland nurses*. Paper presented at the Australian Business & Behavioural Sciences Association (ABBSA) Conference, Cairns, Australia.

Gururajan, R., Quaddus, M., Fink, D., Vuori, T., & Soar, J. (2005). *Drivers and Barriers to adoption of wireless handheld system in WA healthcare: Selected views*. Paper presented at the HIC 2005, Melbourne, Australia.

Gururajan, R., Toleman, M., & Soar, J. (2004). *Necessity for a new technology acceptance model to predict adoption of wireless technology in healthcare*. Paper presented at the Let's Make a Difference with Health ICT, HIC Conference, July 25-27.

Horan, T. A., Tule, B., & Hilton, B. N. (2006). Understanding physician use of online systems: An empirical assessment of an electronic disability evaluation system. In T.A.M. Spil & R.W.Schuring (Eds.), *E-Health Systems Diffusion and Use: The Innovation, the User and the USE IT Model*. London: Idea Group Publishing.

Howard, A., Gururajan, R., Hafeez-Baig, A., & Howard, S. (2006). *Clinical Usefulness of Wireless Technology in Healthcare: An Indian Study.* Paper presented at the Australasian Conference on Information Systems, University of South Australia, Australia.

Hu, P. J., Chau, P. Y. K., & Liu Sheng, O. R. (2002). Adoption of telemedicine technology by health care organisations: An exploratory study. *Journal of Organizational Computing and Electronic Commerce*, *12*(3), 197–222. doi:10.1207/S15327744JOCE1203_01

Hu, P. J., Chau, P. Y. K., & Tam, K. Y. (1999). Examining the technology acceptance model using physician acceptance of telemedicine technology. *Journal of Management Information Systems*, *16*(2), 91–112.

Ivers, B., & Gururajan, R. (2006). *Management issues in telecommunications: videoconferencing & telehealth.* Paper presented at the International Conference on Recent Trends in Information Systems Proceedings, India.

Jayasuriya, R. (1998). Determinants of microcomputer technology use: Implications for education and training of health staff. *International Journal of Medical Informatics*, *50*, 187–194. doi:10.1016/S1386-5056(98)00067-7

Lapointe, L., Lamothe, L., & Fortin, J. (2006). The dynamics of IT adoption in a major change process in healthcare delivery. In T.A.M. Spil & R.W. Schuring (Eds.), *E-Health Systems Diffusion and Use: The Innovation, the User and the USE IT Model*. London: The Idea Group Publishing. Mingers, J. (2001). Combining IS research methods: Towards a pluralist methodology. Information Systems Research, 12(3), 240-259.

Myers, M. D. (1997). Qualitative research in Information Systems. *MIS Quarterly*, *21*(2), 241–242. doi:10.2307/249422

Reinecke, I. (2004) *Managing Information in Health*. Melbourne National Health Information Summit.

Rogoski, R. (2005). Wireless by Design. *Health Management Technology*, (January): 1–7.

Sausser, G. D. (2003). Thin is in: web-based systems enhance security, clinical quality. *Healthcare Financial Management*, *57*(7), 86–88.

Sax, U., Kohane, I., & Mandl, K. D. (2005). Wireless Technology Infrastructures for Authentication of Patients: PKI that Rings. *Journal of the American Medical Informatics Association, 12*(3), 263–268. doi:10.1197/jamia.M1681

Simpson, R. L. (2003). The patient's point of view—IT matters. *Nursing Administration Quarterly, 27*(3), 254–256.

Smith, C. (2004). New Technology Continues to Invade Healthcare: What are the Strategic Implications/Outcomes? *Nursing Administration Quarterly, 28*(2), 92–98.

Spil, T. A. M., & Schuring, R. W. (2006). E-Health system Diffusion and Use. Hershey, PA: Idea Group Publishing.

Stuart, D., & Bawany, K. (2001). *Wireless Services: United Kingdom* (Operational Management Report No. DPRO-90741). Gartner.

Suomi, R. (2006). Introducing electronic patient records to hospitals: Innovation adoption paths. In T.A.M. Spil & R.W.Schuring (Eds.), *E-Health Systems Diffusion and Use: The Innovation, the User and the USE IT Model*. Hershey, PA: IGI Global.

Turisco, F. (2000). Mobile computing is next technology frontier for health providers. *Healthcare Financial Management, 54*(11), 78–82.

Venkatesh, V., Morris, M. G., Davis, G. B., & Davis, F. (2003). User Acceptance of Information Technology: Toward A Unified View. *MIS Quarterly, 27*(3), 425–478.

Wisnicki, H. J. (2002). Wireless networking transforms healthcare: physician's practices better able to handle workflow, increase productivity (The human connection). *Ophthalmology Times, 27*(21), 38–41.

Zikmund, W. (1994). *Business research methods* (International Ed.), Orlando, FL: The Dryden Press.

Chapter 8
HealthGrids in Health Informatics:
A Taxonomy

Aisha Naseer
Brunel University, UK

Lampros K. Stergioulas
Brunel University, UK

ABSTRACT

Healthcare is a vast domain encapsulating not only multiple sub-domains or sub-sectors but also many diverse operations and logistics within each sub-sector. This diversity needs to be handled in a systematic and well-characterized manner in order to maintain consistency of various healthcare tasks. Integration of health information systems within each healthcare sub-sectors is crucial for ubiquitous access and sharing of information. The emerging technology of HealthGrids holds the promise to successfully integrate health information systems and various healthcare entities onto a common, globally shared and easily accessible platform. Many different types of HealthGrids exist but there lacks a taxonomy to classify them into a hierarchical order. This chapter presents a well-characterized taxonomy of different types of HealthGrid and classifies them into four major types, namely BioGrid, MediGrid, PharmaGrid and CareGrid. Each of these HealthGrids possesses dedicated features and functionalities. The proposed taxonomy serves to better understand the realtionship among various HealthGrid types and would lay a basis for future research.

INTRODUCTION

Healthcare is currently going through a series of technological advancements and modifications. Health information has always been of great importance to society and has a strong impact on various social aspects. Due to its nature, health information has to be dealt with great care and confidentiality. At the same time, it has to be shared and exchanged across various organizations or individuals to provide improved healthcare service. Two of the most important disciplines in Health Informatics today are bioinformatics and medical informatics. As Computer Science and Biotechnology communities join forces to create new technologies for the advancement of medical science and improvement

DOI: 10.4018/978-1-60566-030-1.ch008

of medical service delivery (Stewart, 2004), this might prove to be promising for enabling people to lead normal, healthy lives.

It is widely recognised today that the healthcare industry requires customized solutions with respect to information integration. The information sharing techniques currently available are not sufficient to meet the requirements of an integrated health care system. The state of electronic information integration in healthcare lags noticeably behind other business domains such as banking, insurance and electronic commerce (Bilykh et al., 2003). There is a need for health information systems to be fully integrated with each other and provide interoperability across various organizational domains for ubiquitous access and sharing. Moreover, due to rapid progress of biotechnology an increasing number of life science databases are becoming available that are being operated and managed individually (Tohsato et al., 2005). Many existing solutions still do not offer the desired levels of utility/functionality or sophistication that a health information system demands.

The emerging Grid technologies hold out the promise of a global information channel that is far more powerful and uniquely distinct from the existing internet framework (Naseer and Stergioulas, 2006b). By definition:

"Grid is a large-scale, high-performance, always-on and dynamic, although geographically distributed yet networked, infrastructure that comprises and seamlessly unifies a variety of autonomous, heterogeneous components such as processes, resources, network layers, interfaces, protocols and services, with strong, consistent and controlled relationships among them." (Naseer and Stergioulas, 2006b)

HealthGrid is a Grid used in the context of healthcare. HealthGrids are expected to successfully integrate health information systems and various healthcare entities, including humans and non-humans, such as scientists, scientific tools, medical instruments, physicians, patients and all types of healthcare data or medical information, onto a common (global) platform that would be shared and easily accessible (Breton et al., 2005). In such a scenario, each health information system is composed of various distinct components, which are integrated in a way that each component has its well-defined semantics and ontology and is well-aware of all other components.

Considering the vast nature of the heathcare domain (Alexopoulos et al., 2007), it can not be assumed that only one HealthGrid would be sufficient for the entire healthcare domain. However, many small HealthGrids could be combined together to form a giant HealthGrid infrastructure in order to facilitate collaborative work and resource sharing. There are several existing medical classifications, terminologies and taxonomies (Alexopoulos et al., 2007) but such a taxonomy that illustrates how the various HealthGrids could be classified does not exist yet. Therefore a taxonomy is needed that classifies various types of HealthGrids and lays-out a hierarchical structure that is simple to understand but is yet systematic & well-characterized. Such a taxonomy would be beneficial for understanding, in detail, the realtionship among various HealthGrid types and would lay a basis for the future research.

This chapter offers a systematic taxonomy of the HealthGrids. It first outlines the characteristic features and functionalities of HealthGrids, and reflects on the need for Grid technology in healthcare. The taxonomy of HealthGrids is proposed, based on their functionality, purpose, and application area. Finally, this chapter reflects on the future of HealthGrids in Health Informatics and draws some conclusions.

HEALTHCARE NEEDS GRID TECHNOLOGY

The case for the use of Grid technology in healthcare arises mainly from the need to improve, safeguard and effectively exploit the available *life-significant medical information*, the need to protect the privacy of *personal, life-sensitive health information*, and the need to provide *integrated healthcare services* and have in place effective, global *channels of collaboration*.

Health-related information is important for the well-being of society and has to be accurate and consistent. Medical information provided over the internet often suffers from ambiguity and contradiction that would increase the complexity and confusion of medical issues instead of solving them. Moreover, anyone can publish or post material of their choice over the internet without any peer review or checking, which makes open internet an unreliable source of healthcare information.

Information available on HealthGrids can initially be peer reviewed once before uploading, but even more importantly, it can be constantly and continuously checked and revised appropriately, thus making HealthGrids an accurate and reliable source of health information that can be accessed any time from any place.

Blake and Bult (2006) stated: "One of the major challenges faced by the biomedical research community is how to access, analyse, and visualize heterogeneous data in ways that lead to novel insights into biological processes or that lead to the formulation of a hypothesis that can be tested experimentally". In order to exploit effectively the wealth of medical information, there is an urgent need to *integrate, manipulate, process, and analyse* huge heterogeneous datasets from disparate sources. More systematic use of Grid technology in healthcare will not only help meet the current needs for data processing, but will ensure that future demand for even more capacity to deal with far larger volumes of data can be met (Breton et al., 2005).

Moreover, whenever *confidential medical information* is shared among health organizations, security and privacy are critical issues (Bilykh et al., 2003), since HealthGrids contain 'life sensitive data'. The information content in a healthcare system is related to various entities, such as hospitals and their staff, stakeholder organisations and their members, medical equipment/devices, medicines, diseases, patient information records and healthcare operations (pathways). Amongst all the entities, the *patient record* is the most prominent, since it encapsulates information on most other entities (some of which is personal, and should be kept private to the patient).

On another level, HealthGrids can prove to be an *effective channel for international collaborations* where the world's scientific minds can collectively work, such as to conduct a group-wise analysis, and might produce solutions that would effectively address complex medical problems (for instance, a disease or remedy).

There are many *other reasons* why the healthcare industry needs Grid technology, such as to:

1. provide more computational power
2. make network resources readily available
3. better utilise system resources, and reduce wastage by eliminating idle resources
4. create new business opportunities and exploit economies of scale
5. enable faster problem solving
6. support multiple operations by concurrent and ubiquitous access
7. provide the massive data storage spaces required in healthcare
8. make healthcare solutions/systems more efficient
9. facilitate collaborations and integration among various healthcare resources and stakeholders

All of the above and many more emerging issues demand to be addressed in a sophisticated manner by an advanced and reliable solution and a systematic, well-characterized taxonomy of different types of HealthGrids is expected to facilitate these operations. A study by Estrella et al. (2007) discusses that Grid computing holds the promise of harnessing extensive computing resources located at geographically dispersed locations that can be used by a dynamically configured group of collaborating institutions. It defines a suitable platform on which distributed medical informatics applications could be based. Particularly, HealthGrids are expected to address issues such as data distribution, data processing, data analysis, data sharing, data security, resource heterogeneity and interoperability.

HealthGrids might prove to be a good way to address these needs and provide reasonable solutions the challenges of modern healthcare. A study by Piggott et al. (2004) explores the potential use of Grid technology in Healthcare, such as integration of heterogeneous data sets from multiple diverse sources systems. Thus, if successfully implemented, the HealthGrid will have a high impact towards lower costs and greater benefits for healthcare in the long run. In this respect, the HealthGrid could be the driver of Health Informatics and which is the next generation of healthcare IT and a taxonomy of various HealthGrid types would be of significance at this stage in order to have a better idea of how the various types are classified in order of their hierarchy.

TAXONOMY OF HEALTHGRIDS TYPES

There are various types of HealthGrids defined in the healthcare sector. Each has been devised for a dedicated purpose, so as to provide special services and to support the performance monitoring of specialized tasks in a particular healthcare sector. A taxonomy of HealthGrids types is proposed based on their functionality, purpose, and application area. This must be kept in mind that all HealthGrids are mainly DataGrids.

Considering the vast nature of the heathcare domain (Alexopoulos et al., 2007), it can not be assumed that only one HealthGrid would be sufficient for the entire healthcare domain. However, many small HealthGrids could be combined together to form a giant HealthGrid infrastructure in order to facilitate collaborative work and resource sharing. There are several existing medical classifications, terminologies and taxonomies (Alexopoulos et al., 2007) but such a taxonomy that illustrates how various HealthGrids could be classified doesnot exist yet.

This chapter presents a taxonomy of HealthGrids (Figure 1) and classifies them into four major types, namely BioGrid, MediGrid, PharmaGrid and CareGrid, where the BioGrid and the MediGrid merge into the BioMedicalGrid, which combines the features and functionalities of both Bio and Medi Grids. The BioGrid is sub-categorized into representative examples such as ProGrid for Proteomics and GeneGrid for Genomics, both of which merge into the ProGenGrid. The MediGrid is also further sub-categorized into typical implementations, such as Medical Imaging (Visual) grids (e.g. MammoGrid) for the management and processing of medical images, scans or DICOM (Digital Imaging and Communications in Medicine) files, NeuroGrid for neurologists and SimGrid for medical simulations and modelling (another example of a Visual Grid). There is a need for the HealthGrids to be integrated and possess strong interactions among themselves in order to facilitate data sharing. For example, although GeneGrid does not have a direct link with the CareGrid as shown in Figure 1, however, data from both these domains could be made available for accessing & sharing over these Grids, if needed.

The various types of HealthGrids, along with characteristic applications, are examined and discussed further in this section. Each of the HealthGrids described in this section is effectively a DataGrid and could also be a SemanticGrid (Semantic grid project, 2007) if it is based on semantic principles. For example, in a similar fashion to NeuroGrid, there can be a dedicated HealthGrid for each medical domain, such as CardioGrid, OptiGrid, OrthoGrid, GynaecologyGrid or OtolaryngologyGrid and many others.

Figure 1. Taxonomy of HealthGrids types

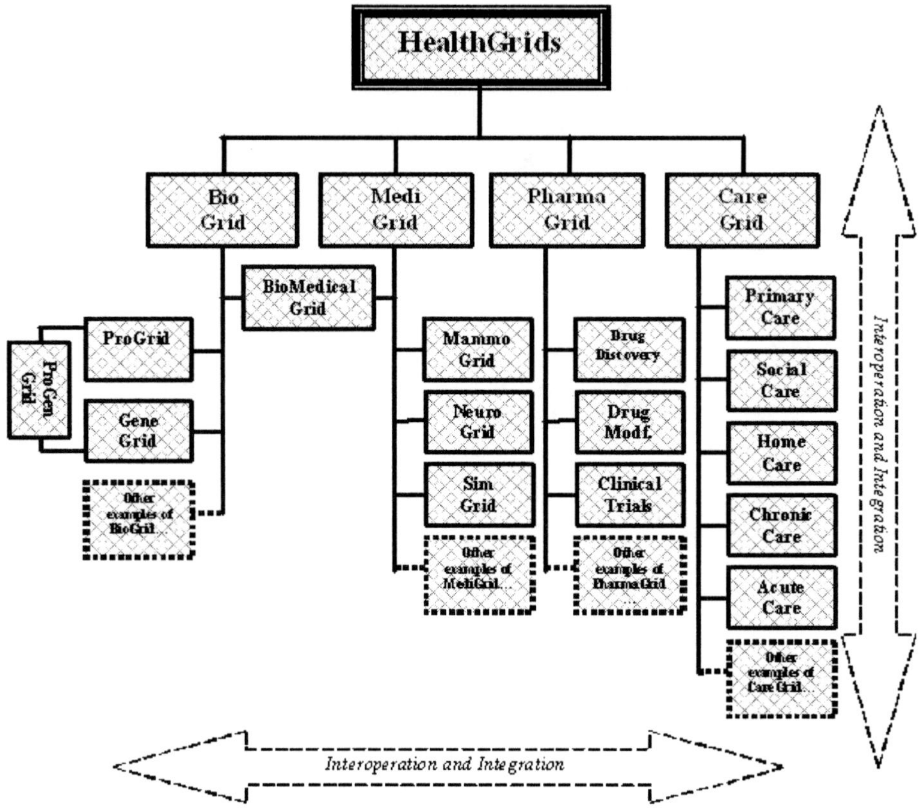

BioGrid

BioGrid is a type of HealthGrid designed specifically for accessing and sharing biological information, often around the globe, by authorized individuals and/or organizations. Information related to biological components at the molecular level such as genes, proteins, DNA, RNA, chromosomes and other molecular biological structures need to be critically analysed for further biological research purposes. BioGrids are increasingly important in the development of new computing applications for the life sciences and in providing immediate medical benefits to individual patients. They have significant potential to support the offering of personalised medical care and to be able to target only those at risk (Ellisman et al., 2004). Examples of BioGrid are shown in Figure 2.

OGSA-DAI (Open Grid Service Architecture Data Access and Integration) have been used in ChemBioGrid by bringing Data Management tools into collaborative environment. The mechanism has been studied, for supporting Digital Libraries in High-Performance Computing environment based on Grid technology. OGSA-DAI have been implemented to provide abilities to assemble heterogeneous data from distributed sources into integrated virtual collections (Zhuchkov et al., 2006). The BioGrid is sub-categorized into the ProGrid and the GeneGrid, which are also the applicable examples of BioGrids and are described below:

Figure 2. Examples of BioGrid

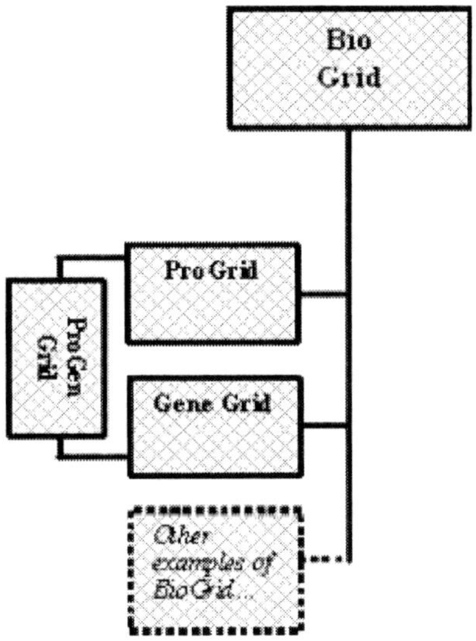

a. ProGrid

ProGrid is a practical example of BioGrid that is specialized in the management of all types of information related to proteins, such as proteomic and proteo-type data, protein structures, protein identification, protein analysis, protein expression level, protein mutation, protein screening and classification.

The human body is incredibly complex and consists of roughly 50 trillion cells, each consisting of an enormous number of components (of the order of 10^{13}), many of which are proteins. It normally takes months on a Peta-flop class computer (one capable of performing 10^{15} calculations per second) to simulate the activity of a single protein, taking into account each atom in the protein. No such computer systems exist today, and designing one remains a formidable challenge (Stewart, 2004).

The ProGrid will be able to address this issue by making available enormous computation resources for highly complex computational operations. A recent study (Cannataro et al., 2005) presents MS-Analyzer, a tool for the management processing and analysis of proteomic Mass Spectrometry data. It is a specialized version of PROTEUS (Cannataro et al., 2004), which is a Grid-based Problem Solving Environment for bioinformatics applications that uses (a) domain ontologies to design complex in silico experiments by modelling basic software tools, data sources and workflow techniques and (b) data mining software tools to provide proteomics facilities. Its main requirements include interfacing with proteomics facilities, storing and managing proteomic Mass Spectrometry data, and interfacing with off-the-shelf data mining and visualization software tools.

An architecture combining the use of OGSA-DAI, Grid distributed querying (OGSA-DQP) and data integration software tools to support distributed data analysis has been proposed (Zamboulis et al., 2006), for the integration of several autonomous proteomics data resources.

b. GeneGrid

GeneGrid is another practical example of BioGrid that is specialized in the management of all types of information related to genes and of relevance to genomic studies, such as information on genomes & genotype, genetic structures, genetic sequences, genetic mutations, genetic diseases, genetic epidemiology, gene therapy, gene naming, genetic analysis, gene screening, genetic variation and genetic classification. For the purposes of genetic epidemiology GeneGrid can support the unified naming of phenotypes and standardised acquisition and recording of clinical parameters. In genetic epidemiology studies, a clinical annotation service is one of the central services in a Grid for clinical phenotype descriptions (Breton et al., 2005). The GeneGrid project (Jithesh et al., 2005) integrates numerous bioinformatics programs and databases available on different resources across various sites allowing scientists to easily access the diverse applications and data sources without having to visit many web servers. This reduces the overall time for executing the experiment. The

Grid services developed in the GeneGrid project are based on the Open Grid Services Architecture (Foster et al. 2003) and provide scheduled access to resources, data, and applications, using XML-based messages.

The need to have a dedicated GeneGrid arises due to the ever-increasing volumes of genomic data and ever more demanding complex computations for genetic operations.

c. ProGenGrid

The ProGrid and GeneGrid merge into the ProGenGrid which is dedicated to perform management of data related to the sequence and structure of both the genome and proteins. Operations carried out on a ProGenGrid could include the aggregation, selection, retrieval, analysis, filtration and sharing of proteomic and genomic data for concurrent access and collaboration. The ProGenGrid, developed at the University of Lecce (Aloisio et al., 2005a), is intended to provide a practical solution to specific HealthGrid problems. This Grid aims at providing a virtual laboratory where e-scientists can simulate biological experiments, compose existing analysis and visualization tools, monitor their execution, store the intermediate and final output and finally save the model of the experiment for updating or reproducing it. Another study (Aloisio et al., 2005b) introduces the ProGenGrid workflow that comprises a semantic editor for discovering, selecting and composing bioinformatics tools available in a Grid environment, and a workflow scheduler for running the composed applications. The workflow editor uses an ontology of tools for the bioinformatics domain and employs the Unified Modeling Language (UML) for modelling the workflow. The UML graphical notation is stored as an XML file. On running the application, the workflow scheduler takes activities from the XML file and runs them, taking into account the state and availability of Grid resources and relevant bioinformatics tools. The system also allows monitoring of the job flows.

MediGrid

The MediGrid (Medical Grid) is a type of HealthGrid designed specifically for accessing and sharing medical information around the globe by authorized individuals/organizations. Examples of MediGrid are shown in Figure 3.

It is expected to contain all levels of medical information from tissue, organ, and patient to population and public health, including various types of scans, mammograms, simulations and models of different body organs and other medical domains. All this information needs to be shared and critically analysed for further medical research purposes. A paper proposes a MediGrid (Boccia et al., 2005) which has been designed specifically for the aggregation and integration, analysis and visualization, and processing and management of biomedical images for nuclear doctors. It is a distributed, user friendly GUI-based application that uses the First In First Out (FIFO) algorithm for job scheduling and follows the Grid Application Development Software (GrADs) Project workflow (Berman et al., 2001), (Vadhiyar and Dongarra, 2005). It focuses on complex Grid-

Figure 3. Examples of MediGrid

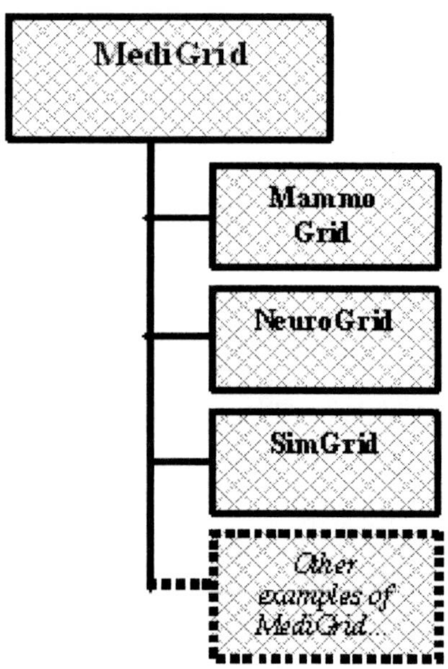

enabling parallel algorithms for the examination of medical images.

Amongst others, the MediGrid can be subcategorized in terms of its practical application; representative examples include the MammoGrid, the NeuroGrid and the SimGrid, which are next described:

a. MammoGrid

The MammoGrid (Mammography Grid) (MammoGrid, 2007) is one of the most important practical examples of a MediGrid designed particularly for the access, storage, retrieval, analysis, management, manipulation and sharing of various types of digital images, medical scans, or DICOM (Digital Imaging and Communications in Medicine) files. Some computationally intensive image analysis algorithms often devised to assist clinicians to make decisions in diagnosis and therapy are known to produce better results, but are not used in practice due to the lack of computing power (Breton et al., 2005). The MammoGrid is expected to provide enormous computing and storage resources so as to make feasible and to support distributed image analysis.

A recent study (Scheres et al., 2005) presents an interface between Grid computing middleware and a three-dimensional electron microscopy (3D-EM) image processing package ("Xmipp") (Sorzano et al., 2004). Results showed clearly that 3D-EM image processing can greatly benefit from the resources offered by Grid computing. Another study (Glatard et al., 2005) produced a generic, Grid-enabled workflow framework, to be deployed on the computational Grid infrastructure provided by the EGEE European project (EGEE, 2008). It encompasses image registration algorithms wrapped in standard Web-Services, a Grid enabled workflow manager, and Grid middleware for performing the distributed computations. The framework developed could easily be adapted to a wide variety of medical applications. However, one of the limitations stems from the *stateless nature* of Web Services.

e-Diamond, a UK e-Science project (Brady et al., 2003), is a Grid-enabled prototype system (medical image database) that aims at supporting breast cancer screening by maintaining a national database for digital mammograms. In the development of e-Diamond, an object-relational approach to the storage of DICOM files has been taken (Power et al., 2004). Other work carried out within the context of the e-Diamond research project (Power et al., 2005), (Simpson et al., 2005) addresses the challenges of patients' data security and confidentiality via employing query modification. Query modification is also used in GIMI (Simpson et al., 2005) to restrict access to the data in Grid-enabled medical research databases for the sake of patients' data security.

A MIP-Grid (Grid-enabled Medical Image Processing Application System) is presented (Huang et al., 2006), that is based on OGSA-DAI middleware. It aims at providing high performance medical image process services in a large distributed grid computing environment. OGSA-DAI allow uniform access to and integration of data held in heterogeneous data resources.

b. NeuroGrid

The NeuroGrid (Neurology Grid) is another example of a MediGrid that is designed to support neurologists worldwide in their collaborative work. A recent study (Geddes et al., 2005) has proposed the implementation of a NeuroGrid, i.e. a Grid dedicated to neuro-scientific studies. It is intended to be built on the experience of other UK e-science projects aiming to assemble a Grid infrastructure, and apply this to three exemplar areas: (a) stroke, (b) dementia and psychosis, and (c) generic collaborative neuroscience research. Grid-enabled sharing of data, experience and expertise will facilitate the archiving, curation, retrieval and analysis of imaging data from multiple sites and enable large-scale clinical studies in neurology. To achieve this goal, the NeuroGrid seems to be built upon existing Grid technologies and tools (developed within the UK e-Science programme), aiming to integrate image acquisition, storage and analysis, and to support collaborative working within and between neuro-imaging medical centres. Moreover, the Biomedical Information Research Network (BIRN) (Ellisman and Peltier, 2004) is devoted to neurology and is exploring the use of Virtual Data Grid (VDG) to support multiscale brain mapping. BIRN currently participates in three testbed projects; namely Function BIRN, Morphometry BIRN and Mouse BIRN (Stewart, 2004).

In the not too distant future, a dedicated NeuroGrid will address the need to support the computation and monitoring of various neurological functions, for both humans and animals, such as brain histology, MRI (Magnetic Resonance Imaging), neurological disorders, electron microscopy and brain imaging.

c. SimGrid

The SimGrid (Simulation Grid) is also an example of MediGrid designed specifically for providing special simulation and modelling services for various types of medical treatments and analysis such as surgery, radiotherapy, chemotherapy, endoscopy, electrocardiography, osteotomy and bio-fluids simulation. Thus SimGrid encapsulates all simulation levels from Proteomics and Genomics up to overall body-level simulation. The SimGrid can be of importance not only in planning surgeries but also in training surgeons (Breton et al., 2005). The simulation process is quite time consuming and might require millions (or even billions) of computation cycles and terabytes of storage space, depending upon the nature of the specific simulation task. However, using Grids for this purpose could resolve the problem of computation speed to a considerable extent.

A recent study (Gonzalez-Velez and Gonzalez-Velez, 2005) presents a stochastic simulation of L-type Ca^{2+} current assuming thousands of calcium channels on the membrane of a spherical cell. The simulation runs on a dedicated Grid and employs structured parallelism techniques. Results showed hours of time saved using a computational Grid for simulation (compared to single-machine simulation runs).

GEMSS (Grid-enabled Medical Simulation Services) (Jones et al. 2004), (Benkner et al. 2005) that is concerned with the Grid-provision of advanced medical simulation applications and aims to provide a transparently accessible health computing resource suited to solving problems of large magnitude. The viability of this approach is currently being evaluated through six diverse medical applications, including maxillo-facial surgery planning, neuro-surgery support, medical image reconstruction, radiosurgery planning and fluid simulation of the airways and cardiovascular system. Without using a Grid, an accurate nonlinear simulation takes a considerably longer time (up to several hours), whereas, by allowing access to high performance computing through the Grid, the simulation time can be reduced to a level acceptable for clinical implementation (less than one hour), with the potential to improve the outcome of the surgical procedure. The GEMSS Grid infrastructure is based on standard Web Services technology with an anticipated future transition path towards the OGSA (Foster et al. 2003) standard proposed by the Global Grid Forum.

A new execution and simulation procedure for two dental applications, namely Computational Fluid Dynamics (CFD) and Computational Aero Acoustics (CAA) is proposed in (Nozaki et al., 2005), which can reduce the implementation time via Grid-enabled parallel processing. The study also reports on the design, implementation and performance evaluation of the optimal CPU resource allocation based on the total computation time of the dental application, which combines CFD and CAA as a part of a DentGrid system. The data for both the simulations is obtained by Magnetic Resonance Imaging (MRI). This DentGrid system aims to be a computation and storage power supplier for dental clinics and hospitals. Simulating dentistry operations is highly beneficial, in the sense that dentists can examine visually the post-effects of dental surgery.

The modelling of individuals is an ongoing research topic and involves the complete simulation of the human body, which is a computationally intensive task. In the field of modelling and simulation, Grid computing has the capability to accelerate the pace of the analysis/discovery process and to deliver the new results quickly and efficiently to the medical user community (Berti et al., 2003).

The application of OGSA-DAI in Simulation Grids has been discussed (Xing et al., 2006), to address the issues of integrating, controlling and accessing the different types of distributed data resources in the simulation. The databases in the simulation grid system supported the dynamic distribution of the data and model resources in the simulation environment.

OGSA-DAI has been used also as a middleware in the BioSimGrid project (Wu et al., 2004), that aims to exploit the Grid infrastructure to enable comparative analysis of the results of biomolecular simulations.

BioMedicalGrid

The BioGrid and MediGrid merge into the BioMedicalGrid which encapsulates features of both the Bio and Medi Grids. The main challenge faced in biomedical informatics is the development and maintenance of an infrastructure for the storage, access, transfer and simulation of biomedical information and processes. Moreover, BiomedicalGrids must be able to produce, use and deploy knowledge as a basic element of advanced applications and to achieve this, they are mainly based on Knowledge Grids and Semantic Grids (Breton et al., 2005). BiomedicalGrids will thus provide a universally accessible platform for the sharing of ever-increasing biomedical data pertaining to all the levels of healthcare such as molecule, cell, tissue, organ, patient and public health. They are expected to provide interoperability and sharing/collaboration to both the Biological and Medical domains of healthcare.

Recent research (Tirado-Ramos et al., 2005) has used *on-line application monitoring* for improved computational resource selection and application optimization. A number of user-defined performance metrics within the European CrossGrid Project's G-PM tool (CrossGrid.org, 2008), (Stevens et al., 2004) have been used to run a blood flow simulation application (solver) based on the lattice Boltzmann method for fluid dynamics. Results showed that online monitoring gives a more accurate view of computational resource status than the regular resource information provided by standard information services to resource brokers. Moreover, on-line monitoring has good potential for optimizing biomedical applications for more efficient computational runs. Other work (Alonso et al., 2005), (Tirado-Ramos et al., 2005) has shown how a BioMedicalGrid can enhance the processing of a biomedical application as well as the respective image analysis. The integration of a bio-physical model into a clinical augmented reality system is another challenging task, where Grid technology could be the key (Breton et al., 2005).

PharmaGrid

Another important type of HealthGrid is the PharmaGrid (Pharmaceutical Grid), which focuses on the management and sharing of drug-related data to support operations such as clinical trials, dose computation, drug discovery, drug development, drug interactions, pathology and genomics that could be carried out in a collaborative environment to advance the quality of healthcare. Examples of PharmaGrid are shown in Figure 4.

The pharmaceutical industry is a distinct domain with specific operations and processes, and is currently faced with many challenges. There is an increasing need for more innovative products that can target more effectively today's critical

Figure 4. Examples of PharmaGrid

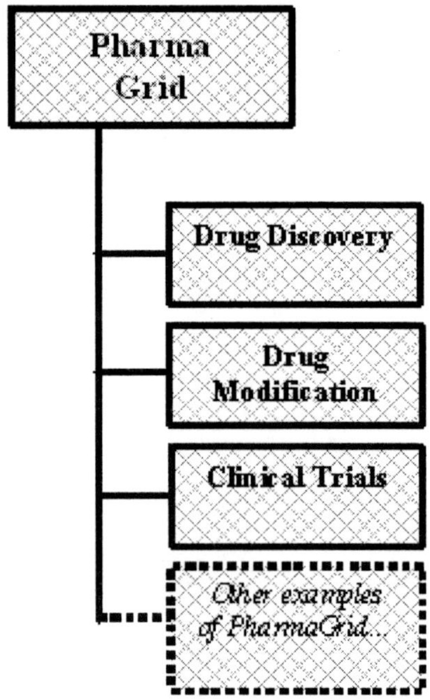

diseases. At the same time, there is a growing pressure for personalised medication (by using both phenotype and genotype), a move which will increase both the effectiveness and safety of medicines, but which will eventually shrink the scale of economy and create a much more fragmented market. Furthermore, the data produced by the pharmaceutical industry is of the order of terabytes or petabytes in size and needs massive storage capacity. Moreover, various operations to do with the manufacturing of drugs and the dissemination of drug information need huge numbers of computational cycles. The results obtained from various drug experiments and clinical trials are of crucial importance and need to be delivered in a consistent and timely manner to the healthcare professionals and patients.

One of the key challenges of the pharmaceutical sector today is to manage, share and understand the medicines information in a way that facilitates and accelerates the Research & Development process. This progress suffers from poor information management due to inflexible, closed, heterogeneous, unconnected and segregated sources of information. It has now been widely recognised that Grid technology holds out the promise for a more effective means of sharing and managing information and enhancing knowledge-based processes in the Pharma R&D environment. The emerging PharmaGrid is a powerful new technology set to revolutionise the way medicines-related ("Pharma") information is used. The PharmaGrid has the potential to address the "information" problem, with many benefits for the industry, in terms of boosting innovation in drug discovery, shaping clinical trials, reducing time to market, and reducing costs. (see Figure 4)

Furthermore, Grid technologies have the potential to provide transparency and integration of information, break communication barriers, enhance communication and collaboration between the various actors (industry, regulators, healthcare and insurance providers, doctors and patients), and as a result to accelerate a large number of healthcare processes to do with pharmaceutical therapies.

Other benefits from the use of PharmaGrids include (Houghton, 2002):

- substitution of in silico for in vitro and in vivo testing;
- operation and management of clinical trials;
- monitoring post-launch usage and outcomes;
- marketing and distribution of medicines;
- e-commerce and total quality management in healthcare supplies and procurement;
- regulatory and watchdog activities;
- financial planning and cost efficiency in healthcare;
- health information services for all stakeholders;
- electronic prescription and clinical decision support tools.

Even more crucially, the Pharma industry and researchers are faced with a continuously growing amount of distributed heterogeneous information, a real explosion of experimental data, documents, article, patents, with rapidly changing terminology and analysis approaches. In order to adequately fulfil such requirements, the PharmaGrids have to meet the following challenges:

- Intelligent middleware that facilitates the user transparent access to many services and execution tasks
- High quality security features, enabling large databases to be accessed via Grid solutions
- Sophisticated semantic and contextual systems to enable diverse sources of data to be related to knowledge discovery

Thus PharmaGrids are expected to deal with all types of drug-related information such as drug features, design specifications, safety, success rate, purpose and usage, and complex operations such as clinical trials, evaluation process, experimental results, treatment, and effective trails. This information should be shared across various organizational boundaries and manipulated online.

The development of PharmaGrids is instrumental in meeting the current industry challenges, as it will provide an efficient way of exchanging and managing knowledge in a shared environment in the areas of discovery, development, manufacturing, marketing and sales of new drug therapies. Grid infrastructures are currently built upon different architectures, designs, technologies, open standards, and operating systems. PharmaGrid development is a highly complex and technically challenging activity and it should address many different problems to do with Pharma information, including knowledge-representation and integration, distributed architectures, search and access controls, data mining and knowledge management, real-time modelling and simulations, algorithm development and computational complexity. PharmaGrids will need to be scale-independent/scalable, adaptive, secure and dependable Grid infrastructures that enable the management of large networked distributed resources across different platforms of stakeholders, such as pharmaceutical companies, policy makers, R&D development companies. The required enabling technologies include amongst others semantic web and agent-mediated approaches, peer-to-peer technologies and self-organising architectures.

PharmaGrids can be part of or closely integrated with other HealthGrids. For reasons of competitiveness and intellectual property protection, PharmaGrids are predominantly private, enterprise IntraGrids with strict access and authentication controls, but there is a recognised need for cross-industry platforms (InterGrids), whereby the resulting integration will lead to more efficient coordination of activities.

Moreover, PharmaGrids open up the perspective of cheaper and faster drug development and may enable parallel processes in drug development, away from the traditional approach where the full cycle of target discovery, target validation, lead discovery, lead optimization and transition to development takes on average 12 years (Breton et al., 2005). PharmaGrids hold the promise to provide improved and efficient drug design and better control of diseases and to improve *patient safety* and *quality of healthcare*. Examples of PharmaGrids could include dedicated Grids for Drug Discovery, Drug Modification, Management and/or Running of Clinical Trials.

Another study (Tohsato et al., 2005), uses Globus Toolkit 3 and OGSA-DAI, for the federation of heterogeneous databases, for supporting a drug discovery process. Due to the rapid progress of biotechnology, there are an increasing number of life sciences databases, which need to be shared in order to conduct research collaborations, and OGSA-DAI could make this feasible.

CareGrid

The CareGrid is designed specifically for the general public healthcare services such as patient-centred or virtual healthcare services, dose computation, self-assessment, and online health management. Services on the CareGrid could be customized according to the individual patient needs so as to provide personalized healthcare services. Moreover, the CareGrid aims to provide data management facilities and improved diagnosis.

Figure 5. Examples of CareGrid

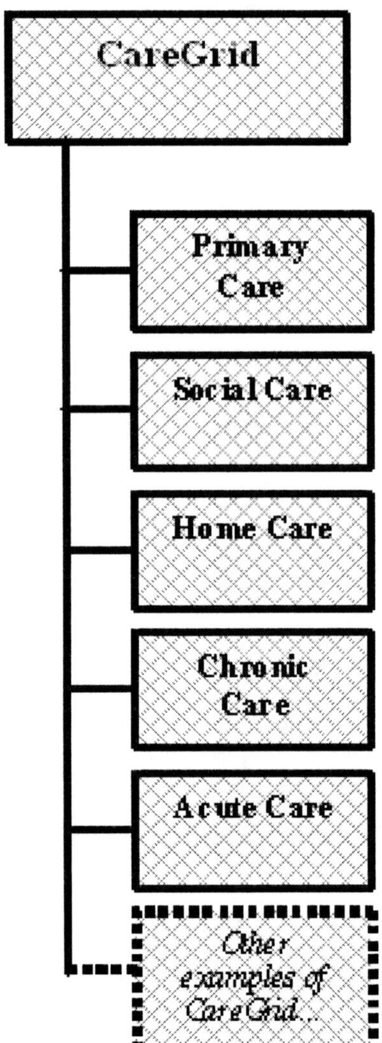

A typical example of CareGrid is a recently implemented prototype for HealthInfoGrid (Bilykh et al., 2003). The HealthInfoGrid can also be viewed as a Service Grid and its services are designed for sharing and distributing medical information, at times of critical importance and under strict privacy and security regulations. Formalization of the interaction semantics of the HealthInfoGrid components is based on coloured Petri-nets (Jensen 1997). HealthInfoGrid has various components such as organization, staging area, initiator, translator, and merger/adder. Examples of CareGrid are shown in Figure 5.

CareGrids represent a new facet of advanced and improved healthcare that can provide personalized healthcare services at a cost-effective price. Patients can access the CareGrid to retrieve information about their own health, such as clinical tests and diagnosis, dose composition and recommendation, precautions and preventions. This would save them the time and effort spent in waiting to book appointments and all the hassle that goes with such processes.

Examples of CareGrids could include dedicated Grids for Primary Care, Social Care, Home Care, and Chronic Care.

WHAT'S NEXT IN HEALTH INFORMATICS WITH HEALTHGRIDS?

As we have seen, HealthGrids can be used to support many kinds of healthcare operations and tasks. As such, they can be made to adapt to the lifestyle choices of the patients. Patients should be more and more able to choose their living styles, keeping in mind their persistent health conditions. The future of Health Informatics with HealthGrids implementations would allow patients to take control of their own health by personalized healthcare or illness management programs, thus improving healthcare provisioning quality while lowering the costs. Particularly, future HealthGrid applications will:

- provide secure access to medical data/information distributed globally
- free-up doctors' time and provide healthcare to patients at their doorsteps
- enhance the use of various health monitoring devices, which can be plugged together via Grids to provide better quality of care
- provide active interoperability & collaboration among the various healthcare stakeholders, which is needed for the success of Health Informatics
- facilitate resource sharing

The main problems with medical information or healthcare data are that it is:

- difficult to access
- not always available
- lacks integrity & interoperability
- difficult to understand or data being obscure
- lacks sharing of distributed resources (including healthcare data)

These problems are magnified due to the dynamic nature of healthcare data which is always being modified, and changes to one part are not updated or reflected onto other parts of the system. Moreover, in Health Informatics massive datasets and heavy computation make things even more complicated. Also the health information systems need to be inter-connected. As HealthGrids are mainly DataGrids, they provide platform for data integration and facilitate interoperability among various healthcare data sources. Thus changes to one would automatically be reflected in other and healthcare information would be accessed in a timely and seamless manner.

The case for the use of Grid technology in healthcare arises mainly from the need to improve, safeguard and effectively exploit the available *life-significant medical information*, the need to protect the privacy of *personal, life-sensitive health information*, and the need to provide *integrated healthcare services* and have in place effective, global *channels of collaboration*. To do all this effectively, different types (the most suitable ones) of HealthGrids should be employed to perform different dedicated tasks with specialized features and functionalities and for this purpose a taxonomy of various HealthGrid types, described earlier in this chapter, would prove to be very useful. For long-term future, there is a need for designing various Grid-enabled applications specifically for HealthGrids. Moreover, there is a diverse range of many other services (Naseer and Stergioulas, 2006a), which can be provided on HealthGrids.

Future of Health Informatics lies in the integration, not only among various types of HealthGrids but also among the various healthcare stakeholders, in order to conduct collaborative research. It also lies in constructing new types of specialized HealthGrids, i.e. HealthGrids dedicated for specialized tasks such as anatomy, morphology, and epidemiology. Integration among various HealthGrids would allow information sharing at an advanced level where information related to one classified domain would be accessible by other domains. Future trends also follow that Grid technologies get tightly integrated with Web Services technologies (Naseer and Stergioulas, 2007).

However, the case for HealthGrid implementation in Health Informatics is not that obvious. Learning new Grid-enabled techniques, procedures, and know how about the HealthGrids applications and confidentiality of the medical data remains a challenge. Thus, if HealthGrids can take-on this challenge and provide easy and secure accessibility to the physically distributed heterogeneous data sources with simple user-friendly interfaces, then the future of Health Informatics is secure and very promising through the implementation of specialized HealthGrids.

CONCLUSION

In order to fully benefit from Health Informatics there is a need for the Healthcare data to be available, accessible, readable, understandable and most importantly reliable. Moreover, Healthcare information needs to be interoperable and shared by integrated channels of collaboration and healthcare stakeholders.

This chapter has reviewed current implementations of HealthGrids, and offered a systematic taxonomy of the HealthGrids. It has outlined the characteristic features and functionalities of HealthGrids and reflected on the need for Grid technology in healthcare. Based on their functionality, purpose, and application area, a taxonomy of HealthGrid types has been proposed constituting of four major categories. It has been shown that each serves a dedicated purpose, so as to provide the required services and to support the performance monitoring of the specified/desired tasks. Furthermore, the various types of HealthGrids have been examined on an individual basis and their representative implementations have been reviewed. In summary, this chapter gives some suggestions about the future of Health Informatics with HealthGrids.

To exploit effectively the wealth of medical information, there is an urgent need to integrate, manipulate, process, and analyse huge heterogeneous datasets from disparate sources. More systematic use of Grid technology in healthcare will not only help meet the current needs for data processing, but will ensure that future demand for even more capacity to deal with far larger volumes of data can be met.

Data security is another major issue, as healthcare data has to be protected through ethical firewalls to ensure the privacy, confidentiality and integrity of patients' data. HealthGrids deal with 'life sensitive data' and patient record is the most sensitive data resource that encompasses many critical elements related to personalized healthcare. As patient record encapsulates instances of various other entities, HealthGrids can help achieve the required levels of robustness and consistency of the patient record by provision of secure access to:

- patient's medical history
- medical images (e.g. mammograms)
- library of examples for training & diagnosis
- health support services
- drug details & clinical trials
- health information systems
- standard formats of files & information for comparative analysis

As HealthGrids can also serve as an effective channel for international collaborations, in order to incur long-term economic benefits from the implementation of HealthGrids, there is a need for interoperation and integration among various HealthGrids as shown in Figure 1. Also constructing new types of specialized HealthGrids dedicated for specific tasks would strengthen the future implementation of Health Informatics. Moreover, it has been witnessed from the study that contemporary Grid technologies such as OGSA-DAI and can prove to be a candidate solution to the problem of data federation or integration. However, work is still going on and efforts are being made towards a modernized facet of future healthcare by using HealthGrids as depicted in a prognosis for year 2013 (Silva and Ball, 2002).

As a final remark, HealthGrids hold the promise to offer accurate and reliable sources of health information that can be accessed at any time and from any place. They can and should become a major driver in the race towards successful e-Health and an important ingredient of Health Informatics which is the next generation of healthcare IT. A successfully implemented HealthGrid infrastructure could support all the facets of healthcare sector, and help realise the vision of personalized healthcare. Successful implementation of HealthGrids will have a high impact towards lower costs and greater benefits for healthcare in the long run, thus facilitating the provision of quality healthcare services cost-effectively.

REFERENCES

Alexopoulos, P., Benetou, X., Tagaris, T., Georgolios, P., & Kafentzis, K. (2007). An ontological approach for fraud detection in the healthcare domain. *In Proceedings of the International Conference on Information Technologies (InfoTech - 2007)*, Vol. 1, Bulgaria.

Aloisio, G., Cafaro, M., Fiore, S., & Mirto, M. (2005a). ProGenGrid: a grid-enabled platform for bioinformatics. *Studies in Health Technology and Informatics*, *112*, 113–126.

Aloisio, G., Cafaro, M., Fiore, S., & Mirto, M. (2005b). ProGenGrid: a workflow service infrastructure for composing and executing bioinformatics grid services. In *Proceedings of the 18th IEEE symposium on computer-based medical systems*, (pp. 555-560). Washington, DC: IEEE Computer Society.

Alonso, J. M., Hernandez, V., & Molto, G. (2005). Experiences on a large scale grid deployment with a computationally intensive biomedical application. In *Proceedings of the 18th IEEE symposium on computer-based medical systems*, (pp. 567-569). Washington, DC: IEEE Computer Society.

Benkner, S., Berti, G., Engelbrecht, G., Fingberg, J., Kohring, G., Middleton, S. E., & Schmidt, R. (2005). GEMSS: Grid-infrastructure for medical service provision. *Methods of Information in Medicine*, *44*(2), 177–181.

Berman, F., Chien, A., Cooper, K., Dongarra, J., Foster, I., & Gannon, D. (2001). The GrADS project: Software support for high-level grid application development. *International Journal of High Performance Computing Applications*, *15*(4), 327–344. doi:10.1177/109434200101500401

Berti, G., Benker, S., Fenner, J. W., Fingberg, J., Lonsdale, G., Middleton, S. E., et al. (2003). Medical simulation services via the Grid. In *Proceedings of HealthGrid Workshop 2003*. Retrieved February 1st, 2008 from http://www.ccrl-nece.de/gemss/Presentations/healthgrid.pdf

Bilykh, I., Bychkov, Y., Dahlem, D., Jahnke, J. H., McCallum, G., et al. (2003). Can grid services provide answers to the challenges of national health information sharing? In *Proceedings of the 2003 conference of the Centre for Advanced Studies on Collaborative research (CASCON '03)*, (pp. 39-53). IBM Press.

Blake, J. A., & Bult, C. J. (2006). Beyond the data deluge: Data integration and bio-ontologies. *Journal of Biomedical Informatics*, *39*(3), 314–320. doi:10.1016/j.jbi.2006.01.003

Boccia, V., Guarracino, M. R., D'Amore, L., & Laccetti, G. (2005). A grid enabled PSE for medical imaging: experiences on MedIGrid. In *Proceedings of the 18th IEEE Symposium on computer-based medical systems*, (pp. 529-536). Washington, DC: IEEE Computer Society.

Brady, J. M., Gavaghan, D. J., Simpson, A. C., Parada, M. M., & Highnam, R. P. (2003). eDiaMoND: A grid-enabled federated database of annotated mammograms. In Berman, F., Fox, G. C. and Hey, A. J. C. (eds.), *Grid computing: making the global infrastructure a reality*, (3rd Ed., pp. 923-943). Hoboken, NJ: Wiley.

Breton, V., Dean, K., & Solomonides, T. (2005). The healthgrid white paper. *Studies in Health Technology and Informatics*, *112*, 249–321.

Cannataro, M., Comito, C., Congiusta, A., & Veltri, P. (2004). PROTEUS: a bioinformatics problem solving environment on grids. *Parallel Processing Letters, 14*(2), 217–237. doi:10.1142/S0129626404001842

Cannataro, M., Guzzi, P. H., Mazza, T., Tradigo, G., & Veltri, P. (2005). Preprocessing of mass spectrometry proteomics data on the grid. In *Proceedings of the 18th international symposium on computer-based medical systems*, (pp.549-554). Washington, DC: IEEE Computer Society.

CrossGrid.org. (2008). *CrossGrid project homepage*. Retrieved February 1st, 2008 from http://www.crossgrid.org/main.html

EGEE. (2008). *Enabling grids for e-science project*. Retrieved February 1st, 2008 from http://www.eu-egee.org/

Ellisman, M., Brady, M., Hart, D., Lin, F., Muller, M., & Smarr, L. (2004). The emerging role of biogrids. *Communications of the ACM, 47*(11), 52–57. doi:10.1145/1029496.1029526

Ellisman, M., & Peltier, S. (2004). Medical data federation: the biomedical informatics research network. In I. Foster, and C. Kesselman, (Eds.), *The Grid: Blueprint for a New Computing Infrastructure* (2nd Ed.). San Francisco, CA: Morgan Kaufmann.

Estrella, F., Hauer, T., McClatchey, R., Odeh, M., Rogulin, D., & Solomonides, T. (2007). Experiences of engineering Grid-based medical software. *International Journal of Medical Informatics, 76*(8), 621–632. doi:10.1016/j.ijmedinf.2006.05.005

Foster, I., Kesselman, C., Nick, J. M., & Tuecke, S. (2003). The physiology of the grid. In F. Berman, G. Fox, and T. Hey, (eds.), *Grid Computing: Making the Global Infrastructure a Reality* (pp. 217-249). New York: John Wiley & Sons.

Geddes, J., Lloyd, S., Simpson, A., Rossor, M., Fox, N., Hill, D., et al. (2005). NeuroGrid: using grid technology to advance neuroscience. In *Proceedings of the 18th IEEE symposium on computer-based medical systems*, (pp. 570-572). Washington, DC: IEEE Computer Society.

Glatard, T., Montagnat, J., & Pennec, X. (2005). Grid-enabled workflows for data intensive medical applications, pp. 537-542. In *Proceedings of the 18th IEEE symposium on computer-based medical systems*, (pp. 570-572). Washington, DC: IEEE Computer Society.

Gonzalez-Velez, V., & Gonzalez-Velez, H. (2005). A grid-based stochastic simulation of unitary and membrane Ca/sup 2+/ currents in spherical cells. In *Proceedings of the 18th IEEE symposium on computer-based medical systems*, (pp. 171-176). Washington, DC: IEEE Computer Society.

Houghton, J. (2002). Information Technology and the Revolution in Healthcare. Working paper 4, Centre for Strategic Economic Studies, Victoria University of Technology, Australia. Retrieved February 1, 2008 from http://www.cfses.com/documents/pharma/04-IT_and_Healthcare.pdfHuang, X., Huang, L. & Li, M. (2006). Grid-enabled medical image processing application system based on OGSA-DAI techniques. In *Proceedings of the International workshops on advanced Web, network technologies and Applications*, (pp. 460-464). In Shen, H. T., Li, J., Li, M., Ni, J. & Wang, W. (eds.). (LNCS, Vol. 3842). Berlin, Germany: Springer-Verlag.

Jensen, K. (1997). A brief introduction to coloured Petri Nets, pp. 203-208. (LNCS Vol. 1217).Berlin, Germany: Springer-Verlag.

Jithesh, P. V., Kelly, N., Donachy, P., Harmer, T., Perrott, R., McCurley, M., et al. (2005). GeneGrid: grid based solution for bioinformatics application integration and experiment execution. In *Proceedings of the 18th IEEE symposium on computer-based medical systems*, pp. 523-528. Washington, DC: IEEE Computer Society.

Jones, D. M., Fenner, J. W., Berti, G., Kruggel, F., Mehrem, R. A., Backfrieder, W., et al. (2004). The GEMSS Grid: An evolving HPC environment for medical applications. In *Proceedings of HealthGrid 2004*. Retrieved February 1, 2008 from http://www.ccrl-nece.de/gemss/Reports/Jones-healthgrid2004.pdf

MammoGrid. (2008). European federated mammogram database implemented on a grid structure. Retrieved February 1st, 2008 from http://mammogrid.vitamib.com

Naseer, A., & Stergioulas, L. K. (2006a). Discovering healthgrid services. In *Proceedings of the IEEE International Conference on Services Computing (SCC'06)*, (pp. 301-306). Washington, DC: IEEE Computer Society

Naseer, A., & Stergioulas, L. K. (2006b). Resource discovery in grids and other distributed environments: States of the art. *Multiagent and Grid Systems - . International Journal (Toronto, Ont.)*, *2*(2), 163–182.

Naseer, A., & Stergioulas, L. K. (2007). Combining web services and grid services: practical approaches and implications to resource discovery. In Periorellis, P. (Ed.), *Securing Web Services: Practical Usage of Standards and Specifications* (pp. 298-317). Hershey, PA: IGI Global.

National Digital Mammography Archive. (2008). Retrieved February 1, 2008 from http://www.hoise.com/primeur/05/articles/monthly/AE-PR-02-05-1.html

Nozaki, K., Akiyama, T., Shimojo, S., Maeda, S., & Tamagawa, H. (2005). Integration of computational fluid dynamics and computational aero acoustics on grid for dental applications. In *Proceedings of the 18th IEEE Symposium on Computer-Based Medical Systems*, (pp. 517-522). Washington, DC: IEEE Computer Society.

Piggott, D., Teljeur, C., & Kelly, A. (2004). Exploring the potential for using the grid to support health impact assessment modelling. *Parallel Computing*, *30*(9-10), 1073–1091. doi:10.1016/j.parco.2004.07.012

Power, D., Politou, E., Slaymaker, M., Harris, S., & Simpson, A. (2004). A relational approach to the capture of DICOM files for Grid-enabled medical imaging databases. In *Proceedings of the 2004 ACM symposium on applied computing*, (pp.272-279). New York: ACM Press.

Power, D., Slaymaker, M., Politou, E., & Simpson, A. (2005). Protecting sensitive patient data via query modification. In *Proceedings of the 2005 ACM symposium on applied computing*, pp.224-230. New York: ACM Press.

Scheres, S. H. W., Merino, A. J., Sorzano, C. O. S., & Carazo, J. M. (2005). Grid computing in 3D-EM image processing using Xmipp. In *Proceedings of the 18th symposium on computer-based medical system*, (pp. 561-563). Washington, DC: IEEE Computer Society.

Semantic grid project. (2008). Retrieved February 1, 2008 from http://www.semanticgrid.org/

Silva, J. S., & Ball, M. J. (2002). Prognosis for year 2013. *International Journal of Medical Informatics*, *66*(1-3), 45–49. doi:10.1016/S1386-5056(02)00035-7

Simpson, A., Power, D., Slaymaker, M., & Politou, E. (2005). GIMI: generic infrastructure for medical informatics. In *Proceedings of the 18th symposium on computer-based medical system*, (pp. 564-566). Washington, DC: IEEE Computer Society.

Sorzano, C. O. S., Marabini, R., Velázquez-Muriel, J., Bilbao-Castro, J. R., Scheres, S. H. W., Carazo, J. M., & Pascual-Montano, A. (2004). XMIPP: A new generation of an open-source image processing package for electron microscopy. *Journal of Structural Biology, 148*(2), 194–204. doi:10.1016/j.jsb.2004.06.006

Stevens, R., McEntire, R., Goble, C., Greenwood, M., Zhao, J., Wipat, A., & Li, P. (2004). myGrid and the drug discovery process. *Drug Discovery Today: BIOSILICO, 2*(4), 140–148. doi:10.1016/S1741-8364(04)02412-6

Stewart, C. A. (2004). Introduction to the edition. *Communications of the ACM, 47*(11), 30–33. doi:10.1145/1029496.1029522

Tirado-Ramos, A., Groen, D., & Sloot, P. (2005). On-line application performance monitoring of blood flow simulation in computational grid architectures. In *Proceedings of the 18th symposium on computer-based medical system*, (pp. 511-516). Washington, DC: IEEE Computer Society.

Tohsato, Y., Kosaka, T., Date, S., Shimojo, S., & Matsuda, H. (2005). *Heterogeneous database federation using grid technology for drug discovery process*, (pp. 43-52). (LNCS Vol. 3370). Berlin, Germany: Springer-Verlag.

Vadhiyar, S. S., & Dongarra, J. J. (2005). Self adaptivity in grid computing. *Concurrency and Computation, 17*(2-4), 235–257. doi:10.1002/cpe.927

Wu, B., Dovey, M., Ng, M. H., Tai, K., Murdock, S., Jeffreys, P., et al. (2004). A web / grid portal implementation of BioSimGrid: A biomolecular simulation database. In *Proceedings of the Information Technology: Coding and Computing*, (pp. 50-54).

Xing, L., Wang, J., & Zhou, B. (2006). Integration and access of data resources in simulation grid system. *Journal of System Simulation, 18*(2), 369–372.

Zamboulis, L., Fan, H., Belhajjame, K., Siepen, J., Jones, A., Martin, N., et al. *Data access and integration in the ISPIDER proteomics Grid.* Retrieved February 1, 2008 from http://www.cs.man.ac.uk/~norm/papers/dils06.pdf

Zhuchkov, A., Tverdokhlebov, N., & Kravchenko, A. (2006). Advancing of Russian ChemBioGrid by bringing data management tools into collaborative environment. *Studies in Health Technology and Informatics, 120*, 179–186.

KEY TERMS AND DEFINITIONS

Grid: a large-scale, high-performance, always-on and dynamic, although geographically distributed yet networked, infrastructure that comprises and seamlessly unifies a variety of autonomous, heterogeneous components such as processes, resources, network layers, interfaces, protocols and services, with strong, consistent and controlled relationships among them

Grid Services: a type of Grid resource (service resource) with special capabilities and features to get tasks successfully accomplished on Grid networks. These are used to access other types of Grid resources

HealthGrid: a type of Grid. It is a Grid infrastructure dedicated to the management of healthcare resources that encompasses and integrates the various Grid components and healthcare components with consistent, compatible and meaningful coordination among them, to facilitate provision of the healthcare services

Heterogeneity: a difference in format, platform, semantics or ontology

Integration or Interoperability: a link or connection that enables communication among two or more resource types

OGSA-DAI: Open Grid Service Architecture Data Access and Integration, it is a powerful technology that possesses strong features for providing interfaces to heterogeneous data sources on Grids in order to integrate them

Resource or Grid Resource: a Grid resource can be any real or conceptual object that is needed to be accessed by other entities, such as human users of the system or programmes that generate requests for accessing particular resources

Taxonomy: a classification

Web Services: considered as the most efficient and reliable communicators of messages from one place to another regardless of geographical or technological heterogeneity

Chapter 9
Improving Patient Safety with Information Technology

James G. Anderson
Purdue University, USA

ABSTRACT

Over three-quarters of a million people are injured or die in hospitals annually from adverse drug events. The majority of medication errors result from poorly designed health care systems rather than from negligence on the part of health care providers. Health care systems, in general, rely on voluntary reporting which seriously underestimates the number of medication errors and adverse drug events (ADEs) by as much as 90%. This chapter reviews the literature on (1) the incidence and costs of medication errors and ADEs; (2) detecting and reporting medication errors and related ADEs; (3) and the use of information technology to reduce the number of medication errors and ADEs in health care settings. Results from an analysis of data on medication errors from a regional data sharing consortium and from computer simulation models designed to analyze the effectiveness of information technology (IT) in preventing medication errors are summarized.

INTRODUCTION

Adverse drug events resulting from medication errors are a significant problem in the U.S. (Bates, 1996; Classen, Pestotnik, Evans, Lloyd, & Burke, 1997). Traditionally hospitals have relied on voluntary reporting of errors. As a result it is estimated that only 5-10% of medication errors that result in harm to patients are reported (Cullen, Bates, Small, et al., 1995). Most of these errors result from deficiencies in system design (Leape, Bates, Cullen, et al., 1995; Gwande, Thomas, Zinner, et al., 1999; Anderson, 2003). Based on these studies, the Institute of Medicine recommended that confidential voluntary reporting systems be adopted in all health care organizations and that information technology be implemented to reduce medication errors (Kohn, Corrigan & Donaldson, 2000). However, little progress has been made since the IOM report (Leape & Berwick, 2005).

DOI: 10.4018/978-1-60566-030-1.ch009

This chapter reviews the literature on: (1) the incidence and costs of medication errors and ADEs; (2) detecting and reporting medication errors and related ADEs; (3) and the use of information technology (IT) to reduce the number of medication errors and ADEs in health care settings. The methodology includes: (1) a review of the literature on the incidence of medication errors and the use of IT to detect and reduce medication errors; (2) analysis of data from a regional data sharing system; and (3) the results of computer simulation models designed to analyze the effectiveness of IT in preventing medication errors.

BACKGROUND

It is estimated that three quarters of a million people are injured or die each year from adverse drug events (ADEs) (Bates, 1996: Classen, Pestotnik, Evans, Lloyd, & Burke, 1997: Lazarou, Pomeranz & Corey, 1998). One study of medication errors in 36 hospitals and skilled nursing facilities in Georgia and Colorado found that 19% of the doses were in error; seven percent of the errors could have resulted in adverse drug events (ADEs) (Barker, Flynn, Pepper, Bates, & Mikeal, 2002). Overall it has been estimated that adverse drug events (ADEs) occur in from two to seven out of every 100 patients admitted to a hospital in the USA (Bates, Cullen, Laird, et al.., 1995; Classen, Pestotnik, Evans, Lloyd, & Burke, 1997). Medication errors and associated ADEs increase the cost of hospitalization by about $4,700 per incident (Bates, Spell, Cullen, et al., 1997). The increased costs for a 700-bed hospital due to ADEs were estimated to be $2.8 million annually. Johnson and Bootman (1995) estimated the annual cost of morbidity and mortality due to drug therapy in 1995 for the U.S. to be $76.6 billion.

ADEs also occur among outpatients at an estimated rate of 5.5 per 100 patients (Honigman, Lee, Rothschild, et al., 2001). A recent analysis of hospital emergency departments in the U.S. estimated that ADEs account for 2.4 out of every 1,000 visits (Budnitz, Pollock, Weidenbach, Mendelsohn, Schroeder, & Annest, 2006).

Most errors are not reported making it difficult to ascertain the true rate of medication errors. Hospitals generally rely on voluntary reporting, which may result in the detection and reporting of as little as 10% of ADEs (Cullen, Bates, Small et al., 1995). One study of hospital units found that only 36 errors were reported on incident reports and 84 errors were reported on anonymous questionnaires over a period of 59,470 patient days (Barker & Allan, 1995). It was estimated that as many as 51,200 errors may have occurred in dispensing and administering medications over this period of time.

Over 24 states have mandated some form of medical error reporting (Comden & Rosenthal, 2002). Many of these reporting systems are internet-based and differ in the data that is shared (from specific processes/outcomes such as medication errors and/or nosocomial infections or infections resulting from treatment to a broad range of incidents); the participants (individual clinicians to entire healthcare organizations); geography (regional, state, and national); technology (paper-based to online); and regulatory expectations about participation (voluntary or mandatory) (Rosenthal & Booth., 2004; Flowers & Riley, 2001). To date there is little evidence of the effectiveness of these error reporting systems in reducing medication errors and ADEs.

A study analyzed data from 25 hospitals in Pennsylvania that agreed to share data on medication errors and organizational actions taken to prevent a reoccurrence of these errors (Anderson, 2008; Anderson, Ramanujam, Hensel and Siro, 2008). The Pittsburgh Regoinal Healthcare Initiative was predicated on a learning chain model where reporting and sharing information on errors will lead to organizational program solving. Identifying system failures and unsafe practices and procedures will then result in improved patient safety (Siro, 2003, 2005). Over a 12 month period the hospital reported approximately 17,000 medication errors. An examination of the longitudinal trends in the data indicated that error reporting increased at a statistically significant rate over the 12 month period. At thie same time reported corrective organizational actions remained unchanged during this same period.

Information technology is also being used to detect adverse drug events (Bates, Evans, Murff, Stetson, Pizziperri, and Hripcsak, 2003). For example, pharmacy data and clinical laboratory data that are available in electronic form can be screened for adverse drug events (Jha, Kuperman, Teich et al., 1998). Another study found that hospital information systems that monitor medication orders for drug-drug interactions and drug-allergy problems and provide drug-dose checking, cumulative dose checking, dose algorithms and detection of transcription errors identified approximately 89% of adverse events. (Bates, O'Neil, Boyle et al., 1994).

In another application of IT to detect ADEs a computerized system developed at LDS Hospital in Salt Lake City, Utah was programmed to generate a daily list of potential ADEs from data contained in an integrated hospital information system such as sudden medication stop orders, ordering of antidotes, and abnormal laboratory values. During an 18 month period 631 of 731 verified ADEs were detected by the automated system compared to only nine ADEs that were identified by the traditional reporting system. (Classen, Pestotnik, Evans & Burke, 1991).

Information systems are also being used to detect ADEs in an ambulatory setting (Honigman, Lee, Rothschild et al., 2001). One study compared several methods of detecting ADEs based on searching for International Classification of Diseases, 9th edition (ICD-9) codes previously associated with ADEs, violations of allergy rules, monitoring of events generally associated with ADEs, and text searches of visit notes (Honigman, Lee, Rothschild et al., 2001). The study concluded that computerized search programs can be used in quality improvement efforts to detect ADEs.

MAIN FOCUS OF THE CHAPTER

About 50 percent of medication errors result from a lack of information when the provider is ordering drugs for a patient. A second major source of errors is the transcription process (Leape, Bates, Cullen, et al., 1995). Studies have shown that information technology and decision support can reduce errors and resulting adverse effects by reducing these sources of errors (Bates, 2000; Bates & Gawande, 2003). System applications of IT rather than individual applications are most likely to be effective in reducing medication errors (Anderson, 2003; Leape, Bates, Cullen, et al., 1995). Kaushal, Shojania and Bates (2003) reviewed five trials that evaluated the effects of computerized physician order entry (CPOE) and seven trials that evaluated clinical decision support systems (CDSS). The investigators concluded that use of CPOE and CDSS can significantly reduce medication errors. For example, the implementation of a computerized physician order entry system reduced medication-related errors between 55 percent and 83 percent depending upon the level of decision support (Bates, Leape, Cullen, et al., 1998; Bates, Tecih, Lee, et al., 1999).

Computerized decision support systems have also been shown to be effective in improving medication safety. A study by Evans, Pestotnik, Classen and others (1998) found that use of a computer-based anti-infective drug management program resulted in a 70 percent decrease in ADEs caused by anti-infective drugs.

Also, computerized alerting systems have been shown to decrease error rates, delays in treatment, hospital length of stay and costs (Jha, Kuperman, Teich, Leape et al., 1998). The HELP system at LDS Hospital in Salt lake City, Utah automatically identifies patients who are at risk for adverse drug events by continuously monitoring electronically stored patient data. Hospital staff is alerted to take action to prevent harm to the patient when potential ADEs are detected (Evans et al., 1994).

However, experience with early hospital and ambulatory care medical information systems suggest that major organizational changes are frequently required to successfully implement information technology especially physician order entry systems (Anderson, 2007; Dorman, Muth-Selbach, Krebs, Criegee-Rieck et al., 2000). Studies such as the one reported by Anderson and others (2002) and the Institute for Safe Medication Practices (1999) suggest that piece-meal implementation of information systems may fail to detect and prevent errors.

Anderson and others (2002) developed a computer simulation model representing the medication delivery system in a hospital. Parameters of the model were estimated from a study of prescription errors on two hospital medical/surgical units and used in the baseline run. The model simulates the four stages of the medication deliver system: prescribing, transcribing, dispensing and administering drugs. In this study interventions that have been demonstrated in prior studies to decrease error rates were simulated. The results suggest that a computerized information system that detected 26 percent of medication errors and prevented associated ADEs could save 1,226 days of excess hospitalization and $1.4 million in hospital costs annually. The results suggest that clinical information systems are potentially a cost-effective means of preventing ADEs in hospitals and demonstrate the importance of viewing medication errors from a systems perspective. Prevention efforts that focus on a single stage of the process had limited impact on the overall error rate. This study suggests that system-wide changes to the medication deliver system are required to significantly reduce medication errors that may result in adverse drug events in a hospital setting (Anderson, Jay, Anderson and & Hunt, 2002).

FUTURE TRENDS

Surveys of U.S. hospitals show that less than 15 percent of hospitals have implemented an electronic medication order-entry system (Ash, Gorman & Hersh, 1998; Pederson, Schneider & Santell, 2001). Anderson and Balas (2006, 2008) surveyed primary care physicians in the U.S. to determine their use of electronic medical records, electronic prescribing, use of decision support tools and electronic communication with patients. Overall 20% to 25% of physicians reported using each of these IT applications in practice. While the majority of physicians perceived benefits of IT they cited costs, vendor inability to deliver acceptable products and concerns about potential violation of the confidentiality of patient data as major barriers to implementation of IT applications.

An Institute of Medicine report stated that the development of a national health information network is critical for advancing patient safety in U.S. health care (IOM, 2001). However, incentives will have to be provided to increase the rate of adoption of IT in health care. One study estimates that the development of a national IT network will initially cost $156 billion and $48 billion annually in operating costs (Kaushal et al., 2005). The report concludes that the private sector is unlikely to rapidly adopt IT without public investment and incentives. The Medicare Payment Advisory Commission (1999) in a report to congress proposed that financial incentives be provided for the implementation of computerized physician order entry systems. Legislation has been introduced into the U.S. Congress that that would provide grants for hospitals to implement information technology (Medication Error Reduction Act, 2001). At the state level California enacted legislation requiring hospitals to implement information technology in order to reduce medication errors (California Senate Bill 1875, 2000).

Medical errors occur in ambulatory care settings and nursing homes as well as in hospitals

(Gurwitz, Field, Avorn, McCormick, Jain, Eckle, et al. 2000; Gurwitz, Field, Harrold, Rotthschild, Debellis, Seger, et al., 2003). To date most information technology applications designed to detect and prevent medication errors have been developed for inpatient hospital settings. An important area for research and development is the design of systems for ambulatory settings. It has been estimated that universal adoption of computerized physician order entry in the ambulatory setting could prevent as many as 2.1 million ADEs a year resulting in annual savings of $34 billion (Johnston, Pan, Walker, Bates & Middeleton, 2004).

The process of reporting medication errors and ADEs needs to be significantly improved. At present only about 10% of medication errors are reported using a voluntary reporting system. In recent years, about one-half of the states have implemented mandatory reporting systems for adverse events (Comden & Rosenthal, 2002). Moreover, the Joint Commission on Accreditation of Healthcare Organizations (JCAHO) requires hospitals to conduct root-cause analyses of adverse events and encourages healthcare organizations to report them to the JCAHO. The usefulness of these reporting systems in reducing medical errors has been limited to date. Lessons learned from error reports generally do not result in organizational changes required to prevent future errors from reoccurring (Anderson, Ramanujam, Hensel, & Siro, 2007).

Currently there is a mismatch between patient safety goals and hospital actions to reduce the risk of future medication errors. Hospitals increasingly seem to recognize the need to implement voluntary error reporting systems in order to gather information needed to reduce errors. At the same time, they fail to initiate organizational changes that are needed to improve patient safety. Typically hospitals narrowly focused on communicating information about errors to health care providers. However, more than the implementation of voluntary reporting systems is required. Significant reductions in errors will also require that organizational changes consistent with the improvement of patient safety be carefully institutionalized and integrated into long-term plans.

CONCLUSION

In order to achieve an acceptable level of patient safety, the Institute of Medicine has called for a national health information infrastructure that will provide complete patient information and decision support tools to health care providers and will capture patient safety information (Aspden, Corrigan, Wolcott & Erickson, 2004). Also the President's Information Technology Committee (2004) has recommended the adoption of electronic health records to provide information to providers at the point of care, computer-assisted decision support based on evidence-based medicine, electronic order entry and interoperability in exchanging health information.

There is considerable evidence that medication errors that result in ADEs can be detected and prevented (Agency for Healthcare Research and Quality, 2001). Information systems that include physician order entry, decision support, and alerting systems can significantly reduce errors and adverse events that result in injury to or the death or patients. However, information technology in order to be effective must be implemented using a systems approach. Also implementation will require organizational commitment to the use of information technology to improve patient safety (Glasser, 2002).

ACKNOWLEDGMENT

Portions of this chapter are taken with from Anderson (2004a) with permission from Campden Publishing Ltd. and from Anderson (2004b) with permission from Ashley Publications. I wish to acknowledge the assistance of Marilyn Anderson with the preparation of this chapter.

REFERENCES

Agency for Healthcare Research and Quality. (2001). Reducing and preventing adverse drug events to decrease hospital costs. *Research in Action, 1*. Rockville, MD: AHRQ Publication Number 01-0020.

Anderson, J. G. (2003). A systems approach to preventing adverse drug events. In S. Krishna, E.A. Balas, & S.A. Boren (Eds.), *Information technology business models for quality health care: An EU/US dialogue* (pp. 95-102). Amsterdam: IOS Press.

Anderson, J.G. (2004a). Using IT for medication safety: systems available. *Hospital Pharmacy Europe, July/August, 1-2*.

Anderson, J. G. (2004b). Information technology for detecting medication errors and adverse drug events. *Expert Opinion on Drug Safety, 3*(5), 1–7. doi:10.1517/14740338.3.5.449

Anderson, J. G. (2008). Regional patient safety initiatives: the missing element of organizational change., In A. Kushniruk and E.M. Borycki (Eds.), *The human and social Side of health information systems*. Hershey, PA: Idea Group Publishing.

Anderson, J. G., & Bales, E. A. (2006). Computerization of primary care in the United States. *International Journal of Healthcare Information Systems and Informatics, 1*(3), 1–23.

Anderson, J. G., Jay, S. J., Anderson, M. M., & Hunt, T. J. (2002). Evaluating the capability of information technology to prevent adverse drug events: A computer simulation approach. *Journal of the American Medical Informatics Association, 9*, 479–490. doi:10.1197/jamia.M1099

Anderson, J. G., Ramanujam, R., Hensel, D., Anderson, M., & Siro, C. A. (2006). The need for organizational change in patient safety initiatives. *International Journal of Medical Informatics, 75*(12), 809–817. doi:10.1016/j.ijmedinf.2006.05.043

Anderson, J. G., Ramanujam, R., Hensel, D., & Siro, C. A. (In Press). Reporting trends in a regional medication error data-sharing system. *Health Care Management Science*.

Ash, J. S., Gorman, P. N., & Hersh, W. R. (1998). Physician order entry in U.S. hospitals. *Proceedings of the AMIA Symposium* (pp. 236-239).

Aspden, P., Corrigan, J. M., Wolcott, J., & Erickson, S. M. (Eds.). (2004). *Patient safety: Achieving a new standard for care*. Washington, DC: The National Academies Press.

Barker, K. N., & Allan, E. L. (1995). Research on drug-use-system errors. *American Journal of Health-System Pharmacy, 52*, 400–403.

Barker, K. N., Flynn, E. A., Pepper, G. A., Bates, D. W., & Mikeal, R. L. (2002). Medication errors observed in 36 health care facilities. *Archives of Internal Medicine, 162*, 1897–1903. doi:10.1001/archinte.162.16.1897

Bates, D. W. (1996). Medication errors: How common are they and what can be done to prevent them? *Drug Safety, 5*, 303–310. doi:10.2165/00002018-199615050-00001

Bates, D. W. (2000). Using information technology to reduce rates of medication errors in hospitals. *British Medical Journal, 320*, 788–791. doi:10.1136/bmj.320.7237.788

Bates, D. W., Cohen, M., & Leape, L. L. (2001). Reducing the frequency of errors in medicine using information technology. *Journal of the American Medical Informatics Association, 8*, 299–308.

Bates, D. W., Cullen, D., & Laird, N. (1995). Incidence of adverse drug events and potential adverse drug events: implications for prevention. *Journal of the American Medical Association, 274*, 29–34. doi:10.1001/jama.274.1.29

Bates, D. W., Evans, R. S., Murff, H., Stetson, P. D., Pizziferri, L., & Hripcsak, G. (2003). Detecting Adverse Events using information technology. *Journal of the American Medical Informatics Association, 10*, 115–128. doi:10.1197/jamia.M1074

Bates, D. W., Evans, R. S., Murff, H., Stetson, P. D., Pizziperri, L., & Hripcsak, G. (2003). Policy and the future of adverse drug event detection using information technology. *Journal of the American Medical Informatics Association, 10*, 226–228. doi:10.1197/jamia.M1268

Bates, D. W., & Gawande, A. A. (2003). Improving safety with information technology. *The New England Journal of Medicine, 348*(25), 2526–2534. doi:10.1056/NEJMsa020847

Bates, D. W., Leape, L. L., & Cullen, D. J. (1998). Effect of computerized physician order entry and a team intervention on prevention of serious medication errors. *Journal of the American Medical Association, 280*, 1311–1316. doi:10.1001/jama.280.15.1311

Bates, D. W., O'Neil, A. C., Boyle, D., Teich, J., Chertow, G. M., Komaroff, A. L., & Brennan, T. A. (1994). Potential identifiability and preventability of adverse events using information systems. *Journal of the American Medical Informatics Association, 1*, 404–411.

Bates, D. W., Spell, N. S., & Cullen, D. J. (1997). The costs of adverse drug events in hospitalized patients. *Journal of the American Medical Association, 277*, 307–311. doi:10.1001/jama.277.4.307

Bates, D. W., Teich, J. M., & Lee, J. (1999). The impact of computerized physician order entry on medication error prevention. *Journal of the American Medical Informatics Association, 6*, 313–321.

Budnitz, D. S., Pollock, D. A., Weidenbach, K. N., Mendelsohn, A. B., Schroeder, T. J., & Annest, J. L. (2006). National surveillance of emergency department visits for outpatient adverse drug events. *Journal of the American Medical Association, 296*(15), 1858–1866. doi:10.1001/jama.296.15.1858

California Senate Bill 1875 (2000). Chapter 816, 1393.63.

Classen, D. C., Pestotnik, S. L., Evans, R. S., & Burke, J. P. (1991). Computerized surveillance of adverse drug events in hospital patients. *Journal of the American Medical Association, 266*, 2847–2851. doi:10.1001/jama.266.20.2847

Classen, D. C., Pestotnik, S. L., Evans, R. S., Lloyd, J. F., & Burke, J. P. (1997). Adverse drug events in hospitalized patients: excess length of stay, extra costs, and attributable mortality. *Journal of the American Medical Association, 277*, 301–306. doi:10.1001/jama.277.4.301

Comden, S. C., & Rosenthal, J. (2002). *Statewide Patient Safety Coalitions: A Status Report.* Portland. ME: National Academy for State Health Policy.

Cullen, D. J., Bates, D. W., & Small, S. D. (1995). The incident reporting system does not detect adverse drug events: A problem for quality improvement. *Journal of Quality Improvement, 21*, 541–548.

Dormann, H., Muth-Selbach, U., Krebs, S., & Criegee-Rieck, M. (2000). Incidence and costs of adverse drug reactions during hospitalization: Computerized monitoring versus stimulated spontaneous reporting. *Drug Safety, 22*(2), 161–168. doi:10.2165/00002018-200022020-00007

Evans, R. S., Classen, D. C., Pestotnik, S. L., Lundsgaarde, H. P., & Burke, J. P. (1994). Improving empiric antibiotic selection using computer decision support. *Archives of Internal Medicine*, *154*, 878–884. doi:10.1001/archinte.154.8.878

Evans, R. S., Pestotnik, S. L., Classen, D. C., & Horn, S. D. (1994). Preventing adverse drug events in hospitalized patients. *The Annals of Pharmacotherapy*, *28*, 523–527.

Flowers, L., & Riley, T. (2001). *State-based Mandatory Reporting of Medical Errors: An Analysis of the Legal and Policy Issues*. Portland, ME: National Academy for State Health Policy.

Gawande, A. A., Thomas, E. J., & Zinner, M. J. (1999). The incidence and nature of surgical adverse events in Colorado and Utah in 1992. *Surgery*, *126*(1), 66–75. doi:10.1067/msy.1999.98664

Glasser, J. P. (2002). *The strategic application of information technology in health care organizations*, (2nd ed.). San Francisco, CA: Jossey-Bass.

Gurwitz, J. H., Field, T. S., Avorn, J., McCormick, D., Jain, S., & Eckler, M. (2000). Incidence and preventability of adverse drug events in nursing homes. *The American Journal of Medicine*, *109*(2), 87–94. doi:10.1016/S0002-9343(00)00451-4

Gurwitz, J. H., Field, T. S., Harrold, I. R., Rotthschild, J., Debellis, K., & Seger, A. C. (2003). Incidence and preventability of adverse drug events in among older persons in the ambulatory setting. *Journal of the American Medical Association*, *289*(9), 1107–1116. doi:10.1001/jama.289.9.1107

Health Care Financing Administration. (1997). Medicare and Medicaid Programs; hospital conditions of participation; provider agreements and supplier approval. *Federal Register*, *62*(244), 66726–66757.

Honigman, B., Lee, J., & Rothschild, J. (2001). Using computerized data to identify adverse drug events in outpatients. *Journal of the American Medical Informatics Association*, *8*, 254–266.

Institute for Safe Medication Practices. Overreliance on computer systems may place patients at great risk. *ISMP Medication Safety Alert, Feb.12,1999*. Huntingdon Valley, PA: ISMP.

Institute of Medicine. (2001). *Crossing the Quality Chasm: A New Health System for the 21st Century*. Washington, DC: National Academy Press.

Jha, A. K., Kuperman, G. J., Teich, J. M., & Leape, L. L. (1998). Identifying adverse drug events: Development of a computer-based monitor and comparison with chart review and stimulated voluntary report. *Journal of the American Medical Informatics Association*, *5*, 305–314.

Johnson, J. A., & Bootman, J. L. (1995). Drug-related morbidity and mortality: A cost of illness model. *Archives of Internal Medicine*, *155*, 1949–1956. doi:10.1001/archinte.155.18.1949

Johnston, D., Pan, E., Walker, J., Bates, D. W., & Middleton, B. (2004). *Center for Information Technology Leadership: Patient Safety in the Physician's Office: Assessing the Value of Ambulatory CPOE*. Oakland, CA: California HealthCare Foundation.

Kaushal, R., Blumenthal, D., Poon, E. G., Jha, A. K., & Franz, C. (2005). The costs of a national health information network. *Annals of Internal Medicine*, *143*, 165–173.

Kaushal, R., Shojania, K. G., & Bates, D. W. (2003). Effects of computerized physician order entry and clinical decision support systems on medication safety. *Archives of Internal Medicine*, *163*, 1409–1416. doi:10.1001/archinte.163.12.1409

Kohn, L. T., Corrigan, J. M., & Donaldson, M. S. (Eds.). (1999). *To Err is Human: Building a Safer Health System*. Washington, DC: National Academy Press.

Lazarou, J., Pomeranz, B. H., & Corey, P. N. (1998). Incidence of adverse drug reactions in hospitalized patients: a meta-analysis of prospective studies. *Journal of the American Medical Association*, *279*, 1200–1205. doi:10.1001/jama.279.15.1200

Leape, L. L., Bates, D. W., & Cullen, D. J. (1995). Systems analysis of adverse drug events. *Journal of the American Medical Association*, *274*, 35–43. doi:10.1001/jama.274.1.35

Leape, L. L., & Berwick, D. M. (2005). Five years after To Err is Human: What have we learned. *Journal of the American Medical Association*, *293*, 2384–2390. doi:10.1001/jama.293.19.2384

Leape, L. L., Cullen, D. J., & Clapp, M. D. (1999). Pharmacist participation on physician rounds and adverse drug events in the intensive care unit. *Journal of the American Medical Association*, *272*, 267–270. doi:10.1001/jama.282.3.267

Medicare Payment Advisory Commission. (1999). *Report to the Congress: Selected Medicare Issues*. Washington, DC: Medicare Payment Advisory Commission.

Medication Errors Reduction Act of 2001 (2001). S 824, 107th congress. 1st Session.

Pederson, C. A., Schneider, P. J., & Santell, J. P. (2001). ASHP national survey of pharmacy practice in hospital settings: prescribing and transcribing – 2001. *American Journal of Health-System Pharmacy*, *58*, 2251–2266.

President's Information Technology Advisory Committee, Health Care Delivery and Information Technology (HIT) Subcommittee. (2004, April 13). *Draft Recommendations*., Retrieved from www.nitrd.gov/pitac

Rosenthal, J. & Booth, M. (2004, October). *State Patient Safety Centers: A new approach to promote patient safety*. Portland, ME: National Academy for State Health Policy.

Siro, C. A., Segel, K. T., Keyser, D. J., Harrison, E. I., & Lloyd, J. C. (2003). Pittsburgh regional healthcare initiative: a systems approach for achieving perfect patient care. *Health Affairs*, *22*(5), 157–165. doi:10.1377/hlthaff.22.5.157

KEY TERMS AND DEFINITIONS

Adverse drug events (ADE): A medication that results in unintended harm to a patient

Computerized Decision support systems: A computer-based system that consists of a knowledge base and an inference engine that generates advice to the providers

Computerized physician order entry (CPOE): Clinical systems that electronically relay the physician's or nurse practitioner's diagnostic and therapeutic plan for action

Electronic health record (EHR): An electronic repository of information about a patient's health care and clinical information management tools that provide alerts, reminders and tools for data analysis

Medical alerts: a computer generated message to the provider that is created when a record or event meets prespecified criteria

Chapter 10
Managing ICT in Healthcare Organization:
Culture, Challenges, and Issues of Technology Adoption and Implementation

Nasriah Zakaria
Universiti Sains, Malaysia

Shafiz Affendi Mohd Yusof
Universiti Utara, Malaysia

Norhayati Zakaria
Universiti Utara, Malaysia

ABSTRACT

The objective of this chapter is to illustrate a case study of a medical research institute in Malaysia in order to discuss issues pertaining to ICT adoption in healthcare organizations, in particular exploring the culture, challenges, and issues of ICT adoption among medical teams, patients, etc. In this chapter, we examine the question of 'What are the challenges of implementing ICT in healthcare organizations?' Some of the lessons learned from the case study were: ICT was successfully adopted and implemented based on several factors such as supportive organizational culture, competent IT workers, committed IT department and heavy investment on ICT infrastructure. Yet challenges also arise which hinges upon factors like initial deployment of outside IT resources or expertise for ICT implementation, lack of user training and continuous communication between involved parties in the initial stage.

INTRODUCTION

This chapter consists of six sections highlighting issues on information and communication technology (ICT) adoption and implementation. The first section discusses the phenomenon of ICT adoption in healthcare institution. Second, we include literature reviews based on three perspectives that oftentimes pose challenges to the deployment of ICT: (1) organizational, (2) people, and (3) technology. Third, we highlight the methodology of the study in this chapter which is a case study. In this section, we provide the background of a single case study -- a medical research institute in Malaysia -- to illustrate

DOI: 10.4018/978-1-60566-030-1.ch010

lessons learned and challenges of ICT adoption and implementation. Fourth, we present our findings which is the detailed descriptions of the issues and challenges based on an analytical framework called 5Ws (what, when, why, where, and who) as well as from the three perspectives mentioned above. Fifth, we provide the discussions in light of lessons learned and the contribution of the study. Lastly, the chapter concludes by summarizing the findings for healthcare institutions that intend to adopt and implement ICT in their organizations and presents the directions for future research undertakings.

In the era of globalization and information age, healthcare industries are intensely promoting and adopting ICT to improve patient care. When more and more patients as health consumers seek and prioritize quality in their lives through enhanced healthcare treatments and services, it places great demands on the health care industry's information-handling abilities and infrastructure (Bodenheimer, 1999). As supported by a recent World Bank (2006) report, "Reliable information and effective communication are crucial elements in public health practices. The use of appropriate technologies can increase the quality and the reach of both information and communication."

In line with this, Malaysia as a developing country has invested heavily in ICT with the mission and vision to improve patient care. Malaysia realizes that patients with healthy lives are better able to maintain healthy minds, healthy lifestyles, and a balance between work and family. In a similar vein, healthcare service organizations also seek for optimal strategies and solutions to increase their medical services. When introducing ICT, these organizations need to consider carefully the challenges that arise from it such as whether the organizational culture is supportive towards any ICT adoption and implementation, whether the organization can build ICT infrastructures that are efficiently and effectively, and whether the organization is willing to recruit, select, and employ competent human resources to use ICT as tools.

For example, according to the study by Mass and Eriksson (2006), when ICT was introduced and hospital staff were unprepared for changes because there was no adequate information given by the technology providers, the immediate result was a lack of knowledge of the new clinical requirements, and users who were ignorant of how to use the new technology; the larger consequence, was a slowed process of implementation and adoption. On the other hand, organizations like hospitals have now realized the potential of integrating ICT into their organization. Technology is reshaping organizations by blending their information systems with rapidly advancing telecommunication technology (Frenzel & Frenzel, 2004). In addition, management teams feel that having ICT integrated into their systems will improve and strengthen healthcare systems in the future. Ragam (2007) asserts that successful ICT adoption will lessen errors considerably, if not totally eliminate them. In addition, according to the World Health Organization, technologies form the backbone of services to prevent, diagnose and treat illness and disease. ICTs are only one category of the vast array of technologies that may be of use, but given the right policies, organization, resources and institutions, ICTs can be powerful tools in the hands of those working to improve health (WHO, 2004).

Besides ICT becoming the catalyst factor for economic growth, it serves as an essential medium of communication between patients and medical teams. Studies have shown that in face-to-face encounters, patients often refuse to share or disclose their illness to support groups such as medical teams, family or friends, even when such disclosure can help them cope with terminal illness. Whether ICT will make patients more or less willing to disclose their information to the support group or family members is still unknown. Hence, the main purpose of this chapter is to understand ICT adoption and implementation issues in one case study of a Malaysian hospital as an example of a health-care institution. In this chapter, we will investigate one overarching research question: What are the challenges of implementing ICT in healthcare organizations?

CULTURE AND CHALLENGES OF ICT ADOPTION AND IMPLEMENTATION

In this section, we first provide some definitions on basic concepts such as culture, organizational culture, and information system culture. We also provide the linkages between these different layers of culture. Second, we also present some literature reviews on ICT adoption and implementation based on the conceptual framework (see Figure 1). In specific, we investigated the culture of ICT adoption among the medical teams and support staff in the hospital environment. Culture can be defined as the way of life or the way things are done. Cultural values are usually associated with nations, though a particular nation may consist of subcultures and even subcultures (Holt & Wigginton, 2002). In addition, Robbins (1996) defines national culture as "the primary values and practices that characterize a particular country" (p.48). Culture differs in many aspects and exists between countries based on cultural dimensions introduced by several theorists. The following paragraphs explore in more detail the three types of culture with which we are concerned: national, organizational, and IS.

A cross-cultural theorist, Geert Hofstede (1980) has conducted hundreds of studies to examine the impact of cultural values on many aspects of organizational behaviors and management practices. His study illustrates national culture based on four dimensions--power distance, uncertainty avoidance, individualism vs. collectivism, and masculinity vs. femininity. Each dimension describes a different area of the cultural impact on management practices. For example, power distance illustrates the willingness of a person to accept the inequality of power in an organization. The second cultural value, individualism vs. collectivism, refers to the 'sense of belonging' a person feels when it comes to job satisfaction and tasks. Third, uncertainty avoidance explains the level of risk and uncertainty that people are willing to accept and undertake. The last dimension, femininity and masculinity, describes the difference between people who are ambitious, hardworking, committed and task oriented as opposed to people who are caring, and relationship-oriented.

Organizational culture comprises the atittudes, experiences, beliefs and values of an organization. According to Schein (1992), organizational culture can be defined as "A pattern of shared basic assumptions that the group learned as it solved its problems of external adaptation and internal integration, that has worked well enough to be considered valid and, therefore, to be taught to new members as the correct way you perceive, think, and feel in relation to those problems" (p.34)."Thus the impact of organizational culture is extensive and intense in organizations where it is manifested in concepts such as 'the way we do things around here,' or certain rites and rituals of the company, 'our company climate,' 'our common practices and norms', and 'our core values.' Schein (1985) suggests three levels of culture: artifacts, espoused values, and basic underlying assumptions. These organizational levels definitely overlap with the national background of an individual, which might create conflicts.

Besides organizational culture, another layer of cultural values that need to be emphasized is the information system (IS) culture. What is an IS culture? There is no clear distinction of this type of culture since it overlaps with national and organizational culture. To avoid any confusion with the already multifaceted cultural values in this chapter, we will limit our definition of IS culture to one particular instance, that of the organizational culture of the developer of the ICT and the users who either adopt or reject the technology that he or she uses in an organization. Extending the work of Hofstede, IS culture can be defined as the set

Figure 1. Conceptual framework of challenges in managing ICT in healthcare organizations

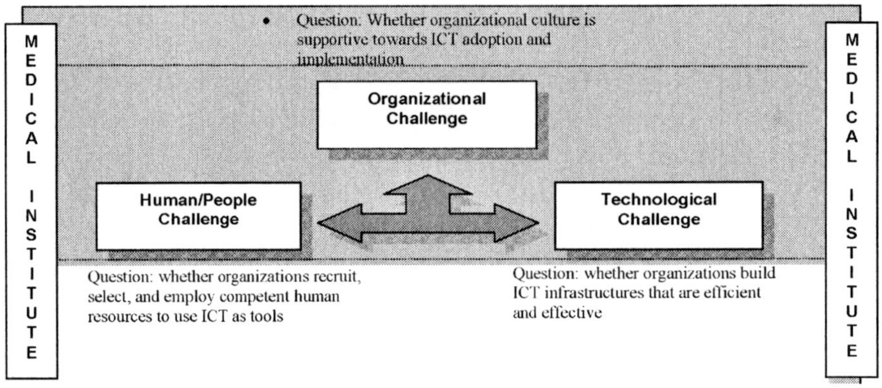

of values and practices shared by the members of an organization involved in information activities; this includes people like IT professionals, managers, and end-users. IS culture is thus a subset of an organizational culture, with unique values that are attached to the IT department. IS culture might resist technologies which threaten to change their current status, power, and working habits, especially when they may violate some of the groups' shared values. IS culture may also be more or less compatible with certain forms of IT; when that is the case, the result can be resistance to IT changes, failure in ICT adoption, and lack of implementation. In other words, the way people perceive the usefulness and ease of use of a given ICT will be impacted by the existing national culture – in this case, that of the medical teams as well as the support staff – together with the common practices, artifacts, espoused values and underlying assumptions of the developer(s) in an organization.

On the overall, culture is complex and multifaceted (Fan, 2000). As such, national culture is interrelated to organizational culture, professional culture (e.g. medical teams as doctors and nurses), as well as the IS culture. All these layers of cultural values can affect the way people handle innovation and ICT adoption. For instance, a study by Aggouram & Ingham (2003) found that when an organization attempts to standardize their information system, culture plays an important role as it affects the success of such task. Besides the multifaceted layers of culture, we also need to address the challenges that are confronted by people when a new technology is introduced. The key question is whether or not people are able to adopt the newly introduced ICT and if yes, what is the culture surrounding the ICT adoption and what are the challenges encountered by an organization?

Challenges of ICT Adoption

Based on the following conceptual framework (Figure 1), there are three aspects that we examined pertaining to the issue of ICT adoption in the hospital which are (1) organizations, (2) human, and (3) technology. Without a doubt, ICT has played a significant role in organizations such as hospitals and will continue to play a greater role in the aim of enhancing healthcare services. ICT is no longer just a business tool but an integral part of the organization's strategies. ICT impacts not only the IT department but every area or department in the organization since ICT is responsible for the integration of information across the entire organization. Based on empirical studies, the challenges of ICT arise from three barriers: organization, people and technology (Nambisan & Wang, 1999; Lorenzi & Riley, 2003; Nøhr,

2005; Pare, 2007; Tanriverdi & Iacono, 1999). These challenges and issues must be managed critically and effectively in order for an organization to function successfully via the use of ICT tools and applications.

Organizational Challenges

One of the most widely discussed questions on ICT implementation in hospitals is the cost of ICT investment – that is, the cost of the hardware and software needed to run the healthcare system. This could be actually high depending on the latest cost of software on the market, but it can also be relatively high, for example particularly costly to hospitals located in rural areas where not enough investment is made in updating or changing to new healthcare systems. In addition, organizations must consider costs associated with planning, specifying requirements, customizing and re-customizing systems, training providers, and reengineering the delivery of healthcare systems to accommodate hospitals. Miller and West (2007) suggest that the initial cost of implementing an Electronic Medical Record in a health center may be as high as $US54, 000 to $US64,000 per participating physician, with ongoing costs of $US21,000 per physician per year. The key question is thus who will bear the expensive costs of ICT investment?

Another important organizational challenge is the organizational culture. An effective and efficiently managed organization normally ensures that their managers and employees understand the basic beliefs and policies governing behavior both within the organization and in external business relationships. The concept of organizational culture encompasses not only the organization as a whole, but also the individuals who are part of, or interact with it. According to Zakaria and Mohd Yusof (2001), a culture that promotes change is thought to be a more nurturing environment for technology users than a culture that promotes stability and certainty. Resistance towards usage of ICT in healthcare systems will frequently surface unless the culture is receptive towards changes, and unless people are ready to both accept new ideas and, more importantly sustain the changed conditions in the future.

Human/People Challenge

Human resources are the most important assets that contribute to organizational success. With the introduction of complex and rapidly evolving technology, organizations oftentimes are limited by the scarcity of skilled employees and experienced managers needed to operate the newly introduced ICTs. It is recommended that IT managers and their top management have a plan to cope with skill shortages because organizations that fail to manage their present staff stand little chance of obtaining and retaining outstanding individuals. Human resources that are reliable and full of capabilities will also increase the efficiency and effectiveness of the ICT. Therefore, organizations need to ensure they can recruit, train, and retain talented IT experts. This issue is directly related to organizational performance as well as individual performance; significant contributions that materially improve an organization's performance have oftentimes been made by a small number of individuals. Another important aspect is that reliable and competent IT expertise can disseminate operations and services much faster than people who do not know or understand how to use ICTs. Thus user training must be in place in order to bring users up to a tolerable level of competence which in turn increases the user acceptance of technological change. User training must be included in all phases of ICT adoption, from the initial stage up to the implementation stage. As suggested by Johnson (2001), three important tasks need to be included: educating the healthcare professionals, conducting research to understand the importance of ICT to stakeholders, and advocating for ICT use in organizations.

Technological Challenge

Without doubt, ICT is changing the way health care functions. With ICT tools, organizations can enhance healthcare services electronically where barriers like time, distance and space no longer matters. What matters is the quality of services. For instance, health care organizations can offer more efficient and various services for health consumers such as ability to access their own health records, browse the Internet for further information and knowledge about one's illness, communicate freely and speedily between patients and doctors, and reach out to online communities of patients that suffer the same illness for psychological support. However, with the amplified role played by ICT, there are some technological challenges that arise such as ease of use, usability, information security and compatibility of the system with the existing one. All the challenges transpire as a result of the technological change undergone at the organizational as well as individual level. Technological change is defined as "the change period, during which something new is planned and introduced, e.g. the period associated with the introduction of new processes that have major new technological ingredients" (Wild, 1990, p.55). The challenges that stem from such changes need to be managed. According to Benjamin and Levinson (1993), "The greater the functionality of an IT system, the more levels of learning and adjustments are required to use it (p.30)." In support of that, Zakaria and Yusof (2001) suggest that readiness and willingness to learn about the new technology at a greater depth and the customization of each of the processes are key issues that need to be taken into account when planning or undergoing technological change. Only then can the learning and transition processes during ICT adoption and implementation be a success.

METHODOLOGY

A Case Study of a Medical Research Institute in Malaysia

A case study is an ideal methodology when a holistic and in-depth investigation is needed (Feagin, Orum, & Sjoberg, 1991). Following storytelling logic, it seeks a deep understanding of a single organization by analyzing its social context (Dyer & Wilkins, 1991). In order to describe a rich story, case researchers approach the field as closely as possible and apply theoretical constructs in ongoing social settings. The descriptive and interpretive nature of storytelling enables researchers to investigate the process by which an artifact comes to obtain its characteristics (Dyer & Wilkins, 1991). It is a backward tracing of artifact history and an analytical conceptualization of the artifact. In other words, a case study is an act of taking an artifact's history apart and reassembling it within a contextual frame. Through these processes, researchers identify the intricacies of a particular context.

In this study, we use case study as a qualitative method because it is most relevant in exploring ICT adoption in a new setting, in this case--Malaysia. Our case study focuses on one medical research institute (MRI) situated in the northern part of Malaysia. The institute is part of a research university which also has its own teaching hospital located in the eastern part of Malaysia. This research institute's mission is to educate and train more medical and dental professionals in conducting medical research. In addition, the institute also provides outpatient services to the local community. At the same time, the medical research institute is planning to open its own research hospital to be fully operational in the year 2010. They hope to become one of the biggest tertiary and advanced medical centers and to meet the medical demands in the northern part of Malaysia.

In terms of Malaysian healthcare system, there are three types of funding: government, semi-government and private funding. In our case study, the medical research institute is part of a semi-government funding scheme because it is part of a higher learning (university) institution. This means that part of the ICT investment is taken care of by the Ministry of Higher Education, so in our case study, since this is a government run medical institute the medical cost is very minimal. In terms of policy, there is no comprehensive policy in regard to ICT use in hospital or healthcare organizations in Malaysia. In this case, the medical research institute adopts the policies used by the university's teaching hospital. In addition, most clinicians were working with teaching hospitals before they joined the medical research institute and were familiar with the policies.

Using a Malaysian medical institute as a case does not mean that the challenges of medical informatics as illustrated in this chapter are unique to Malaysia. We are more interested in pointing out that implementation and adoption of ICT in hospitals involves challenges and issues that need to be addressed by any organization. Malaysia is just one case in point, and though the case maybe unique to Malaysia it implies that other healthcare organizations may experience the same challenges when implementing and adopting ICT applications.

Data Collection

We began collecting preliminary data with the research objective of exploring the challenges faced by a single healthcare organization during the early stages of ICT adoption and implementation. According to Yin (2003), a case study is a research design that allows a researcher to understand a phenomenon in depth and provides richer insights about the problems being researched. Based on the case study approach, we employed structured interview to elicit as much data as possible pertaining to the phases, challenges, and problems encountered during the technological adoption period.

In order to understand the nature of ICT implementation and adoption in the institute, we had in-depth interviews with two key people in the institute: the clinical director and IT Director. We met the respondents a few times and spent many hours interviewing them to obtain their perspectives on ICT adoption and implementation. The clinical director is responsible for overseeing numerous medical specialties like oncology, psychiatry, dentistry, family health, pediatrics, internal medicine, and obstetrics & gynecology. She is also responsible for providing the space and tools for postgraduate research in the institute. The ICT director oversees all the design, development and implementation of ICT systems within the institute. These include the ICT infrastructure to support information and communication exchange within the institute. In the clinical setting, the IT department is responsible for developing a healthcare information system (HIS) within the institute. The HIS includes patient medical records (e-clinical) linked with the radiology information system (RIS) and laboratory information system (LIS) as well as nurses' station, billing, social work department and inventory. The system was completed and launched on March 2006, the same time as the outpatient clinics began to operate.

Interview Protocol and Validity of Case Study

The process of creating the interview protocol started in a formal researcher's meeting where, we, the researchers brainstormed the main issues pertaining to ICT adoption specifically in Malaysia context. The focus was on the overall picture of ICT adoption that affected different stakeholders in the organization. The researchers then decided that the protocol should be divided into two categories. The first category contained questions related to historical background of the organization. We adopted 5W's type of questioning (what, where, when, how, and why) so that we could explore the organization.

For the second category, we used questions that could address the success and challenges of the organization when adopting ICT. For an example, one of the questions asked the participant to give example of a "success story" during ICT development process. There is also one broad question that deals with "barriers and challenges" faced by the IT department during deployment. The "barriers" question is further expanded by setting probing questions that look into human, technology and organizational issues such as asking *"How, if at all, does the communication between doctors and patients change when ICT is introduced?"*

After the first draft of the protocol was completed, we sent the protocol to several researchers who are expert in the qualitative field. To ensure validity, the panel researchers examine the protocol in terms of clarity, organization, relevancy, accuracy and language-use. Once the protocol was approved, the researcher's team went through a mock interview exercise in order to see the flow of the questions as well to know when to ask the probing questions. We also added some "scenarios" to help the main interviewer understood the meaning of each question in case the interviewer got stuck during the interview. All this exercise had helped the main interviewer to prepare for the interview.

Data Analysis: Content Analysis on the Interviews

Content analysis is an unobstrusive research technique used to explore a phenomenon that yielded rich descriptions (Krippendorf, 2004). Based on the interviews we conducted, we will discuss in detail several challenges surrounding the culture, adoption, design and implementation of Hospital Information Systems in a local context. The transcribed interviews were content analyzed. In the first set of data, since this is a preliminary study attempting to explore and understand the challenges of ICT adoption in a hospital context, we used 5Ws (what, why, when, where and who) analysis to elicit a picture of the overall IT system as well the process of development and deployment of such a system. The 5Ws analysis is a common elicitation tool which enables researchers to get in depth information from research subjects. Then, in the second set, the discussions of the findings center on the three potential barriers: organizational issues, human/people issues and technological issues. The findings are described in the following section.

DISCUSSIONS ON ICT ADOPTION IN HEALTHCARE: A CASE OF A MEDICAL INSTITUTION IN MALAYSIA

Exploring ICT Adoption Using the 5Ws Framework

What is E-Clinical System?

It is crucial to first define the concepts of ICT and electronic healthcare. We suggest using the following definition: *ICTs* are defined as tools that facilitate communication and the processing and transmission of information and the sharing of knowledge by electronic means; this includes the full range of electronic digital and analog ICTs, from radio and television to telephones (fixed and mobile), computers, electronic-based media such as digital text and audio-video recording, and the Internet (Frenzel & Frenzel, 2004). *Electronic healthcare*, or *e-health*, is an emerging field of health informatics that refers to the organization and delivery of health services and information using the Internet and related technologies. In a broader sense, the term characterizes not only a technical development, but also a new way of working, an attitude, and a commitment to networked, global thinking, in order to improve health care locally, regionally, and worldwide by using information and communication technology (World Bank, 2006). For purposes of our case study, we will also talk about the *e-clinical* system which is a healthcare information system (HIS) comprised of seven modules that serve eight clinical subspecialties in the institute. The motivation for creating such a system is to operate a paperless transaction in the medical setting. The development of this software was fully supported by the university's IT department, who provided software and hardware infrastructure as well as manpower for software development.

At this point, e-clinical has five full functioning modules which are registration, patient screening, clinical, laboratories / radiology, and billing / inventory. When patients first enroll in the system, they are entered into the out-patient registration by registration personnel. Next, patients' vital signs are recorded in the patient screening module by nursing staff. During patient-physician interviews, the clinical module is used and the information is dispersed into imaging, laboratory and pharmacy modules for different uses. In each module, all charges are connected with the billing module. The social department reviews cases where patients cannot afford medical care and provides necessary support for those patients. If patients are eligible to receive help, the billing information is sent directly to the social department module. The last module, inventory, is connected to the billing module in order to ensure medications and all other orders are in stock.

Why Develop In-House Electronic Medical Record (EMR)

One of the goals of this medical institution is to operate a paperless hospital. In doing so, the organization planned and developed an in-house EMR by customizing their own system using their local clinical requirements. The initial requirements were generated by the top management of the medical institute followed by a series of user feedbacks after the system was launched. Another motivation for developing the in-house system was to reduce costs. Development was also encouraged by their ability to get technical expertise from the university Information Technology division.

When the Roll-Out Takes Place

The system rollout took place in March 2006. The director of the research institute wanted the system to be available as soon as the outpatient clinic was open. The decision to roll out the system in parallel with the service was quite brave, and was, made even though there were issues in system design at that point. The IT personnel met regularly afterwards and listened attentively to user requests. Changes and modifications to the system were made directly and the IT people took time to sit down and help the users. The local champion participated in the IT daily meeting to report user requests and complaints. In this case, local champions are the first group of people who adopts ICT in this hospital.

Where the ICTs are Introduced in the Institution

E-clinical operates in the outpatient clinic, laboratory, pharmacy and imaging centers.

Who are the Users

The users of the system include clinicians, nurses, and registration, billing, inventory and social department personnel. However, each user has limited access control as assigned by the IT department. For an example, the registration personnel can only enter and view patient registration and cannot access other modules. Most clinicians have direct access to all patient information in order for them to track any patients with multiple diseases and get appropriate care from various medical specialties.

Figure 2. General architecture of e-clinical system

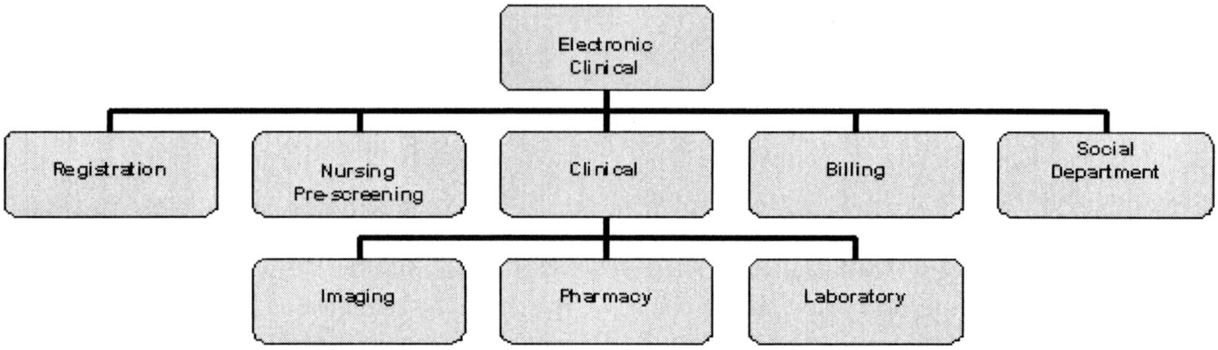

ICT Adoption: Issues on Organizations, Human, and Technology

In the context of the medical institute that we researched, we found that people, especially within the top management, were very receptive to and supportive of the organizational change. In other words, organizational change was part of the culture in which people are not only willing to accept changes but also accepted the role of the ICT and recognized the benefits that they would reap from using it. ICT is expected to facilitate the operations and change the way people in the institute work and the way they provide their medical treatments and services. All members of the board of directors, which is comprised mainly of clinicians, are very open towards ICT implementation in their organization. This is evidence that clinicians are actively accepting ICT in their work flow instead of resisting it, as found in many previous research studies. The institute's director himself made sure the e-clinical system was in place in parallel with the outpatient clinic opening because he wanted to make sure that the transitions went hand in hand. In addition to the sophisticated e-clinical system, the clinical director said that the institution has been using e-mail for their interactions with nurses and students.

Based on our case study, the IT director said one important lesson for future in-patient system development is to include all levels of users at the beginning of system development. For example, the IT department should get insights from registration personnel, nurses and clinicians from different specialties, billing officers, social workers, and any other potential users. The users would be able to give ideas on how to make their workflow as smooth possible, and may be able to see if some design would hinder their work process. In addition, they should review the requirements together with decision makers such as the institute's board of directors. All these inputs are important to ensure that ICT facilitates their daily routine and interaction with patients.

The IT director acknowledged the importance of local champion who becomes a liaison to the development team. During the initial roll-out phase, there were daily meetings among the developers and the clinical side on usage issues from the clinical side; the nurse champion was instrumental in gathering feedback from the clinical side and was able to suggest necessary remedies to the problems that occurred. The IT director mentioned that the local champion understood the day to day challenges in using the system because she was herself an avid user and knew the clinical environment well enough to be able to diagnose the problems faced by other users. The IT director also added that the local champion will be included in the early stage of inpatient system development. The advantages of an in-house development team were that it included knowledgeable end users as well as strong technical support from the university's IT department and an in-house developer that understood the system. The programmers were able to interact with the users and make changes instantly because they understand their own system in depth.

The institute only provided a few sessions of user training at the beginning of system deployment. There was no formal training afterwards. The IT director mentioned that most users refer to their own colleagues if they find problems when using the system. However, we feel that this organization should take extra measures to provide user training. The in-house training should be done in a consistent manner whereby training on the overall system and the potential uses of system would be cleared up among the users in the early stage. In a later phase, training should be provided as a continuous learning and improvement tool for the organization.

There were strong collaborative efforts between the IT department and the clinician side. After the system deployment, the IT people met the clinical end users every day to discuss any issues that arose. After a few weeks of daily meeting, the IT top management asked the programmers to work hand in hand with the users. At this point, all the programmers understood the nature of clinical use of the system. It is important to note that the process of cyclical communication is most important at the early stage of ICT adoption. What is even more effective is that the IT top management takes a leading and proactive role to ensure that the technological as well as organizational change transpires smoothly and effectively.

Based on the case study, one of the main questions during the interview was to understand the technology issues surrounding the development. As mentioned earlier, the medical research institute is part of a research university. The university itself has an established IT department that oversees all IT implementation in the university. The e-clinical system template was taken directly from the university's health center, which had been using an electronic medical record system that was designed by the university IT department. When the medical research institute began their own ICT initiative, they immediately adopted the university's electronic medical record system. However, the IT director said they had to do some minimal modifications because the medical research institute handles more medical specialties compared to the university's health center. For the modification process, MRI had to "borrow" the university's IT department programmers. The migration and modification process took several months during which programmers and MRI IT personnel traveled back forth (the university and MRI are 40 minutes away). This back and forth process was not an easy task, and eventually the top management decided to hire their own programmers to handle e-clinical. Finally, they obtained two full-time programmers to operate e-clinical. In addition, MRI also hired an IT manager to lead the development team. Even though MRI now has its own development team, they still rely on the university's IT department for technical advice. Besides the issue of adapting to the university's electronic medical record format, we also found that MRI did not have to spend any money on the software because all licenses are bought by the university. In this case, MRI was able to cut costs in the development system which is an added advantage to the organization.

In terms of infrastructure, there were some issues of physical layout during the initial phase. For example, there was some discussion about where to place the servers; later on they were able to create a separate space just to store the servers. The IT director added that there was no proper planning of where to install the hardware until later on, when they discovered how disorganized it was to have the servers in various places. In other words, when the decision to adopt ICT was made, people were excited at the idea and accepted the decision without taking into consideration many details like space. In future ICT efforts, they have decided to plan hardware space first. She also mentioned that careful planning has been done in the design of the new hospital building. The institute selected one commercial system, which handles the radiological information system; this commercial system is developed in the USA, thus it incorporates standards like DICOM in the system. The IT department has to take into account these standards when incorporating it with the e-clinical system. In addition, the IT department is exploring other suitable standards for their own system.

LESSONS LEARNED FROM THE CASE STUDY

In this section, we first present several key perspectives based on the lessons learned from the above case study to highlight the critical success factors and best practices of healthcare organizations. Subsequently, we present the contributions based on the case study. The following observations were made:

Plan the ICT Investment More Effectively

Since ICT investment is costly and time consuming, for example in getting the right supplier or vendor, top management needs to plan more proactively by taking factors like time, cost, and benefit into consideration. In the case of MRI, the decisions to invest in ICT applications were not solely made by the top management, particularly the IT Director. Instead, the ICT projects were adopted directly from the University with which the medical research institute has a strong affiliation. Thus in the initial planning stage of buying or adopting ICT and the process of making decisions, questions like what types of ICT to invest, what are the cost and benefits of using one particular or several applications, who are involved in decision making, and timeline to adopt the ICT were not discussed at length. Yet, initial planning is as important as any other stage of the ICT adoption. It is crucial that these issues be addressed at the initial stage of decision making processes and as early as possible so that any problems can be identified and solved much quickly. In the case of MRI, it is fortunate that the adoption of the e-clinical system was not much of a problem.

Recruit, Select, and Retain Local IT Experts

By having the in-house experts as gate-keepers, organizations will benefit by continuous improvements and modifications to suit the needs of the organizations. Additionally, IT experts will also become the main advocates for technological changes as well as the liaisons between users and support staff, because they will learn much faster than others. IT experts are expected to be more equipped with knowledge about the information technology systems and applications. Based on the MRI case, the top management strongly felt that when the IT people, e.g. the programmers, were recruited in-house, it was much easier to manage the time allocated for ICT adoption and to educate other users on the ease of use and usability of the new system. With such recruitment, MRI no longer needs to depend on the vendors for help as their own IT people can handle any 'bugs' or problems that they encounter. As a result, the 'layperson' or non-IT people in the institute have frequently consulted the IT experts for any kinds of problems and difficulties that they encountered not only during the early stage of ICT adoption and implementation, but also on a continuous basis. In essence, IT experts become the main source of reference to help the amateur users in the organizations.

Build a Strong Organizational Culture that Supports Technological Changes

When organizations provide a conducive and supportive environment for ICT, the adoption and implementation process becomes less problematic or challenging. People are more willing to try and use the technology in place. Although in our case study we observed less involvement in decision making and planning in the initial stage of ICT adoption, the organizational culture of the MRI was highly supportive. In fact the IT top management agrees that only with a supportive culture can ICT adoption be successful. As evidence, the processes of adoption and implementation were smooth in the MRI. Personnel at all levels knew that ICT would be part of the normal ways of doing things in the organizations. They welcome such changes because they know that ICT will simplify their work and help them provide their services. Without support, resistance may surface and adoption and implementation will take a longer time.

Involve All Users and Key People in the Organizations

These people can present their needs and provide perspectives on what is desired versus what are the obstacles. By using this strategy, the organization creates an awareness of the change that will take place. When people have first hand information on the changes that will take place, as well as an avenue to voice any grievances, frustrations and anxieties about such changes, they will be more willing and ready to accept such changes. In the end, people will adopt ICT more willingly and become more accountable towards the changes. Our MRI was a unique case because the decision to adopt ICT was not inclusive at the initial planning stage. Rather than "adopt" it was more an issue of "adapt," taking the existing e-clinical system from the other institution -- almost like having a customized system to fit within MRI. But once the e-clinical system was adopted and implemented, the IT director played an active role by ensuring all levels of users participated in the success of the systems. So there are continuous 'loop' feedbacks from end users that provide extensive inputs to programmers on what needs to be done and improved.

Provide Continuous User Training to All Levels of Users

From top management to lower management that will use ICT-- Training is essential at all stages of the transition because educating people on the ICT tools makes them familiar with the new work context, and eventually they become experts in using the tool. Training needs to be given phase by phase, for different people at different times. Top management may take precedence so that they can advocate changes to the subordinates.

Contribution of Study

Without doubt, making investments in ICT can be expensive, for examples in terms of the financial cost, time, and resources. Not only is the infrastructure becomes one of the main concerns for organization, but also the cost of recruiting, training, and sustaining the people as the human resources are as crucial. By looking at the findings based on the lessons learned, there are few implications that can facilitate organizations in managing the rate of ICT adoption among employees. Hence, the contributions of this study come in twofold. First, by looking at the dynamic layers of culture, it helps an organization to fully understand the underlying values of the employees as well as evaluate and improvise the organizational culture, structure, and processes. As such, organizations will incorporate a compatible culture that is consistent with its objectives, vision and mission. Second, organizations can take preventive measurements, proactive plans and strategies to overcome three challenges as previously mentioned (see Figure 1.0). For example, organizations need to invest in training programs for the medical teams and support staffs to use and adopt ICT such administering electronic medical records. Essentially, failure to use and adopt ICT effectively will result in unsuccessful management of patients and its healthcare services.

CONCLUSION AND FUTURE DIRECTIONS

It is obvious that the case study presented in this chapter comprises preliminary data on the practices and lessons learned from an organization that adopts and implements ICT – in this case an e-clinical system. As such, the case provides insights on a Malaysian context in which the effort for ICT adoption is partly supported by the government. In the future, as an emerging healthcare organization, it is expected that the medical research institute will be developing and integrating more ICT applications to support their mission of becoming an excellent medical research center. Although we have presented the issues and challenges surrounding an ICT implementation in the Malaysian health care environment, the challenges can be applied in any other organizational context or in different country-based perspectives. Inherently, there are some important lessons to be learned from this case study as illustrated above. In a nutshell, managing ICT adoption and implementation requires that the organization build effective communication among people who are involved in the technological change processes; create awareness of both the organizational and technological changes that are going to take place; develop continuous and rigorous training to increase familiarity, competency, and knowledge about the ICT to be used; recruit, select, and retain local IT experts to move the ICT adoption processes to success; and promoting supportive organizational culture that supports technological changes. Given these five lessons learned obtained from the case study, we suggest some fruitful questions for future research:

- How, if at all, does ICT change how healthcare delivers its services?
- How has patient care changed, and what are the trends?
- How, if at all, does the work of doctors and nurses change when ICT is introduced in a health care institution?
- How, if at all, does the communication between doctors and patients change when ICT is introduced?
- Does ICT deskill or facilitate doctors and nurses?
- What are the critical success factors for ICT adoption in healthcare organizations?
- How do organizations manage technological changes to ensure effective ICT adoption?

REFERENCES

Aggouram, H., & Ingham, J. (2003). In K. Kangas, (Ed.) National culture and the meaning of information systems success: a framework for research and its implications for IS standardization in multinational organizations, *Business Strategies for Information Technology Management*. Hershey, PA: IGI Global.

Benjamin, R. I., & Levinson, E. (1993). A framework for managing IT-enabled change. *Sloan Management Review*, ▪▪▪, 23–33.

Bodenheimer, T. (1999). The American health care system: The movement for improved quality in health care. *The New England Journal of Medicine*, *340*, 488–492. doi:10.1056/NEJM199902113400621

Dyer, W. G., & Wilkins, A. L. (1991). Better Stories, Not Better Constructs, To Generate Better Theory: A Rejoinder To Eisenhardt. *Academy of Management Review, 16*(3), 613–619. doi:10.2307/258920

Fan, Y. (2000). A classification of Chinese culture. *Cross Cultural Management–An International Journal, 7*(2), 3–10. doi:10.1108/13527600010797057

Feagin, J., Orum, A., & Sjoberg, G. (Eds.). (1991). *A case for case study*. Chapel Hill, NC: University of North Carolina Press.

Fiscella, K., & Geiger, H. J. (2006). Health information technology and quality improvement for community health centers. *Health Affairs, 25*(2), 405–412. doi:10.1377/hlthaff.25.2.405

Frenzel, C. W., & Frenzel, J. C. (2004). *Management of Information Technology*, (4th ed.). Boston: Thomson.

Hofstede, G. (1980). Culture's Consequences: International Differences in Work-Related Values. Beverly Hills, CA: Sage.

Holt, D. H., & Wigginton, K. W. (2002). *International Management* (2nd Ed.). Mason, OH: Thomson Southwestern.

Johnson, K. B. (2001). Barriers That Impede the Adoption of Pediatric Information Technology. *Archives of Pediatrics & Adolescent Medicine, 155*, 1374–1379.

Karahanna, E., Straub, D. W., & Chervany, N. L. (1999). Information technology adoption across time: A cross-sectional comparison of pre-adoption and post-adoption beliefs . *MIS Quarterly, 23*(2), 183–213. doi:10.2307/249751

Lorenzi, N. M., & Riley, R. T. (2003). Organizational issues = change. *International Journal of Medical Informatics, 69*(2/3), 197–203. doi:10.1016/S1386-5056(02)00105-3

Mass, M., & Eriksson, O. (2006). Challenges in the adoption of medical information systems. *Proceedings of the 39th Annual Hawaii International Conference on System Sciences* (HICSS '06), *5*, 95.

Miller, R. H., & West, C. E. (2007). The value of electronic health records in community health centers: Policy implications. *Health Affairs, 26*(1), 206–214. doi:10.1377/hlthaff.26.1.206

Nambisan, S., & Wang, Y. M. (1999). Roadblocks to web technology adoption? *Communications of the ACM, 42*(1), 98–101. doi:10.1145/291469.291482

Nøhr, C., Andersen, S. K., Vingtoft, S., Bernstein, K., & Bruun-Rasmussen, M. (2005). Development, implementation and diffusion of EHR systems in Denmark. *International Journal of Medical Informatics, 74*(2–4), 229–234. doi:10.1016/j.ijmedinf.2004.04.025

Pare', G. & Trudel, M. (2007). Knowledge barriers to PACS adoption and implementation in hospitals. *International Journal of Medical Informatics*, ▪▪▪, 22–33.

Ragam, M. R. (2007). Information technology in healthcare creating a stronger healthcare system. *Asian Hospital & Healthcare Management, 12*, 60–63.

Robbins, S. P., & De Cenzo, D. A. (1996). *Fundamentals of Management* (6th ed.). New York: Prentice Hall.

Schein, E. H. (1992). *Organizational Culture and Leadership*, (3rd ed.). San Francisco, CA: Jossey-Bass

Tanriverdi, H., & Iacono, C. N. (1999). Knowledge barriers to diffusion of telemedicine. In *Proceedings of the 20th International Conference on Information Systems*, Charlotte, NC, (pp. 39–50).

WHO. (2004). *eHealth for Health-care Delivery: Strategy 2004-2007*. Geneva, Switzerland: WHO. Retrieved from www.who.int/eht/en/EHT_strategy_2004-2007.pdf.

World Bank. (2006). *Connecting People, Improving Health: the Role of ICTs in the Health Sector of Developing Countries*, (pp.5-6).

Yin, R. K. (2003). *Case Study Research Design and Methods: Applied Social Research Methods*. Thousand Oaks, CA: Sage.

Zakaria, N., & Mohd Yusof, S. (2001). The role of human and organizational culture in the context of technological change. In *Proceedings of IEMC--Change Management and the New Industrial Revolution.*

Zonabend, F. (1992). The monograph in European ethnology. *Current Sociology*, *40*(1), 49–60. doi:10.1177/001139292040001005

KEY TERMS AND DEFINITIONS

Culture: includes knowledge, belief, art, morals, law, custom, and many other capabilities and habits acquired by a man as a member of a society.

Case study: is defined as a research strategy, an empirical inquiry that investigates a phenomenon within its real-life context. Case study research means single and multiple case studies, can include quantitative evidence, relies on multiple sources of evidence and benefits from the prior development of theoretical propositions.

Electronic medical records (EMRs): are computerized or electronic based health records of a person used by physicians, clinic or hospitals. It is a comprehensive record that combines information across multiple providers.

Information Communication Technology: defined as tools that facilitate communication and the processing and transmission of information and the sharing of knowledge by electronic means which includes the full range of electronic digital and analog ICTs.

Medical informatics: analysis and dissemination of medical data through the application of computers to various aspects of health care and provisions.

Organizational culture: comprises the attitudes, experiences, beliefs and values of an organization. It can also be dfeined as the specific collection of values and norms that are shared by people and groups in an organization and that control the way they interact with each other and with stakeholders outside the organization

Technological change: the change period, during which something new is planned and introduced, e.g. the period associated with the introduction of new processes that have major new technological ingredients.

Chapter 11
Emergency Medical Data Transmission Systems and Techniques

Junaid Ahmed Zubairi
SUNY at Fredonia, USA

Syed Misbahuddin
University of Hail, Kingdom of Saudi Arabia

Imran Tasadduq
FAST – National University of Computer & Emerging Sciences, Pakistan

ABSTRACT

Patients in critical condition need Physician's supervision while they are in transit to the hospital. If the ambulance is linked to the emergency room, the physician can monitor patient's vital signs and issue instructions to the paramedics for stabilizing the patient. When a disaster strikes, scores of people are transferred to the hospital in ambulances. During an emergency situation, the number of patients in critical condition reaches overwhelming proportions. In this chapter, we discuss the state of the art in transferring emergency medical data from the disaster site or ambulance to the hospital and outline some case studies. We present a scheme called MEDTOC (Medical Data Transmission Over Cellular Network) for transferring in-ambulance multiple patients' data to the hospital by UMTS. This system enables the transfer of vital signs to the hospital in reduced and packed format using limited bandwidth wireless network. Medical data can be transmitted over 3G cellular network using various modes and quality of service parameters available in UMTS. This could help the physicians in monitoring several patients who are either in transit or at a triage unit on a disaster site. Results of the application of data reduction algorithm over CAN packets and feasibility studies in transfer of data over UMTS are presented and discussed.

DOI: 10.4018/978-1-60566-030-1.ch011

INTRODUCTION

Use of information technology (IT) in almost all the sectors of every day life including medicine has prompted the advent of telemedicine that is providing high-tech solution to the universal problem of access to health care. Now geographical isolation is no longer a barrier to timely and quality provision of medical care. Telemedicine can be defined as diagnosis, consultation, treatment, education and the transfer of medical data (i.e. high resolution images, sounds, live video and patient records) using interactive audiovisual and data communications (Jerant et. al. 1998). Hence, physicians located with the patient can consult their colleagues remotely in order to solve a difficult case, supplemented with continuing education course over the Internet, or access medical information from digital libraries or provide immediate assistance during disasters.

Disasters can strike any time at any place. Earthquake, fire, building collapse, massive food poisoning and other such disasters need on-time medical response. First responders include ambulances besides fire brigades and elite emergency response teams. Disaster management relies greatly on effective emergency medical care arrangements. During an emergency, scores of people in critical condition are transported to the hospital where expert medical care is provided by the physicians. Sometimes several patients can be moved in large ambulances. Ambulance crew consists of paramedics and driver. Their job is to bring the patient to the hospital alive and stable so that the physician can attend to the patient. If the vital signs (blood pressure, pulse, blood oxygenation and respiration) and additional diagnostic medical data (e.g. EKG) of patients can be transferred to the physician in real-time, then chances of saving patient's life improve considerably. This is due to the fact that the first 60 minutes are the most critical for patients suffering from heart attack or other life threatening situations. If the ambulances are linked to the hospital via wireless network, vital signs and one dimensional (1-d) medical data can be transferred to the hospital in real time.

Many schemes have been proposed to transfer emergency medical data to the hospital using wireless networks. The wireless transmission of 12-lead EKG was demonstrated by Grim in 1987. Majority of work done uses GSM/GPRS to transmit medical information while some people have used 3G systems (Campbell 2005), (Giovas et. al. 2006), (Nakamura et. al. 2003), (Reponen et. al. 2000), (Sillesen et. al. 2006), (E-Health Insider 2006). The focus of most of the researchers has been on the transmission of the medical data of a single patient being transported to the hospital. Some schemes have proposed the tracking of several patients using a laptop computer while the patients are in an on-site triage unit.

The chapter is divided into four sections. Section 1 presents various schemes in literature for transmission of emergency medical data. We have investigated the feasibility of transmitting aggregated vital signs of several patients to the hospital via cellular network. The data is reduced before transmission using a novel data reduction algorithm. The details of the proposed MEDTOC (Medical Data Transmission Over Cellular Network) system are given in section 2 and data reduction algorithm and its application to the aggregated data are described in section 3. In section 4, the results of OPNET simulation of aggregated data transmission using 3G UMTS cellular network are highlighted.

EMERGENCY MEDICAL DATA TRANSMISSION TECHNIQUES

This section gives an overview of the various emergency medical data transmission techniques that have either been proposed or reported in literature As reported in (Kyriacou et. al. 2007), a literature search shows that the work done in wireless transmission techniques of emergency medical data can broadly be divided into GSM/GPRS, 3G, satellite and wireless LAN. Further, majority of the work focuses on the GSM/GPRS network while a lot of others use wireless LAN to transmit data. Very limited work is available in categories of 3G and satellites. Personal Digital Assistants (PDAs) have also been proposed for handling emergency medical data at the prehospital stage and a few systems have also been developed, for example, see (Fontelo et. al. 2003) and (Bolaños et. al. 2004).

Since ad-hoc and sensor networks do not require an infrastructure they can be a useful alternative for medical data transmission especially during disasters (Lorincz et. al. 2004). Such types of networks are particularly useful when either there is no infrastructure such as in remote rural areas or there is no time available to set up a network such as during natural calamities that have destroyed the wired infrastructure.

We now summarize some of the significant work done in various wireless transmission categories for emergency medical data transmission. Later, we will present two case studies in a little more detail that were reported recently and use 3G technology for medical data transmission.

GSM/GPRS FOR EMERGENCY MEDICAL DATA TRANSMISSION

Systems that use GSM/GPRS technology for medical data transmission have recently been proposed/reported in (Hall et. al. 2003), (Kyriacou et.al. 2003), (Pavlopoulos et. al. 1998), (Salvador et. al. 2005) and (Voskarides et. al. 2003). In (Pavlopoulos et. al. 1998), the researchers have developed a portable medical device that allows telediagnosis, long distance support, and teleconsultation of mobile healthcare providers by expert physicians. The device allows the transmission of vital biosignals and still images of the patient from the emergency site to the consultation site using GSM. The device allows a doctor to remotely evaluate patient data and issue directions to the emergency personnel until the patient is brought to the hospital. The system comprises of two different modules; the mobile unit, which is located in an ambulance vehicle near the patient, and the consultation unit, which is located at the hospital site and can be used by the experts in order to give directions. Authors have also developed software that follows the client server model; the mobile site is the client, and the consultation site is the server.

An experimental evaluation of the performance of GSM and GPRS in the transmission/reception of X-ray images and video in emergency orthopedics cases has been carried out in (Voskarides et. al. 2003). It has been observed that FTP transfer rate over GPRS through hand held computers and laptops is in the range of 32 kbps. The download time for typical **X**-ray images of a file size of 200 kilo bytes to the mobile device is in the range of 60 seconds. The researchers report similar performance in the case of simulating an ambulance for the biggest part of the journey.

In (Kyriacou et. al. 2003), a combined real-time and store and forward facility has been developed that consists of a base unit which is fixed and a mobile telemedicine unit. The mobile telemedicine unit is located at the emergency site and the base unit at the physician's office or hospital. Vital biosignals (3–12 lead EKG, SPO2, NIBP, IBP, and Temp) and still images of the patient can be transmitted from the mobile unit. The transmission is performed through GSM, or satellite links, or through Plain Old Telephony Systems (POTS) whichever is available. The mobile unit consists of four modules: the biosignal acquisition module, a digital camera responsible for image capturing, a processing unit which is a PC, and a communication module (GSM, satellite or POTS modem). The base unit is equipped with a modem-enabled PC responsible for data interchange and for displaying incoming signals from the telemedicine unit.

The work reported in (Salvador et. al. 2005) describes a platform built around three information entities namely, patient, health-care agent, and central station. It was designed to enable patients with chronic heart disease in stable condition to complete specifically defined protocols for out-of-hospital follow-up and monitoring. The equipment mainly performed three tasks: i) recording of the desired cardiovascular parameters, ii) incorporation of a configurable questionnaire, and iii) transmission of all the information via GSM. The patients were provided with portable recording equipment and a cellular phone that supported data transmission and wireless application protocol (WAP). However, the system has not been designed to support emergency situations.

In (Hall et. al. 2003), the authors describe a system that they name *Poket Doktor*. This system allows a user to store electronic medical record (EMR) data on a personal electronic device and wirelessly (i.e., through GSM, Wi-Fi or Bluetooth) communicate this data to medical professionals when treatment is required. In a disaster or other emergency situation, medical workers can access a patient's Poket Doktor device without physical access to the device itself. The Poket Doktor system consists of the following: a) the architecture for a wireless, power-efficient smart card to store and communicate medical information, b) through Bluetooth wireless technology with RFID wakeup on the smart card to enable a fast wireless connection to a healthcare provider's device; and c) a platform and application software for a handheld computing device used by healthcare providers.

SATELLITE LINKS FOR EMERGENCY MEDICAL DATA TRANSMISSION

Mobile Tele-Echography Using an Ultralight Robot (OTELO) is a project that provides a fully integrated end-to-end communication between patient and expert stations. It consists of a robot, an interface for displaying images and other information, and a communication link that could be satellite or terrestrial that allows information exchange between two sites (Canero et. al. 2005). The authors in (Canero et. al. 2005) have developed a user interface of the OTELO system in order to provide an end-to-end communication between the patient and the sonographer to facilitate transmission of ultrasound images. Evaluation of these images would enable the physician/sonographer to ascertain the degree of emergency. The system developed consists of a) an ultrasound video transmission system providing real-time images of the scanned area, b) an audio/video conference to communicate with the paramedical assistant and with the patient, and c) a virtual-reality environment, providing visual and haptic feedback to the expert, while capturing the expert's hand movements. The system also provides the facility of processing the received images so as to enhance all or part of the image to get more information.

The system proposed in (Kyriacou et. al. 2003) and described in Section 1.1 also has the provision of transmitting the data via satellite links.

EMERGENCY MEDICAL DATA TRANSMISSION VIA SENSOR NETWORKS

Wireless sensor network (WSN) is an emerging class of systems made possible by low-cost hardware, advanced programming tools, complex algorithms, long lasting power sources and energy efficient radio interfaces. Wireless sensor network is a new paradigm in designing fault tolerant mission critical systems, to enable varied applications such as threat detection, environmental monitoring, traditional sensing and actuation and much more (Wiki 2008).

A software infrastructure that uses sensor networks has been developed in (Lorincz et. al. 2004) and named "CodeBlue". The designed infrastructure integrates sensor nodes and other wireless devices into a disaster response setting and provides facilities for ad hoc network formation, resource naming and discovery, security, and in-network aggregation of sensor-produced data. They have also developed a robust radio frequency (RF)–based localization system – MoteTrack – that lets rescuers determine their location within a building and track patients. Although, the work presented is only preliminary, it opens a number of exciting opportunities and challenges in the use of sensor networks for emergency data transmission. For example, as has been mentioned in (Lorincz et. al. 2004), wireless vital sign monitoring of multiple victims at a disaster scene is of utmost importance. Those reaching first at the disaster scene could place wireless, low-power vital sign sensors on each patient. Nearby physicians and technicians could receive continuous data relayed by these sensors and could get additional information via mobile computers or PC-based systems. Hence, it would be possible for the field personnel to monitor several patients at a time in the light of the instructions they receive from paramedics (Frykberg and Tepas III 1988), (Flint and Milligan 1999).

OTHER EMERGENCY MEDICAL DATA SYSTEMS

A Personal Digital Assistant-based (PDA-based) electrocardiogram (EKG)/blood pressure (BP) telemonitor has been developed in (Bolaños et. al. 2004). A number of instrumentation modules have been developed and integrated to realize a compact system that could be deployed to assist in telemedicine applications and heart rate variability studies. The device can acquire EKG/BP waveforms, transmit them wirelessly to a PDA, save them onto a compact flash memory, and display them on the LCD screen of the PDA.

An interesting wrist ambulatory monitoring and recording system with a smart glove with sensors has been developed in (Axisa et. al. 2004) for the detection of the activity of the autonomic nervous system. It is composed of a smart T-shirt, a smart glove, a wrist device and PC. Smart clothes enable the development of ambulatory measurement and user-friendly monitoring devices. Technologies for integration of smart clothes with human body are now available and sensor's integration in the textile frame is now possible. The software developed with the proposed system records real time data that can either be displayed in the form of graphs or be recorded for later analysis or transmitted to a remote location.

In order to give an opportunity to the developing countries that cannot afford telemedicine due to the expensive equipment and high connectivity costs involved, a low-cost portable telemedicine kit has been developed in (Adler 2000) that allows a health practitioner in a remote area to capture patient data in the form of audio, video, and images in an asynchronous fashion and forward them over the Internet to a doctor for a diagnosis. The kit consists of a digital stethoscope, an EKG recorder and a medical imaging system. A prototype has been developed and several images and medical data have been captured and shown as examples. In the later part of this work, quality trade-offs with cost have also been discussed. The author also argues the quality of the audio/video captured with such devices that would be acceptable to the physician before he/she could give an expert advice and/or arrive at a conclusion.

A pre-hospital patient care system is presented in (Gao 2006) with the design goals of being scalable, reliable and user-friendly. This system enables medics to efficiently track location, monitor the vital signs and notify the change in the status of patients. They called this technology "Vital Mote". The system consists of multiple components namely electronic triage tags with sensors, a wireless ad-hoc mesh network, pre-hospital patient care software, a secure web portal and a handheld PDA.

All the sensors and probes are integrated in the "mote" which was originally developed at university of California with functionalities of vital signs monitoring (pulse oximeter, blood pressure, and a three-lead EKG) location tracking, medical record storage and triage status tracking. VitalMote builds upon the CodeBlue project of Harvard University which is a wireless network for sensing and transmitting vital signs and geo-location data. The connectivity to the system was provided by using Verizon's EVDO coverage in Washington DC.

A wearable computer "mote" attached to the wrist of patient continuously transmits information via ad-hoc mesh network to pre-hospital patient care software package (MCCHALES by OPTIMUS Corporation) running at portable tablet PC where the responder may respond accordingly using the tablet PC. The tablet PC is harnessed to the first responder in a waterproof and anti-glare casing. The information is also transmitted to a central database system in real time. A web portal was also built so that other responder from the responding team and responders from other departments could respond over internet. To detect the anomalies, vital signs monitoring algorithm was also developed. When an anomaly is detected in the patient vital signs, the medic's software application generates an alert in the user interface.

The benefits of the system are low setup time, reliable connectivity, optimized time utilization of responders and more than 90% survival rate in worst case. The distinction of this system to previously developed similar systems is that it uses electronic triage tags in place of paper based tags thus saving sufficient processing time of recording data manually and converting that into electronic format.

EMERGENCY MEDICAL DATA TRANSMISSION VIA 3G TECHNOLOGIES (CASE STUDIES)

3G is emerging as a promising technique for emergency medical data transmission. In this section, we present two case studies on the usage of 3G technology for medical applications. Five case studies based upon technologies other than 3G have been presented in (Pattichis et. al. 2002) while two have been presented in (Kyriacou et. al. 2007).

Mobile Teletrauma System (Chu and Ganz 2004)

A cost effective teletrauma system that uses 3G networks has been introduced in (Chu and Ganz 2004). This system comprises two units namely the trauma-patient unit and the hospital unit have been developed using LabView professional platform. The system allows multiple threads to handle multiple data streams concurrently. Both the units are synchronized to cater the critical responses. The communication in the system is based on client server model.

The trauma-patient unit runs on a highly powerful laptop or a tablet PC (may reside in the ambulance) that is directly connected to medical devices such as vital sign monitoring, portable ultrasound and video camera for data acquisition and a wireless transceiver to send and receive data over a 3G wireless link while the hospital unit resides in the hospital on another PC (may be at physician's desk) connected to the Internet. The hospital unit has access to the trauma-patient unit by virtue of the interconnectivity of the wireless network and the Internet.

The trauma-patient unit processes the data acquired through the connected devices in the form of bio-signals, images and video streams. It extracts the parameters of bio-signals and analyses them, compresses the JPEG images and processes them, and compresses and selects parameters from video stream. To reduce the information that is to be transmitted, it processes the data such that it could fit the narrow bandwidth. This process of reduction has been named transcoding and includes three submodules as shown in Figure 1.

The hospital unit receives, decompresses and de-multiplexes information transmitted by the

Figure 1. Trauma-patient unit software architecture (© 2004, Chu and Ganz. Used with permission)

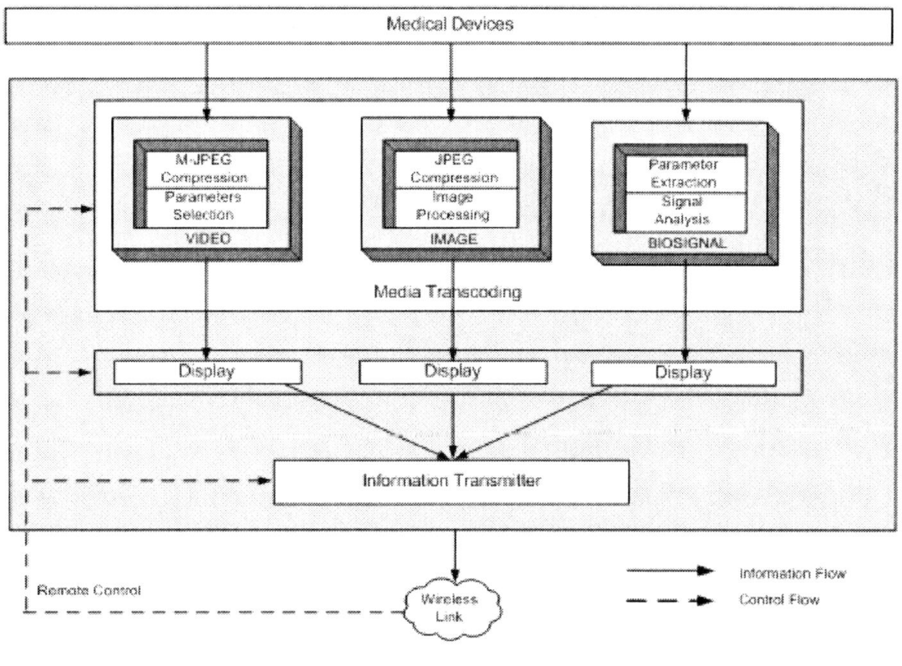

trauma-patient unit. It then stores and displays the received information. It also provides functions for analyzing medical images and EKG signals such as "R-interval extraction", region of interest (ROI), and the edge detection by using the control parameters available at this unit. If needed, more focused information of image is transmitted by the trauma-patient unit for the critical area determined by the physician at the other unit.

In order to avoid congestion in the network, the authors suggest prioritizing the data streams according to the requirement of a particular stream. For example, EKG signal could be at the highest priority and video at a lesser priority. Further, authors suggest using TCP socket to transmit more critical information (such as the EKG signal) while UDP socket to transmit the information that can afford losses (such as video). Frame losses can be minimized by adjusting the frame-rate based on an algorithm proposed in the paper.

Figure 2 shows the experimental test bed used for the proposed system.

MobileRobotic Tele-Ultrasonography Systems (Garawi et. al. 2006)

In this work, performance analysis of a fully integrated end-to-end mobile tele-sonography system has been carried out for remote services mobile tele-echography using an ultra-light robot (OTELO). OTELO was a European Information Society funded project. It comprises a fully portable tele-operated robot that allows a specialist sonographer to perform real time robotized tele-echology. Three main parts of this system are the expert station, the communication links and the patent station.

At the expert station, a medical expert handles a pseudo haptic fictive probe to control the positioning of the remote robot. The communication links vary. This may be satellite, 3G or terrestrial link depending upon which geographical area the system is located in.

The patient station is composed of six degrees of freedom (DoF) lightweight robotic system and has its own control unit. This robot physically

Figure 2. Experimental test bed (© 2004, Chu and Ganz. Used with permission)

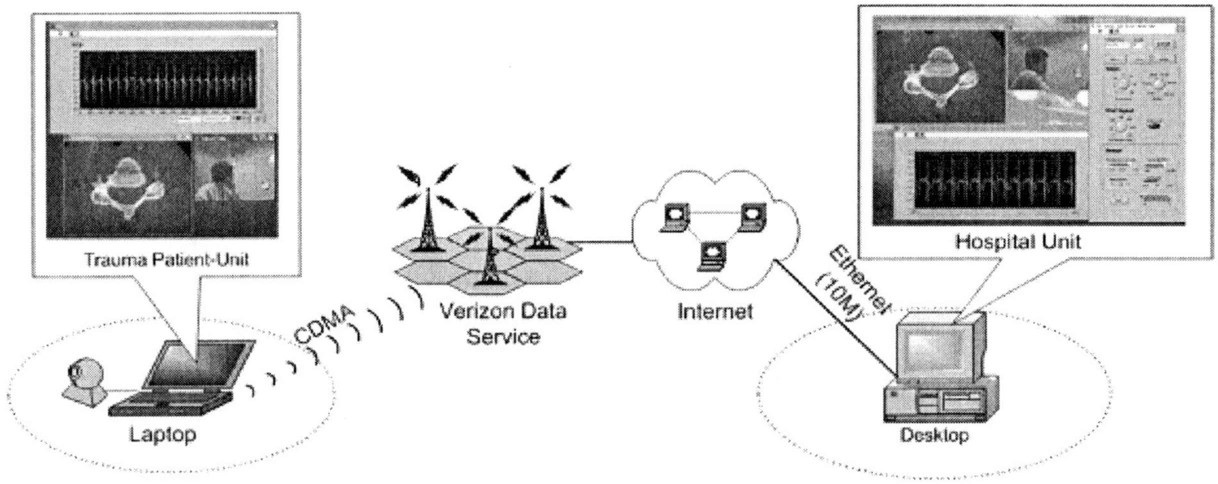

manipulates the ultrasound probe in response to the expert's directives. The expert can move the fictive probe and controls the distant probe holder through forced feedback mechanism.

Since in ultrasound scan, voice is rarely needed by the patient or the doctor, the system sends both ambient video plus voice (videoconference) following the reception of ultrasound data by the expert station. However, if sufficient 3G bandwidth is available, simultaneous ultrasound stream and videoconferencing data transmission can be accommodated.

There are three types of data streams communication in OTELO system; one is the robotic control data, second is ultrasound still images and the third is the medical ultrasound streaming data. The patient station transmits ultrasound images, ultrasound streams, ambient voice and video, and robot control data while it receives robot control data, and ambient voice and video from expert station. Robot control data stream is identified as the most critical type of data.

An experimental setup was used to measure the end-to-end performance using 3G links. The patient station is connected to a 3G terminal via wireless card connected to a laptop PC. This uses the client server model for inter- communication between expert and patient stations. UDP has been employed as the transport protocol for video streaming on the fading channel while RTP has been employed to support real time full duplex data transmission. Performance has been evaluated in terms of average throughput, end-to-end packet delay and delay jitter under different load conditions. The ultrasound data was acquired at the rate of 13 frames/sec in Quarter Common Intermediate Format (QCIF).

The robotic data bursts flow from the expert system at 16 bytes payload on 70 ms time interval. For video compression at low bit rate, H263 codec has been used. Reliable functioning of the robotic system has been achieved using an uplink of 64 kbps with a minimal packet loss of less than 0.5%.

G Embedded Communication System (Issa et. al. 2008)

One of the most recent work reported in (Issa 2008) is the transmission of multimedia medical data through a novel system architecture that chooses the best wireless connection from amongst the various available heterogeneous options. Proposed application is capable of sending signals from ECG, vital signs (such as temperature and heart rate etc.), audio data, still-images and real-time video streaming from a mobile terminal to a receiving facility. The authors claim increased reliability of their system and secure transmission of the data.

A multi-layered communication architecture is proposed that is based upon TCP. These have been defined as Network Interfaces, Connection Layer, Session Layer and Messages. The authors then describe the various operations that involve session manager and connection manager. Session establishment and resumption, switchover and recovery, and scheduling and prioritization have all been described in detail. Proposed system is validated by conducting tests on a commercial CDMA 2000 1x–EVDO network.

INTRODUCING MEDTOC

In this section, we describe our proposed MEDTOC (Medical Data Transmission Over Cellular Network) system. The ambulances are required to be equipped with cellular (3G UMTS) links and MDN (medical data network). Even if the ambulance is at a considerable distance from the hospital, it can use the cellular network for transmission of vital signs and additional data. The data can be aggregated to include vital signs of several patients being transferred to the same hospital. The maximum number of patients can be modified based on the demand of the situation.

The medical instruments collecting patients' vital signs such as EKG, heart rate, temperature and oxygenation are connected to the medical data network. These instruments inject digitized vital signs on MDN. The medical instruments generate Controller Area Network (CAN) formatted data over medical Data Network (Bosch 1991), (Kempf et. al.). Controller Area Network Protocol is a serial communications protocol originally designed for the automotive industry. However, due to its inherent robustness, the CAN protocol has also become popular for embedded control in medical environment. In MEDTOC, the ambulance is equipped with a gateway that would convert the CAN messages to IP packet to be transmitted over the cellular network. Figure 3 and Figure 4 illustrate the MDN, gateway and links for the ambulance to the hospital via cellular network.

AGGREGATED DATA FORM AND DATA REDUCTION

The aggregation of medical data for several patients is desired when an ambulance is carrying

Figure 3. MEDTOC Architecture: Ambulance

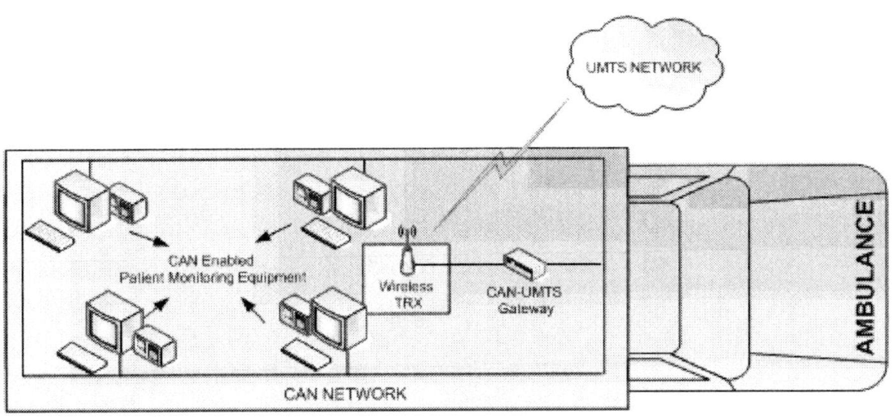

Figure 4. MEDTOC Architecture: Hospital

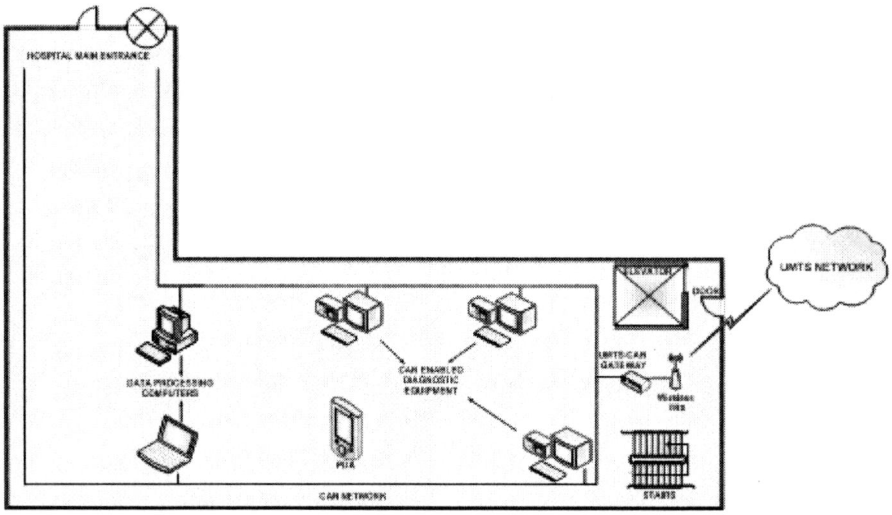

several patients. This aggregation is achieved by using special packet format that puts the data in order. We describe the packet header and payload formats in this section.

Data Aggregation and Packet Formats

CAN header can be manipulated to aggregate medical data for patients. There are two versions of CAN protocols in use. They are called CAN 2.0A and 2.0B. Main difference between these versions is the length of message identifier. Versions 2.0A and 2.0B have 11 and 29 bits message identifiers respectively as shown in Figure 5 (Bosch 1991).

We have selected CAN version 2.0A as we do not need the extra header bytes in MEDTOC system. The base identifier in Figure 5 in a CAN message determines the priority of the message. To achieve dynamic priority for all CAN bus nodes, 11-bits base identifier (BID) can be segmented in the following format: $x_1x_2x_3y_1y_2y_3y_4z_1z_2z_3z_4$. The first three bits $x_1x_2x_3$ represent CAN message type. CAN message types for medical data payload are shown in Table 1.

If first three bits of identification field are "000" then next three bits of BID (BID3 BID4 and BID5) will describe the patient information type as shown in Table 2.

Each patient will be assigned a 2 bits Patient Identification (PID) code and will be defined in BID's bits BID6 and BID7. The patient's name will be sent in 8 bytes in CAN's message's data field. If patient information type field is equal to 001 (Medical data) then patient's medical data will be described in the format shown below:

Age: 2 bytes
Gender: 1 byte (M/F)
Pre-existent health condition: 2 bytes: Diabetic/Non-Diabetic (DB/ND)

In our scheme it is suggested that each CAN enabled medical equipment send patient's digitized vital signs in 16 bits along with patient ID and code of the vital sign as shown in Figure 6.

CAN-UMTS gateway gathers messages from CAN-enabled medical equipment from In-ambulance CAN network and keeps them in relevant buffers such as EKG buffer, BP buffer etc. The data field of a CAN message is up to 64

Figure 5. CAN Version 2.0A and 2.0B

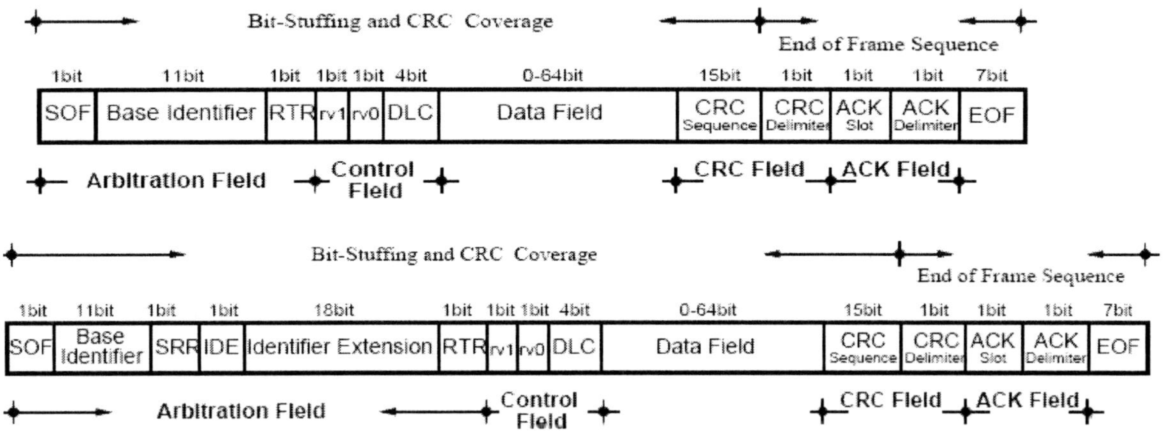

Table 1. Medical data payload types for CAN message

BID0	BID1	BID2	Message definition
0	0	0	Patient information
0	0	1	Blood Pressure
0	1	0	EKG
0	1	1	Pulse Rate
1	0	0	Blood oxygenation

Table 2. Additional message types

BID3	BID4	BID5	Message definition
0	0	0	Patient name
0	0	1	Medical data

bits long, therefore, one CAN message can carry vital signs data of up to 4 patients. To distinguish the EKG data for different patients, it sets 2 bits patient's ids in patient's identification field. For example, EKG data of four patients with ids 00, 01, 10 and 11 is shown in Figure 7.

CAN-UMTS prepares packets of aggregated data and generates IP packets in which aggregated CAN message is treated as IP payload.

Data Reduction Algorithm

The medical data for the patients in critical condition is transmitted over Cellular Network. There are strong chances that due to the mass emergency situation, the number of phone calls and the load over the network would leave very little bandwidth free. It is therefore required to compress the data so that the vital signs of large number of patients can be accommodated over a single UMTS connection. Furthermore, several patients'

Figure 6. CAN message with compression code and non-repeated data bytes

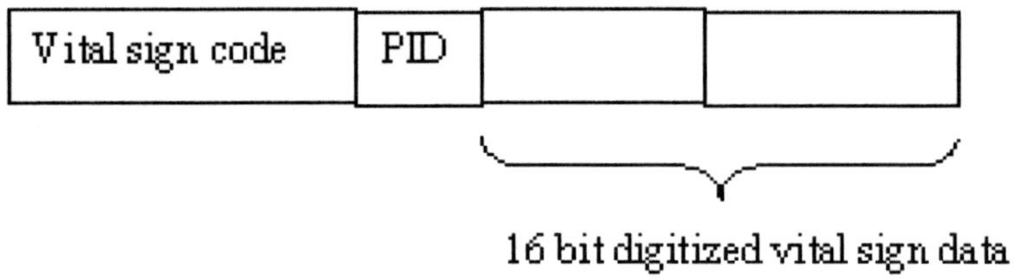

Figure 7. Results for compression of 12-channel 2-byte EKG Data

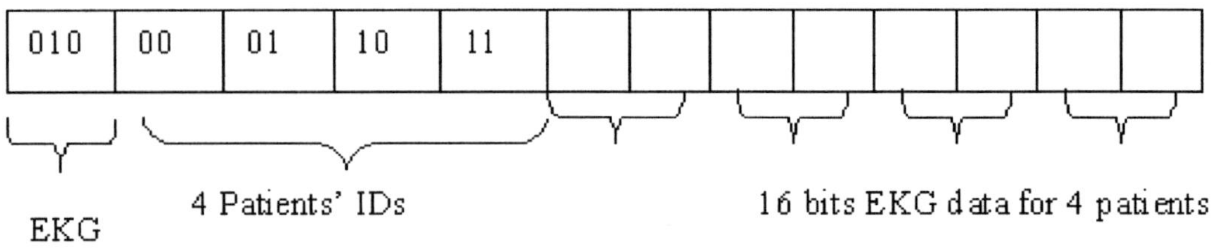

vital signs data over MDN may lead to network saturation over In-Ambulance data network. Accordingly, the number of waiting messages will increase austerely.

It has been suggested that patients' medical information be represented by CAN message's payload as explained in section 3.1. It is very likely that a considerable portion of message payload may remain constant depending upon the message type. For example, if a message represents patient's temperature information, then there are good chances that the temperature may remain constant for a considerable amount of time. Therefore, the data bytes representing the temperature information will remain constant for that period of time. Based upon the "non-variability" feature of some of CAN messages, a data reduction (DR) algorithm for CAN network was developed in (Misbahuddin and Al-Holou 2003). In the DR algorithm, it is assumed all CAN messages have fixed payload size of 64 bits. The transmitting and receiving CAN controller chip maintains a history of recently sent or received N CAN messages in buffers T_BUF and R_BUF respectively. Whenever the transmitting CAN chip schedules a previously sent message, its payload is compared with the payload of message saved in the T_BUF. If some data bytes in the newly generated message are found repeated, then the CAN controller prepares an 8 bit compression code (CC) to indicate this repetition. Eight bits of CC correspond to 8 bytes of CAN's payload size. If i_{th} data byte is repeated, the i_{th} bit in compression code is set to "1". On the other hand, if i_{th} data byte is not repeated, the i_{th} bit in the compression code is set to "0". Non-repeated data bytes will follow the compression code. For example, if in a CAN message bytes 0, 1, 2 and 3 have been repeated and bytes 4, 5, 6 and 7 are new then the compressed CAN message will be as shown in Figure 8.

In a CAN message, the compression code's absence or presence depends upon the repetition of data bytes. To indicate the existence and non existence of compression code, one of the reserved bits (r_0) in the CAN message's control

Figure 8. EKG Data for One Second at 500 Hz

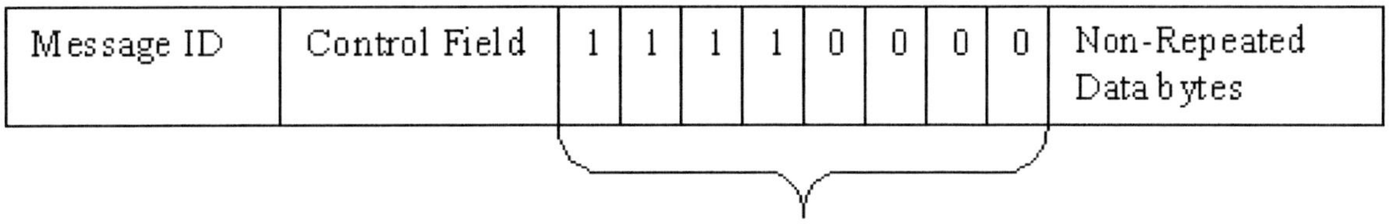

field may be used (Bosch 1991). If the CAN chip includes a compression code, bit r_0 is set to "1". The receiver CAN chip monitors r_0 bit. If it finds r_0 as 1, it will interpret very first byte in data field as compression code. The CAN chip will recover the repeated bytes from the buffer inside the CAN chip and non-repeated bytes from the received message.

The compression code and non-repeated data bytes are sent in the data portion of the message. If there is no repetition of data bytes, no compression code is generated and message is treated as normal CAN message. If a message arrives at a CAN controller with compression code, then the repeated data bytes are recovered from the R_BUFF and the new bytes are extracted from the data field of the arrived message. Actual message is reconstructed by combing the repeated and non-repeated message bytes and handed over to the host system.

We have studied the data pattern in 12 channel EKG data and came to the conclusion that EKG digitized with 2 bytes is attributed with significant non-variability features. This observation encourages us to apply the DR algorithm to ambulatory EKG data. All the medical equipment is CAN enabled. Therefore, DR algorithm can be applied to MDN and is executed by CAN-UMTS gateway to the aggregated CAN messages. We have applied DR algorithm to EKG data and computed the compression ratio. Figure 9 indicates the resulting reduction ratio for the 12-channel EKG data. For MIT heart rate series (MIT-BIH 2008), the data for "hr7257.dat" was compressed to 85% of the original size and the data for "hr11389.dat" was compressed to 89% of the original size. The lower compression ratio for heart rate series is because of the fact that the heart rate value is rounded from floating point representation to one byte integer format and CAN protocol carries 8 readings per packet that differ in small amounts.

SIMULATION RESULTS FOR AGGREGATED DATA TRANSMISSION

We have worked on evaluating the performance and feasibility of transmitting vital signs of multiple patients via single UMTS connection. The patients could be located in large ambulances that can take multiple injured or sick patients from a disaster site to the hospital. Alternatively, the patients could be placed in different ambulances moving in close proximity to each other towards the same hospital. In the latter case, the ambulances are assumed to be equipped with localized wireless connections using Wi-Fi or Wi-Max based MANET.

The one dimensional medical data must be multiplexed for each patient and then the data for different patients can be aggregated into packets that can be transferred over the UMTS network to the hospital. The type of vital signs data, identification and rate of measurement is given in Table 3. The aggregate bandwidth required for transmission of data for one patient is 8900 bps, inferred from the last column of Table 3. For 16 patients' data, the raw bandwidth required is 142,400 bps (or 142 kbps). The multiplexing

Figure 9. Results for compression of 12-channel 2-byte EKG data

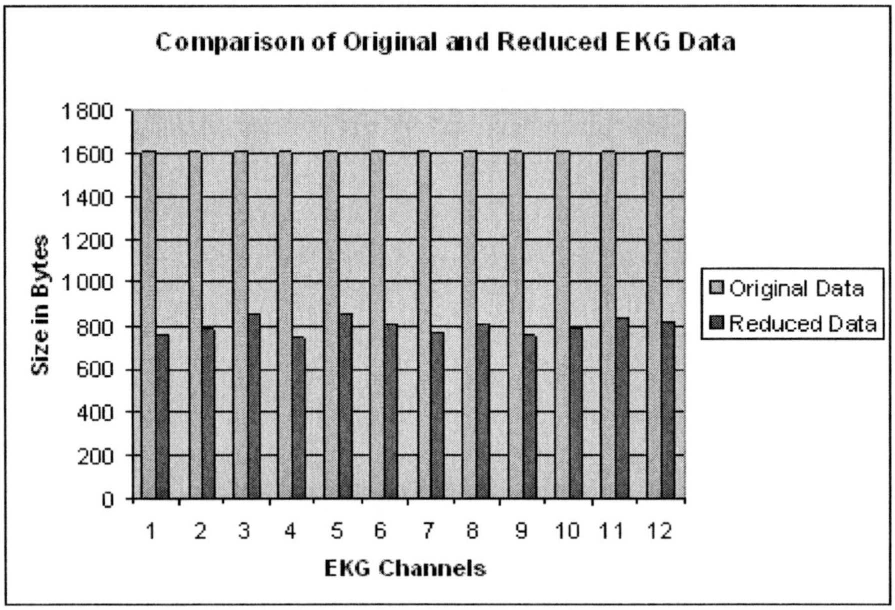

Table 3. Medical data sampling requirements

S.No.	Data Title	Data ID	Sample Rate	Bandwidth consumed
1.	EKG	0	125 to 500 samples per second	2kbps to 8kbps (based on 2 bytes per sample)
2	Blood pressure	1	1 sample every 2 minutes	16 bits per 60 seconds
3	Pulse	2	2 samples per second	32 bits per second
4	Respiration (tidal volume)	3	50 samples per second	800 bits per second
5	SpO2 (blood oxygen-ation)	4	2 samples per second	32 bits per second

and aggregation overhead is negligible as the number of different data types and the number of patients can be encoded within very small bit range.

For the purpose of medical data transmission, we have selected an EKG sample that has been measured at 500 Hz. Figure 10 shows the plot of one second of data. There is one QRS complex per second, indicating normal heart rate.

A simulation scenario was developed in OP-NET in which one mobile node travels across several node-B stations in its journey from point 'A' (disaster site) to point 'B'(hospital) while transmitting aggregated medical data to the hospital. We simulated various conditions including light load and heavy load on the network to study the loss and delay parameters when the medical data is transferred. Figure 11 shows the simulation scenario and Figure 12 shows total traffic received at the hospital.

Figure 13 depicts the end to end delay as recorded at the hospital node.

Figure 10. EKG Data for one second at 500 Hz

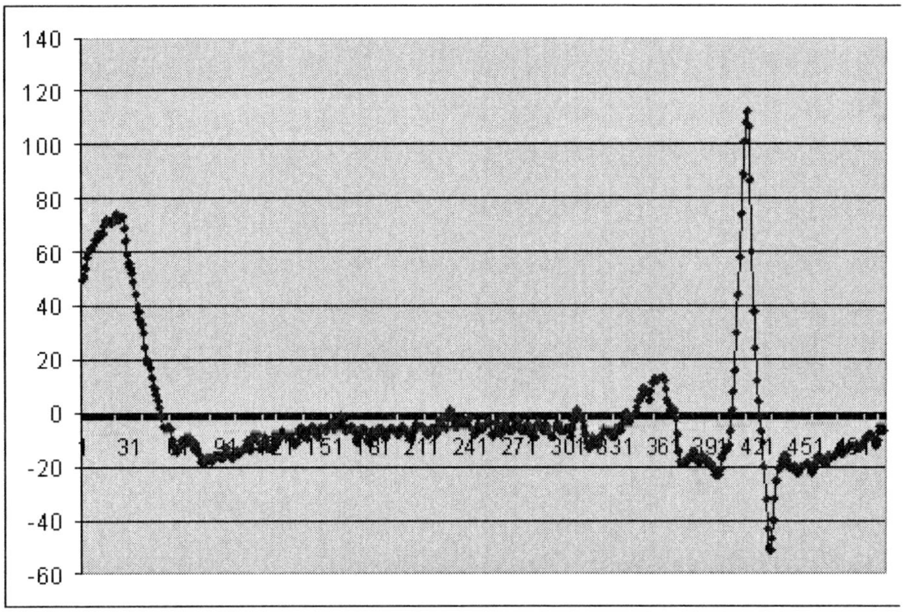

Figure 11. OPNET Simulation of Ambulance Journey to Hospital

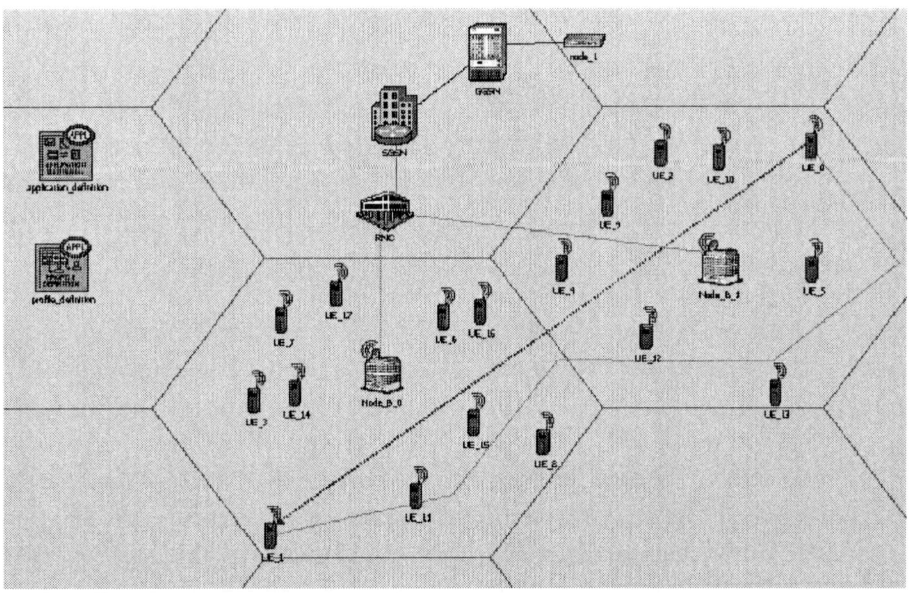

It is clear that the end to end delay is maintained within 0.8 seconds and no traffic was dropped. Thus the UMTS network demonstrates superior performance in forwarding the simulated traffic to the destination. This is despite the fact that no QoS was applied to the traffic and it was considered as best effort traffic.

FEASIBILITY OF EMERGENCY MEDICAL DATA TRANSMISSION

In this section, we briefly discuss the results of a feasibility study undertaken for the implementation of MEDTOC in developing countries. Since the hospitals cannot afford very expensive equipment in such countries, cost plays a major role in the decision to adopt a new technology. Due to shortage of funding and infrastructure to face mass disasters in developing countries, loss of human lives is significant. Therefore any new solution must bear a low cost so that it can be adopted widely for saving lives.

Figure 14 shows our proposed solution for cost effective emergency alert transportation of patients. We propose to use the "Vital Mote" wrist band sensors (Gao 2006). These sensors can transmit the blood pressure, SpO2 (blood oxygenation), heart rate and three lead EKG automatically to a PC or notepad computer within a short distance of 10-20 meters. One Vital Mote can transmit all the data continuously for up to 6 hours on two AA batteries. In Figure 14, it is shown that there are four patients per ambulance and the motes, attached to their wrists, transmit data to a central PC or notepad computer. The computer carries out necessary processing of data to convert it to CAN standard format. It transmits the data to the CAN network through a CAN-USB interface (www.emicros.com) card that plugs into the USB port.

The CAN format data transmitted by CAN-USB interface is received by the CAN-UMTS gateway and controller. CAN controllers are implemented in FPGA/ASIC for low volume/high volume applications. The same chip with send/receive buffers and peripheral connections can function as a bridge between the CAN and UMTS networks. This gateway places a call on UMTS network to the hospital and transmits the data through the high priority QoS class of the UMTS transmission. Table 4 indicates approximate cost of the equipment to be installed in one ambulance. It is obvious that the system is affordable for low budget hospitals as up to four patients can be monitored while on way to the hospital with equipment costing around $2,100.

CONCLUSION

In this chapter, we have focused on enabling technologies for real-time transmission of emergency medical data to hospitals. This matter has recently drawn attention due to sudden and massive calamities that have been occurring at various places. This issue has also become conspicuous due to present challenges and recent natural disasters such as tsunami, earthquakes, fires and disasters etc. We have provided an overview of the current state of the art in this field of real-time transmission of emergency medical data and presented a solution considering the issue not addressed by other researchers. Two case studies are highlighted in which cellular 3G system has been used in transmission of medical data to the physician. These systems are known as Mobile Tele Trauma System and OTELO (mObile Tele-Echography using an ultra-Light rObot). Most of the work done has covered the case of single patient or the data is transmitted locally within an on-site triage unit. We have introduced our novel technique of aggregating and compressing emergency medical data of several patients and its transmission to the hospital using 3G cellular network for analysis and monitoring by the physicians. In our scheme, the data consisting of vital signs is formatted and compressed over the CAN

Figure 12. Traffic for one patient and 16 patients' data received at the hospital

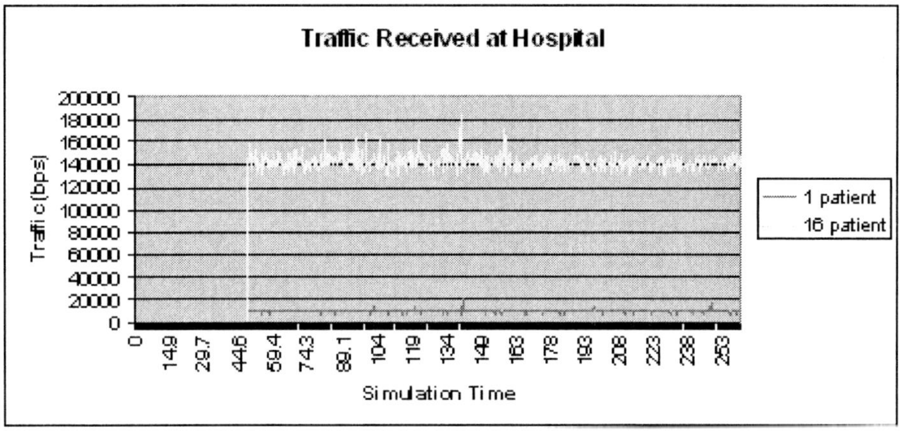

Figure 13. End to end delay

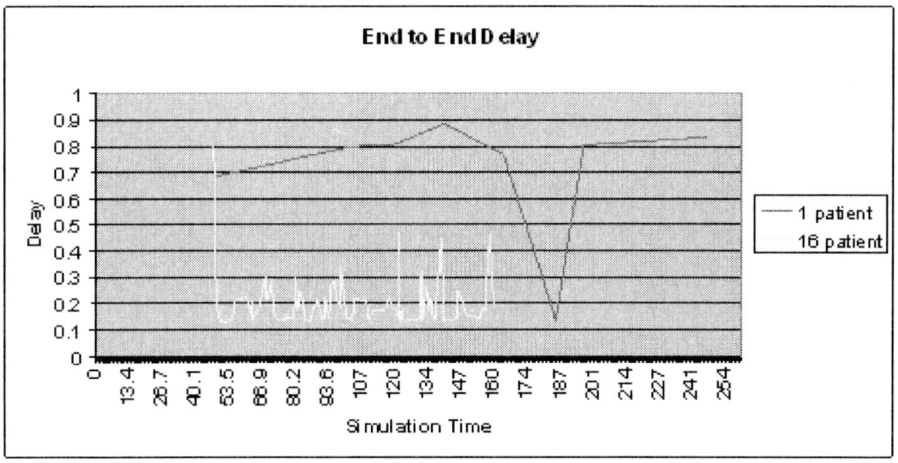

Figure 14. Mote data transmission from ambulance via UMTS to hospital

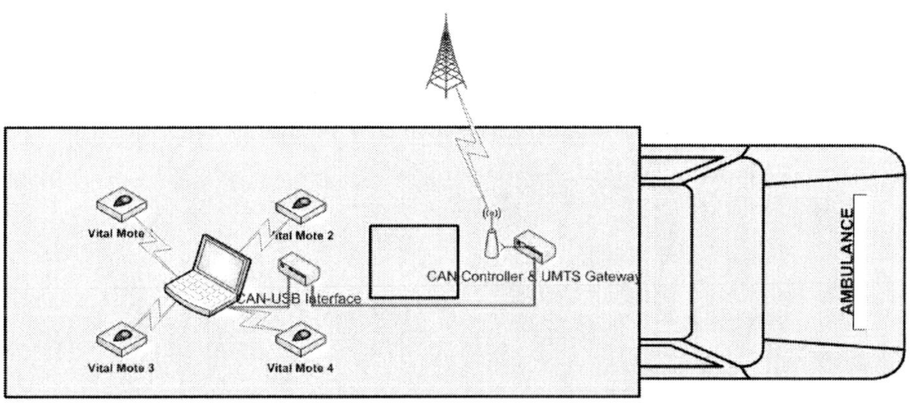

Table 4. Approximate cost of the equipment installed in ambulance

S.No.	Equipment	Quantity	Approximate Cost per Unit in US Dollars	Total Cost in US Dollars
1.	Vital Mote wrist band with HR, EKG, BP and SpO2 Sensors	4	$300	$1,200
2	CAN-USB Interface	1	$100	$100
3	Notepad or Personal Computer	1	$600	$600
4	CAN-UMTS gateway and controller	1	$200	$200
	Total Equipment Cost Per Ambulance			$2,100

network and passed through the CAN – UMTS gateway before being delivered to the hospital. The format fields are outlined and the performance of data reduction algorithm is measured in terms of percentage saving in data size. Our proof of concept simulation in OPNET sets the ambulance in motion and passes it in a loaded network with at least one handover between two node B stations. The data transmitted by the ambulance simulates the bandwidth required by vital signs of one patient and 16 patients. The results indicate no loss and minimal delay in the transfer of data from the ambulance to the hospital. Future work includes design of complete MEDTOC protocol including the transfer of actual medical data with customized software within highly congested 3G network as per mass disaster scenarios. The data may be bound with the QoS classes available in the UMTS network.

REFERENCES

Adler, A. (2000). *A Cost-Effective Portable Telemedicine Kit for Use in Developing Countries*", Unpublished masters thesis, Massachusetts Institute of Technology, Cambridge.

Axisa, F., Gehin, C., Delhomme, G., Collet, C., Robin, O., & Dittmar, A. (2004). Wrist Ambulatory Monitoring System and Smart Glove for Real Time Emotional, Sensorial and Physiological Analysis. In *Proc. of the 26th Annual Int. Conf. of the IEEE EMBS,* (pp. 2161-2164). San Francisco, CA.

Bolaños, M., Nazeran, H., Gonzalez, I., Parra, R., & Martinez, C. C. (2004). A PDA-based Electrocardiogram/Blood Pressure Telemonitor for Telemedicine. In *Proc. of the 26th Annual Int. Conf. of the IEEE EMBS* (pp. 2169-2172). San Francisco, CA.

Bosch (1991). CAN specification Ver 2.0, Robert Bosch GmbH, Stuttgart, Germany.

Campbell, P. (2005). Prehospital triage of acute myocardial infarction: wireless transmission of electrocardiograms to the on-call cardiologist via a handheld computer. *Journal of Electrocardiology*, *38*(4), 300–309. doi:10.1016/j.jelectrocard.2005.05.003

Canero, C., Thomos, N., Triantafyllidis, G. A., Litos, G. C., & Strintzis, M. G. (2005). Mobile tele-echography: user interface design. *IEEE Transactions on Information Technology in Biomedicine*, *9*(1), 44–49. doi:10.1109/TITB.2004.840064

Chu, Y., & Ganz, A. (2004). A mobile teletrauma system using 3G networks. *IEEE Transactions on Information Technology in Biomedicine*, *8*(4), 456–462. doi:10.1109/TITB.2004.837893

E-Health Insider. (2006). *Virgin to upgrade telemedicine across fleet*. Retrieved January 23, 2008, from http://www.e-health-insider.com/News/1925/virgin_to_upgrade_telemedicine_across_fleet.html

Flint, A., & Milligan, S. (1999, 10 December). Your Tragedy Is Ours: President Joins Thousands in Saluting Fallen Firefighters. *Boston Globe*.

Fontelo, P., Ackerman, M., Kim, G., & Locatis, C. (2003). The PDA as a portal to knowledge sources in a wireless setting. *Telemedicine Journal and e-Health*, *9*(2), 141–147. doi:10.1089/153056203766437480

Frykberg, E., & Tepas, J. J. III. (1988). Terrorist Bombings: Lessons Learned from Belfast to Beirut. *Annals of Surgery*, *208*(5), 569–576. doi:10.1097/00000658-198811000-00005

Gao, Tia, Logan K. Hauenstein, Alex Alm Daivid Crawford, Cassius K. Sims, Azmat Hussain & Daivid M. White (2006). Vital Signs Monitoring and Patient Tracking Over a Wireless Network. *Johns Hopkins APL technological Digest, 27*(1), 66–74.

Garawi, S., Istepanian, R. S. H., & Abu-Rgheff, M. A. (2006). 3G wireless communications for mobile robotic tele-ultrasonography systems. *IEEE Communications Magazine*, *44*(4), 91–96. doi:10.1109/MCOM.2006.1632654

Giovas, P., Thomakos, D., Papazachou, O., & Papadoyannis, D. (2006). Medical aspects of prehospital cardiac telecare. In R.H. Istepanian, S. Laxminarayan, C.S. Pattichis, (Eds.), *M-Health: Emerging Mobile Health Systems*, (pp. 389-400) New York: Springer.

Hall, E., Vawdrey, D. K., Knutson, C. D., & Archibald, J. K. (2003). Enabling remote access to personal electronic medical records. *IEEE Engineering in Medicine and Biology Magazine*, *22*(3), 133–139. doi:10.1109/MEMB.2003.1213636

Issa, O., Grégoire, J.-C., Belala, Y., & Wong, J. (2008). 3G Embedded Communication System for Medical Applications. In *IEEE International Systems Conference (SysCon 2008*(pp. 1–8). 7–10 April 2008

Jerant, A., Schlachta, L., Epperly, T. D., & Barnes Camp, J. (1998). Back to the Future: The Telemedicine House Call. *Family Practice Management, 5*(1) Retrieved Jan 23, 2008, from http://www.aafp.org/fpm/980100fm/lead.html

Kempf, G., M. Eckrich & O. Rumf (n.d.). Data Reduction in Automotive Multiplexing Systems., (SAE No. 940135, pp. 45-50).

Kyriacou, E., Pattichis, M. S., Pattichis, C. S., Panayides, A., & Pitsillides, A. (2007, February). m-Health e-Emergency Systems: Current Status and Future Directions. *IEEE Antennas and Propagation Magazine*, *49*(1), 216–231. doi:10.1109/MAP.2007.371030

Kyriacou, E., Pavlopoulos, S., Berler, A., Neophytou, M., Bourka, A., Georgoulas, A., et al. (2003). Multi-purpose HealthCare Telemedicine Systems with mobile communication link support. *BioMedical Engineering OnLine, 2*(7). Retrieved 22 August, 2008 from http://www.biomedical-engineering-online.com

Lorincz, K., Malan, D. J., Fulford-Jones, T. R. F., Nawoj, A., Clavel, A., & Shnayder, V. (2004, October-December). Sensor networks for emergency response: challenges and opportunities. *IEEE Pervasive Computing / IEEE Computer Society [and] IEEE Communications Society*, *3*(4), 16–23. doi:10.1109/MPRV.2004.18

Misbahuddin, S., & Al-Holou, N. (2003, July 14–18). Efficient communication techniques for Controller Area Network (CAN) protocol. In *Proceedings of ACS/IEEE International conference on computer and their applications*, Tunis.

MIT-BIH. (2008). *Database Distribution Series, Heart Rate Time Series*. Retrieved on Jan 23rd 2008, from http://ecg.mit.edu/

Nakamura, M., Yang, Y., Kubota, S., Shimizu, H., Miura, Y., & Wasaki, K. (2003). Network system for alpine ambulance using long distance wireless LAN and CATV LAN. *Igaku Butsuri*, *23*(1), 30–39.

Pattichis, C., Kyriacou, E., Voskarides, S., Pattichis, M. S., Istepanian, R., & Schizas, C. N. (2002). Wireless Telemedicine Systems: An Overview. *IEEE Antennas & Propagation Magazine*, *44*(2), 143–153. doi:10.1109/MAP.2002.1003651

Pavlopoulos, S., Kyriacou, E., Berler, A., Dembeyiotis, S., & Koutsouris, D. (1998). A novel emergency telemedicine system based on wireless communication technology – AMBULANCE. *IEEE Trans. Inform. Tech. Biomed., – . Special Issue on Emerging Health Telematics Applications in Europe*, *2*(4), 261–267.

Reponen, J., Ilkko, E., Jyrkinen, L., Tervonen, O., Niinimaki, J., Karhula, V., & Koivula, A. (2000). Initial experience with a wireless personal digital assistant as a teleradiology terminal for reporting emergency computerized tomography scans. *Journal of Telemedicine and Telecare*, *6*(1), 45–49. doi:10.1258/1357633001933943

Salvador, C., Pascual Carrasco, M., Gonzalez de Mingo, M. A., Munoz Carrero, A., Marquez Montes, J., & Sosa Martin, L. (2005). Airmed-cardio: a GSM and Internet services-based system for out-of-hospital follow-up of cardiac patients. *IEEE Transactions on Information Technology in Biomedicine*, *9*(1), 73–85. doi:10.1109/TITB.2004.840067

Sillesen, M., Ripa, M. S., Strange, S., Nielsen, S. L., Jorgensen, E., Lippert, F. K., & Clemmensen, P. M. (2006). Telemedicine in the transmission of pre-hospitalization EKGs of patients with suspected acute myocardial infarction. *Ugeskrift for Laeger*, *68*(11), 1133–1136.

Voskarides, S., Pattichis, C. S., Istepanian, R., Michaelides, C., & Schizas, C. N. (2003). Practical evaluation of GPRS use in a telemedicine system in Cyprus. In *CD-ROM Proceedings of the 4th Int. IEEE EMBS Special Topic Conference on Information Technology Applications in Biomedicine,* Birmingham.

Wiki (2008). *Wireless Sensor Networks.* Retrieved on Jan 23, 2008, from http://en.wikipedia.org/wiki/Category:Wireless_sensor_network

KEY TERMS AND DEFINITIONS

Aggregated Data Transmission: A technique to transfer data after aggregating multiple data samples.

CAN Protocol: Controller Area Network protocol originally designed for Automotive application, which allows data communication in the form of short messages over a serial bus.

CAN-enabled medical equipment: Medical equipment which inject medical data over a CAN bus.

Emergency Medical Data: Patients' vital medical records.

Medical Data Network: In-Ambulance data network to carry patients' medical data.

OPNET Application: Application of OPNET simulation software.

UMTS: Universal Mobile Telecommunication System, a mobile phone technology which will include Internet access, video and SMS along with traditional phone services.

Vital Biosignals: 3–12 lead EKG, SPO2, NIBP, IBP, Temperature.

Section 3
Health Informatics and E-Health Applications

Chapter 12
Developments in Modelling Organisational Issues in Healthcare:
Multi Method Modelling

Kirandeep Chahal
Brunel University, UK

Herbert Daly
Brunel University, UK

Tillal Eldabi
Brunel University, UK

Ray J. Paul
Brunel University, UK

ABSTRACT

Healthcare organisations increasingly use simulation and modelling techniques to analyse their procedures and policies. Modelling activities attempt to help meet the challenges, constraints and requirements for efficiency encountered in the modern healthcare environment. A variety of techniques are used, often applied in different roles and by different functions in the organisation. Recent research has investigated the benefits of considering multiple approaches in the analysis of problems. This chapter briefly introduces the use of simulation and modelling in healthcare and the factors driving the increasingly widespread use of these techniques. Simple examples show how individual methods may be applied to model healthcare problems. The recent emergence of multi method approaches to modelling is examined and, focusing specifically on healthcare, examples of how these new ideas may also be applied in healthcare modelling are presented. Finally the challenges to implementing such new approaches effectively in a healthcare environment are discussed.

DOI: 10.4018/978-1-60566-030-1.ch012

INTRODUCTION

Studies in Healthcare Informatics propose a wide range of new technologies and techniques for use in modern healthcare environments. Many applications of Information and Communications Technology (ICT) in healthcare focus on using information systems, innovative devices, and specialised learning environments for medical practitioners to support the delivery of healthcare services. An area occasionally overlooked in healthcare informatics literature however is the use of computer based modelling to investigate the organisational and policy issues which underlie effective healthcare service delivery. In 2006 the UK organisation the Royal Society produced a report on the future impact of ICT in UK healthcare (The Royal Society 2006). Among the available technologies and changing trends, the report identified simulation and modelling as an effective tool that may be used to predict demand, evaluate costs and improve service overall. This chapter highlights the use of computer based modelling on organisational problems in healthcare and focuses on how a recently proposed approach to developing models, multi method modelling, can enhance the effectiveness of their application.

Until recently the subject of organisational and policy modelling has enjoyed a low profile in healthcare informatics literature. Some older texts such as Sheaff & Peel (1995) and van Bemmel & Musen et al. (1997) make no reference to the topic at all, however, as Eldabi & Paul et al. (2007) indicates, the number of published studies in this area has grown rapidly in recent years. In some health informatics texts, such as Davies & Bensley (2005), modelling is grouped in the wider category of decision support techniques. This has sometimes served to obscure the role of organisational modelling and the particular differences between the methods applied. Some common approaches used in modelling the problems of healthcare organisations include Econometrics, Discrete Event Simulation, System Dynamics and Markov Modelling. While each is individually effective, recent developments in modelling methodology propose that an integrated perspective of the methods may address the challenges of healthcare modelling particularly well.

This chapter provides an introduction to organisational modelling techniques for readers of healthcare informatics literature who are unfamiliar them. By way of illustration, two simple examples of how organisational healthcare issues may be formulated for analysis using simulation techniques are presented. For those familiar with such studies an emerging strand in modelling methodology, multi method modelling, is introduced with a review of key literature and results in this area. The application of multi method modelling to healthcare issues is discussed in detail. Factors which make this approach particularly appropriate for healthcare problems are presented as well as how features of the models may influence their effective deployment. Five examples of recent healthcare studies which have used multi method approaches successfully are briefly reviewed. Finally the future challenges to applying this approach in healthcare modelling are presented. References to key literature are provided throughout to support the reader in further research.

THE CHANGING PROFILE OF MODELLING IN HEALTHCARE

Using abstract models to understand the behaviour of a subject is common in disciplines such as economics and engineering, as a result where these disciplines overlap with healthcare, models are often used. Increasingly however models are also being applied to issues of process, organisation and cost in healthcare using a wide range of techniques. Briggs & Claxton et al. (2006) presents some approaches for evaluating costs including decision trees, Markov modelling and simulation techniques. Morris & Devlin et al. (2007) discusses economic and statistical models.

Fone & Hollinghurst et al. (2003) provides an extensive survey of healthcare modelling studies, particularly where simulation methods are used, and identifies four main areas for their application; hospital scheduling and organisation, infections and communicable diseases, costs and economic evaluation and screening.

Several different influences are reported as making healthcare modelling increasingly attractive. Davies & Bensley (2005) cites the new challenges for healthcare providers driven by changing demographics and social trends. Young & Brailsford et al. (2004) suggests that the high expectations of service expected from healthcare users may interest policy makers in established modelling approaches. Briggs & Claxton et al. (2006) cites the policy of public health bodies in Australia and Canada requiring the systematic evaluation of all new devices, procedures and pharmaceuticals prior to their approval and adoption.

Increasingly institutional factors in healthcare organisations, such as mandatory requirements for data collection and performance reporting, also support the use of modelling. The widespread availability of on site computing capacity, via workstations and an hand held devices and increasing levels of computer literacy in the workforce mean that models can be readily implemented and their findings easily presented to policy makers.

The Varied Role for Modelling in Healthcare

The general benefits of modelling are the ability to investigate the effects of different decisions on a problem or system without committing significant resources or affecting the real situation adversely. As such, using organisational models it is possible to investigate the behaviour of healthcare systems in different circumstances, applying possible policy responses and reviewing the consequences.

Because of the scale of healthcare organisations the financial and resource costs of poor policy or decision making can be significant. The critical role of healthcare in providing medical treatment means that the evaluation of risk is of the upmost importance. The high cost of failure for healthcare organisations also requires that risk is reduced where possible.

Modelling in healthcare therefore is used to support four main areas of interest for policy makers and professionals:

- Planning and design of services
- Investigation of observed behaviour
- Building descriptions of processes
- Evaluation of financial and resource costs

Service organisation and delivery schemes can be planned and tested using modelling techniques. This may be required in the planning of new services; for example new departments or wards. It may be used to plan the reorganisation of existing services. Once represented using an appropriate model the design may be tested with data to ensure that it meets performance targets. Rohleder & Klassen (2002) provide an example of such a modelling study for clinics investigating prospective systems of appointment scheduling.

Healthcare processes and systems may be studied in order to make predictions about their behaviour or investigate unexpected performance. Models may be used to predict outcomes based on a number of relevant factors or possibly suggest areas in the system where improvements may have the most effect. Lane & Monefeldt et al. (2000) provides an example of this kind of study, investigating the dynamic behaviour of an Accident and Emergency Department.

Modelling may also be used to understand or document an existing process or system. In some circumstances healthcare organisations act as complex systems, evolving to solve problems and sometimes producing counterintuitive behaviour. Creating models provides an opportunity to investigate and document how a system works; which may be a valuable training tool for the professionals who must manage the system in future. Conrick & Dunne et al. (1999) describes the use of simulation models in the education of nurses.

Some modelling studies focus specifically on the costs, benefits and resource allocation problems of healthcare processes including the implications of different choices and policies. Briggs & Claxton et al. (2006) describes a number of such studies, including principles and techniques for carrying them out. Briggs & Claxton et al. (2006) also contrasts modelling with use of experimental trials.

SIMULATION MODELLING IN HEALTHCARE STUDIES

Simulation models use software to recreate the activities or structure observed in the problem, in order to generate outcomes which are comparable with the behaviours in the problem. In practice the implementation of most models is computer based, including the Markov models described in Briggs & Claxton et al. (2006). However the relationship between simulation models and computer implementation is different in that, although they may be conceptualised to some extent, they are entirely impractical without, computing resources.

The use of simulation approaches for modelling healthcare issues has received a great deal of attention recently. Eldabi & Paul et al. (2007) describes a dramatic increase in healthcare simulation studies since 2000. Two styles of simulation modelling, System Dynamics (SD) and Discrete Event Simulation (DES), well established in other disciplines have been used widely in healthcare studies. Another emerging form of simulation, Agent Based modelling (ABM), less widespread due to its relative immaturity has also been used in healthcare studies; Kanagarajah & Lindsey et al. (2006) provides an example. This section briefly introduces SD and DES modelling.

Discrete Event Simulation Modelling in Healthcare

Discrete Event Simulation modelling is a technique well established in disciplines such as manufacturing and scheduling. Some key texts include Banks (2001) and Law & Kelton (2000). DES models attempt to imitate the observed behaviour of the problem, typically by using stochastic distributions to generate events and quantities typical for the system. Problems are often conceptualised as networks of queues and servers. The behaviour of the real system is imitated by estimating distributions for the arrival of entities at the queues and the dispatch of entities by the servers. A number of notations may be used to describe their logic including queuing diagrams, flowcharts and Activity Cycle Diagrams (ACDs) described in Paul & Balmer (1993). Consider the example of a treatment ward A with regular patient admissions. Patients wait for treatment, after treatment they enter a recovery ward B until they are ready to leave. The treatment requires one senior professional and two specialists in order to go ahead. An ACD of this problem may be described by Figure 1.

The three entities move between the states defined in the ACD. Service processes require all related entities to be available in order to begin and release them when complete. The simulation reproduces behaviour observed in the real system. An investigation of the problem may proceed by varying factors such as the arrival rate for the patients, the distribution of time required for treatment or recovery and the number of specialists and professionals available. The output of the model is monitored to establish how performance is affected as the variables are changed. Jun & Jacobson et al. (1999) provides an extensive review of some recent healthcare studies using DES.

Figure 1. Simple DES model of a healthcare problem

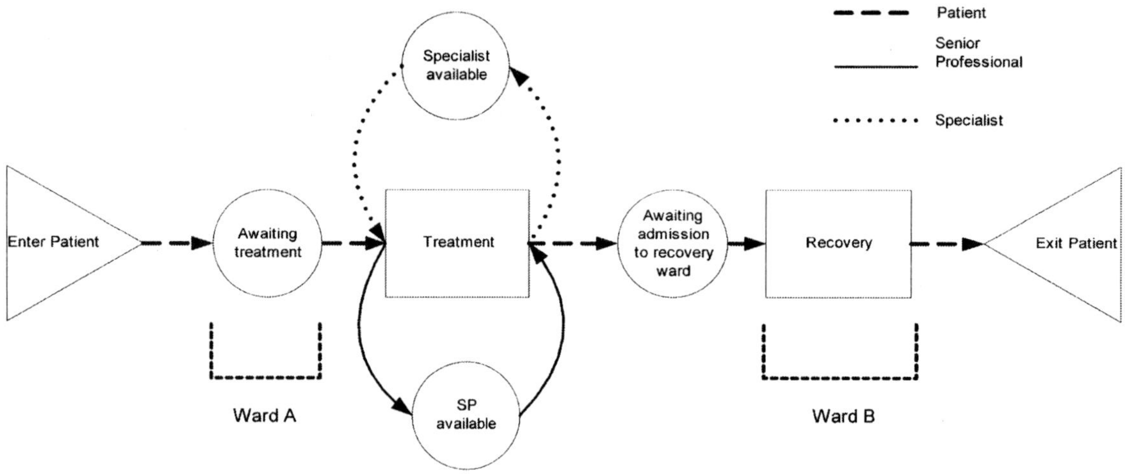

System Dynamics Modelling in Healthcare

System Dynamics modelling is a technique well established in disciplines such as socio-economic and business modelling. Some key texts include Forrester (1961) and Sterman (2000). SD models attempt to reproduce the causal structure of the problem, identifying components and feedback loops that are the cause the dynamic behaviour observed in the system. Models attempt to focus on the systemic properties of the problem caused by the interaction of flows, interdependencies and delays. They may also include "soft variables", qualities that are not measured directly yet are proposed to influence behaviour. There are two common forms of notation Causal Loop Diagrams (CLDs), which capture the conceptual relationships in the problem, and Stock-Flow diagrams which describe the structure in the model in more detail. Only Stock-Flow diagrams are implemented as simulations. Both are described in detail by Sterman (2000).

Consider the simple example of a hospital operating on a fixed level of external funding. Patients may chose the hospital due to its reputation based on a combination of the treatment outcomes and waiting times reported. Treatment outcomes are influenced by the level of funding per patient and waiting times by the current size of the population. CLD and stock flow models of this problem may be described by Figure 2.

Figure 2. Simple SD model of a healthcare problem

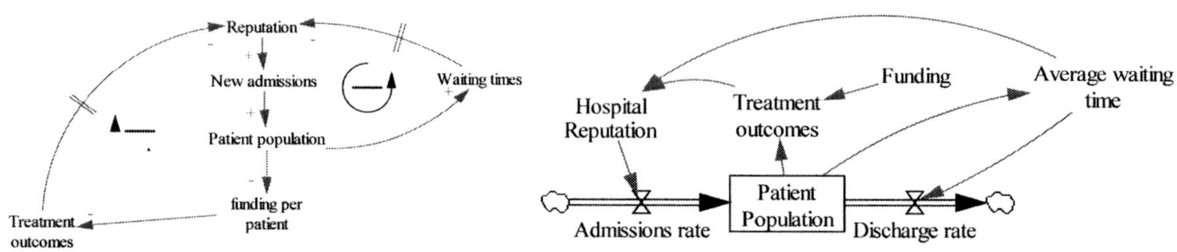

The description shows how quantities flow through the system in feedback loops and the active mechanisms which may produce interesting dynamic behaviour. The model is intended to provide an impression of the dynamic trends resulting from the system structure rather than reproduce observed behaviour exactly.

An investigation of the problem may vary parameters such as the starting population, the length of the delay in affecting hospital reputation and the effect of the two influences on that factor. The output of the model is used to discuss long term behaviour and the consequences of structural change. Dangerfield (1999) provides an extensive review of some recent healthcare studies using SD.

REALISING EFFECTIVE HEALTHCARE MODELLING

Modelling techniques are usually applied to large or sophisticated problems perhaps containing hundreds of variables. Although the two simulation examples presented are very simple they illustrate the impact models may have in the four areas of interest described previously:

Changes to either service could be planned using the models as prototypes to determine the likely effects. For example the effect on patient throughput of using two recovery wards could be planned using the DES model and then perhaps compared with the effect of adding an extra specialist alternative. The models could be used to recreate unexplained behaviour observed in the problem and investigate their likely causes. For example if an increase in funding leads to an unexpected decline of the hospitals reputation the SD model could be used to investigate whether the effects of delays in the system could provide an explanation and what the long term consequences may be.

The process for providing the service in each case is documented by the models and they may provide an aid to discussion in reviewing the processes which, unlike a written description, is dynamic and pliable. Simulation models can therefore communicate the problem effectively to those familiar with the problem yet uninitiated in any modelling technique. With regard to financial evaluation; as with all models containing quantitative variables cost predictions based on the output are fairly straightforward so long as both overheads and unit costs can be accurately established.

The simple descriptions presented above also illustrate well the role played by those making the model. The individual or team responsible for creating the model must investigate the problem and formulate its detail into an abstract form which can be simulated appropriately. Evidence collected from the primary sources is used to develop the basic structure of the model but also to determine and the refine quantitative aspects of the model too. This may require interacting with personnel, studying key documents, taking measurements first hand and conducting experiments. Through the process of modelling, modellers are able to develop, and perhaps disseminate, a detailed and insightful understanding of the problem. The acquisition of this knowledge is considered to be a powerful indirect benefit of modelling.

Also apparent from the two studies is their difference in approach; The DES model emphasises the effects of the stochastic qualities of a problem, whereas the SD model emphasises the endogenous feedback properties. As a result of these differences, the investigation and analysis required for each of them focuses on different parts of the problem. Each approach is considered to be independently effective and as a result modellers using different systems rarely question the framework of assumptions contained within the approach they are most familiar with.

Considering trends in healthcare modelling, Eldabi & Paul et al. (2007) note an interest among subject experts to combine the different methods in their studies. For example one respondent of the authors, when asked to identify current trends, states the "need for much greater integration between disciplines". This chapter now considers this idea in more detail by discussing the basic principles requires as well as practical issues and developments.

THE MULTI METHOD APPROACH TO MODELLING

The requirement for modelling techniques to be used combined and used together has caused a new and interesting theme in modelling methodology to emerge. Described simply as Multi Method Modelling, its roots lie in early discussions between groups of modelling practitioners, their search for the fundamental basis of their own method and comparisons with other approaches. Recent developments in this theme have been stimulated by the widespread use of modelling techniques and a new generation software tools offer more flexible modelling solutions.

Distinctions between methods, it is argued, has led to a separation of modelling specialists into method oriented groups which has affected the field to the extent that communication across method boundaries becomes difficult, if not entirely unproductive. Meadows & Robinson (1985) describe this as paradigmatic relationship between practitioners. The multi method research them aims to clarify and evolve the relationship between different modelling methods.

Multi Method Modelling: Background and principles

The key premise of the multi method approach is that understanding more than one method can help improve the practice of modelling. This requires, at least, an understanding of how approaches differ fundamentally, that is often uncommon for subject specialists to posses. Several authors have attempted to address this issue and have included a variety of methods in the discussion. The subject of their work is summarised in Table 1.

Lane (2000) focuses on communication between communities of modellers who use different systems, identifying differences between the two methods and also how different modes of communication can benefit practitioners in areas of common interest. Meadows & Robinson (1985) examine the assumptions underlying different methods and their modelling process using a number of case studies. Morecroft & Robinson (2005) focuses on differences in the features and properties of models created using two different systems. They provide a detailed example of the two methods at work on a single problem by way of illustration. Schieritz & Milling (2003) compare two different methods and the contrasting ways in which they attempt to achieve similar ends. This list of studies is by no means exhaustive but represents a range of starting points in the comparison of systems that covers a variety of methods. Table 2 briefly describes five different

Table 1. Methods compared by four multi method studies

	Meadows & Robinson	Lane	Morecroft & Robinson	Schieritz & Milling
SD	•	•	•	•
DES		•	•	
ABM				•
Econometrics	•			
I/O analysis	•			
Optimisation	•			

Table 2. Summary descriptions of five different modelling methods

Modelling Paradigm	Realisation	Description
Agent Based Simulation	Simulation	Imitating the behaviour of a problem using granular entities with encapsulated behaviour
Discrete Event Simulation	Simulation	Imitating the behaviour of a problem using processes and passive entities, based on events
Markov modelling	Stochastic	Using a state based view of a problem and the probability of transition between states to analyse potential behaviour
System Dynamics	Simulation	Identifying flows, stocks, and feedback in a problem in order to analyse systemic behaviour
Econometrics	Statistical	Applying statistical techniques to test relationships between problem data variables or analyse problem variables variation over time.

modelling methods that have recently been used to model problems in healthcare.

Realisation refers to the mechanism by which implemented models to produce their results. It is often the case that where the same realisation mechanism is used the process may differ significantly. For example Discrete Event Simulation (DES) typically uses stochastic simulation with variable time steps, System Dynamics (SD) uses deterministic simulation with fixed time steps, whereas Agent Based Modelling (ABM) may use either method. In practice computer based modelling is used to implement all five systems.

The comparisons of four studies use a wide range of criteria to isolate distinct properties for different methods, however at present there is no widely agreed definitive list; perhaps because the properties identified are so dependant on what they are compared with. However it is generally recognised that different kinds of models have different properties and the methods propose a different conceptualisation of the problem. Comparisons usually focus on issues such as the use of random variables, the use of data, representing feedback and verification. Some general themes in modelling are also revealed, for example, the role of models in communication, qualitative and quantitative properties of modelling and the benefit of the model as a product compared with modelling as a process. As this strand of research develops it has been proposed that the multi method approach may lead to the development of new integrated forms of modelling where the properties of the model are determined strictly by the properties of the problem.

Practical Applications

A number of studies have been made based on multi method ideas. These range from general developments in for methodology to studies focusing on a particular application area such as manufacturing, supply chain management or healthcare. Themes in these studies may differ considerably; Lorenz & Jost (2006) and Chahal & Eldabi (2008) analyse the choice between different methods, whereas Borshchev & Karpov et al. (2002) discuss the use of an integrated software platform which supports three different modelling methods. However from these and other studies two main practical strands are notable. The first is studies which provide a considered approach to choosing an appropriate modelling method for a given problem. The second are studies which attempt to combine different kinds of model into a hybrid form either by logical partition of the problem or joining existing models. (see Figure 3)

Figure 3. Common modes of multi method modelling from literature

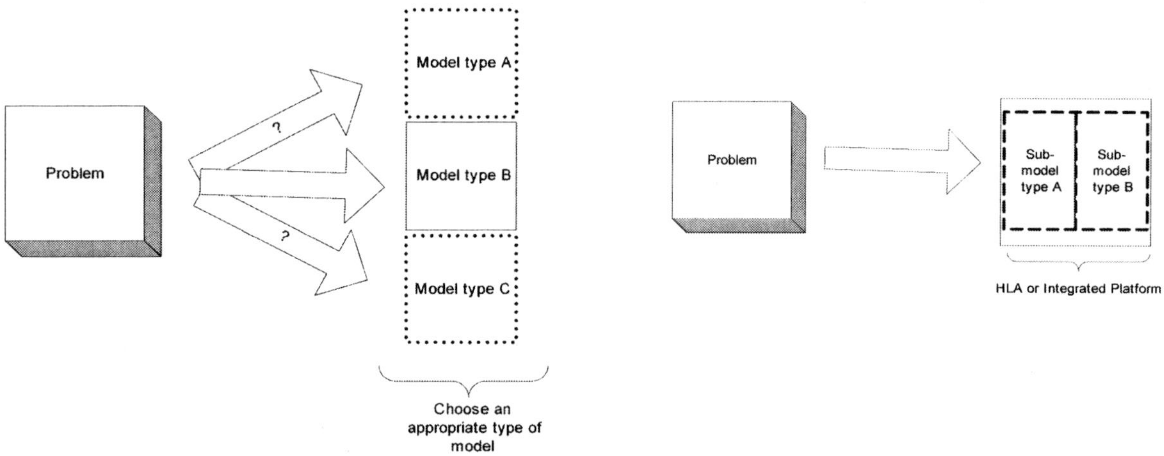

APPLYING MULTI METHOD MODELLING TO ISSUES IN HEALTHCARE

Considering the developing profile of healthcare modelling and the relative immaturity of multi method approaches it may be expected that each may be of little benefit to the other at their current stages of development. On the contrary, to date, the ideas have aroused considerable interest in healthcare modelling circles. This section discusses some of the reasons that a multi method approach has the potential to deliver significant benefits for modelling in healthcare. Some existing work on multi method modelling in healthcare is also reviewed.

Why Healthcare?

A number of factors account for the interest in using a multi method approach to model healthcare problems and in different organisations the reasons vary. However four reasons it may be especially relevant are listed below and described in turn:

- Variety of healthcare modelling problems
- The benefits of integrating functional views
- Requirements for data and analysis
- Issues of scale and limitations of technology

Healthcare modelling embraces a wide variety of problems. Healthcare organisations are very rich in terms of the types of properties that may usefully be modelled. For example modelling the probabilities of events in one area may be as important as modelling paths through a system or modelling population sizes and costs in another. In each case the nature of the problems differs significantly and an appreciation of several methods equips healthcare modellers to deal with each problem effectively by using an appropriate method.

Healthcare organisations are often complex and contain many different functions focusing on their own targets and goals. An integrated view of problems is often useful but unavailable. The different models functions use, often reflect their different view of the problem. For example an

Figure 4. Composite models combine the views of different functions

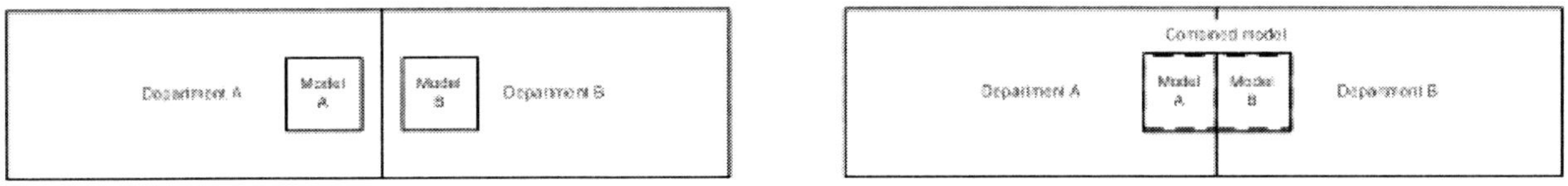

economic policy function may rely on econometric modelling, while an operational policy function may use DES modelling. A multi method approach provides a framework for integrating views and exploring how different functions relate to each other, for example by creating a single composite model from those used by two different functions; illustrated in Figure 4.

Different methods have different requirements for the use of formal numerical data and different problems may differ in the amount of formal data available. For example Econometric modelling requires high quantities of formal data in the conceptualisation and construction of models though more moderate quantities are required for validation. SD modelling typically relies on a mixture of formal and informal data in conceptualisation with more formal data used in model construction and validation. Similarly DES may rely on a variety of information sources in conceptualisation with more formal data required in construction, for example in determining appropriate distributions and significantly more, generated by the model, being used in validation. These properties are described in Table 3. The choice of an appropriate modelling method may be based on the alignment of the data available from the problem and the data requirements of the method.

Due to their diversity, issues in healthcare may vary in the scale and level of detail required to analyse them effectively. Problems may be considered over different organisational boundaries. For example models may examine at ward level, department level or hospital level. Problems may be defined in terms of the individuals, generalised behaviour or wider trends. Modelling may cover different time periods such as short, medium and long term scenarios. All these factors determine how actors or entities in the problem are represented. Entities in a healthcare model, for example, may represent beds, patients, ambulances or staff.

Although different models may require a similar level of effort to conceptualise, in implementation the resources required for the same problem in terms of memory, processor time and mass storage may be significantly different. The factors determining the overall resource requirements for a model are a combination of the level of detail required for each entity, the total number of entities required typically determined by the problem scope and the timescale considered by the model. This relationship is represented in Figure 5.

In this respect different models have different characteristics; ABM typically uses a very high

Table 3. Comparing requirements for numerical data at different stages in the modelling process

	Conceptualisation	Construction	Validation
Econometrics	High	High	Moderate
SD	Low	Moderate	Moderate
DES	Low	Moderate	High

Figure 5. Factors determining modelling resource load

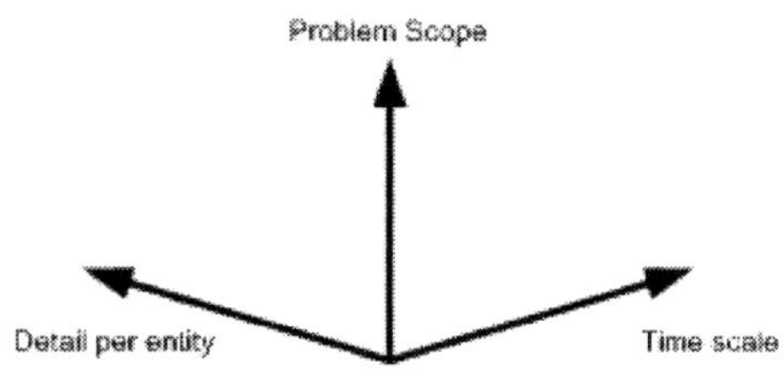

level of resources per entity, modelling the state and processing the actions of each entity in the problem individually. Modelling the same problem in DES would typically use simpler passive entities with behaviour defined in terms the service processes, requiring fewer resources. Even fewer would be required in the SD model where entities typically would be modelled as continuous streams without individual states or behaviour.

One solution to very high resource requirements is to increase the computing resources available until the problem becomes tractable. This is often proposed in healthcare modelling using GRID computing techniques. An alternative solution to applying raw computing power is the use of a multi method approach to conceptualise the problem using a different modelling system. Due to the difference in resource requirements, problems which are intractable using one approach may be tractable by applying another where the overall resource requirement is lower.

Review of Existing Projects

This section briefly reviews some existing and notable multi method studies which focused on healthcare problems. The studies use a variety of methods to achieve range of modelling goals.

Smith, van Ackere (2002) demonstrates an integration of SD and Econometric modelling. The study reviews an NHS problem of understand issues of supply and demand in elective surgery and how behaviour is affected by waiting times and the cost of private treatment. The paper describes how an SD model is developed based on the concepts of the econometric model. The study notes how the difference in approach provides a view of the problem which includes its previously unappreciated dynamic qualities.

Karnon (2003) compares an evaluation of a healthcare treatment using both Markov modelling and DES. Different characteristics of the methods are noted and an example is used to illustrate their different conceptualisation of patient pathways. The problem of evaluating adjunct therapy in the treatment of breast cancer is described. Two models are developed and compared. The conclusions of the paper remark on the differences in their flexibility and resource requirements of the two methods.

Brailsford & Lattimer et al. (2004) describe the analysis of capacity in emergency departments based on SD and DES models. The study describes the problems of resource allocation and capacity facing an emergency unit and explains the choice of SD and its benefits for the main modelling activity, the process and the findings of the study. The paper explains how a DES model was used to examine a particular feature of the problem in more detail which would not have been practical using SD alone.

Cooper & Brailsford et al. (2007) reviews three methods used in the economic evaluation of healthcare problems; DES, decision trees and Markov models. The different properties of the three approaches are described as well as criteria for choosing between them based on the properties of the problem. The study produces a flow chart describing a process for determining which method is most appropriate to a given problem.

Rohleder & Bischak et al. (2007) describes the use of DES in the design for the performance of several patient servicing centres. The study notes that despite the accuracy of the DES modelling on implementation the centres could not sustain the planned capacity. The paper demonstrates how a complementary SD study could have highlighted this issue from the outset.

CONSIDERING FUTURE CHALLENGES

As the use of modelling becomes more widespread in healthcare the potential to adopt a multi method approach increases. This section is concerned with some of the challenges for the successful use of multi method modelling in the future. As work in this area is ongoing it is not possible at this stage to present solutions, simply outline the obstacles to be overcome.

A fundamental challenge to multi method working is overcoming poor communication between subject specialists. Integrated views of modelling require an understanding of the principles and benefits of different approaches. Where this understanding is superficial the resulting studies may be poor and lack validity. This may be addressed though education and the development of guidelines for multi method teams that work to establish the necessary skills.

A key factor in the development of multi method modelling for healthcare applications is the awareness of good practice. It is a challenge to find an effective platform to communicate successes and failures of the approach to the modelling community. An important benefit of recording the practical experiences of applying these methods may be an appreciation of where they are best not applied. It is also a challenge therefore to establish the situations where multiple models can genuinely add value to a study rather than merely cost and complexity.

A practical challenge is the development of integrated tools that support multi method studies. Currently few tools exist which provide a common platform for the development and comparison of multi method models. Specialist tools currently offer superior ease of use in most cases. An important focus for multi method tools may be features for comparing the output of the different models and navigating the modelling structures, in particular mapping between equivalent structures in the different models.

Multi method modelling is occasionally presented as a revolutionary approach that will eventually unify other methods. It has also been proposed that a standard notation for unifying modelling systems may be developed. This position is very much in advance of current state of research and it is questionable whether such a development would either feasible or beneficial. As with all innovative methodological developments, it is a challenge not to inflate the potential benefits of the approach beyond those that can be supported in fact.

CONCLUSION

This chapter has examined the use of modelling to explore the issues that effect healthcare organisations. The application of modelling and simulation to organisational issues in healthcare is sometimes overlooked by healthcare informatics literature. An overview was provided of the role for modelling studies in healthcare and current developments shaping the practice. Some of the principles, applications and key approaches used were reviewed and number of studies and texts are referenced, providing examples of how modelling methods are used in healthcare. The emerging practice of multi method modelling was presented, including some examples of the approach in healthcare. Future challenges to exploit this new approach effectively were also presented.(Explain what went on and th e lessons learned)

The current interest of public health policy-makers in measuring performance and evaluating the effectiveness of healthcare processes makes the modelling of organisational issues increasingly relevant. As new projects are undertaken and healthcare models routinely commissioned, familiarity with modelling methods may become a core skill for healthcare managers and model processing a major use of informatics in healthcare. The realisation that the choice of model significantly influences the perspective on the problem is becoming established. Coiera (1997) recognises this to be a basic principle of healthcare informatics and as such devotes to the whole first chapter to basic concepts in models and modelling. As the use of modelling techniques becomes more common throughout healthcare organisations, the benefits of a multi method approach may increase in significance.

REFERENCES

Banks, J. (2001). *Discrete-event system simulation* (3rd Ed.). Upper Saddle River, NJ: Prentice Hall.

Borshchev, A., Karpov, Y., & Kharitonov, V. (2002). Distributed simulation of hybrid systems with AnyLogic and HLA. *Future Generation Computer Systems*, *18*(6), 829–839. doi:10.1016/S0167-739X(02)00055-9

Brailsford S. C., Churilov L. & Liew S-K., (2003). *Treating ailing emergency departments with simulation: an integrated perspective.*

Brailsford, S. C., Lattimer, V. A., Tarnaras, P., & Turnbull, J. C. (2004). Emergency and on-demand health care: modelling a large complex system. *The Journal of the Operational Research Society*, *55*(1), 34–42. doi:10.1057/palgrave.jors.2601667

Briggs, A., Claxton, K., & Sculpher, M. J. (2006). *Decision modelling methods for health economic evaluation*. Oxford: Oxford University Press.

Coiera, E. (1997). *Guide to medical informatics, the internet, and telemedicine.* New York: Chapman & Hall.

Conrick, M., Dunne, A. & Skinner, J., (1999). *Learning together: Using Simulation to foster the integration of theory and practice.*

Cooper, K., Brailsford, S. C., & Davies, R. (2007). Choice of modelling technique for evaluating health care interventions. *The Journal of the Operational Research Society*, *58*(2), 168–176.

Dangerfield, B. C. (1999). System dynamics applications to European health care issues. *The Journal of the Operational Research Society*, *50*(4), 345–353.

Davies, R., & Bensley, D. (2005). Editorial. *The Journal of the Operational Research Society*, *56*(2), 123. doi:10.1057/palgrave.jors.2601930

Eldabi, T., Paul, R. J., & Young, T. (2007). modelling in healthcare: reviewing legacies and investigating futures. *The Journal of the Operational Research Society*, *58*(2), 262–270.

Fone, D., Hollinghurst, S., Temple, M., Round, A., Lester, N., & Weightman, A. (2003). Systematic review of the use and value of computer simulation modelling in population health and health care delivery. *Journal of Public Health*, *25*(4), 325–335. doi:10.1093/pubmed/fdg075

Forrester, J. W. (1961). *Industrial dynamics*. Cambridge MA: M.I.T. Press.

Jun, J. B., Jacobson, S. H., & Swisher, J. R. (1999). Application of discrete-event simulation in health care clinics: A survey. *The Journal of the Operational Research Society*, *50*(2), 109–123.

Kanagarajah, A. K., Lindsey, P., Miller, A., & Parker, D. (2006). An explorarion into the uses of Agent-Based modeling to Improve Quality of Health Care. In Minai, A., Braha, D. and Bar-Yam, Y., *Proceedings of the 6th International Conference on Complex Systems. 6th International Conference on Complex Systems*, Boston, MA, (1-10). 25-30 June, 2006. Cambridge, MA: The New England Complex Systems Institute.

Karnon, J. (2003). Alternative decision modelling techniques for the evaluation of health care technologies: Markov processes versus discrete event simulation. *Health Economics, 12*(10), 837–848. doi:10.1002/hec.770

Lane, D. C., Monefeldt, C., & Rosenhead, J. V. (2000). Looking in the wrong place for healthcare improvements: A system dynamics study of an accident and emergency department. *The Journal of the Operational Research Society, 51*(5), 518–531.

Law, A. M., & Kelton, W. D. (2000). *Simulation Modelling and Analysis.* New York: McGraw Hill Higher Education.

Lorenz, T. & Jost, A., (2006). *Towards an orientation framework in multi-paradigm modeling.*

Meadows, D. H., & Robinson, J. (1985). *The electronic oracle: computer models and social decisions.* Chichester, UK: Wiley.

Morecroft, J. & Robinson, S., (2005). *Explaining puzzling dynamics: Comparing the use of system dynamics and discrete event simulation.*

Morris, S., Devlin, N. J., & Parkin, D. 2007. *Economic analysis in health care.* Hoboken, NJ: J. Wiley & Sons.

Paul, R. J., & Balmer, D. W. (1993). *Simulation modelling.* Bromley, UK: Chartwell-Bratt.

Rohleder, T., & Klassen, K. (2002). Rolling Horizon Appointment Scheduling: A Simulation Study. *Health Care Management Science, 5*(3), 201–209. doi:10.1023/A:1019748703353

Rohleder, T. R., Bischak, D. P., & Baskin, L. B. (2007). Modeling patient service centers with simulation and system dynamics. *Health Care Management Science, 10*(1), 1–12. doi:10.1007/s10729-006-9001-8

Schieritz, N. & Milling, P.M., (2003). *Modeling the Forest of Modeling the Trees: A comparison of System Dynamics and Agent-Based Simulation,* July 20-24.

Sheaff, R., & Peel, V. J. (1995). *Managing health service information systems: an introduction.* Buckingham, UK: Open University Press.

Smith, P. C., & Van Ackere, A. (2002). A note on the integration of system dynamics and economic models. *Journal of Economic Dynamics & Control, 26*(1), 1–10. doi:10.1016/S0165-1889(00)00025-7

Sterman, J. (2000). *Business dynamics: systems thinking and modeling for a complex world.* London: Irwin/McGraw-Hill.

The Royal Society, (2006). *Digital healthcare: the impact of information and communication technologies on health and healthcare.*

Van Bemmel, J. H., Musen, M. A., & Helder, J. C. (1997). *Handbook of medical informatics.* Heidelberg, Germany: Bohn Stafleu Van Loghum; Springer Verlag.

Young, T., Brailsford, S., Connell, C., Davies, R., Harper, P., & Klein, J. H. (2004). Using industrial processes to improve patient care. *British Medical Journal, 328*(7432), 162–164. doi:10.1136/bmj.328.7432.162

KEY TERMS AND DEFINITIONS

Agent Based Modelling: A simulation based modelling approach, where the problem is represented the using software entities with some degree of autonomy. The behaviour observed in the problem is recreated through the interaction of the entities, known as agents, which are typically modelled using data objects with encapsulated behaviour. Models may exhibit complex emergent behaviour even where the rules governing individual behaviour are relatively simple. They are sometimes considered to combine the analytical features of both system dynamics and discrete event modelling.

Discrete Event Simulation: A simulation based form of modelling in which patterns of events in the problem are recreated so that the timing and resource implications can be examined. The events generated usually include the arrival and departure of entities from the system or one of its sub processes. Timing and quantities in the model are typically generated by implementing appropriate stochastic distributions. Law & Kelton (2000) provides a comprehensive introduction to this form of modelling.

Econometric Modelling: A form of modelling based on the integration of statistical measurements of problem variables with economic theory. Models are based on empirical data collected from the problem and variables may be treated as deterministic or stochastic. A wide variety of statistical techniques are used to measure the quantities in the problem and assess their underlying distributions. These may be used to test hypotheses about the problem and make predictions about future behaviour or the likely effects of policy changes.

Multi Method Modelling: An emerging area in modelling methodology where techniques from different modelling disciples are combined inorder to analyse a single problem. The premise of this approach is that different methods have different features which can, in some cases, be used to support a more effective study. There is particular interest in applying this approach to healthcare problems because of the potential to extend existing model, integrate different stakeholder views and overcome technical limitations in some studies.

Modelling Resource Load: A concept used to compare the relative resource costs of modelling studies using different methods. For small scale studies the difference in resources required may be negligible, however in large studies this factor may be used to determine the most appropriate choice of modelling method. The differences in between methods in problem conceptualisation and model implementation determine the resources necessary to implement the model. In assessing the scale three key factors are relevant; the scope, or size of the problem; the required amount of detail per entity; the time scale considered by the study.

Markov Modelling: A form of modelling based on stochastic processes where the discrete states of a problem and the possible transitions between them are analysed. Systems represented as a network of states with paths between nodes weighted according to their probability of their occurrence. Paths and cycles in the system can be analysed mathematically to determine the likelihood of overall outcomes. The Markov property requires that the probability of transition between two states is dependant only on the current state and the problem must be formulated accordingly.

Organisational Modelling: Modelling undertaken to understand or analyse the effects of the structure, processes, and policies of an organisation. The role of organisational modelling is typically to understand complex observed behaviour, to prototype new policies and configurations or to document existing processes. In healthcare organisations such studies are increasingly used to investigate costs, patient flows and the utilisation of scarce resources. These studies may be contrasted with problems where organisational issues have negligible or no impact; in healthcare these may include anatomical and epidemiological modelling.

System Dynamics Modelling: A systems-oriented simulation based modelling approach first proposed in Forrester (1961). Models are based on the causal structure of the problem including the perceptions of the actors. Two levels of modelling are possible; Qualitative modelling using influence diagrams and causal loop analysis or quantitative modelling using Stock-Flow diagrams and computer simulation.

Chapter 13
Investigating Trust Relationships in a Healthcare Network[1]

Stefanie Kethers
Monash University, Australia

Günter Gans
RWTH Aachen University, Germany

Dominik Schmitz
Fraunhofer FIT, Germany

David Sier
CSIRO Mathematical and Information Sciences, Australia

ABSTRACT

Public hospitals currently face an ever increasing demand on their resources, and there are many attempts at streamlining processes and patient flows. However, in many cases, optimizing processes is not enough, as 'soft' factors such as the relationships between hospital wards influence how efficiently the resources needed to treat patients are utilized. These factors are often ignored when attempting to improve patient flows. In this chapter, the authors describe a case study investigating the relationships between an acute stroke ward and a specialist stroke rehabilitation ward of a large metropolitan health service. The motivation for this study was the hospital management's interest in improving communication and collaboration across wards as a means to optimize hospital processes, and thus, patient care. To assess the relationships between the two wards, the authors examined the patient handover process that links the wards' activities and applied the Trust-Confidence-Distrust (TCD) framework of Gans et al. (2003), which was developed to model trust relationships in social networks, to examine the trust relationships between the wards.

DOI: 10.4018/978-1-60566-030-1.ch013

INTRODUCTION

Public hospitals are under a lot of pressure to improve both their efficiency and service quality, and many hospitals have therefore been spending time and effort to optimize their processes. For example, Ramakrishnan et al. (2005) note that attempts to reduce the lengths of waiting lists for elective procedures and long stays in emergency departments often focus on policy setting, clinical process mapping, or capacity models of patient flows. However, perfectly well-designed processes can run less than smoothly if they fail to address the human side of patient movement through a hospital. In many cases 'soft' factors such as the relationships between hospital staff in different wards along a clinical pathway will determine how efficiently the resources needed to treat patients are utilized. In many situations these factors are ignored when attempting to improve patient flows.

In this paper, we describe the application of the Trust-Confidence-Distrust (TCD) framework defined by Gans et al. (2003) to the investigation of trust relationships between two hospital wards engaged in a patient handover process. This case study represents one of the first applications of the TCD framework to a real-life situation with real-life data. Given that the two wards were part of a large metropolitan health service which is more similar to an organization than to the social network described by Gans et al. (2003), we were particularly interested to see which aspects of the framework were still applicable, and which ones were not.

This paper is structured as follows: In the subsequent section, we outline the background of our study. Then, we briefly describe the TCD framework for analyzing trust relationships. Afterwards we give an overview of the case study we performed, including the setting. Having introduced the research methodology, especially the data capture process, we describe our analysis of the trust relationships using the TCD framework. Eventually, we evaluate the applicability of the TCD framework to the context of our case study and briefly sketch future trends.

BACKGROUND

In health informatics, clinical, organizational processes are mainly investigated in regard to how they can be supported or improved by information technology. Even though this is not the focus of our contribution, such analyses presuppose means to describe and model these processes. Due to the focus on information systems, typical process modelling notations such as event-driven process chains (Scheer, 1994), Petri net based workflow notations (van der Aalst and van Hee, 1996), or languages like the business process modelling notation BPMN (www.bpmn.org) are commonly used. In (Framinan et al., 2005) some have been investigated in the context of business process reengineering of clinical processes. They allow capturing the timely relation of activities and the assignment of resources and responsibilities of involved actors. Also Saboor et al. (2007) propose a method, named MedFlow, to support the systematic assessment of clinical processes focusing on the quality of information logistics. They derived relevant quality criteria from literature, developed an extended process modelling notation based on UML activity diagrams, and evaluated the method in a preliminary case study. Their analysis distinguishes four different process aspects, i.e. control flow, data flow, tool usage, and organizational information. For each of them, a rule-set that represents a "pattern of critical cross-points" was used, to detect weak points within these views. A shortcoming of these modelling means is that the human side of the process, the social interaction of the people that carry out these processes and for example, trust issues that are involved, are neglected. When trust is investigated in the context of health informatics, mostly three fields are considered: how to build up trust in online communities or health information on the web (Luo and Najdawi, 2004; Song and Zahedi, 2007), trust issues in the context of electronic health records (Smit et al., 2005), or regarding the physician-patient relationship.

Networked organizations in health care have already been explored by Peterson et al. (2000). They focused on the foundational constitution and enabling conditions. From their observations they derived that networks "develop through different phases of maturity and network-ability". While the study concerned IT as the enabler, they emphasized that IT is a facilitator but not the major driver for the direction and development of the network. "[It] is the organisation, its professionals and management that ultimately drive networking." Similarly when Avison and Young (2007) investigated the failures of ICT projects in the field of health care, they identified two main reasons: For one, health care should not be treated at an enterprise level but on a national scale. For another, they emphasized that "better person-to-person models are needed to understand how the collegiate and interpersonal elements of care delivery could be embodied better in the systems used for care delivery." Thus, while focussing IT support they again also emphasize the need to consider social interactions.

We thus agree with the views expressed by Avison and Young, and Peterson et al. and others, e.g. (Coiera, 2004): "Since health systems are sociotechnical systems, where outcomes emerge from the interaction of people and technologies, we cannot design organisational or technical systems independently of each other". Therefore, we have employed the Trust-Confidence-Distrust (TCD) framework, as described in the next section, to investigate the social interactions in the transfer of stroke patients from an acute ward to a rehabilitation ward. We have paid special attention to the perceptions that the people involved have of this process; in particular, how staff members of the two wards see the other ward's goals and priorities. As Wachter and Shojania (2004) state, "Psychologically, human beings simply communicate better and more often with people they know than with strangers—particularly if they feel those others are on the same team, have the same interests, and share the same goals".

The next section describes the Trust-Confidence-Distrust (TCD) framework in more detail.

THE TCD FRAMEWORK

The TCD framework was developed for application in a social network, which Gulati (1998) defines as "a set of nodes (e.g., persons, organizations) linked by a set of social relationships (e.g., friendship, transfer of funds, overlapping membership) of a specified type". Weyer (2000) expands on this idea by defining a social network as an autonomous form of coordination of interactions whose essence is the trusting cooperation of autonomous, but interdependent agents who cooperate for a limited time, considering their partners' interests, because they can thus fulfil their individual goals better than through non-coordinated activities. The "agents" in this definition can be organizations or people, or people representing, or working for organizations. According to Powell (1990), networks rely on reciprocal patterns of communication and exchange, and reciprocity and complementarity are essential for the success of a network: "In essence, the parties to a network agree to forego the right to pursue their own interest at the expense of others". As Powell (1990) states, networks are well suited for situations where there is "a need for efficient, reliable information."

In contrast to those of a network, Powell (1990) lists stability, reliability, and accountability as the main strengths of an organization (also called a hierarchy). In an organization, management defines work roles and administrative procedures. Work is often highly specialized and therefore interdependent. As Powell (1990) states, "relationships matter and previous interactions shape current ones, but the patterns and context of intraorganizational exchange are most strongly shaped by one's position within the formal hierarchical structure of authority". In an organization, there is less freedom of choice for the individual agents, as they are constrained by organizational rules and policies. Given that our case study took place in an organizational, rather than a network, environment (cf. next section), we were particularly interested to see whether the TCD framework was applicable to our setting.

In our investigation of trust, confidence, and distrust, we stay in accordance with the definitions given by Gans et al. (2003): We follow the definition of Mayer et al. (1995) of trust as "the willingness of a party to be vulnerable to the actions of another party based on the expectation that the other will perform a particular action important to the trustor, irrespective of the ability to monitor or control that other party". Trust thus occurs between two agents, the trustor and the trustee, and has an element of risk, since the trustor cannot ensure that the trustee will perform the action. In social networks, trust needs to be distinguished from what Gans et al. (2003) call confidence, and Luhmann (1988) calls system trust, in the network as a whole. This is because a network's mesh of dependencies is not completely visible to, let alone manageable by, the trustor. Thus, participation in a social network results in a double vulnerability: to identifiable opportunists, and to the generally incomprehensible mesh of dependencies between all the network partners. Participation in such a network therefore requires confidence in the network (e.g. its rules and stability) as a whole. The third relevant concept described by Gans et al. (2003) is distrust, which the authors distinguish from lack of trust; cf. also Lewicki et al. (1998). For example, a dissatisfied network member can cultivate, but hide her distrust while still exhibiting trustful behaviour. This means that the agent continues as a network member, postponing her decision for voicing dissatisfaction or exiting the network, but starts to collect information (which can be costly and time-consuming), by, for example, monitoring other network members' actions. The agent then typically interprets this information in a subjective way that is strongly influenced by her distrust. According to Luhmann (1988), distrust therefore has an inherent tendency to become stronger.

Gans et al. (2003) call the model describing the interplay of trust, confidence, and distrust, and its effects on the relationships within the network the TCD framework. Figure 1 shows how the TCD framework can be formalized as a multi-perspective framework based on formalisms taken from requirements engineering and computer science at large. By managing the static and dynamic interrelationships through reasoning and/or simulation, the possibly conflicting perspectives and viewpoints can be dealt with. The left side of Figure 1 depicts the intra-agent modelling aspects of the framework, that is, an agent's goals, which are represented by i* strategic rationale models described by Yu (1995), and plans. Plans are based on the strategic rationale diagrams together with pre- and post-conditions using the ConGolog formalism. ConGolog, described in De Giacomo et al. (2000), is a logic-based high-level planning language used in artificial intelligence approaches which is suitable for describing and representing processes. The right hand side of Figure 1 shows the inter-agent aspects, namely, the strategic dependencies between agents, represented as Yu's (1995) i* strategic dependency diagrams, and the implementation of these dependencies in delegation processes formalized as Speech Act diagrams (see Schäl (1996)). We prefer the i* formalism (strategic rationale (SR) and strategic dependency (SD) models) to other languages like UML, ER diagrams, or Petri nets, because it is explicitly designed to cope with strategic goals and agents' intentions, and furthermore is equipped with formal semantics. Thus, as a main feature, it allows not only to reason about the "how" but also about the "why" of different alternatives. The solid lines in Figure 1 indicate the nature of the interrelationships between these different perspectives. For

Figure 1. Interplay between modelling perspectives

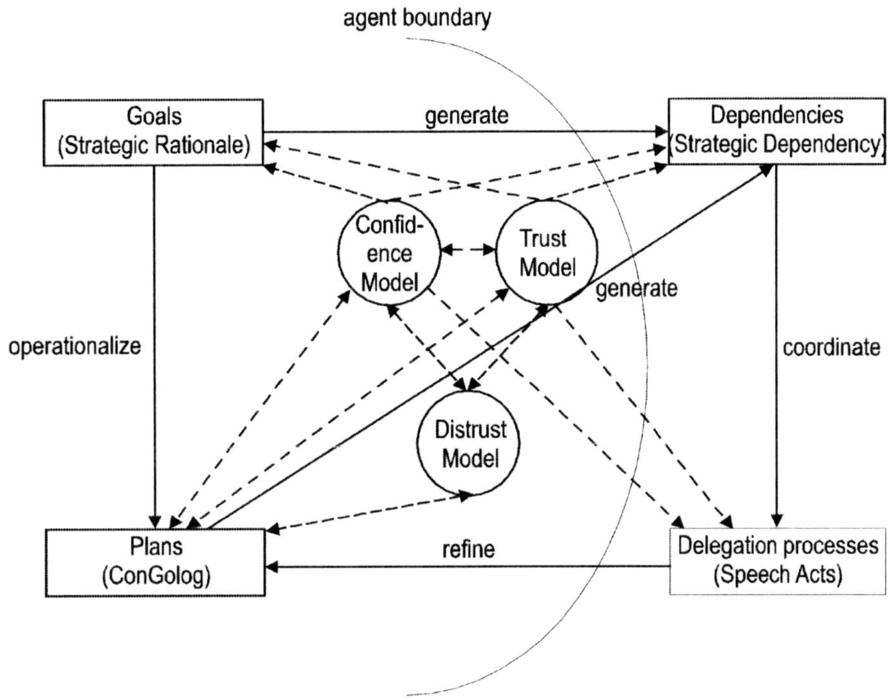

example, strategic dependencies shape and lead to delegation patterns, and the latter are evaluated partially with respect to the former. Conversely, strategic goals lead to operational plans, which then potentially generate strategic dependencies on other agents. Trust, confidence, and distrust, depicted in the middle part of the figure, influence the four main components of the framework, as well as each other (represented as broken lines). For example, the level of trust between agents will influence one agent's propensity to become dependent on the other, say for specific tasks or resources, and the level of distrust can lead to the addition of monitoring tasks to the operational plans. These monitoring tasks may increase or decrease the level of distrust felt by the agent.

While trust has been studied in the social sciences for many years, its formalization from a computational point of view has not been studied for very long. Some approaches like us, view trust as a subjective probability or provide logical approaches to modelling trust. None of the approaches in the literature seem to give distrust a special status. In (Gambetta, 1988), the prevalent view of trust is that of a subjective probability, which, roughly, amounts to the likelihood (assigned by the trusting agent) that another agent will perform a task or bring about a desired situation on which the trusting agent depends. Other work along this line includes (Coleman, 1990; Marsh, 1994; Witkowski et al., 2000). Game-theoretic approaches analyze trust using the iterated Prisoner's Dilemma as a benchmark (Axelrod, 1984; Boon and Holmes, 1991). Castelfranchi and Falcone (1999; 2001) propose a more fine-grained model. It takes into account the agent's mental attitudes such as the trusting agent's beliefs about the trustee's opportunity, ability, and willingness to perform a desired task. A quantitative measure of trust has the advantage that it lends itself nicely to computing a decision whether to delegate a task to a trustee or to update the level of trust depending on the outcome of an interaction with the trustee. Gans et al.'s method for modelling trust is also different from Yu and Liu (2001)'s approach to describe trust relationships in i*. Yu and Liu (2001) propose a purely qualitative approach using softgoals with corresponding contributions.

THE CASE STUDY: TRANSFER OF STROKE PATIENTS BETWEEN WARDS

The goal of this case study was to investigate trust relationships between wards along a clinical pathway with the aid of the TCD framework described in the previous section. The study was commissioned by Southern Health, a large metropolitan health service in South Eastern Melbourne, Victoria, Australia. Southern Health provides public hospital services, aged inpatient, community and home care services, and inpatient and community mental health services across an area in excess of 2,800 square kilometres with a population of over 700,000 people (see http://www.southernhealth.org.au/). Southern Health services are provided through five major hospitals and nine community health services centres. Two clinical services directors together with operations directors at each location manage the different services. Each director reports to the chief executive, who reports in turn to the hospital board. Thus, Southern Health can be classified as a (distributed) organization rather than a network of independent partners. Our study involved the investigation of stroke patient transfers between an acute ward and a rehabilitation ward located on different sites. A mix of medical and allied health staff are involved in the transfers. These people report to different program managers, although ultimately the management responsibility for both the acute and sub-acute patients lies with the head of the Neurology program.

Stroke is the third highest cause of death, and the leading cause of chronic disability in adults in Australia (see Pollack and Disler (2002)). In our investigation we focused on the handover process of stroke patients from the acute ward (AW) to a specialized rehabilitation unit (RW). This unit is the major stroke rehabilitation facility. Stroke patient rehabilitation is a scarce resource needing a coordinated, multi-disciplinary team approach (Pollack and Disler (2002) give an overview of the different roles and stakeholders in stroke patient rehabilitation), so there is a significant amount of cooperation required within a ward, and between wards such as AW and RW. AW and RW are physically located in two different hospitals, separated by a 30-minute drive. Patel et al. (2000) claim that, given that face-to-face communication is an important part of developing and maintaining a shared understanding of team goals and maintaining trust, geographical separation is a potential obstacle to implementing good team processes. Consequently, we were interested in finding out whether the two wards managed to see each other as a team working together towards the shared goal of caring for the patient, or whether there were significant misconceptions about the other ward's work. As Suchman (1995) notes, "work has a tendency to disappear at a distance, such that the further removed we are from the work of others, the more simplified, often stereotyped, our view of their work becomes" (see also Wachter and Shojania (2004)).

Because our focus was on the trust, confidence, and distrust relationships between wards AW and RW, we wanted to capture the stakeholders' perceptions of the handover process. In this context, the stakeholders are the wards; specifically, the health professionals in the acute ward who prepare patients for discharge to the sub-acute area and those in the rehabilitation ward who carry out the patient admission procedures. Stakeholder perceptions are an important indicator of the performance of the transfer processes; in particular, the perceptions in one ward can identify failures in the process not evident to the other ward.

RESEARCH METHODOLOGY

To collect the required information, we followed the Co-MAP method described by Kethers (2002) to obtain the process information for the "a priori goal and capability analysis" postulated by Gans et al. (2003). The main advantage of this method is the strong semantic model underlying the captured data, which allows formal mapping of the data into different perspectives on the investigated process. After an initial meeting with the Nursing Director and members of the Allied Health Rehabilitation and Aged Services Program, we conducted two focus group meetings, each with a team from one ward, to capture that ward's view[2] of the interactions within the ward and with external units, including the other ward. In these meetings, the group developed informal process diagrams (see Figure 2 for an example) that focus on the interactions and information flows within and between the two wards. Information flows between agents are captured as arrows between ovals representing sender and receiver of the information. Graphical symbols are used to represent the media for information flows (for example, phone, formal document, or meeting), and the recipient's perception of the quality of the information flow (e.g., a tortoise for "too slow", or a stop sign for "does not occur at all"). A more detailed description of the different graphical symbols is given by Kethers (2002). During one of the focus group meetings, we became aware of the role of the Rehabilitation Liaison Officer (RLO) who acts as an interface between the wards, so we conducted an additional interview with her.

Based on the informal process diagrams, meeting notes, and additional information collected, we developed the different perspectives on the process shown in Figure 1. As a first step, we developed two strategic dependency (SD) models (see Yu (1995)), one for each ward's perspective concerning the patient transfer process. In a second step we refined our models to strategic rationale (SR) models in order to regard the actors' internal actions as well as their interactions. To identify trust, confidence, and distrust issues in a third step, we then analyzed the different diagrams by regarding the different stakeholders' (the two wards' and the RLO's) perceptions of the process, identifying conflicting views of what is really happening in the scenario, tracking the effects on trust relationships between the wards, and recognizing the effects of these relationships on the process.

APPLICATION OF THE TCD FRAMEWORK

The SD model (a detailed description is given in Yu (1995)) describes the network of relationships among agents (nodes) by specifying dependencies (links) between them. A dependency relationship enables the depender to do things that she would otherwise not be able to, but also makes her vulnerable if the dependee does not fulfil the dependencies. The model offers four dependency types: goal, task, resource, and softgoal dependencies, which differ according to the degree of freedom they leave for the dependee.

The SD models shown in Figure 3 are structured as follows: The circles show the two wards, the arcs show what one ward wants or needs from the other ward. The direction of the 'D's on an arc shows the direction of a dependency. For example, the lowermost arc in the left half of Figure 3 (RW's view) shows that RW depends on AW for a "quick reaction if a patient is unwell". Rectangles represent a resource, such as a piece of information, for example "Feedback about patient" as shown in Figure 3 (AW's view). Boxes with rounded edges represent goals that can be measured, for example in Figure 3 (RW's view), the need expressed by RW for "one contact person for each discipline" at AW. The irregular shapes represent so-called "soft goals" – goals that are subjective and cannot be precisely measured, for example RW's requirement for a "quick reaction

Figure 2. Informal process diagram

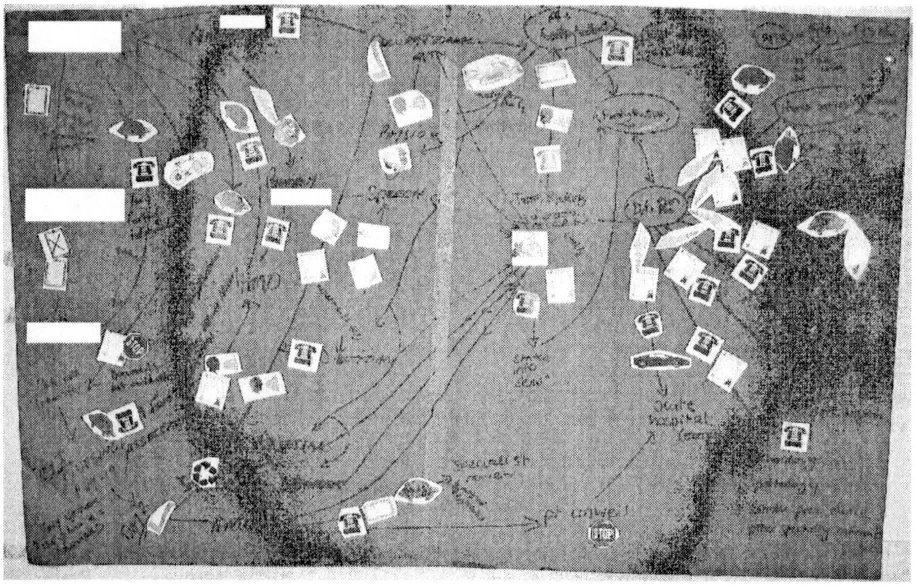

if patient unwell" from AW. In this case, does 'quick' mean 5 minutes or 2 hours?

The SD models show that each ward attributes different and sometimes very stereotyped goals and intentions to the other, even though the main goal for both wards should be (and is!) the welfare of the patient. As an example taken from Figure 3, for the patient transfer process, RW sees AW as trying to move patients out as fast as possible (RW's view, softgoal: "Transfer patients at short notice"), whereas AW sees RW as expecting patients to be handed over at very short notice (AW's view softgoal: "Patient delivery at short notice"); sometimes, we were told, in as little as three hours. Because the discharge documentation that has to accompany the patient has to be compiled by different staff members, by the pharmacy, etc., this extreme time pressure can lead to a lack of coordination in the collection of discharge documents. As a result, incomplete or outdated information can be transmitted from the acute to the rehabilitation ward, which is not what RW expects or wants (RW's view, resource: "Complete / correct / up-to-date patient & assessment info").

Based on the dependency diagrams, and the additional information obtained in the focus group meetings and interviews, we developed extended SR models as described by Gans et al. (2003) for AW, RW, and the RLO. SR diagrams (see Yu (1995)) describe the intentional relationships that are internal to actors, so that they can be reasoned about. Nodes of the model represent goals, tasks, resources, and softgoals, respectively, while links represent either means-ends links, or task decomposition links. The original SR models contain only strategically relevant elements; hence, Gans et al. extended them for operational use. For example, in Figure 4, the task "Transfer patient" is decomposed into five subtasks which are timely ordered. Negation dots, e.g., at the resource "Correct, complete information", stand for a missing resource or the logical negation of a precondition, goal, or softgoal. Contribution links are labelled according to their effects on softgoals (make, break, help, hurt) and finally only if the "Deadline reached" precondition holds the "Transfer patient" task can be initiated.

Relevant excerpts from the three different views of the patient transfer process as held by

Figure 3. Strategic dependency diagrams

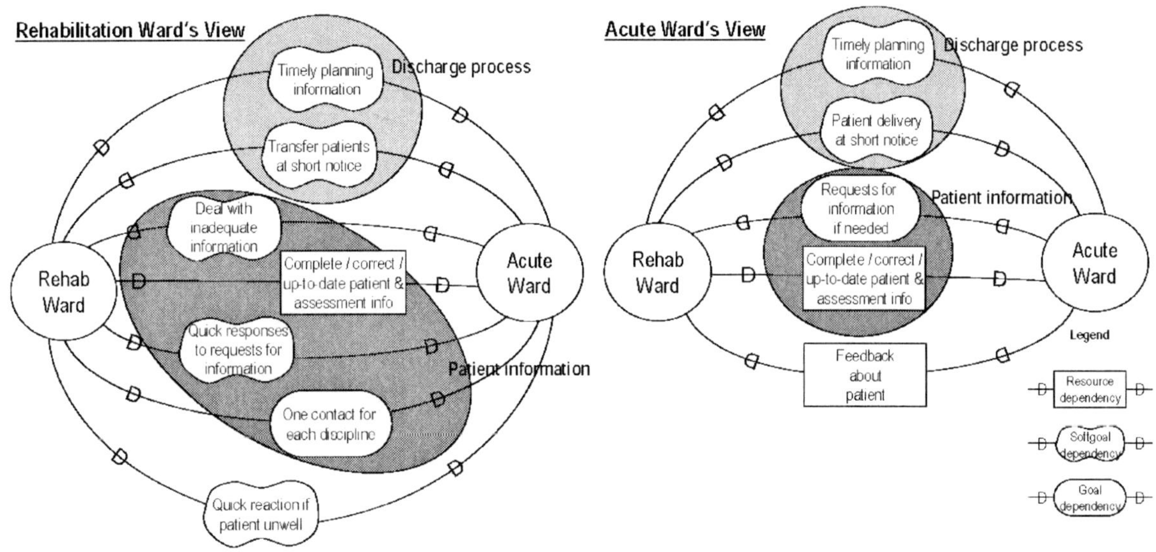

AW, RW, and the RLO, respectively, are integrated into a combined SR model shown in Figure 4. Interestingly, as can be seen in Figure 4 and was stated by the RLO in the interview, AW should know in advance which patients will need to be handed over within the next few days, since a list of those patients is faxed to the wards. Thus, AW should be able to compile the discharge documentation with sufficient prior warning. In addition, the patients' complete medical record is sent, together with the discharge documents, to the rehabilitation hospital's administration, where it would be available to RW staff for a few days before admission. Also, given that the rehabilitation hospital administration receives the list of patients, RW does – at least in theory – have access to timely planning information, as well. Unfortunately, however, neither AW nor RW seem to be able to make use of this information.

The conflicts which were identified on the strategic dependency and strategic rationale diagram level, of course, affect the trust relationships. First of all, the models reveal that there was little direct and positive interaction between AW and RW, and there were no trust-building or relationship-building activities planned into the process. Information flowed from AW to RW, but there was almost no information flowing back from RW to AW. In particular, although AW mentioned that they would like to hear about "their" patients' progress in the rehabilitation ward (see the "Feedback about patient" resource dependency in Figure 3), there is no communication of patient status information from RW to AW unless something untoward happens to the patient, when RW expects (and gets) a quick reaction from AW. This is not conducive to establishing trustful relationships between the wards. In contrast to this, the physical proximity of team members within each ward (including, in the case of AW, the location of the RLO in the same building) leads to good relationships, trust, and understanding, resulting in extremely good (ad-hoc) communication and cooperation.

A main source of distrust in the patient transfer process results from the accompanying patient information documents. There are conflicting ideas about who is actually responsible for ensuring that the patient information is complete (cf. Figure 3). RW staff members consider it their right to receive

Figure 4. Combined extended SR mode: Patient transfer between wards

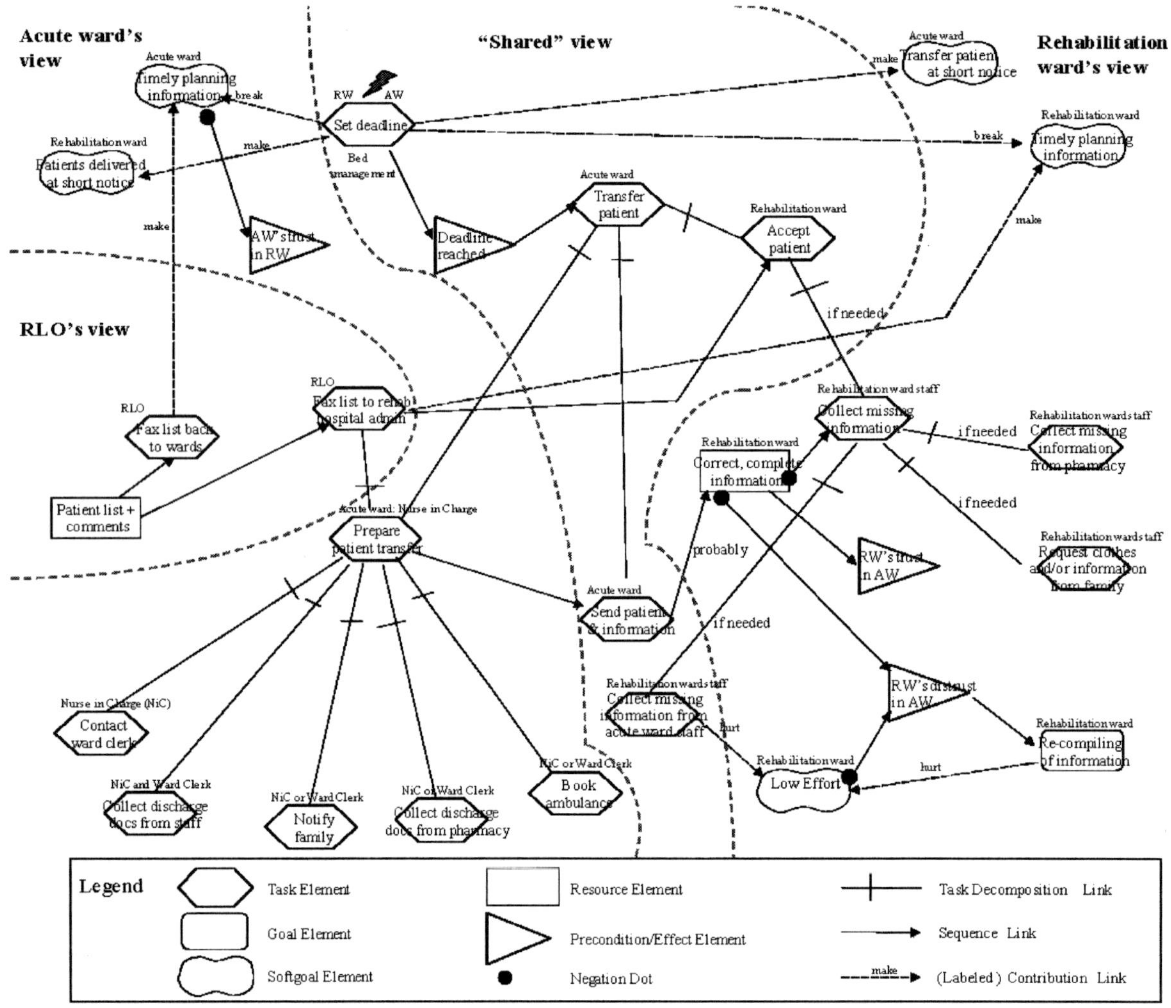

complete, correct, and up-to-date information; and chasing up what is missing takes up a large amount of time, which is seen as frustrating. AW on the other hand holds the opinion that RW receives as much information as is possible under the circumstances (remember that AW sees RW as driving the timeframes for the transfer process). Thus, RW staff should be able to cope with the information they receive, and, if not, it is their responsibility to request additional information that is required. This difference in expectations creates resentment and increases distrust on both sides. For RW, this distrust means that the information coming from AW is often not trusted, even when apparently correct patient information is provided. Instead, RW duplicates AW's work by compiling the information again. As another example, consider the extended SR model of the patient assessment shown in Figure 5. The assessment of a patient is performed by RLO and a rehabilitation physician, who visit the patient on the acute ward. The outcome of that assessment determines whether the patient is send to a rehabilitation ward. RW sometimes considers some of the patients that AW sends them unsuitable. However, RW does not seem to discuss these cases with AW, and has

Figure 5. Combined extended SR model: Patient assessment

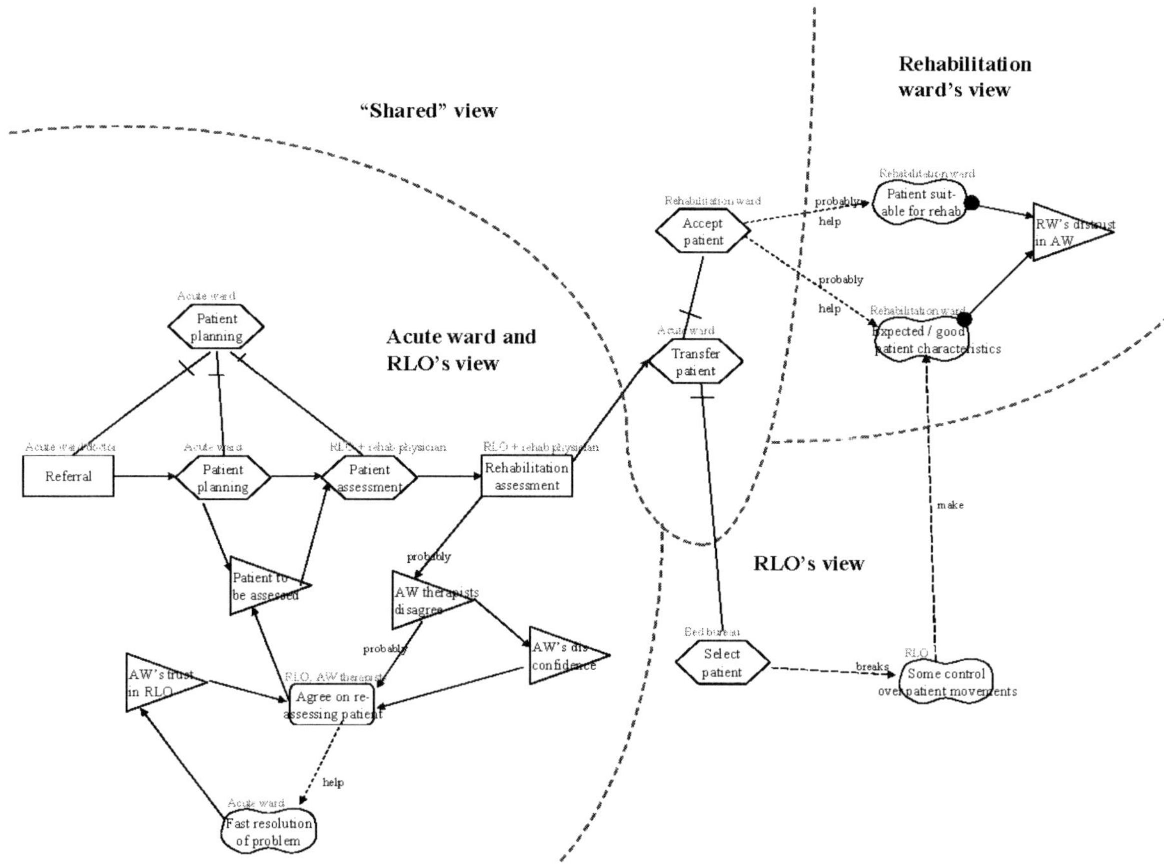

no direct access to the RLO, who is located in AW's hospital. In fact, RW staff did not mention the RLO at all during the focus group meeting. Instead, RW can get frustrated at seemingly unsuitable patients being sent from AW, and RW's distrust in AW increases.

Confidence is a less important issue here, because the metropolitan health service is a stable organization with less choice for the agents involved, and more rules and constraints than the social networks described by Gans et al. (2003). However, due to dis-confidence, by which we mean dissatisfaction with these rules and constraints, agents sometimes circumvent those rules and processes that are seen as producing the wrong results. In the patient assessment example (see Figure 5), AW therapists sometimes disagree with the patient assessment results. The therapists feel that they know the patient better, due to their long-term observation, than a doctor could from a short visit, especially if the patient has a bad day. In these cases, the therapists often use the strong relationship they have with the RLO to voice their concerns and initiate a reassessment at short notice (see the bottom left corner of Figure 5), which is not intended to happen in the clinical process. As described above, RW does not have that option.

EVALUATION AND CONCLUSION

In this evaluation of the applicability of the TCD modelling approach, we applied the framework in a more organizational setting than described by Gans et al. (2003). This means that there are more rules, constraints, and procedures than in a typical social network. This in turn leads to less freedom for the agents (individuals or wards) to change their work processes, for example by changing their delegation behaviour, according to their level of trust, confidence, or distrust in the other agents. In addition, the delegation processes were predetermined due to lack of alternatives, as well, so they did not provide many insights, either. From this it follows that we do not need to apply the more dynamic perspectives from the TCD framework, namely plans and speech acts. In this case study, SD and extended SR diagrams are sufficient to extract information on the trust relationships between the wards.

The data capture method we employed focused on recording the different parties' perceptions of the patient handover process, which we later found very useful in understanding the trust and distrust relationships between the people involved. The information flow diagrams (Figure 2) indicated not just the different agents' activities, but also, for example, where information was perceived as being too late, or of too low quality. The SD and SR diagrams (Figure 3, Figure 4, and Figure 5) resulting from the initial process diagrams, together with our meeting notes, indicated (real and perceived) conflicting goals and expectations that were not met. These lead to manifestations of distrust, which in turn lead to re-work, e.g. recompilation of information by RW, and dis-confidence, e.g. when AW staff exploit their good relationship with the RLO to circumvent the defined patient assessment process. Thus, generally, we found the TCD framework to be applicable also in this more organizational setting.

We believe that understanding and evaluating trust relationships is crucial to supporting people's work processes, and that, ultimately, any ICT aimed at improving the performance of people working together will need to take such 'soft factors' into account to be truly effective. While many aspects of this problem are still open research questions, we hope that our case study has provided some validation of the TCD framework as one methodology for investigating trust relationships in both organizational and network settings preceding, and complementing, the development of any ICT support.

FUTURE TRENDS

An integration of the findings of research on trust, distrust, and confidence in cooperation processes – as it has been presented here – into environments for computer-supported cooperative work (CSCW), such as shared workspaces (e. g. see BSCW (http://www.bscw.de)), seems a logical next step. A key point in this regard concerns addressing awareness issues (Dourish and Bellotti, 1992). Recent approaches try to tailor the awareness notifications to the current, situation-dependent needs of each collaborator (Wang et al., 2007). This fits quite well with the consideration of monitoring within the TCD framework. Gans (to appear) describes a framework of monitoring in social networks that is mainly controlled by distrust and dis-confidence. He states that discrepancies between expectations on one hand and objective as well as subjective experiences on the other hand combined with current distrust and dis-confidence steer the wish to monitor or observe ongoing activities or processes. Comparing this wish to monitor with the costs of monitoring, it leads to real monitoring activities by gathering information that are beyond the usual information flow. The new information firstly is added to the experiences made in this context, secondly influences distrust and dis-confidence, and thirdly leads to activities, for example activities that should change misleading processes.

Hence, in distrust and dis-confidence related parts of our health care domain (for example, the patient transfer) it could be interesting to ask questions of the following kind: How important could it be to observe the activities between AW and RLO? How costly is monitoring in this context and therefore how efficiency-reducing? Which conclusions can be drawn by RW besides the cultivation of distrust and dis-confidence, for instance, to what extent can RW influence, and therefore improve, the patient transfer process? Is the level of distrust or dis-confidence already above a certain threshold where self-strengthening effects take place? Here, the more dynamic parts of the TCD methodology could also provide viable input.

Furthermore, social network analysis is recently gaining more and more attention. Westbrook et al. (2007) use it as a means to understand how the impact of information and communication technologies in health care organizations can be investigated. Ongoing work tries to integrate social network analysis with the i* modelling language and the TCD approach in particular (Jarke et al., 2008). Of particular interest are the extensions that are able to take the dynamics of evolving relationships into account. First approaches (Klamma et al., 2006) that match expectations in regard to emerging structures modelled with i* with the outcome of social network analyses via a suitable pattern language already exist, but have not yet been applied to a health care setting.

REFERENCES

Avison, D., & Young, T. (2007). Time to Rethink Health Care and ICT? *Communications of the ACM, 50*(6), 69–74. doi:10.1145/1247001.1247008

Axelrod, R. (1984). *The Evolution of Cooperation*, New York: Basic Books.

Boon, S. D., & Holmes, J. G. (1991). The dynamics of interpersonal trust: resolving uncertainty in the face of risk. In: Hinde, R.A., & Groebel, J. (eds.), *Cooperation and Prosocial Behaviour*, (pp. 190-211). Cambridge, UK: Cambridge University Press.

Castelfranchi, C., & Falcone, R. (1999). *Social Trust: A Cognitive Approach.* Presentation at the International Workshop on Agent-Oriented Information Systems, CAiSE 1999, Heidelberg. Retrieved from http://www.aois.org/99/ castelfranchi-Social-Trust-paper.doc

Castelfranchi, C., & Falcone, R. (2001). Social Trust: A Cognitive Approach. In Castelfranchi, C., & Tan, Y.-H. (Eds.), *Trust and Deception in Virtual Societies* (pp. 55-90). Norwell, MA; Kluwer Academic Publisher.

Coiera, E. (2004). Four rules for the reinvention of healthcare . *BMJ (Clinical Research Ed.), 328*, 1197–1199. doi:10.1136/bmj.328.7449.1197

Coleman, J. S. (1990). *Foundations of Social Theory*. Cambridge MA: Harvard University Press.

De Giacomo, G., Lespérance, Y., & Levesque, H. J. (2000). ConGolog, a concurrent programming language based on the situation calculus. *Artificial Intelligence, 121*(1-2), 109–169. doi:10.1016/ S0004-3702(00)00031-X

Dourish, P., & Bellotti, V. (1992). Awareness and Coordination in Shared Workspaces. *ACM Conference on Computer Supported Cooperative Work*, New York, NY, (pp. 107-114).

Framinan, J. M., Parra, C. L., Perez, P., & Montes, M. (2005). Guidelines for conducting Business Process Modelling as support to healthcare process management. In *Int. Conf. on Industrial Engineering and Systems Management (ISEM)*.

Gambetta, D. (Ed.). (1988). *Trust: making and breaking cooperative relations*. Oxford, UK: Department of Sociology, University of Oxford.

Gans, G. (n.d.). *An Agent-Based Modeling- and Simulation-Methodology for Strategic Inter-Organizational Networks*. Ph.D. Thesis, RWTH Aachen University, Germany.

Gans, G., Jarke, M., Kethers, S., & Lakemeyer, G. (2003). Continuous requirements management for organisation networks: a (dis)trust-based approach. *Requirements Engineering*, *8*(1), 4–22. doi:10.1007/s00766-002-0163-8

Gulati, R. (1998). Alliances and networks. *Strategic Management Journal*, *19*(4), 293–317. doi:10.1002/(SICI)1097-0266(199804)19:4<293::AID-SMJ982>3.0.CO;2-M

Jarke, M., Klamma, R., Lakemeyer, G., & Schmitz, D. (2008). Continuous, Requirements-Driven Support for Organizations, Networks, and Communities. In *3rd Int. i* Workshop*, CEUR Workshop Proceedings (Vol. 322, pp. 47-50).

Kethers, S. (2000). *Multi-Perspective Modeling and Analysis of Cooperation Processes*. Ph.D. Thesis, RWTH Aachen University, Germany.

Kethers, S. (2002). Capturing, Formalising, and Analysing Cooperation Processes: a Case Study. *10th European Conf. on Information Systems (ECIS)*, Gdańsk, Poland, (pp. 1113-1123).

Kethers, S., Gans, G., Schmitz, D., & Sier, D. (2005). Modelling Trust Relationships in a Healthcare Network: Experiences with the TCD Framework. *13th European Conf. on Information Systems (ECIS)*, Regensburg, Germany, (pp. 1321-1328).

Klamma, R., Spaniol, M., Cao, Y., & Jarke, M. (2006). Pattern-based cross media social network analysis for technology enhanced learning in Europe. *Innovative Approaches for Learning and Knowledge Sharing, First European Conference on Technology Enhanced Learning (EC-TEL)*, Crete, Greece, Springer, LNCS 4227, (pp. 242–256).

Lewicki, R. J., McAllister, D. J., & Bies, R. J. (1998). Trust and distrust: New relationships and realities. *Academy of Management Review*, *23*(3), 438–458. doi:10.2307/259288

Luhmann, N. (1988). Familiarity, confidence, trust: problems and alternatives. In Gambetta, D. (Ed.), *Trust: Making and Breaking Cooperative Relations*, (pp. 94-107). Oxford.

Luo, W., & Najdawi, M. (2004). Trust-building measures: a review of consumer health portals. *Communications of the ACM*, *47*(1), 108–113. doi:10.1145/962081.962089

Marsh, S. (1994). Trust in Distributed Artificial Intelligence. In Castelfranchi, C. & Werner, E. (Eds.), *Artificial Social Systems*, (pp. 94-112). Berlin: Springer.

Mayer, R. C., Davis, J. H., & Schoorman, F. D. (1995). An integrative model of organizational trust. *Academy of Management Review*, *20*(3), 709–734. doi:10.2307/258792

Patel, V. L., Cytryn, K. N., Shortliffe, E. H., & Safran, C. (2000): The Collaborative Health Care Team: The Role of Individual and Group Expertise. *Stanford Medical Informatics Report* (No SMI-1999-0768). Retrieved from http://smi-web.stanford.edu/pubs/SMI_Abstracts/SMI-1999-0768.html

Peterson, R. R., Smits, M., & Spanjers, R. (2000). Exploring IT-Enabled Networked Organisations in Health Care: Emerging Practices and Phases of Development. *8th European Conf. on Information Systems (ECIS)*, Vienna, Austria, (pp. 1253-1260).

Pollack, M. R. P., & Disler, P. B. (2002). Rehabilitation of patients after stroke. *The Medical Journal of Australia*, *177*(8), 452–456.

Powell, W. (1990). Neither Market Nor Hierarchy: Network Forms of Organization. *Research in Organizational Behavior*, *12*, 295–336.

Ramakrishnan, M., Sier, D., & Taylor, P. G. (2005). A two-time-scale model for hospital patient flow. *IMA Journal of Management Mathematics*, *16*, 197–215. doi:10.1093/imaman/dpi014

Saboor, S., Chimiak-Opoka, J., & Ammenwerth, E. (2007). Supporting the Systematic Assessment of Clinical Processes: the MedFlow Method. *Methods of Information in Medicine*, *46*(5), 586–594.

Schäl, T. (1996). *Workflow Management Systems for Process Organisations*, (2nd Ed.) (LNCS 1096). Berlin: Springer Verlag.

Scheer, A.-W. (1994). *Business Process Engineering – Reference Models for Industrial Companies* (2nd Ed.). Berlin: Springer Verlag.

Smit, M., McAllister, M., & Slonim, J. (2005). Public Trust and Electronic Health Records. *Conf. on Privacy, Security and Trust (PST)*.

Song, J., & Zahedi, F. (2007). Trust in health infomediaries. *Decision Support Systems*, *43*(2), 390–407. doi:10.1016/j.dss.2006.11.011

Suchman, L. (1995). Making work visible. *Communications of the ACM*, *38*(9), 56–65. doi:10.1145/223248.223263

van der Aalst, W. M. P., & van Hee, K. M. (1996). Business process redesign: A Petri-net-based approach. *Computers in Industry*, *29*(1–2), 15–26. doi:10.1016/0166-3615(95)00051-8

Wachter, R. M., & Shojania, K. (2004). Handoffs and Fumbles. In Wachter, R. & Shojania, K. (Eds.), *Internal Bleeding: The Truth Behind America's Terrifying Epidemic of Medical Mistakes*. New York: Rugged Land, LLC.

Wang, Y., Gräther, W., & Prinz, W. (2007). *Suitable notification intensity: the dynamic awareness system.* ACM SIGGROUP Conference on Supporting Group Work (GROUP), Sanibel Island, Florida, USA, November 4-7, pp. 99-106.

Westbrook, J. I., Braithwaite, J., Georgiou, A., Ampt, A., Creswick, N., Coiera, E., & Iedema, R. (2007). Multimethod Evaluation of Information and Communication Technologies in Health in the Context of Wicked Problems and Sociotechnical Theory. *Journal of the American Medical Informatics Association*, *14*(6), 746–755. doi:10.1197/jamia.M2462

Weyer, J. (Ed.). (2000). *Soziale Netzwerke. Konzepte und Methoden der sozialwissenschaftlichen Netzwerkforschung*. München/Wien, Germany: Oldenbourg.

Witkowski, M., Artikis, A., & Pitt, J. (2000). Trust and Cooperation in a Trading Society of Objective-Trust Based Agents. In Falcone, R., Singh, M., & Tan, Y.H. (Eds.), *Autonomous Agents Workshop on Deception, Fraud and Trust in Agent Societies*. Barcelona, Spain.

Yu, E. S. K. (1995). *Modeling Strategic Relationships for Process Reengineering* (Tech. Rep. No. DKBS-TR-94-6). Ph.D. Thesis, University of Toronto, Canada. Yu, E. S. K., & Liu, L. (2001). Modelling trust for system design using the i* strategic actors framework. In Falcone, R., Singh, M., & Tan, Y. H. (Eds.). *Trust in Cyber-Societies. Integrating the Human and Artificial Perspectives* (LNAI 2246, pp. 175-194). Berlin, Germany: Springer Verlag.

KEY TERMS AND DEFINITIONS

Confidence (also system trust): Trust in the network/organization as a whole that is due to the mesh of dependencies neither completely visible nor manageable by the trustor. (Luhmann, 1988)

Cooperation: Cooperation denotes the relationships between two or more organizations or parts thereof, which aim at fulfilling some shared goal, are based on written or oral (legal) agreements, and keep the partners legally independent. (Kethers, 2000)

Distrust: "The expectation of opportunistic behaviour from partners" (Gans et al., 2003)

Process: A process is a set of identifiable, repeatable actions which contribute to the fulfilment of the objective (or goal) for which the process was designed. Actions are in some way ordered, performed by actors, and possibly subject to limitations or constraints. Actions can be activities (tasks), or be related to information flows or communication. (Kethers, 2000)

Social network: An autonomous form of coordination of interactions whose essence is the trusting cooperation of autonomous, but interdependent agents who cooperate for a limited time, considering their partners' interests, because they can thus fulfil their individual goals better than through non-coordinated activities. (Weyer, 2000)

Strategic Dependency model: "The Strategic Dependency (SD) model provides an intentional description of a process in terms of a network of dependency relationships among actors. [...] [It] consists of a set of nodes and links. Each node represents an "actor", and each link between two actors indicates that one actor depends on the other for something in order that the former may attain some goal." (Yu, 1995)

Strategic Rationale model: "The Strategic Rationale (SR) model provides an intentional description of processes in terms of process elements and the rationales behind them. [...] [It] describes the intentional relationships that are "internal" to actors, such as means-ends relationships that relate process elements, providing explicit representations of "why" and "how" and alternatives." (Yu, 1995)

Trust: "The willingness of a party to be vulnerable to the actions of another party based on the expectation that the other will perform a particular action important to the trustor, irrespective of the ability to monitor or control that other party." (Mayer and van der Hoek, 1995)

ENDNOTES

1 An earlier version of this paper was published in (Kethers et al., 2005).

2 Note that the ward's view expressed in the process diagrams is not a given, but evolves as the result of much discussion during the focus group meeting, as different staff members discuss their different views of what is happening.

Chapter 14
Resource Alignment of ICT in Taiwanese Small Dialysis Centers

Yu-An Huang
National Chi Nan University, Taiwan

Chad Lin
Curtin University of Technology, Australia

ABSTRACT

The literature on cooperative alliances has been criticized for its relatively narrow concentration on large firms and for ignoring small and medium-sized enterprises (SME) alliances where large firms do not operate in similar ways. Due to their size SMEs are more likely to seek external expertise. For small dialysis centers, they often form alliances to obtain these scarce resources. Unlike large firms which own a lot of slack resources to be able to form alliances with many partners, these small dialysis centers tend to form alliances with only a small number of partners and therefore, their dependence on these partners is higher than large firms. Hence, we conducted case study to investigate the use of complementary and supplementary information communication technology (ICT) resources among several small healthcare centers in Taiwan and evaluated how different types of resource alignment affect the performances of alliances. One contribution of the chapter is that the contribution of dissimilar ICT resources by both the focal and partner firms has a significant positive impact on alliance sustainable commitment. The results also reveal that there is a positive relationship between the contribution of dissimilar ICT resources by the partner firms and alliance performance. However, the contribution of dissimilar ICT resources alone by the focal dialysis centers has no significant impact on alliance performance.

INTRODUCTION

Many smaller dialysis centers are turning to cooperative alliances as a strategy to confront a competitive environment that is characterized by blurring industry boundaries, fast-changing technologies, and global integration. According to Lambe et al. (2002), alliance is broadly defined as the "collaborative efforts between two or more firms in which the firms pool their resources in an effort to achieve mutually compatible goals that they could not achieve easily alone" (p. 141). Cooperative alliance is often

DOI: 10.4018/978-1-60566-030-1.ch014

adopted by small and medium-sized enterprises (SMEs) as a competitive strategy and is also an important strategic choice because it allows SMEs to obtain necessary complementary resources in ICT. This is often carried out to overcome the problems of resource scarcity by entering into an alliance with other firms in order to create excess value relative to their value before the pooling by combining all their resources together (Dymsza, 1988; Nohria and Garcia-Pont, 1991). However, according to Beamish (1987) and Das and Teng (2000b), around 60% of alliances between firms resulted in failure. Needless to say, this is a particularly worrying trend for SMEs which are widely recognized as having important roles to play in emerging economies and are generally characterized by resource constraints (Lee et al., 1999; Weinrauch et al., 1991; Zineldin, 1998). Hence, the choice of partners and resource fit of alliance partners are of great importance for SMEs (Grant et al., 1999). For those SMEs without much ICT resources, the formation process of alliance can be partly viewed as a process to increase both of their tangible and intangible ICT resources. Value generated from alliances is enhanced when partners have different ICT resource profiles and contribute these ICT resources into the alliance. These partner characteristics are important since they help in the evaluation of optimum allocations of ICT resources for potential alliances to achieve suitable alliance resource alignments.

Thus, the objective of this chapter is to examine how the alignment of different types of ICT resources affects the performance of alliances. The research to date has only examined complementarity in terms of dissimilar resources whereas in this study, we aim to measure resource alignment (Das and Teng, 2000a; 2003) by examining the alliance partners' contribution in terms of both supplementary (similar) and complementary (dissimilar) resources. The focus of this study is the small dialysis centers in Taiwan. These small dialysis centers have formed alliances to confront the fierce competition as well as to absorb the regulatory pressure from the regulatory authority. The literature on inter-organizational collaborations has been criticized for its relatively narrow concentration on large firms and for ignoring SMEs' alliances where large firms do not operate in similar ways (Prater and Ghosh, 2005). These cost pressures together with the general dynamic nature of the healthcare industry require a significant change in approaches to utilize ICT resources by these small dialysis centers. Therefore, these small dialysis centers must form alliances to obtain scarce ICT resources. Unlike large firms which own a lot of ICT resources to be able to form alliances with many partners, these small dialysis centers tend to form alliances with only a small number of partners and therefore, their dependence on these partners is higher than large firms. In this regard, these small Taiwanese dialysis centers offer an appropriate context for research.

BACKGROUND

Resource Supplementarity and Resource Complementarity

According to Parkhe (1991) and Sarkar et al. (2001), there are two types of interorganizational diversity. Type I diversity refers to the differences in complementary resources and capability profiles of the alliance partners in a search for synergy (Parkhe, 1991). As noted by Harrigan (1985), resource complementarity refers to both the uniqueness and symmetry of resources and is related to each partner's resource contribution to the alliance. Uniqueness is the most often mentioned characteristic of complementarity and relates to each partner's unique contribution to the alliance. If the resource contribution from each partner is too similar (overlapping), it will not be able to complement the other's weakness (Hamel, Doz, and Prahalad, 1989). Beyond the role of resource complementarity in successful cooperative alliances, each partner has to provide symmetric resource contributions. This is often referred to as "strategic symmetry" where partner interdependence is created by a balanced contribution of unique strengths from each partner (Harrigan, 1985). Strategic symmetry also implies: (a) equal risk sharing (Luo, 1999); (b) partner perceptions of equal costs and benefits in alliances (Dymsza, 1988); and (c) the presence of power and status balance increases commitment in sharing both the costs and benefits (Bucklin and Sengupta, 1993; Chung et al., 2000).

Type II diversity relates to the social dimensions and deals with interorganizational cultural and processual differences between partners within the alliance (Parkhe 1991). Incompatibilities or dissimilarities between alliance partners can negatively affect the interactions quality and hamper the conversion of tacit know-how into value creation within a partnership (Sarkar et al., 2001). We have adapted the definition of resource supplementarity from Das and Teng (2000a) and defined it as the contribution of similar resources that are symmetric by two partners in an alliance. Resource similarity, defined by Chen (1996: 107) as "the degree to which two partner firms contribute resources compatible, in terms of both type and amount, to an alliance", plays a critical role in the alliance formation because partners which possess similar resources can decrease interorganizational rivalry (Chen, 1996). Moreover, resource similarity can also assist in interorganizational learning among alliance partners.

Resource Alignment

According to Das and Teng (2000a), four types of partner resource alignments can be derived by looking at the two dimensions of resource similarity and resource utilization: supplementary, surplus, complementary, and wasteful. Moreover, Das and Teng (2000a; 2003) argue that resource alignment is related to alliance condition and performance. However, there is little research to prove or evaluate Das and Teng's (2000a; 2003) framework of resource alignment. Therefore, it is impossible to establish the relationship between the four types of partner resource alignments and the alliance performance. SMEs are particularly in need of finding suitable partners with the dissimilar resources since they possess a lot less resources than large firms. According to Srinivasan et al. (2005), SMEs require both dissimilar resources and similar resources via equal contribution due to their insufficient slack resources. However, Olk (1997) has pointed out that the benefits of similar resources' contribution in alliances formation have not been adequately researched and recognized in the literature. Chen (1996: p107) has defined resource similarity as "the degree to which two partner firms contribute resources compatible, in terms of both type and amount, to an alliance". The understanding of resource similarity is very important because the firms which have possessed similar resources can potentially be the fierce rivals (Chen, 1996). Therefore, forming alliances is one way for firms which have possessed similar resources to decrease interfirm rivalry. According to partner's similar and dissimilar resources contribution level, supposed interpartners only hold two kinds of resources, partner resource alignment can be classified into two types: supplementarity and complementarity (Das and Teng, 2000a).

Resource Alignment of Supplementarity and Complementarity

The key to the successful resource alignment of supplementarity and complementarity within an alliance is about not only the inter-partners' contribution of similar and dissimilar resources but also the attention paid by the alliance partners on the symmetric resource contribution. This is because symmetrically similar resource contribution can bring in mutual learning and cultural similarity whereas symmetrically dissimilar resource contribution can lead to similar status and creation of synergy. Thus, the partner resource alignment can be classified into four types: supplementarity, asymmetric supplementarity, complementarity, and asymmetric complementarity.

Supplementarity in resource alignment between partners is when the focal firm (the firm under study) and its partner firm contribute similar resources symmetrically. This can be an equally high or equally low contribution of similar resources by each partner firm. For example, dialysis centers may expect their hospital alliance partners to contribute equally for the procurement of expensive medical equipment. Another instance is that dialysis centers may expect to enlarge both in-patients inflow through mutual transfer and introduction of in-patients.

In addition, when the similar resources contribution of focal firm is not equal to the contribution the partner firm, the alignment is called asymmetric supplementarity. This is often caused by status dissimilarity (Chung et al., 2000: p 4). For example, when the partner firm has greater status or power, the focal firm is often forced to pour in more similar resources to the alliance than the partner firm. In general, the focal firm in this situation tends to be dissatisfied with the amount of resources contributed by the partner firm. Asymmetric supplementarity in resource alignment will result in a lack of understanding of inter-partners' knowledge and culture base. In this situation, the opportunistic behavior and the lack of understanding in inter-partners' knowledge and culture base within an alliance will often cause conflicts. This paper argues that higher resource supplementarity can increase the levels of fairness and interorganizational learning of alliance partners and, therefore increase the alliance satisfaction. On the other hand, lower resource supplementarity (asymmetric supplementarity) can cause conflicts between inter-partners and lead to lower alliance commitment and satisfaction.

Complementarity alignment has been the most widely researched and recognized type of resource alignment in alliances (Das and Teng, 2000a). Under complementarity alignment, both partners within the alliance contribute a fair share of dissimilar resources. When the focal firm provides a high contribution in one particular type of resource, the partner firm should provide a relatively high contribution in another type of resource. Similarly, when the focal firm provides a low contribution towards one type of resource, the partner firm may follow suit by providing a relatively low contribution in another type of resource. Therefore, higher resource complementarity is likely to lead to higher alliance satisfaction.

On the other hand, when different resources are not comparably or not equally contributed, it is called an asymmetric complementarity alignment. One reason why asymmetric complementarity can happen is because of status dissimilarity (Chung et al., 2000). That is, one partner within the alliance contributes more unique resource than the other. Another reason is due to SMEs having a general lack of resources. Many SMEs may not be able to fulfill the promise of resources contribution that was agreed when the alliance was initially established (Hyder and Abraha, 2004). This also shows the inability of SMEs to locate the required resources (Prater and Ghosh, 2005). However, there is also a risk of power and status asymmetry when SMEs form alliances with large firms. Under asymmetric complementarity when one or both partners cannot contribute enough unique resources to satisfy the others' needs, there is likely to be higher resource allocation disagreements, greater inter-partner conflicts, and lower alliance satisfaction.

RESEARCH METHODOLOGY

The focus of our study is small dialysis centers in Taiwan. The dialysis industry in Taiwan has two main characteristics. First, more than 97% of health care providers in Taiwan are contracted with a government sponsored agency, BNHI. Due to the financial difficulties within the national health care system in Taiwan, the costs and revenues of these small dialysis providers have been closely monitored by BNHI (Lee and Jones, 2004). BNHI's fixed-budget policy has resulted in reimbursements at lower rates. As a result, the payments to these small dialysis centers have been decreasing markedly each year while, at the same time, their costs have been increasing rapidly. Second, the supply of nephrologists and dialysis centers, and the demand from the end stage renal disease (ERSD) patients have been growing at a steady rate. However, most ERSD patients prefer to go to large hospitals for long-term treatment. In order to survive, many of these small dialysis centers have resorted to forming alliances with medium-sized hospitals or large healthcare service providers. In recent years, most of these small dialysis centers have realized that they can only compete with major hospitals through cooperative alliances.

The objective of this research is to establish whether greater deployment of resource alignments leads to more satisfactory alliance. Two research questions are proposed:

1. Do organizations which use supplementarity alignment more likely to be satisfied with their alliance activities compared with those which have adopted asymmetric supplementarity alignment?
2. Do organizations which use complementarity alignment more likely to be satisfied with their alliance activities compared with those which have adopted asymmetric complementarity alignment?

In an attempt to answer the above two research questions, several mini-case studies involving Taiwanese small dialysis centers were conducted by the authors. The case study method was chosen because it enables the researcher to examine the context of the resource alignment and better understand the responses given in the interviews through observation. In addition, the researchers examined organization documents and annual reports of these dialysis centers. Some patients and medical staff of these dialysis centers were also contacted to confirm some of the materials collected via the case study. This serves as a method of triangulation of research data and ensures that the questions and answers are properly understood by repeating or rephrasing the questions and through paraphrasing the responses back to the interviewee (Silverman, 2001). This reasoning has been supported by Rouse and Dick (1994) who have stated that many information systems practices are difficult to investigate using only survey approaches.

IS/IT managers from these small Taiwanese dialysis centers were interviewed during 2006. Structured interviews were used as one of the data collection methods for the case study. According to Burns (1994), structured interviews are repeated face-to-face interactions between the researcher and participants and allow the researchers to focus on certain themes and issues with rich insights for exploring, identifying, and understanding participants' viewpoints and opinions. The case study approach allowed the researchers to interview a range of IT specialists in each organization, observing practice and analyzing company reports. The findings from these information gathering approaches were analyzed iteratively by the researchers on an individual level, differences reconciled and then a judgment made on each of the major constructs. The responses to interview questions were rated by the researchers relative to the pool of responses. For example, interviewees were asked about the economic satisfaction with their resource alignment in alliance. Their answers were judged in terms of the financial significance of the organization contribution and were then compared with the results for the other organizations resulting in the categories of *low, medium and high*.

ICT ALIGNMENT

This study has defined the inter-organizational resource cooperation among the healthcare centers as the unique and valuable ICT resources contribution by both the focal and partner firms. According to the resource-based viewpoint, ICT resources (for a healthcare center) can be categorizes as intangible resources (specialized IS support), physical resources (medical IS support services) and organizational capabilities (IS management systems) (Chatterjee and Wernerfelt, 1991; Short et al., 2002).

The *satisfaction* scale was based on Cullen et al.'s (1995) perceptual measure of assessing satisfaction with both the relationship and performance between international joint venture (IJV) partners. Geringer and Hebert (1991) have found that subjective satisfaction is positively related to the objective measures of IJV performance (i.e. survival, stability and duration). Therefore, in this study, *satisfaction* was used as an indicator for alliance performance.

Participants interviewed were from different levels of management to provide different managerial perspectives. Questions relating to a particular research theme, for example, level of satisfaction with resource alignment, were examined as a cluster. This was done as a form of in-case analysis and to develop general explanations and interpretations (Eisenhardt, 1989). These steps enhance the construct validity, reliability, and overall quality of the research (Yin, 2002).

All the organizations that took part in the research have been trading for more than five years and are obtained from the Taiwan National Kidney Foundation database. Extensive notes were taken during the interviews. The questions asked during the interviews were related to the inter-partners' contribution volume and types, alliance benefits, reasons for alliance, and their alliance. Other data collected for this research included organization documents and annual reports. Qualitative content analysis (Miles and Huberman, 1994) was used to analyze the data from the case study using the constructs identified in the literature analysis. These included: ICT resource contribution, ICT resource type, supplementarity, complementarity, and overall satisfaction with alliance. Where there were discrepancies in the interpretation of responses to the questions these were resolved by consultation between the researchers and in some cases further explanation from the interviewees. Both researchers evaluated the responses from the interviews and classified them according to the research themes. The Cohen's Kappa statistic was used to analyze the level of correspondence between the researchers and there was a high degree of reliability between the researchers in relation to the interpretation (0.87). This is well above the 61% level suggested for a substantial strength of agreement (Fleiss, 1981). The analysis of the case study results was also conducted in a cyclical manner and the results were checked by co-researchers and other alliance experts. The guidelines set out by Klein and Myers (1999) for conducting and evaluating interpretive field studies in information systems were followed to improve the quality of the research.

RESEARCH FINDINGS

Research Question One

The first research question relates to the deployment of supplementarity alignment and its relationship with alliance satisfaction (see Table 1). Better relationships with partners, greater business growth, and improved sales growth are the most often mentioned benefits in relation to the alliance satisfaction. Please note that each dot denotes one organization.

Research Question Two

The second research question relates to the deployment of complementarity alignment and its

Table 1. ICT resource supplementarity vs. alliance satisfaction

••••λ	
•	••
	••••

Table 2. ICT resource complementarity vs. alliance satisfaction

••••	
•••	•
	•••••

relationship with alliance satisfaction (see Table 2). Better relationships with partners, greater business growth, and improved sales growth are the most often mentioned benefits in relation to the alliance satisfaction.

DISCUSSIONS

Case study was conducted and the respondents were asked to answer the questions in relation to the cooperative relationship with their most important alliance partner. One contribution of the chapter is that the contribution of dissimilar ICT resources by both the focal and partner firms has a significant positive impact on alliance sustainable commitment. The results also show that there is a positive relationship between the contribution of dissimilar ICT resources by the partner firms and alliance performance. However, the contribution of dissimilar ICT resources alone by the focal dialysis centers has no significant impact on alliance performance.

This research has provided several insights for the ICT resource alignment model selected by alliance partners in the dialysis industry. First, past research did not find empirical support that there was a positive relationship between ICT resource complementarity and alliance performance (Das and Teng, 2000a; Hill and Hellriegel, 1994). We had suspected that this had something to do with the measurement of complementarity. Through the use of our measurement, the results indicated that both resources supplementarity and complementarity were positively and significantly related to alliance commitment and satisfaction. Our results had not only confirmed with previous research findings (Lambe et al., 2002) but also provided the possible means of measuring resource alignment (Das and Teng, 2000a; 2002; 2003). The results had shown that the small dialysis centers were more likely to select partners which had owned the requisite complementary resources. The success of the alliance can only be achieved through this sort of resource fit. Second, past research findings suggested that the criteria for complementary resource depended heavily on uniqueness and symmetry of ICT resources (Johnson et al., 1996). In this research, it was found that the criteria could be applied to resource supplementarity in small dialysis centers. Therefore, the establishment of successful alliance depended not only on partners' ability to contribute unique and performing resources but also on the perception of fair dealing of these resources by the small dialysis centers.

CONCLUSION

Previous research has concentrated on large firms and assumed that they paid particular attention to their partners' ability to contribute complementary resources within the alliance, regarding supplementary resources as surplus or slack resources. The research measures and items adopted by our research have provided the means to evaluate complementarity and supplementarity in terms of dissimilar and similar resources. The research measures and items could be applied to both large firms and SMEs in other industries in the future. Moreover, previous research had not examined in detail the relationship between resource alignment and alliance performance in addition to the mediating factors that determine the effect of resource alignment towards alliance satisfaction. This research has made a significant contribution by examining the specific theoretical meaning and role that resource alignment plays within cooperative alliances.

Furthermore, past research findings suggested that the criteria for complementary resource depended heavily on uniqueness and symmetry of resources (Johnson et al., 1996). In this research, it was found that the criteria could be applied to ICT resources supplementarity. Therefore, the establishment of successful alliance depended not only on partners' ability to contribute unique and performing ICT resources but also on the perception of fair dealing of these resources by the focal SMEs in the healthcare industry.

This is especially true when both focal and partner firms have perceived that synergies (1+1>2) have been created by the alliance (see quadrant 9, Table 3). The alliance is also likely to continue in quadrants 6 and 8. Similarly, if both focal and partner firms have not perceived any gains (1+1<2) from forming the alliance then the alliance will be discontinued (quadrant 1). Alliance is also not likely to continue in quadrants 2 and 4. None of the alliance partners are satisfied with the performance of the alliance. Furthermore, one party is likely to withdraw from the alliance while the other party is likely to want to hold on to the alliance in quadrants 3 and 7. For example, in quadrant 7, focal firm has nothing to gain from the alliance and has perceived partner firm as not contributing its fair share of resources to the alliance whereas partner firm would want to hold on to the alliance as it is benefiting greatly from it. Finally, alliance needs to be re-evaluated when both focal and partner firms are indifferent (1+1=2) about the performance of the alliance (quadrant 5).

Second, previous research findings suggested that the criteria for complementary resource depended heavily on uniqueness and symmetry of resources (Johnson et al., 1996). In this research, it was found that the criteria could be applied to

Table 3. The level of synergies created by the cooperative alliance

Perceptions of Focal firm				
	Level of Synergies	*1 + 1 < 2*	*1 + 1 = 2*	*1 + 1 > 2*
Perceptions of Partner firm	*1 + 1 < 2*	1. The alliance is a complete failure and should be discontinued immediately. Both focal and partner firms are very dissatisfied with the performance of the alliance.	2. Both focal and partner firms need to re-evaluate the alliance. Partner firm is very likely to pull out from the alliance.	3. Partner firm is very likely to pull out from the alliance whereas focal is very likely to want to hold on to the alliance. Focal firm has been perceived as not contributing enough of its resources to the alliance.
	1 + 1 = 2	4. Both focal and partner firms need to re-evaluate the alliance. Focal firm is very likely to pull out from the alliance.	5. Both focal and partner firms need to re-evaluate the alliance.	6. The alliance is somewhat successful and is likely to continue. Focal firm is more enthusiastic than the partner firm about the alliance.
	1 + 1 > 2	7. Focal firm is very likely to pull out from the alliance whereas partner is very likely to want to hold on to the alliance. Partner firm has been perceived as not contributing enough of its resources to the alliance.	8. The alliance is somewhat successful and is likely to continue. Focal firm is not as enthusiastic as the partner firm about the alliance.	9. The alliance has been very successful and is very likely to continue. Both focal and partner firms are likely to be very satisfied.

resource supplementarity as well. This research had found that resource supplementarity and complementarity not only can assist in improving reciprocal strengths of alliance partners (Contractor and Lorange, 1988), but also can provide them with means to achieving similar status (Chung et al., 2000) as well as enhancing interorganizational learning (Lane and Lubatkin, 1998; Nonaka and Takeuchi, 1995). This can assist in establishing successful alliances. Third, the effect of resource alignment in relation to alliance satisfaction is likely to be dependent on the commitment to investing the required resources into the alliance. The fact that alliance commitment was found to be a mediating factor of resource alignment on alliances satisfaction is due to the high correlation between the alliance commitment and the alliance satisfaction. Consistent with Sarkar's et al. (2001) findings, this research had found that alliance commitment had a positive mediating effect between partners' resource supplementarity, complementarity, and alliance satisfaction. Therefore, it could be said that successful alliances depend on a partner's willingness to contribute a fair share of the similar and dissimilar resources. Sincere commitment by all partners would likely result in the alliance satisfaction. Thus, the commitment to the alliance was the dominant factor for resource alignment on alliance success.

MANAGERIAL AND PRACTICAL IMPLICATIONS

This study has several managerial and practical implications. First, the results show the relative importance of key factors in choosing appropriate alliance partners. The results from this study indicate that small dialysis centers should be careful in selecting their alliance partners and in evaluating the amount of complementary and supplementary resources the partners are prepared to contribute to the alliance. Instead of focusing only on complementary resources, it is vital to estimate the amount of supplementary resources the partners are able to bring to the alliance. An insufficient contribution of supplementary resources to the alliance can often lead to failure. These criteria can guide small dialysis centers in the partner selection process and in establishing cross-border alliances. Second, for small dialysis centers, commitment is a critical factor that needs to be carefully managed to avoid the possible negative effects of an asymmetric contribution of specific supplementary and complementary resources. The selection of partners who are able to contribute fairly to both the requisite complementary and supplementary resources is of great importance. This will ensure the fair share of any future benefits by all partners and this will ultimately lead to alliance satisfaction and success.

LIMITATIONS AND FUTURE DIRECTIONS

The major limitation of the present study relates to the generalizability of the research findings. The study involved SMEs in Taiwan and the findings are based on the Taiwanese context. It would be interesting to conduct the research in other countries and with different business applications. This research has relied on the information provided at a particular point in time. Further research could take a longitudinal approach as the perception and management of benefits and resource contributions is likely to change over time. Alternatively, our study could be replicated in a few years time to examine how resource alignment and related benefits have changed and are being managed in light of new or emerging alliances.

FUTURE TRENDS

It has been argued that user satisfaction on the use of ICT resources is a more accurate reflection of contentment (Scheepers et al., 2006). Clinical workers within these healthcare centers should welcome the utilizing of ICT resources as long as it provides direct clinical benefits to their work and ease their work practices (Jensen and Aanestad, 2007). However, they tend to harbor negative reactions towards the ICT resources if it implies new mechanisms for administrative control of their work and introduce new tasks previously performed by others (Jensen and Aanestad, 2007). For example, mandatory IS use among doctors has far more implications compared to other professional groups (e.g. nurses and clinicians) because of their traditional autonomy, legitimacy and status (Kohli and Kettinger, 2004). Therefore, it is critical for these healthcare centers undertaking cooperative alliances to implement the ICT resources carefully and appropriately in the future.

Third, it is also crucial for the senior managers of the healthcare centers to examine the implementation issues after obtaining the requisite ICT resources from their alliance partners in the future. Other issues such as behavioral, attitudinal and organizational considerations should not be neglected as well (Thomas et al., 1995). From a practical standpoint, understanding the reactions of their clinical workers toward the newly acquired ICT resources and their subsequent behavior can help healthcare centers devise appropriate intervention strategies and programs to maximize their use and their effects on the firms (LeRouge et al., 2007a). This is important given that most healthcare firms, from our own observation, still pay little attention toward the effective utilization of ICT resources. According to Davidson and Heineke (2007), stakes are too high to be content with gradual diffusion of the healthcare ICT resources and therefore, deliberate steps must be identified to achieve desirable outcomes and increase the pace of dissemination. One way of doing it is to identify the relevant opinion leaders who can serve to reduce the uncertainty of others in adopting new ICT resources (Cain and Mittman, 2002).

Intervention programs aimed at assisting small healthcare centers to overcome learning barriers to adopt ICT resources may also be needed (Reardon and Davidson, 2007). For example, programs to develop community-based knowledge and ICT resources could complement financial incentives programs and might increase their efficacy (Davidson and Heslinga, 2007). A better understanding of the use of such resources may help design better systems, strategies, and programs that are necessary to deliver a higher quality of healthcare services. Finally, it is also important to examine the roles played by doctors, nurses and clinicians in the ICT resource alignment among healthcare centers as they have the power to hold back the adoption or even lead to system's failure (Mantzana et al., 2007). The decision-making process for such ICT resource alignment must be taken into account of these healthcare players' points of view.

REFERENCES

Burns, R. B. (1994). *Introduction to Research Methods,* (2nd Ed.). London: Longman Cheshire Pty Ltd.

Cain, M. & Mittman, M. (2002). Diffusion of Innovation in Health Care. *iHealth Reports*, May, 1-20. California HealthCare Foundation.

Chatterjee, S., & Wernerfelt, B. (1991). The Link between Resources and Type of Diversification: Theory and Evidence. *Strategic Management Journal, 12*, 33–48. doi:10.1002/smj.4250120104

Chen, M.-J. (1996). Competitor Analysis and Interfirm Rivalry: Toward a Theoretical Integration. *Academy of Management Review, 21*(1), 100–134. doi:10.2307/258631

Chung, S., Singh, H., & Lee, K. (2000). Complementarity, Status Similarity and Social Capital as Drivers of Alliance Formation. *Strategic Management Journal, 21*, 1–22. doi:10.1002/(SICI)1097-0266(200001)21:1<1::AID-SMJ63>3.0.CO;2-P

Contractor, F. J., & Lorange, P. (1988). *Cooperative Strategies in International Business.* Lexington, MA: Lexington Books.

Cullen, J. B., Johnson, J. L., & Sakano, T. (1995). Japanese and Local Partner Commitment to IJVs: Psychological Consequences of Outcomes and Investments in the IJV Relationship. *Journal of International Business Studies, 26*(1), 91–115. doi:10.1057/palgrave.jibs.8490167

Das, T. K., & Teng, B. S. (2000a). A Resource Based Theory of Strategic Alliances . *Journal of Management, 26*(1), 31–61. doi:10.1016/S0149-2063(99)00037-9

Das, T. K., & Teng, B.-S. (2000b). Instabilities of Strategic Alliances: An Internal Tensions Perspective. *Organization Science, 11*, 77–101. doi:10.1287/orsc.11.1.77.12570

Das, T. K., & Teng, B.-S. (2002). The Dynamics of Alliance Conditions in the Alliance Development Process. *Journal of Management Studies, 39*(5), 725–746. doi:10.1111/1467-6486.00006

Das, T. K., & Teng, B.-S. (2003). Partner Analysis and Alliance Performance. *Scandinavian Journal of Management, 19*, 279–308. doi:10.1016/S0956-5221(03)00003-4

Davidson, E., & Heslinga, D. (2007). Bridging the IT Adoption Gap for Small Physician Practices: An Action Research Study on Electronic Health Records. *Information Systems Management, 24*(1), 15–28. doi:10.1080/10580530601036786

Davidson, S. M., & Heineke, J. (2007). Toward an Effective Strategy for the Diffusion and Use of Clinical Information Systems. *Journal of the American Medical Informatics Association, 14*(3), 361–367. doi:10.1197/jamia.M2254

Dymsza, W. A. (1988). Success and Failures of Joint Ventures in Developing Countries: Lessons from Experience. In F. J. Contractor, P. Lorange (Eds.) *Cooperative Strategies in International Business* (pp. 403-424). Lexington, MA: Lexington Books.

Eisenhardt, K. M. (1989). Building Theories from Case Study Research. *Academy of Management Review, 14*(4), 532–550. doi:10.2307/258557

Fleiss, J. L. (1981). *Statistical Methods for Rates and Proportions* (2nd Ed., pp. 38-46). New York: John Wiley.

Geringer, J. M., & Hebert, L. (1991). Measuring Performance of International Joint Ventures. *Journal of International Business Studies, 22*(2), 249–263. doi:10.1057/palgrave.jibs.8490302

Grant, M., Preece, S. B., & Baetz, M. C. (1999). Dangers of Dependence: The Impact of Strategic Alliance Use by Small Technology-based Firms. *Journal of Small Business Management, 37*(2), 20–29.

Hill, R. C., & Hellriegel, D. (1994). Critical Contingencies in Joint Venture Management: Some Lessons from Managers. *Organization Science, 5*(4), 594–607. doi:10.1287/orsc.5.4.594

Hyder, A. S., & Abraha, D. (2004). Product and Skills Development in Small-and Medium-sized High-tech Firms through International Strategic Alliances. *Singapore Management Review, 26*(2), 1–24.

Jensen, T. B., & Aanestad, M. (2007). Hospitality and Hostility in Hospitals: A Case Study of an ERP Adoption Among Surgeons. *European Journal of Information Systems*, *16*(6), 672–680. doi:10.1057/palgrave.ejis.3000713

Johnson, J. L., Cullen, J. B., Sakano, T., & Takenouchi, H. (1996). Setting the Stage for Trust, and Strategic Integration in Japanese-U.S. Cooperative Alliances. *Journal of International Business Studies*, *27*(4), 981–1004. doi:10.1057/palgrave.jibs.8490160

Klein, H. K., & Myers, M. D. (1999). A Set of Principles for Conducting and Evaluating Interpretive Field Studies in Information Systems. *MIS Quarterly*, *23*(1), 67–94. doi:10.2307/249410

Kohli, R., & Kettinger, W. J. (2004). Informating the Clan: Controlling Physicians' Costs and Outcomes. *MIS Quarterly*, *27*(2), 197–235.

Lambe, C. J., Spekman, R. E., & Hunt, S. D. (2002). Alliance Competence, Resources, and Alliance Success: Conceptualization, Measurement, and Initial Test. *Journal of the Academy of Marketing Science*, *30*(2), 141–158. doi:10.1177/03079459994399

Lane, P. J., & Lubatkin, M. (1998). Relative Absorptive Capacity and Interorganizational Learning. *Strategic Management Journal*, *19*, 461–477. doi:10.1002/(SICI)1097-0266(199805)19:5<461::AID-SMJ953>3.0.CO;2-L

Lee, K. S., Lim, G. H., & Tan, S. J. (1999). Dealing with Resource Disadvantage: Generic Strategies for SMEs. *Small Business Economics*, *12*(4), 299–311. doi:10.1023/A:1008085310245

Lee, M.-C., & Jones, A. M. (2004). How Did Dentists Respond to the Introduction of Global Budgets in Taiwan? An Evaluation Using Individual Panel Data. *International Journal of Health Care Finance and Economics*, *4*(4), 307–326. doi:10.1023/B:IHFE.0000043760.57999.36

LeRouge, C., Mantzana, V., & Wilson, E. V. (2007b). Healthcare Information Systems Research, Revelations and Visions. *European Journal of Information Systems*, *16*(6), 669–671. doi:10.1057/palgrave.ejis.3000712

Mantzana, V., Themistocleous, M., Irani, Z., & Morabito, V. (2007). Identifying Healthcare Actors Involved in the Adoption of Information Systems. *European Journal of Information Systems*, *16*(1), 91–102. doi:10.1057/palgrave.ejis.3000660

Miles, M. B., & Huberman, A. M. (1994). *Qualitative Data Analysis: An Expanded Sourcebook.* Thousand Oaks, CA: Sage Publications.

Nohria, N., & Garcia-Pont, C. (1991). Global Strategic Linkages and Industry Structure. *Strategic Management Journal, 12*(Summer Special Issue), 105-124.

Nonaka, I., & Takeuchi, H. (1995). *The Knowledge-creating Company.* New York: Oxford University Press.

Olk, P. (1997). The Effect of Partner Differences on the Performance of R&D Consortia. In P. W. Beamish, & J. P. Killing (Eds.), *Cooperative Strategies: North American Perspectives* (pp. 133-159). San Francisco, CA: New Lexington Press.

Prater, E., & Ghosh, S. (2005). Current Operational Practices of U.S. Small and Medium-Sized Enterprises in Europe. *Journal of Small Business Management*, *43*(2), 155–169.

Reardon, J. L., & Davidson, E. (2007). An organizational learning perspective on the assimilation of electronic medical records among small physician practices. *European Journal of Information Systems*, *16*, 681–694. doi:10.1057/palgrave.ejis.3000714

Rouse, A., & Dick, M. (1994). The Use of Computerized Tools in Qualitative Information Systems Studies. *Proceedings of the 5th Australasian Conference on Information Systems (ACIS 1994),* (Vol. I, pp. 209-220), Monash University, Melbourne, Australia.

Sarkar, M. B., Echambadi, R., Cavusgil, S. T., Preet, S., & Aulakh, . (2001). The Influence of Complementarity, Compatibility, and Relationship Capital on Alliance Performance. *Journal of the Academy of Marketing Science*, *29*(4), 358–373. doi:10.1177/03079450094216

Scheepers, R., Scheepers, H., & Ngwenyama, O. K. (2006). Contextual Influences on User Satisfaction with Mobile Computing: Findings from Two Healthcare Organizations. *European Journal of Information Systems*, *15*, 261–268. doi:10.1057/palgrave.ejis.3000615

Short, J. C., Palmer, T. B., & Ketchen, D. J. Jr. (2002). Resources-Based and Strategic Group Influences on Hospital Performance. *Health Care Management Review*, *27*(4), 7–17.

Silverman, D. (2001). *Interpreting qualitative data* (2nd Ed.). London: Sage.

Srinivasan, R., Rangaswamy, A., & Lilien, G. L. (2005). Turning Adversity into Advantage: Does Proactive Marketing during a Recession Pay Off? *International Journal of Research in Marketing*.

Thomas, R., Robinson, J., Waring, T., Wainwright, D., & Maguire, S. (1995). Information Management and Technology in England's Large Acute NHS Hospitals. *Journal of Management in Medicine*, *9*(1), 40–49. doi:10.1108/02689239510080476

Weinrauch, D. J., Mann, O. K., Robinson, P. A., & Pharr, J. (1991). Dealing with Limited Financial Resources: A Marketing Challenge for Small Business. *Journal of Small Business Management*, *29*(4), 44–54.

Yin, R. K. (2002). *Case Study Research, Design and Methods*, (3rd Ed.). Newbury Park, CA: Sage Publications.

Zineldin, M. A. (1998). Towards an Ecological Collaborative Relationship Management. *European Journal of Management*, *32*(11/12), 1138–1164.

KEY TERMS AND DEFINITIONS

Alliance: The collaborative efforts between two or more firms in which the firms pool their resources in an effort to achieve mutually compatible goals that they could not achieve easily alone.

Alliance Satisfaction: The contentment the alliance partners feels when the alliance has achieved its aims or objectives.

Dialysis Center: A facility that provides the diagnostic, remedial, and rehabilitative services to care for the dialysis patients.

Resource Alignment: The resource alignment can be classified into four types: supplementarity, asymmetric supplementarity, complementarity, and asymmetric complementarity.

Resource Complementarity: The degree to which two partner firms symmetrically contribute dissimilar resources, in terms of both type and amount, to an alliance.

Resource Supplementarity: The degree to which two partner firms symmetrically contribute similar resources, in terms of both type and amount, to an alliance.

SMEs: Small to median enterprises. The European Commission has defined SMEs as organizations which employ less than 250 people.

Chapter 15
Guideline Representation Ontologies for Evidence-based Medicine Practice

Kai Zheng
The University of Michigan, USA

Rema Padman
Carnegie Mellon University, USA

Michael P. Johnson
The University of Massachusetts Boston, USA

Sharique Hasan
Carnegie Mellon University, USA

ABSTRACT

An ontology in the context of guideline representation is a specification of conceptualizations that constitutes evidence-based clinical practice guidelines. It represents the elements of a guideline by specifying its attributes and defining the relationships that hold among them. For example, a guideline representation ontology would define a set of medical decisions and actions (concepts), as well as a set of rules (relationships) that relate the evaluation of a decision criterion to further reasoning steps or to its associated actions. A rigorously defined computational ontology provides considerable promise of producing computable representations that can be visualized, edited, executed, and shared using computer-based systems. A widely acknowledged ontology, or standard representation schema, is the key to facilitating the dissemination of guidelines across computer systems and healthcare institutions. The first part of this chapter presents the evolution of ontology research in guideline representation. Several representative ontologies are reviewed and discussed, with in-depth analyses of two popular models: GLIF (Guideline Interchange Format) and PROforma. The second part of the chapter analyzes seven key elements constituting a guideline representation. It also discusses the criteria for evaluating competing ontologies and some known limitations in the existing models. At the end of this chapter, four key steps are outlined that converts a guideline into computerized representation, which can be then used in Clinical Decision Support Systems (CDSSs).

DOI: 10.4018/978-1-60566-030-1.ch015

INTRODUCTION

Evidence-based medicine is "the conscientious, explicit, and judicious use of current best evidence in making medical decisions about the care of individual patients" (Sackett, Rosenberg, Gray, Haynes, & Richardson, 1996). Evidence-based clinical practice guidelines, a condensed form of evidence-based medicine, are published and maintained by professional organizations. For example, the National Guideline Clearinghouse[1] currently hosts over 1,700 active guidelines, spanning a wide variety of disease areas and conditions. However, these guidelines are usually prepared and disseminated as unstructured, descriptive textual documents that are primarily intended for human readers, inhibiting their automated use within Clinical Decision Support Systems. In addition, the lack of a standard schema also impairs the interoperability of guideline representations, resulting in a waste of implementation time and resources, and potentially increased error rates. To alleviate the problem, the development of standard, structured guideline representation ontologies is of vital importance.

The contemporary usage of the term *ontology* is derived from its much older usage in philosophy, in which it studies existence, its component entities, and the relationships between them. A contemporary ontology can be defined as "a formal, specific conceptualization of a domain; by adopting an ontology, an agent makes an ontological commitment to use only the vocabulary the ontology provides, and to use it only to denote the concepts provided" (Gruber, 1993). This definition articulates the concepts existing in a domain as well as its taxonomy, rules, and the relationships existing between them. These concepts are usually abstract, simplified views of the knowledge existing in a domain, such as medicine or biology. They do not necessarily represent complete knowledge of that domain, but can be composed of a subset, required for a specific application[2].

The main purpose of introducing the concept of ontology into knowledge representation is to enable knowledge sharing and reuse. Rigorously defined ontologies---with computer-recognizable semantics and structure that support some level of computation---are called *computational ontologies*. Computational ontologies are pivotal component of computer systems designed for intelligent reasoning, for example, Clinical Decision Support Systems.

The concept of ontology has been widely adopted in many disciplines such as computer science, information science, medicine, and genomics. Well known examples are 1) the semantic web ontologies that provide a universally accessible platform for data to be shared and processed by automated tools over web[3]; and 2) the gene ontologies that provide controlled vocabularies to describe gene and gene product attributes in any organism[4]. Not surprisingly, every knowledge-base or knowledge-based expert system should implement an ontology, explicitly or implicitly (Gruber, 1993).

In the context of clinical practice guideline representation, an ontology is a specification of concepts and relationships that constitute an evidence-based clinical practice guideline. It conceptualizes the elements of a guideline, their properties, and defines the relationships that hold among them. For example all guideline representation ontologies have a set of medical decisions and relevant actions (*concepts*), and a set of temporal rules that relate decision evaluation results to associated actions (*relationships*). A well established and generally acknowledged guideline representation ontology ensures that the resulting representations can be easily understood by non-authoring human readers, therefore facilitates the dissemination of guidelines across institutions. Well defined computational ontologies also provide considerable promise of enabling automated guideline acquisition, visualization, execution, and sharing. Such characteristics are prerequisites for a computer-recognizable, interchangeable guideline format. Without these features, it is difficult to enable automated knowledge acquisition and execution for Clinical Decision Support Systems designed to enhance evidence-based practice (Wang et al., 2002; Zielstorff, 1998).

EXISTING GUIDELINE ONTOLOGIES

The Evolution of Guideline Ontologies

There have been numerous efforts to represent medical knowledge to support computerized decision support. Among them, the Arden Syntax introduced in 1989, was the first and has become a certified standard of HL7[5]. Arden Syntax provides a specification for encoding medical knowledge as individual rule-based procedures, also known as Medical Logic Modules (MLMs). These MLMs each contains sufficient logic to make a single medical decision. Arden Syntax, however, is not designed to represent comprehensive clinical practice guidelines. It is up to the adopter's judgment to link individual MLMs in order to construct complex logic representing a full guideline. Extensions of Arden Syntax have been developed to accommodate this limitation, for example Interacting MLMs (Kuhn & Reider, 1994), which specifies how to use multiple MLMs as a set to mimic guideline behavior; and Augmented Decision Tables, which implements algorithms for additional capacities, such as probabilistic reasoning (Shiffman, 1997). Nevertheless, it has been a well known issue that the Arden Syntax is inadequate to represent complex guidelines that have advanced medical decision algorithms or multiple steps that unfold over time (Peleg et al., 2003).

This realization has led to the development of more comprehensive models. Among them well known and still existing ones include Asbru, EON, GLIF (Guideline Interchange Format), and SAGE (Sharable Active Guideline Environment), developed in the United States; and GASTON, GUIDE, PRODIGY and PRO*forma*, developed in Europe. Some of these ontologies, such as GLIF and SAGE, aim to achieve a general, interchangeable format; others such as PRODIGY3, focus on representing guidelines in certain disease areas such as chronic disease management and preventive care procedures.

Most of the existing guideline ontology models were independently developed. Nevertheless, they share many common characteristics, reflecting synthesized views of prior modeling work as well as the inherent nature of the evidence-based clinical practice guidelines these models attempt to represent (Peleg et al., 2003). While distinct design choices are made along many dimensions, ultimately these efforts attempt to achieve an guideline representation ontology that can:

- Represent and execute various types of guidelines with varying levels of complexity;
- Efficiently represent guidelines with minimal, reusable constructs;
- Provide visual tools that allow none-expert users to directly create, modify, compile, and execute computer algorithms that implement clinical practice guidelines;
- Support seamless integration with heterogeneous CDSSs for automated guideline execution;
- Provide a mechanism to minimize the amount of work in adapting generic guideline representations to intuitional requirements or other local contexts.

Because of many common shared characteristics, the existing models are reasonably interchangeable. Researchers have shown that a generic comparison model can be developed in order to map different guideline representation models to a set of generalized guideline execution tasks (Peleg et al., 2003). Being aware of the existence of such common characteristics, newly initiated projects, such as SAGE, aim to develop mechanisms to inherit the relevant features of existing ontologies to achieve a unified format for guideline representation.

In the next section we review several representative guideline ontology models: GLIF, SAGE, PRO*forma*, EON, PRODIGY, Asbru, and GUIDE. Two popular models, GLIF and PRO *forma*, are also selected for in-depth analyses.

Major Ontologies in Use

Approximately thirty ontologies have been developed for representing and executing medical knowledge. The ontology models included in this section are typically comprehensive ontologies that can be used to represent a full guideline. Information contained in this section is obtained from research publications or the project websites of these ontologies, unless otherwise specified.

GLIF

Unlike many other ontologies, the principle motivation for the development of the Guideline Interchange Format (GLIF) is to achieve a standard, sharable language for modeling and disseminating clinical practice guidelines. GLIF is developed by the InterMed Collaboratory, a joint project of the medical informatics laboratories at Harvard, Stanford, Columbia, and McGill Universities. Its research and implementation work is currently overseen by the HL7 Clinical Guidelines Special Interest Group. The first published version of GLIF, version 2, was released in 1998. The latest one, version 3, was released in 2000. An in-depth analysis of the GLIF3 format is presented in Section 3.2.

TOOLS: GLIF uses Protégé as its authoring tool[6]. GLIF3 develops an object-oriented query and expression language, GELLO, for encoding medical decisions. The GLIF3 Guideline Execution Engine (GLEE) is the tool for executing the guidelines encoded in the GLIF3 format.

IMPLEMENTATION: GLIF3 encoded guidelines are being used at Columbia University for post-CABG (Coronary Artery Bypass Grafting) patient care planning. A diabetes foot guideline is used in Israel at several primary care outpatient clinics.

URL: http://www.glif.org/

SAGE

Similar to GLIF, the SAGE (Sharable Active Guideline Environment) is proposed to inherit features of the existing ontologies as well as established medical standards to achieve a mechanism for interoperable distribution of guideline-based decision support systems. The ultimate goal of SAGE is to create an infrastructure that allows guideline execution across heterogeneous clinical information systems. The project started in 2002, as a collaboration between the IDX Corporation, Stanford Medical Informatics, Mayo Clinic (Rochester), the University of Nebraska, Intermountain Health Care, and Apelon. The most recent internal release is version 1.57, updated in September, 2005 (Tu et al., 2007).

TOOLS: SAGE also uses Protégé as its authoring tool, with a customized plug-in called *Kwiz* that extends Protégé's ability for guideline modeling in SAGE.

IMPLEMENTATION: SAGE encoded guidelines have not been used in practice; nevertheless there are plans to use SAGE to implement guidelines for immunization, diabetes, and community-acquired pneumonia in simulated environments at Mayo Clinic and University of Nebraska Medical Center.

URL: http://sage.wherever.org/

*PRO*forma

PRO *forma* aims to provide a specification and a knowledge representation language for authoring, publishing, and executing clinical guidelines. It is developed at the Advanced Computational Laboratory of Cancer Research in the United Kingdom. Starting in 1999, PRO*forma* was commercialized by *Infer*Med Ltd, under the brand name *Arezzo*. PRO*forma* is essentially a first-order logic (FOL) formalism[7] to support medical decision making and plan execution. In addition, it supports a number of non-classical logics, such as temporal logic. An in-depth analysis of the PRO *forma* is presented in Section 3.3.

TOOLS: *Tallis Composer* is developed to author and execute guidelines encoded in the PRO*forma* format. It is available at no charge for collaborative research use. *Arezzo*, a commercial product, provides dedicated authoring and execution environment for PRO *forma*.

IMPLEMENTATION: PRO *forma* has been used to develop a wide range of prototype and routinely used clinical applications. Some examples are CAPSULE, providing advice on prescribing in general practice, and Bloedlink, providing advice on laboratory tests, management of chronic diseases such as dyspepsia, asthma, and depression.

URL: http://www.acl.icnet.uk/lab/proforma.html

EON

EON is a guideline representation ontology that seeks to "create an architecture made up of a set of software components and a set of interfaces that developers can use to build robust decision-support systems that reason about guideline-directed care" (Musen, Tu, Das, & Shahar, 1996). It was developed by Stanford Medical Informatics. The project was initiated in 1996, ended in 2003, and the results are carried over to the SAGE project. Its guideline model, called *Dharma*, defines guideline knowledge structures such as eligibility criteria, abstraction definitions, guideline algorithms, decision models, and recommended actions. The EON execution system obtains patient data through a specified temporal database manager or from user input, and then generates guideline based recommendations.

TOOLS: EON uses Protégé as its authoring tool. *Padda* is the environment for executing guidelines encoded in EON, based on CORBA[8] architecture in a client-server fashion.

IMPLEMENTATION: EON is mainly used in the ATHENA project[9] to provide hypertension advisories at a number VA sites. An application called T-HELPER (Therapy-Helper) also uses EON for data management of patients with HIV.

URL: http://www.smi.stanford.edu/projects/eon/

PRODIGY

PRODIGY (Prescribing RatiOnally with Decision Support In General Practice study) is a clinical decision support system that integrates with the commercial primary care information systems in the UK. It is developed by the Sowerby Centre for Health Informatics at Newcastle. PRODIGY aims to facilitate knowledge engineering by producing a simple, understandable model sufficiently expressive in order to represent chronic disease management guidelines. PRODIGY I includes a guideline representation model, which was used in PRODIGY II to implement guidelines for the management of acute diseases. PRODIGY3 is designed to model guidelines for more chronic diseases management areas.

TOOLS: PRODIGY uses Protégé as its authoring tool. Dedicated PRODIGY3 execution environments are required in local adaptation.

IMPLEMENTATION: PRODIGY3 has been used in the UK to implement several chronic disease guidelines including hypertension, asthma, and angina.

URL: http://www.prodigy.nhs.uk/

Asbru

Asbru was developed as part of the Asgaard project by the Vienna University of Technology and Stanford Medical Informatics. It is a time-oriented, intention-based, skeletal plan-specification representation language to embody clinical guidelines as skeletal plans. These skeletal plans are typically used by human executing agents other than the original plan designer, although they also provide promise to represent guidelines in a computable format (Shahar, Miksch, & Johnson, 1998).

TOOLS: *AsbruView* is a graphical tool that supports visualization and understanding of Asbru encoded guidelines. *CareVis* is an integrated visualization of Asbru guidelines and temporal patient data. Finally *DELT/A* is a tool to edit Asbru guidelines in *XML* format, and to link to the original HTML guideline documents.

IMPLEMENTATION: Asbru has been used in the Asgaard project to create prototypes for a number of guidelines such as diabetes, jaundice, and breast cancer.

URL: http://www.asgaard.tuwien.ac.at/

GUIDE

GUIDE is a component-based, multi-level architecture that is designed to represent and execute guidelines with both workflow management systems and EMR technologies. GUIDE is developed by the Laboratory for Medical Informatics, Department of Computer and System Science at the University of Pavia, Italy. The GUIDE framework includes a Virtual Electronic Medical Record (vEMR)[10] and a logging system that allows all details of the health care process to be traced.

TOOLS: *Guide Editor* is a tool for editing guidelines encoded in GUIDE format.

IMPLEMENTATION: GUIDE is used in an application to support management of stroke patients in four hospitals in the Lombardia region. An application to support the management of patients with heart failure is being evaluated by general practitioners in the Trentino Alto Adige region.

URL: http://www.labmedinfo.org/research/dsg/decision_support.htm

TWO ONTOLOGIES IN DEPTH

In this section we will take a closer look at two of these seven ontologies. These two ontologies are selected because 1) they are comprehensive ontologies that can be used to represent a full guideline; 2) they significantly leverage on prior modeling work; 3) they are under continued development; 4) they are balloted to be standards under auspices of standard organizations such as HL7; and 5) they are being used, or under evaluation, to implement evidence-based guidelines in practice.

A number of comparison studies have been conducted to examine the differences and common characteristics of the existing models (Peleg et al., 2001; Peleg et al., 2003; Wang et al., 2004); among these studies the Peleg et al's paper on comparing computer-interpretable guideline models (Peleg et al., 2003) is most widely cited. In the paper the authors compared several competing models, including Asbru, EON, GLIF, GUIDE, PRODIGY, and PRO*forma*. The authors concluded that all current guideline ontologies attempt to "hierarchically decompose a guideline into networks of component tasks that unfold over time, and define rules and relationships, typical temporal sequences, among these component tasks" (Peleg et al., 2003). The resulting representations usually consist of networks of component tasks and the ability to express various arrangements of these components and interrelationships between them, also known as Task-Network Model (TNM).

In Peleg et al's paper the side-by-side comparisons were conducted among eight dimensions: organization of guideline plans, representation of goals or intentions, representation of guideline actions, models of decision-making, expression language, data interpretation, medical concept model, and patient information model. The authors concluded that consensus was found along a number of dimensions including plan organization, expression language, conceptual medical record model, medical concept model, and data abstractions; differences were most prominent in their underlying decision models, goal representation, use of scenarios, and structured medical actions (Peleg et al., 2003).

Analysis Dimensions and Evaluation Criteria

In this section we extend the analysis of GLIF (GLIF3 primarily) and PRO*forma* to include additional dimensions that reflect key components found common across major guideline ontology models. In representing clinical guidelines in a clinical decision support system, we found that these dimensions are essential to the effectiveness and feasibility of implementing an ontology model in practice. These dimensions are:

- **Level of Knowledge Acquisition**: Steps from acquiring medical knowledge from guideline publications to modeling and executing the computerized representations within heterogeneous computer systems;
- **Component Tasks**: Specification of concepts that constitute a guideline representation;
- **Expression Language**: Specification of how to express various concepts in a computer-recognizable format, with rigorously defined semantics and structures;
- **Medical Concept Model**: A layer that enables an ontology model, or its execution engine, to acquire patient data in order to provide case-specific advisories. The patient data may be coded using different medical controlled vocabularies;
- **Automated Execution**: The ability of supporting automated execution of the guideline representations;
- **Level of Sharing**: At what level the encoded guidelines can be shared: at the design level as conceptual representations, at the encoding level as sharable, computer-recognizable documents, or at the execution level that allows software agents to interact over networks;
- **Tools**: Tools developed or used for authoring, visualizing, executing, and disseminating guideline representations;
- **Applications**: Applications implemented in practice that use these ontology models to represent and execute evidence-based clinical practice guidelines;
- **Limitations**: Limitations that may prevent the wide-spread use of an ontology model. In particular we examine a model's ease of use, amount of work required for local adaptation, and its track record of being used and evaluated in practice.

For a guideline ontology model to be successful, it must be 1) comprehensive, so it can be used to map out complex clinical guidelines; 2) efficient, so a guideline representation can be derived through a small number of steps with a small number of conceptual constructs; and 3) flexible, so that the resulting representations can be easily localized or further modified. To assess the completeness, efficiency, and flexibility of an ontology model, we developed the following evaluation criteria used for the in-depth analyses:

1. Whether the model can be incorporated into computer-based systems for effective clinical decision-support;
2. Whether the model is comprehensive enough to represent complex guidelines, such as diabetes treatment recommendations;
3. Whether the model is simple enough to represent guidelines with minimal constructs;
4. Whether the model allows clinicians with no advanced programming knowledge to revise and customize the guideline representations. The updated guidelines should be executable in a hosting decision support system with no or minimal reconfiguration;
5. Whether the model provides an execution environment that supports automated

guideline execution;

6. Whether exchange of guidelines can be performed at the execution level, i.e., computerized guideline representations can be directly shared across execution environments. It should also provide a mechanism to facilitate communications across execution environments;
7. The amount of work needed in local adaptation. To minimize the localization effort, the model should provide an abstract layer that separates site-specifics from generic guideline representations[11];
8. Whether the resulting guideline representations can be used for different purposes, for instance issuing physician-oriented reminders or generating administration-oriented reports for quality assurance;
9. Whether the model supports established medical terminologies and standards. It should also be extendable in order to accommodate future terminologies and standards;
10. The model should leverage the existing guideline modeling methods.

GLIF3

GLIF3 is the most recent release of GLIF, the Guideline Interchange Format. This in-depth analysis is conducted based on GLIF-related research publications (Boxwala et al., 2004; Boxwala et al., 2001; Ohno-Machado et al., 1998; Patel, Branch, Wang, Peleg, & Boxwala, 2002; Wang et al., 2004), and the *GLIF3 Specifications* available at the GLIF project website (http://www.glif.org/).

Overview

GLIF3, developed by the InterMed Collaboratory, is a specification for structured representation of guidelines that aims to facilitate sharing of clinical guidelines (Ohno-Machado et al., 1998). The

Figure 1. Sample guideline diagram modeled with GLIF3

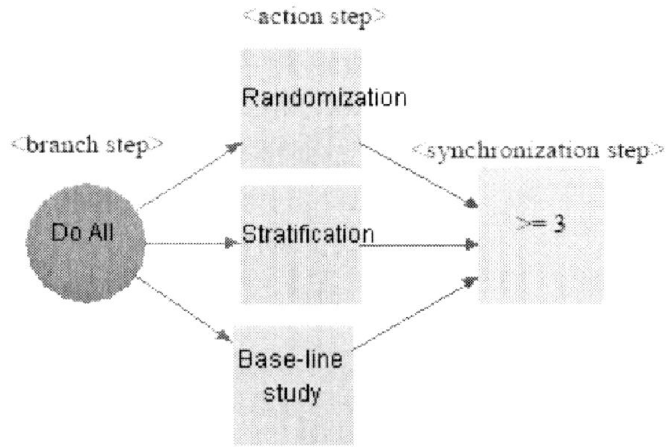

objective of the GLIF3 specification is to provide a representation for guidelines that is precise, unambiguous, human-readable, computable, and independent of computing platforms. The goals of GLIF3 are to 1) enable viewing of GLIF3-formatted guidelines by different software tools, and 2) enable adapting the guidelines to a variety of local uses (Peleg et al., 2000). A sample guideline diagram modeled with GLIF3 is shown in Figure 1[12].

Level of Knowledge Acquisition

GLIF3 enables guideline knowledge acquisition at three levels: 1) *Conceptual Flowchart*, a human-readable flowchart of clinical decisions and actions that captures the essence of a guideline specification, typically prepared by medical experts; 2) *Parseable Specification*, typically encoded by GLIF3 informaticians to define details of the representation such as patient data types, algorithms of each medical decision, and clinical recommendations (this level of specification can also be used to verify logical consistency and completeness of a guideline representation); and 3) *Implement-able Specification*, comprising none-shareable, institution-specifics, which can be used in local adaptation to map guideline logic and instructions to the medical records stored in an operational clinical information system.

Component Tasks

In GLIF3, guidelines are represented as flowcharts of temporally sequenced nodes called *Guideline Steps*. Different classes of guideline steps are used for modeling different constructs. Nesting of steps is allowed, which is used to represent recursive specifications of actions and decision. The guideline steps consist of:

- *Decision Step*: Used to represent medical decisions contained in a guideline, for example "check to see whether the patient's recent cholesterol test is under 160 mg/dL". A hierarchy of decision classes provides the ability to represent different decision models. A decision step has a *Name* attribute, describing the criterion in text, and a *Specification* attribute, specifying the decision criterion in a formal expression language;
- *Action Step*: Use to represent actions to be performed, typically medical recommendations. An action step can be either automated ones (*Case Steps*), or ones that have to be made by a physician or other health worker (*Choice Steps*);
- *Branch Step and Synchronization Step*: Used to model multiple simultaneous paths through the guideline. A branch step directs flow to one or more of a number of guideline steps, according to a non-Boolean selection method. A synchronization step is used in conjunction with branch steps to synchronize flow of control through multiple, possibly parallel paths. When the selection method on a branch step is parallel, the synchronization step is placed further along each possible path exiting the branch step, in order to resynchronize the flow of control before additional steps in the guideline can be visited;
- *Patient State Step*: Entry point into a guideline, which also allows for labeling distinct patient states;
- *Macro Step*: A special class whose attributes define the information that is needed to instantiate a set of underlying GLIF3 steps that represent a pattern appeared in guidelines.

The GLIF3 classes above are specified using Unified Modeling Language (UML) class diagrams. Additional constraints on represented concepts can be described using Object Constraint Language (OCL), a subset of the UML standard. The Resource Description Framework (RDF) is the infrastructure the GLIF3 uses for the encoding, exchange, and reuse of structured metadata.

Besides the classes mentioned above, GLIF3 also introduces several new concepts, such as *Iterations* and *Conditions* that control the iteration flow, *Events* that trigger guideline steps, *Exceptions* that handle exception conditions, and a keyword *Didactic* for adding keywords to the constructs.

Expression Language

GLIF3 has its own expression language, GELLO, which is an object-oriented expression language derived from the logical expression grammar of Arden Syntax. GELLO can be used for representing logical criteria, numerical expressions, temporal expressions, and text string operations. GELLO has been balloted to be an HL7 accredited standard in 2004.

Medical Concept Model

GLIF3 has three layers for acquiring patient data from institutional information systems. The first layer, *Core GLIF*, defines a standard interface to medical data items and the relationships among them. The second layer, the *Reference Information Model (RIM)*, defines the basic data model for representing medical information needed in specifying protocols and guidelines. It includes high-level classification concepts, such as medications and observations about a patient, as well as their attributes, such as units of a measurement and dosage for a drug and other medical concepts and medical data may have. GLIF3's RIM uses HL7 Reference Information Model[13], also known as the Unified Service Action Model (USAM). The third layer, *Medical Knowledge Layer*, is still under development. It will specify the methods for interfacing with controlled vocabularies, medical knowledge bases, and heterogeneous EMRs.

Automated Execution

The GLIF3 Guideline Execution Engine (GLEE) is the execution environment for executing GLIF3 encoded guideline representations. It is built as a middleware that can be integrated with clinical information systems at a local institution. However the flexibility and generality of GLEE, and its capacity of being integrated with local infrastructures, have not yet been adequately evaluated. Integration of GLEE with a specific event monitoring application or computerized physician order-entry system is not supported.

Level of Sharing

In GLIF3 the *Parseable Specification* results in a structured format that can be directly shared. However, local adaptors need to convert this level of specification to an *Implement-able Specification* in order to integrate the guideline representations with local workflow and institutional information systems. The guideline execution engine, GLEE, is still in its primitive development stage and sharing at the execution level is not available. The developers of GLIF3 have set this level of sharing as their next project target.

Applications

GLIF3 and GLEE are being used at Columbia University to reinforce the guideline coherence for post-CABG (Coronary Artery Bypass Grafting) patient care planning. They are also used to implement a diabetes foot guideline at several primary care outpatient clinics in Israeli. The integration of GLIF and GLEE with the clinical information system at the New York Presbyterian Hospital for clinical event monitoring is currently being explored.

Limitations

While GLIF3 is the most comprehensive guideline representation ontology currently available, it remains an experimental language with inadequate support of automated execution and lack of proven capacity of integration with institutional information systems. Although GLIF3 aims to define a standard for the computer-interpretable, sharable format, it has not yet been adopted by the vast health informatics community. To date GLIF3 and its execution engine, GLEE, are only used in prototype demonstrations in research settings.

GLEE, the GLIF3 Guideline Execution Environment, has been developed to facilitate execution of GLIF3-encoded guideline representations; however, it is still in the development stage and does not assure guideline sharing at the execution level. The value of having a standard, interchangeable format is largely diminished if tremendous work will be involved in local adaptation. This problem is not unique to GLIF though. It has been a widely acknowledged issue that reflects the lack of standard medical terminologies and communication protocols. HL7 and other standard developing organizations have made considerably efforts to address the issue. With the concept of Virtual Electronic Medical Record (vEMR), the release of HL7's new RIM standard, and other alternative technologies such as Unified Medical Language System (UMLS)[14], the problem may be eventually solved. However, how to integrate ontology models with heterogeneous clinical information systems remains a challenge.

PRO*forma*

We analyze the PRO *forma* ontology based on the project's academic publications (Fox & Bury, 2000; Fox et al., 1997; Fox, Johns, & Rahmanzadeh, 1998; Sutton & Fox, 2003) and the PRO *forma* language specifications available at http://www.acl.icnet.uk/lab/proforma.html.

Overview

PRO *forma*, developed at the Advanced Computational Laboratory of Cancer Research in UK, is a formal knowledge representation language designed to capture the content and structure of a clinical guideline in a form that can be interpreted by a computer. It has been successfully used to build and deploy a wide range of decision support systems, guidelines and other clinical applications (Sutton & Fox, 2003). PRO *forma* is essentially a first-order logic (FOL) formalism extended to support decision making and plan execution. In addition it supports a number of non-classical logic, such as temporal logic and modal logic, and two novel logic, LA, Logic of Argument, and LOT, Logic of Obligation and Time.

Applications built using PRO *forma* can be used to support the management of medical procedures and clinical decision making at the point of care. The *Infer*Med Ltd has commercialized PRO *forma* under the brand name *Arezzo*. This product has been successfully implemented in practice and has been integrated in many European EMR systems. *Infer*Med Ltd's current clients include Hoffman la Roche, the European Society for Cardiology, and the European Society for Research in the Treatment of Cancer.

The goals of the PRO *forma* development are to achieve a guideline representation language 1) be sufficiently expressive to fully represent a range of clinical processes; 2) be sufficiently general to describe processes in any clinical specialty; in addition it 3) use concepts that are intuitive for clinical users; 4) processes specified in the language can be enacted by machine; 5) the semantics of the language are demonstrably sound; and 6) applications can be automatically checked for consistency and other properties.

Level of Knowledge Acquisition

Converting a guideline into a PRO *forma* representation takes three steps. First a high level diagram that describes the outline of guideline (in terms of set of tasks) is developed. Next, this graphical structure is converted into a database, with detailed procedural and medical knowledge required to execute the guideline. Finally, the resulting computerized clinical guidelines are tested and executed using a PRO *forma*-compatible engine, such as *Arezzo Performer*.

Component Tasks

PRO *forma* decomposes a clinical guideline hierarchically into task networks representing plans or procedures carried out over time. Logical constructs, such as situations, constraints, pre- and post-conditions, allow the details of each task and inter-relationships between the tasks to be defined. The PRO *forma* model classifies tasks into four different classes: *Plans*, *Decisions*, *Actions*, and *Enquiries*.

- *Plans*: Sets of tasks to be carried out to achieve a clinical goal. Plans are the basic building blocks of a guideline, and may contain any number of tasks of any type, including other plans;
- *Decisions*: Points at which choice has to be made, such as a choice of investigation, diagnosis or treatment. A PRO *forma* decision task defines the decision options, relevant information, and a set of argument rules which determine the options to be chosen according to current data values;
- *Actions*: Procedures that need to be executed in the external environment, such as

the administration of an injection or updating a database. An action can be either an operation to be performed by a person, or SQL statements that describe data manipulation procedures in a database, along with identifying information of the database in which the action is to be performed;

- *Enquiries*: Represent information needs to be acquired from a person or an external source. Enquiries may be associated with the location of a database and SQL queries that can return desired data. If automated information acquisition is not available, some external human or software agent must take the appropriate action.

All PRO *forma* tasks have several common attributes, including *Pre-Conditions*: logical conditions that must be true in order for the task to start; *Post-Conditions*: logical conditions that may be assumed to be true after the task has finished; *Goal*: a logical condition expressing the situation that the task is intended to bring about; *Caption and Description*: documents what the task does and may refer to external sources of information justifying and explaining the operations described by the task; *Trigger*: a message that may be passed to the task in order to start it even if its parent plan has not scheduled it to start; and finally *Task Scheduling Constraints*: logical constraints that prevent one task from starting before another task or set of tasks has been completed.

The PRO *forma* processes can be represented diagrammatically as directed graphs in which nodes represent tasks and arcs represent scheduling constraints. A guideline itself contains a single root plan, which may be recursively divided into sub plans. A sample diagram modeled using PRO *forma* is shown in Figure 2[15].

Expression Language

PRO *forma* is a first-order logic formalism expressed in Backus-Naur Form (BNF) notation[16].

Figure 2. Sample guideline diagram modeled with PROforma

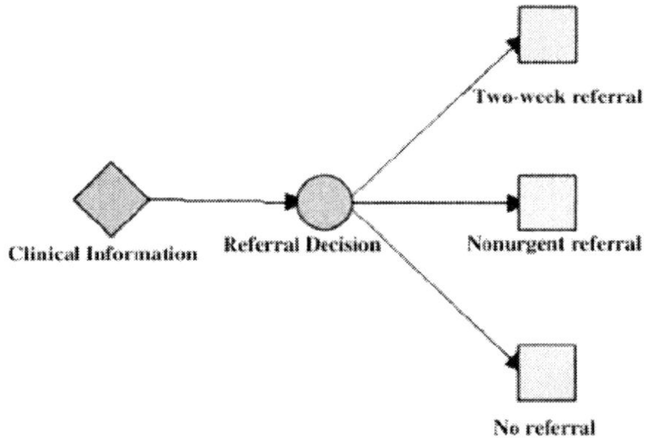

In the BNF form the PRO *forma* defines a set of proprietary operators and operations that can be used to sufficiently model medical decisions[17]. It can be used to model complex medical decision and processes such as temporal reasoning.

Medical Concept Model

PRO *forma* does not define an abstract medical concept model, instead it relies on the logic and queries embedded in each task for acquiring patient data needed in decision-making. In other words, PRO *forma* requires a tight integration---customized database connection strings and queries---in order to be integrated with heterogeneous clinical information systems. *Arezzo*, the commercialized counterpart of PRO *forma*, provides such integration solutions for major European EMR systems.

Tools

Arezzo Composer and *Arezzo Performer* are dedicated authoring and execution environments for working with PRO *forma*-encoded guidelines. They are commercial products of the *Infer*Med Ltd. The Advanced Computational Laboratory of Cancer Research also develops a similar counterpart, *Tallis Composer*, which is freely available for collaborative research use. The *Tallis* toolset is also an enactment engine, which can be used to publish package for making applications available over internet.

Automated Execution

The resulting computerized "enactable" clinical guideline representations can be tested and executed using a PRO*forma*-compatible engine. PRO*forma* also defines public operations that an external system may request the engine to perform, for instance an external system may invoke a public operation with patient information as inputs and receive action recommendations as outputs. The guideline representations (tasks and their properties) are stored in a database which allows the enactment engine to retrieve and execute.

Level of Sharing

Although it is possible to transfer the guideline representations from one enactment engine to another, the PRO*forma* is simply not a language specification designed for guideline sharing. It does not make use of the standards for storage and interchange of structured information, such as *XML* and RDF, and it does not comply with any of the health information exchange standards, such as HL7. Developers of PRO*forma* are currently working on *XML* semantics that can be used to represent tasks and data items defined in PRO *forma*, in order to achieve certain level of interchangeability.

Applications

PRO *forma* has been used to develop a wide range of prototype and routinely used clinical applications to provide advice on prescribing and aid in management of chronic disease conditions. *Infer*Med Ltd, that commercializes the PRO*forma* technology under the brand name of *Arezzo*, has been a successful startup with many European clients.

Limitations

First, PRO*forma* is not an representation language that is designed to enable guideline sharing. While PRO *forma* and its commercial version *Arezzo* have been routinely used in a number of applications, they do not provide a sufficient platform and accompany toolsets for representing and disseminating guidelines. The PRO *forma* model has many proprietary specifications of tasks and data items, which do not make use of any of the existing standards for structured data storage and exchange. In addition its guideline representations are stored in a relational database with proprietary schemas.

Second, the PRO*forma* model does not have an abstract layer representing patient data elements and their properties, which in turn requires customized interfaces to be built in order to retrieve patient data for effective decision-making. The PRO*forma*-based systems largely relies on rules embedded in properties of each task for data acquisition, for example the *Enquiries* task and the *Actions* task keep track of external sources and methods of data acquiring or manipulating, either by issuing SQL queries to a database system or raising the event to a person. This architecture requires tremendous effort in revising PRO*forma* guideline representations in order to incorporate site-specific details.

ONTOLOGIES AND CLINICAL DECISION SUPPORT SYSTEMS

Based on the review of several representative ontologies and the in-depth analyses of GLIF3 and PRO *forma*, this section summarize the ontology approach by conceptualizing common elements constituting a guideline representation, and outlining general steps for computerizing an evidence-based clinical practice guideline using formal ontologies.

Deconstructing Clinical Guidelines

While different ontology models take different design choices, their common characteristics collectively reveal the underlying structure of the descriptive guideline publications. In general, most clinical guidelines can be decomposed into the following seven major concepts:

1. **Triggering Criteria**: Initial screening to determine whether a patient should enter the guideline protocol. It provides general guidance on patient population or geographic region that the guideline can be applied to. It may also be relevant to its intended practice environments, such as children care providers or specialists of a certain type of disease;
2. **Information Flow**: An overall structure of a guideline, typically temporal sequences that connect various elements;
3. **Decisions**: Logic of evaluating criterion for making a medical decision;
4. **Actions**: Actions to be taken based on results of evaluating a decision criterion, typically treatment plans to be recommended;
5. **Exceptions**: Plans when statements specified in a guideline cannot be performed or are not valid under certain circumstances;
6. **Medical Terminologies, Data Structure, and Data Acquiring Methods**: How to map a statement such as "check the asthma severity" to computer-interpretable queries that typically lead to a database lookup;
7. **Relationships among Guidelines and Guideline Components**: A virtual construct that enables an guideline to contain other guidelines or a subset of another guideline. For example an estimation of ten-year risk of fatal cardiovascular disease can be included in several chronic management guidelines.

Implementing a Guideline using a Formal Ontology

Since many of the existing guideline ontologies share similar components, the procedures for representing an unstructured, descriptive guideline in computer-interpretable format can be generalized. We describe below a general four step process for implementing a computer-interpretable guideline using a formal guideline ontology. The resulting guideline representations can be then incorporated into Clinical Decision Support Systems to support medical decision-making.

1. **Knowledge Acquisition**: A conceptual level, preliminary flowchart is created by a panel of medical experts. This flowchart captures the basic elements and flow of information of a guideline, such as the one illustrated in Figure 3;
2. **Medical Terminology Mapping**: Based on the preliminary flowchart, a panel of medical experts and informaticians needs to determine medical terminologies that can be used to represent the narrative statements of medical concepts, for instance "diabetes diagnosis" should be translated into "250.*" (ICD-9-CM is used here for illustration). Because a variety of controlled vocabularies are available, the panel needs to make a decision about which vocabulary to use if ambiguity exists.(see Figure 4) In addition, the medical concepts in a guideline statement may contain composite elements. Such concepts must be decomposed to a level that matches the structure in which these concepts are stored in EMRs. For example, a short-acting beta-agonist treatment contains a class of drugs such as Albuterol, Proventil, and Ventolin; and a Lipid Profile test may include individual tests of HDL, LDL, Triglycerides, and Total Cholesterol. There exist other considerations that may further complicate the situation, for instance the panel needs to

Figure 3. A sample preliminary flowchart capturing the basic concepts of a clinical guideline

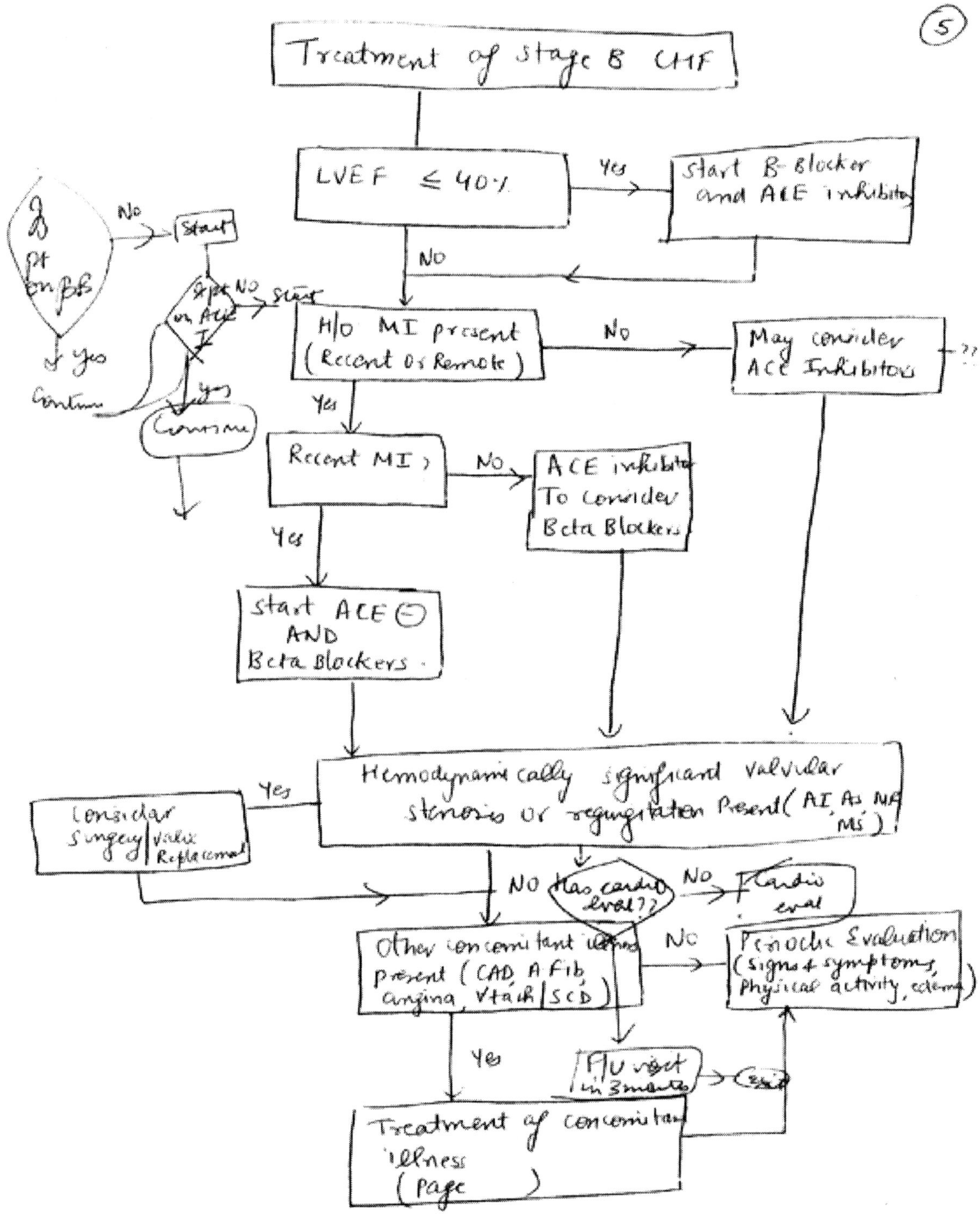

Figure 4. A sample worksheet for medical terminology mapping

GUIDELINE NAME: OSTEOPOROSIS GUIDELINE CODER'S INITIAL: ______ DATE: ______

description	data item	data item code	logic pseudo code	exception
On Corticosteroids for 3 or more months?	☐ Medication ☐ Diagnosis ☐ Laboratory Test ☐ Procedure ☐ Other ______			
Testosterone done within last year?	☐ Medication ☐ Diagnosis ☐ Laboratory Test ☐ Procedure ☐ Other ______			
Testosterone result normal?	☐ Medication ☐ Diagnosis ☐ Laboratory Test ☐ Procedure ☐ Other ______			
Bone density done with 1 year?	☐ Medication ☐ Diagnosis ☐ Laboratory Test ☐ Procedure ☐ Other ______			
On >= 7.5mg/day Prednisone or an equivalent?	☐ Medication ☐ Diagnosis ☐ Laboratory Test ☐ Procedure ☐ Other ______			
On Bisphosphanate?	☐ Medication ☐ Diagnosis ☐ Laboratory Test ☐ Procedure ☐ Other ______			
Bone density < -3.5?	☐ Medication ☐ Diagnosis ☐ Laboratory Test ☐ Procedure ☐ Other ______			
Had a spine or hip fracture?	☐ Medication ☐ Diagnosis ☐ Laboratory Test ☐ Procedure ☐ Other ______			
On Estrogen?	☐ Medication ☐ Diagnosis ☐ Laboratory Test ☐ Procedure ☐ Other ______			

Figure 5. A sample visual diagram

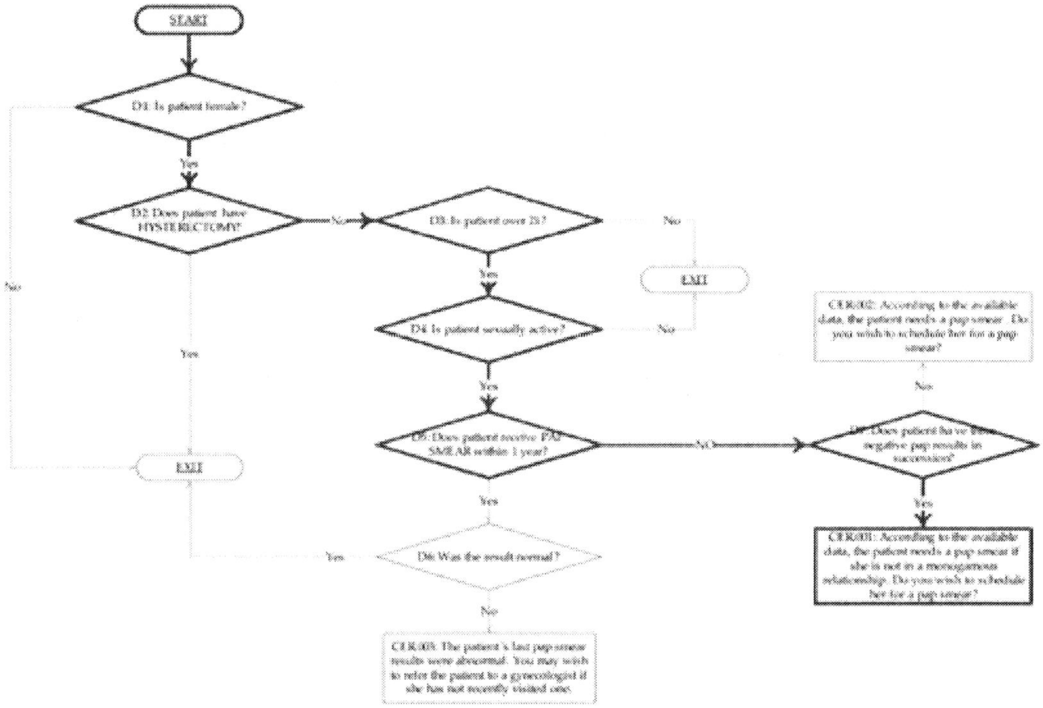

determine whether "Albuterol" represents a generic drug name, or a name of a drug class, or an ingredient contained in a drug formula.

3. **Guideline Encoding**: This step is performed by a trained modeler who is familiar with the specifications of the ontology being used. The modeler uses the associated guideline encoding tool which typically supports visualized guideline encoding, to computerize the conceptual flowchart created in the knowledge acquisition step. More specifically, the modeler draws a set of defined shapes to represent various entities and connects them with unilateral lines to represent temporal sequences of execution. Next the modeler defines the vocabulary choices and advanced rules determined in the medical terminology mapping step. The modeler finally specifies data elements that are needed for executing the current guideline. Although this step requires significant amount of effort by a modeler, it is one-time investment and the resulting representation is straightforward and it hides most of the details at various layers of abstraction. This representation, essentially a flowchart that looks no different from the conceptual flowchart created in step 1, can be directly edited by clinicians for customization or incremental updates (such as change of a threshold value based on newly published evidence). Figure 5 shows an example of the resulting visual diagram, where the highlighted path illustrates a possible decision-making pathway.
4. **Guideline Execution**: Depending on the nature of the tool, the encoding converts the computerized guideline representations into a programming language and compiles it into executable which can be used by the system in which the guideline is implemented. The Guideline Execution Engine (GLEE),

for example, is the tool for executing the guidelines encoded in the GLIF3 format.

CONCLUSION

This chapter introduces the concept of guideline representation ontology, which is a specification of conceptualizations that constitutes evidence-based clinical practice guidelines. The main purpose of introducing the concept of ontology into knowledge representation is to enable knowledge sharing and reuse. Over the past several years, many ontology models for representing clinical practice guidelines have been developed, and become more expressive and powerful over time. However, there are several outstanding issues that must be resolved before any specific ontology can become widely adopted. The most critical prerequisite for wider acceptance of a guideline ontology is that it should be comprehensive enough to represent complex guidelines. Second, the guideline ontology should be simple enough to represent guidelines with a minimal set of constructs. Furthermore, since medical professionals are integral members of the guideline development and revision process, the ontology and related tools should be developed so clinicians with no advanced programming knowledge can revise and customize the guideline representations. To achieve this goal, the model must be accompanied by user-friendly tools for modification, and execution.

This chapters reviews several reprehensive ontologies, and presents in-depth analyses of two popular models: GLIF (Guideline Interchange Format) and PRO*forma*. These ontology models have advanced the state of knowledge on how to represent clinical practice guidelines in computer-interpretable format; however, they all share certain limitations that have prevented their widespread use. First, most of these models are experimental ontologies that lack proven validity and effectiveness in practice. Second, many of the existing ontology models do not support automated guideline execution: while these representations of clinical practice guidelines are stored in a structured, computer-interpretable format, they are not algorithms that may be programmed directly into CDSSs. Third, some of the existing models are specialized in certain disease areas, i.e. their knowledge domains may be too narrow to represent generic types of guidelines. On the other hand, more generalized ontology models are often too complex to be used by clinician users who have little or no advanced computer knowledge. Finally, software tools provided to support editing, visualizing, and executing guideline representations encoded in these ontologies are not user-friendly.

A second set of major considerations revolves around a guidelines ability to be exchanged without significant effort, both for the distributor and the receiver. Exchange of guidelines can be performed at execution level, i.e., computerized guideline representations can be directly shared across execution environments. For a receiver, adaptation of the guideline to the specific constrains of the implementation site, should require minimal redesign. To fulfill this requirement the model should provide an abstract layer that separates site-specifics from generic guideline representations. In addition to an ontology's ability to represent complex logic and its ability to be distributed without significant modification, it should have enough flexibility so that it can be used for different purposes and allows for future expansions. Furthermore, it should support established medical terminologies and standards data exchange standards.

Currently, there are a significant number of solid guideline ontologies to choose from when developing Clinical Decision Support Systems. However, the field is still active and much progress can be expected in the coming years, both in the improvement of existing ontologies as well as the development of novel ontologies and methods for representing clinical knowledge and decisions in computerized clinical decision support systems.

REFERENCES

Boxwala, A. A., Peleg, M., Tu, S., Ogunyemi, O., Zeng, Q. T., & Wang, D. (2004). GLIF3: a representation format for sharable computer-interpretable clinical practice guidelines. *Journal of Biomedical Informatics*, *37*(3), 147–161. doi:10.1016/j.jbi.2004.04.002

Boxwala, A. A., Tu, S., Peleg, M., Zeng, Q., Ogunyemi, O., & Greenes, R. A. (2001). Toward a representation format for sharable clinical guidelines. *Journal of Biomedical Informatics*, *34*(3), 157–169. doi:10.1006/jbin.2001.1019

Fox, J., & Bury, J. (2000). A quality and safety framework for point-of-care clinical guidelines. *Proc AMIA Symp*, 245-249.

Fox, J., Johns, N., Lyons, C., Rahmanzadeh, A., Thomson, R., & Wilson, P. (1997). PROforma: a general technology for clinical decision support systems. *Computer Methods and Programs in Biomedicine*, *54*(1-2), 59–67. doi:10.1016/S0169-2607(97)00034-5

Fox, J., Johns, N., & Rahmanzadeh, A. (1998). Disseminating medical knowledge: the PROforma approach. *Artificial Intelligence in Medicine*, *14*(1-2), 157–181. doi:10.1016/S0933-3657(98)00021-9

Gruber, T. R. (1993). A translation approach to portable ontology specifications. *Knowledge Acquisition*, *5*(2), 199–220. doi:10.1006/knac.1993.1008

Kuhn, R. A., & Reider, R. S. (1994). A C++ framework for developing Medical Logic Modules and an Arden Syntax compiler. *Computers in Biology and Medicine*, *24*(5), 365–370. doi:10.1016/0010-4825(94)90003-5

Musen, M. A., Tu, S. W., Das, A. K., & Shahar, Y. (1996). EON: a component-based approach to automation of protocol-directed therapy. *Journal of the American Medical Informatics Association*, *3*(6), 367–388.

Ohno-Machado, L., Gennari, J. H., Murphy, S. N., Jain, N. L., Tu, S. W., & Oliver, D. E. (1998). The guideline interchange format: a model for representing guidelines. *Journal of the American Medical Informatics Association*, *5*(4), 357–372.

Patel, V. L., Branch, T., Wang, D., Peleg, M., & Boxwala, A. (2002). Analysis of the process of encoding guidelines: a comparison of GLIF2 and GLIF3. *Methods of Information in Medicine*, *41*(2), 105–113.

Peleg, M., Boxwala, A. A., Bernstam, E., Tu, S., Greenes, R. A., & Shortliffe, E. H. (2001). Sharable representation of clinical guidelines in GLIF: relationship to the Arden Syntax. *Journal of Biomedical Informatics*, *34*(3), 170–181. doi:10.1006/jbin.2001.1016

Peleg, M., Boxwala, A. A., Ogunyemi, O., Zeng, Q., Tu, S., Lacson, R., et al. (2000). GLIF3: the evolution of a guideline representation format. *Proc AMIA Symp*, 645-649.

Peleg, M., Tu, S., Bury, J., Ciccarese, P., Fox, J., & Greenes, R. A. (2003). Comparing computer-interpretable guideline models: a case-study approach. *Journal of the American Medical Informatics Association*, *10*(1), 52–68. doi:10.1197/jamia.M1135

Sackett, D. L., Rosenberg, W. M., Gray, J. A., Haynes, R. B., & Richardson, W. S. (1996). Evidence based medicine: what it is and what it isn't. *BMJ (Clinical Research Ed.)*, *312*(7023), 71–72.

Shahar, Y., Miksch, S., & Johnson, P. (1998). The Asgaard project: a task-specific framework for the application and critiquing of time-oriented clinical guidelines. *Artificial Intelligence in Medicine*, *14*(1-2), 29–51. doi:10.1016/S0933-3657(98)00015-3

Shiffman, R. N. (1997). Representation of clinical practice guidelines in conventional and augmented decision tables. *Journal of the American Medical Informatics Association*, *4*(5), 382–393.

Sutton, D. R., & Fox, J. (2003). The syntax and semantics of the PROforma guideline modeling language. *Journal of the American Medical Informatics Association*, *10*(5), 433–443. doi:10.1197/jamia.M1264

Tu, S. W., Campbell, J. R., Glasgow, J., Nyman, M. A., McClure, R., & McClay, J. (2007). The SAGE Guideline Model: achievements and overview. *Journal of the American Medical Informatics Association*, *14*(5), 589–598. doi:10.1197/jamia.M2399

Wang, D., Peleg, M., Tu, S. W., Boxwala, A. A., Greenes, R. A., & Patel, V. L. (2002). Representation primitives, process models and patient data in computer-interpretable clinical practice guidelines: a literature review of guideline representation models. *International Journal of Medical Informatics*, *68*(1-3), 59–70. doi:10.1016/S1386-5056(02)00065-5

Wang, D., Peleg, M., Tu, S. W., Boxwala, A. A., Ogunyemi, O., & Zeng, Q. (2004). Design and implementation of the GLIF3 guideline execution engine. *Journal of Biomedical Informatics*, *37*(5), 305–318. doi:10.1016/j.jbi.2004.06.002

Zielstorff, R. D. (1998). Online practice guidelines: issues, obstacles, and future prospects. *Journal of the American Medical Informatics Association*, *5*(3), 227–236.

KEY TERMS AND DEFINITIONS

Guideline Representation Ontology: An Guideline Representation Ontology is a specication of conceptualizations that constitutes evidence-based clinical practice guidelines.

Computational Guideline Representation Ontology: A Computational Guideline Representation Ontology provides computable representations that can be visualized, edited, executed, and shared using computer-based systems.

ENDNOTES

1. http://www.guideline.gov/.
2. The concept of ontology pervades our life. For example, a natural language is analogous to an ontology, in which nouns and verbs are concepts and grammar defines the relationships. A taxonomy or hierarchy is also a simple kind of ontology, in which concepts are arranged according to only one relation: ``is a kind of''.
3. Web Ontology Language (OWL) is an ontology that facilitates information sharing between intelligent applications (instead of just presenting information to humans). It explicitly represents the meaning of terms in vocabularies and the relationships between those terms. It is a standard under development by W3C. http://www.w3.org/2001/sw/.
4. Gene Ontology (GO) is an ontology that facilitates information sharing and machine reasoning, by providing a controlled vocabulary for the description of cellular components, molecular functions, and biological processes. It is a standard under development by Open Biological Ontologies (OBO). http://www.geneontology.org/GO.doc.shtml.
5. Health Level Seven (HL7) is an ANSI accredited standards developing organization

in the health domain. It is an international community of healthcare subject matter experts and information scientists collaborating to create standards for the exchange, management and integration of electronic healthcare information. http://www.hl7.org/.

6 Protégé is an open source ontology editor for constructing domain models and knowledge-based applications with ontologies, maintained by Stanford University. http://protege.stanford.edu.

7 First-order logic, or first-order predicate logic, is symbolized reasoning in which each sentence, or statement, is broken down into a subject and a predicate. The predicate modifies or defines the properties of the subject. First-order logic is very useful in the creation of computer programs for in artificial intelligence reasoning.

8 CORBA (Common Object Request Broker Architecture) is an Object Management Group (OMG) standard that enables software components written in multiple computer languages and running on multiple computers to interoperate.

9 ATHENA (Assessment and Treatment of Hypertension: Evidence-Based Automation), a research project conducted by Stanford Medical Informatics and several participating VA hospitals.

10 vEMR is an abstract collection of patient care related information. It is a widely adopted concept to enable data exchange across health care applications, and platform-independent application development.

11 One time local adaptation to reflect site-specifics may be required; however, the model should minimize the local adaptation effort by allowing configurable site profiles

12 Reprint of Peleg et al., Guideline Interchange Format 3.5 Technical Specification, http://www.glif.org/.

13 HL7 Reference Information Model (HL7 RIM) expresses the data content needed in a specific clinical or administrative context and provides an explicit representation of the semantic and lexical connections that exist between the information carried in the fields of HL7 messages.

14 Unified Medical Language System (UMLS) is a software tool designed to facilitate the development of computer systems for use of terminologies of biomedicine and health. It is used by system developers in building or enhancing electronic information systems that create, process, retrieve, and aggregate biomedical and health data and information. http://umlsinfo.nlm.nih.gov/.

15 Reprint of Sutton DR and Fox J, The syntax and semantics of the PROforma guideline modeling language, Journal of American Medical Informatics Association. 2003;10:433--443.

16 BNF is a formal notation to describe the syntax of a given language, such as temporal and argumentation logic.

17 Syntax specification is available at: http://www.acl.icnet.uk/.

Chapter 16
Speeding Up Decision Support:
Investigating the Distributed Simulation of a Healthcare Supply Chain

Navonil Mustafee
Warwick Business School, UK

Simon J.E. Taylor
Brunel University, UK

Korina Katsaliaki
Middlesex University, UK

Sally Brailsford
University of Southampton, UK

ABSTRACT

Discrete-Event Simulation (DES) is a decision support technique that allows stakeholders to conduct experiments with models that represent real-world systems of interest. Its use in healthcare is comparatively new. Healthcare needs have grown and healthcare organisations become larger, more complex and more costly. There has never been a greater need for carefully informed decisions and policy. DES is valuable as it can provide evidence of how to cope with these complex health problems. However, the size of a healthcare system can lead to large models that can take an extremely long time to simulate. In this chapter the authors investigate how a technique called distributed simulation allows us to use multiple computers to speed up this simulation. Based on a case study of the UK National Blood Service they demonstrate the effectiveness of this technique and argue that it is a vital technique in healthcare informatics with respect to supporting decision making in large healthcare systems.

INTRODUCTION

Computer simulation, or just simulation, is a decision support technique that allows stakeholders to conduct experiments with models that represent real-world systems of interest (Pidd, 2004a). It has been widely used for many years in domains such as manufacturing, logistics and telecommunication.. However, its use in healthcare is comparatively new. It is only really during the last decade that the application of simulation in health care has grown

DOI: 10.4018/978-1-60566-030-1.ch016

substantially (Fone et al, 2003). Healthcare needs have also grown in the same period and healthcare organizations become larger, more complex and more costly. There has never been a greater need for carefully informed decisions and policy. Computer simulation is valuable as it can provide evidence of how to cope with these complex health problems. It can be used as an alternative to "learning by doing" or empirical research (Royston, 1999). Furthermore, if carried out correctly, simulation modelling gives stakeholders the opportunity to participate in model develop and, hopefully, gain deeper understanding of the problems that they face. As a result, decision-makers and stakeholders can gain a new perspective on the relationships between the available resources, the level of the system's performance and the overall quality of the healthcare provision.

Many successful studies have been reported using simulation to address health care system problems (Jun et al, 1999; Cooper et al 2007). Of these, four simulation approaches have been used. These are Monte-Carlo Simulation, Agent-Based Simulation, System Dynamics and Discrete-Event Simulation. Monte-Carlo Simulation has its roots in World War Two and is a simulation technique that uses a sequence of random numbers according to probabilities assumed to be associated with a source of uncertainty, for example, stock prices, interest rates, commodity prices, etc. (Rubinstein, 1981). In healthcare, Monte-Carlo Simulation has been used to evaluate the cost-effectiveness of competing technologies or healthcare strategies that require the description of patient pathways over extended time horizons. It is the main approach to modelling used in economic evaluations in health care interventions when there is a need to increase the number of states in the model to overcome the homogeneity assumptions inherent in Markov models and decision trees (Barton et al., 2004). Agent-Based Simulation is a computational technique for modelling the actions and interactions of autonomous individuals in a network, called agents, with a view to assessing their effects on the system as a whole but not independently. It is a technique used since the mid-1990s to solve a variety of financial, business and technology problems. Its application in the healthcare sector is not yet widespread but is has been used to study problems such as the spread of epidemics (Bagni et al., 2002). System Dynamics comes from Industrial Engineering in the 1950's and is a modeling approach that takes a holistic view of the problem. In healthcare, Systems Dynamics is used to model health systems from a more integrated or top-level approach. This simulation technique can assist the design of healthcare policies by examining how the fundamental structure might influence the progressive behaviour of a system. It takes into consideration factors such as the time variation both of tangible elements, such as waiting times and health care costs, as well as intangible, such as patient anxiety and the effects of various pressures on purchasing decisions (Taylor and Lane, 1998). In Discrete-Event Simulation, a technique that emerged in the UK in the late 1950's, systems are modeled in greater detail than with Systems Dynamics and with more complex temporal dependencies than with Monte-Carlo Simulation. It involves the modelling of a system as it progresses through time and is particularly useful for modelling queuing systems (Robinson, 1994). Discrete-Event Simulation is therefore particularly well-suited to tackle problems in healthcare where, for example, resources are scarce and patients arrive at irregular times (for example in A&E departments). Some of the applications of Discrete Event Simulation is therefore to forecast the impact of changes in patient flow, to examine resource needs (either in physical capacity of beds and equipment or in staffing), to manage patient scheduling and admissions or to investigate the complex relationships among the different model variables (for example, rate of arrivals or time spent in the system). Discrete-Event Simulation therefore allows decision makers (namely, health policy makers, administrators and hospital managers) to effectively assess the efficiency of existing health care delivery systems, to improve system performance or design, and to plan new ones. An extensive taxonomy of discrete event simulation studies in healthcare over the past twenty years is presented in Jun et al. (1999) and Fone et al. (2003). It has been shown that Discrete-Event Simulation can create significantly more insight than Monte-Carlo Simulation in areas such as health economics (Eldabi et al, 2000).

To recap, healthcare systems are becoming larger and more complex. Of our computer simulation approaches, Discrete-Event Simulation (DES) is the most suitable technique to capture these complexities for to support meaningful decision making as it allows appropriate levels of detail and dynamic, stochastic behaviour to captured. However, a knock-on effect of this is that DES models are becoming larger, more complex, and significantly more computationally demanding. In some cases, the time taken to run the simulation of a single scenario can take over a day. These long run-times can make the whole simulation project untenable. However, research has shown that it is possible to reduce these run-times by using a technique called *distributed simulation* that utilises multiple computers to share the processing load. This is, however, not at all easy! This chapter therefore reports on this recent, exciting advance in healthcare informatics that could widely benefit many large-scale modelling projects and, ultimately, broaden the application of this technique.

The chapter is structured as follows. In section 2 we present more details on DES. Section 3 gives an overview of *distributed simulation*, the approach to sharing the processing load of large models over several computers. Section 4 reports on our case study, the National Blood Service simulation. Section 5 presents some results from our case study that compares our work on the performance of the simulation running a single computer system against a simulation running on multiple computers using distributed simulation techniques. Section 6 discusses the implications of these results. Section 7 discusses some important future trends emerging from our demonstration of the benefits of distributed simulation. Section 8 draws the chapter to a close.

DISCRETE EVENT SIMULATION

A Discrete-Event Simulation (DES) model encompasses a number of important concepts, namely entities, state, events and logical relationships, which define the overall behaviour of the abstract representation of the real system being studied. Entities are the elements of the system that can be individually identified and processed (e.g., patients, orders, documents, etc.). These "flow" through the system requiring resources (e.g., nurses, beds, etc.) in order to perform activities (e.g., prognoses, operations, etc.). Waiting lines (queues) (e.g., reception areas, waiting rooms, clinics, etc.) are where entities wait for needed resources to become available or for events to take place (e.g., hospital admissions, doctor assessment, etc.). Logical relationships link the different entities together and make them behave in a certain way. While a complete introduction to DES is outside the scope of this paper, excellent background literature includes Pidd (, 2004a), Law (2007) and many papers from the Winter Simulation Conference series (www.wintersim.org).

The process of building DES models usually involves some form of software. The software can either be a high level programming language or a data-driven software system in which the model is specified using user-defined and default data items. These computer packages are described as Visual Interactive Modelling Systems (VIMS) (Pidd, 2004a), or Simulators (Law, 2007). Most of these have evolved into "black box" or "shrink wrapped" software with user interfaces that are familiar to users of Microsoft Windows™ packages such as Office™. We therefore refer to these as Commercial Off-The-Shelf (COTS) Simulation Packages (CSPs). Examples include AnyLogic™

(XJ Technologies), Arena™ (Rockwell Automation), Flexsim™ (Flexsim Software Products, Inc), Simul8™ (Simul8 Corporation) and Witness™ (Lanner group). Moreover, some CSPs are specifically aimed at the health care industry, such as MedModel™ (ProModel Corporation) and Arena™ (Rockwell Automation) with a health care template.

The CSPs allow the users to create and experiment with simulations visually and interactively. They are easy and intuitive to use and are popular among modellers. They enable relatively unskilled users to develop useful simulations in a short period of time without the need for detailed computer programming (Pidd and Cassel, 2000). Furthermore, the introduction of visually oriented graphical outputs not only aids in the verification and validation of models and results (Gipps, 1986), but also in the communication of results to decision makers. In addition, once the model is set and enhanced with user-friendly mechanisms for running different scenarios, these systems can be easily be reused by end-users alone. The number of health care organisations and government agencies using these advanced simulation packages has grown (Jun et al., 1999).

These CSPs, although suitable for most systems that are modelled in industry (which includes the healthcare sector), may lack the capability to simulate large and complex models (Pidd, 2004b). Moreover, "there remain systems that cannot be sensibly simulated in this way, either because the application logic is too detailed or obscure for the simulators, or for other reasons such as the need to run an extremely fast or large simulation" (Pidd and Cassel, 2000). Therefore, there are still occasions that may justify the development of simulation programs from scratch using general-purpose programming languages (such as Java or C++). However, since these bespoke simulation programs are usually tailor-made to investigate specific problems (i.e. lack flexibility) and because they usually lack in visual interaction and animation capabilities (i.e. CSPs have evolved over the years to give quite sophisticated capabilities that bespoke solutions typically cannot afford), they may not appeal to healthcare managers.

Nevertheless, as healthcare systems become more complex to manage there is a greater demand for quantifiable evidence to assist decision making. Within the healthcare sector, only a limited number of simulation models have been developed to analyse complex multi-facility healthcare delivery systems (Jun et al., 1999). Most simulation models report on individual or local in scale units of healthcare facilities or problems in general. There is an emerging need for the development of more powerful high speed distributed simulations which will could facilitate the creation of complex, but tractable, models of large integrated systems, with the results implemented more easily and frequently (Baezner et al., 1990). This book chapter therefore focuses on an approach to *distributed simulation* that is making the high speed simulation of large and complex healthcare systems using CSPs more possible.

Distributed simulation refers to the execution of a DES comprising two or more models, each of which runs on a separate processor or computer (the distinction is made as some computers have multiple processors). However, the CSPs do not have inbuilt support for distributed simulation. *The objective of this chapter is therefore to propose and demonstrate a solution which enables the execution of large and complex healthcare models, developed in CSPs via the use of distributed simulation.* We demonstrate via a case study how this approach has been used to support the National Blood Service (NBS) supply chain simulation in the Southampton area of the UK. This is arguably the first attempt to create a distributed simulation in healthcare. This research assumes added significance because a CSP (Simul8™ from Simul8 Corporation) has been used to create and execute the NBS models. This is unlike the majority of distributed simulations, in domains such as the military, where the models themselves are coded using a general purpose programming language.

We now introduce the technique of distributed simulation.

DISTRIBUTED SIMULATION

This section will outline the motivations of using distributed simulation and highlight its application areas. It will discuss the theory behind it and present an overview of different middleware being used to executing such simulations, in particular the High Level Architecture (HLA), which is increasingly becoming the *de facto* standard for distributed simulation.

Definition

In a distributed simulation, a large computer model is executed over several processors. These processors can be a part of a multiprocessor computer or may belong to multiple PCs that are connected over a network. Parallel Discrete Event Simulation (PDES) usually refers to the execution of such distributed DES on parallel and distributed machines (Page and Nance, 1994).

In the context of PDES, Fujimoto (2001) distinguishes between parallel and distributed simulation based on the frequency of interactions between processors during the simulation execution. A parallel simulation is defined as running a simulation on a tightly coupled computer with multiple central processing units (CPUs) where the communication between the CPUs can be very frequent (e.g., thousands of times per second). A distributed simulation, on the other hand, is defined as executing simulations on multiple processors over loosely coupled systems (e.g., a network of PCs) where the interactions take more time (e.g., milliseconds or more) and occur less often. Sometimes the terms parallel simulation and distributed simulation are used interchangeably (Reynolds, 1988). Fujimoto (2003) uses the term distributed simulation to refer to both the parallel and distributed variants of PDES. The rationale presented is that, although historically, the terms "distributed simulation" and "parallel simulation" referred to geographically distributed simulations and simulations on tightly coupled parallel computers respectively, new distributed computing paradigms like clusters of workstations and grid computing has made this distinction less obvious. This research takes a similar view and therefore does not distinguish between the parallel and distributed variants of PDES. We will therefore use "*distributed simulation*" to refer to the execution of simulations on both multiprocessor machines and over a network of PCs.

Motivations

Some of the reasons for using distributed simulation are as follows (Fujimoto, 1999a; Fujimoto, 2003).

- Distributed simulation can facilitate model reuse by "hooking together" existing simulations into a single simulation environment. It is usually far more economical to link existing simulations to create distributed simulation environments than to create new models within the context of a single tool or piece of software.
- A large simulation may have memory and processing requirements that cannot be provided by a single system. Distributing the simulation execution across multiple machines may allow the memory and processors of many computer systems to be utilized. Thus, distributed simulation may enable large simulations to be executed that could not be executed on a single computer. This may also lead to the distributed model running faster than the single "standalone" alternative.
- Executing simulations on a set of geographically distributed computers facilitates wider user participation in the simulation experiments. This also alleviates the

cost and time that is normally associated with bringing participants to one physical place in, for example a joint training exercise or decision making in a supply chain.

Application Areas

The current and potential application areas for distributed simulation are presented in Table 1 (Fujimoto, 1999b).

Although the table lists only some of the application areas of distributed simulation, the fact that CSP-based simulation has not been identified as either a current or potential distributed simulation application area may seem to suggest that there is very little work done in the area of CSP-based distributed simulation.

Distributed Simulation Theory

A simulation has to process events in increasing timestamp order (the "timestamp" of an event is the time at which the event is scheduled to occur). Failure to do so will result in *causality errors*. A causality error occurs when a simulation has processed an event with timestamp T1 and subsequently receives another event with timestamp T2, wherein T1 > T2. Since the execution of the event with timestamp T1 may have changed the state variables that will be used by the event with timestamp T2, this would amount to simulating a system in which the future could affect the past (Fujimoto, 1990). For a serial simulator that has only one event list and one logical clock it is trivial to avoid causality errors. In the case of distributed simulation, the avoidance of causality is a lot more difficult because it has to deal with multiple event lists and multiple logical clocks that are assigned to various processors. The reason for this is explained below.

The system being modelled (e.g., a hospital) may be composed of a number of physical processes (e.g., clinics and operating theatres within the hospital). In a distributed simulation, each physical process is usually mapped to a logical simulation process running on a separate machine. All the interactions between the physical processes (e.g., transfer of patients from clinic to the operation theatre) are modelled as messages that are exchanged between their corresponding logical

Table 1. Application areas of distributed simulation

Applications	Type of Simulation
Military applications	Analytical war game simulations are performed to evaluate different strategies for war. These simulations are typically composed of individual models that represent different military divisions and use algorithms for synchronisation of the models (discussed in section 3.3). Another application of distributed simulation in the military is for training, and Test and Evaluation (T&E). These are conducted in Distributed Virtual Environments (DVE) where both humans (human-in-the-loop) and devices (hardware-in-the-loop) take part in the simulation.
Telecommunication networks	Analytical PDES have been used widely to evaluate networking hardware, software, protocols and services in the telecommunication industry.
Social interactions and business collaborations	Distributed Virtual Environments allow people to interact socially and to develop business collaborations on the Internet. Note: This was identified as a potential application area of distributed simulation in 1999, but today it has become a reality with popular Internet-based 3-D social networks like Second Life (Linden Research, 2007).
Medical application (potential area)	Computer generated virtual environments have been created both for doctors (to practice surgical techniques) and for patients (to treat various phobias). However, most of this work is currently limited to non-distributed virtual environments.
Transportation (potential area)	PDES (multiprocessors) can reduce the time taken to experiment with different strategies for responding to unexpected events like congestion resulting from weather conditions, etc. This will help take decisions faster.

processes. Each message will have a timestamp associated with it.

In figure 1, the simulation represents a physical system that has two physical processes, say, PP1 and PP2. Logical simulation processes LP1 and LP2 model the two physical processes. The logical processes have their own simulation executive, simulation clock and an event list. During simulation initialisation the event lists of both LP1 and LP2 are populated with the events E1 and E2 respectively. The timestamps for E1 and E2 are 10 and 20 respectively. It will be possible for LP1 to process event E1 without any causality error since the timestamp of E1 is less than the timestamp of E2. However, LP2 will not be able to execute event E2 at time 20 because causality error may then occur. The reason for this is that execution of E1 might schedule another event E3 for LP2 at time 15. In such a case, if LP2 had been allowed to execute E2 at simulated time 20 then it would have resulted in a causality error because the timestamp of E3 is less than the timestamp of E2. Different synchronisation protocols exist for distributed simulation that prevent or correct such causality errors.

Synchronisation protocols are one of the most important research areas of distributed simulation. They can be broadly divided into conservative (pessimistic) protocols and optimistic protocols.

Figure 1. Execution of events in a distributed simulation (Fujimoto, 1990)

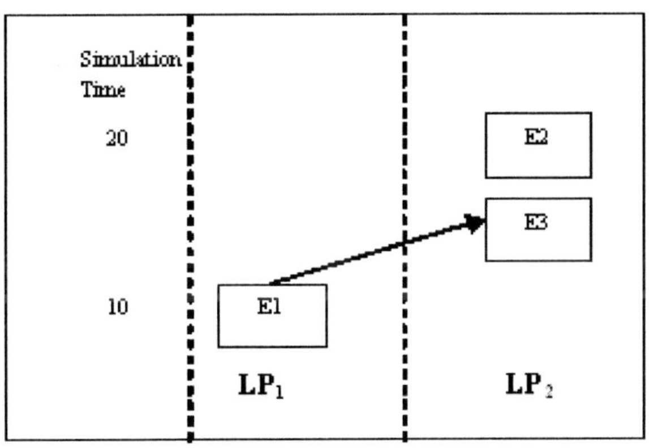

In a conservative protocol a processor is never allowed to process an event out of order; whereas in an optimistic protocol a processor is allowed to process an event out of order, provided it can revert back to its previous state in the case of a causality error (Nicol and Heidelberger, 1996). Chandy and Misra (1979) created one of the first pessimistic approaches that implements the conservative synchronisation protocol. An optimistic synchronisation protocol like Virtual Time, and its implementation called the Time Warp mechanism, executes events without considering the event time ordering (Jefferson, 1985). It has to save its state frequently so that a rollback to a previous state can occur when an event with a time stamp less than the current simulation time is received. Today, synchronisation protocols are usually implemented through supporting software termed distributed simulation middleware. These are discussed next.

Distributed Simulation Middleware

A distributed simulation middleware is a software component that implements the distributed simulation algorithms to achieve synchronisation between individual running simulations (or LPs). Middleware such as HLA-RTI (IEEE 1516, 2000), FAMAS (Boer, 2005), GRIDS (Taylor et al., 2002) and CSPE-CMB (Mustafee, 2004), can be used to facilitate distributed execution of CSP-based simulations. Distributed simulation protocols such as Aggregate Level Simulation Protocol (ALSP) (Fischer et al., 1994) and Distributed Interactive Simulation (DIS) (Miller and Thorpe, 1995) have been used widely in defence training simulations. However, there has been no reported application of these technologies to CSP-based simulations. As such they fall outside the scope of this book chapter.

The our healthcare case study uses the HLA-RTI middleware to couple together models created using the CSP Simul8™ and executed on different computers. As such, the next section of this chapter discusses the HLA-RTI middleware for distributed simulation.

The High Level Architecture

The High Level Architecture (HLA) (IEEE 1516, 2000) was originally proposed to support distributed simulation between existing and new simulations within the U.S Department of Defense (DoD). This came from the need to reduce the cost of training military personnel by reusing computer simulations linked via a network. HLA is now a IEEE standard. In the HLA, a distributed simulation is called a *federation*, and each individual simulation is referred to as a *federate*. A HLA Runtime Infrastructure (HLA-RTI) is a distributed simulation middleware, conforming to the HLA standards, that provides facilities to enable federates to interact with one another, as well as to control and manage the simulation.

The HLA is composed of four parts: a set of compliance rules, the Federate Interface Specification (FIS), the Object Model Template (OMT), and the Federate Development Process (FEDEP). The rules are a set of ten basic conventions that define the responsibilities of both federates and the federation in the context of their relationship with the HLA-RTI. The FIS is an application interface standard which defines how federates interact within the federation. The FIS standard is implemented by the HLA-RTI. The HLA-RTI, thus, forms a base into which existing simulations (federates) can be "plugged into" to form a large distributed simulation (Fujimoto and Weatherly, 1996). There are several implementations of HLA-RTI available, for example, DMSO HLA-RTI and Pitch pRTI (Karlsson and Olsson, 2001). The OMT provides a common presentation format for HLA federates. FEDEP defines the recommended practice processes and procedures that should be followed by users of the HLA to develop and execute their federations.

For models created using CSPs to interoperate using the HLA standard, some of the FIS-defined interfaces have to be implemented. The FIS organises the communication between federates and the HLA-RTI into six different management groups. These are:

- **Federation management:** HLA-RTI calls for the creation and deletion of a federation, the joining and resigning of federates from the federation, etc.
- **Declaration management:** These pertain to the publication and subscription of messages between federates.
- **Object management:** Calls that relate to the sending and receiving of messages to and from federates.
- **Ownership management:** Calls for transfer of an object and attribute ownership.
- **Time management:** These provide synchronisation services.
- **Data distribution:** For efficient routing of data between federates.

Mustafee and Taylor (2006a) have shown that a HLA-based CSP interoperability solution is possible by using services defined in at least four of these six management groups, viz., federation management, declaration management, object management and time management.

The time management component of the HLA supports interoperability among federates that use different time management mechanisms. These include federates executing simulations using both conservative and optimistic synchronisation protocols (Fujimoto and Weatherly, 1996). However, almost all research in CSP interoperability using the HLA standard is concerned with conservative synchronisation. For example, HLA-RTI has been used with CSPs AnyLogic™ (Borshchev et al., 2002), AutoSched™ (Gan et al., 2005) and Witness™ (Taylor et al., 2003). However, these individual research projects developed different and incompatible approaches to using CSPs together with HLA standard for distributed simulation.

Building on the lessons learnt from these work,

a standardization effort, described in Taylor et al. (2006), specifically addressing the problems of HLA-based distributed simulation and CSPs began in 2002. This has led to the development of a suite of CSP Interoperability (CSPI) standards under the Simulation Interoperability Standards Organization's (SISO) CSPI Product Development Group (CSPI PDG). The CSPI PDG's standards are intended to provide guidance on how specific requirements of HLA-based distributed simulation can be supported with CSPs.

This section has presented a detailed discussion on distributed simulation and the HLA-RTI middleware. In the next section the authors discuss the case study, the National UK Blood Service distributed simulation, wherein the HLA-RTI middleware has been used to execute a large and complex healthcare simulation model that was created using the CSP Simul8™.

THE HEALTHCARE SIMULATION CASE STUDY

Our blood supply chain study was carried out with the collaboration of the UK National Blood Service (NBS) and its main concern has been the analysis of policies for managing the blood inventory system in typical UK hospitals supplied by regional blood centres (Katsaliaki and Brailsford, 2007; Katsaliaki et al., 2007). The model was built using the CSP Simul8™. In order to overcome time execution problems of this large and complex healthcare model the researchers had to interface different copies of Simul8™, each executing part of the model in separate computers, with the HLA-RTI middleware for distributed simulation.

Background to the Blood Supply Chain

The NBS consists of 15 Process, Testing and Issuing (PTI) Centres which together serve 316 hospitals across England and North Wales. Each PTI Centre serves around 20 hospitals. Our case study was performed with the Southampton PTI Centre.

The NBS schedule collections of whole blood from voluntary donors in local, community venues or places of employment. The blood is transported back to the nearest PTI Centre where it is tested for ABO and Rhesus grouping and infectious diseases such as HIV. A unit (450ml) of whole blood is then processed into around 115 different products, of which the main three are red blood cells (RBC), platelets and plasma. RBC have usually a shelf life of 35 days and platelets of 5 days. Plasma can be frozen and stored for up to a year. In this study we consider only RBC and platelets which together comprise 85% of issues and are the chief source of wastage and shortages.

Blood products are stored in the PTI Centre's blood bank until they are requested by the hospitals served by that Centre. There are mainly three types of delivery. Routine scheduled deliveries are usually made on a daily basis on milk runs and are free of charge. The NBS also makes additional deliveries to an individual hospital in response to specific requests by charging a small fee. These are: emergency deliveries, which are prioritised on receipt for immediate dispatch and transportation and ad-hoc deliveries, which are additional to routine deliveries. There is also a nationally coordinated scheme for transferring excess stock between PTI Centres.

The blood remains in the hospital bank until it is cross-matched (tested for compatibility) for a named patient after a doctor's request. Individual doctors are responsible for the quantity of blood products ordered for each patient in the hospital. It is common place for doctors to over-order to be on the safe side although there is some guidance from the Maximum Surgical Blood Ordering Schedule (MSBOS) which specifies how much blood is required for a given operation.

After cross-matching, blood is then placed in the "assigned inventory" for that patient for some time until the transfusion and for some "safety" time after if not used at that instant. If unused, it returns to "unassigned inventory" and is cross-matched to another patient. Blood units are usually sorted in a FIFO order (not age-based) in the hospital bank and issued accordingly. Ideally the oldest units should be issued first but this is not always the case since doctors prefer to use fresher blood, and moreover sorting the stock according to its age, especially in a big blood bank, is a painstaking procedure to which not all the hospitals devote the necessary time. In practice, only just above half of the cross-matched blood is actually transfused, and on average a unit will be cross-matched around three times before it is used or outdated. This clearly represents a huge potential for savings since the cost of a single unit of RBC is around £132 and for platelets is £214. Moreover, patients should ideally be given blood of the same type (a blood component is a set of eight products specified by the ABO and Rhesus group) but "mismatching" is possible in emergencies; for example, O-negative blood can be given to anybody. However, this practice is prohibited and is perceived as poor quality service.

Overall, there are two mechanisms for placing orders for blood; doctors who place orders to the hospital blood bank for their patients and hospital blood bank managers who place orders to the NBS Centre for stock replenishment. There are also two stocking processes; one at the central blood bank and one at the hospital bank; in the latter, stock can be either assigned or unassigned. Figure 2 illustrates all these processes in a flowchart.

The Standalone NBS Model

The blood supply system described above is undoubtedly a stochastic system with variable demand for blood (even for elective surgery) depending on the number of patients, type of operations and the occurrence of complications requiring extra transfusions. The supply is variable too since it relies on volunteers showing up to donate. Organisational issues also arise from the fact that the NBS manages the supply side and the hospitals manage the demand side of the logistics chain. As discussed earlier, DES was

Figure 2. Lifecycle of a blood unit (Katsaliaki, 2008)

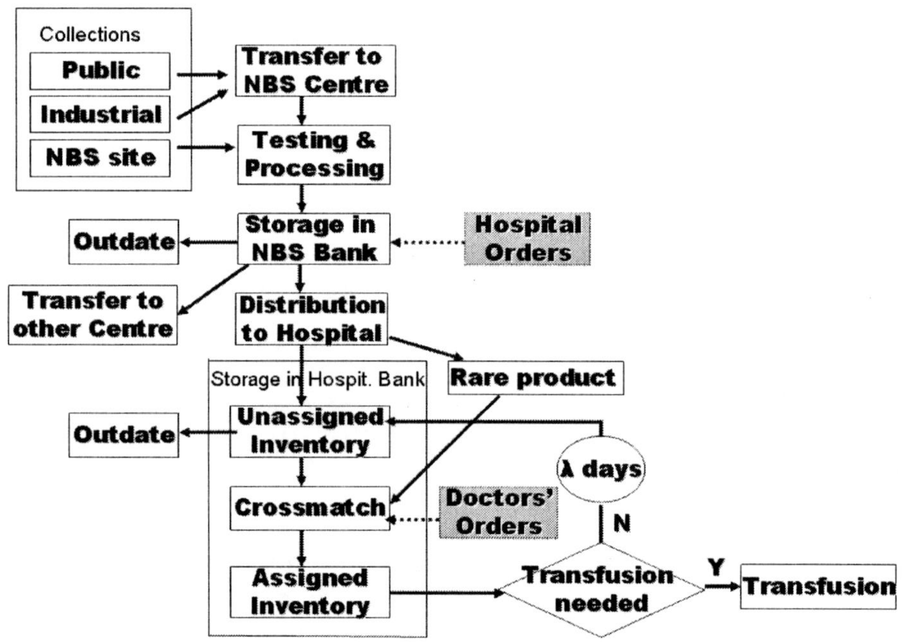

chosen to investigate the problems of this supply chain as complex stochastic multi-product, multi echelon perishable inventory problems have been shown to be intractable by analytic techniques (Donselaar et al, 2006; Goyal and Giri, 2001) or other simulation methods. DES was also the technique which the majority of the researchers have adopted to tackle parts of this problem since some decades ago.

The model was built using the CSP Simul8™. The supply chain model is very large and complex, and as such requires extensive data. Up to nineteen months' data were acquired for the years 2003 and 2004 by the NBS information system (PULSE) providing details about collections, processed and issued units, stock holding and discards. This gave details of the products supplied to each hospital, by date, time, delivery type, quantity and blood group. Questionnaires were also sent to the hospitals supplied by the Southampton centre, and interviews conducted with NBS staff and hospital blood bank managers. There are two main categories of entities in the model; items and orders. Items are the individual blood units (RBC and platelets) delivered from the NBS Centre to the hospitals in a one-way direction, since returns of products are not allowed. Items are also delivered internally from the hospital bank to the patient changing their stage in the system. In the latter returns within the hospital bank are allowed. Orders are placed both by the doctors to the hospital blood bank and by the hospitals' blood bank managers to the NBS Centre for blood products, and represent the backwards flow of information. Requests are matched with items according to their characteristics (attributes) as in a Kanban system and delivered as appropriate.

While the model runs, data are reported in an Excel file, such as the day and time of placing an order with the Centre, the type of order (routine, ad-hoc or emergency), the requested product and the amount by blood group. The model time units are minutes, and the remaining shelf-life of blood products is counted in minutes. However, the hospitals' blood bank stock for placing orders to the NBS is checked only every hour. Moreover, the decision to run the model in minutes was enforced by the fact that many processes, such as physician requests and delivery times, could be better approximated in small units of time. In

Figure 3. Screenshot of a simplified version of the Simul8 model showing one hospital

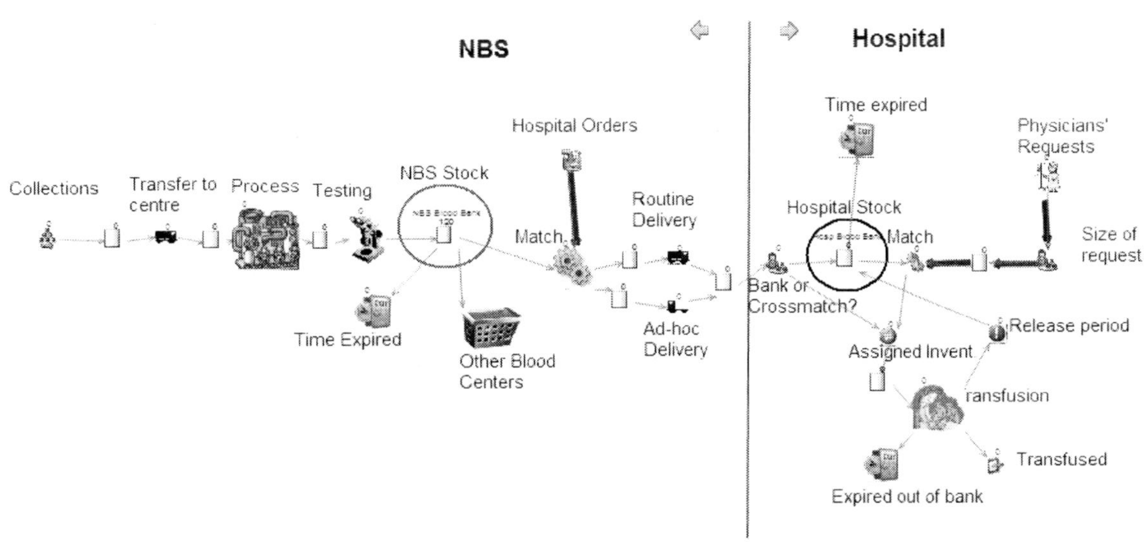

addition, an attempt to run the model in hours did not significantly accelerate the overall running time.

The basic version of the model contains the processes of the NBS Centre, from collection of whole blood to delivery of blood products, and the processes within a single medium-volume hospital. The model captures all the main processes of the supply chain. Figure 3 shows a simplified illustration of this simulation model. The black arrows represent blood units flow and the thick blue arrows represent information flow, i.e. orders.

The expanded version of this model incorporates the Centre's supply of multiple hospitals. Figure 4 shows an example of the relationships between the NBS supply centre and hospitals it serves, which in the "conventional" approach is simulated on a single computer. Note that this shows four hospitals. Ideally, there should be up to twenty!

In our "conventional" or standalone single computer approach the execution times increased dramatically when the number of hospitals increased in the model (see section 5). We now

Figure 4. NBS conventional model with the NBS PTI and four hospitals

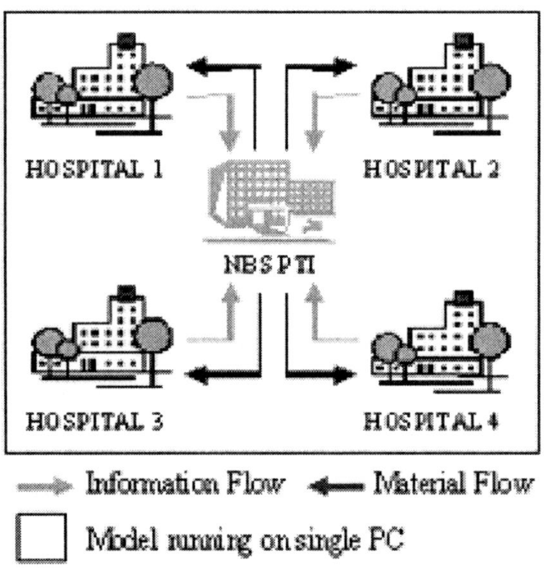

describe our distributed simulation approach to this problem.

The Distributed NBS Model

In our distributed simulation of the NBS supply chain, we (1) divided up the conventional NBS model into different model elements, (2) used the HLA-RTI middleware and (3) interfaced different copies of CSP Simul8™ with the HLA-RTI. The version of the HLA-RTI we have used for our research is the DMSO RTI 1.3NG *(Rtiexec.exe)*. Figure 5 shows the logical relationship between the different parts of the distributed NBS model.

The model decomposition creates individual models of the Southampton PTI and hospitals (in this example four different hospitals were used). These models run in separate copies of Simul8™. Together they form federates that interact by time-stamped messages that represent the interaction

Figure 5. NBS distributed model with NBS PTI and four hospitals

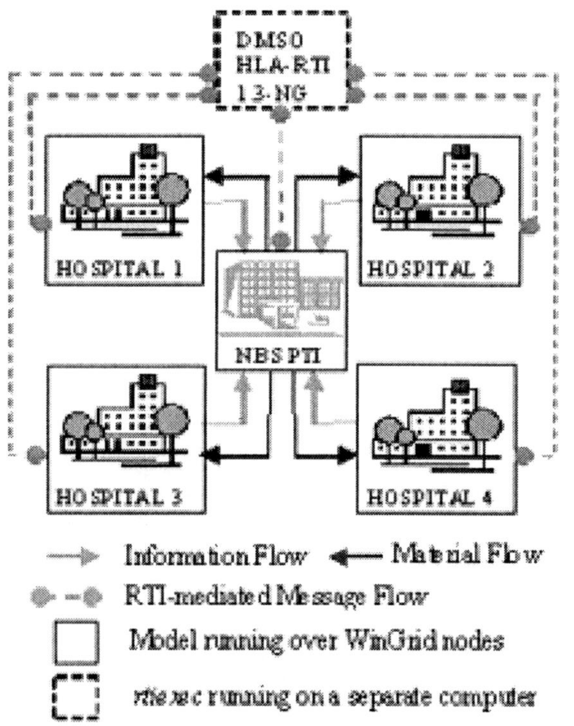

of one model part with another (e.g., when an entity leaves one part of a model and arrives at another). These are mapped onto HLA interactions. The complete model, constituted of distributed federates, form our NBS supply chain federation. Note that in this work, Simul8™, like most of the other CSPs, does not provide inbuilt support for distributed simulation. The modifications made to the Simul8™ CSP are described in Mustafee and Taylor (2006).

In this investigation, to make our approach as easy to use and support as possible, interaction between the models/Simul8 and the HLA-RTI is via an Excel file. For example, entities representing orders are written into the file by Simul8 during the execution of hospital models. The HLA-RTI then correctly transfers this information to the NBS model by means of HLA interactions. This approach was adopted as it did not require special modifications to the CSP and modellers are typically skilled to use the CSP with Excel (the HLA-RTI/Excel link is very simple). The incoming orders from each hospital are collected into their corresponding queues in the NBS model and the orders are matched with the available stock of blood. The resulting matched units are written into an Excel spreadsheet in the NBS federate. This information is then sent to the different hospital models in a similar manner. As mentioned above, the decision to implement the distributed supply chain in this manner was motivated by issues of end user transparency and ease of implementation.

EXPERIMENTS AND RESULTS

To investigate the distributed approach against the conventional approach, four scenarios were investigated. These were one NBS supply centre serving one, two, three and four hospitals respectively. The hospitals which were added to the models were all of the same size. For instance, physician requests were around 1000 blood units for each hospital per month, with each hospital diverging by a small percentage (≤6%) from the mean. Before experimentation commenced, the outputs for the conventional and distributed models were compared to check that the same results for a year's run was produced. This was done to validate the minor modifications to link Simul8/Excel/HLA-RTI in the distributed model did not artificially increase/decrease the workload. All experiments were conducted on Dell Inspiron laptop computers running Microsoft Windows XP operating system with 1.7GHz processors and 1GB RAM connected through a 100Mbps CISCO switch. The same computer specifications were used to guarantee consistency in runtimes. The results of the execution times for each of the models are based on the average of 5 runs (selected as an isolated network was used – low variance).

Figure 6 shows the execution time in seconds for both conventional and distributed approaches as the NBS simulation progress, month by month. The results show that the conventional model with one hospital took approximately 14 minutes to run for a whole simulated year. The run time rose to 78 minutes when the model ran with two hospitals and to approximately 17.5 hours with three hospitals. The addition of the fourth hospital increases the execution time to 35.8 hours. The distributed model with one NBS supply centre and one hospital ran in approximately 8.5 hours, with two hospitals in 9.8 hours, with three hospitals in 12.7 hours and with four hospitals in 16.5 hours.

DISCUSSION

The NBS simulation is representative of a large model. Looking at the results as the system size grows, runtimes increase rapidly from the trivial (for one hospital) to the extravagant (for only four hospitals!). From the results it is apparent that the versions with one or two hospitals are less time consuming to run using the conventional approach. Conversely, when a third and fourth

Figure 6. Runtimes of conventional (s) and distributed method (d) for one NBS PTI centre with one to four hospitals

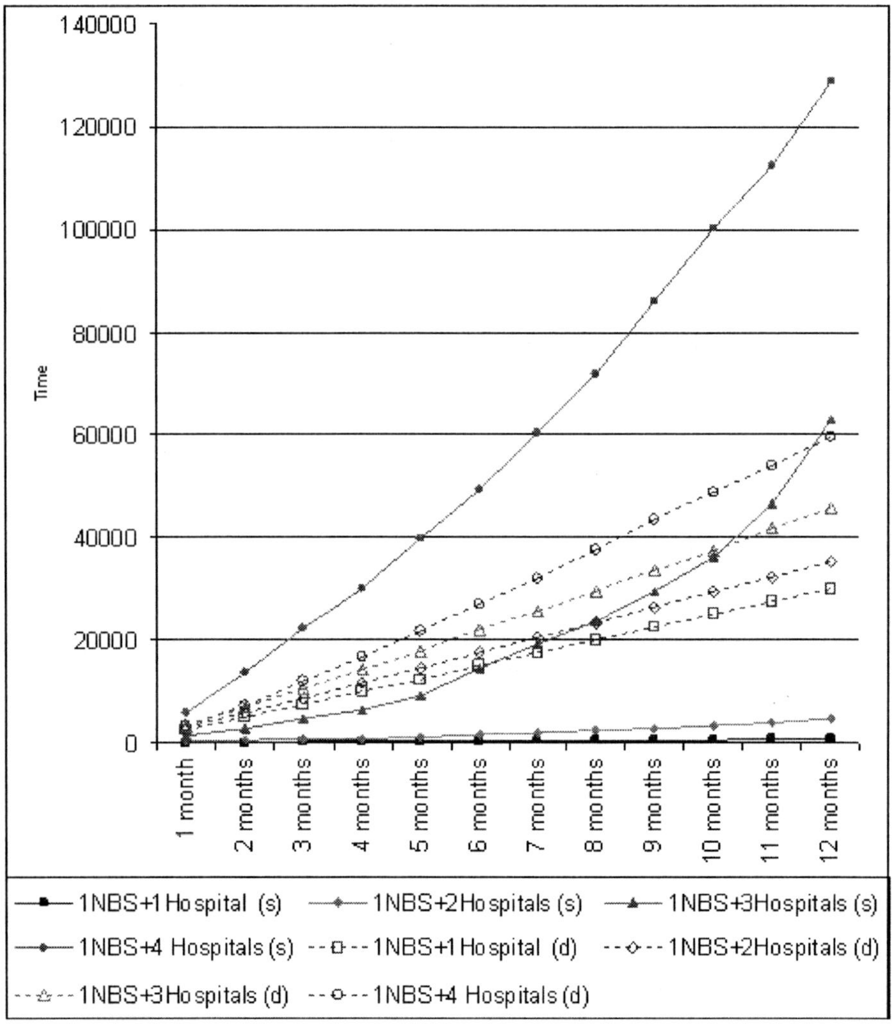

hospital are added then the distributed method bests the runtime of the conventional approach. There also appears to be an exponential escalation of the runtime in the conventional version while increasing the number of hospitals in the model. This is quite a contrast to the substantially smaller and smoother rise in the runtime in the distributed method.

The enormous number of entities in the system, each of which carries many attributes, increases the computation time of the conventional model exponentially even though there is no exponential element in the functions of the model. This exponential increase appears to result from a combination of two different factors. Firstly, the massive amount of information generated by the model cannot be accommodated in the random access memory (RAM) alone, and hence the operating system has to keep swapping information to the hard disk. The part of the hard disk which is kept aside for use as swap space is called virtual memory. It takes much more time for the processor to recall information from the virtual memory when compared to RAM. Thus, as the models get bigger, more information is generated resulting in more swaps between the RAM and the virtual memory, thereby contributing to an increase of execution time. Secondly, the behaviour of the system being modelled is such that all entities (blood units) in the system have a limited shelf life. This behaviour is modelled in the NBS simulation by continually scheduling events that decrease the shelf life of each entity by the minute. This results in more computations as the number of entities flowing through the system increases. Thus, the increase in runtime appears to be primarily due to a large event list caused by a combination of the volume of entities and the "counting down" of the shelf life. The large event list in turn causes swapping between RAM and virtual memory which further causes long runtimes. Our results suggest that the distributed approach allows the processing and memory demands made by large event lists to be shared over several computers.

What does this mean overall? In this particularly large scale simulation, our distributed simulation effectively halved the time taken to perform a single of the NBS simulation with four hospitals. The trend appear to indicate that this performance gain will become better with more hospitals. The *magnitude* of the problem means that runtimes will never be trivial. However, our approach to using distributed simulation, one that is generalizable to many different CSPs and large scale simulations, means that one may expect large runtimes to be reduced. As mentioned previously, this work is important as it is the first demonstration that an effective distributed simulation technique *can* help in the reduction of unrealistic runtimes and thus make possible decision support systems for large scale problems that were hitherto unfeasible.

FUTURE TRENDS

To introduce this problem we commented that CSPs, although suitable for most simulations that are modelled in industry, may be unable to simulate large and complex models (Pidd, 2004b), as was the case with our NBS simulation. Arguably, one reason for this is, the larger the model, the greater the processing power and memory required to simulate the model. Simulation is a computationally intensive technology that has benefitted from increasing processor speeds made possible through advances in computer science; and with ever increasing processing speeds, the CSPs, in future, will possibly provide features that may not presently seem possible (for example, dramatic decrease in model runtime, execution of increasingly large and complex models, etc.) (Hollocks, 2006).

However, it is also true that with more processing power available the simulation user may tend to develop even larger and more complicated models simply because it is possible to do so (Robinson, 2005). This, in turn, may again mean that standalone CSPs will not be able to support execution of some user models because of their sheer size and complexity. We have demonstrated that distributed simulation can be used to help reduce the impact of size and complexity in terms of reducing runtimes. Our approach involved interfacing to the CSP via an Excel spreadsheet. However, if it was possible to interface directly to the CSP, then further performance gains could be made. Thus, CSPs that implement synchronisation algorithms or which allow interfacing with distributed simulation middleware like HLA-RTI, could make possible the simulation of large complex systems that are currently beyond the capability of many CSPs and thus beyond the reach of health care management.

CONCLUSION

This chapter has described an investigation into the decision support of large healthcare systems. The chapter has presented Discrete-Event Simulation (DES) as an approach to decision support but suffers from long runtimes when large systems are simulated. The chapter also introduce COTS Simulation Packages (CSPs) as the main tools used for DES. We then introduced distributed simulation as a possible technique for sharing the processing load of large healthcare systems simulations. A case study comparing conventional and distributed approaches to simulating the supply chain of blood from a National Blood Service Centre to hospitals with the simulation package Simul8™ was then presented. Our results show that it is possible to use multiple computers to reduce the runtime of large simulations using distributed simulation. Further performance gains could be made if this technique and its associated technologies are directly integrated into the CSPs used for simulation. We therefore argue that Discrete-Event Simulation, supported by CSPs with integrated distributed simulation technology, could make possible a range of large scale decision support tools for healthcare that are currently not possible. As healthcare systems are growing, and the need for carefully considered decisions increase, the lack of such technology could place a significant barrier to effective healthcare in the future. We hope that our demonstration shows that this barrier could be overcome and that it is entirely possible that healthcare systems, and healthcare informatics as a field, could widely benefit from this complex, but simply realised, technique.

REFERENCES

Baezner, D., Lomow, G., & Unger, B. W. (1990). Sim++: The transition to distributed simulation. In D. Nicol (Ed)., *Proceedings of the 1990 SCS Western Multiconference on Simulation: Distributed Simulation,* January 17-19 (pp. 211-218). San Diego, CA: Society for Computer Simulation.

Bagni, R., Berchi, R., & Cariello, P. (2002). A comparison of simulation models applied to epidemics. *Journal of Artificial Societies and Social Simulation*, *5*(3).

Barton, P., Bryan, S., & Robinson, S. (2004). Modelling in the economic evaluation of health care: selecting the appropriate approach. *Journal of Health Services Research & Policy*, *9*(2), 110–118. doi:10.1258/135581904322987535

Boer, C. A. (2005). *Distributed simulation in industry*. PhD thesis, Erasmus Research Institute of Management (ERIM), Erasmus University Rotterdam, The Netherlands. Retrieved February 4th, 2008 from https://ep.eur.nl/handle/1765/6925.

Borshchev, A., Karpov, Y., & Kharitonov, V. (2002). Distributed simulation of hybrid systems with AnyLogic and HLA. *Future Generation Computer Systems*, *18*(6), 829–839. doi:10.1016/S0167-739X(02)00055-9

Chandy, K.M. & Misra, J. (1979). *Distributed Simulation: A Case Study in Design and Verification of Distributed Programs, 5*(5), 440-452.

Cooper, K., Davies, R., & Brailsford, S. (2007). Choice of modelling technique for evaluating health care interventions. *The Journal of the Operational Research Society*, *58*, 168–176.

Eldabi, T., Paul, R. J., & Taylor, S. J. E. (2000). Simulating economic factors in adjuvant breast cancer treatment. *The Journal of the Operational Research Society*, *51*(4), 465–475.

Fischer, M. C., Adams, A., & Miller, G. (1994). Aggregate level simulation protocol (ALSP) - training for the future. In *Proceedings of the 1994 Military Operations Research Symposium*. Military Operations Research Society (MORS), USA. Retrieved February 15th, 2008 from http://ms.ie.org/alsp/biblio/mors_94_fischer/mors_94_fischer.html

Fone, D., Hollinghurst, S., Temple, M., & Round, A. (2003). Systematic review of the use and value of computer simulation modelling in population health and healthcare delivery. *Journal of Public Health Medicine*, *25*(4), 325–335. doi:10.1093/pubmed/fdg075

Fujimoto, R. M. (1990). Parallel discrete event simulation. *Communications of the ACM*, *33*(10), 30–53. doi:10.1145/84537.84545

Fujimoto, R. M. (1999a). Parallel and distributed simulation. In P. A. Farrington, H. B. Nembhard, D. T. Sturrock, & G. W. Evans, (Eds.), *Proceedings of the 31st Winter Simulation Conference*, (pp. 122– 131). New York: ACM Press.

Fujimoto, R. M. (1999b). *Parallel and distributed simulation systems*. New York: John Wiley & Sons.

Fujimoto, R. M. (2001). Parallel and distributed simulation systems. In B. A. Peters, J. S. Smith, D. J. Medeiros, & M. W. Rohrer (eds.), *Proceedings of the 33rd Winter Simulation Conference*, (pp. 147-157). Washington, DC: IEEE Computer Society.

Fujimoto, R. M. (2003). Distributed simulation systems. In S. Chick, P. J. Sánchez, D. Ferrin, & D. J. Morrice (Eds.) *Proceedings of the 35th Winter Simulation Conference*, (pp. 124-134). Winter Simulation Conference, USA.

Fujimoto, R. M., & Weatherly, R. M. (1996). Time management in the DoD high level architecture. In *Proceedings of the 10th Workshop on Parallel and Distributed Simulation Workshop* (pp. 60-67). Washington, DC: IEEE Computer Society.

Gan, B. P., Lendermann, P., Low, M. Y. H., Turner, S. J., Wang, X., & Taylor, S. J. E. (2005). Interoperating Autosched AP using the high level architecture. In M. E. Kuhl, N. M. Steiger, F. B. Armstrong, & J. A. Joines (Eds.) *Proceedings of the 37th Winter Simulation Conference*, (pp. 394-401). Winter Simulation Conference, USA.

Gipps, P. J. (1986). The role of computer graphics in validating simulation models. *Mathematics and Computers in Simulation*, *28*, 285–289. doi:10.1016/0378-4754(86)90049-2

Goyal, S., & Giri, B. (2001). Recent trends in modeling of deteriorating inventory. *European Journal of Operational Research*, *134*(1), 1–16. doi:10.1016/S0377-2217(00)00248-4

Hollocks, B. W. (2006). Forty years of discrete-event simulation - a personal reflection. *The Journal of the Operational Research Society*, *57*(12), 1383–1399. doi:10.1057/palgrave.jors.2602128

IEEE. 1516 (2000). *IEEE standard for modelling and simulation (M&S) high level architecture (HLA)*. New York: Institute of Electrical and Electronics Engineers.

Jefferson, D. R. (1985). Virtual Time. *ACM Transactions on Programming Languages and Systems*, *7*(3), 404–425. doi:10.1145/3916.3988

Jun, J. B., Jacobson, S. H., & Swisher, J. R. (1999). Application of discrete-event simulation in health care clinics: A survey. *The Journal of the Operational Research Society*, *50*, 109–123.

Karlsson, M., & Olsson, L. (2001). pRTI 1516 - rationale and design. In *Proceedings of the 2001 Fall Simulation Interoperability Workshop* (01F-SIW-038). Orlando, FL: Simulation Interoperability Standards Organization.

Katsaliaki, K. (2008). Cost effective practices in the blood service sector. *Health Policy*.

Katsaliaki, K., & Brailsford, S. B. (2007). Using Simulation to Improve the U.K. Blood Supply Chain. *The Journal of the Operational Research Society*, *58*, 219–227.

Katsaliaki, K., Mustafee, N., Taylor, S.J.E., Brailsford, S. (2007). Comparing Conventional and Distributed Approaches to Simulation in a Complex Supply-Chain Health System. *Journal of the Operation Research Society*.

Law, A. M. (2007). *Simulation Modelling & Analysis*. New York: McGraw-Hill International Edition.

Linden Research. (2007). *Second Life*. Retrieved February 9th, 2008 from http://secondlife.com/.

Miller, D. C., & Thorpe, J. A. (1995). SIMNET: the advent of simulator networking. *Proceedings of the IEEE*, *83*(8), 1114–1123. doi:10.1109/5.400452

Mustafee, N. (2004). *Performance evaluation of interoperability methods for distributed simulation*. MSc. thesis, Department of Information Systems, Computing and Mathematics, Brunel University, UK.

Mustafee, N., & Taylor, S. J. E. (2006). Investigating distributed simulation with COTS simulation packages: experiences with Simul8 and the HLA. In J. Garnett, S. Brailsford, S. Robinson, & S. Taylor, (Eds.) *Proceedings of the 2006 Operational Research Society Simulation Workshop (SW06)*, (pp. 33-42). Birmingham, UK: Operational Research Society.

Nicol, D., & Heidelberger, P. (1996). Parallel Execution for Serial Simulators. *ACM Transactions on Modeling and Computer Simulation*, *6*(3), 210–242. doi:10.1145/235025.235031

Page, E. H., & Nance, R. E. (1994). Parallel discrete event simulation: a modeling methodological perspective. In *Proceedings of the 8th Workshop on Parallel and Distributed Simulation*, (pp. 88-93). New York: ACM Press.

Pidd, M. (2004a). *Computer simulation in management science* (5th Ed.). Chichester, UK: John Wiley & Sons.

Pidd, M. (2004b). Simulation worldviews: so what? In R. G. Ingalls, M. D. Rossetti, J. S. Smith, & B. A. Peters, (eds.) *Proceedings of the 36th Winter Simulation Conference*, (pp. 288-292). Winter Simulation Conference, USA.

Pidd, M., & Cassel, R. A. (2000). Using Java to develop discrete event simulations. *The Journal of the Operational Research Society*, *51*, 405–412.

Reynolds, P. F. (1988). A spectrum of options for parallel simulation. In M. Abrams, P. Haigh, and J. Comfort (Eds.), *Proceedings of the 20th Winter Simulation Conference*, (pp. 325 –332). New York: ACM Press.

Robinson, S. (1994). *Successful Simulation: A Practical Approach to Simulation Projects*, Maidenhead, UK: McGraw-Hill.

Robinson, S. (2005a). Discrete-event simulation: from the pioneers to the present, what next? *The Journal of the Operational Research Society*, *56*(6), 619–629. doi:10.1057/palgrave.jors.2601864

Royston, G. (1999). Commentary: trials versus models in appraising screening programmes. *British Medical Journal*, *318*, 360–361.

Rubinstein, R. Y. (1981). *Simulation and the Monte Carlo Method.* New York: John Wiley & Sons.

Taylor, K., & Lane, D. (1998). Simulation applied to health services: opportunities for applying the system dynamics approach. *Journal of Health Services Research & Policy*, *3*, 226–232.

Taylor, S. J. E., Sharpe, J., & Ladbrook, J. (2003). Time management issues in COTS distributed simulation: a case study. In S. Chick, P. J. Sánchez, D. Ferrin, & D. J. Morrice, (Eds.) *Proceedings of the 35th Winter Simulation Conference*, (pp. 838-846). Winter Simulation Conference, USA.

Taylor, S. J. E., Sudra, R., Janahan, T., Tan, G., & Ladbrook, J. (2002). GRIDS-SCF: An infrastructure for distributed supply chain simulation. *Simulation*, *78*(5), 312–320. doi:10.1177/0037549702078005553

Taylor, S. J. E., Wang, X., Turner, S. J., & Low, M. Y. H. (2006). Integrating heterogeneous distributed COTS discrete-event simulation packages: an emerging standards-based approach. *IEEE Transactions on Systems . Man and Cybernetics: Part A*, *36*(1), 109–122. doi:10.1109/TSMCA.2005.859167

van Donselaar, K. H., van Woensel, T., Broekmeulen, R. A. C. M., & Fransoo, J. C. (2006). Inventory control of perishables in supermarkets. *International Journal of Production Economics*, *104*(2), 462–472. doi:10.1016/j.ijpe.2004.10.019

KEY TERMS AND DEFINITIONS

COTS: Commercial, Off-The-Shelf (COTS). This term is used to refer to software applications that can be purchased from software vendors.

CSP: COTS Simulation Package (CSP). In this thesis the term CSP is used to refer to simulation packages for both Discrete-Event Simulation (DES) and Monte Carlo Simulation (MCS).

HLA: The High Level Architecture (HLA) is an IEEE standard for distributed simulation.

HLA-RTI: The High Level Architecture-Run Time Infrastructure (HLA-RTI) is distributed simulation middleware that implements the interface specifications outlined by the HLA standard.

Rtiexec: rtiexec.exe is the HLA-RTI middleware program.

Discrete Event Simulation (DES): DES is an approach to modelling using interconnected blocks to represent interaction between specific processes and is run on a computer using mathematical models. The latter are stochastic, that is they involve input generated according to probability distributions. A discrete model assumes that the state of the system changes only at specific times, often referred to as events.

Chapter 17
Information Security and Privacy in Medical Application Scenario

Sigurd Eskeland
University of Agder, Norway

Vladimir Oleshchuk
University of Agder, Norway

ABSTRACT

This chapter discusses security and privacy aspects for medical application scenario. The chapter analyze what kind security and privacy enforcements would be needed and how it can be achieved by technological means. Authors reviewed cryptographic mechanisms and solutions that can be useful in this context.

INTRODUCTION

With the emergence of information technology in health care, there has been much focus on security and confidentiality issues of electronic patient records (EPR) in medical environments. Medical records contain confidential personal information which may include sensitive data about AIDS/HIV status, sexual transmittable diseases, emotional problems, psychiatric illnesses, sexual divergences, genetic predispositions to diseases, information about toxic addictions, and so on (Rindfleisch, 1997). It is therefore essential that such information is protected from disclosure except when medical practitioners require access to patient records in order to provide proper medical care to patients. An important issue here concerns proper authorization of access to EPRs. A basic criterion for this should be legitimacy, meaning that only medical personnel providing medical care to a given patient (or patients) should be granted only access to the necessary medical data of the concerning patient they are providing care to. Another significant security issue concerns secure and confidential management, handling and storage of personal medical information (Serour, 2006).

Security of medical networks and privacy of medical data have long been topics of great concern, since almost every person would have at least one patient record containing personal and confidential medical information. The manual record keeping systems of the past lacked automatic enforcement

DOI: 10.4018/978-1-60566-030-1.ch017

of access control. Medical practitioners would necessarily not be prohibited to access arbitrary patient records, meaning that the confidentiality of patients was resting considerably on the discretion of each individual medical practitioner and legal enforcement. Today, medical data is in general managed by networked computer systems which have replaced paper-based patient records and manual record keeping systems. Health organizations and hospitals are administrating large databases of such personal electronic patient records (EPR). Computerized medical databases have a number of advantages compared to paper-based systems concerning flexibility, functionality and a more effective data management due to the possibly ubiquitous accessibility of data, independently of location and time. This complies well with decentralized organizations since data can be easily transferred within and across health establishments by means of wired and wireless computer networks.

In agreement with common medical ethics and due to the confidential nature of medical data, access to medical data should rest on a "need-to-know"-basis and legitimacy. In other words, the medical data of a patient should only be disclosed to medical personnel that have a legitimate need to access the medical data of the patient, which would be due to providing medical care to that patient. Proper measures should be taken to confine the availability of the data in agreement with the "need-to know"-principle. The increased accessibility of medical data due to digitalized data management and networked computing, rise important needs and requirements concerning the security and privacy of medical data and confidentiality of patients. Threats and violations to the privacy medical data could just as well come from within the health organization than from outside, and it is essential that proper access control mechanisms and data protection should be facilitated.

In this chapter we discuss security and privacy aspects for medical application scenario. We look at what kind of security and privacy enforcements would be needed and how it can be achieved by technological means. We review relevant issues in this context such that authorization and granting of EPR access, patient consent, access acquisition, teams, hierarchy, and related cryptographic issues.

PATIENT CONFIDENTIALITY

The confidentiality of the patient is a focal point of importance. The same applies to patients' medical records that may contain very sensitive information such as AIDS/HIV status, sexual transmittable diseases, emotional problems, psychiatric illnesses, genetic predispositions to diseases, drug addictions, etc. Electronic medical databases and networking provide an efficient data management and availability but may create needs for strengthening ethical and legal requirements correspondingly.

Patients' Rights

A significant factor related to patient confidentiality is the right the patient has to decide the course of action to be undertaken by medical practitioners or others in relation to the patient. With respect of patient confidentiality and patient consent, American Medical Association (AMA) states that "the physician's duty to maintain confidentiality means that a physician may not disclose any medical information revealed by a patient or discovered by a physician in connection with the treatment of a patient. The physician generally should not reveal confidential communications or information without the patient's express consent" (American Medical Association, 2008). Patients' right for self-determination could include:

1. An informed basis for medical treatment and medical procedures to be undertaken.

2. An informed basis of who is requesting access to the EPR of the patient, and having the right to grant or deny it.
3. An informed basis of the motivations and purpose for medical and scientific research that involves access to medical data including the identities of the individuals undertaking the inquiry.

In the latter case, patient anonymity would be useful to protect the confidentiality of the concerning patients. By means of anonymization, public patient identities such as names, addresses, social security numbers, etc., would be hidden and replaced by pseudonyms that could be randomly selected. Pseudonyms could be issued on a long-term basis, but a long-term association between a pseudonym and an EPR would lower the patient confidentiality in the long run. Temporary or session-wise pseudonyms would effectively prevent that any association between an EPR and a pseudonyms can take place over time.

Issues Relevant to Patient Confidentiality

A security system with proper access control facilities would be required to ensure a minimum level of patient confidentiality. Access control would, however, raise questions such as what would be the criteria for access to patient records to be granted? Who should grant access? Should the patient be able to influence how and to who access to his or her EPR is to be granted? Should user roles or the job position of the user, for example whether the user is a nurse, doctor or specialist, infer restrictions on what parts or data modules of a granted EPR that the user may be allowed to access, or which operations (read, write, etc.) that he or she may apply on the granted data? How should access control be managed regarding medical teams? Concerns should also to be made about the confidentiality of stored medical data, and the confidentiality and integrity of data that is in transfer over networks. We attempt to provide some views on these questions in the following sections.

PLAYERS IN THE MEDICAL SCENARIO

In the medical scenario considered in this chapter, we recognize the main players to be as follows:

- The owner of the EPR, i.e., the patient. Each patient is represented by one EPR that he or she imposes ownership onto.
- Medical practitioners like doctors and nurses. Two or more medical practitioners can be associated, forming medical teams. We distinguish between ad hoc (short-term) medical teams, and long-term medical teams.
- Information security administrators. The medical practitioners providing care to a patient are to be assigned or granted access to the electronic patient record of this patient. Such assignments form short-term, temporary relationships between a given EPR and the pertaining medical practitioners, whereof the duration would be in accordance to the period of treatment.

ACCESS CONTROL BY DELEGATION AND SEPARATION OF DUTY

As pointed out, the "need-to-know" principle is a proper criterion for authorization of EPR access to medical practitioners and teams, since only those who are providing care to a certain patient should be granted access to the patient's medical data. Although given such a criterion, somebody has to be in position of granting medical practitioners access to relevant medical data. The principle of separation of duty (SoD) states that a minimum number of participants performing some partial task are required to carry out this task or transaction (Botha & Eloff, 2001). Enforcement of separation of duty would prevent individuals to carry out this task or transaction on their own.

A typical example would be in banking where for example two employees, one manager and one clerk could be required to carry out some financial transaction. Access to the bank vault is also a good example. It may not be desirable that individuals could solely access the vault due to the risk of fraud, robbery and extortion. The safety would be considerably improved by a threshold-based security system, where partial unlocking of least 2 or 3 arbitrary persons out of for instance 4, each holding a unique and secret key, should be required in order to unlock the vault. Corresponding security mechanisms would be threshold-oriented cryptosystems, which requires the collaboration of t arbitrary participants out of n to carry out some cryptographic computation. A threshold security requirement could be a desirable property in many security systems involving collaboration of several participants. The threshold requirement is an enforcement of the principle of separation of duty. Examples of threshold-oriented cryptosystems can be found in (Desmedt & Frankel, 1989; Pedersen, 1991; Harn, 1994; Li & Pieprzyk, 1999; Eskeland & Oleshchuk, 2007; Saeednia & Ghodosi, 1999).

In our opinion, the consent or agreement of a minimum number of relevant participants is a useful criterion for authorizing access to medical data. Patients, medical practitioners and security administrators are relevant for filling this granting role. This yields the following arrangements in which such a consent criterion for EPR access authorization could be accomplished:

- Medical practitioners or a medical team can obtain access to a relevant EPR due to the consent of the concerning patient to whom they are going to provide medical care.
- A medical team can obtain access to a relevant EPR due to the consent of a minimum number of security administrators.
- A medical team can obtain access to a relevant EPR due to the consent or agreement of a minimum number of its members.

Patient Consent

EPR access could be granted based on patient consent. This has become an important principle in medical ethics (American Medical Association, 2008) and it has been broadly recognized that the patients have a right to exert control over who is to access their own medical data. It would therefore be reasonable that patients should have a right to decide who should (and should not) be able to access their EPR by means of consent. That is, patients should be allowed to exert control over their respective EPRs. This would be consistent to data access delegation, permitting the patient to delegate access of his or her EPR to specific medical personnel. This has in the past been implemented manually by means of written consent from the patient in many health establishments. Such manual practise would rely on individuals' discretion with no automatic control enforcement of the delegation. In EPR data systems, patient consent could be securely enforced by means of an automatic security system and cryptographic methods. See (Bergmann, Bott, Pretschner, & Haux, 2007; Coiera & Clarke, 2004; Galpottage & Norris, 2005; Eskeland & V. Oleshchuk, 2007a) for further discussion and examples of such schemes.

Delegation by Third Parties

Security administrators are trusted parties that may authorize medical personnel access to EPRs on behalf of patients. However, such an arrangement would entail that the administrators would have access to all patient records at that given institution, or even worse, to a number of associated institutions due to networking. Such unconditional access to highly confidential information of a large number of people is in general an undesirable situation. This possible security weakness would be minimized by introducing a separation of duty. This would require the participation of a minimum number of security administrators in order to grant one or more specific medical practitioners access to an EPR on behalf of the pertaining patient.

It should be noted that a patient consent-based delegation system, as discussed in the previous subsection, should support the possibility of third party delegation due to the emergency case. In emergency situations, the patient may be unconscious and would thus be unable to actively consent to EPR authorization. Threshold-based delegation could thus be an appropriate alternative solution for ensuring patient confidentiality.

Data Access Acquisition

In agreement with the principle of separation of duty, a threshold requirement could be a useful security requirement for allowing medical teams to acquire access to relevant medical data. Medical care is typically provided by medical personnel organized in teams. Since a team consists of a number of associated medical practitioners, this by itself could be recognized as a proper basis for trust. Mutual consent and agreement among a given minimum number of team members should be a proper basis for medical personnel to acquire EPR access and a reasonable criterion for meeting the objective of legitimacy, since that the team members would be working for the same cause. Enforcement of such a requirement would accordingly prevent that individuals may snoop and arbitrarily read personal medical data unless holding special privileges. A cryptographic scheme that enforces a team-based EPR acquisition is proposed in (Eskeland & Oleshchuk, 2008).

Threshold-Oriented Cryptosystems

Threshold secret sharing is a cryptographic approach that provides one way of enforcement of the separation of duty principle. According to this method, a secret number (for example, a cryptographic key) is split into n unique secret user "shares". One such user share is handed to one person so that in a group of n persons, each is holding a share. The secret number can only be computed by means of at least t arbitrary such shares and less than t shares reveal nothing of the secret number. The term *threshold* denotes the minimum number of participants of the group that is required to collaborate in order to reveal the secret number. Such a scheme increases the flexibility in contrast to requiring all n participants, i.e., a fixed set of participants, to carry out this computation. This is desirable in scenarios where some sort of separation of duty is required, for example that an originator of some sensitive information like a secret key, is only willing to let it be disclosed as result of the agreement of a given number of pre-designated individuals. Accordingly, it is precluded that single individuals can obtain the secret on their own.

An instance of a threshold secret sharing scheme is basically useful only once, since the participants have to reveal their secret user shares in order to compute the shared secret. And once the shared secret is computed, it is revealed once and for all. Nevertheless, threshold secret sharing in practise mostly used as a building block in threshold-oriented cryptographic schemes such as threshold decryption (Desmedt & Frankel, 1989; Pedersen, 1991; Eskeland & Oleshchuk, 2007; Saeednia & Ghodosi, 1999), threshold signatures (Harn, 1994) and multi-party key establishment (Li & Pieprzyk, 1999), enforcing a minimum number of participants to collaboratively carry out the cryptographic function. In such schemes, the secret user share of each participant and the shared secret are protected from being revealed to the other participants. Threshold cryptosystems are commonly based on the Shamir secret sharing scheme (Shamir, 1979). Threshold decryption is a class of cryptosystems where an arbitrary composed subset of a minimum number of participants of a given group is required to collaboratively carry out decryption. Each such group is represented by a public key which allows encryption. The encrypted data can only be decrypted due to the partial computations of *t* such participants in agreement with the threshold requirement. Threshold signatures is another class of threshold cryptosystems that enforce that minimum *t* participants are required to compute such signatures in agreement with the threshold requirement.

HIERARCHICAL ASPECTS

In the medical scenario, the medical practitioners and employees are hierarchically ranked according to their job positions and duties, so that a medical doctor would have higher ranking than a nurse. Hierarchical organization implies that higher ranking correspond to more privileges and responsibilities. Medical practitioners of higher ranking would accordingly be in position to be entrusted access to more confidential information than the practitioners of lower ranking. Electronic patient record systems provide opportunities for fine-grained access control with regard to the sensitivity of the data. Depending on the desired level of fine-graininess, each data field, data block or data module of the EPR, could be each assigned a confidentiality level from a small range, for instance [0-3] where 0 denotes none or low confidentiality level and 3 corresponding to high confidentiality level. Alternatively, the confidentiality levels could be classified as open, non-sensitive, sensitive, and highly sensitive. Each data item could be individually marked according to its sensitivity level, or grouped into modules according to confidentiality level.

It is necessary to have a reasonable agreement between the ranking of the medical practitioners and the confidentiality levels of the medical data, where participants are only granted access to data (of a given EPR) whose confidentiality level is in agreement with their ranking and to data of underlying confidentiality levels. It must accordingly be prohibited that participants may obtain access to data whose sensitivity level is above the privilege level of that participant.

An example is showed in Figure 1, where each EPR is categorized into three confidentiality levels. There are three levels of user rankings; nurse, general physician and chief physician, which agree with the EPR confidentiality levels. The structure is a totally-ordered, meaning there is only one class of users for each level. Alternatively, since there may be a number of types of medical specialists, compartmentalization of a given level into two or more user classes could be useful. An example is showed in Figure 2, where level 4 is compartmentalized into two classes. Accordingly, confidential data pertaining to one specialist area would not be accessible to specialists of other areas. Also note that chief physicians would have access to all of the EPR data. Thus a proper permissions assignment is needed to provide permitted to process data of each data level. Typical permissions would be read, write and delete. A cryptographic EPR access control scheme based on patient consent for hierarchical medical teams is presented in

Figure 1.

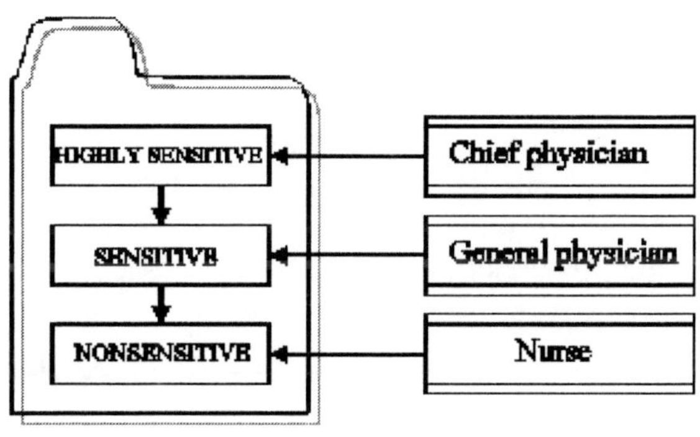

Figure 2.

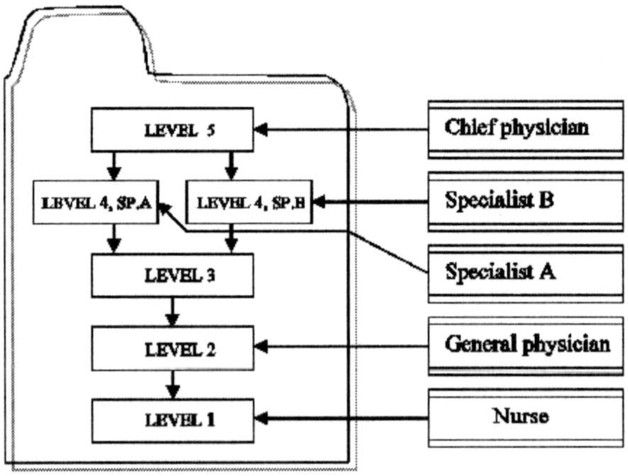

(Eskeland & Prasad, 2006).

SECURING MEDICAL DATA

Problems to overcome in insecure networks would be to provide user-oriented security and data oriented security:

- Data-oriented security includes preservation of secure communication, secrecy and confidentiality of data, integrity of data, data authentication and non-repudiation of data.
- User-oriented security includes secure communication, user authentication and ensuring proper access control.

A user would be represented by a cryptographic user key he or she is holding. An important issue here relates to secure association between users and data, which means secure binding between data and the cryptographic key of a user. This can be realized by encryption and digital signatures, whereof cryptographic algorithms are the basic building blocks. As discussed in subsequent subsections, cryptographic algorithms are basically classified as public key (asymmetric key) and shared key (symmetric key).

User Authentication

A user that is going to communicate with one or more users over an insecure network needs to make sure that the other users are really those who he or she thinks they are. Otherwise, an adversary may successfully masquerade as a peer user, and thereby obtain confidential information. A server needs to authenticate users logging on before confidential access can be provided. Likewise, a user needs to make sure the authenticity of a server when logging onto the server before supplying personal credentials like passwords or pin-codes. Since the users cannot see each other physically, cryptographic means can be taken to provide secure user authentication. In the medical scenario, after a medical practitioner has been successfully authenticated by an EPR server, it has to validate the credentials of the person to decide whether access to the requested data can be granted or not. This would also include determining what operations that the user would be allowed to perform on the data.

If the authentication succeeds, the subsequent communication should be made secure. This is achieved by cryptographic key establishment protocols that securely establish secret session keys shared among the pertaining parties for encryption of the communicated data (Boyd & Mathuria, 2003; Rafaeli & Hutchison, 2003). However, many cryptographic key establishment protocols also provide user authentication. In the following sections, we will look at two aspects of data confidentiality:

- The confidentiality of the communication of data between two entities.
- The confidentiality of the data at the server.

Secure Communication

It is essential that data in transfer are protected to prevent the data from being obtained by unauthorized individuals or intruders, for example by eavesdropping. Secure communication would require the use of security protocols that have to provide relevant security properties. Security protocols assume that computer networks are insecure, with the possible presence of a passive or active adversary. This is a reasonable assumption for wireless networks due to the broadcast-orientation, where any message can be intercepted by anyone present in the location. A passive adversary would have the ability to eavesdrop the communication over the network. An active adversary would be able to manipulate, i.e., change, replace and suppress data that is in transfer. An important type of attacks is the replay attack where an adversary attempts to subvert a security protocol by replaying former messages. Measures like incorporating MACs or digital signatures should be taken to ensure that the integrity of data is intact.

Secure Data Storage

It could be desirable to provide a more overall level of information confidentiality, not only with respect to access control mechanisms and on what basis should granting of EPR access take place (i.e., what should be the criteria and conditions for granting EPR access), but also concerning the long-term storage of the medical data. For example, it could be argued that long-term encryption of medical data may provide an increased level of confidentiality than if stored as plaintext. Nevertheless, this assumes that the corresponding cryptographic keys would have to be "out of reach" since encryption imposes the problem of secure key management and key storage. If a cryptographic key is compromised, its encrypted data would correspondingly be considered compromised. Storage and management of cryptographic keys would therefore impose a potential security risk since that whoever that is controlling the cryptographic keys also controls the corresponding data. However, in (Eskeland & Oleshchuk, 2007a) a cryptographic method is proposed that provides security scheme where EPRs are stored encrypted at the EPR server, where each EPR is encrypted with a unique secret key. There are no cryptographic key tables and no one, including patients, hold or can obtain the cryptographic key pertaining to his or her encrypted EPR. The protocol enables secure reconstruction of a secret EPR cryptographic key at the EPR server due to the interaction between the EPR server and the consenting patient granting a specified medical team access to his or her EPR. This allows the EPR server to subsequently decrypt the pertaining EPR. The EPR key is thus reconstructed out of reach of pertaining and other participants.

Shared Key Cryptography

Symmetric key ciphers (i.e., shared key ciphers) have the advantage of relatively short keys and the ability of high rates of throughput. In such systems, cryptographic keys must be shared among those entities that are to communicate confidentially, so regarding two-party communication the key must remain secret in both ends. In large networks, there would be many key pairs to be managed, and each user would have to securely manage a list containing the keys for each of his or her contacts.

Sharing long-term secret keys among a number of users is an impractical and troublesome assumption due to increased vulnerability from the aging of keys, and lack of flexible user constellations due to the shared keys. This could be mitigated by an online trusted third party (TTP) so that all communication goes through the TTP that shares a secret key pair with all relevant users. Nevertheless, this would in many cases be undesirable. It would correspondingly be a problem to distribute and establish new shared keys to new contacts over an insecure network if the key distribution protocol (i.e., the key establishment protocol) is based on symmetric key ciphers, since this would require that a symmetric key is already shared between the distributor and the receiver.

In practice, symmetric key ciphers are mostly applied session-wise due to their capabilities of high throughput and efficiency, where shared session keys would be established session-wise by means of some secure key establishment protocol. Such protocols could be based on symmetric key or public key systems. Key establishment protocols based on public key cryptosystem eliminate the disadvantages of sharing long-term secret keys.

Public Key Cryptography

In public key systems, each user has a personal public/private key pair where the public key is publicly representing the pertaining user. This eliminates the disadvantage of sharing long-term secret keys. However, the downside of such systems would be lower throughput rates than those based on symmetric key schemes, and relatively large key sizes. Secure data transfer is achieved by means of encrypting a message with the public key of the receiver. By means of the corresponding secret key, the receiver would be the only who can decrypt the pertaining cryptotext. Examples of popular public key cryptosystems are RSA and ElGamal (Rivest, Shamir, & Adleman, 1978) and (ElGamal, 1985).

For efficient and communication a prior agreement of a secret shared key would be more practical. The authenticity of public keys should nevertheless be provided, so that it can be certified that a given public key is actually representing the users as it is claimed to do. Otherwise, an adversary could substitute such a key with his or her own public key, and could subsequently decrypt the confidential information that was intended for another person. Digital certificates are means for establishing the authenticity of public keys. Digital signatures basically contain the identity and the public key of the user, and a digital signature of a trusted third party (TTP), typically the party issuing the keys.

Cryptographic Protocols

Cryptographic protocols are a wide range of methods that provide two or more participants with secure computation for various purposes. More precisely, a cryptographic protocol is a distributed algorithm defined by a sequence of steps precisely specifying the actions required of two or more entities to achieve a specific security objective. Such actions would require use of cryptographic primitives. There are cryptographic protocols for secure user authentication, secure key establishment, secure voting, electronic cash, and anonymous transaction schemes and so on. See for example (Boyd & Mathuria, 2003; Schneier, 2006; Rafaeli & Hutchison, 2003) for overviews. Many times, the objective for data security could also include the issue of user security. For example in the case of secure communication where two users would like to communicate securely over an insecure network, each of them would first have to make sure that the other party is who he or she claims to be. Since the parties cannot meet each other physically, user authentication has to be performed over the network. The parties would have to agree on some secret shared cryptographic session key for subsequent secure communication. Most practical user authentication schemes and key agreement schemes with user authentication are based on public key cryptographic schemes.

Due to the necessity of preserving patient confidentiality, such properties of cryptographic protocols are very relevant issue for the medical scenario. This includes aspects concerning the three types of players (patients, medical practitioners, and security administrators), medical teams, hierarchical aspects, access control and granting, patient consent, patient anonymity; secure communication and key establishment, hierarchical access control issues, secure data management and storage, and more.

Security Issues

The purpose of cryptographic protocols is to provide secure and confidential communication on insecure computer networks. This is achieved due to a number of relevant security properties provided by such protocols. Wireless networks is regarded insecure in the sense that communicated messages could easily be eavesdropped by an adversary (passive attack), or even modified or replaced (active attack). In general, an active adversary could be capable to suppress, replace, replay and modify messages over the network. Cryptographic protocols have to ensure that two-party or multi-party computations can be carried out in agreement with some given security requirements. This would typically include confidentiality, preventing that other than the participants from obtaining the inputs (e.g., the cryptographic user keys) and the computed results. Thus, an essential security requirement is long-term user key confidentiality. It must be prevented that any participant or outsider can obtain long-term secret user keys.

Secure Key Establishment

Secure communication over computer networks is usually achieved by means of encrypting the exchanged messages. The messages could be encrypted by means for long-term public keys (or long-term shared keys). However, the last case would require that they share the same secret key. It can be done by means of some secure key establishment protocol.

By means of such protocols, two or more individuals can establish shared secret cryptographic keys over insecure networks. The protocols can be based on secret key cryptography or public key cryptography. Due to sharing of long-term secret keys among a number of users is an impractical assumption, most key establishment protocols that is based on shared key cryptography require an online TTP. Hence, each user would share a secret key with the TTP, and all key establishment messages would go through the TTP. Kerberos (Steiner, Neuman, & Schiller, 1988) and the shared key protocol of Needham-Schroeder (Needham & Schroeder, 1978) are two well-known examples of key establishment protocols based on shared keys.

Clearly, it would be a problem to distribute and establish new shared keys to new users over an insecure network if a key is not already shared between the new user and the TTP. The advantage of public key based solutions is simplification of key management and eliminating the need for an online TTP. This increases considerably the usability for public key protocols, and public key protocols have therefore become far more important than shared key protocols. For example, the RSA public key cryptosystem (Rivest et al., 1978) is based on the Factorization Problem (i.e., the difficulty of factorizing integers composed of two very large primes), and the ELGamal public key cryptosystem (ElGamal, 1985) is based on the Diffie-Hellman Problem (Diffie & Hellman, 1976), which is a variant of the Discrete Logarithm Problem. Key establishment protocols can basically be divided into key transfer protocols and key agreement protocols. Key transfer protocols are where one entity generates the secret key and distributes it confidentially to one or more users. Key agreement is where two or more participants that "agree" on one secret key by equally contributing to the value of the established key. Depending on the number of participants, such protocols are categorized as two-party and multi-party protocols.

Group-Oriented Cryptographic Protocols

Secure group communication refers to the scenario in which a group of participants can communicate securely over some computer network in such a way that the exchanged messages would be unintelligible for outsiders and non-pertaining users

(Boyd & Mathuria, 2003; Rafaeli & Hutchison, 2003). Conference key establishment protocols (also known as multi-party key establishment protocols) allow a number of users to establish a shared session key whereof secure communication over insecure computer networks can be achieved by encrypting the exchanged messages. Group-oriented key agreement is a special case of secure multi-party computation, where n participants compute the result of some function $f(x_1, x_2, \ldots, x_n)$ and where each participant holds a secret input x_i. The problem is how to compute f without revealing their secret inputs to any other party, including the other participants. The function could be any function taking any inputs where the computations are conducted over a distributed network. No information about the inputs should be learned beyond what is absolutely necessary in order to conduct the computations. Strictly speaking, any participant that is legitimately included in the execution of a security protocol should not learn about the private inputs of the other participants. All that may be learned is the result of the protocol, in agreement to whom the result is designated to. Most protocols distribute the same result for all participants, i.e., the participants collaboratively compute one result that is to be shared among them. In addition to key transfer and key agreement, such protocols can also be classified according to the nature of the user composition, that is whether the team composition is ad hoc or predefined (long-term).

Earlier in this chapter, we pointed out the hierarchical aspects of the medical context where medical teams are composed of hierarchically ranked medical personnel like doctors and nurses. Secure hierarchical group communication could be achieved due to using hierarchical key establishment protocols. Such protocols would facilitate secure establishment of a number of session keys in agreement with the given number of user levels. An essential security property is that users of a given level can compute the hierarchical session keys pertaining to their own and underlying security levels, while it is computationally infeasible to compute hierarchical session keys of overlying security levels. An example of such protocol is presented in (Eskeland & Oleshchuk, 2007b), although the key establishment protocols found in the literature are generally non-hierarchical.

However, a relatively large class of hierarchical cryptographic schemes is known for hierarchical access control. (See (Kuo, Shen, Chen, & Lai, 1999; Lin, 1997; Zou, Ramamurthy, & Magliveras, 2001) for examples of such schemes.) The main difference between hierarchical key establishment protocols and hierarchical access control protocols is that the former provide secure establishment of hierarchically-arranged short-term session keys, while the latter provide secure distribution of hierarchically-arranged long-term, predefined keys.

Patient Anonymity

Due to the sensitive nature of medical information like information about AIDS/HIV status, sexual transmittable diseases, emotional problems, psychiatric illnesses, genetic predispositions to diseases, toxic addictions, etc., it may be desirable that identities (names, addresses, personal security numbers, etc.) of patients associated with it are hidden to prevent them from being associated with their physical disabilities. A common way of obtaining anonymity is by means of pseudonyms. A pseudonym is an identity that is a means of referencing, and can be long-term (fixed) or temporary. A temporary pseudonym is preferred since it would prevent that association between a fixed pseudonym and the medical data of the pertaining patient can build up. Nevertheless, there should be no deducible association between the real identities and the pseudonyms of the patients. A cryptographic scheme that enables patients to anonymously grant medical teams' access to their EPRs without revealing their true identities to the medical practitioners is proposed in (Eskeland & Oleshchuk, 2006). A non-cryptographic patient anonymization scheme can be found in (Sweeney, 1997).

CONCLUSION

In this chapter, we have discussed security and privacy issues related to medical scenario. We reviewed relevant aspects like patient confidentiality, patient anonymity, medical teams, user and data hierarchy, various types of authorization and granting of EPR access (e.g. by patient consent, trusted third parties or team-based access acquisition), and cryptographic issues like authentication, secure communication and secure preservation of data in the context of medical scenario.

REFERENCES

American Medical Association. (2008). *Patient confidentiality.* Retrieved from http://www.ama-assn.org/ama/pub/category/4610.html

Bergmann, J., Bott, O. J., Pretschner, D. P., & Haux, R. (2007). An e-consent-based shared EHR system architecture for integrated healthcare networks. *Journal of Medical Informatics*, 2-3.

Botha, R. A., & Eloff, J. H. P. (2001). Separation of duties for access control enforcement in workflow environments. *IBM Systems Journal*, *40*(3), 666–682.

Boyd, C., & Mathuria, A. (2003). *Protocols for Authentication and Key Establishment.* Berlin, Germany: Springer-Verlag.

Coiera, E., & Clarke, R. (2003). e-Consent: The Design and Implementation of Consumer Consent Mechanisms in an Electronic Environment. *Journal of the American Medical Informatics Association*, *11*(2), 129–140. doi:10.1197/jamia.M1480

Desmedt, Y. G., & Frankel, Y. (1989). *Threshold cryptosystems.* Paper presented at the Advances in Cryptology.

Diffie, W., & Hellman, M. (1976). New directions in cryptography. *IEEE Transactions on Information Theory*, *22*(6), 644–654. doi:10.1109/TIT.1976.1055638

ElGamal, T. (1985). A public key cryptosystem and a signature scheme based on discrete logarithms. *Information Theory . IEEE Transactions on*, *31*(4), 469–472.

Eskeland, S., & Oleshchuk, V. (2006). *Anonymity authorization granting in medical information networks* Paper presented at the European Conference on eHealth 2006, Fribourg, Switzerland.

Eskeland, S., & Oleshchuk, V. (2007). *Collusion-resistant threshold decryption.* Paper presented at the Communication, Network, and Information Security CNIS 2007, Berkeley, California, USA.

Eskeland, S., & Oleshchuk, V. (2007a). *EPR Access Authorization of Medical Team Based on Patient Consent.* Paper presented at the Conference on eHealth 2007, Oldenburg, Germany

Eskeland, S., & Oleshchuk, V. (2007b). *Hierarchical Multi-Party Key Agreement for Wireless Networks.*

Eskeland, S., & Oleshchuk, V. (2008). Secure Team-Based EPR Access Acquisition in Wireless Networks. *Availability, Reliability and Security, 2008. ARES 08. Third International Conference on*, 943-949.

Eskeland, S., & Prasad, N. (2006, July 17, 2006,). *A Novel Decentralized Hierarchical Access Control Scheme for the Medical Scenario.* Paper presented at the International Workshop on Ubiquitous Access Control, San Jose, CA, USA.

Galpottage, P. A. B., & Norris, A. C. (2005). Patient consent principles and guidelines for e-consent: a New Zealand perspective. *Health Informatics Journal*, *11*(1), 5–18. doi:10.1177/1460458205050681

Harn, L. (1994). Group-oriented (t, n) threshold digital signature scheme and digital multisignature. *IEE Proceedings. Computers and Digital Techniques*, *141*(5), 307–313. doi:10.1049/ip-cdt:19941293

Kuo, F., Shen, V., Chen, T., & Lai, F. (1999). Cryptographic key assignment scheme for dynamic access control in auser hierarchy. *IEE Proceedings - Computers and Digital Techniques (Now: Iet Computers and Digital Techniques)*, *146*(5), 235-240.

Li, C.-H., & Pieprzyk, J. (1999). *Conference Key Agreement from Secret Sharing.* Paper presented at the Proceedings of the 4th Australasian Conference on Information Security and Privacy.

Lin. (1997). Dynamic key management schemes for access control in a hierarchy. *Computer Communications, 20*(15), 1381.

Needham, R. M., & Schroeder, M. D. (1978). Using encryption for authentication in large networks of computers. *Communications of the ACM*, *21*(12), 993–999. doi:10.1145/359657.359659

Pedersen, T. (1991). A Threshold Cryptosystem without a Trusted Party. In *Advances in Cryptology — EUROCRYPT '91* (pp. 522-526).

Rafaeli, S., & Hutchison, D. (2003). A survey of key management for secure group communication. *ACM Computing Surveys*, *35*(3), 309–329. doi:10.1145/937503.937506

Rindfleisch, T. C. (1997). Privacy, information technology, and health care. *Communications of the ACM*, *40*(8), 92–100. doi:10.1145/257874.257896

Rivest, R. L., Shamir, A., & Adleman, L. (1978). A method for obtaining digital signatures and public-key cryptosystems. *Communications of the ACM*, *21*(2), 120–126. doi:10.1145/359340.359342

Saeednia, S., & Ghodosi, H. (1999). A Self-Certified Group-Oriented Cryptosystem without a Combiner. In *Information Security and Privacy* (pp. 192-201).

Schneier, B. (2006). *Applied Cryptography.* Hoboken, NJ: Wiley.

Serour, G. I. (2006). Confidentiality, privacy and security of patients' health care information: FIGO Committee for the Ethical Aspects of Human Reproduction and Women's Health. *International Journal of Gynaecology and Obstetrics: the Official Organ of the International Federation of Gynaecology and Obstetrics*, *93*(2), 184–186. doi:10.1016/j.ijgo.2006.03.011

Shamir, A. (1979). How to share a secret. *Communications of the ACM*, *22*(11), 612–613. doi:10.1145/359168.359176

Steiner, J. G., Neuman, B. C., & Schiller, J. I. (1988, February). *Kerberos: An Authentication Service for Open Network Systems.* Paper presented at the Winter 1988 Usenix Conference.

Sweeney, L. (1997). Guaranteeing anonymity when sharing medical data, the Datafly System. *Proceedings/AMIA Annual Fall Symposium*, (pp. 51-55).

Zou, X., Ramamurthy, B., & Magliveras, S. (2001). Chinese Remainder Theorem Based Hierarchical Access Control for Secure Group Communication. In *Information and Communications Security* (pp. 381-385).

KEY TERMS AND DEFINITIONS

Access Control: This includes authentication, authorization and audit with measures such as physical devices, biometric control and monitoring.

Anonymity: The property of not being identifiable that is personal identity, or personally identifiable information of that person that can be used to identify that person is not known.

Electronic Patient Records (EPRs): An individual patient's medical record in digital format.

Group-Oriented Cryptography: A class of cryptographic schemes to provide security in scenarios where a group of participants can communicate securely over some computer network in such a way that the exchanged messages would be unintelligible for outsiders and non-pertaining users.

Information Privacy: The ability of an individual or group to control revealing information about them.

Information Security: A set of means for protecting information and information systems from unauthorized access, use, disclosure, disruption, modification, or destruction.

Key Management: Any method in information security by which cryptographic keys are exchanged or established between users based use of some cryptographic schemes.

Patient Consent: This principle means that patients have a right to choose whether or not to accept your advice or treatment, and control access to his/her private medical data.

Public Key Cryptography: A form of cryptography in which the key used to encrypt a message differs from the key used to decrypt it.

Secret Key Cryptography: A form of cryptography in which the key used to encrypt a message is identical (or trivially related) to the key used to decrypt it.

Threshold Cryptosystem: A cryptosystem where in order to decrypt an encrypted message a number of parties exceeding a threshold is required to cooperate.

Section 4
Health Informatics and E-Health Impact

Chapter 18
A Process Architecture Approach to Manage Health Process Reforms

Christine Stephenson
Emirates Airlines, Dubai, UAE

Wasana Bandara
Queensland University of Technology, Brisbane, Australia

ABSTRACT

Business Process Management (BPM) is often perceived as a top priority concern in organisations; both in public and private sectors. This has been clearly noticed in the Australian health care sector, evidenced by the Australian Government's commitment to pursuing a reform agenda that reflects a new approach to improving health and aged care services. The adoption of a business process management approach can be a key tool to facilitate health reform in the public and private sectors. This approach provides a structured and hence rigorous approach to ensure that health processes are reviewed, improved and implemented consistently throughout the organisation, especially where public health services are provided from multiple service points. Process modeling is an embedded component of most BPM initiatives, yet a resource intensive task. How process models can be derived efficiently (i.e. with less resources and time) and effectively (at a high quality to meet the specific needs) is an integral element of interest to most organisations, however, this area of research is still in its infancy. This paper aims to address this gap by proposing a 'process-pattern' based approach to process modeling where models are created and managed within a 'process architecture'. The process pattern approach is explained with evidence from a large state based health organisation using an integrated risk management process for health care service management as an example. The study employed an action research approach and the chapter unfolds its findings around the main phases of the research method. The contributions from this work are twofold. From the perspective of practice, it offers a validated high level example of a process pattern for an Integrated Risk Management Program for health. From an academic perspective: it presents a validated Risk Management process pattern for delivering health services which can be used as or a benchmark in further research.

DOI: 10.4018/978-1-60566-030-1.ch018

INTRODUCTION

Australia's growing health demands are creating new challenges for governments at the national, state, territory and local levels (Minister of Ageing, 2008). The Australian Federal Health Department intends to spend $51.8 Billion dollars on National Health initiatives in 2008-2009 through the National Health and Hospitals Reform Plan. The aim is to improve the capacity of the states and territories to deliver health services when and where the citizens (in particular, working families) need them. The current Australian Health Care Agreements will be extended for 12 months with an extra $1 billion in provided funding. New agreements will be finalised by the end of 2007, with opportunities for major reform (Department of Health and Ageing, 2007). One of the major challenges to implement the intended reforms relates to how Hospitals are currently organized using logical groupings (functions) of clinical specialties instead of being grouped according to process groupings. Taking a process-oriented approach to improving processes can be challenging as these processes need to cross the traditional functional boundaries in order to realize process efficiencies (Vera, A. & Kuntz, L. 2007).

The adoption of a Business Process Management (BPM) approach can be a key tool to facilitate health reform in the public and private sectors. Business Process Management (BPM) provides a structured and consequently a rigorous approach to ensure that health processes are reviewed, improved and implemented consistently throughout the organisation, especially where public health services are provided from multiple service points.

BPM in general, includes methods, techniques, and tools to support the design, enactment, management and analysis of business processes (van der Aalst et al., 2003). One of the key concerns and challenges when applying BPM is the lack of accepted methodologies, and resources to guide these initiatives (Larsen and Myers, 1998; Murphy and Staples 1998; Amoroso, 1998; Indulska et al., 2006). A common BPM methodology that can be utilised and catered for all specific contexts is yet to be derived; and may not be feasible due to the complexities that each individual context brings in. However, a common aspect of all BPM approaches is the orientation towards understanding the current-processes and aim towards an improved better-process. Business process articulation in the form of high-level and detailed process models is a common component of most process improvement projects (Indulska et al., 2006; Bandara 2005). Process Modeling provides a structured and consequently a rigorous approach to ensure that all required aspects of processes are reviewed, improved and implemented consistently. However, detailed process modeling can be an expensive exercise (Becker et al, 2003), and also complex in terms of managing all the different types and levels of processes (and their models), their relationships and interdependencies. While Process Architectures are highly recommended for this (Davis and Bradander, 2007), there is a dearth of examples and information on how to implement such an approach. Addressing this gap is the main aim of this chapter.

In this chapter, we propose a Process Architecture approach where Process Patterns are used at different levels to capture and deploy s for health processes. A risk management process in the health arena is selected to demonstrate the design and application of the proposed Process Architecture concept. This research combines diverse concepts in the area of risk management, business process analysis and health treatments services. The remainder of the chapter commences by first briefly introducing these concepts. The chapter then introduces the Organisation in which this research was designed and implemented at. The paper then proceeds to provide a detailed example which demonstrates how a Process Architecture is designed and implemented (by using process patterns). The details are presented in the form of empirical evidence gathered through an action research approach Finally, the chapter concludes with a discussion of the limitations, of this work as well as a preview of future activities.

INTRODUCING KEY CONCEPTS

This section is dedicated to describing the many terms and concepts used later in the chapter during the overall research process and findings discussions that are followed.

The term best practice is used to describe the process of developing and following a standard way of doing things that can be used (i.e. for management, policy, and especially software systems development) multiple times. Even though the term best practice has now become a buzz word within organizations, it is not a new notion. For example, Frederick Taylor (1911) stated that *"Among the various methods and implements used in each element of each trade there is always one method and one implement which is quicker and better than any of the rest"* (Taylor, 1911). is ideally, defining ways that can be used to get things done based on past experience. Organizations benefit by adapting these, as they assure quality results and consistency when the process is followed. Today, 's' are documented in various forms, such as in reference models and information libraries (i.e. SCOR, ITIL, PMBOK, ETOM etc) and are accepted more as 'better-practice' that can assist organizations to define, design, implement and monitor business process improvement initiatives. These documented s often use graphical models to illustrate the methods to follow.

Process Modeling

Process modeling is an approach for visually depicting how businesses conduct their operations by defining the entities, activities, enablers and further relationships along control flows (Curtis et al., 1988; Gill, 1999). It is widely used to increase awareness and knowledge of business processes, and to deconstruct organizational complexity (Davenport, 1993; Hammer and Champy 1993; Smith and Fingar 2003). The visualization of business processes in the form of process models has increased in popularity and importance (Bandara et al., 2005). Process modeling is an embedded component of most BPM initiatives, yet a resource intensive task (Becker et al., 2003). *"The importance of business processes has been amplified by being in the centre of late technological inputs in the form of ERP and workflow systems that aim at increasing productivity and functional interconnectivity by automating internal and external transactions"* (Adamides and Karacapilidis, 2006). Thus, how process models can be derived efficiently (i.e. with less resources and time) and effectively (at a high quality to meet the specific needs) is an integral element of interest to most organisations. This area of research is still in its infancy, with only a few studies conducted on critical success factors of process modeling (e.g. Bandara et al, 2005). Even these, (while they depict what the critical success factors are with empirical evidence) do not provide procedural guidelines on how to achieve these success factors, to improve the efficiency and effectiveness of process modeling initiatives.

Process Pattern

A pattern in general is *"an abstraction from a concrete form which keeps recurring in specific non-arbitary contexts"* (Riehle and Zullighoven, 1995). Patterns have been usefully applied across different disciplines in the past. Alexander et al., (1977) describes how patterns can be used for building architectural designs. Patterns have been widely applied in the Software development arena since the "Gang of Four" (GoF) patterns were introduced by Gamma et al., (1995), they have also been widely applied in the workflow management arena[1]. Recent research (i.e. Van der Aalst et al, 2003) has proposed the use of patterns for the description and evaluation of workflow management technologies. Forster (2006) describes potential business process improvement options across different layers of an organisation using a pattern approach. Literature predicts the high proliferation of patterns within the BPM arena (Harmon, 2003).

The basic benefit of a pattern is that the fundamental elements can be reused and hence better knowledge management, efficiency and effectiveness reached, when they are applied within projects. Patterns can be seen as *building blocks*, which when put together form a meaningful entity with minimal effort. However, the knowledge (held by the person applying the patterns) of how to, and when to bring them together, plays a critical role for its success. Patterns can also be perceived as *standard recipes*, where the basic fundamental concepts can be adapted and catered for to meet specific needs.

Within a BPM context, a pattern is "*an idea that has been useful in one practical context and will probably be useful in others*" (adopted from Fowler, 1997, p.8). Hence patterns are not invented, rather discovered by observing its success over a number of applications. In other words, a process-pattern is a common approach to solve problems that are proven to work in practice (adapted from Ambler, 2000). Process patterns are different to reference models (such as SCOR, ITIL, PMBOK etc) – which have been applied widely for process improvement projects. "*A reference model is an abstracted depiction of reality that serves as a standardised or suggestive conceptual basis for the design of enterprise specific models, usually within a like domain*" (Taylor, 2003, p. ii). A pattern has a much smaller focus, and can be a part of a reference model. While process patterns may inherent some features of reference models, they do not provide 'enterprise' solutions, rather provide process specific solutions, which are much smaller in scope. Process patterns can be usefully applied across the various phases of a BPM project.

Enterprise Business Architecture and Process Architecture

An Architecture illustrates the relationships between parts that create a whole; however, they do not illustrate flow, sequence or timing of events (Whittle and Myrick, 2005). Therefore, an Enterprise Business Architecture provides the guiding framework that describes the relationship between all the parts of the organisation from the strategy to implementation[2]. The Enterprise Business Architecture is made of a number of facets of the organisation as shown in Figure 1.

The Zachman framework for Enterprise Architecture developed by John Zachman, provides a guide for how information about an Enterprise should be organised. The purpose of Zachman's framework was to provide a simple structure that supports the enterprise to access, interpret, develop, manage and change descriptions of the organisation (The Open Group, 2007). The framework proposed above in Figure 1 aligns well with the Zachman approach by providing multiple perspectives of the organization from the contextual, conceptual, logical and physical layers of the enterprise (Figure 1- section A) which also describes the what, how, where, who, when and why in the Zachman model (Figure 1- section B) for each perspective outlined in the figure below.

The process architecture is one of the facets of the Enterprise Business Architecture, where it provides the framework by which the organisation's processes can be structured. The process architecture more importantly provides the relationship between the processes to the other facets of the Enterprise Business architecture such as the People, Finance, Location, Governance etc. In general terms, process architecture is the structural design of general process systems.

"*A business process architecture is a hierarchical structure of process description levels and directly related views covering the whole organisation*

Figure 1. Facets of enterprise business architecture

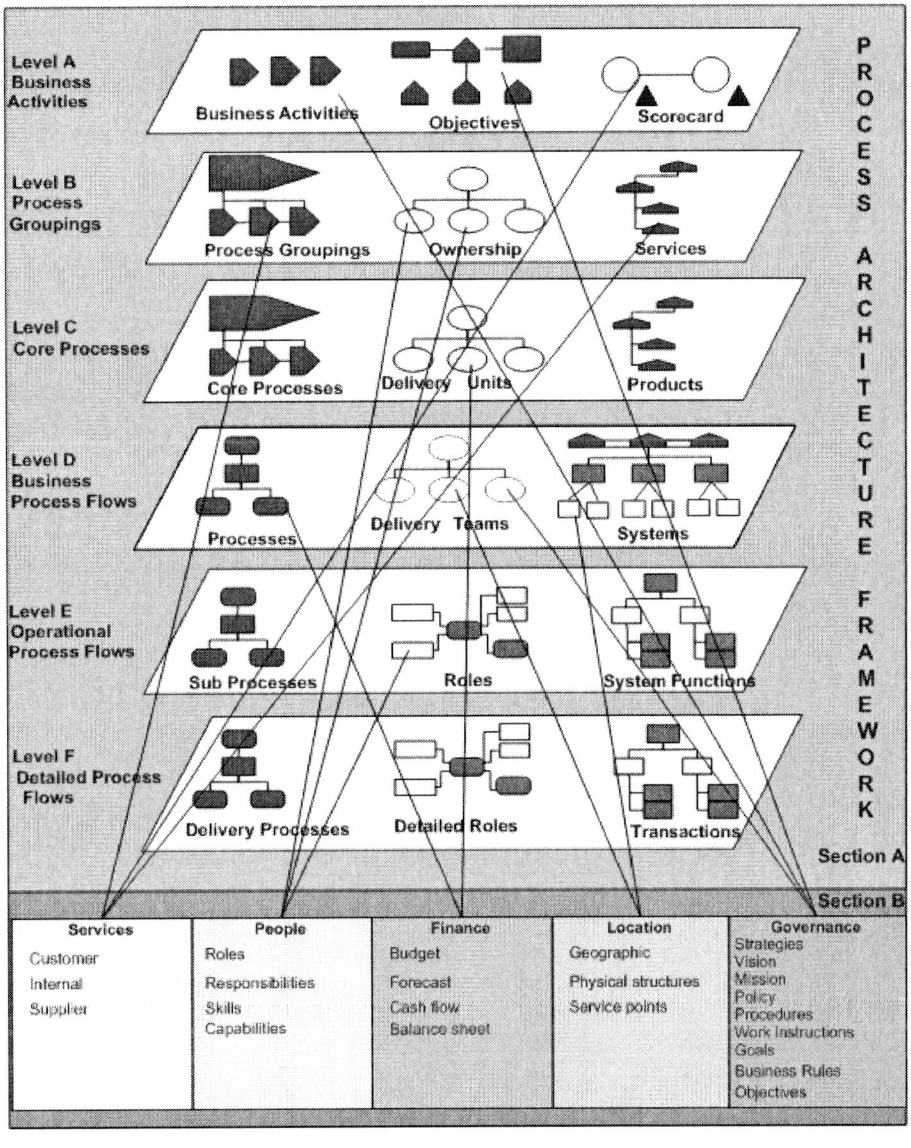

from a business process point of view. It starts with high-level process maps representing a conceptual business view down to the detailed process flow descriptions describing specific tasks and their relation to roles, organisation, data and IT systems." (Davis and Brabander, 2007, p.50). This process architecture defines a framework for organising, deriving, managing and maintaining the process pattern.

A process architecture organises the processes so that staff can easily adopt a pattern based approach to their work as this provides them with a structure to manage their business analysis and improvement projects. The process architecture model adopted in this study is shown in Figure 1 Section A. This is the architectural process modeling approach proposed by Davis (2006) which is also applied across British Telecom. This model provides a top down approach using six layers

Table 1. Process architecture hierarchy descriptions (adapted from Davis and Brabander, 2007)

Process Architecture Framework Levels	Definitions
Level A: Enterprise Map	This may be represented as three fundamental activities that are carried out to run the organisation's business: • Direct the Business; • Manage the Business; and • Operate the Business. It distinguishes operational customer oriented processes from management and strategic processes.
Level B: Process Groupings	The level defines different views of how the processes are structured to deliver the three business activities at Level A, which are to Direct, Manage and Operate the Business. These Processes may be structured from: • A process execution perspective showing standard end-to-end processes (e.g. Service Fulfilment); or • A functional perspective (e.g. Value Domains such as Emergency Services, Health Services)
Level C: Core processes	These are recognisable sub-processes of end-to-end Processes. They can generally be carried out by a Business Unit or a Line of Business functional area. These types of models define those activities that deliver services that are unique to an organisation and that no other organisation delivers, as distinct from supporting processes. Level C Process Models are normally modelled as Value Chains and are comprised of tasks that are defined in detail in the Business Process Flows at Level D.
Level D: Business Process Flows	This level defines the process flows of the core processes defined at Level C and are comprised of tasks. They are normally defined generically (i.e. not specific to a particular product, service, customer, geographical operation, etc). It often will only show the 'Happy Case' (the most common) scenario and exclude the detail of alternative actions, failures and error recovery. Tasks can be decomposed into more detail if required in Level E Operational Process Flows.
Level E: Operational Process Flows	These process models define in more detail the Business Process Flows defined at Level D. It is comprised of steps, normally specific to an operational environment and will be characterised by the Application Systems and Organisational Units or Positions that support and execute them. These types of models typically will include the 'Sad Case' scenario showing the detail of alternative actions, failures and error recovery. The 'Happy Case' and 'Sad Case' scenarios comprise the Business Rules of the organisation. These steps can be decomposed into more detail if required in Level F; Detailed Process Flows.
Level F: Detailed Process Flows	This level defines in more detail the Operational Process Flows defined at Level E. It is comprised of operations and may be used to generate workflows or be used as detailed requirements for systems development. An example of an operation is to describe program logic using pseudo code which can then be coded in the specific programming language. This is embedding the operation logic into the software.

from A to F (see Figure 1 section A and Table 1 for details on each layer) where the level of detail represented by the process models increases from top to bottom. Process patterns can be identified at each level of the model which is actually the 'design' of the organisation and how it is meant to operate.

THE CASE ORGANIZATION

A major Australian Health organization[3] provides public health treatment services to a geographically dispersed population of nearly 4 million people. These services are provided through a number of tertiary hospitals, clinics, aged care facilities and community health centers in metropolitan, rural and remote regions. Table 2 provides a brief overview of the case organization under investigation.

This large state-wide Health Services organization has introduced a major program of improvement and transformation which is supported by funding provided under the Australian Health Care Agreement 2003 – 2008 (Department of Health and Ageing, 2008). As a result of this initiative, a business unit was established – its focus being on innovation and reform in the workplace. The objective of the new business unit was to develop a culture of safety and standardize systems and clinical practice to ensure . These goals align well with the concept of using a pattern-based approach

Table 2. Brief overview of the of the case organization

Population Serviced	**3.9 Million**[4]
Annual Budget (as of 2007)	Approximately $8.3 Billion
Hospitals	38
Number of Public Health Service Centers including hospitals	Approximately 160
Number of Beds	Approximately 10,000
Key Stakeholders	• Members of the Public – Health Service Consumers • Primary Health Care Providers • Specialists • Non-Government Organizations • Health Service Industry Partners such as Diagnostic Service Providers
Number of employees (including full-time, part-time and contractors)	• Approximately 75, 000
Types of services provided	• Public Health Services • In-Patient and Outpatient Clinical and Non-Clinical Health Services • Aged Care • Community Health
Number of IT Systems	Approximately 45 Statewide systems with over 25, 000 localized systems
Number of IT Staff, full-time, part-time and contractors	Approximately 900

to achieve. The Integrated Risk Management (IRM) program was identified as a key strategic initiative that would ensure that a approach was taken to ensure patient safety and support a culture of risk management where staff are encouraged to report clinical incidents and ensure that risk management strategies are implemented to minimize risk. The overarching goal of the Integrated Risk Management program was to document a set of Business Requirements to review the current business processes and define a set of Functional Requirements for an ICT solution to facilitate the capture and management of risk information.

A number of projects commenced as a result of this IRM program which was to define an enterprise-wide Risk Management policy, standards, guidelines and the implementation of an IT system within all Health Service Centers from hospitals to clinics and other health facilities. The IRM Program consisted of three major projects; (i) to define an IRM Framework for the enterprise, (ii) define business requirements for a Complaints Management system, and (iii) define business requirements for a Clinical Incident Management system. Each of the three projects required a detailed review of the current (As-Is) business

Table 3. Brief descriptions of the three risk management projects

Projects	**Description**
Clinical Incident Management	The proactive identification and treatment of hazards before they can lead to patient harm. This also includes the minimization of harm when it does occur and corrective action to minimise the risk of the incident occurring again.
Complaints Management	The management of complaints made by members of the public. This process identifies the incident(s) which lead to the complaint and ensures that an investigation is conducted ending in feedback being provided to the complainant on the corrective action taken.
Integrated Risk Management	The integration of risk management at each level of management into all business activities including strategic planning and decision-making processes

processes where workshops were conducted with key stakeholders.

The Clinical Incident Management project commenced first due to critical strategic and political pressure resulting from negative press reports in the local paper reporting stories of negligence by clinical staff. The objective of the project was to improve the management of clinical incident reporting at health service centers and restore confidence in the public. The Complaints Management project commenced shortly after, followed by the Integrated Risk Management framework which was meant to integrate the risk areas across the Enterprise.

These three projects, in the Integrated Risk Management Program, were implemented sequentially where the intention was to incrementally build on the lessons learnt from each implementation phase. At the time of commencement, similarities between each project were not clear and the objective was to leverage any synergies identified between them.

PROJECT DESIGN AND FINDINGS

An action research method was chosen for this project, which was conducted as a combined consulting and research project, with the goal of producing immediate practical and academic outcomes. Action research is proposed as a useful methodology when the goal is the inquiry into a particular situation and the development of a solution to a problem. It is a form of research that is not a separate, specialised technical activity but one which is closely linked to practice and which can be comfortably undertaken by practitioners. This is particularly valid for the nature of research conducted in the health services sector (Winter and Munn-Giddings, 2001).

The principal researcher led the proposed Process Architecture design and pattern design and played an integral role within the project settings. "*Action research aims to contribute both to the practical concerns of people in an immediate problematic situation and to the goals of social science by joint collaboration within a mutually acceptable ethical framework*" (Rapoport, 1970, p.499). It also assists to "*develop self-help competencies of people facing problems*" (Susman, and Evered, 1978, p.588). It is a scientific research method that has its roots and methods well established since Kurt Lewin (1946) first introduced the term 'action research' as the pioneering approach towards social research (cited in Susman, and Evered, 1978, p. 586).

While different studies classify action research in various ways, most action research follows the traditional 'plan-do-check' approach (Chein et al., 1948). We have adapted the Susman, and Evered (1978) five phased action research model, following an 'experimental action research' approach (Chein et al, 1948; Susman, and Evered, 1978). The five core phases are; (i) diagnosing, (ii) action planning, (iii) action taking, (iv) evaluating, and (v) specifying learning. The next sections will describe each of these phases in detail.

Diagnosing

This phase primarily identifies and defines and problem. Health administrations are increasingly experiencing the need for disclosing their processes and proving the efficiency of their occupation. Process modeling methods have proven to be an adequate mechanism in order to achieve transparency, but process modeling projects can be very expensive and time consuming, often with many external consultants involved (Becker et al, 2003). Thus, a high level framework (pattern) to depict the major process tasks and flows is proposed as a useful way to get started (Davis and Bradander, 2007).

Aligning organisation strategy and the implementation of the strategy is a challenge faced by all organisations (Smith, 2007). The public sector in Australia is faced with an increase in demand for health services, combined with an ageing population and an acute skills shortage[5]. Overseas trained specialist skills are being sourced to fill this gap, but with such a strategy come complications in terms of culture, language etc[6]. It is critical that processes are put in place to ensure that health services are delivered safely and patient care is optimal. In order to implement an Integrated Risk Management strategy, it is therefore important to ensure the implementation of the strategy is structured and closely aligned to achieving the right outcome.

Many organisations in Australia and New Zealand adopt the ASNZS4360:2004 standard as the framework to manage risk which can be applied to a wide variety and wide range of activities from the public, private or community organisations and by groups and individuals (AS-NZS4360:2004). The risk management framework consists of a number of steps which is shown in summary through Figure 2. Appendix 1 provides an overview of the standard and its core steps. This framework has been adopted by the case study organisation as the standard approach to managing risk in clinical and non-clinical areas. Subsequent policies, procedures and governance processes have been implemented by hospitals, clinics and other health treatment service centres to ensure compliance.

It is expected that the implementation of the Risk Management Framework would provide a systematic process to ensure that all internal systems promote evidence-based strategies to minimizing risk across the entire organization increasing patient safety and reducing the risk of harm.

Action Planning

Alternative courses of action for solving a problem are considered in this phase. The Program Manager provided the Program Management Steering Committee, as the Governance Authority, with two alternative approaches to implement the Integrated Risk Management Program. The alternatives endorsed by the Steering Committee were two fold:

Approach 1: Establish a Risk Management Policy and Allow Each Business Unit to Implement the Policy Independently

This would be a typical approach adopted in a large federated organisation where the head of each federated unit is accountable for implementing the policy. Such an approach would require each jurisdiction to report their alignment with the policy but manage risk independently within their area. The problem with such an approach is that it becomes difficult to manage risk consistently across the organisation with varying levels of maturity, budget pressures, skills etc. The policy is open to interpretation and hence implementation becomes inconsistent.

This approach has been used in the past in the Case Study organisation and was the current approach before the IRM Program was proposed. During the development of the Business Case for the IRM Program a significant issue observed was the inconsistent interpretation of the current State-wide policy across the Health Service Centres.

Approach 2: Implement a Process Architecture Approach

A process architecture approach will provide the structure required to ensure that there is clear alignment between the policy, procedures, work instructions, business and system requirements definition. This approach will use process patterns to facilitate the implementation of the IRM framework independent of business context areas of Clinical Incidents, Complaints Management and Risk Management.

The contexts for each of the three projects was observed by the business to be very different processes and not related to each other. Clinical Incident staff such as Nurses and Doctors believed

Figure 2. Risk management framework (Adopted from the Australian and New Zealand Standard on Risk Management ASNZS 4360:2004)

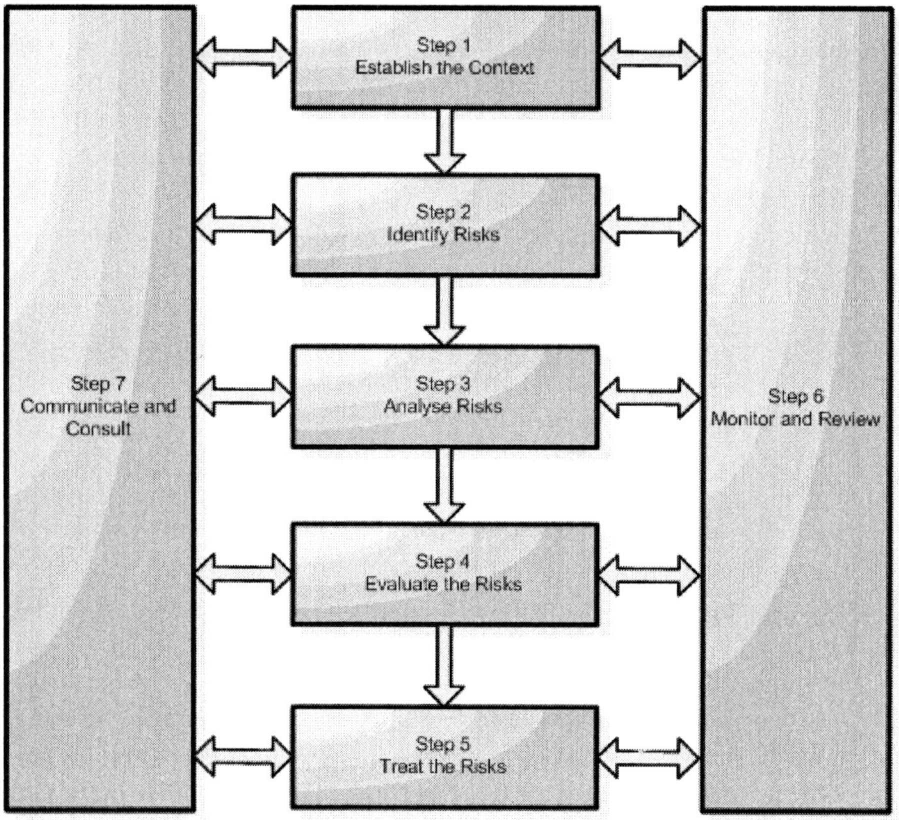

that they were responsible for ensuring that clinical incidents did not occur while treating patients. Patient Liaison staff responsible for managing complaints made by members of the public (including patients), felt their objective was to investigate complaints and provide feedback in a timely manner. The only similarities observed by these staff were when it came to assessing the risk of each clinical incident or customer complaint, the investigator identified process patterns for each business context area to demonstrate that by using a process pattern approach, it was possible to identify other areas of process synergy and view all three contexts from the same process pattern. These demonstrations lead to an increased understanding of all the stakeholders of how the overarching Risk Management Policy applied equally to Clinical Incident, Complaints and Risk Management.

Action Taking

This phase deals with the selection of some form of action and the actual implementation of it. Reforming and aligning the organisation's services, processes, people, budgets, location to the new Integrated Risk Management Policy required a Process Architecture approach to ensure alignment from the Conceptual to the Physical Implementation level in the organisation.

Given that it is challenging to align policy and outcomes, the process pattern approach taken will allow for the effective implementation of strategic policy and operational outcomes. This approach

Figure 3. Applied six level process hierarchy (adopted from Davis and Bradander, 2007)

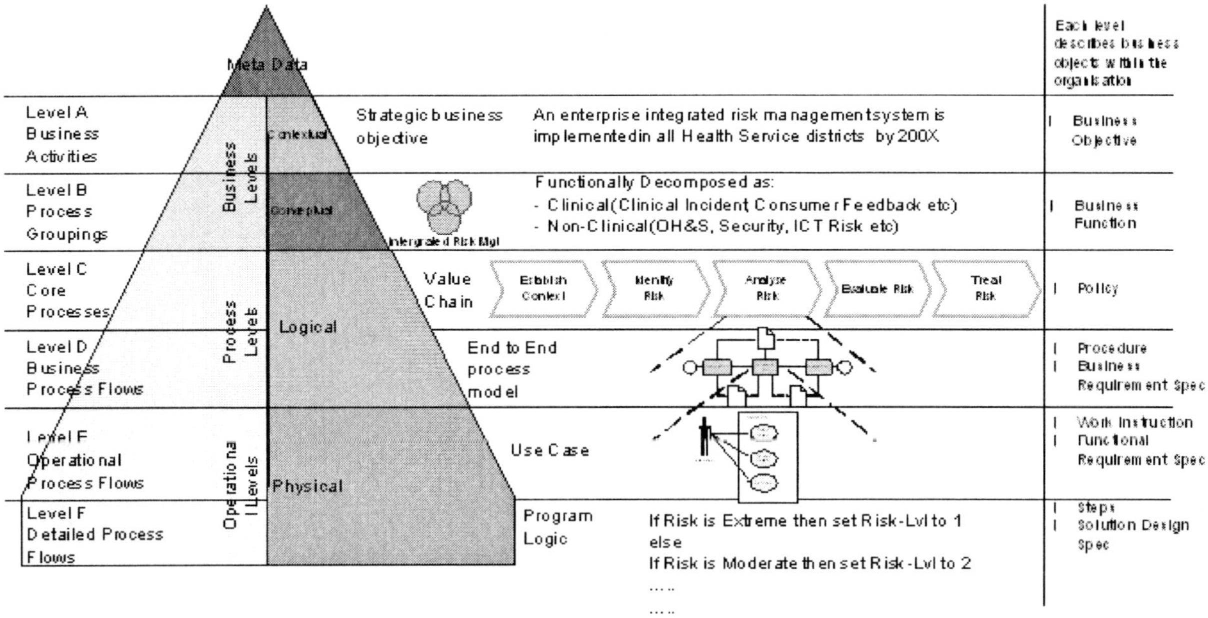

involved a detailed review of the different business context areas within the organisation and a top-down approach was designed for this purpose. Figure 3 (accompanied with Table 4) depicts the overall approach taken in graphical form.

The researcher reviewed the Health organisation's strategic information to firstly understand how the organisation currently implemented Risk Management Policy. Standards, procedures, work instructions, information system solutions relevant to risk management were examined to get an understanding of how the staff within the organisation enacted the processes which manage risk within the organisation constraints (business rules). It soon became apparent that managing risk was a high level corporate goal to provide safe and quality health services to the public. Each federated health service centre was responsible for interpreting the enterprise risk management policy to define internal risk management standards, policies, procedures and work instruction. Federated information systems were also built within each area to support the capture of incident data for analysis and reporting. Appendix 2 depicts in detail the business objects that were looked at each main level of the Process Architecture, demonstrating the artefacts that were reviewed and the model types that were use to depict these (within the Process Architecture). Appendices 3 to 8[8] contain example models used to document each of the Process Architecture levels.

The levels depicted above in the Process Architecture hierarchy in Figure 3, provides levels of abstraction (the ability to decompose a concept, in a structured way to manage the complexity more effectively) in this case within the Risk Management pattern. Enterprise Architects frequently use these levels of abstraction to develop and use models of the organization (Aitken, 2007). In this case study, business process models have been used to provide these levels of abstraction within the Clinical Incident, Complaints and Integrated Risk Management business context areas. Each of these levels of abstraction are described in the Table 4.

The Risk Management process pattern is embedded from the strategy, policy and procedure levels right down through to the lowest program

Table 4. Levels of abstraction of the process architecture (Aitken, 2007)

Model type[7]	Purpose	Alignment attribute type	Description
Contextual	Provides a description of the goal or purpose of the process	Goal Requirements	Consists of the Business Vision, Mission, Goals, Objectives etc. that describe the motivation of the organisation
Conceptual	Describes what the process must achieve in order to satisfy the high level goal	Objectives Constructs	The way the organisation is structured to support the strategic objectives
Logical	Describes the implementation criteria for the process - the logic for implementing the processes in a particular manner	Design principles and assertions Logical components and implementation criteria	The Policies and Procedures provide the guiding logic for who is responsible for enacting a process and how it should be enacted.
Physical	An exact description of what is to be implemented	Measures Physical components	The instantiation of the processes which are guided by the work instructions. Detailed business rules provide guidance on what should be done to complete a process.

logic level to transparently align the organization from the top to the bottom. The statewide IRM policy (Level C in Figure 3) and procedures (Level D in Figure 3) are issued as corporate governance documents to every Health Service Centre. Alignment with the policy is monitored through planned audits of each Health Service Centre's implementation of the corporate policy. The IRM policy is also used to articulate a set of business requirements for ICT solutions to support Clinical and Non-Clinical Risk Management areas. The business processes are embedded in these business requirement specifications to communicate how the Risk Management policy and procedures are to be implemented by other business solutions providers such as trainers, change managers etc.

Based on the preliminary research conducted at the early stages of this phase (refer to Appendix 2 for details), a process pattern was documented, that described the 'Integrated Risk Management Framework' that describes the essential steps involved in managing risk in the organisation (see Appendix 5) . Although the research was a time consuming exercise, the development of the pattern was relatively quick as a Risk Management expert was approached to support the documentation and validation of the pattern. As mentioned earlier, Appendix 2 provides a list of documents that were provided by the Risk Management expert and reviewed through out the exercise. The pattern was then tested during the phased implementation of the Clinical Incident and Complaints Management projects assigned to the researcher with the various stakeholder groups identified in the process pattern, who came from an a variety of service areas within the business.

It was important to ensure that this process architecture and pattern approach could be applied independent of the context of the risk being managed. The areas reviewed as part of the exercise were from within hospital administration, clinical service, occupational health and safety, fire safety and building management.

Instead of drawing separate process models for each of the three areas reviewed, the risk management process pattern was used to validate the process within each risk context area. Typically such projects take life between three to six months (as evidence from archived past project documentation), however, the process pattern approach enabled the researcher complete the project in one month. Adopting a pattern-based approach allowed one model (pattern) to be used to validate the process at each area with the analysis focusing on the similarities and differences between them.

Evaluating

This phase is dedicated to studying the consequences of the action(s) taken. As discussed earlier, the pattern based approach was very effective to meet with accelerated time frames and provide quality process models.

Figure 4 (together with Table 5) below describes the high level approach taken to implement and evaluate the three projects. Things were implemented in 6 core role-out phases, each phase having an evaluation and feedback loop (as described in column 3 of Table 5).

However, this is not to say that the approach is without its limitations. Some of the limitations identified through reflection and observation were as follows:

Figure 4. Project implementation steps

- **Low level of process architecture maturity:** The non existence of a process architecture meant that the researcher had to develop the process architecture as the project evolved. The process of discovering and developing patterns would have been more efficient if an architecture and hence, a structure, defined for discovering and developing patterns was already in place.
- **Organizational cultural hindrances:** Typically in large organisations, stakeholders believe that their process is 'different' or unique and thus, do not lend itself to things that may seem 'generic'. Patterns on the other hand are generic forms of information (derived through the extraction on what keeps on recurring within certain contexts). A process pattern is a successful tool to initially focus on the similarities in the process (and not the differences). When the pattern based approach was applied with each risk context areas stakeholders, the idea of being too unique hindered its acceptability and created resistance. However, once it was shown that only the terms used to describe incidents and risk were different, but the process was essentially the same, the pattern based approach was accepted and adapted. In addition to self reflection and observations, evaluative data were gathered through formal feedback through a series of interviews. Clients were asked to provide feedback on the approach taken during the project and post-project. Clinical and non-clinical staff positively commented on the reduction in time taken to complete workshops without the need to consume significant amounts of Subject Matter Expert time. Remarks were made on the quality of the business analysis artefacts, mainly due to the fact that the researcher could spend more time on reviewing the process models, conducting

Table 5. The project implementation approach

Step	Description of each step	Evaluation Technique(s) used
Project Scope	Project scope was defined with key stakeholders such as the Project Sponsor, Steering Committee and Subject Matter Experts. Three health service centres were identified as representative sites from which to gather data.	Face-to-face meetings Scoping Workshops Review of Strategic Documents, standards, external legislation
Define Business Baseline	The As-Is business processes were defined and issues identified based on input from subject matter experts at each of the three sites. Process Pattern for Risk Management Documented.	Workshops Interviews with frontline staff On the Job observations Review of Policies, Procedures and Work Instructions Review of current Information Systems used
Analyse Process Synergies	The As-Is processes at each site were compared against the Process Pattern to identify process synergies.	Workshops with Subject Matter Experts.
Document Target Business Processes	Target business processes were defined for each business context area highlighting the processes that were in common – Risk Identification, Risk Analysis, Risk Evaluation, Risk Treatment and Monitoring and Review	Workshops with Subject Matter Experts
Design New Business Solution	The Target business processes provided the functional business requirements which were described using Use Cases and the Solution Requirement Specification which used UML models to describe the interactions of the user with the software system	Workshops and documentation of the functional requirements by the business analyst Joint Application Development workshops with the Super User, Business Analyst and Systems Analyst Development and User Acceptance testing of the software system
Implement the New Business Solution	The new system was rolled out across the organisation and is current in use today. Change management techniques were used to train staff to use the new system.	State wide Training sessions Communication of the updated policy, procedures and work instructions through the Intranet website Link to the web-enabled software system with a User Manual

detailed analysis and providing recommendations for improving the business. A range of specific organisational benefits of using a pattern approach were stated during these interviews. They are briefly summarised below.

- ***Better control on how things are done:*** An organisation can reduce overhead costs by analysing the most efficient and effective way to implement a business process to ensure alignment of the business with the strategic objectives. This process pattern can then be implemented right across the organisation to conduct business in a consistent way.
- ***Clearer requirements definitions for Enterprise solutions:*** An organisation should first document the current business process for the ideal scenario (in a pattern) and use this model (the pattern) to examine the differences between business areas to the pattern/ideal scenario. Significant differences can then be analysed and decisions made to standardise the processes (to-be pattern) and define requirements for the Enterprise solution.
- ***Audit for Compliance*:** Quality management systems typically use policy, procedures and work instructions to conduct audits. Audits consist of

checks to see if a process has been implemented the way it is supposed to. A pattern repository can enable the organisation to assign benchmarks to the pattern and assist audit the business area based on the benchmark.

- ◦ ***Communication and transparency on how things are done***: Training staff consistently to do the same thing the same way can be challenging, especially in large organisations. A pattern based approach can be adopted where the process pattern is used to develop training material.

Specifying Learning

The goal of this phase is to use a process architecture to implement process patterns so that these patterns may be used as a solution to realise an organisation's strategic objectives using a structured top-down approach. Eight main issues were identified as major areas to be addressed when applying a pattern based approach. They were classified as Process Architecture requirements and high and low level project requirements. *Process Architecture requirements* related to (i) Defining a process architecture framework, (ii) establishing standard terms and definitions. *High level project requirements* related to the elements that were important at a project level when implementing a pattern based approach and included (iii) the creation of a pattern repository, and (iv) the documentation of pattern governance and ownership. The *low level project requirements* were those elements that related to the individual patterns and consisted of; (v) having different levels of abstraction, (vi) fragmentation, (vii) embedded flexibility and (viii) context specification.

Process Architecture Requirements

- ***Defining a process architecture framework:*** In the absence of literature or empirical evidence, there is very little guidance on what a good process architecture framework looks like, leave alone what a process architecture framework should be. It is critical however to define such a framework in order to represent the different levels of abstraction in the organization and the relationships between the variety of process perspectives.
- ***Establishing standard terms and definitions:*** There is a significant amount of ambiguity in the Business Process Management domain where terms and definitions are confusing. It is important therefore, for an organization to establish a standard set of terms and definitions to reduce ambiguity and establish a common language prior to proceeding with projects as these.

High Level Project Requirements

- **The creation of a pattern repository:** The processes and the frameworks have to be stored somewhere in order for people to access them. These repositories should store the pattern models, the meta models and the processes on how to use the meta models.
- **Pattern governance and ownership:** Governance processes should dictate who the pattern owners are and ensure that the patterns are reviewed regularly, so that they don't end up becoming shelfware. Changes in the business environments are inevitable, the impact of these changes on the process patterns should be evaluated periodically to ensure the pattens continue to be ".

Low Level Project Requirements

- **Maintain different levels of abstractions:** Every process pattern has to fit with the process architecture, otherwise its applicability within the organisation becomes vague. Thus, each pattern must be within the layers of the process architecture, with clear meta-data on which perspectives it captures and the degree of detail it entails.

- **Maintain fragmentation (for reuse):** Large scale process modeling projects are often conducted in a piece mental manner (Green and Ould, 2004). End to end processes can be broken down to fragments, where each fragment can be depicted by a process pattern, which can be adapted separately. While fragmentation, and structured layering of process patterns is important, an overarching structure (a high level pattern) to depict how these fragments fit together is very important.
- **Allow flexibility and context specification:** Flexibility has to be maintained within the patterns to allow minor changes to fit the process/ context . Issues related to flexibility has to be integrated into the guidelines on how to use the patterns (i.e. *'how can one expand and edit the models*?' has to be described within the pattern deployment guidelines). What is a detailed pattern within a certain context can be extracted at a higher level, which can be then used as a pattern at a higher level across any context (e.g. delivering a treatment in health vs a generic delivery of service). The higher the pattern sits in the Process Architecture (refer to figure 2, Level (i.e. A, B C) compared to lower levels (i.e. D, E, F), the more context free it is and hence the more flexible it should be.

FUTURE TRENDS

There are numerous opportunities for organizations to adopt a business process management approach that includes process architecture to enable the successful implementation of organization strategy that is aligned from the top level to the implementation level. Organizations using a process architecture approach to link the various facets of the business to processes will provide the linkage required to align strategy with outcomes. This approach can also be used to provide a common platform to lead valuable discussions between various functional areas of the organisation and to identify how each functional area relates and their contribution to the common goals and objectives.

Further research could be conducted to populate process repositories consisting of process models at each level in the organization where these patterns could then become 'free ware' and re-usable in the truest sense of a pattern in any organization. The identification of these process patterns is worthy of research as business context patterns such as health, manufacturing, research etc could be shared amongst organizations especially in areas where there is a high degree of commonality in business processes (e.g. Governance, HR, Finance, Quality Management etc).

CONCLUSION

This chapter proposed a pattern based modeling approach for health services to enhance related business processes. It depicted an example of deploying an Integrated Risk Management Program within a large health organisation. The study followed an action research approach within a reputed public heath organisation, in Australia. It first presented an introduction to the research context, with an overview on the key concepts applied and a brief introduction to the case organization. The research design and findings within each phase were then presented unfolding the story of how the research conclusions were obtained.

The study's findings are of benefit to both the research and practicing communities. In particular, the paper depicted how process patterns can be implemented using Process Architecture framework to (i) align organisations strategies to the actual implementation of these strategies, and (ii) derive a 'standard' to the services across federated organizational units.

The study is not without its limitations. Process patterns are presented here as best practice (or 'better practice'); as a possible 'standard' that can be followed within a particular setting or context. Past evidence has shown that the adoption of such standards is hindered by lack of stakeholder awareness and lack of perceived usefulness. Furthermore, process patterns are relevant only to document a certain limited high-level process flow, and there is a fair amount of skill that is required by the adoptee of the patterns to usefully apply it in a given context. Process patterns can have embedded constraints based on organisational policies, legislations, culture and varying structures. The notion of 's' does not commit people or companies to one inflexible, unchanging practice, instead, s is a philosophical approach based around continuous learning and continual improvement, hence the process patterns need to be continuously reviewed and updated.

The results reported in this paper are the first steps towards depicting the value of a pattern based approach for better process management and reform within the health context, and further improvements to the reported findings are underway. Means of increasing the awareness of the benefits and buy-in for process patterns (to increase their adoption and proliferation) has to be conducted. More empirical data can to be collected for triangulation purposes in the evaluation phase of the study design. 'Usability' testing (in the form of extended empirical tests) to identify what further details can be provided to support the adoption of these patterns within specific contexts needs to be addressed. In particular, the integration of context specific information within the process patterns (Rosemann, 2006) will be useful to support the adoption of these high-level process patterns within the specific, detailed processes of an organization. While the process patterns provide a useful body of knowledge, this should be owned and managed by a process-pattern-owner in order to sustain its currency and usefulness in this ever - changing environment.

For Health Reform Managers, there is an opportunity to take a holistic approach to reform by identifying process patterns before embarking on a reform project. Process patterns can help manage behavior and enforce compliance by demonstrating similarities between seemingly disparate groups to encourage the organisation and staff adopt the process pattern as a tried and tested method to achieve an objective. Managers can sell their business case for reform more effectively by being able to identify areas of synergy through the use of the pattern and demonstrating the cost effectiveness of using a uniform approach to manage the reform. The added advantage, of course, is being able to demonstrate the linkage between reform in practice to the overall organisation goals and objectives.

REFERENCES

Adamides, E. D., & Karacapilidis, N. (2006). A knowledge centred framework for collaborative business process modeling. *Business Process Management Journal, 12*(5), 557–575.doi:doi:10.1108/14637150610690993

Aitken, C. J. (2007). Design integrity and EA governance. In P. Saha (Ed.) *Advances in Government Enterprise Architecture.* Hershey, PA: Idea Group

Alexander, C., Ishikawa, S., & Silverstein, M. (1977). *A Pattern Language: Towns, Buildings, Construction.* New York: Oxford University Press.

Ambler, S. (2000). Reuse patterns and antipatterns. *Software development.*

Amoroso, D. L. (1998). *Developing a model to understand Reengineering project success*. Washington, DC: IEEE.

Bandara, W., Gable, G. G., & Rosemann, M. (2005). Factors and measures of business process modeling: Model building through a multiple case study. *European Journal of Information Systems, 14*, 347–360. doi:10.1057/palgrave.ejis.3000546

Becker, J., Kugeler, M., & Rosemann, M. (2003). Process Managament - a guide for the design of business processes. Berlin, Germany: Springer.

Chein, I., Cook, S. W., & Harding, J. (1948). The field of action research. *The American Psychologist, 3*, 43–50.doi:doi:10.1037/h0053515

Curtis, B., Krasner, H., & Iscoe, N. (1988). A field study of the software design process for large systems. *Communications of the ACM, 31*(11). doi:10.1145/50087.50089

Davenport, T. (1993). *Process innovation: Reengineering work through information technology*. Cambridge, MA: Harvard Business School press.

Davis, R. (2006). British Telecom - Six-Level Process Hierarchy. In *Proceedings of the Process days conference*, Sydney Australia, August 22-24.

Davis, R., & Bradander, E. (2007). *Aris Design Platform: Getting Started with BPM*. Berlin, Germany: Springer-Verlag.

Department of Health and Ageing. (2007). *Budget statements for 2008-09.* Retrieved July 7th 2008, from http://www.health.gov.au/internet/budget/publishing.nsf/Content/2008-2009_Health_PBS/$File/Department_Overview.pdf

Department of Health and Ageing. (2007). *2003-08 Australian Health Care Agreements- Information sheet number 1 - April 2007.* Retrieved July, 2008, from http://www.health.gov.au/internet/main/publishing.nsf/Content/ahca0308-infosheet1.htm

Forster, F. (2006). The idea Behind Business Process Improvement: Towards a Business Process Improvement Pattern Framework. *Business Process Trend Advisor,* 04-06.

Fowler, M. (1997). *Analysis Patterns: Reusable Object Models*, (Vol. Reading). Reading MA: Addison- Wesley.

Gamma, E., Helm, R., Johnson, R., & Vlissides, J. (1995). *Design Patterns: Elements of Re-usable Object- Oriented Software.* Reading, MA: Addison – Wesley.

Gill, P. J. (1999). Application Development: Business Snapshot -Business Modeling Tools Help Companies Align Their Business and Technology Goals. *Information Week.*

Green, S., & Ould, M. (2006). *The primacy of process architecture*. Retrieved Nov 22nd from http://www.csm.uwe.ac.uk/~sjgreen/paper2.pdf

Hammer, M., & Champy, J. M. (1993). *Reengineering the corporation: a manifesto for business revolution.* London: Nicholas Brealey Publishing, Allen and Urwin.

Harmon, P. (2003). "Business Process Change: A Manager's guide to improving redesigning, and automating processes". Amsterdam, Boston: Morgan Kaufmann.

Indulska, M., Chong, S., Bandara, W., & Sadiq, S. (2006). *Major Issues in Business Process Management: An Australian Perspective*. Paper presented at the Australian Conference on Information Systems (ACIS 2006).

Larsen, M. A., & Myers, M. D. (1998). BPR Success or failure? A business Process reengineering project in the financial services industry. *Communications of the ACM*, 367–381.

Minister of Ageing. (2008, June 12th). *Historic meeting of ministers for ageing/seniors – responding to Australia's changing demographics*. Retrieved July 7th 2008, from http://www.health.gov.au/internet/ministers/publishing.nsf/Content/A58A5B08571D0BDDCA2574650024A4C1/$File/JE082.pdf

Murphy, F., & Staples, S. (1998). Reengineering in Australia: Factors affecting success. In *Proceedings of the Australasian Conference of Information systems*, Sydney, Australia.

Rapoport, R. N. (1970). Three dilemas of action research. *Human Relations*, *23*, 499–513. doi:10.1177/001872677002300601

Reihle, D., & Zullighoven, H. (1995). A pattern Language for tool construction and integration based on the tools and materials metaphor. In J.O Coplian & D.C Schmindt (Eds.), *Pattern Languages of Program Design*. Reading, MA: Addison Wesley Professional.

Rosemann, M. (2006). *Understanding Context-awareness in buisness process design*. Paper presented at the Australasian Conference on Information Systems, Dec 6-8, Adelaide.

Smith, H., & Fingar, P. (2003). Business Process Management. *The Third Wave*. Tampa, FL: Meghan-Kiffer Press.

Smith, R. (2007). *Business Process Management and the Balanced Scorecard: Using Processes as Strategic Drivers*. Hoboken, NJ: John-Wiley and Sons.

Susman, G., & Evered, R. (1978). *An assessment of scientific merits of action research* (Vol. 25, pp. 582-603).

Taylor, C. (2003). *Reference Models for IT service Provision*. Masters dissertation, Queensland University of Technology, Brisbane, Australia.

Taylor, W. F. (1911). *Modern History Sourcebook: The Principles of Scientific Management*. Retrieved November 22nd, 2006 from http://www.fordham.edu/halsall/mod/1911taylor.html

The Open Group. (2007). The Open Group Architecture Framework (TOGAF 8.1.1). Retrieved July 14th 2008 from http://www.opengroup.org/bookstore/catalog/g063v.htm

Van der Aalst, W. M. P., ter Hofstede, A. H. M., & Weske, M. (2003). Business Process Management: A Survey. In *Proceedings of the International conference of Business Process Management*, Eidhoven, The Netherlands, June 26-27.

Vera, A., & Kuntz, L. (2007).Process-based organization design and hospital efficiency . *Health Care Management Review*, *32*(1), 55–65.

Whittle, R., & Myrick, C. (2005). Enterprise Business Architecture: The formal results between strategy and results. Boca Raton, FL: Auerbach Publications.

Winter, R., & Munn-Giddings, C. (2001). *A handbook for action research in health and social care*. New York: Routledge.

KEY TERMS AND DEFINITIONS

Best Practice: The term best practice is used to describe the process of developing and following a standard way of doing things that can be used (i.e. for management, policy, and especially software systems development) by multiple times.

Business Process: A business process is a collection of tasks that produce something of value to the organisation, its stakeholders or its customers.

Business process architecture: A business process architecture is a hierarchical structure of process descriptions levels and directly related views covering the whole organization from a business process point of view. It starts with high-level process maps representing a conceptual business view down to the detailed process flow descriptions describing specific tasks and their relation to roles, organization, data and IT systems. (Davis and Brabander, 2007).

Business Process Management: Refers to aligning processes with the organization's strategic goals, designing and implementing process architectures, establishing process measurement systems that align with organizational goals, and educating and organizing managers so that they will manage processes effectively. (http://www.bptrends.com/resources_glossary) last accessed 9/7/2008

Business Process Modeling: Business process modeling includes techniques and activities used as part of the larger business process management discipline. Business process modeling is an activity performed by business analysts within an organisation. Analysts use modeling tools to depict both the current state of the business and the desired future state.

Business Requirement: A method of describing in business terms of what an organisation does and how it does it in order to achieve a business objective.

Enterprise Business Architecture: Enterprise Business Architecture provides the guiding framework that describes the relationship between all the parts of the organisation from the strategy to implementation[9].

Pattern: A pattern in general is "an abstraction from a concrete form which keeps recurring in specific non-arbitrary contexts" (Riehle and Zullighoven, 1995).

Policy: A policy is a deliberate plan of action to guide decisions in order to achieve an organisation's objective.

Process Architecture: The process architecture is one of the facets of the Enterprise Business Architecture, where it provides the framework by which the organisation's processes are structured. The process architecture more importantly provides the relationship between the processes to the other facets of the Enterprise Business architecture such as the People, Finance, Location, Governance etc.

Process Modeling: Process modeling is an approach for visually depicting how businesses conduct their operations by defining the entities, activities, enablers and further relationships along control flows (Curtis et al., 1988; Gill, 1999).

Risk Management: Is the culture, processes and structures that are directed towards realizing potential opportunities whilst managing adverse effects.

Work Instruction: The detailed description of the steps person, robot or a computer system must complete in order to fulfill a task.

Value Chain: A value chain is a sequence of activities that is initiated by a firm's customer and ends when that customer receives an outcome (service or product).

Task: A task is an atomic activity that is included within a process.

Business Rules: Business rules describe how an organisation operates and the constraints under which the operations are performed.

Operations: Operations are ongoing recurring activity that a business is involved in. Business operations deliver direct or indirect value to the organisations customers.

ENDNOTES

1. See http://workflowpatterns.com for further details. Last accessed, 14th of July, 2008.
2. See The Business Analysis Body of Knowledge www.theiiba.org. Last accessed on 14th of July, 2008.

3 Please note that the organisation is kept anonymous in this paper for confidentiality purposes.

4 Office of Economic and Statistical Research Information Brief, released 24 March 2005. Australian Demographic Statistics September Quarter 2004

5 See http://www.anu.edu.au/aphcri/Domain/Workforce/Thistlethwaite_3_FINAL.pdf, for further details on the Health related skills shortage in Australia. Last accessed July 14th, 2008.

6 See http://www.humanresourcesmagazine.com.au/articles/59/0c028f59.asp for further details on issues with filling the gap with overseas employees. Last accessed July 14th, 2008.

7 This also relates to the levels of abstraction of the Process Architecture.

8 **Appendix C:** ***Level A***: Sample Contextual Model of the Integrated Risk Management function **Appendix D:** ***Level B***: Sample Conceptual Model of the Complaints Management function **Appendix E:** ***Level C:*** Sample Process Models (related to Integrated Risk Management) which shows the application of the ASNZS4360:2004 Risk Management framework in the case study organization. **Appendix F:** ***Level D***: Sample Business Process Flow Model which shows how risks are treated **Appendix G:** ***Level E***: Sample UML Use Case description that was used to document how Risks are assessed. **Appendix H:** ***Level F***: Sample Operational Process Flow Model (in BPMN) that depicts the recording of potential and actual incident and intervention information These clearly demonstrate the funnel like decomposition of complex concepts within each level of abstraction.

9 See The Business Analysis Body of Knowledge www.theiiba.org. Last accessed on 28 Jan 2008

APPENDIX A: EXTRACT FROM THE ASNZS:4360:2004 RISK MANAGEMENT STANDARD

Risk management involves managing to achieve an appropriate balance between realizing opportunities for gains while minimizing losses. It is an integral part of good management practice and an essential element of good corporate governance. It is an iterative process consisting of steps that, when undertaken in sequence, enable continuous improvement in decision-making and facilitate continuous improvement in performance.

Risk management involves establishing an appropriate infrastructure and culture and applying a logical and systematic method of establishing the context, identifying, analysing, evaluating, treating, monitoring and communicating risks associated with any activity, function or process in a way that will enable organizations to minimize losses and maximize gains.

To be most effective, risk management should become part of an organization's culture. It should be embedded into the organization's philosophy, practices and business processes rather than be viewed or practiced as separate activity. When this is achieved, everyone in the organization becomes involved in the management of risk.

Although the concept of risk is often interpreted in terms of hazards or negative impacts, this Standard is concerned with risk as exposure to the consequences of uncertainty, or potential deviations from what is planned or expected. The process described here applies to the management of both potential gains and potential losses.

Organizations that manage risk effectively and efficiently are more likely to achieve their objectives and do so at lower overall cost.

The Main Elements of Risk Management are as follows:

- **Establish the context:** Establish the external, internal and risk management context in which the rest of the process will take place. Criteria against which risk will be evaluated should be established and the structure of the analysis defined.
- **Identify Risks:** Identify where, when, why and how events could prevent, degrade, delay or enhance the achievement of the objectives.
- **Analyse Risks:** Identify and evaluate existing controls. Determine consequences and likelihood and hence the level of risk. This analysis should consider the range of potential consequences and how these could occur.
- **Evaluate Risks:** Compare estimated levels of risk against the pre-established criteria and consider the balance between potential benefits and adverse outcomes. This enables decisions to be made about the extent and nature of treatments required and about priorities.
- **Treat Risks:** Develop and implement specific cost-effective strategies and action plans for increasing potential benefits and reducing potential costs.
- **Monitor and Review:** It is necessary to monitor the effectiveness of all steps of the risk management process. This is important for continuous improvement. Risks and the effectiveness of treatment

measures need to be monitored to ensure changing circumstances do not alter priorities.
- **Communicate and Consult:** Communicate and consult with internal and external stakeholders as appropriate at each stage of the risk management process and concerning the process as a whole.

The Risk Management Standard provides a generic guide for managing risk in any organisation context whether it is public, private, community, enterprise or individual. It is thus a scalable framework that can be applied quite successfully independent of industry or economic sector.

APPENDIX B: CASE STUDY SAMPLE DOCUMENTS

The table below catalogs the documents that were reviewed as part of the research project. When conducting a document review, each document was categorized into the relevant Process Architecture Levels to identify what type of business object needed to be identified and reviewed. The principal researcher then selected the appropriate model type to be used to capture the relevant information about the business object. Adopting this approach provided a structured method for gathering and analysing information that is relevant to the exercise and supports the implementation of a Process Architecture approach.

Process Architecture Levels	Business Objects	Artifact Reviews – Content Extracted	Model Type
A	Business Objective	Strategic Plan - Provide safe and sustainable services	• Contextual Model drawn using blocks, arrows, triangles • Organisation function chart
B	Business Functions	Function Groupings from Organisation Charts: Clinical Incident Management Complaints Management Integrated Risk Management	• Service groupings • Functional perspective • Conceptual models
C	Policy	Review of Policy Document to extract Value Chains and IDEF0 models: Clinical Governance Policy Consumer Complaints Management Policy Integrated Risk Management Policy	• Value Chains • End-to-end processes using BPMN or IDEF0 • Logical models
D	Procedure Business Requirement Specifications	For each Business Context Area IDEF0 models were drawn: - Implementation Standards and Procedures e.g. Management of Clinical Adverse Events Procedure, Consumer Feedback Management Procedure - Business Requirements Specification consisting of AS-IS process models	BPMN Process Model, IDEF0 or IDEF3, UML Workflow
E	Work Instructions	For each Business Context Area at each Health Service Centre an example of the Work Instruction artifacts observed to define Use Cases: - Incident Reporting using the Central Information System Database - Receiving a Complaint Work Instruction - Pressure Area Care Work Instruction As part of the Business Analysis activities, Functional Requirements Specifications were created for each of the three Business Context Areas.	BPMN Activity Model, Use Cases
F	Steps	UML Workflow models were used to depict workflow: The Corporate Integrated Risk Management Solution was built based on detailed Solution Requirement Specifications defined for each of the three Business Context Areas.	Flowcharts, System Flow Chart, Data Flow Diagram

APPENDIX C: LEVEL A CONTEXTUAL MODEL: INTEGRATED RISK MANAGEMENT

The Model shown in Figure 5 was used to show conceptually how the Integrated Risk Management function collectively supports the achievement of the case study organisation's strategic objective. The model also shows how the Integrated Risk Management function is structured within the organisation.

Figure 5.

APPENDIX D: LEVEL B CONCEPTUAL MODEL: COMPLAINTS MANAGEMENT

The IDEF0 High-Level A0 model (see Figure 6) was used to define the scope of the Complaints Management function. The same approach was taken to identify the scope of the Clinical Incident and Integrated Risk Management functions.

Figure 6.

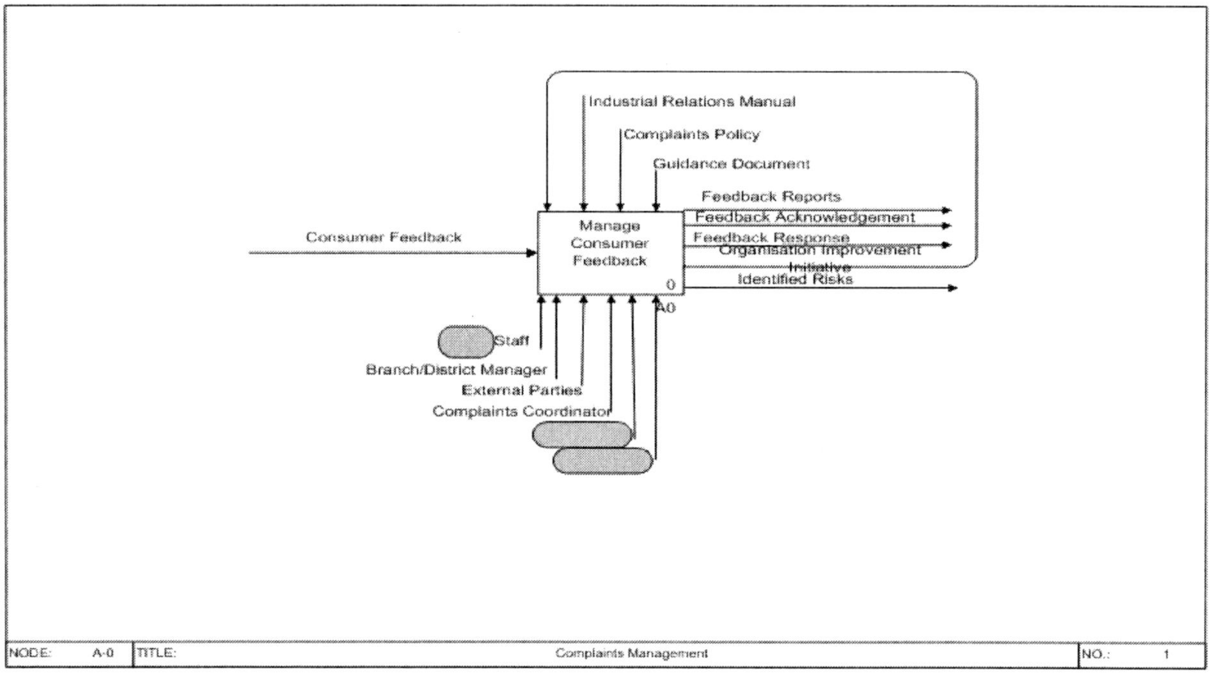

APPENDIX E: LEVEL C PROCESS MODELS – INTEGRATED RISK MANAGEMENT

IDEF0 was used as the notation to document the end-to-end process (value chain) for all three projects. Figure 7 is an example of the IDEF0 model which shows the application of the ASNZS4360:2004 Risk Management framework as it is implemented in the case study organisation. The same pattern was used to document the Clinical Incident and Complaint Management Processes.

Figure 7.

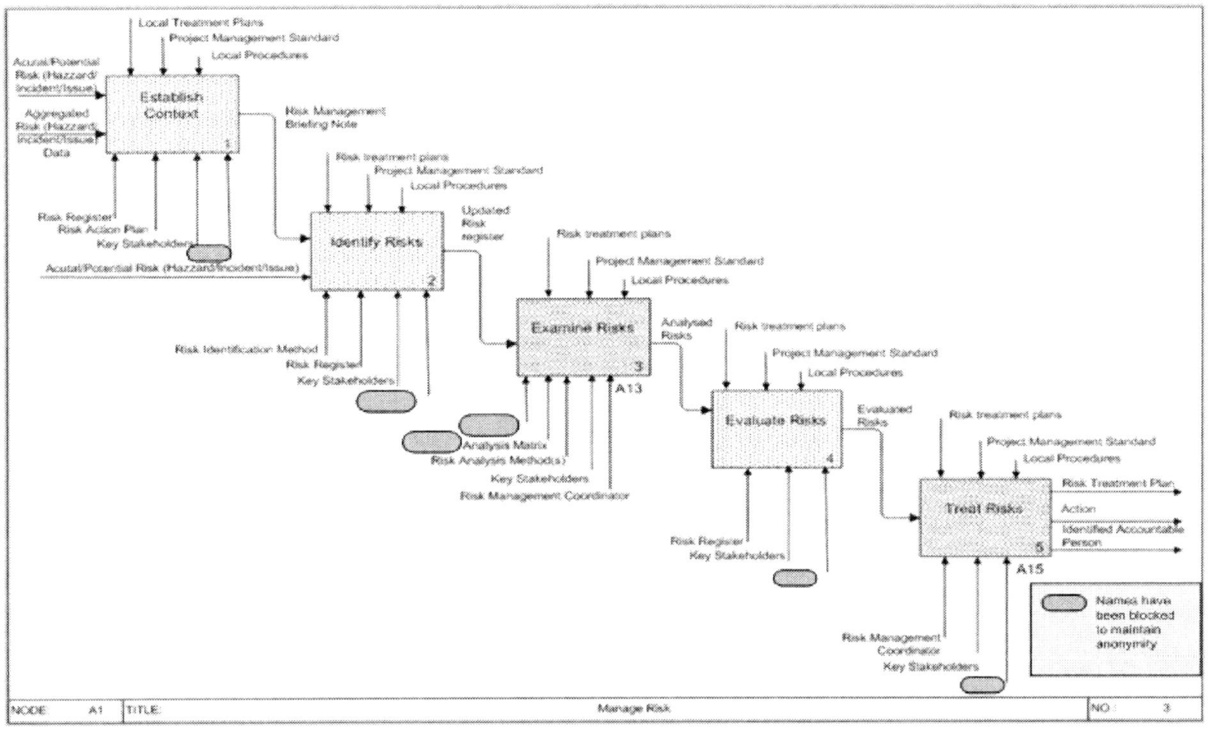

APPENDIX F: LEVEL D BUSINESS PROCESS FLOW MODEL – TREAT RISKS

The IDEF0 business process flow model shown in Figure 8 was used to document how Risk is treated within the case study organisation. This pattern was used to validate that risk is treated the same way in Clinical Incident, Complaints and Risk Management.

Figure 8.

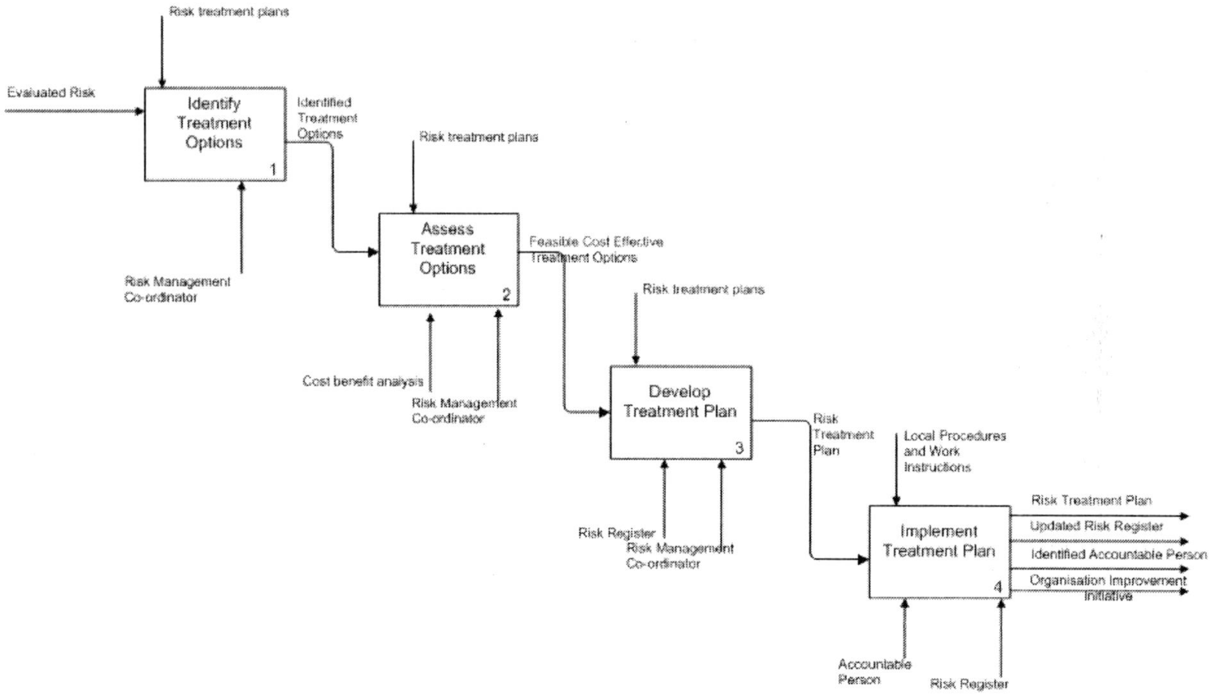

APPENDIX G: LEVEL E USE CASE – COMPLAINTS MANAGEMENT – ASSESSING RISK

Figure 9 is an example of the UML Use Case that was used to document how Risks are assessed. This Use Case is meant to show how business rules are applied and cause branches in logical flow. Use Case provided the Solution Requirement specifications to the IT software development group on how a solution is required to interact with the User/Actor.

Figure 9.

<table>
<tr><td>Use Case ID:</td><td colspan="2">UC-04</td></tr>
<tr><td>Process Number</td><td colspan="2">A44 Output Update Complaints Risk Register</td></tr>
<tr><td>Use Case Name:</td><td colspan="2">Update Complaints Risk Register – Assess Risk</td></tr>
<tr><td>Actors:</td><td colspan="2">Executive Officer</td></tr>
<tr><td>Description:
Preconditions:</td><td colspan="2">Add an actual or potential consequence to the Complaints Risk Register.
1. Open complaint issues have not been risk assessed</td></tr>
<tr><td>Postconditions:</td><td colspan="2">1. Issues are added to the Risk Register</td></tr>
<tr><td>Normal Flow:</td><td colspan="2">1. The Executive Officer selects to update the Complaints Risk Register
2. System displays a list of Feedback Forms and open complaint issues sorted in Date Received order (most recent last) – see Appendix O.
3. The Executive Officer selects to view one of the listed Complaint Issues.
4. The Executive Officer requests a new consequence type be added to the Complaint Issue
5. The Executive Officer selects a consequence type
6. The Executive Officer selects a degree of severity
7. The Executive Officer repeats steps 4 to 5 until all consequence types are entered
8. The Executive Officer selects a likelihood
9. The system generates an overall risk rating
10. The system records the details of the person updating the risk register</td></tr>
<tr><td>Alternative Flows:</td><td colspan="2">10a The Executive Officer wants to add comments for the risk assessment
1. The Executive Officer selects to add comments to the risk register
2. The Executive Officer enters in comments for the risk register</td></tr>
<tr><td>Business Rules:</td><td colspan="2">• Every complaint issue must be risk assessed
• The history of risk rating changes will be stored.</td></tr>
<tr><td rowspan="4">Data Elements:</td><td>Entered (Represented in the order entered by the actor)</td><td>Accessed by system</td></tr>
<tr><td rowspan="3">UC-04.1 Risk Consequence Type
UC-04.2 Likelihood
UC-04.3 Degree of Severity
UC-04.4 Risk Assessment Comments</td><td>Feedback Number
Issue Number</td></tr>
<tr><td>System Generated</td></tr>
<tr><td>Risk Assessment Date
Overall Risk Rating
Issue Status
Risk Recorded by First Name
Risk Recorded by Surname
Risk Recorded by Position</td></tr>
</table>

APPENDIX H: LEVEL F OPERATIONAL PROCESS FLOW MODEL

Figure 10 is an example of a detailed Operational Process Flow Model. Typically, Systems Analysts use these types of model to document how a software developer will convert the business logic and business rule into software syntax. The human-computer interaction is also depicted in these models to clearly demonstrate when the user is required to interact with the software system.

Figure 10.

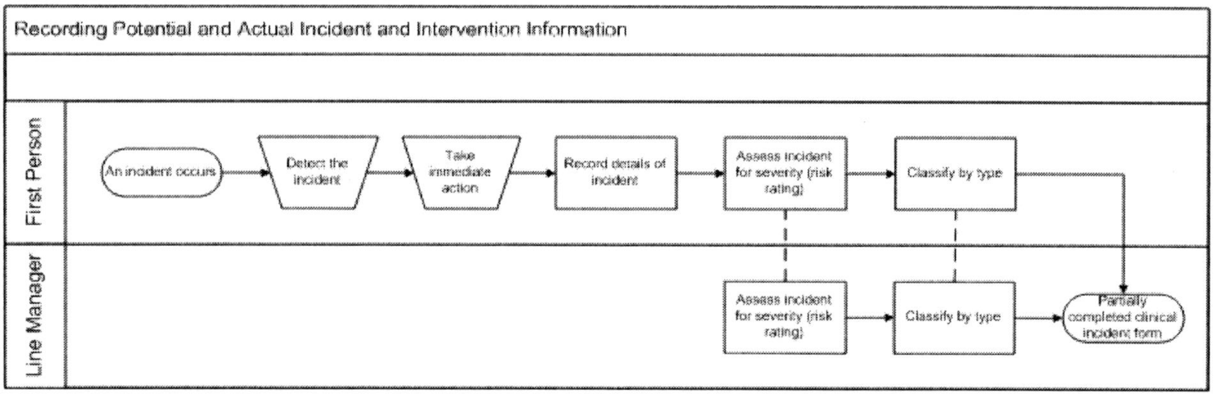

Chapter 19
Replacing an Old Functioning Information System with a New One:
What Does it Take?

Hans Kyhlbäck
Blekinge Institute of Technology, Sweden

Berthel Sutter
Blekinge Institute of Technology, Sweden

ABSTRACT

This chapter addresses a problem that is often experienced when ICT systems are being implemented in a work practice. Posed as a question, it might be formulated like this: What does it take to replace an old functioning information system with a new one? Findings are grounded on a long-term case study at a community elder care. This chapter used the Development Work Research (DWR) approach that is an interventionist methodology comprising ethnography as well as design experiment. During the case study, a new digital case book for the community wound care was developed. However, as it turned out, the nurses' established practice favored the old-fashioned mobile information system. First conclusion of this chapter is that an old-fashioned information system within health care work will not successfully be replaced by a new one, unless the new is better "as a whole", that is, better supports work practices of a range of occupational and professional workers. Second conclusion is that when designing information system for the public sector, system designers will almost always face dilemmas based on a contradiction between central, high level interest and local level work-practice perspectives. The third conclusion is that in order to succeed in the design of new information and communication system, the distinctive features of the work activities in question have to be delineated by ethnographic studies, and taken into consideration in the design process.

DOI: 10.4018/978-1-60566-030-1.ch019

OVERVIEW

In this chapter we want to address a problem that is often experienced when ICT systems are being implemented in a work practice. Posed as a question, it might be formulated like this: What does it take to replace an old functioning information system with a new one? Our findings are grounded on a long-term case study, using interventionist methodology comprising ethnography (about ethnography, see (Krippendorff, 2006; Suchman, 1987)) as well as design experiment. In spite of its local origin and the diverse particularities it contains, we claim that the findings from the case study have a more general interest and validity.

The point of departure of our discussion is a case study. It is about the development of a new Information and Communication Technology (ICT) system, where a digital case book for the wound care was developed. The development was carried out in a joint project using the Developmental Work Research approach (a kind of action research, see (Engeström, 1993)) in which an evolutionary system development practice was incorporated. Developmental Work Research is a methodology within the framework of cultural-historical activity theory. It comprises ethnographic investigation, reflection on the history of the work and designing solutions to identified need problems. This methodology for creation of a new tool, such as a computer system, includes gathering of qualitative data to be analysed and used as raw material input in transformation of the investigated work practice. Nurses, computer system developers and researchers joined in the activity for analysis and design of a new digital case book. The first outcome was a rough prototype of the to-be-designed system.

Interestingly the nurses´ established work practice favoured their old-fashioned mobile information system, a bag on wheels loaded with binders together with other material including the paper case books on wounds. In the further course of the study, we learned to know why the new design did not match as a deployed system. We reminded as what Thomas Kuhn (1962) has pointed out: a paradigm would not be abandoned just because it faces many anomalies; an alternative paradigm, regarded as better, must be available. Something similar seems to be valid for the replacement of an old-fashioned, albeit functioning, activity system, including its information and communication facilities. A better one has to be presented, received and realised in practice. In our case of wound care practice, this seems to require that new software and hardware are developed to be immediately accessible for the nurses in performing their everyday work.

The main reason is that the computer system did not match the work practice of the municipal nurses, a work practice that is characterised by three distinctive features: High mobility, the need for face-to-face interaction in different locations, and a great variety of artefact usage. From the perspective of the nurses the new information system was not "better as a whole" than their old-fashioned bag-on-wheels system was. Here we realised that we have design lessons to learn. This chapter is an elaboration of those lessons learned.

FEATURES OF A COMMUNITY WOUND CARE ACTIVITY

The long term case study that forms the empirical ground for our argumentation in this chapter was conducted in a small municipality in the south of Sweden. There community elder care is given to about 400 people living in eleven special accommodation units where they receive help with everyday things, like getting dressed, taking medicine, and some having their wounds cared for. A number of assistant nurses, nurses, managers and other personnel work and provide round-the-clock service.

Although the treatment of wound is only one of many things the nurses have to take care of, this sub-activity of their work has been the point of departure of our R&D project. Its first concrete aim was to design a digital case book to be used as a tool by the nurses in their wound care practice.

What has emerged as particularly important to us as co-developers of a work activity and designers of a new ICT system is that office work - the imagined use situation for most ICT system design - has expanded. More and more administrative work, the diverse use of documents of all kinds, has become decentralised at the same time as the centres that orchestrate and eventually sum up or supervise the spread-out office work have grown. (See (Latour, 1987; Latour, 1990)) The main reason why that is happening seems to be the growing connection between more and more activities (globalisation, networking, or what to call it). (See (Smith, 2005))

Because office work has grown and are being spread out and has become an aspect of shop floor work, we have to rethink office work. What is it? Is it still a straight administrative practice performed in special localities, or is it also a more interwoven activity, where document handling and shop floor work are interconnected in complex ways? And consequentially, what will it mean for the design of computer support for also "blurred uses" of documents? From questions like those arises our particular interest in office work of wound care activity on, and close to, the shop floor.

The wound care activity of the nurses comprises two parts, an office part and a shop floor part. The nurses not only plan, delegate, supervise, and assess the wound care activity as in traditional office work. They also do the treatment of the elderlys′ wounds. So, they do craft as well as office work, and they often do it simultaneously. Typically, regular office work is dominating in the beginning of the working-day as well as in the end of the day - with, for example, planning, prioritising, communication with doctors and other staff, and evaluation. In between, there is time for the shop floor work of wound caring. Even if this is the overall pattern of work of the nurses, the picture is more complex.

Only a few individuals suffer from wounds that are hard to heal. Nonetheless, it is a very painful, time demanding and a taboo issue to experience. Each wound is a unique challenge of getting hold of and making into progressive healing and well-being. Both planned and emerging treatment tasks of a great diversity are necessarily provided in close contact with many individuals, where each situation needs assessment, communication, decision making and sometimes hands-on work.

The use of clusters of artefacts (Bertelsen & Bødker, 2002a; Blomberg, Suchman, & Trigg, 1996) are constitutive of most work practices, among them the wound care work of nurses. The artefacts are brought into the activity, made accessible and often re-designed to make a better fit to the work to be done. In the set up and configuration of each cluster the nurses take into account that the artefacts make some operations and actions possible but restrict some others. In the actual case there are medical materials, medicine and aids for remembering and documentation of provided care. In addition, there is a specific clustering of artefacts a nurse selects in the beginning of each working shift: a set of medical instruments, treatment materials, a diary, a note pad or a deck of small slips of paper, one to five ordinary paper binders with documents, as well as other things. The artefacts are then packed into a *bag-on-wheels* if the nurse need to travel in a car, or put into a *tray* or *basket* if she (mostly the nurse is a "she") prepares for only in-door mobility. Thus, those clusters of artefacts make up the current mobile ICT system in use by the nurses. (see Figure 1)

The shop floor documentation work in community elder care looks like this: In conjunction with a performed action, the nurse makes use of a table or a furnish detail to temporarily rest their slip of paper, diary or check-list in order to document an event with a pen. If needed the binders are consulted during the time of giving

Figure 1. The old functioning information and communication system used in wound care activity (©2008 Hans Kyhlbäck. Used with permission)

treatment. Notes on slips of papers are put in the nurse´s pockets or notes are made on the note pad. Occasionally, the nurse withdraws to a more "office like" place for a refined documentation. She translates her first hand notes from the slip of paper into the regular paper forms stored in the binders. Still, most of the documentation work results in lines of free text descriptions on paper stored in binders. This means that the artefacts that she brings along and accesses when needed, form an extensive mobile information system. This information and communication system is designed and redesigned by the practitioners themselves as a part of their community care work activity. The nurses actively construct the nearest context of their own work. As already mentioned, their everyday practice is characterised by intensive, and sometimes rapidly on-going, interactions with care recipients and other health care staff. This trait of the practice of the nurses puts a heavy demand on their technical support systems. In order to function, the technical systems have to be available for immediate access.

Our study reveals that municipal nurses work practice can be characterised as heavily *on the go and on the move*. Work actions in elderly care are typically an unforeseen mix of planned events and dealing with a diversity of emerging cases. Since the practice involves a diversity of people to interact with, it also means shifting of locations for meeting the care recipients in their homes. Because the nurse has to embody a vast set of operations in performing actions suitable to the situations, she must bring along necessary artefacts, in her hands and pockets, or in the bag on wheels or in the tray or basket. Closer to the care recipient, artefacts are made ready. Other artefacts, specific for each individual care recipient, are found in a cup-board at each individuals home. To make those needed tools, medicine and other materials accessible, the nurse has to choose tools and items. Indeed, she makes a redesign every time at every location where she provides health care.

To sum up, the practice of wound care work is, in our case at least, characterised by three things. First, the nurses are on the go and on the move as they regularly are interacting face to face with a lot of people in different places. Second, they use a variety of artefacts, the combination of which they most often design themselves. And third, the nurses are mixing office work and shop floor work in intricate ways. The bag-on-wheels, tray or basket, provide them with the most needed artefacts as well as allowing for rapid shifts between various places. In the municipal elderly care, this cluster of artefacts has still shown to be a reliable mobile information and communication system as well as a container for medical materials.

A NEW ICT SYSTEM: FOR WHICH PURPOSE?

There are diverse motives for the introduction of a new ICT system in an organisation. But an ICT system is seldom a peripheral artefact. Incorporated into an activity it will surely have a great impact on the organisation and the ongoing work activities. Many voices and interests might be challenged, but most often the inertia of the organisation will go for business as usual. We find it important to question: For whom will a new ICT system be beneficial?

Wound treatment has significantly changed during the last decades. Compared to a few decades ago it has improved substantially: wounds are systematically diagnosed and a more advanced treatment is provided (Öien, 2002; Öien & Ragnarson Tennvall, 2006). The potential to initiate a healing process has become the guiding principle in municipal health care. New challenges regarding continuity of care, new division of labour between the nurses and their colleagues, better documentation practices to support assessment of the status of a particular wound and refinements of a shared memory among the practitioners, and perhaps digital photos add to better documentation of the wound healing process.

In short - new knowledge about wound care mean new prospects. So, there is a new priority: not just wait and see, but go for active treatment for healing and not only pain reduction. This new perspective on and promises of new wound care methods, calls for better documentation practices of which for example digital pictures can be an important feature. An obvious fact is however that the nurses have an essential interest to co-operate through documents within their own practice field but also to extend and maintain relations with many others. Consequently, with regard to the complex character of wound treatment, it is obvious that demands of remembering, assessment and information sharing among all involved in giving care are urgent.

Typical for the nurses is that they are generalists in providing a huge number of different care treatments tasks of which some are planned and others appear as urgent cases. The division of labour among the nurses is mainly based on allocation to a set of accommodation units where 30 to 50 individuals live in their own flat. One nurse is assigned the formal responsibility for a number of individual elderly tenants but they form a group of 3 to 4 nurses, who replace each other on the same care recipients but on different work shifts. The documentation work as a whole is shared among the groups of nurses. The system of different paper forms, collected in regular binders, stored on shelves and placed in bag-on-wheels for transportation, is in a way "home-made", that is, designed by the nurses themselves. Their everyday practice will be affected by changes of the cluster of artefacts made integral to the activity system. This means that if the nurses were forced to switch to a new computerised wound care documentation system, the whole set of remaining paper forms would still be there, requiring the nurses to keep up with the old regular binders, with hand-written reports and at the same time learn to use the new digital system and adapt it to the local activity system. We encounter an upcoming contradiction between the old and a new way to document work that takes more time and an extended set of skills to perform. The benefit would probably not, even if we could disregard the prototypes' weakness when seen in isolation, outweigh the cost caused by the new case book. To make a switch seems to make necessary a one-time exchange of most of the paper document work in favour of an all-embracing computer system.

With the introduction of a new ICT system, an old computer system (or a wholly paper-based information system) will become (partly) substituted. This was the case when our design project started. Only few network connected standard desk-top computers were available for the nurses, either at the administration centre or at the elderlys' accommodation units. Furthermore, the computers were second hand equipment, out-dated in administration work. Consequently, a major shift to a large new software system, would make it necessary to upgrade and extend the number of computer hardware units as well. The existing mobile bag-on-wheels and tray/basket system makes documentation forms available close to the care recipient's home. A computer network can not to be expected to be available on that many places, if restricted to standard desk-top computers. Hence, there is an obvious contradiction between the old systems′ accessibility in different locations and the network computers spatially restriction to office and co-ordination centres. A changeover to mobile devices would be an option, but it would face an obvious problem: the size of a standard paper form, which roughly comply with a standard desk-top screen, and the size of standard hand-held computers. Particularly when it comes to digital photos on wounds, the height and width do matter, "one-size does not fit all", but a convenient hand-held computer with not to small screen and keyboard could be a solution. However, hand-held or other general purpose computers supporting the nursing practice in bedside or "direct treatment" of the ailing individual are not (yet) established in elder care. Some first advances are typically made in laboratory experiments (see e.g. (Bång, Larsson, & Eriksson, 2003; Dahl, Svanaes, & Nytro, 2006)) or at clinical practice considered as "the most wired" (Hendrich, Chow, Skierczynski, & Lu, 2008). In nursing homes ICT use is still a scarce resource but is seen as key to future care (Conn, 2007).

Security matters are also an important aspect of this documentation work. Information on wounds has to be restricted to only those who have a legitimate interest and are involved in providing treatment to the care recipients. Each nurse has the formal responsibility for a number of individuals. She is the one who sets up new documentation paper work containing references to physicians diagnosis, and descriptions on treatment. Besides, she maintains proper reports on current status and also reports on taken measures in the provided health care. Ordinary binders as containers for documents are artefacts with a physical, three-dimensional property. In the hands of the nurse, there is no doubt where the information is and who has access. The nurse is in full control and can protect unauthorised people from getting access. At the same time she has an interest to share the information with her colleagues. When this occurs through non-planned actions, and that happens frequently in the nursing activity that requires a lot of improvisation, the drawback of paper documents becomes obvious: it is not within reach from several places.

On the other hand, a problem emerges in transforming the paper forms into a digital computer network because established routines and rules for access are jeopardised. The nurse with former control of each paper within her sphere of control is now experiencing that "it is somewhere in the computer". That means a digital space with many individual accounts and access relations, all of which are not established and controlled by the nurse herself. A key aspect of the prototype designed by our group was the attempt to map the nurses' control of the paper work into the digital casebooks. Through a particular software architectural solution, the nurse who has the formal responsibility for a care recipient, is the only one with superior control of the digital wound care documentation (Kyhlbäck & Persson, 2003). This design was in accord with the nurses' way of preserving security matters but it does contradict the way control is established and maintained in the prevailing power paradigm of client-server network architecture. A solution to that difficulty might be a specific implementation of control, as in this prototype, not with a single centre of power, but to realise a competing order compared to the structure of the actual operative system.

Another dilemma when replacing the old paper based system is one of human power relations and parallel ways of organising municipal health care (Westerberg, 2000). The investment in a new system requires decisions about scarce economical resources to be taken by executives and politicians in the hierarchical line organisation. According to the social welfare legislation it is the central authority's responsibility to allocate health and elderly care on equity terms in order to fulfil imperative obligations towards the individual citizen. High level management has a rational of keeping up with a budget and a good as possible distribution of resources. However, the horizontal organisation realised by the ordinary local practice of nurses, assistant nurses, other personnel and family relatives who provide the services have wound care on a daily basis in focus. Many things, and especially taboo issues such as wounds and wound treatment, are secured and protected in the interest of the individual. A high rank manager has no identified right or reasons to access specific information about a particular wound. Managers and politicians on executive and central positions are making decisions on overall matters concerning the care recipients in both ordinary housing and in special accommodations, they are not supposed to deal with detailed everyday work tasks. This roughly explains why changes dependent on budget decisions, such as introduction of a large-scale computer system, have to address what is knowledgeably to those in high rank and central positions. A matter like a changed wound care documentation system is likely to be regarded as remote and of minor importance.

THE SHORTCOMING OF THE NEW ICT SYSTEM

The system development process in which the prototype was designed will not be described in this chapter. (But see (Kyhlbäck & Persson, 2003)) Suffice is to say that the prototype was constructed as a network distributed case book in an attempt to make a more unified wound care case book. Two main features of the system was a kind of peer-to-peer network architecture (See for example (Oram, 2001) about the peer-to-peer concept) and a picture archive system made as part of the digital case book.

There seems to be a *mind set* which permeates software development and which is opposed to the essential qualities of the work practice of the nurses. This mind set probably originates from the construction of large scale systems that are satisfying central management interests and the support of resource allocation, follow ups and control. An all embracing computer system supporting working life is a paradigmatic case in a retail store where computing is straight forward to apply on sales of commodities. In charging elderly for provided community care or calculating salaries and wages, there is also an obvious computation potential. However, computer support for health care is a much more delicate matter.

Computer interface design consistent with typical desk work practice in banking and other business areas is not automatically an appropriate solution for nurses and their colleagues. As already have been pointed out, the core work practice of the nurses is characterised by high mobility, close to patient interaction, and discretion in use of a variety of artefacts.

In our case project, we found that the nurses had problems handling the computer system, handling deficiencies that may look trivial for an office white collar worker: spending time to get familiar with small icons, virtual menus, buttons and other standard widgets. Also the task of navigating between logical units, and at a proper point getting "deeper" into the folder structure, proved to be difficult for the nurses because it demands remembering an extensive and murky structure of units, folders and files.

What we have learnt is that for reading and writing when on the go and on the move, size matters, especially when it is about "getting a good picture" or actually integrate photos in a documentation system. It is difficult, probably harder to deal with than often expected because we think we are very well acquainted with photos in our ordinary family life. This is what Bertelsen and Bødker identify as a discontinuity, or a contradiction, between interpretation and implementation (Bertelsen & Bødker, 2002b). In an actual working life context, we interpret the idea to employ digital photos as a promising possibility turning them into tools for support of the work practice. But when really trying to implement these thoughts about integrating the digital images into a computer system, we inevitable close much of the perceived possibilities because the concrete software code need to end in unambiguous statements acceptable for the machine execution. In the process of dealing with this contradiction, a very crucial trade off must be made between on the one hand opening up for a larger size of a photo, and on the other allowing for other widgets, necessary for making meaning out of a two dimensional screen display.

Photos on wounds do have valuable properties in terms of colours and shapes. To make justice to those properties, the display size is significant. In addition, as the above task of photo management reveals, size of text labels, buttons and other widgets is also significant. The nurses are not able to deal with such a smooth performance in navigating and hitting the right spots on the standard screen as they have proved to when taking the still photos with a standard camera at the care recipients' bedside. Probably the interface constructions can be made more logical and perhaps a better file-choosing-window could be realised, but a problem that permeates both the designed prototype and the operative system is a preferred size on a default scale of width and height for all kinds of widgets and text that the interface is built on. If sitting at the desk top computer all day long is the reality for software developers, one small size on the scale is appropriate. If being on the go and on the move – as the nurses are - a larger size is required. This is a problem in architecture and building construction, recognised within other areas but not well grounded in computer interface design. When considering the size of traffic signs, shape and text sizes need to match people's perception constraints when moving at high speed. Apparently the same fundamental principle of choosing the right size within a scale appropriate for humans activities is acknowledge in town renewal projects (Gehl, 2001) and we think it is valid for computer design as well. What we clearly have found in our case is a size problem that gets worse when the target domain practice differs from the design practice of computer system developers.

Another aspect of a supposed "trivial" character is revealed in the joint between different systems. The vast structure of logical units, folders and files is something learnt long ago, and directly a matter to deal with on several occasions a day for desk top workers (like software developers). They have an easy access to some kind of remembering and a mental model of this structure. For the nurses it is hard to recall or imagine such a "good picture" and to make it embodied and easy to reach when needed. The nurses are typically not sitting at desktop work and that is why they often experience breakdowns when trying, for example, to find the small scroll button, to scroll the window, read and correctly interpret the meaning of short small text labels. The whole matter gets even worse when the computer display differs in some aspects compared with last experienced occasion, or when an unintended mouse click cause a window to collapse or in some inexhaustible way change its appearance.

On the level of over-all design, we are able to summarise what it takes to replace an old paper based with a new computer system in community elder care. Close and detailed observations are a way of getting the practitioners' voice being heard. Respecting their experience of realising work is a basis for our problem analysis and way of designing solutions. We find that a design project that takes the unit of the practitioners' work practice as a conceptual framework for the specific design product is in a better position of making the to-be-designed artefact an integral part of the activity system that is to be transformed. In the case of municipal wound care, we suggest that a further initiated system development process has to consider the following aspects:

- The practitioners' participation in a system design is a necessary way of getting a comprehensive understanding of the need problem, which in turn is a prerequisite to make a better artefact replacing the old one(s).
- The software development process organised as re-design of the local activity system(s) is a way of incorporating the most valuable features of the older artefact(s) in use.
- The nurses and other shop floor workers do several kinds of office work, most of which are conducted more or less as an integral part of the shop floor activity. It is a challenge for system development to support also this kind of paper work.
- Power relations between stake-holders in the target domain have to be addressed and investigated as a component of the developmental process. This affects the set up of the design and allows us not to forget the practitioners' work-related interest of elder care.
- Security problems are partly solved in preserving the nurses' superior control of the information.

DISCUSSION

What we now have investigated turns out to be a part of a work practice domain that is very complex in terms of interaction with people, artefacts usage, and mobility. In the first place the nurses are those with main responsibility for providing health care on a day-to-day basis. Through ethnographic studies, participatory design and participatory evaluation, we have found how the nurses' work is essentially different to the work of office workers such as for example computer system developers.

Typically, computer systems have mainly been designed and successfully been deployed in work domains populated with workers like machine operators and office clerks. Typical for the education area of computer science and software engineering is the lagging orientation of text books that draws heavily on machine automation with examples of vending machines, automatic teller machines and similar. The history of developing computer systems is dominated by a motive for automation and where it has been realised, we find paradigm examples in "one- or a few-buttons-push machines". Of course, this is not particularly surprising. A technical development starts where it is most suitable for the technology as such. But today demands on new and better technical solutions require rethinking a lot of what is needed in those other areas.

Donald Schön has taught us about what he calls "reflection in action" as one characteristic of professionals work in complex and less clearly defined practices. He explains why formal computational models generally fail because they do not suit work where a practitioner exerts a diversity of skills in dealing with "complexity, uncertainty, instability, uniqueness, and value conflict" (Schön, 1983, p.18). Examples of architectural design, business management and criminal justice are professions where the practitioners reframe a situation and in reflection, the practitioner makes use of skills acquired in earlier work with similar problems. In many ways, we think his lessons also apply to nurses' work in demanding interaction with people and urgent cases. Possible computer solutions supporting more complex and advanced activity systems, as for example community wound care, require us to take the practitioners daily work seriously. This means gathering and handling opposing and sometimes conflicting requirements, which a future solution needs to accommodate to. In the case of wound treatment, a nurse might have an orientation towards appropriate day-to-day actions, a physician to make precise assessment and prescription, a municipal manager to secure good enough documentation in accordance with legislation statements. Sometimes, any of those people, might have a good reason to step back a bit and reflect on their work and what documents they together design and make use of.

In taking the practitioners seriously in order to find computer system suitable for more complex work practice, we find it important to do ethnographic studies and investigate the ground for forces of change in a local activity system within the work domain. Our method urge us to explore tensions and contradictions as resources for design of new solutions – let it be redesign of practice or creation of new technology. The Developmental Work Research approach implies research in the field, in close contact with practitioners at work. This is true for the gathering of key artefacts in use, but also in development of computer system. The method invites us to do participatory design and participatory evaluation of the new artefact.

To work in a standing position and being on the go and on the move, or to work in sitting position at desk work, makes an important difference. Currently in our case of the community elder care, because of decisions on a high and central position, a major and commercial ICT system has been deployed a few years ago. It is mainly designed for administrative purposes and for the management of community care in a Swedish municipal context. It can be regarded as enforced on the personnel "from above". To some extent, also the nurses in our case are obliged to integrate parts of this all-embracing system into their work. The particular task of making wound care documentation is not (yet) opened up for in the ICT system. However, the nurses have been directed to utilise the system for other documentation purposes. In addition, new computers have exchanged the older ones in the nurses' administration centre. As it seems, this has been for good and the nurses have become more familiar with computing, but certainly it has a cost. A question is if the nurses have become more of typical office clerks as part of their work practice. Will the nurses remain mobile on their shop floor and close to the bedsides or to be seated at the desk top?

SUMMING UP AND CONCLUSION

Our study was propelled by the question of what it takes to replace an old functioning information system with a new one. We claimed that our local study has given an answer beyond the constraints of the local situation, having a more general bearing on the role of ICT in health care. So, what is our answer to that question?

Before we draw our conclusions we will summarise our findings in three headings. First, there are the features of the work activity of the practitioners at the shop floor, in our case the nurses in municipally organised wound care of the elderly. Second, there are other stake-holders too, who influence the introduction and design of the new information system. Third, there is a challenge to align the diverse and conflicting ICT-use interests in the organisation, a challenge that the implementation of a new ICT system cannot avoid.

Features of the Work Activity of the Nurses

The nurses´ work practice is characterised by being *highly mobile*. When meeting the care recipients they mostly are "on the move and on the go", and are bringing their "mobile office", contained in a bag-on-wheels or a tray/basket packed with artefacts for the foreseen doings. In those home located situations it is obvious that office desk top computers do not fit at all. Instead, more basic information and communication technology are used: paper and pen, binders and spreadsheets, post-it notes, mobile phones, et cetera. And when the nurses in the end of the day finally turn up in their more ordinary offices to sum up the work day and transfer their impressions and notes into the available computer system, it becomes clear that "size matters". The small scale icons, menus, buttons, pictures and text, designed for office work, does not fit well into their ICT practices.

Multifarious actions and use of a variety of artefacts make up wound care activity. Like many professionals, nurses use and produce documents as part of their practice, but they are handling more specific or solid artefacts than texts and pictures too: cleaning and dressing materials, specific bandages, support stockings and boots to put on the ailing individual, gloves to put on their own hands, a Doppler device to assess blood pressure, guidelines for nutrition and body movements, stories of care recipients everyday life - a mixture of practical hands-on and theoretical reflections.

High usage of clusters of a variety of artefacts is a distinctive attribute of their work practice. There will be no standard way for how to lay the table for the ever changing situations when the nurses are out on the field and in the home of individuals. The main rule that works is improvisation. The actions and operations to play out are facilitated by a rich set of accessible artefacts.

Face to face (and body to body) interaction is key in the wound care activity with care recipients and close colleagues. The nurses are shop floor workers. More traditional office work is only one part of the nurses´ activity. They perform several other kinds of document handling actions, close to their shop floor activity. Designers of ICT systems have to take that often unnoticed office work seriously when they build systems that are to be supportive.

Other Stakeholders' Influences of the New Information System

The ICT system that the nurses are obliged to use is designed for a large organisation. The opinions of the nurses about what is needed and how to devise it are only some of the voices in a big choir. Experiences from deployment of ICT systems in organisations show that there is a top level dominance in giving voice to the perspectives and priorities of higher and lower administration. One visible consequence is that the office metaphor of ICT use seems to be paramount in this context. Behind the scene, architectural solutions designed elsewhere, may interfere with shop floor workers way of dealing with and securing documents.

Aligning Diverse ICT-Use Interests

There is a tension between a rationalistic, big scale ICT solution to the access of documents, certification control and integrity protection on one side, and a local-oral and paper based old-fashioned but locally well working solution on the other. The challenge is to design for multiple uses and interests, including unanticipated use (Pekkola, 2003; Robinson, 1993). This is easier to say than to do, but a grounding in ethnography is a way to go. From the perspectives of the nurses *it is crucial that the ICT system gets incorporated into their work practice*, taking its distinctive features into account, and not the other way around. In other words, the computer system that is meant to support the informative and communicative actions of the core activity at the shop floor has to be co-ordinated with the professionals′ competency and discretion. But there are also other interests involved in the organisation that decide about and deploy the new ICT system. How to cope with that is a key question for the management of the nursing organisation but also for the specialists involved in the development of the technology.

CONCLUSION

Our first conclusion is that an old-fashioned information system within health care work will not successfully be replaced by a new one, unless the new is better "as a whole", that is, better supports work practices of a range of occupational and professional workers. Our second conclusion is that when designing information system for the public sector, system designers will almost always face dilemmas based on a contradiction between central, high level interest and local level work-practice perspectives. And the third conclusion is that in order to succeed in the design of a new information and communication system, the distinctive features of the work activities in question have to be taken into consideration in the design process.

REFERENCES

Bång, M., Larsson, A., & Eriksson, H. (2003). NOSTOS: A paper-based ubiquitous computing healthcare environment to support data capture and collaboration. *American Medical Informatics Association Annual Symposium Proceedings* (pp. 46-50). Washington DC.

Bertelsen, O. W., & Bødker, S. (2002a). Interaction through multi-artifacts. In S. Bagnara, S. Pozzi, A. Rizzo, & P. Wright (Eds.), *ECCE 11 - Cognition, Culture and Design Eleventh European Conference on Cognitive Ergonomics* (pp. 103-111). Rome: Instituto di scienze e technologie della cognizione consiglio nazionale delle ricerche.

Bertelsen, O. W., & Bødker, S. (2002b). Discontinuities. In Y. Dittrich, C. Floyd, & R. Klischewski (Eds.), *Social thinking - software practice* (pp. 409-424). Cambridge, MA: The MIT Press.

Blomberg, J., Suchman, L., & Trigg, R. H. (1996). Reflections on a work-oriented design project. *Human-Computer Interaction*, *11*(3), 237–265. doi:10.1207/s15327051hci1103_3

Conn, J. (2007). A long-term solution. *Modern Healthcare*, *37*(45), 52–54.

Dahl, Y. Svanaes, D. & Nytro, Ø. (2006). Designing pervasive computing for hospitals: learning from the media affordances of paper-based medication charts. *Pervasive Health Conference and Workshops* (pp. 1-10). Washington, DC: IEEE.

Engeström, Y. (1993). Developmental studies of work as a test bench of activity theory: the case of primary care medical practice. In S. Chaiklin & J. Lave (Eds.), *Understanding practice: perspectives on activity and context* (pp. 64-103). Cambridge, MA: Cambridge University Press.

Gehl, J. (2001). *Life between buildings*. Copenhagen, Denmark: Arkitektens Forlag.

Hendrich, A., Chow, M. P., Skierczynski, B. A., & Lu, Z. (2008). A 36-hospital time and motion study: how do medical-surgical nurses spend their time? *The Permanente Journal*, *12*(3), 25–34.

Krippendorff, K. (2006). *The semantic turn. A new foundation for design*. New York: Taylor & Francis Group.

Kuhn, T. (1962). *The structure of scientific revolutions*. Chicago: University of Chicago Press.

Kyhlbäck, H., & Persson, H. (2003). Wound care documentation project at municipal elder care. In A. Moreno & J.L. Nealon (Eds.), *Application of software agent technology in the health care domain* (pp. 125-141). Basel, Switzerland: Whitestein series in software agent technologies, Birkhäuser.

Latour, B. (1987). *Science in action.* Cambridge, MA: Harvard University Press.

Latour, B. (1990). Drawing things together. In M. Lynch & S. Woolgar (Eds.), *Representation in scientific practice* (pp. 19-68). Cambridge, MA: The MIT Press.

Öien, R. F. (2002). *Leg ulcer management in primary care with special reference to pinch grafting.* Doctoral thesis Malmö University Hospital, Lund University, Lund, Sweden.

Öien, R. F., & Ragnarson Tennvall, G. (2006). Accurate diagnosis and effective treatment of leg ulcers reduce prevalence, care time and costs. *Journal of Wound Care, 15*(6), 259–262.

Oram, A. (Ed.). (2001). *Peer-to-peer: harnessing the benefits of a disruptive technology.* Sebastopol, CA: O'Reilly.

Pekkola, S. (2003). Designed for unanticipated use: common artefacts as design principle for CSCW applications. *ACM SIGGROUP conference on Supporting group work table of contents* (pp. 359-368). Sanibel Island, FL: ACM.

Robinson, M. (1993). Design for unanticipated use.... In G. de Michelis, C. Simone, & K. Schmidt (Eds.), *Third European Conference on Computer Supported Cooperative Work (ECSCW'93)* (pp.187-202). Amsterdam, the Netherlands: Kluwer Academic Publishers.

Schön, D. (1983). *The reflective practitioner – how professional think in action.* New York: Basic Books.

Smith, D. E. (2005). *Institutional ethnography. A sociology for people.* Lanham, MD: Altamira Press.

Suchman, L. (1987). *Plans and situated actions: the problem of human-machine communication.* Cambridge, UK: Cambridge University Press.

Westerberg, K. (2000). *The important activity - work, tools and tensions of municipal middle managers in elder care.* Doctoral thesis: Department of Applied Psychology, Umeå Universitet, Umeå, Sweden.

KEY TERMS AND DEFINITIONS

Artefacts: Man made things, that is things that are culturally and socially produced/brought about (in contrast to natural things).

Clusters of artefacts: In work practices most often several artefacts, or clusters of artefacts, are used in ways determined by the practitioners′ discretion.

Case book: Less formal document created and used for the main purpose to support a particular practice (in our case it is wound care). It shall not be confused with the formal medical or other kind of record required by legislation.

Community elder care: In Sweden the local government provides help and service to elderly. On criteria of national legislation and the individual′s actual needs, an agreed set of provisions are given by municipal employees. Usually once or several times each day at the elderly′s home.

Cultural-historical activity theory (CHAT): Founded by Vygotsky, Luria, and Leontiev, and built on the assumption that an activity is artefact-mediated and object-oriented.

Developmental work research (DWR): A kind of interventionist or action research guided by cultural-historical activity theory. Researchers and practitioners jointly investigate the work practice, analyze the empirical data and do design for change of the actual work practice.

Ethnographic investigation: Observation in practice of those people who actually carry out any activity that is of interest. Ethnographic techniques involve the use of video or audio recording devices and/ or taking field notes. The collected material is the empirical data used for producing research reports.

Participatory design (PD): Joint design involving design specialists plus practitioners such as graphic, metal and other shop floor workers. The rational is to take advantage of the "content" knowledge of the practitioners, to preserve skills and to promote a democratic development of working life.

Shop floor work: In the context of health care, shop floor work is work practice directly related to the patients´ wounds or other health problems. It is front line work, in contrast to office work or management work.

Chapter 20
A Quality Assurance Approach to Healthcare:
Implications for Information Systems

Mark C. Shaw
De Montfort University, UK

Bernd Carsten Stahl
De Montfort University, UK

ABSTRACT

Despite decades of research, healthcare information systems have been characterised by cost over-runs, poor specifications and lack of user uptake. A new approach is required which provides organisations with a reason to invest in this type of software. W Edwards Deming argues that quality is not an entity but derives from using feedback, iteratively to seek improvement to processes, in order to increase productivity and to make better use of resources. The authors propose that supporting this form of quality assurance (QA) using information systems (IS) has the potential to deliver a return on investment. An object-oriented analysis, where healthcare is viewed as the delivery of interdependent processes to which Deming's form of QA is applied, results in a class model of data types that has some useful characteristics. It is able to store data about medical and non-medical events; to save descriptions of procedures and to represent the QA process itself. With software based on the model, organisations will have a memory of previous attempts at making improvements as well as data about feedback from patients and staff to drive future change. A critical research in information systems (CRIS) analysis of this model proposes a number of criticisms deriving from theories about rationality; concepts of technology; politics and hidden agendas, as well as the social consequences of technology. The view that QA is a standardised, ongoing conversation about the important characteristics of a process pre-empts many of these counter arguments. The CRIS critique also highlights the need to ensure that development is in harmony with the needs of the many stakeholders in healthcare IS. These concepts lead to new directions in healthcare IS research. The class model needs to be tested against clinical and non-clinical use-cases for its viability not only as support for QA but also as an electronic patient record. A standard terminology is required for processes and for how objects from the model should be used to represent them. The model predicts that user interfaces will have to collect more detailed data than hitherto. Also use of the software should be tested in controlled trials to demonstrate whether the required improvements in quality not only benefit the patient but also the organisations managing their care.

DOI: 10.4018/978-1-60566-030-1.ch020

INTRODUCTION

The primary aim of W. Edwards Deming's approach to QA is to improve productivity by avoiding re-work, thereby making better use of man-hours and machine-time (Deming, 1990e). The effect is a reduction in the costs of manufacture of good product. The method requires an organisation continuously to seek improvement to processes as a result of systematically obtaining feedback. We propose that the delivery of health care can be modelled as a set of interdependent procedures and that there is every reason to apply Deming's ideas, even though they were developed for manufacturing industries.

What are the implications for healthcare information systems and their fundamental data structure - the electronic patient record - of being designed to support Deming's form of QA? By drawing on the theories that underpin his approach, the meaning of QA in the context of healthcare is examined and a generic class model that supports the process is developed, using object-oriented analysis.

If an information system is created using our set of classes, what factors will influence its success? A step back is taken and a judgmental eye cast on the model from the perspective of CRIS. We argue that even when a completely different interpretation of the nature and purpose of QA and healthcare IS is adopted, there remain good arguments to support our approach. Having outlined our concepts, we conclude by proposing new directions for research.

BACKGROUND

Why Invest in Health Information Systems?

Reviews of individual health information systems for the management of patients with chronic diseases are positive (Dorr et al., 2007) as are those of computer based nurse documentation (Ammenwerth et al., 2001). There is agreement that the overall costs and benefits have rarely been fully assessed (Herbst, Littlejohns, Rawlinson, Collinson, & Wyatt, 1999; Shekelle, Morton, & Keeler, 2006) but none-the-less Shekelle (2006) states that:

"Despite the heterogeneity in the analytic methods used, all cost-benefit analyses predicted substantial savings from [Electronic Health Record implementation.] The quantifiable benefits are projected to outweigh the investment costs. However, the predicted time needed to break even varied from three to as many as 13 years."

This conclusion is open to question because an understanding is required of how different research methods influence results (Moehr, Anglin, Schaafsma, Pantazi, & Grimm, 2006; Wyatt & Wyatt, 2003; van't Riet, Berg, Hiddema, & Sol, 2001). Consequently some authors have suggested the need for a broadly accepted, standard evaluation framework (Rahimi & Vimarlund, 2007; Ammenwerth, Graber, Herrmann, Burkle, & Konig, 2003; Ammenwerth et al., 2004).

An overview of academic medical informatics (Jaspers, Knaup, & Schmidt, 2006) suggested that:

"The computerised patient record ... is playing a growing part in medical informatics research and evaluation studies, but the goal of establishing a comprehensive lifelong electronic health record ... is still a long way off."

Why should healthcare organisations invest in information systems that are yet to provide an electronic health record and which offer, at best, a modest economic benefit? We propose that they are most likely to gain if they establish a QA process and use software to support it.

What is Quality?

The concept of 'quality' has been criticised because the meaning is elusive. A narrow definition focussed mainly on customer satisfaction, has been used to legitimate increasing managerial control over healthcare professionals (Palfrey, Thomas, & Phillips, 2004b). On the other hand, making 'quality' synonymous with high professional standards is seen as forcing staff to adhere to yardsticks imposed by senior management (Palfrey, Thomas, & Phillips, 2004a).

Additional barriers to the success of QA in the British National Health Service (NHS) have been: lack of resources; lack of expertise or advice on project design and analysis; lack of an overall plan for audit; organisational impediments and problems between groups and group members (Johnston, Crombie, Alder, Davies, & Millard, 2000). It is no surprise that the effects of quality improvement projects are variable, depending on the context in which they are used and the way they are implemented (Walshe & Freeman, 2002).

Quality Assurance

We avoid arguments over the meaning of the word: 'quality' by proposing that healthcare can be modelled as a set of interdependent processes. Viewed this way, we can apply Deming's ideas about: 'seeking continuously and forever, iteratively to improve process and product' (Deming, 1990d).

Deming suggested that each process should be described in terms of a specific test of its action and a pass/fail criterion (Deming, 1990b). When tracked over time, the proportion of failures to meet these 'operational definitions' will fluctuate and statistical boundaries can be set for the extent of the variation.

When the proportion of failures lies outside pre-defined, statistical limits: 'special causes' are said to be present. These require to be investigated and to be remedied on a case by case basis as soon as possible after they are detected. Often they represent rare or exceptional circumstances, such as equipment failure.

When the proportion of failures lies within pre-defined statistical limits, a process is said to be in statistical control and variation is due to: 'systematic causes', which require management to improve the method of working.

As part of an agenda to avoid developing better systems, management may argue that each patient is 'one-of-a-kind' due to biological variation. This logic is faulty because it is likely that patients can be classified into one of a set of variants and care tailored accordingly.

A consequence of defining healthcare as a sequence of interdependent processes is that errors in preceding activities, if left unaddressed, will accumulate and affect the correct performance of their dependants. This is another reason for management not to avoid its responsibilities.

For manufactured goods, quality may be defined in terms of improvements in three areas: the product; the customer's use of the product and the requirements for maintenance of the product. In contrast, we propose that the quality of a service may be defined in terms of improvements to the design of its constituent processes. Enhancements should be sought in the actions undertaken and the operational definitions needed, using feedback from patients about the process and its effects and from staff about the resources needed to keep consistently delivering without fault.

Meaningful feedback needs to be obtained in a systematic way. The plan, implement, observe and review approach suggested by Shewhart and popularised by Deming (1990c) offers a useful methodology. Planning defines the process and desirable changes. Implementation executes the alteration on as small a scale as can be demonstrated to provide meaningful results. Observation gathers data about the effects of the modification. Review examines what was learnt and what can be predicted regarding future operations. This should be an iterative process which acts as a permanent driver for improvement.

Continuous Quality Improvement

Continuous quality improvement (CQI) is the application of Deming's form of QA to healthcare. It has been used to improve cardiac care in a hospital, over a 10 year period (Brush et al., 2006), as well as in an emergency department to reduce complaints and increase patient satisfaction (Welch & Allen, 2006). Without a control group however, it is difficult to ascertain whether these reported changes follow from the QA process or other factors such as better technology.

Data collected before and after the CQI implementation of a number of care pathways, showed that most lead to better treatment (Panella, Marchisio, & Di Stanislao, 2003). The investigators reported difficulty obtaining results from existing information systems and pathway failures were attributed to the inability to engage clinicians in the process of quality improvement because of a lack of timely statistics about changes to care.

A randomised controlled trial demonstrated that CQI had no effect on the care delivered to patients with asthma in two geographic areas of the United States. There were methodological problems with the assessment of effect and external factors such as financial stringency and organisational change confounded the results (Homer et al., 2005). In contrast a second trial examining the effect of CQI on the management of depressed patients, demonstrated modest improvements in the process and outcome of care: more completed the required programme and more functioned better socially (Rubenstein et al., 2006).

Deming (Deming, 1990a) suggested that initial change will be dramatic as special causes are removed. What is left thereafter is the need to change the methods of work, which is altogether a more difficult and longer-term undertaking. The results reported in the research on CQI are to be expected because the investigators have yet to take full account of this possibility.

IMPLICATIONS FOR INFORMATION SYSTEMS

Object-Oriented Analysis

In order to examine the effects on information systems design, we performed an object-oriented analysis (Booch, 1994) of Deming's form of QA as applied to healthcare.

When dealing with health, it is useful to be able to follow the patient for long periods of time. We argue that this can only be achieved only if there is knowledge of data type and location. These pre-requisites ensure that the correct comparison procedure can be applied.

In quantitative research, classification of data into groups, using the appropriate comparison operation, leads to the ability to count them and thereby to the performance of statistical analyses. In qualitative research, comparison permits identification of terms used to describe themes of interest.

In our analysis, we have attempted to apply these principles to arrive at a description of QA that avoids the need for free-text, wherein the location and the type of the data are unknown (at least until there is reliable, automated natural-language comprehension).

Class Model

In the following section, the classes of information employed in the model are written in capital letters, when they are first mentioned.

Processes may be represented as combinations of ACTIONs, performed by ACTORs.

The test component of an operational definition may be represented as an action from which an OBSERVATION may result.

The 'pass/fail criterion' of an operational definition requires classifying observations according to some standard. We propose that an

ANALYSIS type of action should be used to represent this and other methods of summarising and interpreting data.

Groups of analyses may be recognised as forming a set. The resulting HYPOTHESIS about the cause of a problem may lead to the PLANNING of remedial TASKS. Each task will require a set of CAPABILITIES, such as a person's SKILLs or a machine's FUNCTION, for its successful conclusion. Part of planning will be to choose appropriate actors to fulfill the requested capabilities.

An advantage of real time data gathering is that it is possible to provide people with an opportunity to record why they succeeded or failed to perform a task (Buetow, 2005). The INDICATION class handles both these scenarios, providing the capability to determine whether a hypothesis was "in favour" or "against" a task.

Machines may perform actions on behalf of people, such as monitoring blood pressure. LOCATIONS describe where an event took place in space and may be composed of sub-locations. Arguably, locations may perform actions on behalf of people and so we propose that an actor could be a PERSON, a piece of EQUIPMENT or a LOCATION.

No individual acts in isolation; each lives in a physical and social environment and inherits a genetic legacy. A person has a RELATIONSHIP with other people. This might be genetic, marriage or friendship. Also an actor may have a ROLE within an ORGANISATION. Examples are employment or membership of a sports club. Organisations may themselves be composed of a number of sub-organisations and may have a location in space.

For QA, actors must have the ability to remember PLANs about what tasks to undertake when a particular hypothesis pertains. Plans need to be made sensitive to circumstances by being able to represent decisions. Since tasks can lead to actions which result in observations that are analysed: it can be argued that one or more hypotheses may pertain following a task. Plans may be created to define what to do for each of these expected hypotheses.

Figure 1 shows the class diagram that was created following the above analysis. Links are to be read from left-to-right and from top-to-bottom. The QA feedback loop is characterised by the following relationships:

- An OBSERVATION "resulted-from" an ACTION, which a PERSON "performs".
- An OBSERVATION "is-interpreted-by" an ANALYSIS, which a PERSON "performs".
- A PERSON "performs" an ANALYSIS, which "generates" a HYPOTHESIS.
- A HYPOTHESIS "initiates" PLANNING, which a PERSON "performs".
- A TASK "is-planned-by" PLANNING.
- A PERSON "performs" an ACTION, which "is-realised-by" a TASK.

More About Observations

Deming suggested that operational definitions should be couched in terms of objective tests such as the red, green and blue settings needed to achieve a particular colour. We note that whilst such observations are common in medicine there are many, such as symptoms and signs, which involve a degree of subjectivity on the part of the observer. We propose the use of 'mechanoid' and 'humanoid' observations to distinguish the two.

A mechanoid observation is defined as one where a machine makes a record of a measurement directly from sensor data and provides the same report of previous measurements to multiple independent observers. In contrast, a humanoid observation is one where no data about what the sensor detected are available; only a person's interpretation of what was present. Both types of observation may involve data loss. In the case of mechanoid observations, the nature of the loss and the processing that generated it is, in principle, explicit and available for all to examine and verify.

Figure 1. Class model, showing the QA loop

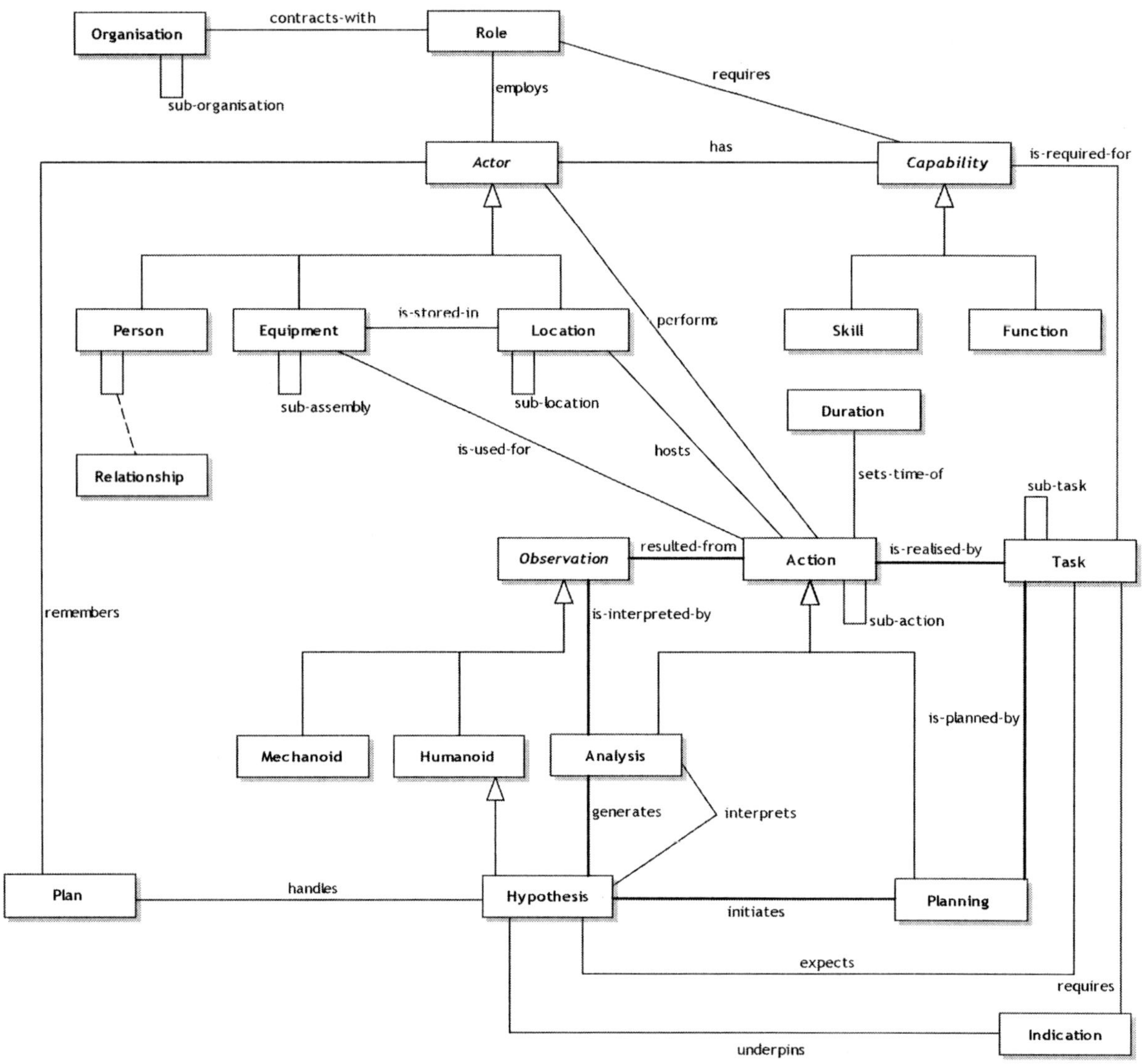

In the case of the humanoid observation, there are no such guarantees.

Modelling Health Care

In the following sections, we demonstrate that useful concepts regarding the management of patients in a healthcare setting can be modelled using the classes and relationships in figure 1. This is not intended as proof of validity but rather as an illustration of potential utility in representing medical and administrative processes.

Risk Factor

A 'risk factor' increases the chances that a person may contract a disease.

In Figure 2, the box surrounding 'smoking:Action' and 'cigarettes:Equipment' is a swim lane. In the diagrams in this section and

Figure 2. Representation of a person smoking

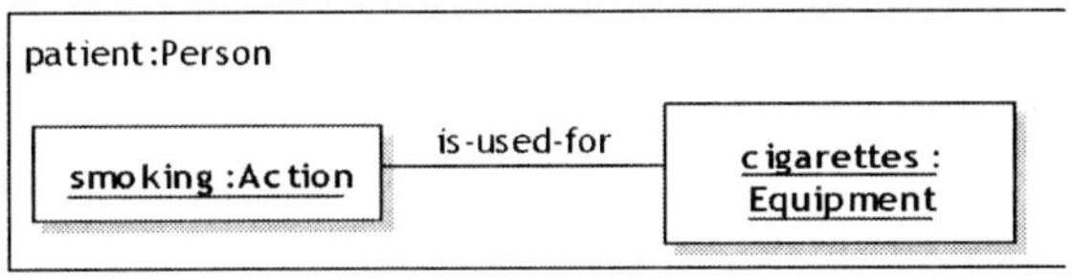

those which follow, swim lanes are used to show an actor performing an action.

Referral

A referral is a request for help made to a health care professional either by a patient or a colleague. One approach to modelling this is to use the idea that a patient consents to the action and that a recipient accepts the request. (see Figure 3)

Figure 3. Representation of a referral

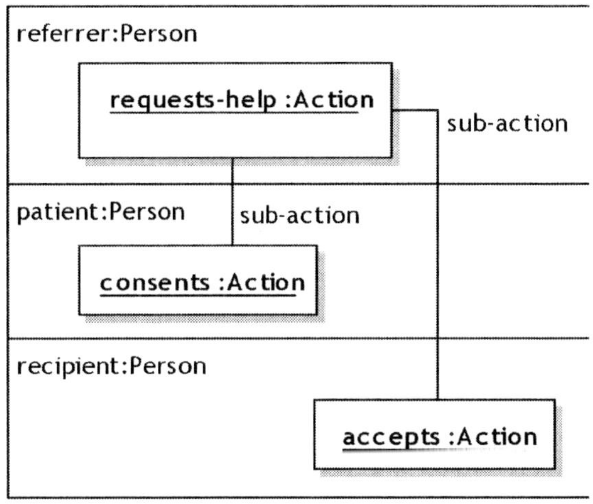

Assessment

Assessment is the process of gathering observations about the patient by listening to a description of the problem (taking a history), by conducting a physical examination and by organising investigations, such as sampling blood, taking x-rays or ultrasound images, measuring physiological parameters or examining tissue samples taken during operative procedures.

While taking the history, the clinician interprets what has been said and applies labels mapping the description to accepted medical terminology for symptoms. During physical examination, the professional's senses (vision, touch, hearing and smell) are used to look for manifestations of disease (Nardonne, 1990). Humanoid observations should be used for symptoms, signs and those physiological measurements where no independent record is taken. The use of mechanoid observations should be reserved for investigations where a record of the sensor's output is kept.

In Figure 4, a health care practitioner takes a history, during which the patient is asked about

Figure 4. Representation of a symptom

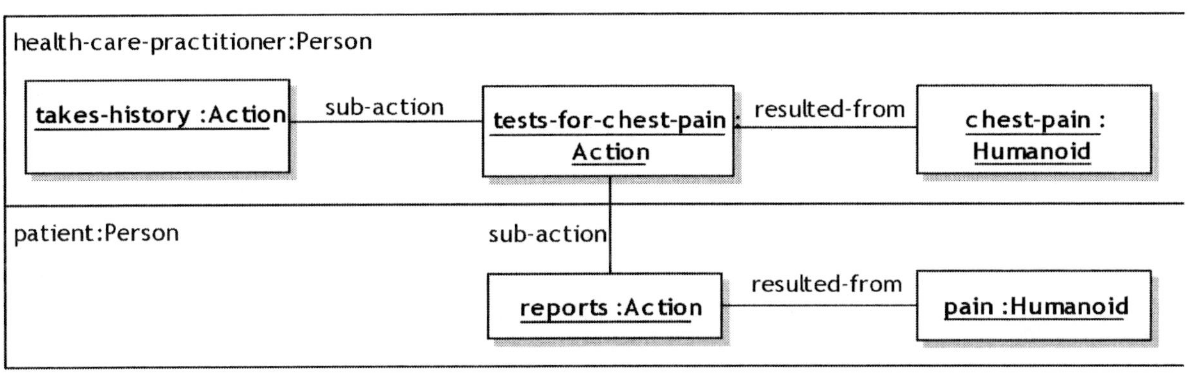

Figure 5. Representation of a sign

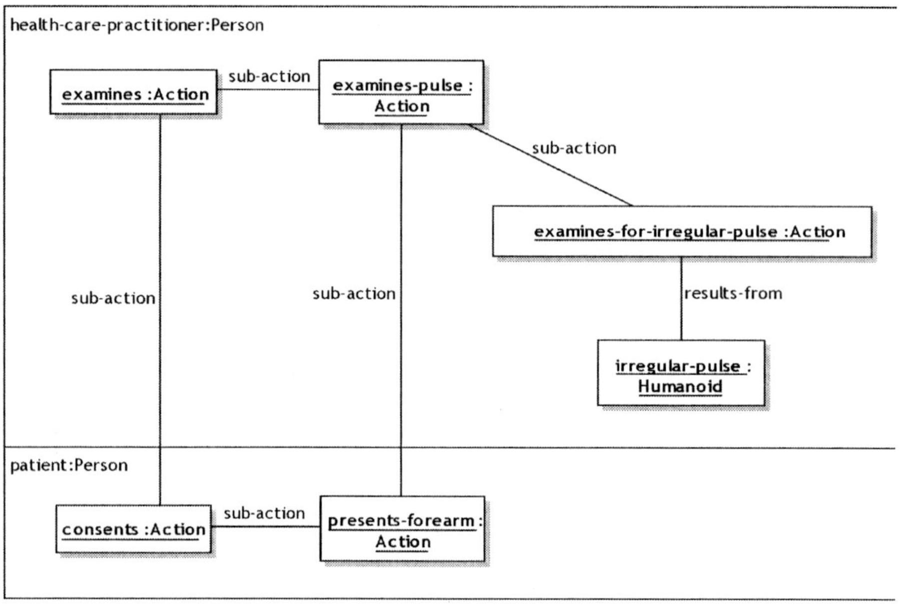

Figure 6. Representation of an investigation

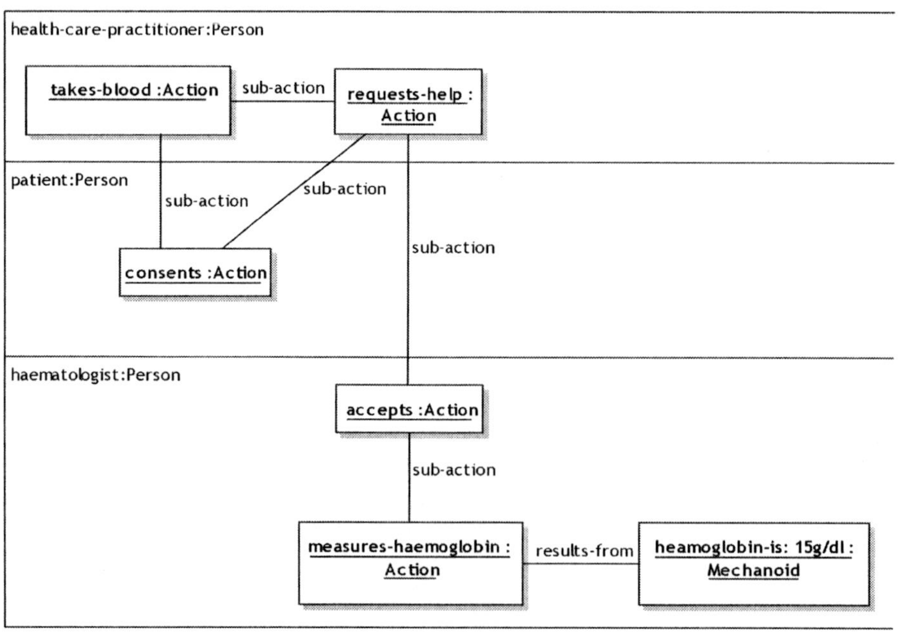

chest pain. Pain is reported, leading to a positive test, represented by the existence of the chest-pain humanoid observation.

In Figure 5, the patient is examined for an irregular pulse. If the humanoid observation were missing, it would be reasonable for an analyst to deduce that the clinician examined the forearm and found nothing. If the examines-for-irregular-pulse action were absent, no such inference could be made. This demonstrates how the class model could handle an important concept in medical diagnosis: the contrary finding (see *Diagnosis*).

Figure 6 presents a simplified view of the analysis of a blood sample. Many details such as the method of taking blood, the administrative procedures, the equipment used and the process of transporting the blood sample, are not shown.

Diagnosis

Diagnosis is the process of labelling clusters of observations; the clinician selects which ones form a set, based on recognised patterns or the characteristics of disease processes (Nardonne, 1990). The technique for synthesising observations into a diagnosis has been described as one of hypothesis generation followed either by refinement or by elimination, as a result of a contrary finding (Nardonne, 1990) making the ability to store the latter important to an electronic patient record. (see Figure 7)

Management

Management is the selection, planning, execution and monitoring of tasks appropriate to the handling of a patient's problems. Usually the diagnosis forms the basis upon which treatment is selected but the clinician may also choose to use symptoms or signs, either because of the distress they are causing or because an urgent intervention is required (Nardonne, 1990).

While planning a task, decisions are made about who will perform the procedure, where, when and how. Clinicians marshal appropriate resources, none of which are under their exclusive control and take account of what skills are available, as well as the patient's circumstances, consent and ability to comply.

Monitoring is a repeated assessment, which takes place after treatment. It is focussed on the set of symptoms, signs and investigations that best indicate progress. During this phase, new problems may come to light, requiring that a new diagnostic review is initiated.

Figure 7. Representation of a diagnosis

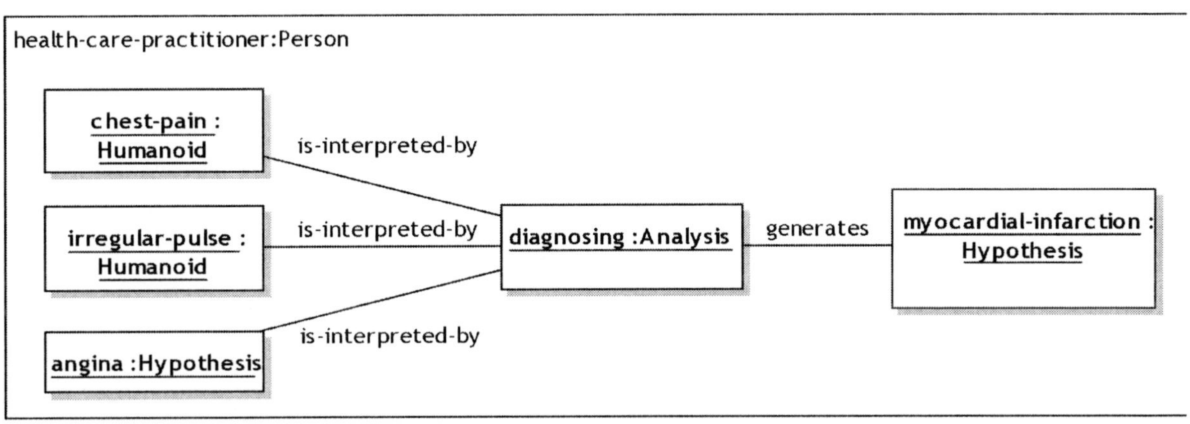

In Figure 8, a diagnosis of myocardial infarction initiates myocardial infarction care planning. This involves two tasks: monitor electrocardiograph (ECG) and administer morphine. The patient consents to receiving morphine and the task is realised by the health care practitioner giving morphine. The monitor ECG task is realised by the ECG machine's leads being attached to the patient's chest and the machine displaying a trace.

Organisational Memory

An example plan is provided for part of the management of ovarian cancer (Shaw, Wolfe, Devaja, & Raju, 2003). The hypothesis that a woman has ovarian cancer initiates the task of planning for a laparotomy (a procedure to assess the presence and extent of disease in the abdomen).

The laparotomy task requires that a midline incision is performed (the details of which are not shown). Next peritoneal fluid or washings should be sampled in order to determine whether the disease has spread from the ovaries to other tissues, which has implications for further treatment. Determining the correct stage requires the surgeon to take a sample of peritoneal fluid or if there is none, to perform a peritoneal lavage and then to take a sample of the resulting fluid in the abomen.

In figure 9, the task to sample peritoneal fluid or washings begins by asking the surgeon to examine for peritoneal fluid. Two possible outcomes are shown by the 'expects' relation: either fluid is present or absent in the abdominal cavity. If fluid is found, a sample is taken. If there is none, peritoneal lavage is performed and a sample of the lavage fluid (washings) taken.

It should be noted that there is a requirement to determine the sequence of peer tasks in a plan. In Figure 9, the tasks should be carried out in left-to-right order.

Whereas the health care practitioner performs actions on a person and gains feedback from observation of that individual, QA performs actions on plans and gains feedback from observation of the results. Figure 10 shows how the QA process might be represented using classes from the model. Initially observations of the process are analysed to generate a hypothesis about how it might be

Figure 8. Representation of the early management of a heart attack

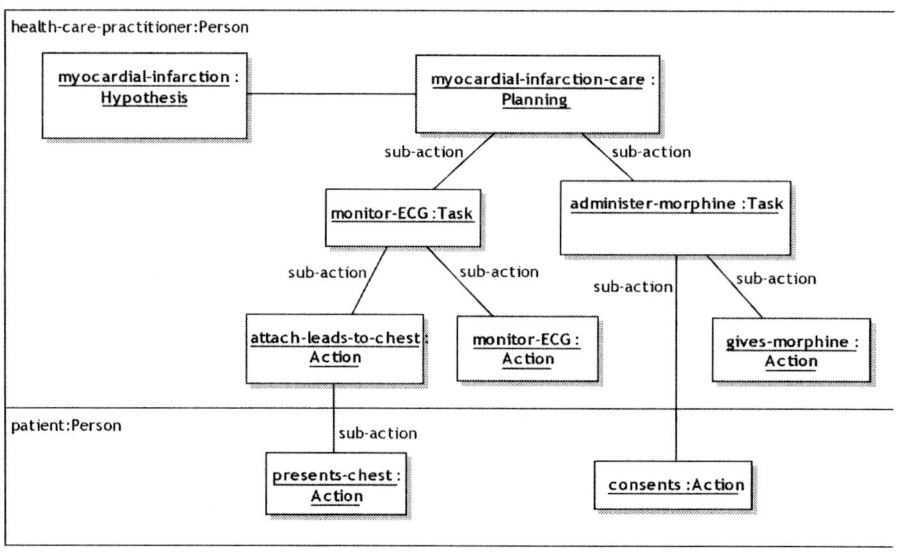

Figure 9. Plan for the early stages of a laparotomy for ovarian cancer

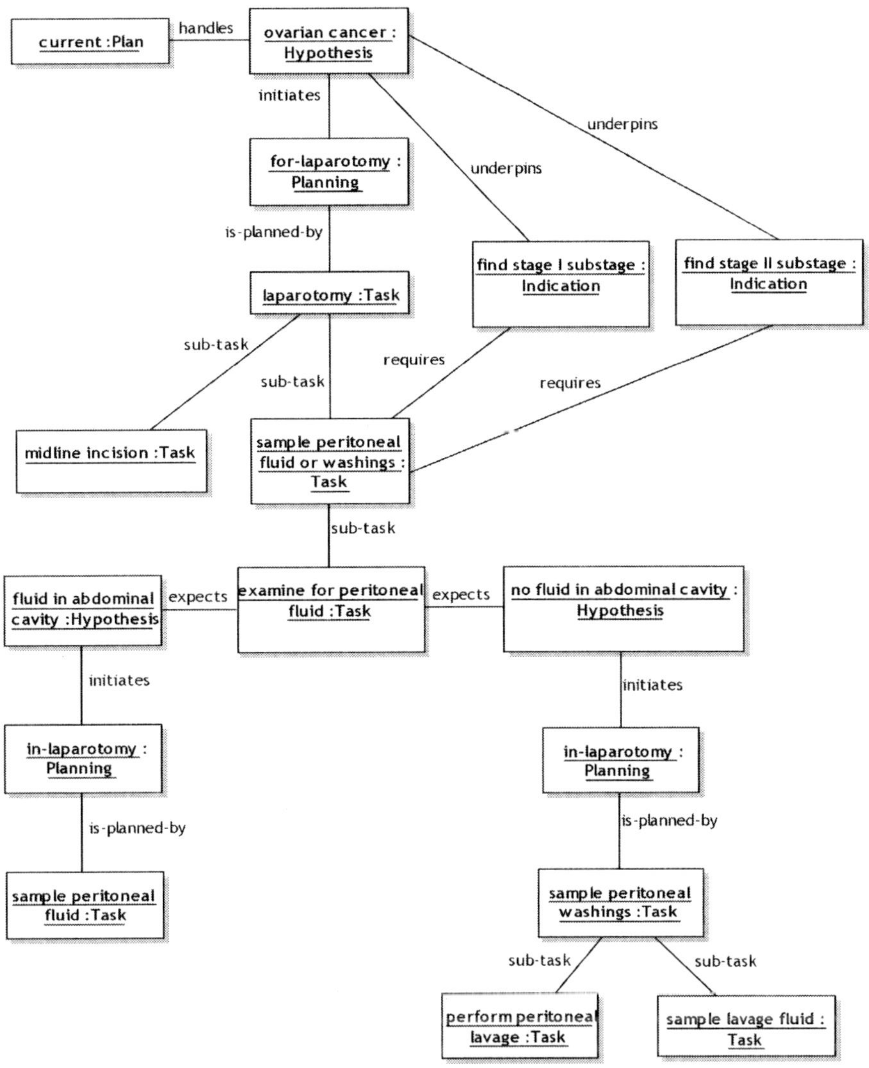

improved. Next the alteration is planned, and a task defined which is realised by an action to change the process. The effects of the alteration are then monitored by gathering further data.

CRITIQUE OF THE QA MODEL

The QA model of healthcare information systems is based on assumptions that may be familiar with medical as well as ICT professionals. It implicitly assumes that reality can be described in a relatively straightforward manner. Patients as well as medical professionals are viewed as rational individuals who seek to communicate in order to achieve a mutually beneficial outcome. The technology required to underpin the QA system has not been considered in any detail and is presumed to be unproblematic. Use of technology follows functional requirements. Briefly, the model we have developed follows the positivist mainstream model of information systems research and practice. This

Figure 10. Representation of the QA process (Note: the vertical swim-lane)

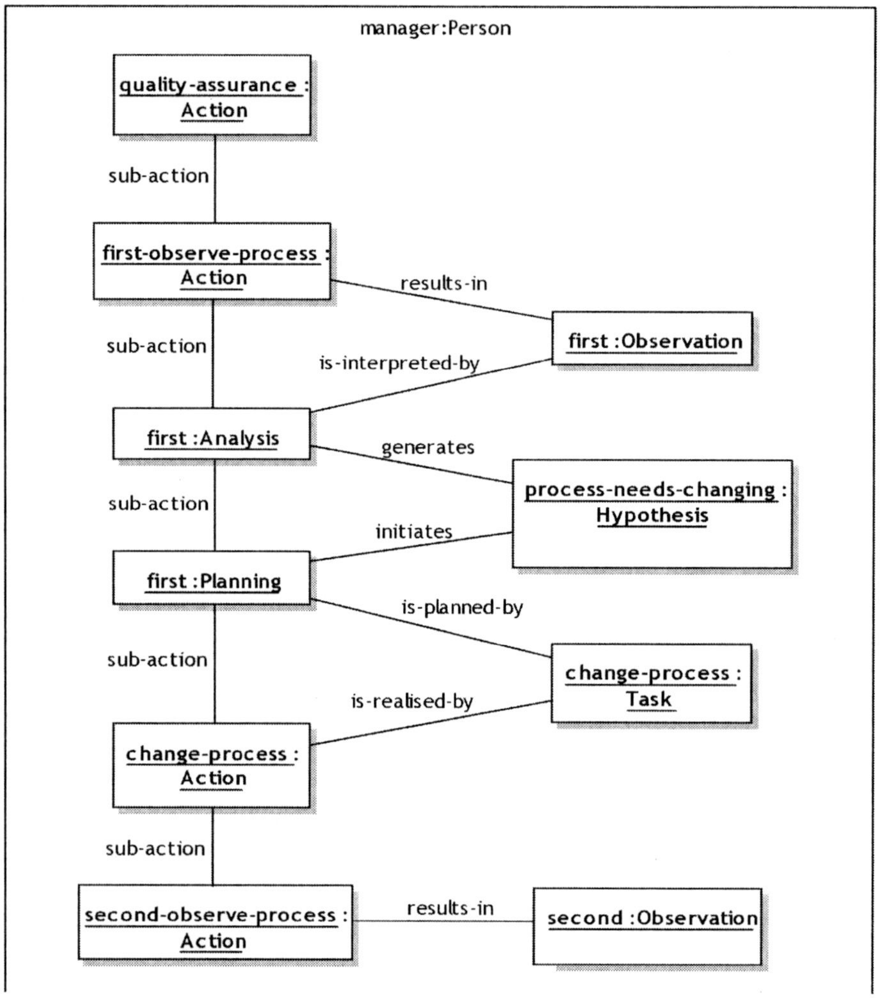

approach has the advantage of being familiar to many of the relevant stakeholders of healthcare information systems. At the same time it may cause problems. A primary indicator of the shortcomings of the mainstream understanding of information systems is the persistently high failure rate. Despite decades of research on information systems, the majority of systems can still be considered failures due to price overruns, poor specifications, lack of user uptake etc. Wilson & Howcroft (2002) have pointed out that the concept of failure is problematic per se. It is probably unproblematic to state that the history of ICT projects in the NHS is a history of failures.

The Critical View

Developing a new approach, such as the QA approach we are suggesting here, should thus consider early on whether there are factors that are likely to cause systems to fail despite sound conceptual underpinnings. We will use this section to sketch a possible counterargument to our QA approach in order to then propose how the model could be used to address these.

For this purpose we will briefly look at the position of Critical Research in Information Systems (Howcroft & Trauth, 2005) and explore which issues this may raise for our model. Critical Research in information systems (CRIS) is an approach to IS that draws from critical theories in the social sciences and attempts to discover angles typically overlooked by traditional research. A main aim of CRIS is to promote emancipation understood as the ability of individuals to live a self-determined life. CRIS is a useful choice of approach to our QA model because it emphasises aspects of social reality that our model so far neglects, such as organisational and national politics, gender, class, conceptualisation of technology and others. Moreover, CRIS, because of its emphasis on emancipation, has an ethical underpinning (Stahl, 2008), which maps well onto the implied ethical dimension of healthcare. The purpose of healthcare provision in general can be seen as emancipatory.

CRIS draws on a range of theoretical roots and it is impossible to undertake a comprehensive analysis of our model from a CRIS point of view. We will therefore draw on the CRIS literature that explicitly refers to healthcare IS in order to identify dominant issues that our approach so far has not covered.

Rationality

A good point to start a critique of mainstream IS that might be applied to our model is the concept of rationality. Like most complex concepts this one is difficult to grasp and define. Its clearest example may be the autonomous individual on whom neoclassical economic theory is built. Such an individual is rational because she has a complete set of preferences and acts in order to maximise her utility according to these preferences. Translated into a healthcare setting, this means that individuals, be they patients, doctors, or any other stakeholders, act in a way to maximise the overall utility. It is easy to see that this will break down at the point where preferences are not identical. The patient may want a maximum of healthcare, whereas the doctor may view this as medically unwarranted and the manager as too expensive. In addition, patients are often described as irrational when their actions do not contribute to their health, or doctors are seen as irrational when they do not follow organisational goals.

The concept of rationality has been critiqued for a variety of reasons. It may simply not be possible for humans to be rational in the sense described above. Our individual preferences are not complete and often contradictory. In addition we lack the knowledge and cognitive capacities to make optimal decisions. A system based on the idea that people are and will be have rationally is thus likely to face problems. An additional problem arises when technical systems are introduced to increase the rationality of healthcare provision. Empirical evidence suggests that the 'irrational' nature of human interaction does not change by the introduction of information systems. In fact the introduction of such systems often introduces new irrationalities (Berg, 1999).

A further problem of rationality arises due to competing demands. We have already indicated that healthcare IS are often seen as ways of saving money (Palfrey et al., 2004a). This is a legitimate aim. However, one should see that it will in many cases conflict with the similarly legitimate aims of other stakeholders (Adams & Fitch, 2006). The use of information systems to promote a financial perspective on rationality can thus be seen as an attempt to promote a particular agenda.

A further problem of rationality is that there are different types of rationality that determine our social reality. Information systems tend to represent an abstract rationality, which is arguably often not compatible with the practical rationality of healthcare practitioners. Hanlon et al. (2005) give an example of the NHS direct system, a nurse-based 24 hour health advice system, whose technical base represents a rationality that is not compatible with the rationality of the nurses operating it. A different example of problems of competing rationality is developed by Klecun & Cornford (2005) who show that a traditional view of rationality when used for evaluating healthcare systems fails to pick up relevant issues.

Concepts of Technology

A central question in critical discourses revolves around the conceptualisation of technology. Critical scholars often draw on other discourses such as the social construction of technology but also on traditional critical theory to develop an account of how the very concept of technology affects social outcomes (Feenberg, 1991; Feenberg, 1999). The point here is that technology is not a neutral tool that can be used to whatever purpose the user decides to employ it. Instead, technology is seen as endowed with certain values and affordances that favour certain uses over others.

This point is linked with questions of technical determinism. Much mainstream work on ICT seems to assume that technologies have certain uses that they are built for and that users will make use of the options of technology in the way they were planned for. On the other hand there are numerous examples of technology either not being used or being used for purposes different from those envisaged. This has to do with what has been termed the "interpretive flexibility" of technology (Doherty, Coombs, & Loan-Clarke, 2006) (or interpretative flexibility (Cadili & Whitley, 2005)).

An important aspect of the concept of technology is the capacity of ICT to capture reality. In our model this issue is highlighted by the distinction between humanoid and mechanoid observations. Technologies are much better at capturing some aspects of reality than humans and vice versa. Healthcare information systems are likely to favour mechanoid observations because they are easier to integrate in technical contexts. This is likely to lead to reductionist perspectives on healthcare which can blend out the immeasurable, which arguably is often an important aspect of medical practice (Hanlon et al., 2005).

The main point here is that a naïve reliance on an intuitive understanding of technology is not likely lead to the success of a new approach. If the QA model is to be successful, then design and implementation should be aware of competing demands on technology but also different users' conception of technology.

Politics and Hidden Agendas

One reason why the above two points are of relevance to our approach is that technology is often used for political purposes. Such purposes can stem from organisational politics as well as national politics. The primary example of this is the growing influence of financial considerations. One main benefit of healthcare IS is that they tend to allow a more detailed breakdown of costs of treatments and a clearer allocation of these costs to different stakeholders. At the same time this leads to a strengthening of cost considerations when compared with others.

The UK government has promoted new ICTs in the NHS partly on the grounds of facilitating more choice for patients. This can be seen as a positive aim as few would dispute that the ability to choose one's doctor is bad. However, one needs to understand that this rhetoric of choice can also lead to a fundamental restructuring of healthcare provision and change the balance between market and state allocation of resources (Mol, 1999).

A different example is the distribution of power in organisations. Traditionally, healthcare in western countries tends to be very much centred on doctors. They hold the knowledge; they make decisions and allocate resources. Doctors' autonomy is a highly valued tradition. However, in complex modern healthcare organisations, power is increasingly taken away from doctors and moved towards managers. Such power struggles are normal and can be found in most sectors and organisations. What is important for us to note is that technology can be used as a tool in such struggles. This can lead to the acceptance or rejection of a technology

Social Consequences of Technology

A final point worth mentioning here has to do with the social consequences of technology. The wide availability of healthcare information via the internet has already started to impact on doctor-patient relationships. Patients are better informed and often have specific demands on doctors. Doctors, on the other hand, often resist this change of role which threatens their traditional position of authority.

A further social consequence of the introduction of ICT into healthcare is that it will inevitably lead to changes in procedures. The mere fact that data is to be recorded changes the way doctors interact with patients. This is of course usually intended and thus not to be lamented. However, the changes will often go beyond what was envisaged. If, for example, a system captures the number of patient a doctor sees, then this is likely to affect management's view of the doctor. As a consequence the doctor is likely to pay attention to the number of patients seen and may make choices on which patients to see. An unintended consequence may be that easier cases will find it easier to be treated than difficult ones because they take less time and improve the doctor's performance record. This is what Zuboff (1988) described as "informating", a property of ICT that not only captures but also produces information, which then changes the original processes.

While the nature of interaction between stakeholders can change, the very practice of medicine can also be changed. Again, this is intended, and our QA model explicitly aims to improve healthcare provision by allowing doctors to better understand the consequences of their decisions. On the other hand, there is a danger that it will lead to increased bureaucracy and medicine by algorithm. The danger of "cookbook medicine" based on standards and protocols developed on the basis of collected data (Berg, 1997) is not to be underestimated.

The QA Model Response

The above critique of the QA model does not claim to be complete. Its purpose is to show that there are aspects of healthcare IS that our model does not capture but that still have the potential to affect its success.

We believe that all of the points are valid and relevant but do not have to lead to the downfall of the QA model. The important point to avoid these issues is to start the QA process with a suitable interpretation of what QA is about. QA is an iterative process that allows continuous interaction with the aim of improving outcomes. This means that it must be open to changes in focus and criteria of quality as well as a shifting view of relevant data and ways of collecting it. Understood this way, QA can be seen as a standardised ongoing conversation about important characteristic of a process.

Such an open understanding of QA would pre-empt much of the critique discussed earlier. It would not make assumptions about appropriate standards of reality and allow for a questioning of implied standards via the QA process. It would be open to different concepts of technology including the resulting means of collecting, formatting, and storing information. These larger contextual issues, including political and social consequences of technology, may be impossible to include in the technical model that we have started to develop in the *Background*. However, the QA process as a whole will have to be sensitive to them, given that they are arguably important not only for user acceptance of technology but for the entire QA process in healthcare.

One could argue that this will require something like a 2nd order QA process. We need to think about some way of continually ensuring that the QA process is of high quality. Again, there is a question whether this can be technically implemented and in what way it will require organisational changes.

A final issue has to do with development and implementation of a QA system. While we have tried to make a sound statement on some of the conceptual basics, the critique has shown that context sensitivity will be required. It is unlikely that the same implementation of the same system in different contexts will lead to comparable results. This is where the socio-technical approach to systems design and development (Mumford, 2003) is likely to be able to address many of the challenges by allowing for participation of a range of stakeholders, most importantly of end users.

CONCLUSION

We have argued that healthcare organisations should focus on establishing QA and then invest in information systems to provide timely data to help engage clinicians in the process. We used object-oriented analysis to develop a class model describing Deming's form of QA, assuming that healthcare can be modelled as a set of interdependent processes.

Our model could provide organisations with a memory of a process's history as well as detailed data about practise and its effects. In conjunction with research, such an information system would deliver timely data to support systematically making changes to healthcare procedures. This should result in care that provides the patient with the solution to their problem and that minimises their contact with health services, thereby increasing capacity and productivity. If this is indeed correct, healthcare organisations should obtain a return on their outlay on IS.

We took a step back to look at possible counterarguments against our approach as might be voiced by critical scholars. We suggest that our model is open to some critical arguments but understanding QA as a standardised, ongoing conversation about the important characteristics of a process overcomes many such objections. This review also highlighted the need to develop information systems in harmony with the needs of their many stakeholders.

Future Research

The class model needs to be validated by examining whether a wide of variety of use-cases induce changes.

How objects in the model are used to represent health care processes needs to be standardised as well as how they are named by terminologies for diagnoses, clinical and administrative procedures.

In principle, the level of detail in the model offers the possibility of defining the meaning of diagnostic codes for diseases, in terms of actions, observations and analyses. The value of this capability in actual use will need to be assessed.

Little in our class model is specific to medicine. It could support comprehensive data collection not only about healthcare but also about the various non-clinical supporting processes. To realise this, collection of data would need to be more detailed and from a wider range of staff than existing systems. Will user interfaces need to change in order to cope? Will the availability of these additional data be useful to healthcare organisations?

The next step of our research will be to examine these questions as well as the effect of the model on clinical processes. We plan to build a prototype and undertake a quantitative and qualitative evaluation in an environment where a comparison can be made with the effects of alternate software systems.

REFERENCES

Adams, C., & Fitch, T. (2006). Social Inclusion and the Shifting Role of Technology: Is Age the New Gender in Mobile Access? In *Social Inclusion: Societal and Organizational Implications for Information Systems* (pp. 203-215).

Ammenwerth, E., Brender, J., Nykanen, P., Prokosch, H. U., Rigby, M., & Talmon, J. (2004). Visions and strategies to improve evaluation of health information systems - Reflections and lessons based on the HIS-EVAL workshop in Innsbruck. *International Journal of Medical Informatics*, *73*, 479–491. doi:10.1016/j.ijmedinf.2004.04.004

Ammenwerth, E., Eichstadter, R., Haux, R., Pohl, U., Rebel, S., & Ziegler, S. (2001). A randomized evaluation of a computer-based nursing documentation system. *Methods of Information in Medicine*, *40*, 61–68.

Ammenwerth, E., Graber, S., Herrmann, G., Burkle, T., & Konig, J. (2003). Evaluation of health information systems-problems and challenges. *International Journal of Medical Informatics*, *71*, 125–135. doi:10.1016/S1386-5056(03)00131-X

Berg, M. (1997). Problems and promises of the protocol. *Social Science & Medicine*, *44*, 1081–1088. doi:10.1016/S0277-9536(96)00235-3

Berg, M. (1999). Patient care information systems and health care work: a sociotechnical approach. *International Journal of Medical Informatics*, *55*, 87–101. doi:10.1016/S1386-5056(99)00011-8

Booch, G. (1994). *Object-Oriented Analysis and Design with Applications*. (2nd Ed.). Redwood City, CA: The Benjamin/Cummings Publishing Company, Inc.

Brush, J. E., Balakrishnan, S. A., Brough, J., Hartman, C., Hines, G., & Liverman, D. P. (2006). Implementation of a continuous quality improvement program for percutaneous coronary intervention and cardiac surgery at a large community hospital. *American Heart Journal*, *152*, 379–385. doi:10.1016/j.ahj.2005.12.014

Buetow, S. (2005). Why the need to reduce medical errors is not obvious. *Journal of Evaluation in Clinical Practice*, *11*, 53–57. doi:10.1111/j.1365-2753.2004.00497.x

Cadili, S., & Whitley, E. A. (2005). On the interpretative flexibility of hosted ERP systems. *The Journal of Strategic Information Systems*, *14*, 167–195. doi:10.1016/j.jsis.2005.04.006

Deming, W. E. (1990a). Common Causes and Special Causes. In *Out of the Crisis* (pp. 309-370). Cambridge, UK: Cambridge University Press.

Deming, W. E. (1990b). Operational Definitions, Conformance, Performance. In *Out of the Crisis* (pp. 276-296). Cambridge, UK: Cambridge University Press.

Deming, W. E. (1990c). Principles for transformation. In *Out of the Crisis* (pp. 18-96). Cambridge, UK: Cambridge University Press.

Deming, W. E. (1990d). Quality, Productivity, Lower costs. In *Out of the Crisis* (pp. 2-17). Cambridge, UK: Cambridge University Press.

Deming, W. E. (1990e). Service Organisations. In *Out of the Crisis* (pp. 183-247). Cambridge, UK: Cambridge University Press.

Doherty, N. F., Coombs, C. R., & Loan-Clarke, J. (2006). A re-conceptualization of the interpretive flexibility of information technologies: redressing the balance between the social and the technical. *European Journal of Information Systems*, *15*, 569–582. doi:10.1057/palgrave.ejis.3000653

Dorr, D., Bonner, L. M., Cohen, A. N., Shoai, R. S., Perrin, R., & Chaney, E. (2007). Informatics systems to promote improved care for chronic illness: A literature review. *Journal of the American Medical Informatics Association*, *14*, 156–163. doi:10.1197/jamia.M2255

Feenberg, A. (1991). *Critical theory of technology*. New York: Oxford University Press.

Feenberg, A. (1999). *Questioning technology*. London: Routledge.

Hanlon, G., Strangleman, T., Goode, J., Luff, D., O'Cathain, A., & Greatbatch, D. (2005). Knowledge, technology and nursing: The case of NHS direct. *Human Relations*, *58*, 147–171. doi:10.1177/0018726705052179

Herbst, K., Littlejohns, P., Rawlinson, J., Collinson, M., & Wyatt, J. C. (1999). Evaluating computerized health information systems: hardware, software and human ware: experiences from the Northern Province, South Africa. *Journal of Public Health Medicine*, *21*, 305–310. doi:10.1093/pubmed/21.3.305

Homer, C. J., Forbes, P., Horvitz, L., Peterson, L. E., Wypij, D., & Heinrich, P. (2005). Impact of a quality improvement program on care and outcomes for children with asthma. *Archives of Pediatrics & Adolescent Medicine*, *159*, 464–469. doi:10.1001/archpedi.159.5.464

Howcroft, D., & Trauth, E. M. (2005). *Handbook of critical information systems research theory and application.* Cheltenham, UK: Edward Elgar Publishing.

Jaspers, M. W. M., Knaup, P., & Schmidt, D. (2006). The computerized patient record: Where do we stand? *Methods of Information in Medicine*, *45*, 29–39.

Johnston, G., Crombie, I. K., Alder, E. M., Davies, H. T. O., & Millard, A. (2000). Reviewing audit: barriers and facilitating factors for effective clinical audit. *Quality & Safety in Health Care*, *9*, 23–36.

Klecun, E., & Cornford, T. (2005). A critical approach to evaluation. *European Journal of Information Systems*, *14*, 229–243. doi:10.1057/palgrave.ejis.3000540

Moehr, J. R., Anglin, C., Schaafsma, J., Pantazi, S., & Grimm, N. (2006). Lest formalisms impede insight and success: Evaluation in health informatics - A case study. *Methods of Information in Medicine*, *45*, 67–72.

Mol, A. (1999). Ontological politics: a word and some questions. In J.Law & J. Hassard (Eds.), *Actor network theory and after* (pp. 74-89). Oxford, UK; Malden, MA: Blackwell/Sociological Review.

Mumford, E. (2003). *Redesigning human systems.* Hershey, PA: Information Science Reference.

Nardonne, D. (1990). Collecting and Analysing Data: Doing and Thinking. In H.K.Walker, W. D. Hall, & J. W. Hurst (Eds.), *Clinical Methods.* Stoneham, MA.: Butterworth Publishers.

Palfrey, C., Thomas, P., & Phillips, C. (2004a). Mulitple Perspectives and Decision Making. In *Effective Health Care Management: An Evaluative Approach* (1st Ed., pp. 55-60). Oxford, UK: Blackwell Publishing.

Palfrey, C., Thomas, P., & Phillips, C. (2004b). Performance management: Concepts and approaches. In *Effective Health Care Management: An Evaluative Approach* (1st Ed., pp. 93-99). Oxford, UK: Blackwell Publishing.

Panella, M., Marchisio, S., & Di Stanislao, F. (2003). Reducing clinical variations with clinical pathways: do pathways work? *International Journal for Quality in Health Care*, *15*, 509–521. doi:10.1093/intqhc/mzg057

Rahimi, B., & Vimarlund, V. (2007). Methods to evaluate health information systems in healthcare settings: A literature review. *Journal of Medical Systems*, *31*, 397–432. doi:10.1007/s10916-007-9082-z

Rogerson, S. (2000), Ethicol: Electronic Patient Records, *IMIS Journal, 10*(5), retrieved from: http://www.ccsr.cse.dmu.ac.uk/resources/general/ethicol/Ecv10no5.html

Rubenstein, L. V., Meredith, L. S., Parker, L. E., Gordon, N. P., Hickey, S. C., & Oken, C. (2006). Impacts of evidence-based quality improvement on depression in primary care: A randomized experiment. *Journal of General Internal Medicine*, *21*, 1027–1035. doi:10.1111/j.1525-1497.2006.00549.x

Shaw, M. C., Wolfe, C. D., Devaja, O., & Raju, K. S. (2003). Development of an evidence-based algorithm for the management of ovarian cancer. *European Journal of Gynaecological Oncology*, *24*, 117–125.

Shekelle, P. G., Morton, S. C., & Keeler, E. B. (2006). *Costs and Benefits of Health Information Technology. (Prepared by the Southern California Evidence-based Practice Center under Contract No. 290-02-0003.)* (Rep. No. 132). Rockville, MD: Agency for Healthcare Research and Quality.

Stahl, B. C. (2008). The ethical nature of critical research in information systems. *Information Systems Journal*, *18*, 137–163. doi:10.1111/j.1365-2575.2007.00283.x

van't Riet, A., Berg, M., Hiddema, F., & Sol, K. (2001). Meeting patients' needs with patient information systems: potential benefits of qualitative research methods. *International Journal of Medical Informatics*, *64*, 1–14. doi:10.1016/S1386-5056(01)00185-X

Walshe, K., & Freeman, T. (2002). Effectiveness of quality improvement: learning from evaluations. *Quality & Safety in Health Care*, *11*, 85–87. doi:10.1136/qhc.11.1.85

Welch, S. J., & Allen, T. L. (2006). Data-driven quality improvement in the emergency department at a level one trauma and tertiary care hospital. *The Journal of Emergency Medicine*, *30*, 269–276. doi:10.1016/j.jemermed.2005.07.007

Wilson, M., & Howcroft, D. (2002). Re-conceptualising failure: social shaping meets IS research. *European Journal of Information Systems*, *11*, 236–250. doi:10.1057/palgrave.ejis.3000437

Wyatt, J. C., & Wyatt, S. M. (2003). When and how to evaluate health information systems? *International Journal of Medical Informatics*, *69*, 251–259. doi:10.1016/S1386-5056(02)00108-9

Zuboff, S. (1988). *In the age of the smart machine the future of work and power*. New York: Basic Books.

KEY TERMS AND DEFINITIONS

Continuous Quality Improvement (CQI): The application of Deming's form of QA to healthcare (see *Quality Assurance* below).

Critical Research in Information Systems (CRIS): An approach that draws from critical theories in the social sciences and attempts to discover angles typically overlooked by traditional research. A main aim of CRIS is to promote emancipation, understood as the ability of individuals to live a self-determined life.

Electronic patient record (EPR): allows health care providers, patients and payers to interact more efficiently and in life-enhancing ways. It offers new methods of storing, manipulating and communicating medical information of all kinds, including text, images, sound, video and tactile senses, which are more powerful and flexible than paper based systems. The policy of governments appears to favour a national healthcare infrastructure with a longitudinal patient record covering a patient's complete medical history from the cradle to the grave. (Rogerson, 2000)

Healthcare Information Systems: An information system (IS) is a system of persons, equipment and manual or automated activities that gather, process and report on the data an organization uses. A healthcare information system is one used by an organisation involved in the delivery of health care.

Object-Oriented Programming: A programming paradigm that uses "objects" and their interactions to design applications and computer programs. Programming techniques may include features such as encapsulation, modularity, polymorphism, and inheritance.

Quality Assurance: W Edwards Deming defined quality assurance as the continuous, systematic, iterative improvement of processes by obtaining feedback from clients and from staff. It may be viewed as a standardised, ongoing conversation about the important characteristics of a process.

Rationality: Best exemplified by the autonomous individual on whom neoclassical economic theory is built. Such an individual is rational because she has a complete set of preferences and acts in order to maximise her utility according to these preferences.

Stakeholder: A person, company, etc., with a concern or (esp. financial) interest in ensuring the success of an organization, business, system, etc. (taken from OED Online: http://dictionary.oed.com/).

Chapter 21
Supporting the Development of Personalized E-Health:
An Insight into the E-Patient Context

Ulrika Josefsson
University of Gothenburg, Sweden

ABSTRACT

The area of E-health development for patient-healthcare interaction has lately received significant attention by the health informatics community. Increasingly healthcare and information technology (IT) developers are proposed to take seriously the needs and preferences of the patients. This chapter explores the multifaceted E-patient context, in an effort to contribute to an increased patient-centeredness of this form of technology development. Patient-centeredness is captured in terms of personalization as an attempt to depart from patients' specific context to contribute to technology design and use. Using a qualitative approach, the chapter reports from 25 in-depth interviews performed with Swedish patients and representatives of patient associations. Six themes of the E-patient context derive from the findings (diagnosis, demographics, access, preferences, coping, and patient role). The results present a fine-grained picture of the E-patient context adding to previous approaches of personalization. The introductory discussion reflects on the themes in relation to their tentative implications for the development of patient-centered personalized E-health for patient-healthcare interaction.

INTRODUCTION

This chapter explores the multifaceted context of E-patients. The aim is to contribute to the ongoing discussion about patient-centered approaches in E-health development. In particular, the text concerns E-health solutions for online patient-healthcare interaction. This form of E-health involves a wide range of technological arrangements including online support for patients to learn about health and illness (Murero & Rice, 2006), or to get informed about the healthcare system and to make choices in healthcare (Ranerup, 2008). Other arrangements are E-health applications for contact with treating clinic (Leimeister & Krcmar, 2006), remote disease management and care assistance (Torp et al., 2008),

DOI: 10.4018/978-1-60566-030-1.ch021

or systems to manage online bookings (McCarthy et al., 2007), etc.

Increasingly the discussion about E-health for patient-healthcare interaction proposes healthcare providers and information technology (IT) developers to take seriously the needs and preferences of the patients (Demiris, 2006; Johnson & Ambrose, 2006; Murero & Rice, 2006). Patient-centeredness considering the wider picture of the patient situation is promoted contrasting previous organization- centered approaches. However, taking the patient perspective seriously requires a detailed picture of the patient context moving beyond general ideas of patients or narrow biomedical perspectives. Therefore, it is here proposed that patients' experiences of illness, their varying needs and preferences should become central components (see Lewin et al., 2001). More specifically, patient-centeredness is here discussed in terms of *personalization*. This involves an intention to depart from patients' specific context to guide technology design and use.

Regarding the emerging forms of E-health for patient-healthcare interaction, two main dimensions characterize personalization. The first dimension departs from individual activities online like patients' seeking of medical information (Adams et al., 2006; Kivits, 2006; Josefsson, 2006; Morahan-Martin, 2004) or seeking of social support (Barnett & Hwang, 2006; Johnson & Ambrose, 2006; Wright & Bell, 2003). In its simplest form, this means personalization when patients (on their own) by means of different sources bring together a personal set of information according to their preferences and needs. This form of personalization is recognized by patients being considered a homogeneous group sometimes grouped together using general terms such as "health seekers" or "healthcare consumers", etc. suggesting that patients have the same or similar needs and preferences.

The second dimension of personalization departs from healthcare providers' information needs in the care process. Here personalization generally refers to E-health applications collecting personal biomedical data for disease management and follow-ups. Often these systems are organization-centered taking a medical and/or a technical interest to gather data. As an example, Benaroia et al. (2007) developed an interactive system (accessed in the waiting room) for patients to enter medical history data prior to appointments. Other examples involve patients' home-based access to the EPR (Electronic Patient Record) (Bergmann et al., 2007; Schabetsberger et al., 2006). Lately a development of this form of personalization has been noticed taking an increased interest in the wider patient situation (Burkow et al., 2008; Leimeister & Krcmar, 2006; Rahimpoura et al., 2008).

Both dimensions of personalization are important to the E-health development in the patient-healthcare relationship. However, to take patient-centeredness seriously and to open up for the Internet to become a more effectively utilized healthcare resource, there is a need for complementing approaches of personalization focusing on the fine-grained picture of the E-patient context. Further, thoroughly considering the E-patient context is here believed to make an important step towards new forms of E-health solutions where patients can contribute as the valuable healthcare resource they truly are (Demiris, 2006; Johnson & Ambrose, 2006).

The following text focuses on chronically ill patients suffering from long-term health conditions such as MS (multiple sclerosis), diabetes, or cancer. This choice is motivated by chronic illnesses being conditions that often develop over time, involve complex information needs, and require recurrent contacts with healthcare providers and professionals (Maes et al., 1996). This makes chronically ill patients important to focus on as potential long-time users of different forms of E-health solutions. In addition, chronic conditions show increasing prevalence in society further stressing the importance to focus on this particular patient group (Wilson et al., 2004).

Furthermore, this chapter addresses patients' actual use of the Internet. This means the text focuses on patients who make use of online solutions to manage issues of their illness. However, this does not mean the participants necessarily are experts on Internet use for medical purposes but rather that they use the Internet in one way or another to deal with illness. Here, these patients are denoted as "E-patients". Focusing on chronically ill E-patients a qualitative approach is applied and the chapter reports from 25 in-depth interviews with Swedish E-patients and representatives of Swedish patient associations.

The chapter opens with an overview of the performed research study followed by a presentation of the results. Six dimensions of the E-patient context, derived from the findings, guide the presentation. Thereafter follows an introductory discussion on the tentative implications of the findings for increased personalization of E-health tools. Conclusions from the study close the chapter.

THE RESEARCH

Aiming to capture the E-patient context this chapter reports from qualitative research work. This involved the intention to search for a broad empirical basis. Therefore, the data were gathered from three related research studies (Table 1).

The purpose of the first study was to get an introduction to the field and to patients as adopters of the Internet for medical information. Therefore, the point of departure was Internet use by patient associations and their contacts with patients. The associations were selected from four lists on the Internet of Swedish patient associations. The associations' use of interactive online facilities together with the idea to involve a broad set of associations guided the selection. Seven associations were contacted each representing a certain diagnosis. The associations are non-profit organizations for patient support. The number of members and financial basis varies with the largest associations having about 50,000 members and the smaller 2,500 members. The larger associations are receiving grants while the smaller are depending on voluntary work. The interviewees serve as chairmen or official informers at the associations.

Table 1. The performed interview studies

Study/ Duration	Diagnosis		Question Areas
1. Representatives of patient associations/ February-March 2000	Diabetes, Hearing Disorders, Psoriasis, Parkinson's Disease	Tourette's Syndrome, Whiplash injury Rheumatism	Purpose of the Internet pages/ patient's use of the interactive facilities/ medical information needs/ opportunities and challenges of Internet use/ future use of the Internet
2. 10 patients running self-help groups on the Internet/ March-May 2002	Whiplash injury, Polycystic Ovarian Syndrome (PCO), Endometriosis, Multiple Sclerosis (MS)	Chronic Fatigue Syndrome, Chronic prostatitis, Fibromyalgia, Panic disorder, Thyroid disease	Patterns of use of the Internet for medical information/ pros and cons/ information-communication needs and demands/ disease specific needs
3. 8 patients using the Internet to cope with their disease/ November 2003-February 2004	Prostate cancer (PC)		The specifics of using the Internet for medical information about PC/ pros and cons/ information-communication needs and demands for patients with PC

In addition, they have personal experiences of the disease/injury and of being a patient using the Internet for medical information.

To get closer to patients and their perspective on Internet use the second study involved patients that share the experience of initiating self-help groups on the Internet. Contrasting patient associations, self-help groups are started and managed by single patients (the owner) and the groups are not formally organized. For instance, they have no chairman, administration, membership fee, or formal rules and regulations as do registered patient associations. In addition, the self-help groups rely on the owners' ability (technical as well as social) to run the groups. Also, the groups provide online activities only. The self-help groups offer a set of web pages containing medical information about a specific disease together with interactive facilities like discussion boards or e-mail lists. The purpose is mainly to provide patients with medical information and the possibility to get contact with fellow sufferers for exchange of experiences on a peer-to-peer basis. The idea of the second study was to capture "patients in action" on the Internet meaning that the interaction and communication activities performed were central. Therefore, the selection of patients as initiators and managers of self-help groups was guided by the interactive facilities provided and the "patient activity" that occurred in the self-help groups. In addition, to get a broad patient perspective the intention was to let the selected patients represent several diseases and health conditions. Using regular search engines 10 self-help groups[1] were selected using search words like "my illness", "my story", "patients tell", and "others' story" together with different diagnoses (from the lists of patient associations).

The third study consisted of interviews with patients suffering from prostate cancer (PC). The aim was to focus on patients with a shared diagnosis to provide a deeper example of the specifics of the situation of facing illness. In short, PC mostly strikes elderly men and more than 2/3 are over 70 years old. This type of cancer is the most common cancer among men. In Sweden, there are about 10,000 new cases each year (Swedish Cancer Society, 2008) and the American Cancer Society (2008) estimates that there will be about 186,320 new cases of PC in the U.S. in the year 2008. The incidence of PC makes the patients an important group to follow also when it comes to Internet use and the specific requirements for online support related to the diagnosis. Cooperating with the Department of Oncology at the Sahlgrenska University Hospital in Göteborg (Sweden), contacts with prostate cancer patients were established.

A semi-structured approach with a few specified question areas guided the interviews and they were performed as a conversation between the researcher and the respondents. The participants were guaranteed anonymity and the names used in the presentation of the data are fictitious. The interviews lasted for 40-75 minutes and were tape recorded and later transcribed.

The collected data were analyzed using an inductive process and the material was read and re-read in search for patterns and features (Hammersley & Atkinson, 1995). Two main stages describe the iterative process. The first stage involved the identification of general patterns and features running through the data. The second stage involved sifting out additional patterns and features on gradually more specific levels. This included both anticipated issues such as general views of patients' different preconditions to make use of the Internet for medical information and emerging issues such as patients' coping behavior related to Internet use. More particular, the analysis focused on regularities of the empirical data as well as on deviant cases in an effort to balance the characterizations (Silverman, 2005). Further, the process of analysis involved the search of patterns within each performed study as well as across the studies. In addition, the analysis was guided by the principal aim to provide significant examples of the phenomena rather than to quantify and to generalize from the collected material.

THE E-PATIENT CONTEXT

The following presents the results of the study and the presentation departs from six themes that derive from the findings. The themes are *diagnosis*, *demographics*, *access*, *preferences*, *coping*, and *patient role*.

Diagnosis

In this section, a number of examples from the empirical study illustrate the diversity of the overall patient situation related to particular diagnoses. The first concerns the severe fatal disease such as different forms of cancer. For instance, patients diagnosed with prostate cancer (PC) are informed that they suffer from a severe and sometimes life threatening disease. If the cancer is in such a stage that treatment is available, the patient is also informed that he is expected to be active in the process of choosing between different forms of treatments (like surgery or radiation therapy). Mike expresses the situation as follows:

"This [prostate cancer] is probably one of the most extreme diagnoses when it comes to information need. When you have been diagnosed, the doctor cannot say what treatment is the most appropriate one. He can very well say which one is directly inappropriate but medical science today cannot say what treatment is best for PC. This means that the patient – without any knowledge about the disease is supposed to decide what treatment he will have. Under such conditions there is an incredible need for information to make a choice so impossible not even the doctor can do it."

A second example is the chronic life long disease. Here Multiple sclerosis (MS) exemplifies this category although several of the diagnoses represented in the study could be used as well. In short, MS often progresses in phases and gradually leads to worsening of several of the central functions of the body often involving cognitive dysfunctions as well (National Multiple Sclerosis Society, 2007). Today, there is no cure for MS and the patient is reduced to take various disease-modifying drugs. Besides the need for social support and human understanding, this particular diagnosis involves information needs of how the development of the disease might turn out and how the patient can be supported in his or her everyday life. Maria was diagnosed with MS in 1996. She was then 26 years old:

"When I was diagnosed I tried to understand it all. I read everything. At the time there was little online information about MS directed towards patients."

Maria's needs for information and contact with others resulted in the online self-help group she is managing. Her web site contains a lot of medical information about MS and provides patients the possibility to interact using the discussion board, the e-mail list, or the chat. Some of the features on the web site mirror the specifics of the disease and related information need. Maria continues:

"In the beginning, I didn't know what could happen and the "symptom list" developed as I experienced my symptoms. It is the same with "treatments" which has been changed as new treatments have become available [...] On the e-mail list people get to know each other more and talk much about practical matters such as social insurance issues, wheel chairs etc. People ask for advice and so on. On the discussion board there is much more about symptoms. People write about there experiences and ask if others have experienced the same".

The third example concerns the specific requirements of stigmatizing diseases. Patients suffering from these types of diseases may benefit from approaching sensitive subjects using individual strategies. Kate running an online self-help group for patients with endometriosis reported about this:

"We noticed that there were many patients who didn't want to join the e-mail list and we realized that this was connected to the stigma of the disease...since endometriosis is related to the more intimate parts of the female body not many women cry out that they have got this disease. It is still shameful. That's why we left the discussion board open so they don't have to sign on to participate".

A fourth example is the type of illness characterized as "less-known" and/or "difficult-to-decide" disease such as chronic fatigue syndrome, fibromyalgia, or whiplash injury. Except the need for additional medical information and facts, the situation also demands for recognition and acknowledgement of personal experiences. Kim (chronic fatigue syndrome) highlights this:

"It is important to remember that many doctors say that this disease does not exist! They just say it is psychological. That's what you say when you don't know. So, for people with chronic fatigue syndrome it is extremely important to find others with the same strange disease".

A final example is diseases involving relatives as main (home) caregivers. The Tourette syndrome (TS) is one example. This disease is a neurological or "neurochemical" disorder characterized by tics, which are "involuntary, rapid, sudden movements or vocalizations that occur repeatedly in the same way" (National Tourette Syndrome Association, 2007). Since the age of onset is before 18, the parents get a central role in the care and treatment of the patient. The parent situation is central for the participating patient association for TS. In their work, they have noticed "*a desire for reliable information in Swedish about TS, specifically for parents of newly diagnosed children*" and that "*parents have a great demand for exchanging experiences with others in the same situation*".

Demographics

Exploring the E-patient context involves the consideration of characteristics such as age and sex. For example, in the study the representative of the association for hearing disorders expressed that "*in the contact with our members we have to consider that some are in their 70-ies not using computers*". Another example is patients with prostate cancer (PC). PC strikes in the ages around 70 and the patients are usually recognized as less frequent users of information technology and/or the Internet. Mike (67 years old) reflected on the use of the Internet by typical PC-patients:

"I get a lot of e-mails and often it is from someone asking about the disease for their father or grandfather. You see, often it is not the patient but the younger generations that use e-mail and Internet for information and communication".

Furthermore, PC strikes men only. However, the treatment processes often involve strains on the general quality of life (with problems such as incontinence and impotence) involving the patient's partner as well. This contributes to specific needs of information and Tom (PC) says:

"About sex and married life...well, it takes two to deal with this disease. It's the man AND his partner".

For women's diseases related to infertility problems (like endometriosis and PCO) there were similar concerns.

In addition, some of the patient associations have acknowledged the role of gender and age as important factors for information needs. For example, the association for Parkinson disease has initiated sub-groups called "Women with Parkinson" and "Young Parkinson". In addition, associations for diabetes, psoriasis, and hearing disorders have similar subgroups for younger patients.

Further, education is often recognized as a crucial variable regarding the extent of patients' use of the Internet. In the reported study, work and education indicated patients' abilities to seek information and to judge the information found. For example, George (PC) is a physician and he reported being offered special online services like "*a web portal for doctors where you can order coverage of articles in your field of interest*". Michael provides an additional example:

"*In my work as a distribution manager in an international company, I'm used to search for information on the Internet and I know that the Internet is a source of knowledge. So for me it was not a big deal to get online. I do that quite a lot at work so it was nothing new". (Michael, PC)*

Besides formal education the patients in the study emphasized the need of language skills, which were considered as crucial when using the Internet to deal with illness. Mike (PC) explained this:

"*The first thing is language skills. You have to know English...well, first you have to know how to handle a computer but then you really must have language skills in order to reach beyond Swedish web sites*".

Access

This dimension concerns access to technology as well as access to online medical information. Regarding technology, patients in the study emphasized the need of general knowledge about computer/IT use (as exemplified by the last quote in the previous section). Naturally, there is also a need of physical access in order to make use of the technology for health purposes. In the study, all of the interviewed patients had Internet access in their homes and none reported using publicly available computers. The interviewed representatives of the patient associations mirrored this situation of physical access although they could not provide a complete picture regarding all their members.

Regarding access to online medical information, patients have different knowledge and experiences of information seeking. In addition, to interpret and to choose among the results can be challenging. The majority of the study participants were Internet literate but some found it problematic to use. For instance, Mark (PC) who is familiar with the use of computers from his work at a bank office still find the medical information online difficult to manage. Therefore, he mainly visits web sites provided by his family or by healthcare even though he knows "*that there is a lot to learn out there but I am not really sure where to go or how to search*".

Finally, there is a social dimension of information access as illustrated by the following excerpts indicating the value of personal information sources like family, friends, and peers: "*I have a friend who has been through the same thing...so I contacted him and he gave me a lot of information and his own story*" (Mark, PC). "*I have two brothers suffering from PC and naturally we have talked a lot about this*" (Michael, PC). Finally, Linda (PCO) continues: "*The best thing is that I have got contact with so many other women. We have exchanged many common experiences. This has really meant a lot to me and I feel that I know so much more from the things I have learned from the others*".

Preferences

Even though the study reveals a general positive view on Internet use there was a common theme among the respondents that "*Internet should be a complementary information source*" (Eric, PC) mirroring the need for personal encounters as well: "*I want to meet and to talk to the doctor in person*" (Ian, PC).

Further, it should be mentioned that some of the patients were hesitant to use the technology for issues concerning their personal health although they had access to the technology and to the knowledge on how to use it.

In addition, ideas about E-patients' preferences for medical information and interaction is often based on the assumption that they are only acting on their own behalf. However, they may also be acting on behalf of a specific patient group, like when participating in online self-help groups. Mary, running a self-help group for whiplash injury illustrates this as follows:

"I think I have learned quite a lot about this [whiplash injury] so I wanted to try to help others as well...I know how bad you feel and this is a good way to help each other".

Coping

For several of the patients in the study the initial way to deal with the disease and the new life situation was to search for medical information. The information seeking seems to have a value in its own right. To search, read, and sometimes to translate and bring information together becomes a strategy to cope with the situation. Michael (PC) describes this as follows:

"I felt good to be out on the Internet. There was so much. I could surf, search, and go through stuff and print it out. I made copies to my own computer so I had several hundred pages about prostate cancer".

Another way to cope involved the search for medical information related to social support. In the study, this involved the search for human understanding and emotional support as well as information about how to manage the everyday life situation. In addition, the results of the study highlight two functions of social support as a coping strategy. The first function means a way to get actual help and support from fellow patients in the same or similar situations. This might occur in a direct way on discussion boards or on e-mail lists where "*they get information and support as well as e-mail friends*" (Lucy, running a self-help group for panic disorder). Additionally, it could be in indirect forms by patients reading others' stories. Sylvia, running a group for fibromyalgia expresses this:

"They look for contact with other patients. Some simply want to read. On the page "Others' stories", they can read about this [fibromyalgia] happening to other people as well. It is most reassuring since you might feel as the loneliest person in the world and you think that this happens only to me".

The second function of social support involves an opportunity for patients to facilitate others. This means that patients are being helped not only by getting support but also by helping others. In the study, Maria suffering from multiple sclerosis describes this as:

"...it makes me happy to be able to help others. For me... I am past the worst... but I know how hard it was and every time I get an e-mail from someone who thanks me it is most rewarding ... it is a very satisfying feeling."

Patient Role

The final theme concerns the E-patient context in a larger perspective. Patients acting on the Internet are influenced by the changing patient role increasingly considering patients as informed partners in the healthcare and in the treatment processes. For instance, the patient associations in the study picture Internet as an important arena supporting this development:

"Naturally we hope that our efforts on the Internet will provide for an increasing number of active members staying informed about healthcare, treat-

ments, research, and policies" (representative of the association for rheumatism).

Additionally, from a patient perspective John (PC) highlights online information and the changing patient role:

"Healthcare must make their web pages clearer and not so anonymous. I mean... healthcare stills see the patient as someone who is coming cap in hand ...the older generation still does... but the younger put new demands..."

DISCUSSION

For patients, personalization of E-health applications involves improved usability and increased possibilities for an effective disease management. For healthcare, it implies a more functional use of the Internet as an efficient healthcare resource. However, earlier work on personalization of E-health applications have mainly focused on patients' opportunities to make their *own* personalization of web resources, or on healthcare providers' possibilities for online collection of personal medical data. This means previous efforts pay limited attention to patients' actual context and their specific illness situation. As a complement, the reported study draws our attention to an additional dimension of personalization. The themes derived from the findings add to other ideas of personalization by providing a fine-grained picture capturing the complexity of the E-patient situation. Departing from the actual patient context the introductory discussion below outlines tentative implications for the development of personalized E-health applications for patient-healthcare interaction.

Supporting the Development of Personalized E-Health

The results provide several examples of differences of required scope of information due to the particular diagnosis. For instance, patients diagnosed with a severe, fatal, and/or chronic disease might demand access to detailed information to make adequate medical decisions as well as access to emotional and social support. For these patients, an online resource that can manage various in-

Table 2. Summary of the themes of the e-patient context in the study

Diagnosis	Severe fatal disease Chronic life-long disease Stigmatizing disease "Lesser Known"/ "difficult to decide" disease Disease involving relatives as main caregivers
Demographics	Age Sex Education
Access	Access to information; personal sources/ knowledge and experiences of medical information seeking online Access to technology; physical access/ knowledge and experiences of IT/Internet use
Preferences	Preferences and attitudes of Internet use in the patient—healthcare relationship Personal interest—group interest
Coping	Seeking online medical information Seeking social support Facilitating others
The patient role	Democratization of healthcare Increasing personal responsibility/ patients as partners in healthcare

formation needs related to different stages of the disease is particularly useful. In addition, patients suffering from stigmatizing conditions may need special attention involving the possibility to share their story with fellow sufferers in a secure way. In similar ways patients suffering from "less-known" or "difficult-to-decide" diseases may benefit from the possibility to get contact with others for recognition and relevant information. Finally, health conditions involving home caregivers put special demands on E-health solutions to meet their needs for contact with others.

When aiming for personalized E-health solutions, these examples highlight a need for a deeper analysis of the particular requirements related to diagnosis. In addition, it indicates the need for increased focus on *the development diagnose-specific E-health*, for more adequate patient support. A few such initiatives have been reported, like the work by Leimeister & Krcmar (2006) who designed and implemented a virtual community for breast cancer patients, involving facilities for medical information, contact with healthcare providers as well as possibilities for interaction with fellow sufferers. An additional example is the work by Herxheimer and colleagues[2] (2000). They developed a web site (www.dipex.org) to support patients with particular diagnoses. The web site mainly focuses on patients' illness stories. The stories on the web site are grouped according to diagnosis and are provided in text, audio, and/or as video recordings.

Besides disease-specific requirements, the demographical factors become important. For instance, elderly people may have other needs and demands of an E-health tool (Hisham & Edwards, 2007) than children and adolescents (Hansen et al., 2003). Similarly, gender has significance for needs and demands of online support (Boiano et al., 2007; Vermaas & Wijngaert, 2005). In addition, education influences patients' use of the Internet (c.f. Morahan-Martin, 2004; Wilson et al., 2004). In the study, participants using their professional competencies to utilize the Internet mirrored this. Together this implies that design of personalized E-health requires a thorough consideration of patients needs related to age, sex, education, and work, as well. Striving for the best possible fit between patients' needs and the E-health application, a promising way would be to *promote patient participation in the design process* (Leimeister & Krcmar, 2006).

Furthermore, the access to technology and to information is a part of the E-patient context. For instance, the patients in the study had physical access to the Internet in their homes although this is not yet the normal situation for the majority (Josefsson, 2006; Morahan-Martin, 2004). In addition, Henwood et al. (2003) argue having a computer at home is not equal to access as general computer and Internet literacy together with social structures affect this as well. Also, access is related to knowledge and experiences of online technology use which calls for further attention to issues of 'digital divide' and a deeper understanding of the meaning of access.

In association, there are social aspects of access that should be considered as well. This involves patients' needs of dialogues with fellow sufferers, friends, family, etc. further enhancing the perceived validity and utility of information. Finally, the study exemplifies patients' varying knowledge and experience of online information seeking and judging of the information.

Together, this implies a wide range of sociotechnical differences of the E-patient context related to access. To meet this diversity one strategy is to develop online tools offering educative functions to *support learning processes* about the Internet as an information resource as well as about medical issues to increase health literacy (c.f. Murero & Rice, 2006; Morahan-Martin, 2004).

In addition, the E-patient context involves preferences for technology use. The findings indicate that even if patients have the necessary resources to use the technology they might be hesitant when it comes to disease management. This implies that we should *take into consideration patients' different views on the role of the human encounter* in the patient-healthcare relationship, and avoid tendencies towards technological determinism (Henwood et al., 2003). This involves taking seriously patients requirements for complementary online resources rather than replacements of existing forms of patient-healthcare interaction. In addition, there are reasons to consider that E-patients sometimes act on the behalf of a group interest (besides their personal interest). In the study, patients' individual information seeking efforts and interests in online support groups exemplifies this. This indicates expectations on E-health to support patients' preferences for medical information, healthcare interaction, *as well as* for interaction with fellow sufferers.

An additional theme of the E-patient context concerns coping strategies. This involves the ways patients cope with the stressful and difficult life situation of facing illness (Snyder, 1999). In the study, patients' extensive online information seeking efforts is one example. The participants indicated that the search efforts are important per se when coping with illness and several of the interviewed patients referred to the information seeking as a form of "therapy". However, the Internet offers vast amount of information of varying quality aggravating patients' possibilities to find useful information (Morahan-Martin, 2004; Josefsson, 2006) to support their coping process. Although the forms of coping are individual and may take different expressions (Snyder, 1999) it is important for healthcare providers and IT developers to reflect upon how to support patients' coping processes as this may affect the overall outcome of care (Maes et al., 1996; Snyder, 1999). Therefore, considering patients' online information seeking as a part of the coping process can further fuel the discussions about the need of healthcare provided online guidance to reliable sources (c.f. Adams et al., 2006; Demiris, 2006; Henwood et al., 2003; Johnson & Ambrose, 2006; Morahan-Martin, 2004). Other ways of coping should be recognized as well. For instance, there are patients resisting additional information and/or just prefer to become informed in line with the development of the disease (Henwood et al., 2003).

Patients' seeking of social support is an additional form of coping exemplified in the study. This further highlights the value of patient-to-patient communication (Barnett & Hwang, 2006; Leimeister & Krcmar, 2006; Snyder, 1999; Wright & Bell, 2003). Among the participants, some seek direct contact with others through discussion boards or e-mail lists while others prefer to follow ongoing discussions without participation, or just to read others' stories. In addition, the patients in the study indicated that social support might have a second meaning as well. This refers to statements about the benefits of being able to facilitate others as well. That is, some patients appreciated the possibility to help others and at the same time help themselves.

Although, information seeking, getting social support, and to help others are well known forms of coping (c.f. Barnett & Hwang, 2006; Leimeister & Krcmar, 2006; Snyder, 1999; Wright & Bell, 2003) there are still few examples of healthcare provided E-health solutions involving facilities to support them. This indicates a need for additional work on how E-health applications can *support coping processes* to increase patients' possibilities for disease management and to enhance healthcare outcomes.

Finally, personalized E-health for patient-healthcare interaction involves the consideration of the changing patient role. In large, this relates to the ongoing process of democratization of the healthcare service and the development of "the informed patient" (Henwood et al., 2003; Kivits, 2006; Ranerup, 2008). The change process aims to strengthen the patients' position and to increase their possibility to participate and to take increased responsibility. This means, the patient role is moving towards an active consumer making his or her own healthcare decisions. However, this calls for a technology development that *supports patients to act according to the new (and still changing) patient role*. For instance, this could include offering online guidance to reliable information sources, possibilities for online dialogues with healthcare professionals (Johnson & Ambrose, 2006; Morahan-Martin, 2004), and/or tools supporting patients' access to healthcare (like information about available choices, etc.) (Ranerup, 2008). In addition, the technology development must take into consideration patients' different information needs and varying care processes and that patients have different preconditions to act the new patient role.

CONCLUSION

The aim of the chapter is to explore the E-patient context to support the ongoing development of personalized E-health for patient-healthcare interaction. The study focuses on patients' actual use of the Internet and six themes derive from the findings: *diagnosis*, *demographics*, *access*, *preferences*, *coping*, and *the patient role*. The themes introduce a fine-grained picture of the E-patient context adding to previous ideas of personalization. It is concluded that a deeper understanding of the context draws attention to areas that are important for healthcare providers and IT designers to consider and further analyze when striving for personalized E-health. The areas include: the development of diagnose-specific E-health, patient participation in the design process, the support of learning processes, the need to take into consideration patients' different views on the role of the human encounter, the support of coping processes, and the need to support patients to act according to the new (and still changing) patient role.

For analytical purposes, the themes are treated in separate although they are intertwined. In addition, aiming for a broad picture and an introductory discussion, many aspects are briefly mentioned though they demand a thorough analysis in their own right. In addition, other factors that due to the nature of the study have not been included might influence the picture (such as financial, technical, and cultural healthcare challenges related to the demands of personalized E-health tools). Finally, using a qualitative approach the presented study involves a limited number of interviews focusing on a specific type of patients and diagnoses. Therefore, complementary methods are required to further explore and understand the phenomenon and to expand on the issues of how to support the development of personalized, efficient, and truly useful E-health solutions in the patient-healthcare relationship.

REFERENCES

Adams, S., de Bont, A., & Berg, M. (2006). Looking for answers, constructing reliability: An exploration into how Dutch patients check web-based medical information. *International Journal of Medical Informatics*, *75*(1), 66–72. doi:10.1016/j.ijmedinf.2005.07.036

Alexander, J., & Ziebland, S. (2006). The web – bringing support and health information into the home: the communicative power of qualitative research. *International Journal of Nursing Studies*, *43*(4), 389–391. doi:10.1016/j.ijnurstu.2005.10.012

American Cancer Society (2008). Retrieved July 12, 2008, from http://www.cancer.org.

Barnett, G. A., & Hwang, J. M. (2006). The Use of the Internet for Health Information and Social Support: A Content Analysis of Online Breast Cancer Discussion Groups. In M. Murero and R. E. Rice (Eds.), *The Internet and Healthcare: Theory, Research, and Practice* (pp. 233-253). Mahwah, NJ: Lawrence Erlbaum Associates.

Benaroia, M., Elinson, R., & Zarnke, K. (2007). Patient-directed intelligent and interactive computer medical history-gathering systems: a utility and feasibility study in the emergency department. *International Journal of Medical Informatics*, *76*(4), 283–288. doi:10.1016/j.ijmedinf.2006.01.006

Bergmann, J., Bott, O. J., Pretschner, D. P., & Haux, R. (2007). An e-consent-based shared EHR system architecture for integrated healthcare networks. *International Journal of Medical Informatics*, *76*(2-3), 130–136. doi:10.1016/j.ijmedinf.2006.07.013

Boiano, S., Borda, A., Bowen, J. P., Faulkner, X., Gaia, G., & McDaid, S. (2007). Gender Issues in HCI Design for Web Access. In S. Kurniawan & P. Zaphiris (Eds.), *Advances in Universal Web Design and Evaluation: Research, Trends and Opportunities* (pp. 116-153). Hershey, PA: IGI Global.

Burkow, T., Vognild, L., Krogstad, T., Borch, N., Østengen, G., Bratvold, A., & Risberg, M. (2008). An Easy to Use and Affordable Home-Based Personal eHealth System for Chronic Disease Management Based on Free Open Source Software. *Studies in Health Technology and Informatics*, *136*, 83–88.

Ridge, D., Ziebland, S., Anderson, J., Williams, I., & Elford, J. (2007). Positive prevention: Contemporary issues facing HIV positive people negotiating sex in the UK. *Social Science & Medicine*, *65*, 755–770.doi:doi:10.1016/j.socscimed.2007.03.049

Demiris, G. (2006). The Diffusion of Virtual Communities in Health Care: Concepts and Challenges. *Patient Education and Counseling*, *62*, 178–188. doi:10.1016/j.pec.2005.10.003

Hammersley, M., & Atkinson, P. (1995). *Ethnography. Principles in practice* (2nd Ed.). London, Routledge.

Hansen, D. L., Derry, H. A., Resnick, P. J., & Richardson, C. R. (2003). Adolescents Searching for Health Information on the Internet: An Observational Study. *Journal of Medical Internet Research*, *5*(4), e25. doi:10.2196/jmir.5.4.e25

Henwood, F., Wyatt, S., Hart, A., & Smith, J. (2003). Ignorance is bliss sometimes: constraints on the emergence of the "informed patient" in the changing landscape of health information. *Sociology of Health & Illness*, *25*(6), 589–607. doi:10.1111/1467-9566.00360

Herxheimer, A., McPherson, A., Miller, R., Shepperd, S., Yaphe, J., & Ziebland, S. (2000). Database of patients' experiences (DIPEx): a multi-media approach to sharing experiences and information. *Lancet*, *355*(9214), 1540–1543. doi:10.1016/S0140-6736(00)02174-7

Hisham, S., & Edwards, A. D. N. (2007). Aging and its Implications for Elderly Web Experience. In S. Kurniawan & P. Zaphiris (Eds.) *Advances in Universal Web Design and Evaluation: Research, Trends and Opportunities* (pp. 97-114). Hershey, PA: IGI Global.

Johnson, G. J., & Ambrose, P. J. (2006). Neo-Tribes: The Power and Potential of Online Communities in Health Care. *Communications of the ACM*, *49*(1), 107–113. doi:10.1145/1107458.1107463

Josefsson, U. (2006). Patients' Online Information Seeking Behavior. In M. Murero and R. E. Rice (Eds.), *The Internet and Healthcare: Theory, Research, and Practice* (pp. 127-147). Mahwah, NJ: Lawrence Erlbaum Associates.

Kivits, J. (2006). Informed Patients and the Internet. *Journal of Health Psychology*, *11*(2), 269–282. doi:10.1177/1359105306061186

Leimeister, J. M., & Krcmar, H. (2006). Designing and Implementing Virtual Patient Support Communities: A German Case Study. In M. Murero and R. E. Rice (Eds.), *The Internet and Healthcare: Theory, Research, and Practice* (pp. 255-276). Mahwah, NJ: Lawrence Erlbaum Associates.

Lewin, S. A., Skea, Z. C., Entwistle, V., Zwarenstein, M., & Dick, J. (2001). Interventions for providers to promote a patient-centered approach in clinical consultations [Review]. *Cochrane Database of Systematic Reviews (Online : Update Software)*, 4.

Maes, S., Leventhal, H., & de Ridder, D. T. D. (1996). Coping with Chronic Diseases. In M. Zeidner and S. E. Norman (Eds.), *Handbook of Coping. Theory, Research, Applications* (pp. 221-251). New York: John Wiley & Sons, Inc.

McCarthy, J., Riaz, K., & Nolan, Y. (2007). An Interactive Outpatient Reminder System. *The Internet Journal of Medical Informatics*, 3(1). Retrieved June 18, 2008, from http://www.ispub.com/ostia/index.php?xmlFilePath=journals/ijmi/vol3n1/outpatient.xml

Morahan-Martin, J. M. (2004). How Internet users find, evaluate, and use online health information: A cross-cultural review. *Cyberpsychology & Behavior*, *7*(5), 497–510.

Murero, M., & Rice, E. R. (Eds.). (2006). *The Internet and Healthcare: Theory, Research, and Practice*. Mahwah, NJ: Lawrence Erlbaum Associates.

National Multiple Sclerosis Society (2007). Retrieved November 20, 2007, from http://www.nmss.org

National Tourette Syndrome Association (2007). Retrieved November 20, 2007, from http://www.tsa-usa.org

Rahimpour, M., Lovella, N. H., Branko, G. C., & McCormick, J. (2008). Patients' perceptions of a home telecare system. *International Journal of Medical Informatics*, *77*(7), 486–498. doi:10.1016/j.ijmedinf.2007.10.006

Ranerup, A. (2008). In What Ways does Web Technology Support the Individual in Choice Reforms in Healthcare? *International Journal of Healthcare Information Systems and Informatics*, *3*(2), 48–68.

Schabetsberger, T., Ammenwerth, E., Breu, R., Hoerbst, A., Goebel, G., & Penz, R. (2006). E-health approach to link-up actors in the health care system of Austria. *Studies in Health Technology and Informatics*, *124*, 415–420.

Silverman, D. (2005). *Doing Qualitative Research*, (2nd Ed.). London: Sage Publications.

Snyder, C. R. (Ed.). (1999). *Coping – The psychology of what works*. New York: Oxford University Press.

Swedish Cancer Society (2008). Retrieved July 12, 2008, from http://www.cancerfonden.se.

Torp, S., Hanson, E., Hauge, S., & Magnusson, L. (2008). A pilot study of how information and communication technology may contribute to health promotion among elderly spousal carers in Norway. *Health & Social Care in the Community*, *16*(1), 75–85.

Vermaas, K., & Wijngaert, L. (2005). Seeking Health Information on the Internet. Different genders, different uses, different risks. In *Proceedings of 13th European Conference on Information Systems*, May 26-28, 2005, Regensburg, Germany.

Wilson, P., Leitner, C., & Moussalli, A. (2004). Mapping the Potential of eHealth: Empowering the Citizen through eHealth Tools and Services. Paper presented at the eHealth Conference, Cork, Ireland, 5-6 May, 2004, European Institute of Public Administration, Maastricht, the Netherlands.

Wright, K. B., & Bell, S. B. (2003). Health-related Support Groups on the Internet: Linking Empirical Findings to Social Support and Computer-mediated Communication Theory. *Journal of Health Psychology*, *8*(1), 39–54. doi:10.1177/1359105303008001429

Ziebland, S. (2004). The importance of being expert: the quest for cancer information on the Internet. *Social Science & Medicine*, *59*(9), 1783–1793. doi:10.1016/j.socscimed.2004.02.019

KEY TERMS AND DEFINITIONS

Chronic: Refers to long-term or life-long health conditions.

E-health: Refers to different forms of online support for disease management and patient-healthcare provider communication.

E-patients: Patients who make use of online solutions to manage issues of their illness.

Illness: Refers to the larger situation of suffering from a particular disease involving medical, social, practical, and psychological aspects.

Patient: Refers to a person diagnosed with a particular disease having recurrent contacts with the treating clinic or doctor.

Patient-centered: Refers to an extended view of patients (beyond the biomedical perspective) with their personal experiences of illness, needs, and preferences for care as central components (Lewin et al. 2001).

Personalization: The idea to depart from the patient's specific context to guide technology design and use.

ENDNOTES

1. For the selection of the self-help groups, it is important to keep in mind that Sweden has a limited self-help tradition. At the time of the study, no lists or registers or the like of self-help groups exists.
2. Additional academic work about the Internet site "Dipex.org" is published in e.g. Damien et al (2007), Alexander & Ziebland (2006), and Ziebland (2004).

Chapter 22
Adoption of Mobile Technology by Public Healthcare Doctors:
A Developing Country Perspective

Nesaar Banderker
University of Cape Town, South Africa

Jean-Paul Van Belle
University of Cape Town, South Africa

ABSTRACT

Doctors working in the South African public healthcare sector are faced with the unique resource constraints prevalent in a developing country. Mobile information and communication technologies (ICTs) hold the promise of improving the quality of healthcare, but this potential can only be unlocked if individuals decide to adopt the new technologies. Understanding the factors that influence the doctor's adoption of a technology is therefore vital. This chapter reports on an investigation into the factors influencing the adoption of mobile devices by doctors in the public healthcare sector in the Western Cape, South Africa. The research methodology was shaped by qualitative enquiry and described through thematic analysis. The authors confirmed the key adoption factors identified in prior research: job relevance, usefulness, perceived user resources and device characteristics. However, some additional adoption factors were uncovered in this research, namely patient influence, support structures from national government and hospital administration, and unease in respect of malpractice legal suits.

BACKGROUND

Healthcare in South Africa

Healthcare is a key component of South African society, socially and economically (Chiasson *et al* 2004). Total healthcare spending in South Africa is 8.7% of GDP which is substantially above the norm of 5% recommended for developing countries by the WHO (Chetty, 2007). The *public* healthcare budget alone totalled R47.8 billion (approximately US$ 6.7 billion) in 2006, representing 4.27% of GDP. This represents a substantial growth compared with 1995 when it stood at only 1.84% of GDP. However, despite these efforts by the new democratically elected government, huge inequalities remain. The budget of the private sector, which services less than 8 million people, exceeds that of the public sector servicing

DOI: 10.4018/978-1-60566-030-1.ch022

38 million (Chetty, 2007). Much of this remains a legacy of the pre-1994 apartheid era inequalities institutionalised through labour laws and highly unequal provision of services for different racial groups (Department of Health, 2004). There is still a movement of skilled resources from areas of poverty and low socio-economic development to more wealthy areas. Doctors who have recently qualified and completed their compulsory two years working for the public healthcare sector are either moving into private practice or leaving South Africa to work in other countries (Padarath *et al* 2003). This results in a scarcity of skilled clinical resources in the public healthcare sector.

Although doctors working in the public healthcare sector are highly skilled, their available time is preciously sliced to try and diagnose and care for as many patients in a day as is possible. 80 to 85% of the South African population has access to public healthcare facilities only (Chetty, 2007). A doctor in the public day hospital environment is expected to diagnose, treat and manage about 40 patients during an 8–hour shift. This means that the doctor spends an average of only 12 minutes with each patient. Doctors in public healthcare also have to work extremely long shifts of sometimes more than 30 hours. Due to this extreme pressure, doctors can easily make an incorrect diagnosis or prescribe the incorrect patient management routine. Patients attending these public hospitals have to wait in long queues to be seen by the doctor. When they finally see the doctor, the visit is rushed. A full examination of the patient is not always possible and this could result in inadequate care of the patient.

ICTs offer tremendous potential in supporting the public healthcare function in the South African society. Although administrative healthcare information systems have been implemented, the shift to systems that support the clinical work performed by healthcare professionals directly has been slow to take off (Andersen 1997). Better ICT support would, in turn, enable doctors to facilitate the provision of high quality, better informed and cost-effective public healthcare to all the citizens of South Africa.

Mobile Technologies in Healthcare

Mobile technologies can bring immense benefits to the healthcare environment (Varshney 2006), because it is so information intensive (Li, Chang, Hung & Fu 2005). Doctors do most of their work at the point of care, which is the patient. This means that they move around between wards, outpatient clinics, diagnostic and therapeutic departments and operating theatres. This movement, together with the fact that most South African public hospitals usually only have one central computer terminal per ward, makes it extremely difficult to service all the needs of the doctor. The use of ICTs in support of this point of care activity of the doctor is what is relevant to this research. Mobile device technologies are quite suitable for supporting the doctor at the point of care. They are small, lightweight, can be carried around with the doctor and usually come with some form of networking protocol built into the device (Porn & Patrick 2002). Mobile devices are also becoming more affordable and offer more processing power and storage capabilities (Varshney 2006). Mobile technology ranges from cellular telephones, pagers and PDAs, to very sophisticated tablet computers. Key benefits, as summarized from a large number of studies, include a reduction in medical errors, time savings, better quality care and higher productivity (Lu, Xiao, Sears & Jacko 2005).

A number of studies have looked at adoption of mobile computing devices. An excellent, systematic analysis of surveys of healthcare providers' PDA adoption is given by Garritty & Emam (2006) who found adoption rates in developed countries to vary between 45% and 85%. For instance, in a longitudinal study of mobile technology 33% of Canadian doctors reported use of a mobile device in their clinical practice in 2003, up from 19% in 2001 and 28% 2002 (Martin 2003). By contrast, a similar study at selected healthcare institutions in Florida revealed that as many as 95% of the respondents to the survey owned a mobile computing device (Joy & Benrubi 2004). The study also showed a pattern of perceived benefit for using the devices to maintain procedural statistic logs, pharmacology reference manuals and personal clinical protocols; but respondents did not perceive a massive time saving. Both studies also show quite a sharp increase in mobile device technology adoption by doctors.

Porn and Patrick (2002) and Hameed (2003) identify a number of healthcare applications that could be run successfully on a mobile device:

- **E-prescription:** This allows doctors to access basic patient information and check formulary compliance before writing the prescription. Potentially harmful drug interactions can be determined and often a patient's personal medication history is available. Prescriptions can be printed or transmitted directly to a pharmacy. The main benefits are a reduction in medication errors and less calls from pharmacies due to illegible handwriting (Berkowitz, 2002).
- **Charge capture:** This application allows a doctor to view schedules, capture patient charges and access or update patient information all at the point of care.
- **Order entry:** Applications to order certain tests could be scheduled, delivered to a central processing unit and acted upon. This will reduce errors due to misplacement of application forms.
- **Test result reporting:** The results of the tests can be delivered directly to the mobile device. This will free doctors from having to refer to a specific PC workstation to retrieve test results.
- **Medical information:** Access to the latest medication formulary, disease description, symptoms and treatment as well as access to clinical procedures can be provided on a mobile device.

More technical descriptions of how mobile technologies can work in healthcare sector can be found in numerous sources, e.g. (Varshney 2006)

Adoption Models and Healthcare

In order to realise the full potential and promise of healthcare information systems, technologies and applications, a better understanding of the organisational context as well as people and social issues is required. The adoption of mobile technologies in the healthcare sector involves both an organisational and an individual aspect. The organisational context or motivational factors that drive mobile ICT adoption is a relatively under-researched field; refer to Khoumbati & Themistocleous (2006) for an overview of relevant research and a comprehensive framework. The focus in this research is on the *individual factors* that drive mobile technology adoption in healthcare, with particularly focus on the doctors.

Because explaining human behaviour in all its complexity is quite a daunting task, a variety of models have been developed to explain and predict user behaviours and intentions. The most widely used of these models are the diffusion of innovation (DOI) theory published by Rogers (1995), the theory of reasoned action (TRA) (Ajzen & Fishbein 1980), the theory of planned behaviour (TPB) (Ajzen 1991) and the technology acceptance model (TAM) (Davis 1989). These models have been well tested, validated and proven to be reliable when used in the evaluation of user acceptance in studies of business organisations, corporations and even students. However, there is less research evaluating technology adoption using TPB, TRA, DOI within a healthcare context.

In validating TAM and its extensions, researchers have determined some key factors that are of significance for use in general technology adoption models. These include perceived ease of use, perceived usefulness, perceived user resources, voluntariness, experience, subjective norm, image and computer self-efficacy. However, doctors are professionals who are particularly highly skilled, knowledgeable, autonomous and pragmatic decision makers. This impacts on the applicability of a number of constructs and causes some of the models not to behave in the way determined by prior research in other contexts. For instance, Hu & Chau & Tam (1999) found that the original TAM did not correlate well with doctor's intentions to use a new technology. When reviewing literature on the adoption of healthcare technologies by medical professionals the majority of the studies found apply to general healthcare systems such as telemedicine, internet health and clinical systems (Chau & Hu 2002, Chismar & Patton 2003, Horan *et. al.* 2004) while some studies were found that applied specifically to mobile healthcare (Wu, Wang & Lin 2005, Harkke 2005, Li *et al* 2005, Lu *et al* 2005, Varshney 2006, Wu, Wang & Lin 2007).

Overall, however, researchers find the TAM-inspired models to be a successful approach to explaining the adoption of mobile technologies in the healthcare sector, with Wu *et al* (2007) purporting to be able to explain up to 70% of the variance in behavioural intention to use mobile healthcare systems. These studies found the following factors to be of relevance when researching adoption in a healthcare setting:

- **Perceived usefulness/Job relevance:** A new technology needs to be useful to its user. Usefulness is defined as causing an increase in the doctor's productivity by being relevant to the doctor.
- **Perceived user resources:** The extent to which an individual believes that they have the personal and organisational support to use the device. This was validated by Horan *et al* (2004) and Lu *et al* (2005) whose research discovered that workplace compatibility played a more important role in predicting user intentions than the current TAM construct of perceived ease of use.
- **Subjective norm:** People who are close to the doctor could influence the doctor by their opinions of whether the device should be used or not.
- **Image:** Doctors will perceive the use of a mobile technology device as enhancing their status within their working environment. This was validated by Succi and Walter (1999) who state that doctors will more likely be influenced by the impact of the use of the new technology on their professional status. Further research has contested the idea that social processes of subjective norm and image would influence the decision to adopt. This is seen to be a result of the pragmatic nature of doctors in decision making, as well as a reliance on their own assessment rather than that of others. However, in the context of South Africa where being a medical doctor is often seen as a status symbol the two factors of subjective norm and image will be retained to ascertain whether they would play a positively influencing role.
- **Task/technology fit:** A study by Chau & Hu (2002), added this factor – defined as alignment with current work practices – to TAM. It was thought that doctors would more likely adopt a new technology if it aligned closely with their current work practices.
- **Result demonstrability:** The technology should visibly improve the doctor's quality of care provided and enhance his effectiveness thus improving the quality of the doctor's work

Furthermore, in the evaluation of TAM2 (Venkatesh & Davis 2000) by Chismar and Patton (2003), it was found that the construct of perceived ease of use showed an insignificant effect when used to predict intention of doctors. It has also been found that for technologies that are not mandated for use by the healthcare institutions,

Figure 1. Significant influencing factors

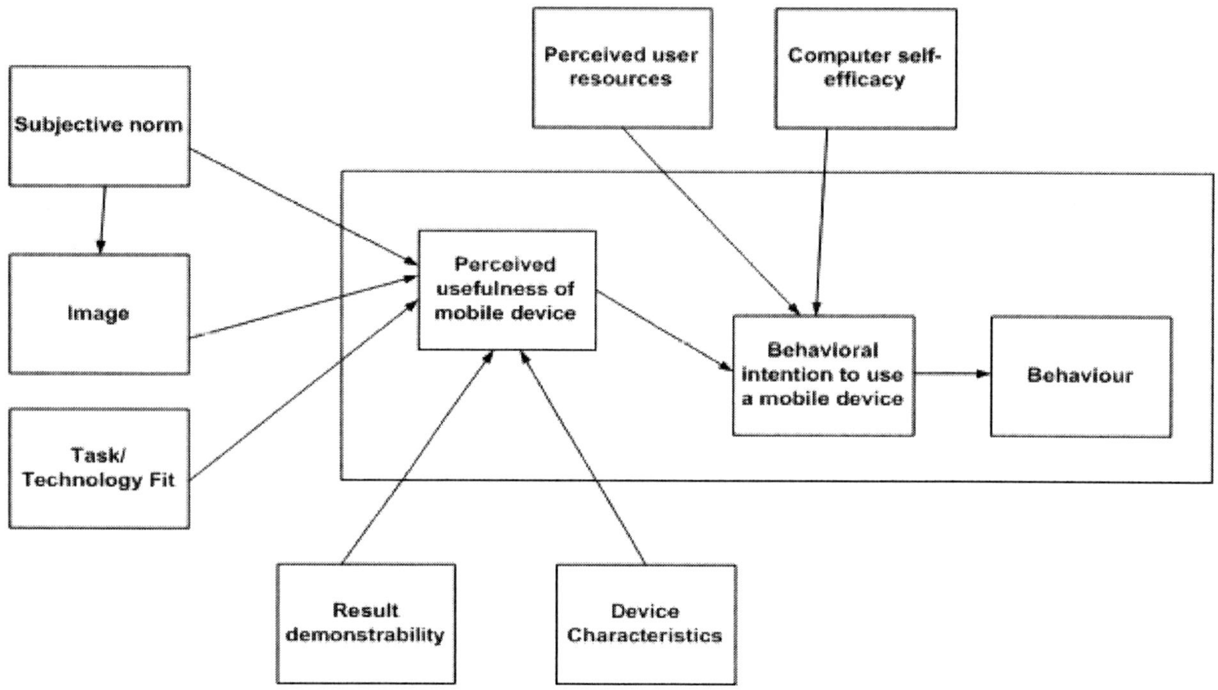

the construct of voluntariness can be removed from the model. In studies of a new technology the construct of experience can also be removed, since it was intended to measure the adoption of existing technologies. Due to the high intellectual and cognitive capacity of doctors, they appear to understand new technologies quicker. Doctors are therefore individuals with a high level of self-efficacy. This makes a good argument for the removal of the computer self-efficacy construct from the model. However, due to mobile technologies being relatively new to the South African market and not being widely diffused this factor will be included in the model developed.

The above research reduces the significant factors in the context of doctors' intention to use a mobile technology device to subjective norm, image, task/technology fit, result demonstrability, perceived user resources, computer self-efficacy and the technology device characteristics. These factors are summarized graphically in Figure 1. These factors form the starting point for the research interviews

RESEARCH OBJECTIVE

Despite the purported advantages of mobile technology there is a distinct lack of adoption of this technology in the public healthcare sector in developing countries in general, and South Africa in particular. The public healthcare sector is recognized as having lagged behind other South African industries, such as the financial sector, in the use and adoption of new information technologies (Bower 2005). ICTs encompass a wide range of technologies.

This research hopes to provide a better view as to *what* the significant factors influencing the adoption of innovative mobile technology solutions by public healthcare doctors to support them in their daily clinical activity are. More specifically, the objective of this research is to identify key factors that hinder or assist doctors' adoption of mobile technologies in healthcare.

Identifying these significant factors of influence will hopefully also provide an *insight* into how ICT solutions for healthcare should be developed, marketed, implemented and who the key stakeholders in the adoption process are. This research is particularly relevant because it cannot be assumed that research conducted in developed world contexts is applicable to developing countries.

RESEARCH METHODOLOGY

The factors identified in the literature (see Figure 1) forms the basis for the framework that could be tested against public healthcare doctors. This section addresses the problems of *who* to test the framework against and *how* it will be tested.

Strategy

This research follows an exploratory qualitative research design strategy. It is exploratory since it is not directly involved with hypothesis testing and theory evaluation. It is more directly involved with laying a basic descriptive foundation to explain and understand the possible factors influencing adoption of a mobile technology device by doctors. A qualitative study was chosen over a quantitative one since the former allows for a better understanding of the people, and the social and cultural context in which the technology adoption can occur. Also, richer data sets from which factors influencing the possible adoption of mobile technologies can be obtained by discourse between people instead of having them complete a questionnaire. We believe that our specific qualitative approach complements the quantitative approach adopted by (Wu *et al* 2007) who summarized a large number of quantitative adoption studies, and the evidence/opinion-based qualitative approach of (Lu *et al* 2005) into adoption factors.

Site Selection and Sampling

The study was conducted in the two largest public healthcare facilities in Cape Town, namely the Groote Schuur Hospital (widely known because of the first heart transplant) and Tygerberg Hospital. These hospital are directly associated with the University of Cape Town and the University of Stellenbosch respectively. They are of similar size, offer very similar services, have similar administrative processes and are analogous to the rest of South Africa's academic public hospitals.

Due to time, resource and financial constraints as well as the limited time availability of doctors, a convenience sampling method was used. Possible doctors were identified by two doctors acting as the researcher's contacts in the hospitals and were selected based on their willingness to take part in the research since all participation was voluntary. Although a convenience sample allowed the researcher to skirt many of the resource issues mentioned, this did come at the expense of possibly compromising the generalisability and representativeness (Pare 2004). In total, twelve doctors were interviewed. The interview sample was made up of doctors from each of the South African racial profiles.

Data Collection

Participant interviews were used as the primary source of gathering data. The interviews were semi-structured, with set questions as well as open-ended questions. Basic demographic data was also collected from the doctors. Key questions were developed around all the significant factors of influence identified during the literature review (Figure 1 above) with additional questions being derived from Chismar and Patton (2003). Questions were not necessarily asked in the order they were set out since the conversation dictated which question would be asked next. The complete list of the questions is available from the authors. A checklist was kept during the interview to ensure that all questions were asked. Interaction and discussion usually led to further follow-up questions of both explanatory and exploratory nature (Ritchie & Lewis 2003).

The interview was recorded on an audio recording device, freeing up the interviewer to more closely observe the interviewee and possibly gain some further insight from the visual clues provided by the interviewee. A protocol for conducting the interview was established. This ensured that each interview process was consistent. It also helped ensure that standard items like obtaining consent, providing the interviewee with basic information about the research and informing them that the interview would be recorded, would not be forgotten.

As a departure point for starting the discussion, pictures of other mobile technology devices were shown to the interviewees. In addition, the interviewees were also shown a physical Nokia 9300 with a demonstration of some of the medical software obtained for the device, namely a drug formulary program, a fracture analysis program and a nutrition analysis program.

Data Analysis

There are many methods of analysis suggested for the interpretation of the data collected. These include Hermeneutics (Klein & Myers 1999), Grounded Theory (Sarker & Wells 2003), Semiotics – which includes content analysis, conversation analysis and discourse analysis – and thematic analysis (Ritchie & Lewis 2003). However, these modes of analysis work to develop theory in most cases and fit closely with the interpretive paradigm (Fitzgerald & Howcroft 1998). A thematic analysis of the textual data was performed, as recommended by Ritchie and Lewis (2003).

The analysis process that was followed can be described as follows:

- The recorded data from the interviews was listened to. While listening to the recording, reflective remarks about the interview and the data from the interview were made. This allowed for the visualization of the researcher's perceptions and ideas (Miles & Huberman 1994).
- A coding scheme that is consistent with the theoretical propositions identified during the literature review was then developed (Hammersley & Atkinson 1983). Additional codes were created for ideas presented by the interviewee that did not fit into the original coding scheme.
- The coding scheme was used to allow the segmentation of the data into units that are easily mapped to the theoretical propositions identified during the literature review. The scheme also allows for easier organization and retrieval of the data.
- These codes were then grouped together in logical units which formed higher order categories.
- For these categories a response from each interviewee was mapped. This formed the basis of a thematic chart. The visual nature of a thematic chart helped in discovering connections between coded segments (Miles & Huberman 1994).
- From this thematic chart, themes were developed by checking the occurrence of a certain idea and the language used by the interviewee.
- These themes were then used to answer the objectives of the study.

FINDINGS AND DISCUSSION

The results obtained by the analysis of the interview data as well as a discussion of these results are presented together in order to maintain a logical flow of information. Since the data analysis was done using a thematic analysis, the findings will be presented in the themes identified. These themes can also be referred to as the adoption factors identified.

Postulated Themes

Perceived Usefulness of a Mobile Device

The doctors agreed unanimously that the mobile technology device would be very useful and relevant to them. Two of the older doctors, however, could only conceptualise the device being useful by providing information to them. This use as an information providing tool was confirmed when a doctor emphatically stated that he "*currently carr[ies] 2 to 3 management reference books around with me. I know that there is an electronic version of all 3 books available for the iPaq.*"

The younger doctors could conceptualise many other exciting uses for the device. A few of the solutions that really excited the doctors are:

- Making paper records of patients obsolete: "*Such a device could make the need for paper records obsolete. All patient information could be stored electronically and accessed from this device and not from the only PC assigned to an entire ward. This will make missing folders and folders not containing up-to-date patient information a thing of the past.*"
- Not having to struggle with reading illegible notes and other information: "*Doctors handwriting is generally quite poor and illegible. This device could make incorrect prescriptions due to bad writing a thing of the past.*"
- Mobility: "*Patient information could be delivered to such a device when you walk into the ward. This would alleviate the need to consult the slow, outdated PC assigned to the floor.*"
- As a decision support tool: "*I will have the latest available patient management information and with this can ensure that the patient is treated correctly.*"

However the doctors did strongly indicate that the device would never be able to replace their skill and training and actually make the decision for them.

Most of the imagined uses envisaged by the doctors are a reality in more developed countries. Examples of mobile electronic patient record systems exist (Turisco & Case 2001). E-prescriptions systems which make the "illegible" handwriting problem of doctors obsolete also exist (Berkowitz 2002). The transmission of real-time patient information using mobile devices and telecommunication infrastructure has been implemented in Sweden and the Netherlands (Wu, Wang & Lin 2005). There are also examples of medical reference material on mobile devices being useful in certain situations (Harkke 2005).

Social Influences

A strong statement *against* the effect of social influences guiding a doctor's decision to use a mobile technology device was made. One of the older doctors hesitated when answering the questions regarding status. When clarifying her hesitation she stated: "*Indian doctors, especially the older ones, were usually recommended by their parents to become a doctor.*" This was usually for the prestige that came with being able to say that one's child is a doctor as well as the desire to have their children "be better off than the parents". This image of the medical profession being one of status was hard to totally avoid for an Indian doctor. The remainder of the doctors did not agree with the statement that status, image or peer influence will have some bearing on their decision to use the device. "*I would not at all be influenced to use this device by my peers nor would I think of it as increasing my status.*"

There was one softly conflicting statement of "*...as more doctors start using these devices you will become the odd one out for not using one...*" but when explored further it developed into the fact that doctors would only use the device when found to be useful and relevant to their daily clinical activity: "*If I see a colleague using such a device and he is able to provide better care to his patients I would most definitely be influenced to get one.*"

Perceived User Resources

When asking the interviewees questions around perceived user resources, they were quite emphatic that they did not believe they would obtain support for the use of a mobile technology device from within the public healthcare environment. There was a feeling of hopelessness when talking about the public hospitals IT support structures. One aspect of the lack of support related to the level of skills: "*I believe that the hospital IT department is not highly skilled and would take some time to adjust to support a more innovative device like this Nokia 9300.*" It was also felt that the hospital IT department was under-resourced and would not be able to cope with the added support required for the mobile technology device: "*They barely cope with just running the daily activities of the hospital. How will they cope with the added support required for this device?*"

Even though doctors felt that public hospitals did not have the resources to support the use of such a device, they would not be negatively influenced by this: "*The hospital might not support the device but that still will not stop me from using it.*"

Computer Self-Efficacy

All the doctors interviewed considered themselves to be highly skilled professionals who had daily interaction with computers. "*I have an interaction with computers throughout my working day.*" The fact that 10 of the 12 doctors did not have much prior experience with mobile technology devices did not scare them away from using the device: "*As a highly skilled professional I think I am capable of learning to use a new technology from a user manual.*"

Device Characteristics

Ten doctors expressed an initial concern that the limited screen size of the handheld devices might make it less useful: "*Perhaps the screen on this device would not be able display information very legibly*" and "*I don't think a web page will display very nice on such a small screen*". However, some were quite surprised at the amount of information displayed with the drug formulary program on the Nokia 9300: "*That displays information in a very comprehensive manner and with one click of page down you can see the rest of the information.*"

Both loss and theft of the device was also a major consideration for the doctors. "*I think such a device would easily be able to get feet.*" However, the two doctors who were high adopters of a mobile technology device said that doctors would have to learn to take care of the device in a similar manner in which they care for their stethoscopes.

The software demonstrated to the doctors was accepted with great enthusiasm. "*That could most definitely help me as a look up when I don't know what the drug does*" and "*You could look up side effects to make certain there will be no complications for the patient.*" The doctors were enthusiastic that the technology would be able to help them deliver better quality care. This is supported by the uses they conceptualised for the device. One of the doctors working in an emergency trauma unit, where rapid diagnosis and accurate patient management are essential, was sure that a mobile device could further ensure that patient management was in line with the diagnosis as well as being the most effective one and aiding in the fight for the patient's life.

Emerging Themes

A number of additional themes were identified during the analysis of the interview data. They do not form part of the original significant factors of influence identified during the literature review and appear to be specific to the healthcare environment.

Patient Influence

An addition to the social influences theme that was not part of the original significant factors was the patients' perceptions of the doctor if they should see the doctor using a mobile technology device. When talking about a patient's perception of the doctor if the patient should see the doctor using a mobile technology device to reference information from, there was a majority consensus that the patient's perception would *not* negatively influence their decision to use the device. This was conveyed strongly through statements like: "*It will help me improve the care and management provided to the patient and result in a much improved patient outcome*"; "*I will not mind at all to use the device to look up information in front of a patient*" or "*Patients should understand or be educated that having the latest information available as a reference tool will be of great benefit to them at the end of the day*".

However, two doctors did say that they would be hesitant to use the device while sitting with the patient: "*The patients might question my competence if they see me looking up information in front of them with this device. The same goes for looking up information from a book.*" However, that would not stop them from using the mobile device to look up information, just that they would not do it while the patient was sitting with them. "*I would most definitely use it when not in front of a patient*" or "*If I needed to look up information then and there I would go to another room and then come back.*"

By contrast, it was also mentioned by one of them that patients are starting to move away from the idea that a doctor should know everything. They are generally starting to ask more questions about the conditions they are diagnosed with. He did say that a mobile device might be useful in explaining conditions graphically to patients, as they would more readily be able to understand a picture than a wordy explanation. "*When patients ask questions about their medical condition, we could perhaps provide a clearer explanation to patients using such a device to display information graphically.*"

Malpractice Legal Suit

Another social influence factor was identified by the pattern of doctors wanting to use the mobile technology device as an information and decision support tool, reflecting the growing unease amongst the doctors of the increasing trend of malpractice legal suits being brought against doctors. This device could help doctors prevent such a situation from arising: "*This will help in action that could be taken against the doctor for incorrect treatment and management.*" If such a device could keep a history of the patient and all decisions made regarding diagnosis and treatment, it could help defend the doctor's decisions: "*An audit of patient information and history, patient management and drugs prescribed could be kept.*"

This unease of legal action being brought against the doctor was also discovered during the discussion on patient influence. So long as the patient knew that the device was being used to make 100% certain that the correct diagnosis and management of the patient takes place, doctors would use the device in front of a patient.

Management and Government Support

Even though these two factors of hospital administration and government help could form part of perceived user resources on a micro-scale it is the macro-scale that was being referred to by the doctors. They were referring to national government and healthcare management and the fact that healthcare could not escape the political reality it found itself in. This is why these two factors are regarded as separate from the de facto definition of perceived user resources.

Support from the managerial structures of the hospital evoked responses tainted with a lot of emotion: "*The people in hospital management have completely forgotten what it is like to be a doctor. They seem to be fighting for some of the wrong things.*" There was a unanimous agreement between all doctors interviewed that absolutely no support would be garnered from the management of public hospitals for the purchase of mobile technology devices: "*Even if we proved to them how useful such a device would be and how it would increase my productivity and improve patient outcomes, I really don't think they would spend money on it.*"

However, this stance is understandable in the context of South Africa as a developing country with more than 70% of working age adults being unemployed, 53% of the population living below the poverty line and 20% of the population being HIV positive (Department of Health, 2004). There are too many needs for the already thinly sliced portion of resources cake provided to the public healthcare sector by the South African government with problems of HIV, TB and inadequate resources deemed to receive more share of the healthcare budget: "*In a developing country like ours we have too many other health concerns to warrant healthcare budgetary expense on such a device*"; "*TB, HIV, infant mortality and cost of health services to the general public all take priority on already scarce financial resources*" and "*Our hospitals are overcrowded and you cannot spend money on a nice-to-have while you do not have beds for patients or doctors to service the patients.*"

These findings show that there is a clear statement being made by the doctors that no support would be given to them by the hospitals in the use of a mobile technology device. However, this lack of support for the adoption of a mobile technology device by the environment doctors find themselves in will not detract from there willingness to use the device. In fact 10 of the 12 said that they would purchase the device from their private funds as they could see many potential uses for the device: "*So long as it does not cost too much and the benefit it will add is quite visible, I will not mind paying for it*"; "*I don't think I would mind paying for such a device out of my own pocket if one can be found for about R3500*" (≈ US$500). It was mentioned that if the use of the device was privately funded, hospital management would grab the opportunity to use the device in the hospital. "*If a company like HP came and privately funded such a device they would jump at the opportunity.*"

SUMMARY AND CONCLUSION

The data analysis revealed that the factors of job relevance, usefulness, task/technology fit, result demonstrability, computer self-efficacy and device characteristics were in agreement with the findings of previous research on ICT adoption in healthcare. The more technically competent doctors are, the more likely their intention to use a mobile technology device. Where doctors found the device relevant and useful to their daily clinical activities, they would use the device. The better the device and its software could support them, the greater would be their intention to use such a device. Table 1 lists the adoption factors identified as significant during this research.

Could these factors form part of a generalised technology acceptance model for innovative technology in the South African public healthcare sector, along the same lines as (Wu, Wang & Lin, 2007)? We suggest that the hospitals from which participants were obtained are comparable to the rest of the South African public hospitals: doctors

Table 1. Adoption factors identified by the research

Factors	Supports the literature?	Comments
Perceived usefulness of a mobile device	Yes	In general a very positive perception of mobile technology devices by doctors was evident even though half of them had never come into contact with one before. They perceived the device being able to provide them with relevant information either via the internet or software for the device. They perceived the device as a reference tool, patient information tool and even contemplated its use as a decision support tool that could help in diagnosis and medication prescription.
Social influences	No	Doctors in public healthcare in the Western Cape display a professional maturity that does not allow factors like image or subjective norm to influence them.
Perceived user resources	No	Lack of resources to support their use of these devices by the hospitals did not negatively influence their intention to adopt. This could be attributed to the social circumstances South African doctors find themselves in, where they have learnt to cope with limited resources on a daily basis. Despite their extremely pressurised work environments, and poor hospital management and administration, patient care is uppermost in their minds.
Computer self-efficacy	Yes	Concurred with previous research (Chismar & Patton 2003), that due to the high self-efficacy beliefs of doctors this factor can be ignored even when researching an innovative technology in a South African context.
Device characteristics	Yes	Doctors would be negatively influenced by characteristics they regarded as being important for them.
Task/technology fit	Yes	The medical profession is a very information intensive one (Harkke 2005) and doctors realised that this device would be able to help keep abreast of the latest information.
Result demonstrability	Yes	Doctors believed that the technology would be able to help them deliver better quality care to their patients.
Patient influence	New	Doctors did not feel intimidated by possible patient perceptions on their doctor's use of the device. Most doctors did however expect that the patient perception would be positive anyway.
Fear of legal action	New	Underlying doctors' perceptions of the device as an information tool was an unease in respect of malpractice legal suits. It was thought that the technology could aid the decisions made. This could help reduce the possibility of incorrect diagnosis and treatment and perhaps legal action against the doctor.
Management and government support	New	Negative sentiments were expressed about the lack of national healthcare structures and government support for the use of such a device. Nevertheless this did not appear to influence their personal intention to adopt mobile technology. It was however felt that these structures should be providing more impetus for the use of these devices.

working in these hospitals face similar working conditions, challenges, administrative tasks and resource shortages. Their opinions could therefore be seen to be fairly representative for the South African public healthcare sector. This would mean that the factors identified could form a revised TAM for South African public hospitals; this could be researched using quantitative means.

In conclusion, the research shows that South African public healthcare doctors are eagerly looking for ways to support themselves in their daily clinical activities. They can conceptualise many uses for a mobile technology device, many of which are already a practical reality in countries like the USA, UK and many countries in Europe. Using the device as an information and decision support tool can be made a reality for public healthcare doctors in South Africa. This will not only provide much needed support to overworked doctors, it will also help improve healthcare outcomes for the majority of the South African public. The key stakeholders involved in the public healthcare function, the government, healthcare management and ICT industry, can help push the adoption of these devices. The ICT industry could get involved by developing strategic partnerships with the public healthcare sector. These partnerships can be used firstly for the showcasing the potential of mobile devices to the public healthcare sector. Once an interest is shown the partnerships can be used for the development of standards, infrastructure and solutions. Government can involve themselves through e-government initiatives and push the concept of mobile technology and healthcare. Hospital management can become involved by starting to support initiatives to help doctors provide better quality care to patients by using these devices as they have envisaged in this research, as a reference-, decision support- and record keeping tool.

The interpretation of the research results should take into account a number of limitations. Firstly, the sample was quite small and, to an extent, self-selected. Also, other stakeholders, especially hospital management and patients, were not interviewed. Finally, the perceptions of mobile technology are influenced by potential and actual use thus many responses could have been based on incorrect or incomplete conceptualisations of potential mobile technology application(s).

ACKNOWLEDGMENT

This chapter is a revised and updated version of a paper presented at the European Conference on Information Systems. The feedback of the anonymous reviewers are hereby gratefully acknowledged.

REFERENCES

Ajzen, I. (1991). The theory of planned behaviour. *Organizational Behavior and Human Decision Processes*, *50*, 179–211. doi:10.1016/0749-5978(91)90020-T

Ajzen, I., & Fishbein, M. (1980). *Understanding Attitudes and Predicting Social Behaviour.* Englewood Cliffs, NJ: Prentice-Hall.

Andersen, J. G. (1997). Clearing the way for physicians' use of clinical information systems. *Communications of the ACM*, *40*(8), 83–90. doi:10.1145/257874.257895

Berkowitz, L. L. (2002). Clinical informatics tools in physician practice. *Healthcare Informatics*, *19*(4), 41–44.

Bower, A. G. (2005). *The diffusion and value of healthcare information technology*. Santa-Monica, CA: RAND Publishing.

Chau, P. Y. K., & Hu, P. J. (2002). Examining a model of information technology acceptance by individual professionals: An exploratory study. *Management Information Systems*, *18*(4), 191–229.

Chetty, K. S. (2007). Equity Promoting Health Care Policies in South Africa. *Report to the Health Systems Knowledge Network*. Retrieved Jan 10, 2008 from http://www.wits.ac.za/chp/kn/Chetty%202007%20Equity.pdf

Chiasson, M., Davidson, E., Kaplan, B., Lau, F., & Reddy, M. (2004, September). *Interdisciplinary windows for studying information systems in healthcare: Challenges and opportunities*. Paper presented at IT in healthcare: Socio-technical Approaches Second International Conference, Oregon, USA.

Chismar, W. G., & Patton, S. W. (2003). *Does the extended technology acceptance model apply to physicians?* 36th Hawaii International Conference on System Sciences, Hawaii.

Davis, F. D. (1989). Perceived usefulness, perceived ease of use, and user acceptance of information technology. *MIS Quarterly*, *13*(3), 319–340. doi:10.2307/249008

Department of Health. (2004). *National HIV and Syphillis Antenatal Seroprevalence Survey in South Africa 2003*. Retrieved January 10, 2008, from http://www.doh.gov.za/docs/2003hiv-f.html.

Fitzgerald, B., & Howcroft, D. (1998, December). *Competing dichotomies in IS research and possible strategies for resolution.* AIS International Conference on Information Systems, Helsinki, Finland.

Garritty, C., & Emam, K. E. (2006). Who's Using PDAs? Estimates of PDA Use by Health Care Providers: A Systematic Review of Surveys. *Journal of Medical Internet Research, 8*(2), e7. doi:10.2196/jmir.8.2.e7

Hameed, K. (2003). The application of mobile computing and technology to health care services. *Telematics and Informatics, 20*, 99–106. doi:10.1016/S0736-5853(02)00018-7

Hammersley, M., & Atkinson, P. (1983). *Ethnography: Principles in Practice*. London: Tavistock.

Harkke, V. (2005). *Physicians' usage experiences of a mobile information system.* 38th Hawaii International Conference on System Sciences, Hawaii.

Horan, T. A., Tulu, B., Hilton, B., & Burton, J. (2004). *Use of online systems in clinical medical assessments: An analysis of physician acceptance of online disability evaluation systems.* 37th Hawaii International Conference on System Sciences, Hawaii.

Hu, P., Chau, P., & Tam, K. (1999). Examining the technology acceptance model using physician acceptance of telemedicine technology. *Journal of Management Information Systems, 16*(2), 91–112.

Joy, S., & Benrubi, G. (2004). Personal digital assistant use in Florida in obstetrics and gynaecology residency programs. *Southern Medical Journal, 97*(5), 430–433. doi:10.1097/00007611-200405000-00002

Khoumbati, K., & Themistocleous, M. (2006). Integrating the IT Infrastructures in Healthcare Organisations: a Proposition of Influential Factors. *The Electronic . Journal of E-Government, 4*(1), 27–36.

Klein, H. K., & Myers, M. D. (1999). A set of principles for conducting and evaluating interpretive field studies in information systems. *MIS Quarterly, 23*(1), 67–94. doi:10.2307/249410

Li, Y. C., Chang, I. C., Hung, W. F., & Fu, H. K. (2005). *The critical factors affecting hospital adoption of mobile nursing technologies in Taiwan.* Proceedings of the 38th Hawaii International Conference on System Sciences, Hawaii, USA.

Lu, Y. C., Xiao, Y., Sears, A., & Jacko, J. A. (2005). A review and a framework of handheld computer adoption in healthcare. *International Journal of Medical Informatics, 74*(5), 409–422. doi:10.1016/j.ijmedinf.2005.03.001

Martin, S. (2003). More than half of MDs under age 35 now using PDAs. *Canadian Medical Association Journal, 16*(2), 952–952.

Miles, M. B., & Huberman, A. M. (1994). *Qualitative Data Analysis: An Expanded Sourcebook*. Beverly Hills, CA: Sage.

Padarath, A., Chamberlain, C., McCoy, D., Ntuli, A., Rowson, M., & Loewenson, R. (2003). *Health personnel in Southern Africa: Confronting maldistribution and brain drain.* Equinet discussion paper no. 4, Health Systems Trust, South Africa.

Pare, G. (2004). Investigating information systems with positivist case study research. *Communications of the Association for Information Systems, 13*, 233–264.

Porn, L. N., & Patrick, K. (2002). Mobile computing acceptance grows as applications evolve. *Healthcare Financial Management, 56*, 66–70.

Ritchie, J., & Lewis, J. (2003). *Qualitative Research Practice: A Guide for Social Science Students and Researchers*. London: Sage Publications.

Sarker, S., & Wells, J. D. (2003). Understanding mobile handheld device use and adoption. *Communications of the ACM, 46*(12), 35–40. doi:10.1145/953460.953484

Turisco, F., & Case, J. (2001). Wireless and Mobile Computing. *Health Reports*. California Healthcare Foundation.

Varshney, U. (2006). Using wireless technologies in healthcare. *International Journal of Mobile Communications, 4*(3), 354–368.

Venkatesh, V., & Davis, F. D. (2000). A theoretical extension of the technology acceptance model: Four longitudinal field studies. *Management Science, 46*(2), 186–204. doi:10.1287/mnsc.46.2.186.11926

Wu, J. H., Wang, S. C., & Lin, L. M. (2005). *What drives mobile healthcare? An empirical evaluation of technology acceptance.* 38th Hawaii International Conference on System Sciences, Hawaii.

Wu, J. H., Wang, S. C., & Lin, L. M. (2007). Mobile computing acceptance factors in the healthcare industry: A structural equation model. *International Journal of Medical Informatics, 76*(1), 66–77. doi:10.1016/j.ijmedinf.2006.06.006

KEY TERMS AND DEFINITIONS

Adoption Model: A model that postulates a number of factors driving or influencing the adoption decision of individuals or organisations, e.g as used in the context of the adoption of a particular technology. Much research has been done around the empirical testing and validation of models proposed by various researchers. Most of the hypothesized adoption factors are typically not directly measurable or observable but are theoretical constructs themselves e.g. usability, user satisfaction. Their influences (or relationships) can be direct or indirect through intermediate factors (such as intention to adopt) and many models indicate that some factors may mediate the relationships between factors rather than exert a direct influence. Some models are multi-stage models. Some of the most widely research adoption models in the field of technology adoption are the TAM (Technology Adoption Model), TAM2 (an extended version) and the UTAUT (Unified Theory of Acceptance and Usage of Technology).

Perceived usefulness/Job relevance: A new technology needs to be useful to its user. Usefulness of a technology can be measured indirectly by checking whether it causes a real (or perceived) increase in the adopter's productivity by being relevant to the adopter.

Perceived user resources: The extent to which an individual believes that they have the personal and organisational support to use the device.

Subjective norm: An adoption factor which looks at the influence exerted by the social environment of the adopter i.e. other people which the adopter may perceive as important. It is really the person's perception of social normative pressures and relevant others' beliefs whether the adopter should adopt or not. These people can be professional peers, colleagues, subordinates, parents, people of authority etc.

Image: This refers to the degree to which the proposed adoption of an innovation is likely to enhance the status or image of the adopter in his/her social environment. Many people are heavily influence by their perceptions of the impression they make, or the status they have obtained within their social or professional circles. E.g. doctors may perceive the use of a mobile technology device as enhancing their professional status within their working environment.

Task/technology fit: The alignment of a technology with current work practices. It was thought that doctors would more likely adopt a new technology if it aligned closely with their current work practices. The task/technology fit is in itself a complex, composite theoretical construct which has to be broken down into a number of sub-constructs or dimensions if one wishes to measure it empirically and a number of task/technology fit models have been proposed in the literature.

Result demonstrability: The degree to which the results or benefits of using the innovation are apparent i.e. how tangible or apparent these benefits are to the adopter. The technology should visibly improve the quality or effectiveness of the adopters' work or processes e.g. the decision making process or the job output quality.

Section 5
Further Reading

Chapter 23
Computerization of Primary Care in the United States

James G. Anderson
Purdue University, USA

E. Andrew Balas
Old Dominion University, USA

ABSTRACT

The objective of this study was to assess the current level of information technology use by primary care physicians in the U.S. Primary care physicians listed by the American Medical Association were contacted by e-mail and asked to complete a Web-based questionnaire. A total of 2,145 physicians responded. Overall, between 20% and 25% of primary care physicians reported using electronic medical records, e-prescribing, point-of-care decision support tools, and electronic communication with patients. This indicates a slow rate of adoption since 2000. Differences in adoption rates suggest that future surveys need to differentiate primary care and office-based physicians by specialty. An important finding is that one-third of the physicians surveyed expressed no interest in the four IT applications. Overcoming this barrier may require efforts by medical specialty societies to educate their members in the benefits of IT in practice. The majority of physicians perceived benefits of IT, but they cited costs, vendor inability to deliver acceptable products, and concerns about privacy and confidentiality as major barriers to implementation of IT applications. Overcoming the cost barrier may require that payers and the federal government share the costs of implementing these IT applications.

INTRODUCTION

The adoption of information technology (IT) to support the delivery of healthcare is recognized increasingly in many countries as an essential tool to improve patient care (Dick & Steen, 1997; Leaning, 1993; President's Information Technology Advisory Committee, 2004). Until recently, IT products available for healthcare providers mostly were designed for large organizations, were business-oriented, complex to implement, and costly. Recent advances in technology have made IT applications more available to primary care physicians in smaller practices. Products are available that are modular; able to be integrated with different systems, and designed to fit the physician's practice pattern without substantial investments in hardware, software, and maintenance (McDonald & Metzger, 2002).

As a result, the introduction of computers and IT applications into primary care in countries with favorable government policies and financial incentives has been rapid (Kidd, 2000; Mount, Kelman, Smith, & Douglas, 2000; Purves, Sugden, Booth, & Sowerby, 1999; Thakurdas, Coster, Guirr, & Arroll, 1996). A number of English-speaking countries has experienced widespread implementation of information technology. The Harvard School of Public Health and the Commonwealth Fund's International Symposium survey of primary care physicians found the following proportions of primary care physicians in the following countries who were using electronic medical records: U.S. (17%); Canada (14%); Australia (25%); New Zealand (52%); and the U.K. (59%). The survey also found the following use of electronic prescribing by primary care physicians: U.S. (9%); Canada (8%); Australia (44%); New Zealand (52%); and the U.K. (87%) (Harris Interactive, 2001a).

The U.S. trails European countries in the use of information technology in patient care. Overall, 29% of general practitioners in the European Union use electronic medical records compared to only 11% in the U.S. Only three countries from the Organization for Economic Cooperation and Development (OECD)—Portugal, France, and Spain—lag behind the U.S. (Harris Interactive, 2002b). Despite its potential to improve efficiency and quality of care, use of information technology in healthcare lags behind other sectors of the economy in the U.S. In 2001, most of the $20 million invested in healthcare information technology was used to computerize financial systems (Goldsmith, Blumenthal, & Rishel, 2003). Less than 10% of U.S. hospitals had adopted electronic medical record systems and less than 5% had implemented computerized physician order entry by 2001.

Given the increasing public attention to the importance of health information technology, the rate of IT adoption among primary care providers is important (Hillestad, et al., 2005). Accurate estimates of the adoption rate for information technology form the basis for policy regarding how to stimulate its use by physicians. The overall aim of this study was to determine primary care physicians' use of information technology in patient care. The specific objectives included the following:

1. Estimating the proportion of primary care physicians who have adopted information technology applications in their practices.
2. Determining physician perceptions of the benefits of these IT applications.
3. Determining physician perceptions of the barriers to the adoption of IT applications in their practices.

Primary care in the U.S. is delivered by physicians who comprise several specialties; namely, family practice (FP), internal medicine (IM), pediatrics (PEDS), and obstetricians and gynecologists (OBGYN). One other group of physicians was included in the survey comprising medical specialties such as geriatrics and occupational medicine.

Four IT applications were selected for investigation. First, electronic medical records (EMRs) are promoted as more comprehensive and accessible to healthcare providers. Studies have shown that EMRs have the potential to reduce medical errors, especially when integrated with other applications such as decision support (Bates et al., 1998). Electronic prescribing involves the use of computers or hand-held devices to submit prescriptions to pharmacies electronically. E-prescribing has the potential to improve efficiency, to reduce prescription errors, and to improve compliance with managed-care formularies (Miller, Gardner, Johnson & Hripcsak, 2005; Schiff & Rucker, 1998). Third, point-of-care decision support tools can improve the quality of patient care; for example, an antibiotic decision support system (Evans et al., 1998) and automated decision support alerts for contraindicated medications (Galanter, Didomenico & Polikaitis, 2005). Fourth, patients consistently have expressed a strong desire for online communication with physicians (Harris Interactive, 2005). This may involve e-mail queries as well as online consultations. Electronic communication allows physicians to deliver better care and patients to assume greater responsibility for their own care.

METHODS

Survey Method

A Web-based survey was developed to investigate primary care physicians' use of the four IT applications described previously. These applications were selected because healthcare providers in the U.S. and the EU find them helpful and effective (Harris Interactive, 2003, 2005). Comparative data also exist from earlier surveys on the use, perceived benefits, and barriers to these applications. At the same time, earlier studies failed to differentiate primary care physicians by specialty.

We describe the design and administration of the survey. A Web-based survey method was chosen, because it permitted us to survey a national sample of primary care physicians with a reasonable budget (Eysenbach, 2005; Lazar & Preece, 1999; Wyatt 2000). Also, we wanted to sample an Internet-literate population that is most likely to be early adopters in their practices (Rogers, 1983).

Survey Design

The study was sponsored by the Quality Improvement Working Group of the American Medical Informatics Association and the School of Public Health at St. Louis University. The e-mail that was sent out inviting primary care physicians to participate in the study contained a link to the Web-based survey (see Appendix).

In order to facilitate comparisons to earlier surveys, items were adapted from other widely cited surveys; in particular, the annual Health Care Information and Management Systems Society (HIMSS) Leadership Survey (HIMSS, 2002) and the Harris Interactive polls that were conducted in the U.S. and the EU (Harris Interactive, 2002b, 2003).

The questionnaire was divided into seven sections. The first section included information about the physician's specialty and practice. The second section asked physicians to rate the priority of a number of Internet technologies. The next three sections listed specific financially focused, clinically focused, and patient-focused IT applications. The physician was asked to indicate for each IT application if he or she (1) had implemented, (2) planned to implement within one year, (3) had no plans to implement but was interested in learning more, or (4) had no interest. Physicians also could respond by indicating that they didn't know or that they chose not to answer that question. The sixth section asked physicians to rate the benefits of using IT applications on a Likert scale. Responses ranged from (1) high benefit to (4) not a benefit. The final section asked about barriers to implementing IT applications. Responses ranged from (1) not a barrier to (5) insurmountable barrier. A copy of the survey is included in the Appendix.

Factor analyses were performed on the items that measured perceived benefits of the IT application and on the perceived barriers to implementation. A single factor accounted for 63% of the variance in the benefits items. The reliability based on Chronbach's Alpha was 0.93. For the barriers items, a single factor accounted for 48% of the variance. The reliability was 0.86 based on Chronbach's Alpha.

Sample

We contracted with SK&A Information Services to broadcast an e-mail invitation to primary care physicians to participate in the study. This company maintains a comprehensive list of physicians based on the AMA Physician Masterfile. The list is updated weekly through the use of surveys, publication mailings, and the U.S. Postal Services Address Correction Services. E-mail invitations to participate in the study were sent out to 31,743 primary care physicians. Of these e-mails, 1,101 were rejected due to invalid e-mail addresses. A total of 2,145 physicians responded, representing a 7.3% response rate to the survey. The software prevented respondents from completing the survey more than one time. Questionnaires from physicians who were not currently practicing or who were not currently engaged in primary care were eliminated as were questionnaires with significant missing data. This resulted in a final sample of 1,665 that was used in the analysis.

Table 1 presents demographic data and practice information about the study sample. Sixty percent of the physicians were between 41 and 60 years of age, while 29% were younger. Three-fourths of the responding physicians were male. Almost 75% practiced family medicine, internal medicine, or pediatrics, while 15% practiced obstetrics and gynecology and 9% other medical specialties. More than 88% of the respondents were primarily clinicians. The other 12% held primarily administrative positions in their practices and were excluded from the final analysis.

About 14% of the respondents were hospital-based. Almost 18% of the physicians were in group practices of 10 or more; more than one-third of the respondents were in small group practices with less than 10 physicians, and 20% of the physicians

Table 1. Physician characteristics of the study sample

Characteristic	N	%
Age		
30 or less	16	1.1%
31–40	259	17.9%
41–50	537	27.0%
51–60	484	33.4%
61–70	108	7.4%
70 or above	46	3.2%
Gender		
Male	1134	74.5%
Female	388	25.5%
Specialties		
Family Practice	448	29.8%
Internal Medicine	368	24.5%
Pediatrics	324	21.5%
Obstetrics and Gynecology	225	15.0%
Other Medical Specialties	138	9.2%
Role		
Physician	1972	88.4%
Administrative	176	11.6%
Type of Organization		
Hospital	232	13.9%
Group: 10 or more	298	17.9%
Group: Less than 10	607	36.5%
Solo	327	19.6%
Other Settings	201	12.1%

were in solo practice. The remaining 12% were in integrated health delivery service organizations, managed care organizations, and so forth.

RESULTS

Use of Information Technology

Table 2 shows the extent to which physicians in each specialty have implemented each of the four IT applications. Overall, only one out of four has implemented electronic medical records and report using point-of-care decision support tools. About 23% communicate electronically with patients. Only one out of five primary care physicians utilizes electronic prescribing. A surprisingly high number of physicians indicated no interest in all of the IT applications. Thirty-six percent indicated no interest in decision support tools, while 31.3% and 23.5% evidenced no interest in electronic prescribing and electronic medical records, respectively. Almost 30% stated that they were not interested in electronic communication with patients.

A greater proportion of internists report having implemented all four of the IT applications in practice ($p<0.05$). Thirty-one percent have implemented electronic medical records; about 26% have implemented electronic prescribing, decision support tools, and e-mail communication with patients. In general, OBGYNs are the least likely to have implemented any of the IT tools with the exception of electronic communication with patients ($p<0.05$). Less than one out of six of these physicians have implemented electronic medical records or electronic prescribing or decision support tools, and only one out of five have implemented electronic communication with

Table 2. Use of information technology by primary care specialty (%)

Application	FP	IM	PEDS	OB/ GYN	Other	Total
Electronic Medical Records						
Implemented	23.2	31.2	23.0	16.4	40.6	25.8
Plan to implement	16.9	13.9	12.5	16.0	12.8	14.4
Interested in	26.7	23.7	33.4	23.7	19.5	26.4
No interest	24.8	21.2	19.7	31.5	21.8	23.5
NA	8.4	10.0	11.5	12.3	5.3	9.5
Electronic Prescribing						
Implemented	17.7	26.4	20.4	13.3	24.0	20.1
Plan to implement	18.2	16.7	13.0	14.3	15.2	16.2
Interested in	21.5	15.5	21.8	17.6	12.0	18.6
No interest	31.1	30.2	30.6	35.2	34.4	31.3
NA	11.6	11.2	14.1	19.5	14.4	13.8
Decision Support Tools						
Implemented	27.6	25.7	24.0	15.6	30.8	25.1
Plan to implement	16.6	11.1	9.4	10.1	8.7	12.0
Interested in	11.2	11.5	9.4	15.6	11.5	12.2
No interest	33.9	35.9	35.6	43.6	35.6	35.9
NA	10.7	15.8	21.5	15.1	13.5	14.8
Electronic Communication						
Implemented	25.5	26.6	20.4	21.2	26.2	23.2
Plan to implement	11.4	7.1	8.2	10.1	1.6	8.7
Interested in	9.3	6.5	12.1	11.1	9.5	9.9
No interest	29.0	28.1	28.9	31.7	29.4	28.9
NA	24.8	31.7	30.4	26.0	33.3	29.4

patients. OBGYNs also expressed the least interest in IT applications ($p<0.05$). More than 30% indicated no interest in electronic medical records, electronic prescribing, and e-mail communication with patients. More than 40% indicated no interest in implementing decision support tools. There may be several major reasons for this low use of IT and lack of interest by OBGYNs. Most of the IT applications are general and may not meet the specific needs of this specialty. Also, there appear to be few published studies involving the use of IT by OBGYNs.

Perceived Benefits and Barriers

Overall, the majority of primary care physicians surveyed perceived benefits from implementing IT applications (see Table 3). Almost 75% indicated that these applications could reduce errors; 70% perceived IT as potentially increasing their productivity; more than 60% indicated that IT tools have the potential to reduce costs and to help patients assume more responsibility. Physicians are less certain about some of the other potential benefits of IT applications. About half of the physicians surveyed evidenced skepticism that IT applications would shorten consultations and reduce the number of patients who seek unnecessary healthcare. More than 40% felt that IT is unlikely to reduce unnecessary tests and treatments.

More than 80% of primary care physicians report the lack of financial support for IT applications as a major barrier to adoption. This is followed by their perceptions that vendors fail to deliver acceptable products as primary barriers to implementing these tools (79.3%) (see Table 4). In general, physicians perceive these barriers as difficult to overcome. Almost two-thirds of the physicians surveyed also cited the lack of a strategic plan for implementing applications and difficulty in recruiting experienced IT personnel as major barriers, while more than one-half cited lack of sufficient knowledge of IT as a barrier to implementation. At the same time, physicians indicated that these last three barriers easily could be overcome.

Predictors of IT Implementation

Table 5 provides the logistic regression models and predictors for implementing each of the IT applications. Demographic factors, specifically age and gender, were not associated significantly with the implementation of the four IT applications. In only one instance was there a significant difference between male and female physicians. Males were almost twice as likely to implement e-prescribing as females.

Physicians' specialties did predict whether or not they had implemented certain IT applications. Pediatricians and obstetricians and gynecologists were significantly less likely to have implemented electronic medical records. In contrast, family practitioners were almost three times more likely to have implemented point-of-care decision support tools. Specialty was not a significant predictor of implementation of electronic prescribing and communication with patients.

Perceived benefits and barriers appear to be consistent predictors of whether or not primary care physicians implemented three of the four IT applications. Physicians who perceived that IT can reduce medical errors were one and one-half times more likely to have implemented electronic medical record, e-prescribing, and decision support tools. In contrast, physicians who cited lack of financial support and the considerable investment required to implement these applications as significant barriers were less likely to have implemented all three of these IT applications. Physicians who perceived vendors as failing to deliver useful and acceptable products were significantly less likely to have implemented decision support tools. The decision to implement electronic communication with patients did not appear to be affected by demographic characteristics, specialty, or perceptions of benefits or barriers.

Table 3. Perceived benefits of implementing IT applications (%)

Benefit	High	Medium	Low	None
Patients assume responsibility for monitoring symptoms/disease	23.6	38.7	22.1	15.6
Shorter consultations	17.0	29.1	20.9	32.9
Patients not seeking medical care when it was not needed	22.5	28.2	24.4	25.0
Patients coming in sooner for necessary treatment	33.8	29.6	18.4	18.3
Fewer unnecessary tests	29.4	27.9	16.1	26.5
Fewer unnecessary treatments	32.8	24.9	16.9	25.4
Fewer errors	53.4	21.4	10.5	14.7
Increased productivity	39.2	30.3	14.2	16.3
Reduced costs	37.5	25.5	15.4	21.6

Table 4. Perceived barriers to implementing IT applications (%)

Barriers	No Barrier	Easily Overcome	Overcome some effort	Overcome great effort	Insurmountable
Lack of financial support	7.6	5.0	35.3	41.3	10.7
Vendors' inability to deliver acceptable products	12.4	8.3	34.8	36.3	8.2
Acceptance by staff	17.8	23.9	41.6	15.3	1.3
Difficulty proving quantifiable benefits	14.8	18.0	38.7	24.6	3.9
Lack of strategic plan for implementing	19.7	15.2	35.7	25.3	4.1
Recruiting experienced IT personnel	22.0	17.6	31.7	24.0	4.8
Retaining experienced personnel	24.6	17.9	36.6	18.1	2.8
Insufficient knowledge of IT applications	15.0	22.5	41.4	19.3	1.7
Considerable investment in IT applications	6.1	6.9	28.8	47.6	10.6

DISCUSSION

Adoption of electronic medical records has been the most widely surveyed IT application. A review of 22 studies of outpatient electronic medical record (EMR) adoption from 1998 to 2002 suggested a utilization rate of 20% to 25% at the time of the surveys (Brailer & Terasawa, 2003). However, data from the U.S. National Ambulatory Medical Care Survey (NAMCS) indicated that in 2001, only 17% of office-based physicians used electronic medical records (Burt & Hing, 2005).

These studies vary considerably in terms of how respondents were selected and their generalizability to a physician population. Many of the studies are unscientific and utilized surveys of meeting attendees. Only three of the 22 studies reviewed were rated as generalizable. Also, most of these studies do not differentiate among physicians by specialty. Consequently, there is

Table 5. Predictors of the implementation of IT applications (odds ratios)

Characteristic	EMR	E-Prescribing	Decision Support	E-Communication
Age				
30 or less	1.000	1.000	1.000	1.000
31–40	0.668	1.474	0.761	1.360
41–50	0.421	0.401	0.760	1.614
51–60	0.568	0.392	0.660	1.157
61–70	0.530	0.503	0.606	1.393
70 or above	0.503	0.706	0.499	1.393
Gender				
Male	1.175	1.942**	1.094	1.066
Female	1.000	1.000	1.000	1.000
Specialties				
FP	1.420	1.433	0.591**	0.924
IM	0.712	1.125	0.957	0.851
Pediatrics	0.513**	0.622	1.206	0.616
OBGYN	0.406**	0.957	1.180	0.586
Other	1.000	1.000	1.000	1.000
Benefits				
Fewer Errors	1.541**	1.574**	1.238*	1.086
Increased Productivity	1.023	1.282*	1.157	0.919
Reduced Costs	0.804*	0.724**	0.788*	0.868
Barriers				
Lack of Financial Support	1.591**	1.452**	1.296*	0.960
Vendors' Failure to Deliver	1.169	1.211*	1.309**	1.108
Considerable Investment	1.207	1.271*	1.221	1.278

$^{**}p<0.01$ $^{*}p<0.05$

only limited data on adoption of EMRs by specialty. The 2002 Health Care Information and Management Systems Society (HIMSS, 2002) survey administered to attendees and exhibitors at the annual conference found that 42% of internal medicine practices and 30% of family medicine practices reported using EMRs. These rates show little change from the HIMSS survey in 2001. However, since only meeting attendees were surveyed, it is impossible to extrapolate these results to the U.S. primary care physician population as a whole.

There are fewer studies of the adoption of other IT applications such as electronic prescribing and online communication between physicians and patients. The National Ambulatory Medical Care Survey (NAMCS) indicated that only 8% of office-based physicians in 2001 ordered prescriptions electronically (Burt & Hing, 2005). The Harris Interactive study that compared use of IT by U.S. general practitioners to European physicians found that 17% of physicians in primary care practices reported that they used EMRs, and 9% reported using electronic prescribing (Harris Interactive, 2002a). This survey also dates back to 2000-2001. Neither study differentiates physicians by specialty.

More recent information is needed about the extent to which primary care physicians use information technology for patient care, patterns of use, and perceived barriers to use of IT. Many of the surveys discussed earlier were undertaken before the year 2000. The NAMCS statistics on uses of computerized clinical support systems in medical settings are based on office-based physician practices rather than only on primary care physicians (Burt & Hing, 2005). The Harris Interactive study reports aggregate statistics for primary care physicians and specialists. Our survey examined IT applications that appear to offer the greatest potential to primary care physicians in providing high-quality patient care. It also differentiates primary care physicians by specialty.

This study provides evidence from a large sample of U.S. primary care physicians that there is limited implementation of clinical and patient care IT applications. Overall, only about 25% of primary care physicians have implemented electronic medical records, e-prescribing, point-of-care decision support tools, or electronic communication with patients. These results are similar to those from a Harris Interactive survey of 400 U.S. physicians conducted in 2001 and other earlier studies indicating a slow rate of adoption However, the proportion of physicians who have implemented e-prescribing has almost doubled from 11% to 20% since 2001. This may be due in part to improvements in the technology, such as the use of wireless devices.

Of concern is the finding that almost one out of three primary care physicians surveyed expressed little or no interest in the four IT applications. This may indicate that while two-thirds of primary care physicians perceive that implementation of IT can reduce costs and errors and help patients assume more responsibility for their medical conditions, a significant number of these physicians does not perceive the advantages of implementing IT technologies to provide patient care. One way of overcoming this barrier may be for medical specialty societies to offer seminars, short courses, and/or Web seminars on IT for CME credit with a focus on those features that are most useful to physicians in that specialty.

Age and gender on the whole do not appear to predict implementation of these four IT applications. However, there are significant differences in implementation among the specialties. A greater proportion of internists report having implemented all four IT applications. Pediatricians and obstetricians and gynecologists are less likely to have implemented EMRs, while family practitioners are more likely to have implemented decision support tools. OBGYNs, in particular, have been slow to adopt IT in practice. Only 16% have implemented EMRs and decision support tools. Even less, 13%, have implemented electronic prescribing. The slow adoption of IT applications by this specialty group may be due to the fact that these tools fail to address the special needs of this group of physicians. Also, OBGYNs may need to see more studies that demonstrate how these tools can help them to improve their practices.

This finding suggests that future surveys that assess adoption of IT applications by physicians need to differentiate by specialty rather than to treat primary care physicians or office-based physicians as homogeneous groups. Efforts to encourage IT adoption by physicians need to be tailored to specific specialty groups by emphasizing features of the technology that are particularly useful to that specialty.

Perceptions of benefits and barriers are significant predictors of implementation of three of the four applications. Physicians who perceive that EMRs, e-prescribing, and decision support tools can help them to reduce medical errors are significantly more likely to have implemented these technologies. At the same time, perception of barriers is a significant impediment to implementation (Anderson, 1997, 1999; Harris Interactive 2001b). Those physicians who perceived lack of financial support and high investment cost required were much less likely to have implemented these three IT applications. Also, physicians cited lack of experience and knowledge of IT as barriers. This may indicate that physicians may feel that learning to use IT applications in practice may require too much time and energy by them and their staff in order to achieve the perceived benefits. Consequently, a key to increased use of patient care IT applications by primary care physicians may be to convince them that the benefits significantly outweigh the barriers, primarily cost. Also, physicians do not perceive vendors as delivering acceptable IT products that meet their needs. More than 70% of physicians who responded to the survey perceived vendors' unresponsiveness as a barrier to implementation of IT. It may be necessary for vendors to examine more thoroughly the needs of primary care physicians and how their IT applications fit into clinical practice in order to convince physicians to adopt them.

Other studies have indicated that lack of funding and costs are the largest barriers to the adoption of EMRs. Surveys have found that 50% or more of respondents cited lack of adequate funding as the major barrier to implementation (HIMSS, 2002; Medical Group Management Association, 2001; Medical Records Institute, 2002; Miller & Sims, 2004). This perception is based on the fact that implementation of some IT applications such as EMRs requires large up-front investment and ongoing maintenance costs. A study by the California Health Care Foundation (2003) estimated that the cost of implementing a computerized physician order entry (CPOE) system in an ambulatory care practice ranges from $15,000 to $50,000 per physician with a median cost of $30,000 per physician.

Overcoming the cost barrier will be difficult and may require incentives by payers and the government. An example is New Zealand, Australia, and the U.K., which have introduced government funding programs to stimulate adoption and use of EMRs (Bates, Ebell, Gotlier, Zapp & Mullins, 2003). Professional associations also can facilitate adoption of IT. The American Academy of Family Physicians, through a nonprofit foundation, is developing low-cost, open-source EMR software that will be available to physicians with no licensing fee.

Decisions to implement electronic communication with patients appear to be independent of perceptions of benefits and barriers. Barriers to electronic communication with patients may be different than barriers to the other IT applications. Physicians generally express concerns about the legal status of these communications and concern about the security of patient information sent over the Internet.

One of the limitations of this study is the low response rate (7.3%). Low response rates are one of the major limitations of Web-based surveys in general (Eysenbach, 2005). A systematic review of 17 Internet-based surveys of health professionals found that reported response rates ranged from 9% to 94% (Braithwaite, Emery, de Lusignan & Sutton, 2003). Most of these studies utilized professional e-directories. Some used commercial organizations' e-mail directories or recruited volunteers via Web sites of electronic discussion groups. Six of the 17 studies reviewed did not report response rates. A meta-analysis of response rates in Web- and Internet-based surveys found that the mean response rate for 68 surveys was 39.6% with a standard deviation of 15.7% (Cook, Heath & Thompson, 2000). Other researchers have reported similarly low response rates of 18% for a study of physicians in Hong Kong (Leung, Johnston, Ho, Wong & Cameo, 2001).

One study of general practitioners' use of decision support for management of familial cancer sent five separate e-mail reminders and achieved a response rate of 52.4% (Braithwaite, Sutton, Smithson & Emery, 2002). In the case of our study, the high cost of sending additional reminders to physicians precluded our doing so.

Since our survey was administered online and did not include an alternative mail survey, there is a risk of over-sampling respondents who are more likely to utilize computers in their practices. Our sample was drawn from physicians with e-mail addresses listed by the American Medical Association (AMA). These physicians may be knowledgeable about IT applications and more likely to implement them in patient care. This sample design was adopted since we wanted to sample an Internet- and computer-literate population of primary care physicians. These physicians are most likely to be early adopters of IT applications in their practices. Consequently, estimates of implementation reported in this study are likely to be higher than for the entire population of primary care physicians.

At the same time, limitations on the generalizability of the results apply to many of the earlier reported studies of IT adoption by physicians (Brailer & Terasawa, 2003). The HIMSS surveys were voluntary surveys administered to conference attendees (HIMSS, 2002). The MediNetwork 2002 Medical Group Office Management Systems Survey was voluntary and reported a 7.52% response rate. The AHA Most Wired Survey 2002 and the Medical Records Institute Survey of Electronic Health Record Trends and Usage sponsored by SNOMED were online voluntary surveys and did not report response rates. Comparative data for the U.S. and the E.U. reported by Harris Interactive did not report response rates. Data on the E.U. countries were based on the EuroBarometer 104 conducted in June/July 2001. U.S data were collected by Harris Interactive. Our study is an improvement over a number of these earlier studies in which there are serious questions about the reliability and the generalizability of results due to flawed study design or industry sponsorship (e.g., the HIMSS Leadership Survey). Also, earlier studies with few exceptions failed to differentiate primary care physicians or office-based physicians by specialty.

In this study, no attempt was made to specify specific features of each of the four IT applications. Physicians simply were asked if they had implemented or intended to implement each application. However, features of each application vary considerably from practice to practice. For example, an EMR in addition to patient problem lists, medications, allergies, tests, and personal information and medical history may be linked to an electronic prescribing system and evidence-based decision support tools.

CONCLUSION

The present study has documented the extent to which primary care physicians use IT in providing patient care. Variation among different primary care specialty groups is an important finding as is the finding that one out of three primary care physicians expressed no interest in using any of the four IT applications for patient care. Moreover, the finding that perceived that benefits and barriers are the most significant predictors of IT implementation has implications for strategies to promote implementation of IT in clinical practice. Primary care physicians will need to be convinced that the benefits of these tools outweigh their costs. Also, vendors will need to be more responsive to the needs of primary care physicians. Finally, overcoming the costs barrier will require incentives and/or cost sharing by payers and the federal government.

ACKNOWLEGMENT

This study was supported by the Center for Education and Research in Information Assurance and Security (CERIAS). Data were collected by the Purdue University Social Research Institute. Marilyn Anderson, Don Malott, and Heather Rodriquez assisted with the data analysis and manuscript preparation.

REFERENCES

Anderson, J.G. (1997). Clearing the way for physicians' use of clinical information systems. *Communications of the ACM, 40*, 83–90.

Anderson, J.G. (1999). Increasing the acceptance of clinical information systems. *MD Computing, 16*, 62–65.

Bates, D.W., Ebell, M., Gotlier, E. Zapp, J., & Mullins, H.C. (2003). A proposal for electronic medical records in U.S. primary care. *Journal of the American Medical Informatics Association, 10*, 1–10.

Bates, D.W., Leape, L.L., Cullen, D.J., Laird, N.,

Petersen, L.A., Teich, J.M., et al. (1998). Effect of computerized physician order entry and a team intervention on prevention of serious medication errors. *Journal of the American Medical Association, 280*, 1311–1316.

Brailer, D.J., & Terasawa, E.L. (2003). *Use and adoption of computer-based patient records*. Oakland, CA: California Health Care Foundation.

Braithwaite, D., Emery, J., de Lusignan, S., & Sutton, S. (2003). Using the Internet to conduct surveys of health professionals: A valid alternative? *Family Practice, 19*, 587–590.

Braithwaite, D., Sutton, S., Smithson, W.H., & Emery, J. (2002). Internet-based risk assessment and decision support for the management of familial cancer in primary care: Survey of GP's attitudes and intentions. *Family Practice, 20*(5), 545–551.

Burt, C.W., & Hing, E. (2005). *Use of computerized clinical support systems in medical settings: United States 2001-03. Advanced data from vital and health statistics, No. 353*. Hyattsville, MD: National Center for Health Statistics.

California Health Care Foundation. (2003, October). *Electronic medical records: Lessons from small physician practices. ihealthreports.*

Cook, C., Heath, F., & Thompson, R.L. (2000). A meta-analysis of response rates in Web- and Internet-based surveys. *Educational and Psychological Measurement, 60*(6), 821–836.

Dick, R.S., & Steen, E.B. (1997). *The computer-based patient record: An essential technology for health care*. Washington, DC: National Academy Press, Institute of Medicine.

Evans, R.S., Pestotnik, S., Classen, D., Clemmer, T., Weaver, L., Orme, J., et al. (1998). A computer-assisted management program for antibiotics and other anti-infective agents. *New England Journal of Medicine, 338*, 232–238.

Eysenbach, G. (2005). Using the Internet for surveys and research. In J.G. Anderson, & C.E. Aydin (Eds.), *Evaluating the organizational impact of healthcare information systems* (2nd ed.) (pp. 129–143). New York: Springer.

Galanter, W.L., Didomenico, R.J., & Polikaitis, A. (2005). A trial of automated decision support alerts for contraindicated medications using computerized physician order entry. *Journal of the American Medical Informatics Association, 12*(3), 269–274.

Goldsmith, J., Blumenthal, D., & Rishel, W. (2003). Federal health information policy: A case of arrested development. *Health Affairs, 22*(4), 44–55.

Harris Interactive. (2001a). U.S. trails other English speaking countries in use of electronic medical records and electronic prescribing. *HarrisInteractive Health Care News, 1*(28), 1–3.

Harris Interactive. (2001b). The increasing impact of eHealth on physician behavior. *HarrisInteractive Health Care News, 1*(31), 1–14.

Harris Interactive. (2002a). The future use of the Internet in 4 countries in relation to prescriptions, physician communication and health information. *HarrisInteractive Health Care News, 2*(13), 1–4.

Harris Interactive. (2002b). European physicians especially in Sweden, Netherlands and Denmark lead U.S. in use of electronic medical records. *HarrisInteractive Health Care News, 2*(16), 1–3.

Harris Interactive. (2003). eHealth influence continues to grow as usage of the Internet by physicians and patients increases. *HarrisInteractive Health Care News, 3*(6), 1–7.

Harris Interactive. (2005). Many nationwide believe in the potential benefits of electronic medical records and are interested in online communications with physicians. *The Wall Street Journal Online Health Care Poll, 4*(4), 1–5.

Hillestad, R., Bigelow, J., Bower, A., Girosi, F., Meili, R, Scoville, R., et al. (2005). Can electronic medical record systems transform health care? Potential health benefits, savings, and costs. *Health Affairs, 24*(5), 1103–1117.

HIMSS 13th annual HIMSS leadership survey. (2002). Retrieved from http://www.himss.org/2002survey

Kidd, M.R. (2000). Clinical practice guidelines and the computer on your desk. *Medical Journal of Australia, 173*, 373–375.

Lazar, J., & Preece, J. (1999). Designing and implementing Web-based surveys. *Journal of Computer Information Systems, 39*(4), 63–67.

Leaning, M. (1993). The new information management and technology strategy of the NHS. *British Medical Journal, 307*(6898), 217.

Leung, G.M., Johnston, J.M., Ho, L.M., Wong, F.K., & Cameo, S.C. (2001). Computerization of clinical practice in Hong Kong. *International Journal of Medical Informatics, 62*, 143–154.

McDonald, K., & Metzger, J. (2002, September). Achieving tangible IT benefits in small physician practices. *California HealthCare Foundation, ihealth Report.*

Medical Group Management Association. (2001). *Medical group management association survey 2001.*

Medical Records Institute. (2002). *4th annual Medical Records Institute's survey of electronic health record trends and usage, 2002.*

Miller, R.A., Gardner, R.M., Johnson, K.B., & Hripcsak, G. (2005). Clinical decision support and electronic prescribing systems: A time for responsible thought and action. *Journal of the American Medical Association, 12*(4), 403–409.

Miller, R.H., & Sims, I. (2004). Physicians' use of electronic medical records: Barriers and solutions. *Health Affairs, 23*(2), 116–126.

Mount, C.D., Kelman, C.W., Smith, L.R., & Douglas, R.M. (2000). An integrated electronic health record and information system for Australia. *Medical Journal of Australia, 172*, 25–27.

President's Information Technology Advisory Committee. (2004). *Revolutionizing health care through information technology.* Arlington, VA: National Coordination Office for Information Technology Research and Development.

Purves, I.N., Sugden, B., Booth, N., & Sowerby, M. (1999). The PRODIGY project—The iterative development of the release one model. In *Proceedings of the AMIA Annual Symposium* (pp. 359–363).

Rogers, E.M. (1983). *Diffusion of innovation* (3rd ed.). New York: Free Press.

Schiff, G.D., & Rucker, D. (1998). Computerized prescribing: Building the electronic infrastructure for better medication usage. *Journal of the American Medical Association, 280*, 516–517.

Thakurdas, P., Coster, G, Guirr, E., & Arroll, B. (1996). New Zealand general practice computerisation: Attitudes and reported behavior. *New Zealand Medical Journal, 109*, 419–422.

Wyatt, J. (2000). When to use Web-based surveys. *Journal of the American Medical Informatics Association, 7*(4), 426–430.

APPENDIX

Dr. <name>

The Quality Improvement Working Group of the American Medical Informatics Association in conjunction with the School of Public Health at St. Louis University is undertaking a survey of physician experience with information technology at the point of care. The survey is being performed under contract with the Social Research Institute at Purdue University and funded by the Center for Education and Research in Information Assurance and Security.

To participate, simply click on the link below and you will be directed to the Social Research Institute Web site at Purdue University. Please complete the short survey. Your responses will be kept strictly confidential and will be used solely for academic research purposes. We are grateful for your willingness to provide your valuable perspective on the real implementation experience of a physician using information technology at the point of care.

If you have any questions, please contact:

James G. Anderson, Ph.D.
Professor of Medical Sociology
Purdue University
Chair Elect, Quality Improvement Working Group
American Medical Informatics Association
Andersonj@soc.purdue.edu

E. Andrew Balas, M.D.
Dean and Professor
School of Public Health
St. Louis University
Chair, Quality Improvement Working Group
American Medical Informatics Association
balasea@slu.edu

CLICK HERE <Web site Address>

Which of the following best describes your role within your Organization:

1. Physician
2. Director
3. Scientist
4. President
5. Chief of Executive officer
6. Medical Director
7. Chief Medical Officer
8. Vice President of Medical Services
9. Other

a. don't know
b. I choose not to answer

Which of the following best describes the environment where you spend most of your workday:

1. Hospital
2. Medium or large group practice or clinic (10 or more physicians)
3. Small group practice or clinic (less than 10 practicing physicians)
4. Solo Practice
5. Integrated Health Delivery Service Organization
6. Long Term Care
7. Managed Care Organization (MCO)
8. Mental and Behavioral Services
9. Other

a. don't know
b. I choose not to answer

Which of the following Internet Technologies are priorities during the next year:

Upgrading Security of medical information for HIPAA compliance
1. High Priority
2. Medium Priority
3. Low Priority
4. Not a Priority

a. don't know
b. I choose not to answer

Reducing Medical Errors
1. High Priority
2. Medium Priority
3. Low Priority
4. Not a Priority

a. don't know
b. I choose not to answer

Promoting Patient Safety
1. High Priority
2. Medium Priority
3. Low Priority
4. Not a Priority

a. don't know
b. I choose not to answer

Reducing Costs
1. High Priority
2. Medium Priority
3. Low Priority
4. Not a Priority

a. don't know
b. I choose not to answer

Increasing Productivity
1. High Priority
2. Medium Priority
3. Low Priority
4. Not a Priority

a. don't know
b. I choose not to answer

Internet Tools

Which of the following financial-focused Internet Technology tools have/ do you plan to implement:

Connectivity to payers
1. Have implemented
2. Plan to implement within 1 year
3. No plans to implement but interested in learning more
4. No interest

a. don't know
b. I choose not to answer

Assistance in coding patient visits
1. Have implemented
2. Plan to implement within 1 year
3. No plans to implement but interested in learning more
4. No interest

a. don't know
b. I choose not to answer

Electronic charge capture
1. Have implemented
2. Plan to implement within 1 year
3. No plans to implement but interested in learning more
4. No interest

a. don't know
b. I choose not to answer

Which of the following clinically focused Internet tool have or do you plan to implement:

Document scanning/imaging
1. Have implemented
2. Plan to implement within 1 year
3. No plans to implement but interested in learning more
4. No interest

a. don't know
b. I choose not to answer

Transcription/voice recognition
1. Have implemented
2. Plan to implement within 1 year
3. No plans to implement but interested in learning more
4. No interest

a. don't know
b. I choose not to answer

Electronic team messaging between clinic staff
1. Have implemented
2. Plan to implement within 1 year
3. No plans to implement but interested in learning more
4. No interest

a. don't know
b. I choose not to answer

Electronic lab order entry
1. Have implemented
2. Plan to implement within 1 year
3. No plans to implement but interested in learning more
4. No interest

a. don't know
b. I choose not to answer

Electronic routing of test results
1. Have implemented
2. Plan to implement within 1 year
3. No plans to implement but interested in learning more
4. No interest

a. don't know
b. I choose not to answer

Electronic medical record
1. Have implemented
2. Plan to implement within 1 year
3. No plans to implement but interested in learning more
4. No interest

a. don't know
b. I choose not to answer

Electronic Prescribing
1. Have implemented
2. Plan to implement within 1 year
3. No plans to implement but interested in learning more
4. No interest

a. don't know
b. I choose not to answer

Point–of-Care decisions support tools
1. Have implemented
2. Plan to implement within 1 year
3. No plans to implement but interested in learning more
4. No interest

a. don't know
b. I choose not to answer

Which of the following patient-focused Internet Tools do you have or plan to implement:

Incoming telephone call management
1. Have implemented
2. Plan to implement within 1 year
3. No plans to implement but interested in learning more
4. No interest

a. don't know
b. I choose not to answer

Automated telephone appointment reminders
1. Have implemented
2. Plan to implement within 1 year
3. No plans to implement but interested in learning more
4. No interest

a. don't know
b. I choose not to answer

Automated patient notification of test results
1. Have implemented
2. Plan to implement within 1 year
3. No plans to implement but interested in learning more
4. No interest

a. don't know
b. I choose not to answer

Automated telephone patient reminders for health prevention
1. Have implemented
2. Plan to implement within 1 year
3. No plans to implement but interested in learning more
4. No interest

a. don't know
b. I choose not to answer

Electronic communication between physicians and patients
1. Have implemented
2. Plan to implement within 1 year
3. No plans to implement but interested in learning more
4. No interest

a. don't know
b. I choose not to answer

Internet site with health information links for patients
1. Have implemented
2. Plan to implement within 1 year
3. No plans to implement but interested in learning more
4. No interest

a. don't know
b. I choose not to answer

In general, what have been the benefits for the health service of your patients using IT applications?

Patients assuming more responsibility for monitoring their symptoms/disease?

1. High Benefit
2. Medium Benefit
3. Low Benefit
4. Not a Benefit

a. don't know
b. I choose not to answer

Shorter consultations

1. High Benefit
2. Medium Benefit
3. Low Benefit
4. Not a Benefit

a. don't know
b. I choose not to answer

Patients not seeking medical help when it was not needed

1. High Benefit
2. Medium Benefit
3. Low Benefit
4. Not a Benefit

a. don't know
b. I choose not to answer

Patients coming in sooner for necessary treatment

1. High Benefit
2. Medium Benefit
3. Low Benefit
4. Not a Benefit

a. don't know
b. I choose not to answer

Fewer unnecessary tests

1. High Benefit
2. Medium Benefit
3. Low Benefit
4. Not a Benefit

a. don't know
b. I choose not to answer

Fewer unnecessary treatments

1. High Benefit
2. Medium Benefit
3. Low Benefit
4. Not a Benefit

a. don't know
b. I choose not to answer

Fewer errors

1. High Benefit
2. Medium Benefit
3. Low Benefit
4. Not a Benefit

a. don't know
b. I choose not to answer

Increased productivity

1. High Benefit
2. Medium Benefit
3. Low Benefit
4. Not a Benefit

a. don't know
b. I choose not to answer

Reduced costs

1. High Benefit
2. Medium Benefit
3. Low Benefit
4. Not a Benefit

a. don't know
b. I choose not to answer

Barriers to Implementation

To what extent are the following barriers to implementing IT applications:

Lack of Financial Support
1. Not a barrier
2. Barrier easily overcome
3. Barrier overcome with some effort
4. Barrier overcome with great effort
5. Insurmountable barrier

a. don't know
b. I choose not to answer

Vendors inability to effectively deliver an acceptable product
1. Not a barrier
2. Barrier easily overcome
3. Barrier overcome with some effort
4. Barrier overcome with great effort
5. Insurmountable barrier

a. don't know
b. I choose not to answer

Acceptance by the staff
1. Not a barrier
2. Barrier easily overcome
3. Barrier overcome with some effort
4. Barrier overcome with great effort
5. Insurmountable barrier

a. don't know
b. I choose not to answer

Difficulty proving quantifiable benefits
1. Not a barrier
2. Barrier easily overcome
3. Barrier overcome with some effort
4. Barrier overcome with great effort
5. Insurmountable barrier

a. don't know
b. I choose not to answer

Lack of a strategic plan for introducing application
1. Not a barrier
2. Barrier easily overcome
3. Barrier overcome with some effort
4. Barrier overcome with great effort
5. Insurmountable barrier

a. don't know
b. I choose not to answer

Recruiting experience IT personnel
1. Not a barrier
2. Barrier easily overcome
3. Barrier overcome with some effort
4. Barrier overcome with great effort
5. Insurmountable barrier

a. don't know
b. I choose not to answer

Retaining experience personnel
1. Not a barrier
2. Barrier easily overcome
3. Barrier overcome with some effort
4. Barrier overcome with great effort
5. Insurmountable barrier

a. don't know
b. I choose not to answer

Insufficient knowledge of IT applications
1. Not a barrier
2. Barrier easily overcome
3. Barrier overcome with some effort
4. Barrier overcome with great effort
5. Insurmountable barrier

a. don't know
b. I choose not to answer

Requirement of a considerable investment in IT applications

1. Not a barrier
2. Barrier easily overcome
3. Barrier overcome with some effort
4. Barrier overcome with great effort
5. Insurmountable barrier

a. don't know

b. I choose not to answer

This work was previously published in International Journal of Healthcare Information Systems and Informatics, Vol. 1, Issue 3, edited by J. Tan, pp. 1-23, copyright 2006 by IGI Publishing (an imprint of IGI Global).

Chapter 24
Open Source Software:
A Key Component of E-Health in Developing Nations

David Parry
Auckland University of Technology, New Zealand

Emma Parry
University of Auckland, New Zealand

Phurb Dorji
Jigme Dorji Wangchuck National Referral Hospital, Bhutan

Peter Stone
University of Auckland, New Zealand

ABSTRACT

The global burden of disease falls most heavily on people in developing countries. Few resources for healthcare, geographical and infrastructure issues, lack of trained staff, language and cultural diversity and political instability all affect the ability of health providers to support effective and efficient healthcare. Health information systems are a key aspect of improving healthcare, but existing systems are often expensive and unsuitable. Open source software appears to be a promising avenue for quickly and cheaply introducing health information systems that are appropriate for developing nations. This article describes some aspects of open source e-health software that are particularly relevant to developing nations, issues and problems that may arise and suggests some future areas for research and action. Suggestions for critical success factors are included. Much of the discussion will be related to a case study of a training and e-health project, currently running in the Himalayan kingdom of Bhutan.

ORGANIZATION OF THIS ARTICLE

This article is organized around a number of sections. The introduction outlines the rationale of the article and deals with some aspects of open source software (OSS) that make it attractive for software development in the health domain for low-income countries. The methodology section then introduces the framework of assessment that is being used. The majority of this article describes a case study of a project run by the authors in Bhutan in the obstetric domain. Critical success factors for such a project are then analyzed and some conclusions are drawn. The discussion covers some of the issues that have arisen from this experience, and articulates some lessons learned.

INTRODUCTION

This project deals with the intersection of a number of domains, as shown in Figure 1.

E-Health

E-health has become a popular term for the transformation of healthcare that has occurred through the use of electronic communications, in a conscious imitation of "e-business." E-health encompasses more than the traditional electronic health record. It involves the use of information and communications technologies in the widest sense, including telemedicine, Web-based health and mobile devices for healthcare. A definition has been proposed, after comprehensive analysis, in Pagliari et al. (2005):

E-health is an emerging field of medical informatics, referring to the organization and delivery of health services and information using the Internet and related technologies. In a broader sense, the term characterizes not only a technical development, but also a new way of working, an attitude, and a commitment for networked, global thinking, to improve healthcare locally, regionally, and worldwide by using information and communication technology.

This definition is actually adapted from a previous one in an editorial which discussed the scope of "e-health" (Eysenbach, 2001). The globalized and networked aspects are particularly important in our case study—the emphasis is on communication and collaboration rather than distance

Figure 1. Research domains

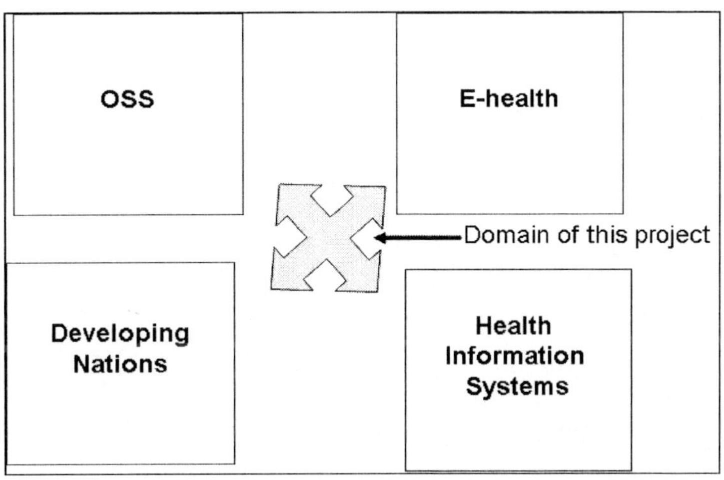

Health Information Systems

Health information systems (HIS) often have three main objectives: to improve patient care, improve management and form part of a quality improvement program. However, these objectives—as described by Littlejohns, Wyatt and Garvican (2003), are not always achieved. As part of a HIS implementation there are often major changes to workflow and practice, large expenditures on hardware including computing and communications, and system integration, as well as software development, training and implementation. Failures occur in HIS development often due to a lack of understanding of the complexity of the project (Littlejohns et al., 2003). Interestingly, OSS appears to answer some of these issues by providing more stable—if less feature-rich—software, and providing a generally larger pool of developers and users than for proprietary software.

Open Source Software

Open source software (OSS) has gained very wide acceptance particularly in the Web server community. Projects such as Apache (Mockus, Fielding, & Herbsleb, 2000) have involved large scale participation, and dominant market share. In the healthcare domain, Sourceforge.net lists 58 applications for download. Many of the applications are extremely specialized, but on the other hand, some like the Web Interface Repository server (WIRM), (Jakobovits, Rosse, & Brinkley, 2002) are effectively complete development environments. This article will argue that successful development and use of OSS in healthcare requires a number of critical "success" factors, and that these reflect both the nature of OSS projects in the wider world and particular aspects relevant to healthcare. OSS can be seen as part of a wider movement that has been characterized as innovation from the user community (Hippel, 2001). This emphasizes the point that OSS is not just "free" but also is able to be modified by the community that uses it.

DEVELOPING NATIONS AND THE CASE OF BHUTAN

Health information systems are important for developing nations as well as industrialized ones. A large review of the use of information technology in primary care in developing countries (Tomasi, 2004) identified five main areas of application—data processing in the healthcare system, decision support, electronic data transmission, electronic patient records and telemedicine. Many developing countries have low levels of trained clinical staff, and this can increase the load on secondary and tertiary providers. In order to audit their performance, and increase efficiency, electronic records and workflow systems can reduce the workload on the staff available.

Both of these aspects are particularly important for developing nations for a number of reasons:

- Developing nations have extremely limited health budgets, but the burden of disease on individual households can be very large. For example, up to 100% of household income being spent on end-stage care for AIDS patients in some nations in Africa (Russell, 2004).
- Developing nations often have a diverse mixture of groups within them, and it cannot be assumed that all citizens have a common language. Even when a common language exists, it may be spoken by a relatively small percentage of the world's population, and commercial development of software using that language may not be feasible.
- Infrastructure and resource constraints, in particular for network connectivity, may reduce the utility of high-performance systems routinely used in the west. For example, PACS systems involving transmission of

large images via network connections may not be practical, but memory stick-based approaches may be feasible (Parry, Sood, & Parry, 2006).

- Open source approaches allow the development of expertise in multiple sites away from large commercial organizations. Therefore, they can encourage the upskilling of software developers in smaller centers. This expertise can be applied to the localization of standard packages and the development of a solid base for software support. In this aspect, both the development and the use of open source software can be beneficial in the education sector. Developing nations often have large and increasing numbers of young, educated people available for project development. OSS tools are attractive for teaching information systems development because of cost, wide availability of documentation and localized versions being available. For example, Debian translators are available in over 80 l language versions including Dzonga—the national language of Bhutan.
- Commercial software suppliers may be reluctant to sell advanced software packages in developing nations because of the difficulty of arranging support and the perceived threat of piracy.
- Developing nations' health systems often have a complex collection of groups working within them including governments, commercial organizations, local and international charities and international official organizations. The requirement for reporting and data analysis may well be more complex than in industrialized nations.
- Infrastructure developed to support call-center development or tourism, including Internet and telecommunications technology, is easily adapted to allow links between nations. Because OSS tools are supported via the Web, this approach avoids the reliance on expensive and out-of-date paper manuals and development kits. OSS's licensing structure allows cross-national projects to be completed much more easily.
- Mobile devices have particular promise for e-health in developing nations (Iluyemi, Fitch, Parry, & Briggs, 2007). Mobile OSS development is a particularly active area of research (Raento, Oulasvirta, Petit, & Toivonen, 2005).

The case study in this article deals with the intersection of a number of research domains, (Figure 1), which means that the choice of methodology for analysis may be challenging. There have been some recent papers on the use of OSS in health information systems, focused mainly on developed country applications (Kantor, Wilson, & Midgley, 2003; McDonald et al., 2003). Interestingly, these papers point out that the use of OSS in healthcare is not new and that although perhaps small-scale, this work has been consistently ongoing. However, these papers do emphasize the potential gains to be had by the use of OSS in healthcare both in terms of health providers and also developers.

Because of the widely varying state of communications infrastructure in developing countries, western models of development which emphasize in-hospital systems linked by fixed line, high-capacity networks may not be appropriate. In the context of less developed countries, there have been a number of telemedicine projects, often concerned with communication from centers of excellence in western nations (e.g., Swinfen, Swinfen, Youngberry, & Wootton, 2005), or within developing countries (Deodhar, 2002), but a shared approach to development is vital (Wooton, 2001).

Methodology

In order to analyze a case study, some sort of framework of analysis should be adopted. The development project was actually quite complex with elements of telemedicine; knowledge man-

Figure 2. Overall system plan

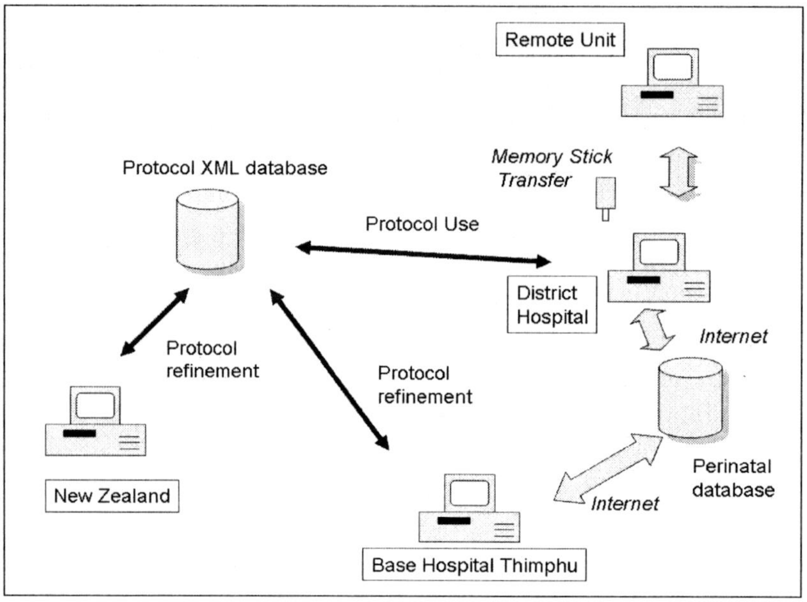

agement and information processing included in the overall design (see Figure 2).

A survey of telemedicine projects in India (Pal, Mbarika, Cobb-Payton, Datta, & McCoy, 2005) identified six critical success factors for telemedicine success; these were used as practical and simple measures that could be applied in this complex, yet small-scale project. The success factors identified were:

1. Set clear program objectives
2. Garner government support
3. Adapt user-friendly interfaces
4. Determine accessibility via telecommunications and Internet access
5. Implement standards and protocols
6. Measure cost-effectiveness and user satisfaction

The case study will deal with these areas, although the project is wider than a simple telemedicine project as it includes database development and integration with the audit system, along with Web-based protocols.

CASE REPORT: E-HEALTH SUPPORT FOR OBSTETRIC SERVICES IN BHUTAN

Bhutan is a small Buddhist kingdom located in the Himalayas, with a population of fewer than 700,000. Land transport is extremely slow because of the geography—for example it takes three days to travel across the country, a distance of around 300km. There is only one airport and no facility for helicopter transport. Seventy percent of the population live in rural areas with 30% more than a one-hour walk from the nearest road head. Bhutan has had major successes in increasing life expectancy and improving healthcare, but avoidable perinatal and maternal mortality and morbidity remains an issue. Current figures for Bhutan suggest an infant mortality rate of 67/1000 and a maternal mortality rate of 4.2/1000—compared with New Zealand's rates of 4/1000 and 0.07/1000 respectively (World Health Organization, 2006a).

Large numbers of preventable neonatal deaths continue to occur in the less developed countries.

However, recent work has suggested (Darmstadt et al., 2005) that evidence- based interventions in antenatal and intrapartum care could reduce these rates by between 37% and 67%. These interventions are not complex and are relatively inexpensive. The overarching imperative is to ensure appropriate care for pregnant women that involves patient education and cooperation with antenatal and intrapartum services. Although there have been many studies on the use of e-health in obstetrics and perinatology and in less developed nations (Deodhar, 2002), there remains relatively little work on the evaluation of these systems. In particular, the outcome and integration of these systems into existing structures, and the changes that occur because of their introduction have not been studied, although the 1 to 45 cost benefit ratio quoted in this study is impressive.

The World Health Organization has been running a "Making Pregnancy Safer" Initiative (World Health Organization) in order to reduce the level of neonatal and maternal mortality. Previous work in Bhutan had developed a protocol book for emergency obstetric care (EmOC). Other countries using EMOC have recorded improvement in outcomes, for example, Bangladesh (Islam MT, 2006) and Peru (Kayango et al., 2006). One of the major lessons learned in these trials was that a record of outcomes via a perinatal database, and the wide dissemination and use of protocols are vital for success. In general it is important that all health workers caring for pregnant women use health information that is based on clear evidence from rigorous studies (Tita, Stringer, Goldenberg, & Rouse, 2007). Surprisingly perhaps, the identification of appropriate procedures for dealing with high-risk patients has been shown to be effective in reducing the demand for interventions (Islam MT, 2006).

The Bhutanese Health System

Healthcare is free in Bhutan, and is delivered via a tertiary structure. The primary healthcare unit is the "Basic Health Unit" (BHU), of which there are approximately 170 around the country. These units do not always have medically qualified staff, but they run outreach and clinic services and usually a number of beds are available. Birthing services, run by nurses, are sometimes available. District health units (around 30) will have at least one generalist medical officer; some of these units have the capacity to perform caesarean sections and ultrasound scanning. There are three referral hospitals in the country which have at least one obstetrician and theatre services. The Jigme Dorji Wanchuck National Referral hospital (JDWNRH) in the capital has four obstetricians and is the tertiary referral unit for the whole country. Because there is no general practitioner service, patients have the opportunity to refer themselves directly to hospital-based consultants even in cases where primary care would be more appropriate. This and the paucity of qualified obstetricians, results in a large workload and the obstetricians are busy and often difficult to contact for advice. A current project is running to introduce the EmOC system to Bhutan, and the protocols are being integrated with these to provide seamless care.

Project Description

The aim of the project described in this article was to collaboratively develop a number of treatment and/or diagnostic protocols to allow the clinical staff to apply appropriate evidence-based care for the major problems that would be dealt with by a perinatal service. The role of the perinatal service is described in Mascarenhas, Eliot and MacKenzie (1992). Essentially, it provides care for mothers and babies from conception to birth, and aims to reduce the risks to mother and baby in this process, by appropriate intervention and monitoring. In addition to the staff applying the protocols in practice, the aim is to raise awareness of the issues that affect perinatal outcomes amongst others, for example, referring to clinicians. The development of a collegial editing and review process involving clinical staff in Bhutan and New Zealand was also seen as a vital part of the project. The project also included the development of a perinatal Web-based database to allow for more effective management of the service on a day-to-day basis and also allow for analysis of clinical performance.

OSS occurs in a number of places in the system. The perinatal database is written in PHP with a mySQL database engine. Web page development was done using open source tools, as was the XML protocol development. However, proprietary products were used for the operating systems and Web server software in Bhutan, along with the Linux/Apache setup for the Web server in New Zealand. In addition, standard proprietary products were used to develop the protocols.

Review of Success Factors

Clear Objectives

The objectives of the project were identified in initial discussions and codified in the agreement signed between the stakeholders. The objectives included the development of a perinatal medicine service, continuing support for this service and standardization of treatment based on the best possible evidence. An additional objective was sustainability of the service. OSS supported this by allowing low- or no-cost technical documentation and development tools to be made available to local staff.

Government Support

The Royal Government of Bhutan (RGOB) is the sole supplier of healthcare in the kingdom. The RGOB runs a series of five-year plans which identify objectives and priorities as well as sources of funding. Plans developed by overseas providers are examined and extensive negotiation takes place to ensure that the country receives appropriate and sustainable help that is consistent with the RGOB objectives. This process began in the case of this project, two years before the initiation, when representatives of the funders—The Magee Family—met with other stakeholders including government representatives, clinical staff from New Zealand and Bhutan associated with the project, and UNICEF. This resulted in a project agreement that was signed off in a formal ceremony. The project composed a number of other elements including funding for hardware and training of clinical workers in the perinatal medicine area. Continuing involvement of the stakeholders has been a great asset to the project. The RGOB department of IT has been running a long-term project to support OSS and is getting closer to the development of a policy on its use (Bhutan Department of Information Technology, 2007).

Adapt User-Friendly Interfaces

The user interface adopted was a standard Web browser, whatever the source of the data—even locally stored protocols would display in a browser. The native protocols were stored as XML documents, which were then displayed in a human-readable format via a Web browser. XML was chosen for ease of updating—in that the editing process could alter content without a great deal of formatting issues and with the awareness that other display methods such as voice responses or mobile devices may be used in the future. As an open standard, XML is very well suited to this approach. The XML design is intended to be expandable and able to represent both diagnostic and therapeutic protocols.

A fragment of the XML representation is shown in Figure 3. The initial outline was based on the PubMED (may need to define this) schema, but simplified to remove excessive bibliographic elements. The XML documents identify the responses to particular diagnoses or symptoms which would be expected to be encountered commonly. The aim is to allow clinical staff, who may be at a remote site, to identify what emergency care is needed, whether the patient needs to be referred or transferred and the degree of urgency of that referral. Also, the protocol can identify

Figure 3. XML protocol fragment

```
<Root_Element>
  <Name>Cord prolapse</Name>
  <Definition>
The cord that normally presents itself is within intact membranes. When the membranes rupture, the cord
      prolapses. This is an emergency as cord compression and/or occlusion can cause fetal asphyxia.
  </Definition>
  <Keywords>
    <Keyword>Rupture of Membrane</Keyword>
    <Keyword>Prolapse</Keyword>
  </Keywords>
  <Diagnosis>
    <Diagnostic_step>Palpable cord on vaginal exam</Diagnostic_step>
    <Diagnostic_step>Observed cord protruding onto vulva</Diagnostic_step>
  </Diagnosis>
</Root_Element>
```

what additional tests or procedures need to be performed.

Determine Accessibility

Although land transport is difficult, Bhutan is in the process of increasing the availability of Internet access. Apart from dial-up connections, there are microwave links and recently the international telecommunications union (ITU) e-post initiative (International Telecommunications Union, 2006) has recently been launched in Bhutan using very small aperture (VSAT) satellite ground stations for rural access to electronic communications, and this may be useful for rollout to remote areas. OSS tools are often very efficient in terms of file size, and machine footprint (use of processor time and memory) so they can be used in a wider range of scenarios than might be possible for the latest proprietary operating systems or applications.

Implement Standards

The protocols themselves were developed in a standard format (Table 1), and as seen above, implemented using XML. In addition to this, an attempt was made to standardize the production of the protocols so that candidate protocols from other sources would go through an editorial process and be routinely revised. This process was formally followed using paper-based systems, but electronic approaches allow instantaneous updating of the live protocol without fear of version control issues and also allow a trail to be kept of previous versions that can be linked to any events linked historically to the implementation.

Measuring Cost-Effectiveness and User Satisfaction

This aspect is perhaps the most difficult part of the project. As part of the process, protocols will be regularly reviewed by stakeholders. In addition, a perinatal database is being implemented in order to record outcomes, and assess performance against that expected in the protocol, in particular, areas where the protocols are not being followed, and whether the protocols or behavior or both should be modified. It is hoped that improvements in the

Table 1. Major elements of the protocol document

Element	Comment
Name	Name of protocol
Definition	
Keywords	Used for searching
Diagnosis	For diagnostic protocols
Diagnostic Step	
Procedure	For procedural protocols
Procedure Step	
Audience	Intended user, includes country and location
Evidence	A small selection of the supporting evidence
Author	Multiple authors possible
Last Update	
Review Date	

mortality and morbidity figures will also be noticeable, because of the currently relatively high rates of morbidity. Substitute measures, such as adherence to protocol may also be used. Finally, a rise in awareness of the general maternity service and increased access to it by women, only half of whom currently have an attended birth, would be expected to accompany improved outcomes among those who have contact with the perinatal service.

Lessons Learned

Integration of protocols from diverse sources was one of the major challenges facing the team. Protocols were sourced from the National Women's Hospital Auckland, New Zealand, the World Health Organization and EmOC protocols in Bhutan.

Collaborative review of protocols was extremely important, as buy-in from clinical staff is vital. However, the process of maintaining a common electronic repository was technically difficult as each of the reviewers tended to work asynchronously using paper copies. The final approach used was to produce paper prototypes and distribute them, collect back annotated versions and then combine them in a final Word document. This was then converted to XML. Development of the perinatal database was restricted by the very small numbers of users available to test and comment on the system, and a wide user community, which may only be available online, may well increase the quality and speed of development..

DISCUSSION AND FUTURE WORK

There are some general issues that affect e-health initiatives, and the use of OSS in the developing world, in particular, connectivity, computing resources and skills.

Connectivity

Less developed nations have generally much lower availability of fixed telephone lines. In addition, geographic, economic and governmental issues often conspire to make conventional dial-up access less common than in western countries. However, wireless and satellite solutions such as VSATS including the international telecommunications union (ITU) e-post initiative (International Telecommunications Union, 2006) are overcoming these issues. It is important to recognize that not every nation's infrastructure is developing in the same way, and many nations may leapfrog to wireless solutions without the use of landline-based solutions. However, high bandwidth solutions may not be appropriate for developing countries. One of the most successful e-health projects has been the Swinfen Project, currently expanding in Iraq (Swinfen et al., 2005). This project uses e-mail in a store-and-forward model, between clinicians in various countries. The prospects of advanced tele-presence approaches being effective in routine care seem slight because of issues concerning quality of service, bandwidth and reliability of connection. Even though the "trauma pod" and other projects financed by the U.S. Department of Defense are beginning to show results (Romano, Lam, Moses, Gilbert, & Marchessault, 2006), costs are likely to render this approach problematic in other contexts.

Computing

Devices such as the Simputer (The Simputer Trust, 2000) and the sub $100 laptop (OLPC, 2006) promise much cheaper access to computing power. It should be emphasized that for e-health applications, the computing device can be fairly simple; indeed mobile devices may become the preferred means of access. Along with cost, the ability to survive rough treatment, extremes of temperature and humidity and long battery life—or even the use of clockwork power in the case of the sub $100 laptop—are more important in developing countries than in the organization for economic cooperation and development (OECD) member countries. Parts supply and transport cost can make the repair of computers extremely expensive. However, organizations such as global assistance for medical equipment (GAME) (http://www.global-medical-equipment.org/whatwedo.html) have established links between professional organizations in the developed and less developed world. These approaches move beyond the shipping of obsolescent equipment to an integrated and well-thought and sustainable out collaboration between donors and recipients.

Skills and Information

At present, consumer e-health is of limited usefulness in the developing world. Low levels of literacy and information literacy cause difficulties. However, the fact that the vast majority of Web resources are written in English and are U.S.-centric in terms of organization of healthcare, availability of drugs and medical devices and naming, makes even materials designed for health consumers in the OECD countries less useful for those in other nations. However, these issues are much less important when the provision of e-health services for medical professionals is considered. Adapting general principles to specific cases is a key skill of medical professionals. Indeed the traffic is not all one-way; less developed nation professionals often have skills that are no longer available in more developed nations. Collaboration in training of medical professionals, where trainees from different nations are exchanged, can improve the training in both systems. This can be supported by the use of e-health tools such as Web sites, e-mail and instant messaging.

Other skills required include the support of the e-health infrastructure in terms of technical support for computing devices and connectivity. Fortunately, the requirement of tourists from western countries for Internet connectivity, wherever they are, along with the burgeoning industries of call centers and 'off-shoring' of software development are providing a strong push for training in these areas.

OSS use in education and training allows nations with limited resources to devote more funding to the human side of education, as well as allowing projects that involve software localization to advance quickly. Open source clinical protocols may become important repositories of clinical knowledge allowing rapid development and input from experience, especially based on standard electronic forms.

Another important aspect of skill transfer and collaboration is the use of early warning networks for disease surveillance such as the Global Outbreak Alert and Response Network (GORAN) that played a very large part in the early detection of SARS (Heymann & Rodier, 2004). Such networks link health workers throughout the world and the transfer of information is by no means one-way.

There remains a dearth of well-controlled studies of e-health initiatives in developing nations, but the need for effective collaboration remains paramount (Wooton, 2001). However, there are a number of pointers to success:

1. The e-health system must be compatible with existing organizational and cultural structures. Some "western" assumptions do not apply in less developed nations and vice versa. For example, routine ultrasound examination in early pregnancy has not been shown to be effective in reducing mortality in a Cochrane review (Neilson, 1998). However, an environment where mortality due to unsuspected problems is much greater, and the availability of on-demand scans is lower, may give different results.
2. Collaboration and training between the professionals involved is vital. This applies to both clinical and technical staff. This may in fact be the area of greatest benefit.
3. Ingenuity is more important than technology. Store-and-forward e-mail may be of greater utility than tele-presence.
4. Open source technology is particularly suited to this area of work. Lower costs, availability of technical skills, greater range of customized languages and often lower technology requirements make open source approaches and especially Web-based open source tools particularly attractive.

FUTURE RESEARCH

Future work in this area will include greater use of multicenter collaboration, both within existing networks such as GORAN and GAME and outside them. Lower bandwidth costs, and easier access to high bandwidths will enable richer media to be used, such as tele-sonography via store-and-forward (Parry et al., 2006). Common health problems are starting to afflict north and south: aging populations, the rapid spread of new infectious diseases and chronic conditions. Common approaches to these issues, including the use of low-cost assistive technology, and offshoring of medical procedures such as radiology (Larson & Janower, 2005), may be controversial, but at least the discussion has started. There are enormous potential benefits in the development of e-health in collaboration with developing nations, and the benefit to the people of world may be immense. An additional benefit of the open source approach may be an increased ability for IT specialists in developed nations to assist people around the world. As virtually every nation now has a Web presence, the technical barriers to such collaboration are much lower than they were even ten years ago. It is hoped that further work will refine the system sufficiently to allow the software to be placed in a repository such as Sourceforge.net. Furthermore, it is hoped that such an approach will encourage increasing collaboration and development in this area.

ACKNOWLEDGMENT

This project would not have been possible without the generosity of the Magee family and the hard work of the representatives of UNICEF and the Royal Government of Bhutan. Staff of Jigme Dorji Wanchuck National Referral hospital, and Thimphu assisted in a very wide range of roles and continue to work on this project

REFERENCES

Bhutan Department of Information Technology. (2007). *Bhutan's journey towards open source.* Paper presented at the DebConf7, Edinburgh, Scotland. https://penta.debconf.org/~joerg/events/25.en.html.

Darmstadt, G., Bhutta, Z., Cousens, S., Adam, T., Walker, N., & Berni, L. (2005). Evidence-based, cost-effective interventions: How many newborn babies can we save?. *The Lancet, 365*(9463), 977-988.

Deodhar, J. (2002). Telemedicine by e-mail—experience in neonatal care at a primary care facility in rural India. *Journal of Telemedicine and Telecare, 8*(Suppl 2), 20-21.

Eysenbach, G. (2001). What is e-health?. *J Med Internet Res, 3*(2), e20.

Heymann, D., & Rodier, G. (2004). Global surveillance, national surveillance, and SARS. *Emerging Infectious Diseases Journal, 10*(2). Retrieved December 1, 2006, from http://origin.cdc.gov/ncidod/EID/vol10no2/03-1038.htm.

Hippel, E. (2001). Innovation by user communities: Learning from open source software. *MIT Sloan Management Review, 42*(4), 82.

Iluyemi, A., Fitch, C., Parry, D., & Briggs, J. (2007). *Health information system for community-based health workers: A case for mobile and wireless technologies.* Paper presented at the IST-Africa, Maputo Mozambique.

International Telecommunications Union. (2006). *Bhutan to be testbed for ITU's e-post venture with universal postal union.* Retrieved April 20, 2006, from http://www.itu.int/newsarchive/press_releases/2002/10.html.

Islam MT, H. Y., Waxman R, Bhuiyan AB. (2006). Implementation of emergency obstetric care training in Bangladesh: Lessons learned. *Reproductive Health Matters, 14*(27), 61-72.

Jakobovits, R., Rosse, C., & Brinkley, J. (2002). WIRM an open source toolkit for building biomedical Web applications. *J Am Med Inform Assoc, 9*(6), 557-570.

Kantor, G., Wilson, W., & Midgley, A. (2003). Open source software and the primary care EMR. *Journal of the American Medical Informatics Association, 10*(6), 616.

Kayango, M., Esquiche, E., Luna, M., Frias, G., Vega-Centeno, L., & Bailey, P. (2006). Strengthening emergency obstetric care in Ayacucho, Peru. *International Journal of Gynecology and Obstetrics, 92*, 299-307.

Larson, P., & Janower, M. (2005). The nighthawk: Bird of paradise or albatross?. *Journal of the American College of Radiology, 2*(12), 967-970.

Littlejohns, P., Wyatt, J., & Garvican, L. (2003). Evaluating computerised health information systems: Hard lessons still to be learnt. *British Medical Journal, 326*(7394), 860-863.

Mascarenhas, L., Eliot, B., & MacKenzie, I. (1992). A comparison of perinatal outcome, antenatal and intrapartum care between England and Wales, and France. *Br.J.Obstet.Gynaecol., 99*(12), 955-958.

McDonald, C., Schadow, G., Barnes, M., Dexter, P., Overhage, J., Mamlin, B., et al. (2003). Open source software in medical informatics—why, how and what. *International Journal of Medical Informatics, 69*(2-3), 175-184.

Mockus, A., Fielding, R., & Herbsleb, J. (2000). *A case study of open source software development: The Apache server.* Paper presented at the Software Engineering, 2000.

Neilson, J. (1998). Ultrasound for fetal assessment in early pregnancy. *Cochrane Database of Systematic Reviews* (4).

OLPC. (2006). *One laptop per child.* Retrieved December 1, 2006, from http://laptop.org/.

Pagliari, C., Sloan, D., Gregor, P., Sullivan, F., Detmer, D., Kahan, P., et al. (2005). What is e-health (4): A scoping exercise to map the field. *J Med Internet Res, 7*(1), e9.

Pal, A., Mbarika, V., Cobb-Payton, F., Datta, P., & McCoy, S. (2005). Telemedicine diffusion in a developing Country: The case of India. *Information Technology in Biomedicine, IEEE Transactions on, 9*(1), 59-65.

Parry, E., Sood, R., & Parry, D. (2006). Investigation of optimization techniques to prepare ultrasound images for electronic transfer [abstract]. *Ultrasound in Obstetrics and Gynecology, 28*(4), 487-488.

Raento, M., Oulasvirta, A., Petit, R., & Toivonen, H. (2005). ContextPhone: A prototyping platform for context-aware mobile applications, *4,* 51-59.

Romano, J., Lam, D., Moses, G., Gilbert, G., & Marchessault, R. (2006). The future of military medicine has not arrived yet, but we can see it from here. *Telemedicine and e-Health, 12*(4), 417-425.

Russell, S. (2004). The economic burden of illness for households in developing countries: A review of studies focusing on malaria, tuberculosis, and human immunodeficiency virus/acquired immunodeficiency syndrome. *Am J Trop Med Hyg, 71*(2_suppl), 147-155.

Swinfen, P., Swinfen, R., Youngberry, K., & Wootton, R. (2005). Low-cost telemedicine in Iraq: An analysis of referrals in the first 15 months. *Telemedicine and Telecare, 11*(Suppl 2), 113.

The Simputer Trust. (2000). *Simputer(TM) - Welcome.* Retrieved December 1, 2006, from http://www.simputer.org/.

Tita, A., Stringer, J., Goldenberg, R., & Rouse, D. (2007). Two decades of the safe motherhood initiative: Time for another wooden spoon award?. *Obstet Gynecol, 110*(5), 972-976.

Tomasi, E., Augusto, L., & Maria de Fatima Santos, M. (2004). Health information technology in primary healthcare in developing countries: A literature review. *Bull World Health Organ, 82*(11), 867-874.

Wooton, R. (2001). Telemedicine and developing countries—successful implementation will require a shared approach. *Telemedicine and Telecare, 7*(Suppl 1), 1-6.

World Health Organization. (2006a). *Estimates of child and adult mortality and life expectancy at birth by country.* Retrieved January 17, 2007, from http://www.who.int/healthinfo/statistics/mortlifeexpectancy/en/index.html.

World Health Organization. (2006b). *Introduction to the 'Making Pregnancy Safer' initiative.* Retrieved October 1, 2007, from http://w3.whosea.org/pregnancy/introf.htm.

This work was previously published in International Journal of Healthcare Information Systems and Informatics, Vol. 3, Issue 3, edited by J. Tan, pp. 1-15, copyright 2008 by IGI Publishing (an imprint of IGI Global).

Chapter 25
Physician Characteristics Associated with Early Adoption of Electronic Medical Records in Smaller Group Practices

Liam O'Neill
University of North Texas, USA

Jeffery Talbert
University of Kentucky, USA

William Klepack
Dryden Family Medicine, USA

ABSTRACT

To examine physician characteristics and practice patterns associated with the adoption of electronic medical records (EMRs) in smaller group practices. Primary care physicians in Kentucky were surveyed regarding their use of EMRs. Respondents were asked if their practice had fully implemented, partially implemented, or not implemented EMRs. Of the 482 physicians surveyed, the rate of EMR adoption was 28%, with 14% full implementation and 14% partial implementation. Younger physicians were significantly more likely to use EMRs (p = 0.00). For those in their thirties, 45% had fully or partially implemented EMRs compared with 15% of physicians aged 60 and above. In logistic regression analyses that controlled for practice characteristics, age, male gender, and rural location predicted EMR adoption. Younger physicians in smaller group practices are more likely to adopt EMRs than older physicians. EMRs were also associated with an increased use of chronic disease management. [Article copies are available for purchase from InfoSci-on-Demand.com]

INTRODUCTION

Electronic medical records (EMRs) have the potential to transform health care in the United States. Achieving the goal of a standardized, inter-operable EMR would offer significant economic and social benefits. An EMR-based health care system would shift the balance away from acute care and specialists and toward primary care and prevention. The experience of the Veterans Affairs (VA) system over the last decade offers some important lessons in this area. In the mid-1990s, the VA invested in a system-wide EMR, eliminated excess hospital beds, and shifted its focus toward health promotion, prevention, and outpatient care. The result has been the transformation into a "full-service" integrated delivery system (Greenfield and Kaplan 2004). One recent study found that VA patients received higher quality care than Medicare patients for 11 out of 11 measures, including preventive services and treatment of chronic diseases, such as diabetes and hypertension (Jha et al., 2003).

A target date of 2014 has been established by President Bush to achieve the widespread adoption of an inter-operable EMR. Yet progress to date has been slow. According to a recent study from the Centers for Disease Control (CDC), only 12.4 percent of physicians nationwide reported using a comprehensive, fully-functional EMR (Hing, Burt and Woodwell 2007). Adoption rates tend to be higher in large academic medical centers and lower in smaller, primary care practices (Rosenthal and Layman, 2008; Hing et al., 2007). Among the reasons given for not adopting EMRs were the following: lack of capital; difficulty finding a system to meet needs; uncertain that EMR investment would produce an economic return; concern that the system would become obsolete; and apprehension over loss of productivity (Conn, 2007).

Historically, some physicians have viewed clinical information technology with skepticism and as a threat to their professional autonomy (Shortliffe, 2005). And whereas some physicians have embraced IT in the clinical setting, others are concerned that IT might interfere with the physician-patient relationship and promote a "cookie cutter" approach to medicine. In a recent editorial, Hartzband and Groopman (2008) warned of the "clinical plagiarism" that occurs when physicians cut and paste each other's notes into the patient's record. They also argued that EMRs would constrain creative thinking and promote a rigid, unreflective approach that they termed "automatization."

Numerous studies have examined the economic aspects of EMR adoption. These include the estimated total savings from a nationwide EMR (Hillestad et al 2005), and the "business case" for adopting EMRs at the practice level (Wang et al. 2003; Miller et al., 2005). Yet the business case alone has proven to be insufficient to bring about widespread adoption (Kleinke, 2005). Smaller practices may lack the resources to implement EMRs, and most of the benefits tend to accrue to other stakeholders, such as insurers, patients, and society.

In smaller practices, physicians are the primary decision-makers on IT investments. Without physician acceptance, a clinical information system will have little chance of success. Yet the role of physicians in EMR adoption decisions and the characteristics of "early adopters" has not been adequately studied and is poorly understood. Our purpose is to address this gap in the literature.

BACKGROUND AND CONCEPTUAL FRAMEWORK

Compared to other OECD countries, the US lags 5-10 years behind in public investment for health information networks. For example, the United Kingdom (UK) has invested $11.5 billion in an enterprise-wide EMR, as compared with $125 million U.S. Federal spending on Health Information Technology (HIT) over a comparable period (Anderson et al. 2006). Hence these countries have moved beyond the planning stage and toward implementation. Patients in the UK can now choose hospitals and make appointments through a national, on-line scheduling system. Canada expects to have EMRs for half its population by 2009.

Policy measures have attempted to address this problem by encouraging EMR adoption through changes in reimbursement. "Pay-for-performance" systems, now being used by both private and public payers, offer bonus payments for reporting and meeting quality targets (Rosenthal et al. 2007). These incentives encourage IT adoption, since the data management and reporting required would be difficult to implement without robust information systems (Shortliffe, 2005). For example, it would be extremely costly and time-consuming for a practice with paper records to report on the immunization status of its patient panel. However, the typical bonus payment is small at only 2 - 3 percent of total reimbursement. Thus it is debatable how much these financial incentives would actually change provider behavior (Berwick 2005). Other policy initiatives include the "Wired for Health Care Quality Act" that would require most providers to adopt EMRs within three years. This bill is currently under consideration in the U.S. Senate, although it is unlikely to be enacted.

Everett Rogers (1995) developed a well-known framework to describe the social process of technology diffusion. Assuming that "innovativeness" follows a normal distribution, then potential adopters can be grouped into five categories, based on how quickly they adopt an innovation (Figure 1). These five categories are the following: Innovators (2.5%), Early Adopters (13.5%), Early Majority (34%), Late Majority (34%), and Laggards (16%). Innovators are the first to adopt and are characterized by their venturesomeness and tolerance of risk. They have the resources to absorb the economic loss of a failed innovation. However, they are often socially disconnected and are rarely opinion leaders. In contrast, Early Adopters are frequently opinion leaders and serve as role models for other members of the social system. The Early Majority are more deliberate and cautious than Early Adopters and more local in their perspectives. They are more likely to adopt an innovation because it meets an immediate need than because it is an interesting idea. The Late Majority adopts only when the innovation has become the norm. They wait until the uncertainty has been removed and the price of adopting has dropped. The choice to adopt may also be the result of network pressure from peers. Laggards are the last to adopt an innovation; they tend to be isolated and localized in their social networks. This group has also been called "traditionalists" in that they swear by the tried and true (Berwick 2003).

Using the framework developed by Rogers (1995), we will, in the first stage, examine the physician characteristics associated with early adoption of EMRs. We will restrict our focus to group practices with five or fewer physicians, since individual physician characteristics are of lesser importance in larger practices, where decisions on IT adoption tend to be more bureaucratic and "top-down." Organizational variables that may influence EMR adoption are also included in the model, such as size of the practice, urban/rural location, and the percentage of Medicaid patients treated (Menachemi et al. 2007). In the second stage, we examine the impact of EMR adoption on disease management and preventive services.

In practice, the conversion to EMRs takes place in stages and over many months or even years (O'Neill and Klepack, 2007). The first stage involves the use of EMRs for internal operations, such as billing, scheduling, patient progress notes, internal communications, and organizing electronic information (Figure 2). The second and third stages involve using EMRs to communicate with clinical partners and for advanced functions, such as preventive services and disease management. Thus we define "Partial EMR Adoption" as Stage 1 implementation and "Full EMR Adoption" as those who have reached Stages 2 and 3. In practice, there is often significant overlap among these stages.

SURVEY DATA AND METHODS

We used a cross-sectional design to survey primary care physicians regarding their practice's use of information technology and practice patterns, in terms of prevention and disease management. The survey was administered in conjunction with the Kentucky Department for Medicaid Services. The initial panel consisted of a statewide random sample of 2,000 providers with at least one Medicaid patient visit in the previous year. The survey methodology followed the Dillman design process (Dillman 2000), with four overall mailings (a pre-survey letter, a survey packet, follow-up postcard, and a final survey packet). After eliminating 62 providers due to bad addresses, 1,928 providers remained in the final sample. The survey process began with mailings in April, 2006, with the final survey coding completed in June, 2006. There were 533 surveys returned for a response rate of 27.6%.

Only 50 out of 533 respondents (9.3%) were in medium-sized or large group practices (those with six or more physicians), and these were excluded from further analysis. Providers were asked if their practice had fully implemented, partially implemented, or not implemented EMRs. Physicians were asked what percentage of their patients received preventive services and disease management in a typical week.

A county was considered "urban" if it was located in a metropolitan area, with the largest city having a population of 50,000 or greater. Six of Kentucky's 120 counties met this criterion; the rest were considered "rural."

Statistical Analysis

Significant differences between EMR adopters (full or partial) and non-adopters were identified using χ^2 tests for dichotomous variables. For ordinal variables, the Mann-Whitney (non-parametric) test was used.

Two separate logistic regression models were used to predict the likelihood of 1) full EMR adoption and 2) full or partial EMR adoption. Candidate variables for the logistic regression models included physician characteristics (age, gender, board certified) and practice characteristics (solo, rural, percentage of Medicaid patients, percentage of managed care patients, and number of physicians in the practice). Variables were selected for the final logistic regression model using the SPSS stepwise procedure (SPSS for Windows, 13.0) and significance was considered at the $p < 0.05$ level.

RESULTS

Of the 482 physicians surveyed, the rate of EMR adoption reported was 28%, with 14% full implementation and 14% partial implementation. This result is consistent with a 2006 nationwide survey of 3,350 office-based physicians conducted by the CDC. In that survey, 29.2% of physicians reported using "any EMR" and 12.4% reported using a "comprehensive EMR", as defined by functionality (Hing et al., 2007).

Physicians who had fully or partially implemented EMRs differed from non-adopters in several important respects (Table 1.) EMR adopters were 5.9 years younger than non-adopters (47.5 vs. 53.4; $p<0.01$). They were also less likely to be in solo practice (65.1% vs. 75.8%; $p<0.01$), more likely to practice in a rural area (79.9% vs. 69.3%; $p<0.05$), and had fewer managed care enrollees (12.5% vs. 17.8%; $p<0.01$).

In terms of practice patterns, physicians who had fully or partially implemented EMRs

Table 1. Physician and practice characteristics associated with use of electronic medical records

Physician Characteristics	Full or Partial EMRs	Non-Adopters	Difference
Sample size	134	348	--
Age (MD)	47.5	53.4	-5.90 **
Male	84.8%	80.1%	4.7%
Board Certified	88.0%	83.9%	4.1%
Disease Management	49.6%	40.6%	9.1% **
Preventive Services	30.1%	25.5%	4.6%
Practice Characteristics			
Solo Practice	65.1%	75.8%	-10.7% *
Size (Number of MDs)	1.67	1.54	0.13 *
Rural	79.9%	69.3%	10.6% *
Medicaid Patients (%)	25.7%	24.4%	1.3%
Managed Care (%)	12.5%	17.8%	-5.3% **

** P-value<0.01
* P-value<0.05.

provided more chronic disease management than non-adopters (49.6% vs. 40.6%; $p<0.01$). Physicians who had fully implemented EMRs provided more preventive services than those who had not adopted or partially adopted EMRs (34.1% vs. 25.5%; $p=0.07$). Further investigation revealed that preventive services differed by specialty ($p<0.001$). For physicians with a specialty of internal medicine or family medicine (n = 109), those with full EMR adoption provided significantly more preventive services than practices with partial or no EMR adoption (46.7% vs. 29.4%; $p = 0.027$).

Two separate multivariate logistic regression models were used to predict full EMR adoption and full or partial EMR adoption, based on physician and practice characteristics (Table 2). Physician age ($p<0.001$), male gender ($p<0.05$), and rural location ($p<0.05$) were significant predictors of EMR adoption. Other physician and organizational characteristics, such as board certified, solo practice, percentage of Medicaid and managed care patients, and the practice size (number of physicians) were not significant.

The relationship between EMR adoption and physician age is clearly shown in Figure 3 and Table 2. For physicians in their thirties, 45% had fully or partially implemented EMRs as compared to less than 15% of those physicians aged 60 or above. The rate of full EMR adoption was 30%

Table 2. Logistic regression equations for predicting emr adoption based on physician and practice characteristics

Full EMRs

Physician Characteristics	Regression Coefficient	Standard Error	Relative Odds	P-value
Constant	0.607	0.799		0.447
Age (10 years)	-0.796	0.150	0.451	0.000
Male	0.912	0.423	2.489	0.031
Rural	0.860	0.376	2.363	0.022

Full or Partial EMRs

Physician Characteristics	Regression Coefficient	Standard Error	Relative Odds	P-value
Constant	0.800			0.178
Age (10 years)	-0.553	0.107	0.575	0.000
Male	0.669	0.307	1.952	0.029
Rural	0.607	0.263	1.834	0.021

for physicians in their thirties and less than 5% for physicians age 60 and older.

This study has several limitations. By design, survey data depend on the ability of participants to give accurate responses. Further, surveys with less than a perfect response rate are subject to response bias. Because the data come from one state, care should also be taken in generalizing the findings to other geographic areas. Overall, EMR adoption was found to be highest in the West and Midwest regions, as compared to the Northeast and South regions (Hing et al., 2007).

Figure 1. Categories of EMR adopters

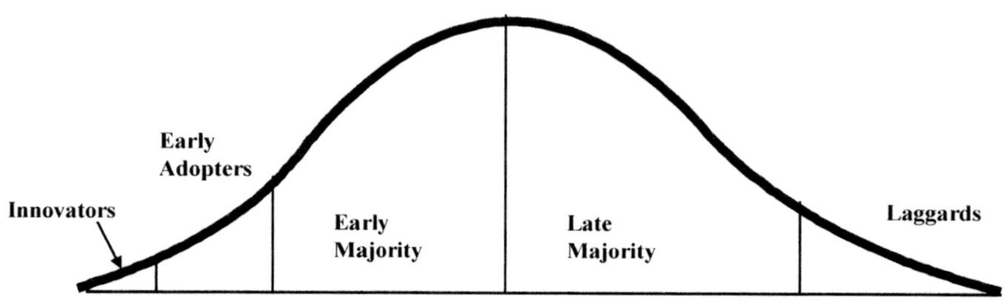

Adapted from Rogers, 1995

Figure 2. Stages of EMR implementation

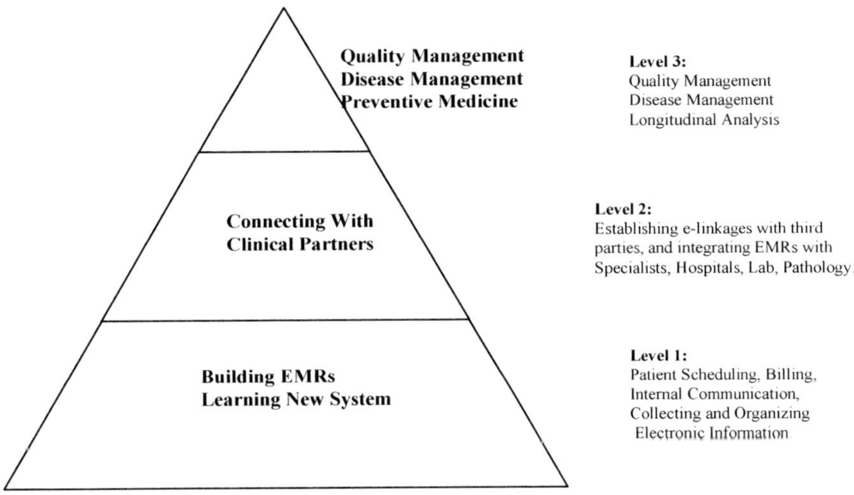

Figure 3. Relationship between EMR adoption and physician age

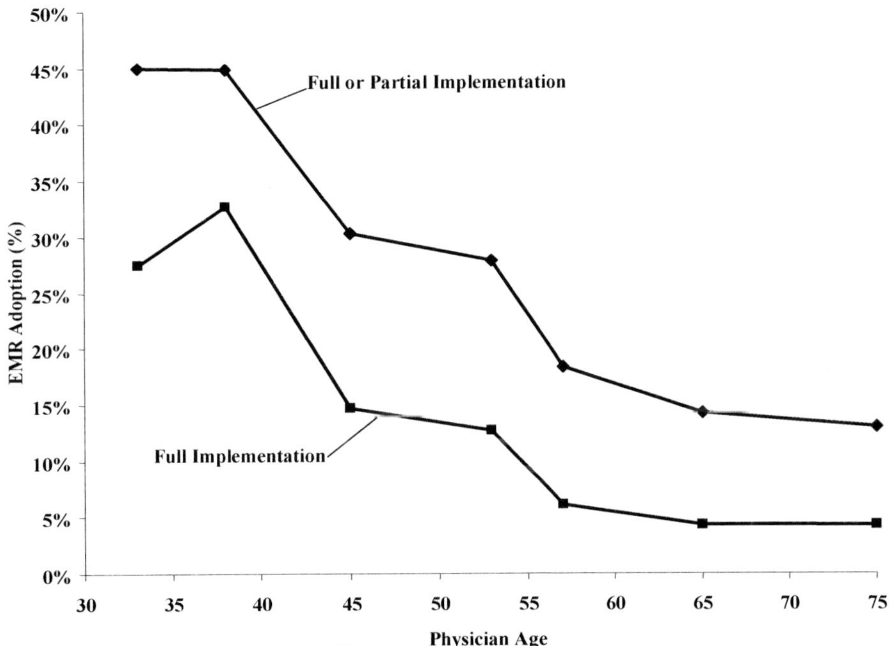

Adapted from O'Neill and Klepack (2007)

DISCUSSIONS AND CONCLUSION

Numerous studies have examined the economic aspects of EMR adoption. Yet few studies have examined the crucial role of physicians in the "social process" of EMR diffusion. This study found that early adopters of EMRs were younger on average than non-adopters and that the likelihood of adopting decreased with increasing age. Previous studies across different industries have found an inconsistent relationship between age and innovativeness (Rogers, 1995). In a survey of office-based physicians, Burt and Sisk (2005) found that physician age was not a significant predictor of EMR adoption. In an e-mail survey of 2,145 primary care physicians, Anderson and Balas (2006) did not find a significant relationship between physician age and clinical IT usage.

Our survey response rate was 27.6%, which is consistent with other published studies with a similar design. For example, three studies on the physician adoption of IT had response rates that ranged from 21 to 28 percent (Gans, Kralewski et al., 2005; Brooks and Menachemi, 2006; Rosenthal and Layman, 2008). For the smaller practices studied, physician rather than organizational characteristics were found to be primary determinants of EMR adoption. Previous studies had found that organizational characteristics, such as the percentage of Medicaid patients, to be significant predictors of EMR adoption (Menachemi et al., 2007). Our study found EMR adoption to be higher in rural areas. A previous study of North Carolina physicians found lower EMR adoption in poorer, rural counties (Rosenthal and Layman, 2008).

According to Rogers (1995), early adopters also serve as opinion leaders who are influential in persuading their peers to adopt the innovation. The advocacy of opinion leaders is often needed to achieve a "critical mass," that is, the tipping point where the process becomes self-sustaining and is typically reached at adoption levels of 10 - 20 percent. Here the diffusion process follows the S-shaped curve, also known as the "epidemic model." According to the CDC, the nation-wide adoption of "comprehensive EMRs" increased from 9.3% in 2005 to 12.4% in 2006. Thus, we appear to be entering Stage 2 of the process in Figure 1. This is a critical phase in that it can determine whether the innovation spreads throughout the population or stagnates. During this phase, Early Adopters can play a pivotal role in facilitating the diffusion of this technology. For example, they can demonstrate to those in the Early Majority how EMRs meet an immediate, practical need.

This approach of enlisting early adopters has been used successfully in other countries. In Australia, "enthusiastic adopters" were identified, and these became local clinical champions and volunteer advocates for Health*Connect,* the country's national health network (Anderson et al., 2006). The NHS in the United Kingdom has also used "pull marketing" techniques to encourage and then leverage these EMR early adopters. Due to its significant ($11 billion) public investment, the UK currently has a national health network for on-line appointment scheduling and electronic prescribing. It plans to achieve full EMR adoption by 2014.

As with other information technologies, such as fax and e-mail, EMRs have significant network effects, in that their utility increases in proportion to the number of other users in the network. In Kentucky, the level of inter-connectivity of health networks remains low. For example, only 27 percent of the physicians in this study who used EMRs reported filing prescriptions electronically. Concerned with this lack of connectivity and the problem of rising Medicaid costs, the Kentucky state government has recently launched an "E-Health Action Plan" that consists of a consortium of purchasers, payors, providers, and practitioners (ehealth.ky.gov). It mission is to increase provider connectivity and lower costs by investing in health information networks. This state initiative can assist the "partial adopters" who are currently in Stage 1 (see Figure 2) to become "full adopters" by establishing electronic linkages with pharmacies, insurers, and hospitals.

We hypothesized that physicians who use EMRs provide more chronic disease management for such conditions as asthma, congestive heart failure, diabetes, HIV, and hypertension, and our results support this hypothesis. Physicians who used EMRs and with a specialty of internal medicine or family medicine also provided more preventive services. In order to check for possible confounding, a two-stage regression analysis was performed, and a propensity score to adopt EMRs was calculated using logistic regression in the first stage, as shown in Table 2. The predicted values from this model were used as a predictor variable in the second stage. "Propensity to adopt EMRs" was not a significant predictor of physician practice patterns, whereas "EMR usage" was significant (p=0.026). This finding further supports the hypothesis by ruling out potential confounders. But whereas these early results are encouraging, they should be interpreted with caution. The learning curve associated with EMRs is long, and the impact of EMRs on these higher level functions (prevention and disease management) may take a year or more to measure (O'Neill and Klepack 2007). Moreover, they require viable "health information networks," that include hospitals, pharmacists, and other providers. Thus the "partial adopters", that is, those in Stage 1 (See Figure 2) cannot expect to realize the full benefits of EMRs.

The impact of EMRs on health care quality as measured by prevention and disease management has significant policy implications. Over the long term, an investment in preventive medicine today can be expected to yield lower costs tomorrow, in the form of fewer hospitalizations and a lower disease burden. Thus, previous studies on "EMR economics" may have underestimated these long-run benefits. Much more research is needed in this area, especially regarding the impact of EMRs on pharmaceutical usage for chronic conditions, such as diabetes and high cholesterol, and their impact on spending for hospital (inpatient) care.

Whereas the costs of EMR adoption in primary care are mostly borne by small group practices, the benefits often accrue to other stakeholders, such as consumers or society. Physicians are not currently reimbursed based on cancer deaths prevented or hospitalizations avoided. Other countries, such as Canada, England, and Australia, have recognized EMRs as a public good that requires substantial public investment (Anderson et al. 2006). "Pay-for-performance" attempts to re-align incentives toward prevention and quality, thereby encouraging EMR adoption.

The identification of early adopters and opinion leaders presents an alternative policy response that could accelerate the uptake of EMRs. Future research could extend this study by examining the needs, attitudes, and beliefs of physicians about the role of clinical information technology in their practice, especially those in the "Early Majority" and "Late Majority" categories.

REFERENCES

Anderson, G. F., Frogner, B. K., Johns, R. A., & Reinhardt, U. E. (2006). Health care spending and use of information technology in OECD countries. *Health Affairs (Project Hope), 25*(3), 819-831.

Anderson, J.G., & Balas, E.A. (2006). "Computerization of Primary Care in the United States." *International Journal of Healthcare Information Systems and Informatics* 1 (3): 1 – 23.

Berwick, D. (2005). 'A deficiency of will and ambition': A conversation with donald berwick. interview by robert galvin. *Health Affairs (Project Hope), Suppl Web Exclusives*, W5-1-W5-9.

Berwick, D. M. (2003). Disseminating innovations in health care. *JAMA : The Journal of the American Medical Association, 289*(15), 1969-1975.

Brooks, R. G., & Menachemi, N. (2006). Physicians' use of email with patients: Factors influencing electronic communication and adherence to best practices. *Journal of Medical Internet Research, 8*(1), e2.

Burt, C. W., & Sisk, J. E. (2005). Which physicians and practices are using electronic medical records? *Health Affairs (Project Hope), 24*(5), 1334-1343.

Gans, D., Kralewski, J., Hammons, T., & Dowd, B. (2005). Medical groups' adoption of electronic health records and information systems. *Health Affairs (Project Hope), 24*(5), 1323-1333.

Greenfield, S., & Kaplan, S. H. (2004). Creating a culture of quality: The remarkable transformation of the department of veterans affairs health care system. *Annals of Internal Medicine, 141*(4), 316-318.

Hartzband, P., & Groopman, J. (2008). Off the record--avoiding the pitfalls of going electronic. *The New England Journal of Medicine, 358*(16), 1656-1658.

Hillestad, R., Bigelow, J., Bower, A., Girosi, F., Meili, R., Scoville, R., et al. (2005). Can electronic medical record systems transform health care? potential health benefits, savings, and costs. *Health Affairs (Project Hope), 24*(5), 1103-1117.

Hing, E. S., Burt, C. W., & Woodwell, D. A. (2007). Electronic medical record use by office-based physicians and their practices: United states, 2006. *Advance Data, (393)*(393), 1-7.

Jha, A. K., Perlin, J. B., Kizer, K. W., & Dudley, R. A. (2003). Effect of the transformation of the veterans affairs health care system on the quality of care. *The New England Journal of Medicine, 348*(22), 2218-2227.

Kleinke, J. D. (2005). Dot-gov: Market failure and the creation of a national health information technology system. *Health Affairs (Project Hope), 24*(5), 1246-1262.

Menachemi, N., Matthews, M. C., Ford, E. W., & Brooks, R. G. (2007). The influence of payer mix on electronic health record adoption by physicians. *Health Care Management Review, 32*(2), 111-118.

Miller, R. H., West, C., Brown, T. M., Sim, I., & Ganchoff, C. (2005). The value of electronic health records in solo or small group practices. *Health Affairs (Project Hope), 24*(5), 1127-1137.

O'Neill, L., & Klepack, W. (2007). Electronic medical records for a rural family practice: A case study in systems development. *Journal of Medical Systems, 31*(1), 25-33.

Rogers, E. M. (1995). *Diffusion of innovations* (4th ed.). New York: Free Press.

Rosenthal, M. B., Landon, B. E., Howitt, K., Song, H. R., & Epstein, A. M. (2007). Climbing up the pay-for-performance learning curve: Where are the early adopters now? *Health Affairs (Project Hope), 26*(6), 1674-1682.

Rosenthal, D. A., & Layman, E. J. (2008). Utilization of information technology in eastern north carolina physician practices: Determining the existence of a digital divide. *Perspectives in Health Information Management / AHIMA, American Health Information Management Association, 5*, 3.

Shortliffe, E. H. (2005). Strategic action in health information technology: Why the obvious has taken so long. *Health Affairs (Project Hope), 24*(5), 1222-1233.

Wang, S. J., Middleton, B., Prosser, L. A., Bardon, C. G., Spurr, C. D., Carchidi, P. J., et al. (2003). A cost-benefit analysis of electronic medical records in primary care. *The American Journal of Medicine, 114*(5), 397-403.

This work was previously published in International Journal of Healthcare Information Systems and Informatics, Vol. 4, Issue 2, edited by J Tan, pp. 69-80, copyright 2009 by IGI Publishing (an imprint of IGI Global).

Chapter 26
An e-Healthcare Mobile Application:
A Stakeholders' Analysis Experience of Reading

Niki Panteli
University of Bath, UK

Barbara Pitsillides
Nicosia, Cyprus

Andreas Pitsillides
University of Cyprus, Cyprus

George Samaras
University of Cyprus, Cyprus

ABSTRACT

This chapter presents a longitudinal study on the implementation of an e-health mobile application, DITIS, which supports network collaboration for home healthcare. By adopting the stakeholders' analysis, the study explores the various groups that have directly or indirectly supported the system during its implementation. The system was originally developed with a view to address the difficulties of communication and continuity of care between the members of a home healthcare multidisciplinary team and between the team and oncologists often hundreds of kilometers away. DITIS evolved to be much more than that and even though it was introduced 5 years ago, it is considered a novel application. Despite this, its implementation has been slow, and several challenges, including the system's sustainability, have to be faced. This chapter aims to understand these challenges and the results of the study point to a diversity of interests and different degrees of support.

INTRODUCTION

Healthcare is an environment that has been experiencing dramatic progress in computing technology in order to process and distribute all relevant patient information electronically and overall to improve the quality of care. In particular, mobile e-health involves a spectrum of information and telecommunication technologies to provide healthcare services to patients who are at some distance from the provider and also to provide supporting tools for the mobile healthcare professional. The benefits of such mobile applications are numerous, with the main one being improvements in access to medical resources and care.

Recently, the healthcare and related sectors have been found to embrace mobile technology in e-healthcare applications. Though there have also been cases of mobile workstations being implemented at small medical units to facilitate easier access to specialist medical advice (e.g., Salmon, Brint, Marshall, & Bradley, 2000), most of the applications have been introduced to support patients at home. These could either be patient centered where patients and/or caretakers are given direct access to a mobile phone for communicating with the provider (e.g., nurse, doctor, counselor, etc.), or nurse centered where nurses who visit and care for patients at home have direct access to mobile applications for communicating with other medical staff.

It follows that the practice of e-health projects is often a collaborative activity requiring extensive and interactive communication within and between members of specialized occupational groups to coordinate patient care services. This becomes necessary when dealing with patients requiring a multidisciplinary team approach to their care, and who are treated outside the hospital environment. In such a case, the team is mostly geographically dispersed and rarely sees the patient together. This requires the creation of virtual multidisciplinary teams of care whose management and coordination can be supported by technology. In the study, we aim to explore the role of diverse stakeholders in an e-health application involving virtual multidisciplinary teams of care. Diverse stakeholders get involved at different stages of the project implementation and may experience different degrees of knowledge about the system itself, its significance, and its novelty. These along with their different backgrounds, interests, and expectations may contribute to different meanings and understanding about the system, its role, and its significance, which will ultimately affect system implementation.

BACKGROUND

Stakeholders' Analysis

The role of stakeholders in IS implementation has long been recognized in the literature, though it has only been during the last few years that the identification of different stakeholders as well as the roles and interrelationships between them was found to be important for uncovering some of the complexity in system implementation (Pouloudi & Whitley, 1997).

Despite this, researchers have given different definitions to stakeholders. Sauer (1993), for example, makes reference to stakeholders as supporters, those who provide funding, information, and influence, whilst Beynon-Davies (1999) argues that there is a need to broaden this definition. As he puts it, "...not all groups with an interest in the development of an information system necessarily support that development. Some stakeholder groups may have a definite negative interest in the success of a given project" (p. 710). Following from these, in this chapter, in an attempt to keep a broad definition, stakeholders are defined as those with a direct or an indirect interest in a project.

According to Mitchell, Agle, and Wood (1997), stakeholders can be distinguished in terms of three relationship attributes: power, legitimacy, and urgency. Power is the ability to impose influence on the relationship; legitimacy is "a generalized perception or assumption that the actions of an entity are desirable, proper, or appropriate within some socially constructed system of norms, values, beliefs, and definitions" (Suchman as cited in Mitchell et al., p. 574). Finally, "[u]rgency is based on time sensitivity and criticality" (Mitchell et al. as cited in Howard, Vidgen, & Powell, 2003, p. 31). A combination of these three attributes contributes to different types of stakeholders who have different roles and expectations.

EMPIRICAL STUDY

In this section, we present the case of an e-health mobile application and adopt a stakeholders' analysis to understand its implementation process and the challenges faced.

Mobile applications are an increasingly important technology for improving the quality of health services, especially at the point of care. They enable the formation of virtual teams of care, and timely, effective, and quality patient management are the expected outcomes. The role of stakeholders in supporting such innovative applications is vital.

The System

DITIS: Virtual Collaborative Teams for Home Healthcare (http://www.ditis.ucy.ac.cy) is an Internet- (Web) based group collaboration system with secure fixed and mobile (GPRS [general packet radio service], GSM [Global System for Mobile Communication], WAP [wireless application protocol]) connectivity (see Figure 1).

It enables the effective management and coordination of virtual collaborative healthcare teams. It provides a secure access to e-records from anyplace and anytime via desktop computers (at work) or a variety of mobile devices (when on the go). It includes a set of tools for effective scheduling and coordination of team members, with features including automatic notification and alerting. It makes use of supportive tools relevant to home care that improve efficiency and minimize errors. The collaboration platform is based on identified roles and scenarios of collaboration, analyzed using the unified modeling language (UML).

The DITIS project was initiated in 1999 to support the activities of the home healthcare service of the Cyprus Association of Cancer Patients and Friends (Pasykaf). The goal of DITIS is to

Figure 1. DITIS system architecture

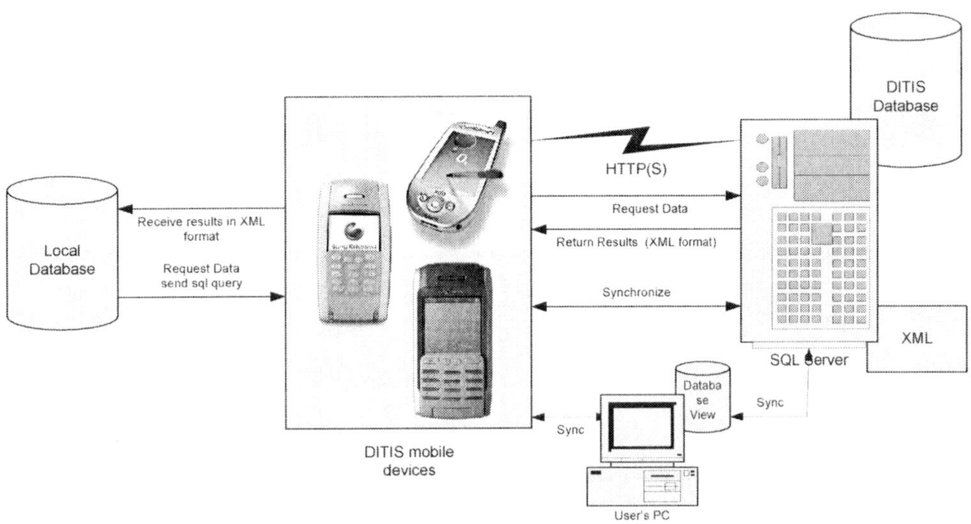

deliver a product that can improve the quality of the citizen's life. Contrary to today's health processing structure, which is, in all practical terms, facility-based care, this project aims to shift the focus onto home-based care, where everything is moving around the patient, supported by a team of multidisciplinary healthcare professionals. Given that the team cannot be by the side of the patient at all times, DITIS developed a collaborative software system to support dynamic virtual healthcare teams, customized for the differing needs of each patient at different times. The virtual healthcare team is supported in its provision of dedicated, personalized, and private service to the home-residing patient on a need based and timely fashion, under the direction of the treating specialist. Thus, it is expected that chronic and severe patients, such as cancer patients, can enjoy optimum health service in the comfort of their home (i.e., a focus on wellness), feeling safe and secure that in case of a change in their condition, the healthcare team will be (virtually) present to support them. The present users of the system include the healthcare professionals treating cancer patients (home-care nurse, oncologist, treating doctor, psychologist, physiotherapist, social worker, etc.) and the Pasykaf administration. It is expected that the system will be extended to other paramedical professionals, as, for example, the Pharmacist and the Cancer Registry, currently located at the Ministry of Health. Furthermore, the system can be adapted to cater to other home healthcare needs, as, for example, cardiac, renal, or diabetic patients.

DITIS deploys a novel networked system for tele-collaboration in the area of patient care at the home by a virtual team of medical and paramedical professionals, implemented using existing networking and computing components (the novelty of the system and competing approaches are briefly discussed in A. Pitsillides et al., 2005; B. Pitsillides et al., 2004). The system was originally developed with a view to address the difficulties of communication and continuity of care between the home healthcare multidisciplinary team (Pasykaf) and between the team and the oncologist often many miles apart. DITIS has through its database and possibility of access via mobile or wire-line computers offered much more than improved communication. Its flexibility of communication and access to the patient's history and daily record at all times, anywhere (in the case of home patients, outpatients, or an emergency hospital admission), has offered the team an overall assessment and history of each symptom. DITIS thus has the potential to improve the quality of life of the patient, for example, by offering the nurse the possibility of immediate authorization to change prescriptions via mobile devices, and the oncologist the possibility of assessment and symptom control without having to see the patient. It also offers the home-care service provider the opportunity to plan future services and lobby for funding by offering audit, statistics, and performance evaluation, and with these in place, the possibility for research.

The User Organization

Pasykaf, the user organization, was founded in 1986 to provide support to cancer patients and their families during their period of rehabilitation and is manned with highly qualified medical, paramedical, and nursing staff. In 1992, it started a home-care service for cancer patients. Specially trained palliative-care nurses in close cooperation with doctors (general practitioners and oncologists), physiotherapists, and psychologists attend and care for patients at home, focusing on maintaining the best possible quality of life, including medical care and psychological support.

In the context of home care, home-care professionals visit patients at home. Traditionally, the team of professionals was (loosely) coordinated by weekly meetings, or in case of some urgent event, information was exchanged by telephone calls or face-to-face meetings. Often, the same information is requested from the patient so each professional can build his or her own medical and psychosocial history and treatment notes (handwritten). Traditionally, these handwritten notes were filed at the Pasykaf district offices once the healthcare professional returned to the office. On a scheduled visit, the file had to be removed from the office and taken with the healthcare professional to the patient's house. This was inflexible and restrictive as there was no possibility of access by another healthcare professional at the same time. Furthermore, after hours, on-call professionals had to make a special visit to the office to collect the patient file (even if there was no other business with the office). For a patient visit to the hospital, especially in an emergency, there was no possibility of immediate access to the patient file from the attending home-care nurse. Therefore, there was limited possibility for continuity of care.

As with every manual system, there was limited possibility for audits and statistics, research was difficult, evidence-based medicine was not supported, dynamic coordination of the team was almost impossible, and communication overheads were very high and extremely costly in human and monetary terms. DITIS aims to address these problems in the provision of home-care services by a team of professionals.

Generally, given the limitations of the existing home-care delivery models, the need for improved ICT-supported practices emerged. Even though the context of health reform may vary across countries, major objectives are similar and include the following:

- A move toward people-centered services.
- A commitment to healthy public policy and a desire to improve the health status and quality of life of individuals and communities.
- Increased emphasis on knowledge- and evidence-based decision making, and efficiency and effectiveness in service delivery.
- A shift from facility-based health services and a focus on illness to community-based health services and a focus on wellness.
- The integration of agencies, programs and services to achieve a seamless continuum of health and health-related services.
- Greater community involvement in priority setting and decision making.

DITIS aims to support the above healthcare reform objectives. We focus our analysis on home healthcare of cancer patients, but expect our results to be applicable to home healthcare in general as well as cross-cultural and cross-border interoperability. Thus, through DITIS, we expect to assist in the delivery of better home care by offering the healthcare team services that are aimed at achieving a seamless continuum of health and health-related services despite the structural problems of home care as compared to facility-based care.

The system was initially deployed in one district, District A, and was gradually implemented in another three districts. The study has adopted the longitudinal approach in data collection for the first 5 years of the system from 1999 to 2004.

Methods and Data Collection

This research is interpretive as our aim is to capture stakeholders' interpretations of the system itself and their use of the system. To this end, our research method is qualitative in nature, examining "humans within their social settings" (Orlikowski & Baroudi, 1991, p. 14).

The fieldwork has taken place in various district sites of Pasykaf. Each site is served by a number of palliative-care nurses who visit patients regularly in their house to offer support. Data on DITIS were collected on different stages of the implementation process.

Phase 1: The preliminary part of the research has studied the use of mobile telephones by a group of palliative-care nurses during the period of August to September 2000. Interviews with three nurses and one doctor in District A have enabled the study of nurse-to-nurse interactions and nurse-doctor interactions via the use of mobile telephones, whilst also contributed to gathering information on their level of awareness about DITIS and its potential use in palliative care.

Phase 2: This part of the study took place in May 2001 and involved the use of a structured questionnaire that was sent to DITIS developers and potential users. It aimed to explore stakeholders' expectations regarding DITIS. A copy of this questionnaire appears in the appendix.

Phase 3: The third phase of data collection took place in April 2003. By this time, DITIS was implemented in four district sites. During this phase, current users of the system in three district Pasykaf offices were interviewed: one psychologist and three nurses. The main issues explored during interviews included the participants' actual use of DITIS, their own explanation of why they use DITIS the way they do, and their understanding of what users' and others stakeholders' role should be for achieving effective DITIS use.

Phase 4: This final part of the study took place in April 2004. Interviews included users (nurses and psychologist) as well as members of other stakeholder teams. During this phase, it was found that even though DITIS has been implemented effectively with the right support from the project team, anxiety was identified at different levels with regard to its future.

Table 1 summarizes the data-collection approach adopted.

RESULTS

Overall, the data reveal that DITIS offers innumerable opportunities for palliative-care nurses and other cancer-care practitioners. DITIS is currently widely accepted as an invaluable tool in palliative care. Nurses, psychologists, and doctors acknowledge that DITIS has numerous advantages and that they are willing to incorporate it in their work activities. DITIS can improve communication, coordination, and collaboration among members. Due to the huge amount of data regarding new and old patient records that need to be handled on a daily basis, DITIS enables users to access data quickly either from their office or remotely. Furthermore, it can be used as a statistical tool for producing internal reports

Table 1. Summary of the adopted data-collection approach

Phase	Time Period	No. of Interviews	Purpose
Phase 1	August-September 2000	4	Understand context of work, users' awareness about DITIS
Phase 2	May 2001	7	Users' expectations
Phase 3	April 2003	4	Level of usage & explanations given
Phase 4	April 2004	5	Stakeholders' own evaluation of DITIS

for the district offices and the head office as well as external reports required by the Ministry of Health and other government departments.

"Pasykaf will be able to extract more information and statistics about cancer symptoms. Information about cancers and their occurrence by region will help to detect possible reasons that may be responsible about cancer (e.g. factories in the areas, etc.)" (Developer, Phase 2).

"Life will be so much easier with DITIS to fill in the gaps from unknown to known" (Nurse, District B).

Interestingly, even though technophobia was identified in Phase 1 of this study as a possible negative factor in the effective implementation of the system, it was later expressed by nurses across different district sites that participated in Phase 3 that users are generally willing to adapt the system in their day-to-day work because they expect that their tasks will be executed faster and easier, saving time and effort.

It was agreed among all participants in the study that the project was a novel one, that it was a radical departure from what existed previously, and that it was designed to be at the core of Pasykaf's activities (i.e., the provision of healthcare to home-based cancer patients).

Implementation Problems

During the first three phases of the study, there was a general feeling that DITIS had not yet been sufficiently incorporated in the daily work activities of the healthcare workers and that this would be a slow process. The main problems identified were with regard to the implementation process. A nurse in District B clearly said that this process "has been slow from all points of view" (Phase 3).

It has been widely recognized that the effectiveness of the system implementation was jeopardized due to financial resources being constrained or at times becoming unavailable. The limited budget that the project development team had to work with mainly had two major implications. First, only a small number of mobile handsets could be acquired. As a result, only nurses in one district office (District A) were given a mobile device with DITIS application, whilst other district offices have to rely only on PC- (personal computer) based applications of DITIS. The latter, however, restricts the use and the potentials of DITIS, which has been developed as a wireless application to promote virtual collaboration in cancer care. Second, limited financial resources have influenced staff availability on the project implementation team. The project has been experiencing staff discontinuities since the early stages of DITIS development. Mainly graduate students have been used for this project under the guidance of two computer-science academics, both members of the DITIS project team. Even though the latter remained the main drivers of the project, DITIS was only one of several projects that they were involved in and therefore could not give their full attention as required by the criticality of the project nature. To quote a nurse, "The system was done on borrowed time" (District A, Phase 3), indicating that for most of the implementation period, there were no full-time project members; rather, even though the system had gained the enthusiasm of several people who committed themselves to the system, none of them could make a full-time commitment. Instead, there were several temporary project members throughout the duration of the implementation process leading to staff turnover. Therefore, the high staff turnover and the lack of full-time staff brought inconsistencies and delays in the project development.

As the psychologist who participated in the study (Phase 3) put it, "There is no person in charge and this leads to communication problems." The same person suggested that there was a need for frequent meetings to keep users informed about the state of the implementation process, alleviate doubts, and improve coordination among cross-groups (e.g., nurses, doctors, psychologists).

Based on the results of the longitudinal assessment, corrective measures were taken, including the creation of a more stable team due to the commitment of all relevant actors and availability of funding. These corrective actions were acknowledged by all the users interviewed in Phase 4 of the study. During this phase, there was a general feeling of satisfaction about the use of DITIS in the day-to-day work practices as users have by now begun seeing the benefits of the system.

> *"The system is more reliable."*
> *"It is 100% better."*

Despite these positive results, there appears to be some anxiety among users about the sustainability of the system. DITIS has been successful in attaining the initial goals set. However, several difficulties, some non-technical in nature, were encountered during the development and deployment of DITIS in Phase I. These are outlined below:

- Underestimation of the workload involved in order to populate the DITIS database, and misjudgment of effort for encouraging users who are used to a paper-based system to switch to a new system, which was in essence still incomplete and under construction
- Network technology limitations (e.g., WAP over GSM). The migration to new technologies (GPRS/UMTS [Universal Mobile Telecommunications System] and ADSL) is resolving many of the original technical problems: Service is always available and bandwidth is much higher.
- Deployment with mobile devices has been limited mainly due to the cost related with having each member of the home-care team have his or her own mobile device, and the pace of new device launches with enhanced functionality. Recently, 30 mobile devices were acquired and are being deployed. This will allow a number of multidisciplinary teams to operate.
- Sustainability of DITIS due to uncertain financial support. Potential funding may derive from the government through its spin-off company initiative. Another one is the Ministry of Health for its planned community-care service.

Stakeholders: Relationships and Roles

The main stakeholders of DITIS derive from inside as well as outside the user organization. A key stakeholder group consists of the nurses and other members of the medical team in the district offices, for example, psychologists who directly use the system. Gradually, the nursing team has begun to embrace DITIS and overcome the initial resistance that was mainly caused due to the delays in implementing the system.

A second group involves the university computer scientists who designed the original system and currently manage the project development and implementation. They have the intellectual property of the system and are the ones who actively promote the system to national and international organizations in order to attract funding that would enable them to continue developing and improving the system. Their interest is in "the expansion of the collaborative system for usage in other fields (e.g., cardiac home care, insurance sales, etc.) and its eventual commercialization" (interview with project leader). The cost of setting up such an infrastructure and supporting it vs. the benefits, such as quality of life and time saved, are difficult to justify in monetary terms; also, there is the potential benefit of using GPRS and ADSL (Asymmetric Digital Subscriber Line) (always connected, higher speeds) vs. the earlier GSM/WAP mobile telephone device and ISDN (integrated services digital network) for the fixed computer lines (dial-up, low bandwidth), and the costs of maintaining such a telecom infrastructure to consider. Another barrier is the high cost of handheld devices and rapid change of technology, which have hindered projects development Cyprus-wide.

An independent commercial software organization that supported the initial idea and design of DITIS has also been a key stakeholder. This organization has recently withdrawn from the project after the first stage of its implementation as they could not see the financial viability and profitability of the project and were no longer interested in investing in mobile-based applications. Another commercial software organization with a focus on mobile e-services has recently joined the project.

Finally, an important stakeholder is Pasykaf as the user organization that hosts the system in its district offices as well as in the headquarters. Pasykaf, a charity organization, is interested in the project as it can see that the system can predominantly enable it to produce national and regional statistical information on cancer and cancer patients, which are required by the government. Our study, however, has shown that the involvement of Pasykaf management in this project has remained limited. Several users recognized that Pasykaf in particular should undertake a more active role in the implementation of the project by investing more time and administrative support.

Accordingly, the stakeholders derive from diverse sectors, and even though they all want DITIS to succeed, their expectations are different. From our data, it was found that all stakeholders agree on the important role that the system could have in cancer support.

In what follows, we describe these different types of stakeholders and identify their relevance to the DITIS project. Based on Mitchell et al.'s model (1997), Figure 2 depicts the stakeholders' relationship attributes and the different types of stakeholders.

Definitive stakeholders possess power, legitimacy, and urgency. The project initiators at the university fall in this group. Due to their active involvement in the design and promotion of the system, they possess both power and legitimacy whilst simultaneously are aware of the risks involved if no funding is secured. For this, they have a clear and immediate mandate to give priority to

Figure 2. Stakeholder typology (Mitchell et al., 1997, p. 874)

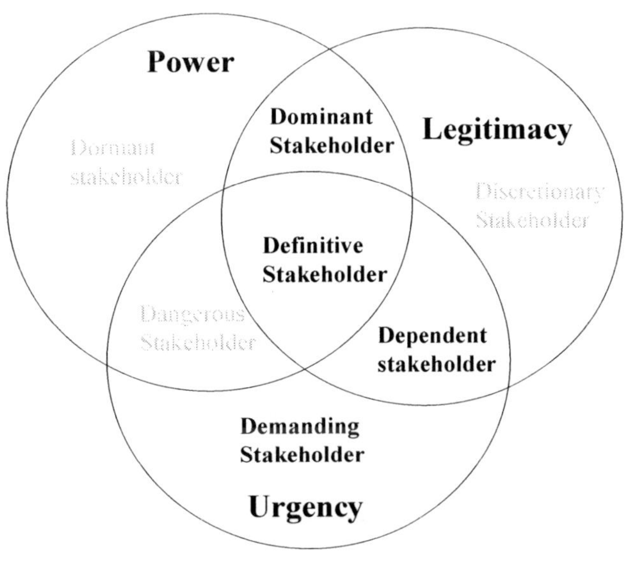

the project and have considered several options, one of which is commercialization.

Demanding stakeholders exist where there is urgency but no other relationship attribute. Within this category, we place the commercial organization that became involved in the initial design of the system. It did so for commercial interests. Due to the financial difficulties that the project faced, the company decided to withdraw their demands for commercialization and thus profitability has not been met.

Dormant *stakeholders* **are the** *stakeholders* who possess power to impose their will, but by not having a legitimate relationship or an urgent claim, their power remains unused...Dormant *stakeholders* have little or no interaction with the firm. However, because of their potential to acquire a second attribute, management should remain cognizant of such *stakeholders*, for the dynamic nature of the stakeholder-manager relationship suggests that dormant *stakeholders* will become more salient to managers if they acquire either urgency or legitimacy. (Mitchell et al., 1997, pp. 874-875)

In the case of DITIS, the dormant stakeholder is the government and other funding bodies that have shown an interest in the system. Because of their potential role in the future of the system, the project management team (university) should remain cognizant of such stakeholders. It is expected that the government's power will be exercised when there is a better recognition of the potentials of the system not only in cancer care but in the other health areas, too.

Dependent *stakeholders* **are those** "who lack power but who have urgent legitimate claims as 'dependent,' because these *stakeholders* depend upon others [e.g., other *stakeholders*] for the power necessary to carry out their will" (Mitchell et al., 1997, p. 877). Nurses represent this type of stakeholders. Their voice has mainly been represented through Pasykaf (management) itself, and, as it was found in the study, their interest in the system is predominantly for efficiency and accuracy in statistical analysis.

Dominant stakeholders are both powerful and legitimate. Their influence in the relationship is assured since by possessing power and legitimacy they form the dominant coalition. In our case, we find that Pasykaf itself belongs to this group of stakeholders as it represents the only host of the system. However, as a charity organization, it has been unable to fund the project itself and therefore its position has remained weak and the management team needs to look elsewhere for financial support. It is expected that when other funders are found, for example, the government, or with the commercialization of the system, the power of Pasykaf will be reduced as other host organizations will emerge, such as those for cardio-care support.

Other stakeholder groups that were identified in Mitchell et al.'s (1997) framework and shown in Figure 2 but not found in our own study are as follows:

- Discretionary stakeholders possess legitimacy, but have no power for influencing the firm and no urgent claims.
- Dangerous stakeholders possess urgency and power but no legitimacy; this may result in the use of coercive power.
- Non-stakeholders possess none of the attributes and thus do not have any type of relationship with the rest of the group.

Accordingly, it is found that in the case of DITIS there were five different distinct types of stakeholders. The diversity in their views, which is expressed in the reasons they give to the legitimacy of the system, as well as the perceived urgency and their ability to influence the system have all contributed to different degrees of support. In this study, apart from the commercial organization, all the other stakeholders have been positively supportive of the implementation process. They have been doing so differently, however, with some, such as the university team, taking a more active role in securing funding and hosting the project team whilst others, such as Pasykaf, remaining more passive. This passiveness is not, however, due to a lack of interest but rather due to other priorities.

FUTURE TRENDS

The potentials of mobile applications in e-health are tremendous. They could be used for supporting health professionals in offering care through improved e-tools (e.g., for improved access to patient records by all health professionals, improved collaboration, and streamlined workflow), which are especially useful for the community-care environment. However, even though mobile technology is a key factor for enabling the formation of geographically proximate medical teams at the point of care, their effective implementation depend not only on the level of support provided to users, but also by the extent to which there is a shared understanding and support among diverse groups of stakeholders.

An important contribution of this study is an examination of the role of diverse stakeholders on the implementation of such a novel e-health initiative. With a growing recognition that e-health can make an impact on the provision of healthcare as well as that e-health applications are becoming even more global, investigating the diversity that may exist among the various stakeholders is becoming vital for their success.

CONCLUSION

This chapter presents a longitudinal study on the implementation of an e-health mobile application, DITIS, which supports network collaboration for home healthcare. Our study has found that users' support has gradually improved over the last years as they have been increasingly exposed to the system capabilities and have recognized the advantages of the system in their day-to-day work for both administrative and consultation purposes. Another reason for this is that the nurses have gained participation in the project team with periodical meetings with the project manager and developers. Yet, the future of the system is uncertain as future funding to gain sustainability may not be available. Such a complex and novel system has not gained shared support by all parties concerned, with one company dropping out (while another one joined) and others not taking an active role. The long-term solution is commercialization, which is currently pursued, but as with any new ideas and products, there is considerable risk involved. The study has adopted the stakeholders' analysis (Mitchell et al., 1997) and found that there are different relationship characteristics among the key stakeholders who show diversity in interests, expectations, and levels of involvement in the system implementation.

DITIS has appeared to act as a useful fuel for improving patient records and promoting an integrated approach that has a direct impact on the quality of treatment and healthcare support to home-based cancer patients. However, even though this is a novel application and despite the fact that it was introduced 5 years ago, the implementation has remained slow and the system has not yet been able to secure its place and its future in the health sector; rather, it has gradually been making an impact on the healthcare support provided by some nurses and medical staff. Lack of organization ownership makes the future of the system uncertain. What has enabled it to survive was the enthusiasm of some key individuals, mainly the university team and those users who could see the direct benefits of the system on the quality of cancer care. Speedy commercialization of the system seems to be the solution for its long-term survivability, and this is the current focus. In the meantime, DITIS is at present being deployed for its healthcare collaboration and patient-management aspects in the context of two EU- (European Union) funded e-TEN (deploying Trans-European e-services for all) market validation projects (HealthService24 and LinkCare) involving trials for cardiac-patient monitoring.

REFERENCES

Beynon-Davies, P. (1999). Human error and information systems failure: The case of the London ambulance service computer-aided dispatch system project. *Interacting with Computers, 11*, 699-720.

DITIS: Virtual Collaborative Teams for Home Healthcare. (n.d.). Retrieved July 2005 from http://www.ditis.ucy.ac.cy

Howard, M., Vidgen, R., & Powell, P. (2003). Overcoming stakeholder barriers in the automotive industry: Building to order with extra-organizational systems. *Journal of Information Technology, 18*, 27-43.

Mitchell, R., Agle, B., & Wood, D. (1997). Towards a theory of stakeholder identification and salience. *Academy of Management Review, 22*(4), 853-887.

Orlikowski, W. J., & Baroudi, J. J. (1991). Studying information technology in organizations: Research approaches and assumptions. *Information Systems Research, 2*(1), 1-28.

Pitsillides, A., Pitsillides, B., Samaras, G., Dikaiakos, M., Christodoulou, E., Andreou, P., et al. (2005). DITIS: A collaborative virtual medical team for the home healthcare of cancer patients. In *M-health: Emerging mobile health* (pp. 247-266). Kluwer Academic/Plenum Publishers. Springer: New York.

Pitsillides, B., Pitsillides, A., Samaras, G., Christodoulou, E., Panteli, N., Andreou, P., et al. (2004). *User perspective of DITIS: Virtual collaborative teams for home-healthcare: Vol. 100. Current situation and examples of implemented and beneficial e-health applications* (pp. 205-216). IOS Press: The Netherlands.

Pouloudi, A., & Whitley, E. A. (1997). Stakeholders identification in inter-organizational systems: Gaining insights for drug use management systems. *European Journal of Information Systems, 6*, 1-14.

Salmon, S., Brnt, G., Marshall, D., & Bradley, A. (2000). Telemedicine use in two-nurse-led injuries units. *Journal of Telemedicine and Telecare, 6*(Suppl. 1), 43-45.

Sauer, C. (1993). *Why information systems fail: A case study approach.* Henley on Thames, UK: Alfred Waller.

Suchman, M. C. (1995). Managing legitimacy: Strategic and institutional approaches. *Academy of Management Review, 20*, 571-610.

APPENDIX

DITIS Implementation Project, May 2001

Please take a few minutes to answer the following questions. I would appreciate if you return the completed questionnaire to me by e-mail.

Thank you very much for your contribution.

Please tick that which most identifies your involvement in the DITIS project.

Designer/Developer: ☐
User (Nurse): ☐
User (Doctor): ☐
Other (please specify): ☐

What do you think the main benefits would be for implementing DITIS within Pasykaf?

After implementation, how do you expect DITIS to be used on a day-day to basis?

What would you expect the results of the pilot study to be? Please identify in your answer those factors that you think might enable or constrain the success of this pilot.

This work was previously published in Web Mobile-Based Applications for Healthcare Management, edited by L. Al-Hakim, pp. 101-117, copyright 2007 by IRM Press (an imprint of IGI Global).

Chapter 27
Mobile E-Health:
Making the Case[1]

Norm Archer
McMaster University, Canada

ABSTRACT

Health care is an industry with a diverse set of stakeholders: governments, private health care providers, medical practitioners (physicians, nurses, researchers, etc.), home health care providers and workers, and last but not least, clients/patients and their families. Overlapping and interacting environments include hospitals, clinics, long-term care facilities, primary care providers, homes, and so forth, involving acute, emergency, chronic, primary, and outpatient care. Patient transitions between these environments are often unnecessarily difficult due to an inability by providers to access pre-existing patient records. Mobile/wireless solutions can play an important role in supporting health care by providing applications that access health care records and reduce paperwork for clinical physicians, nurses, and other workers, community health care practitioners and their patients, or mobile chronically ill patients such as diabetics. This chapter makes the case for mobile health care and its solutions in the non-acute community health care environment, where critical issues include usability, adoption, interoperability, change management, risk mitigation, security and privacy, and return on investment. A proposed community health care application demonstrates how these issues are addressed.

INTRODUCTION

Many individuals receive their care from more than one caregiver or other provider: individual physician, group practice, hospital, long-term care facility, laboratory, pharmacy, walk-in clinic, urgent care center, work-site clinics, school clinics, and so forth. When and where choice is available, clients can select caregivers or other providers based on their proximity, bedside manner, quality and capability, cultural aptitude, or other factors. Clients/patients also must move among health care providers as their state of health changes, creating a need for their health records/histories to move with them, so each provider does not need to prepare a totally new patient history at admission (see Figure 1). Without the general existence of digital health records and some means of integration or interoperability, individual choice and movement leads to fragmentation of the individual's health care experience. Typically, this means that client record transfers are accomplished from one or

Figure 1. Information flows in patient-centred health care (adapted from Krull-Naraj, 2004)

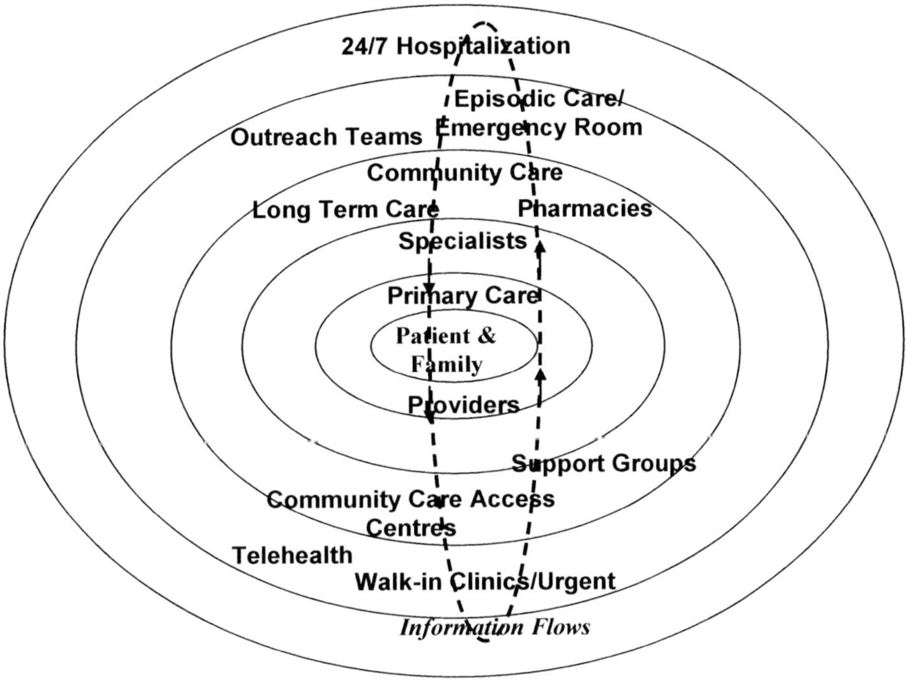

more sources via paper, scanned digital records, and/or fax. The result is that client records may be stored on paper at a number of caregiver institutions or re-keyed into institutional databases, with no possibility of version control or compatibility. This fragmentation of records often leads to errors, duplication, lack of coordination (Brailer, 2005), conflicting approaches to a patient's health care, service and/or resource duplication and many other problems including reduced quality of care, reduced effectiveness, and increased cost to society.

Integration mechanisms have been tried in the past, although none has delivered lasting benefit. These include horizontal and vertical mergers of providers, state-sponsored networks of community care services, and so forth. However, there is theoretically no technical barrier to establishing a network of providers that would use information in an interoperable manner for integrated support of patient care, and this would not require a massive integration of physical assets and the bureaucracy required to operate it. In the U.S. alone, the potential savings from such an approach have been estimated at U.S. $77.8 billion per year (Walker, Pan, Johnston, Adler-Milstein, Bates, & Middleton, 2005). This does not include the substantial clinical and quality of life benefits from this approach. Unfortunately, it has been virtually impossible in most jurisdictions to get broad agreement on a standard and portable electronic health record (EHR) that would support this interoperability. Although the standardized EHR has a continuing focus of the health care community (Berner, Detmer, & Simborg, 2005), the process of adopting a standard would still require large investments in the database conversion process and the necessary secure communications network that would safeguard client privacy and confidentiality. However, without interoperability and health information exchange, health information will remain as it is now, in proprietary and often inaccessible silos.

The lack of a standard EHR definition, and the

lack of interoperability among health care providers are both major strategic issues in information technology support for health care. No doubt at some time in the distant future both these problems will be addressed at a macro-level, but in the meantime, it is essential to make incremental improvements that will adapt to the constantly changing environment in a way that continuously improves health care support at the local level (Lenz & Kuhn, 2004). Such changes may be significant enough to be disruptive to users, so it is critical to plan and implement changes so that already overburdened health care professionals and administrative support receive relief in the most effective and efficient manner possible under the circumstances.

Health delivery practice for non-acute care in many industrialized countries is shifting toward the home. The reasons are the better possibilities for managing chronic care and controlling health delivery costs, but the appropriate infrastructure must be in place in order to maintain client quality of life through quality health services, and the need to predict and thus avoid serious complications. For this potential to be realized, new interoperable telemedicine and information technology (IT) solutions need to be implemented and integrated in the health delivery system, but these solutions need to be assessed through evidence-based medicine in order to provide solid proof for their usefulness. To ensure that quality care delivered efficiently any time and any place requires ready access to patient records and expertise from remote sources such as specialists and online databases, and mobile wireless technology can enable this support. True wireless communities where processes, technology, and people are fully aligned to mobile applications, have a great deal of potential, especially where smooth transitions by patients among the types of care they may experience, including acute, emergency, chronic, primary, and homecare, require continuing coordination among health care institutions, medical practitioners, health care workers, care givers, and the patients themselves. The real benefit of mobility support will come only when technology and process are built around a plan that embraces mobility, and where mobility is not an afterthought.

As mobile wireless unfolds, the health care world must assess both its technical and value propositions, to determine if it has a real value proposition to offer, in terms of quality of life maintenance at lower costs than existing systems. The objective of this chapter is to discuss the roles that electronic mobile solutions can play in health care, and particularly the value propositions and their evaluation that must play a role in the selection of these solutions for efficient and effective use. The concepts presented will be demonstrated by an application in a real mobile health care application.

MOBILITY

Mobility is an aspect of many environments. How mobility affects individuals tends to differ, depending on the nature of what they are doing (working, relaxing, traveling, etc.), their preferences, the form that mobility takes, and the amount of time involved. Supporting mobility through electronic solutions is having a growing impact on individuals by enabling them to carry devices that assist them to stay in constant communication with their organizations, friends, family, and advisors. This may involve using voice or data messages, paging, direct communications by telephone or teleconferencing, and database or document information access, storage, and retrieval. In working environments such as hospitals, such applications are often built upon existing e-business solutions such as corporate and operational databases, along with functional or corporate support areas and their associated networks such as LANs and Internet connectivity. The growing availability of a variety of mobile applications and technologies has encouraged the extension or replacement of existing approaches and business processes. We are only beginning to see true wireless environments where processes, technology, and people are fully aligned to a mobile environment.

Mobile Solutions

The potential selection of systems and devices for mobile support includes voice and data communications, ranging all the way from cell phones to laptop computers and PDAs (personal digital assistants). It will be assumed that end users have ready access to voice communication through cellphones, since these are rapidly becoming as ubiquitous as landline telephones. Mobile or wireless solutions discussed here may use the same networks, including and extending voice cellphone communication. Mobile solutions can be used to support hospital or clinical workers, or community health care practitioners or their patients, where the workers may be away from their home office a high percentage of the time, while traveling or meeting with clients. Others may need to travel occasionally to different sites for meetings, conferences, or training. Clients such as ambulatory care patients may also adopt mobile or monitoring devices, in order to use the services of mobile health care providers. Mobile solutions allow employment hours to be flexible and to extend beyond those hours actually spent in the office, including lunch and break time, traveling to and from work, traveling to meetings, holidays, weekends and evenings. Although this may result in an attendant increase in productivity, working with others through mobile applications may not necessarily fulfill all the needs of workers.

Pervasive Computing

Pervasive computing can be defined as personalized computing freed from the desktop, enabling information access anywhere, anytime, on demand. This provides an apt description of the objective of mobile worker support. Computing devices range from desktop (fixed), to laptops and palmtops (transportable) to handhelds and wearables (fully mobile) (Gorlenko & Merrick, 2003). Mobile devices can be differentiated according to their wireless connectivity. Content transmitted by technological solutions in the mobile wireless world can be mobile (but not wirelessly connected for synchronization with wireline content), wireless (but not mobile), or both mobile and wirelessly connected. Mobile wireless content is converging with the wireline Internet, with the result being referred to as the mobile Internet. The growing mobile wireless market demands both voice and data (text-graphics) communication services. Multimedia content is a suitable mix of the two. The content is carried through the network of a wireless network operator and a service provider. Some mobile devices are unconnected while on the move (e.g. PDAs—personal digital assistants, laptops, and palmtops) although they may be equipped for wireless connectivity in a stationary environment. Clinical, business, and technology functions are usually intertwined in a complex manner in wireless systems, it is essential to maintain patient safety and quality of life, if a health care system is to be implemented acceptably (Scalise, 2005).

Value Proposition for Mobile and Wireless Solutions in Health Care

The business model for adopting mobile solutions is the economic justification for the use of the technology, or the means by which the technology generates a value proposition. In the current wireless marketplace, with an increased system complexity that is driven by the number of players and their interactions (Olla & Atkinson, 2004), (network operators, carriers, content providers, mobile device manufacturers, etc.), the value chain is developing into linkages of partnerships for delivering value to end customers (Sabat, 2002). End customers in e-health may be individual physicians or they may be networks of health care workers who interact in such a way that mobile solutions can assist in improving their interactions cost effectively. Business partnerships involved in supporting mobile solutions continue to evolve, engage, and disengage as new technology evolves and appears, and certain business partners thrive while others fail.

It is often difficult to justify a business case for a mobile project financially. A 2002 survey by *CIO Magazine* (Worthen, 2002) indicated that the two most popular measures of ROI for wireless projects were increased productivity (54%) and improved internal customer satisfaction (40%). For mobile e-health applications, we can add an important constraint which is that the application must not decrease the quality of life of the clients, or ROI justification becomes meaningless.

One framework that has been proposed for value determination of mobile solutions, includes two dimensions: time and place—the work can be either dependent or independent of one or both these dimensions (Wiberg & Ljungberg, 2001). Mobile applications in this framework can be in one of four quadrants: anytime and anywhere; anytime and a particular place; a particular time and anyplace; and a particular time and particular place. Maglaveras et al. (2002) discuss a community-based health care support system that proved the usefulness of wireless technology in providing wireless interactivity anytime and anywhere, but also proved the necessity for restructuring educational medical knowledge for delivery to the patient. An example application of the anytime-anyplace model is in mobile support of chronically ill clients who are still able to work. Here, occurrences could be identified in all four of the quadrants, since clients have particular places where they may spend a considerable amount of time (at work and at home), and certain procedures could be specified at particular times, but there would be value in support in the "anytime and anywhere" quadrant. These concepts help in planning potential mobile support applications.

To justify mobile solutions, health care institutions that deploy wireless data solutions do so on a very selective basis, supporting only those employees who have a demonstrated need for real-time access. There are strong indications that return on investment (ROI) can be most strongly justified for specific classes of tasks in vertical markets such as health care, manufacturing, government, and transportation (Wheelwright, 2002). For example, a recent study of mobile solutions in a variety of applications in 35 major companies found hard benefits that included sales increases of 5-10%, reduced customer wait times by as much as 80%, increases in service calls of up to 32%, and service call responsiveness improvements of up to 7% (Gillott, 2002). Payback periods ranged from a few months to 30 months.

Mobility and flexibility are the biggest drivers of mobile solutions in many institutions and companies (Wheelwright, 2002). Health care companies may choose wireless solutions because they have an outbound workforce that needs to be connected within a corporate environment or when making calls on homecare clients. Cost has slowed the adoption of mobile technology in the past, although it is becoming less of a concern as prices drop and businesses recognize the benefits of offering wireless access to their workforce. Mobile portals provide convenient places where Web users can link to a set of applications that are relevant to their interests and/work (Clarke & Flaherty, 2003). Portals assist the wireless user to interact with Web-based content, and serve a valuable purpose in aggregating multiple applications and/or content providers through one Web site. They also provide a greater degree of personalization and localization than traditional Web portals.

EVALUATION OF MOBILE BUSINESS APPLICATIONS

The novelty of many of the mobile applications currently entering the marketplace, along with inexperience of business with mobile solutions, greatly increases the risks associated with adopting such solutions. For this reason, the business value proposition of proposed mobile applications must be studied with care. To that end, we have developed a process framework (Archer, 2004) that organizes the planning and evaluation process logically. This proceeds from identifying the business goals, defining potential user groups and the applications they would use, and the technical considerations that will lead to the appropriate mobility choice. When implementation issues are factored in, tempered by a variety of moderators, the application can be evaluated, along with its ROI, and compared with the existing application in terms of tangible values such as revenue, cost, and efficiency, and intangibles such as user and customer satisfaction. This process is an essential first phase in any mobile application, since it considers logically the costs and benefits of implementing the planned solution.

Key Issues for Mobile E-Health Applications

A number of key issues can affect the potential for a successful mobile e-health implementation. These include usability, adoption, interoperability, change management, risk mitigation, privacy and security, and return on investment. These are considered in more detail in the following.

- **Usability** can be defined as the quality of a system with respect to ease of learning, ease of use, and user satisfaction (Rosson & Carroll, 2002). It also deals with the potential of a system to accomplish the goals of the user. Usability is a key issue in the adoption of any information system, but it is particularly so for mobile systems, where the end-user device is often hand-held, with limited display and data entry capability (Tarasewich, 2003). Interface design and the design of the device itself have a critical impact on usability.
- **Adoption:** As in any user population, technological changes in the supporting technology for doing tasks make demands on both the quality of user interface and the functionality of mobile devices. Adoption is clearly related to usability, although it involves additional issues. The questions of interest are (Zhu, Nah, & Zhao, 2003): (1) what factors influence users' adoption of mobile computing?; (2) how does the design of mobile devices and interface affect user adoption?; and (3) to what degree do specific factors such as trust and enjoyment (in using mobile devices) play a role in adoption? Zhu et al. (2003) have proposed that perceived ease of use (input and output modalities, navigation, bandwidth), perceived usefulness (service offerings, degree of mobility, compatibility, coverage, reliability), trust (security, privacy, vendor characteristics, perceived ease of use, perceived usefulness), and enjoyment (congruence of skills and challenges, focused attention, interactivity, perceived ease of use, perceived usefulness) will affect intentions to use mobile devices, which will then influence actual usage. Evidence suggests that inadequate access to information and ineffective communication tend to be causes of error and other adverse events for in-patient care (Mendonca, Chen, Stetson, McKnight, Lei, & Cimino, 2004). Information-based handheld wireless applications at the point of care that link to clinical data can help reduce these problems.
- **Interoperability:** Interoperability with existing health care applications and/or databases is necessary, to improve or at least avoid worsening any existing "stovepipe" characteristics that plague the health care IT field. In the absence of compatible databases or health records, separate applications may communicate through messages containing health record information using standard protocols such as HL7.[2] Supporting software could be developed with a messaging toolkit such as Chameleon,[3] or the health record

information may be mapped to a particular database using Iguana.[2] Significant barriers that must also be addressed include policies on accessing and updating existing systems, due to privacy, confidentiality, legal, and regulatory concerns.

- **Change Management:** Many issues arise when technology is changed or introduced to a user population, often transforming the way users must perform their tasks. The manner with which change is introduced, irrespective of the effort invested in enabling it, will impact system adoption. There are multiple obstacles to implementing such a system. These include resistance to change by end users and IT staff, and integration with existing systems. These must be considered in advance in order to mitigate potential risks (Wang & Paper, 2005). There are two important aspects of change that must be considered. The first is in the organizational and business process structures. Not all change can be anticipated and planned in advance. Difficulties in managing change in the introduction of technology arise when the organization does not plan the management of unanticipated change. This increases the complexity of change because the organization unprepared to deal effectively unanticipated complications. For example, new technology often leads to anticipated changes in staffing levels, but there are usually psychological or social dimensions to the remaining jobs that are not anticipated.

Two types of unanticipated change include (Rivard, Aubert, Patry, Pare, & Smith, 2004):

- Emergent change, that may arise spontaneously in response to planned change, with either positive or negative impacts on the organization (for example, a requirement for new skills in analyzing data now being collected that was not previously available).
- Opportunity-based change, introduced intentionally during the change process in response to unexpected impacts. For example, the introduction of mobile technology may create new opportunities for other applications that were not previously considered possible when the mobile infrastructure was not yet in place.

The second major consideration is the technology itself. Even if the new technology offers the full functionality required, with a fully-tested interface, user compliance is far from guaranteed. Studying user interactions with the system, as well as improving it to suit their needs, can be complex, costly, and time intensive but may result in significant rewards. Simple modifications may be introduced to help users to learn and operate the system, thus increasing acceptance. Schoenberg, Safran, and Sands (2000) suggest a functionality for assessing system performance from the user perspective: acquire user information in the background and through direct survey, target population subsets of interest and avoid interrupting those who are not, invoke data acquisition methods "just-in-time" as the user interacts with the system, be as brief and concise as possible during interaction, provide incentives to compensate users for their time, and be consistent across all applications.

- **Risk Mitigation:** End-user adoption is an important issue, and this is addressed by change management, usability, and so forth. Obstacles to end-user adoption of the system must be mitigated, through training and motivation for end users and clients through improved quality of work and life. System reliability is critical in health care, and parallel testing during the test phase until there is sufficient confidence in system reliability (Mikkelsen & Aasly, 2001) is one way to develop confidence in the system.
- **Security and Privacy:** Health record pri-

vacy and confidentiality in many jurisdictions are regulated strictly by government guidelines, in terms of controlling need to know and client permission to access records. Mobile applications must adhere to these guidelines, as well as maintaining security by encoded communications and databases. An additional consideration is the reliability of the system, to ensure that information is not lost and that service interruptions are managed effectively.

- **Return On Investment:** In health service applications, ROI (return on investment) considerations are overridden by a constraint that quality of health care must be improved, or at least not reduced. In calculating ROI, cost considerations include software, hardware, installation, ongoing maintenance, and further development. Savings include some that are more easily quantifiable such as IT staff time, and employee time savings (e.g., time saved when data can be entered directly online, or reduction in errors and the associated time needed to fix them). Virtual office operations and field sales operations tend to have a higher ROI than company groups with little customer-facing work. Health services require a convincing case for the adoption of mobile applications, since there are so many other competing demands on resources. In addition, since there are typically a number of stakeholders (client, physicians and nursing staff, administrative staff, institutions—hospitals, homecare institutions, etc.), each should receive a perceived benefit in order to encourage participation.

CASE EXAMPLE: MOBILE APPLICATIONS IN HOME HEALTH CARE

Health care is the responsibility of the provincial governments in Canada, where the publicly-funded system provides universal access. In the Canadian province of Ontario, health care has been organized into a multi-tiered system. Family physicians provide primary care, typically operate as small businesses, and bill the province for services rendered. They may refer patients to specialists, who may also operate as small businesses or work as hospital employees. Acute care is supported by hospitals. Non-acute care is supported in long-term facilities or in a home environment. Laboratory testing services may be operated privately or in a public hospital. Patients are supported in the home environment by their families and friends, in addition to homecare nursing and housekeeping support that is managed and funded by the Province. To provide homecare and long-term support, the Province has chartered a number of Community Care Access Centres (CCACs) throughout the Province, that contract with private homecare providers for nursing and other patient support.

As demonstrated in Figure 1, information must flow among the various providers in order to provide continuity to patient support, and access to information that exists at many places throughout the system. Unfortunately, the number of Canadian primary care physicians that have fully digitized records is only in the neighbourhood of 5%. Although each of the types of health care institutions (hospitals, CCACs, and homecare providers) has internal digital systems and databases that support its own applications, there are no standards for health records, and little digital communication to support specific clients. Most information flows are on paper forms, usually transmitted by fax, and scanned and stored or transmitted as images. This may serve storage and legal purposes, but the information can not be retrieved in a form that can be used for management or decision support analysis. There are the usual problems in the paper-based system, resulting from delays, errors, and loss of information.

To solve some of the problems associated with current paper-based systems, a project has been proposed for Venus,[4] an Ontario county, to use wireless applications to link mobile homecare workers to centrally supported applications and databases. The Venus County Mobile E-Health Project is being planned through the collaboration of three health care organizations: Mars Home Health (provider of visiting nursing and other services), Venus County CCAC, and Jupiter Hospital. The Aquarius Research Centre plays a role in research and development, and a number of corporate vendors are also involved, including Zodiac Wireless Inc. A carefully researched process will be used to build and trial the system, with the end result being a mobile system that can be easily implemented as an ongoing commercial operation in Venus County and potentially throughout other Canadian jurisdictions.

The project is aimed at improved outpatient quality of care, while eliminating or easing routine work for health care workers. The initial focus will be on reducing or eliminating paperwork by homecare nurses accessing the remote system wirelessly onsite for client details or to enter new data. The project will be led by health care staff and professionals to maximize the chances of successful implementation. The project is incremental in approach, and undertaken in phases, with activities and outcomes carefully researched and evaluated throughout each phase. The project may be terminated or adjusted at the end of each phase. The focus will be on delivering real benefits for clients and health care providers while overcoming the barriers to information exchange among some of the entities indicated in Figure 1, without undue inconvenience to regular health care activities.

An analysis of the business case through a logical process (Archer, 2004) has predicted an approximate reduction of 50% in direct (labour and system) costs by the project. Intangible benefits include: delay until data is available online reduced from 24 to 0 hours, online availability of data increased from 10% to 100%, error rate for data entry reduced from 0.20 to 0.05 per data item, homework by homecare nurses (faxing and other work) reduced from substantial to minimal, time for client-centred care increased during nursing visits, and time required for routine work reduced.

Project Phases

Each phase includes a research component, which will be used to plan the work, collect information, and evaluate results to ensure that the outcome of the phase is optimal from the point of view of the overall project objective. The following describes in limited detail the major phases in the project:

1. A prototype of several mobile wireless applications with a high potential impact on homecare operations, will be designed, tested, and implemented through a trial by a small group of Mars Home Health homecare nurses. Aquarius and Zodiac will be heavily involved in interface design, and a study of usability and user acceptance. The highest impact applications currently in use in paper form by homecare nurses are: supplies ordering, wound care, key path, admission, status change, and discharge. These will be implemented in the first prototype. Technical considerations include the choice of suitable end-user devices to support applications, and wireless network provision. Secure access will be available to data through both wireless mobile and office computers. Linkages to existing databases at Mars Home Health and Venus CCAC will be designed to ensure interoperability. Figure 2 is a conceptual description of the proposed system. Interoperability challenges with existing databases require the development of an interim database for data that does not currently exist in digital form. Decision support applications for clinical and administrative use will be able

Figure 2. Data flows in mobile e-health support system

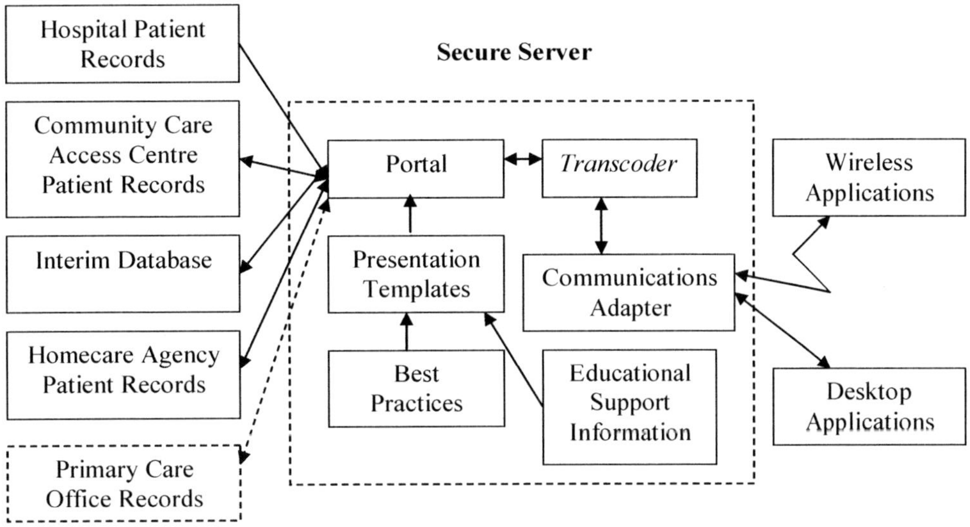

to access all the digital data collected. The secure server provides application support for wireless and desktop devices. Due to the low reliability of access to wireless devices in remote areas (and sometimes in basements or other shielded areas), the devices will need to carry "fat client" applications. That is, applications will run securely on the devices rather than on the server, and data uploads and downloads will occur automatically when wireless access is available.

2. Based on a successful prototype test in phase 1, the prototype will be revised for full operations according to prototype results and learning, and rolled out as a commercial operation to the entire Mars Home Health visiting nurse population of over 120.
3. Further applications specified and required by Mars Home Health and Venus CCAC, will be designed, based on experience in Phase 1, resulting in a suite of applications based on previous and new applications. The full suite will be trialed with a small group of Mars homecare nurses, including an evaluation of the suite (usability and user acceptance) and revisions necessary for commercial operations. This will be followed by a full commercial rollout at Mars.
4. Because there will be a significant increase in data availability online, there will be an investigation into how to make use of the additional information gathered from wireless inputs available online to the health care providers, for managing and decision making. Applications will be designed and developed as appropriate, and the impact on the institutions and clients involved will be studied. An example is improved wound management data collection for monitoring and control purposes:
   - To facilitate a consistent technique in wound assessment;
   - To facilitate a consistent means of documenting wound status;
   - To be a tool to infuse evidence-based practice in wound care management; and
   - To provide a means of data collection that would aid in evaluation and outcome tracking.
5. The final phase will be to design and implement a wireless mobile e-health prototype to assist the three health care institutions to support newly educated Type 2 diabetics.

The client process includes working through an education process in the Jupiter Hospital's Diabetes Education Centre, continuing as the clients move out of the hospital into a normal work and homecare situation over a period of several weeks. The desired end result is client self-management of diabetic condition with integrated back-up support from the health care institutions and primary care physicians.

CONCLUSIONS

Mobile health care technology has the potential for not just supporting health care in any particular health care environment (hospitals, clinics, long term care facilities, homecare), but for more easily managing transitions as patients move from or to acute, emergency, chronic, or primary care. Mobile applications can either eliminate or greatly reduce the use of paper forms, thus reducing system cost, as well as reducing errors and delays in making digital information available online. But if mobile e-health is to be introduced successfully, care must be taken to include all the stakeholders in planning and implementing mobile solutions. Critical issues that have been identified for mobile e-health applications include usability, adoption, interoperability, change management, risk mitigation, security and privacy, and return on investment.

REFERENCES

Archer, N. (2004). *The business case for employee mobility support* (Working Paper No. 9). Hamilton, ON: DeGroote School of Business, McMaster University.

Berner, E. S., Detmer, D. E., & Simborg, D. (2005). Will the wave finally break? A brief view of the adoption of electronic medical records in the United States. *Journal of the American Medical Informatics Association, 12*(1), 3-7.

Brailer, D. J. (2005, January 19). Interoperability: The key to the future health care system. *Health Affairs,* W5-19–W15-21.

Clarke III, I., & Flaherty, T. B. (2003). Mobile portals: The development of m-commerce gateways. In B. E. M. a. T. J. Strader (Ed.), *Mobile commerce: Technology, theory, and applications* (pp. 185-201). Hershey, PA: IRM Press.

Gillott, I. (2002, April). The ROI benefits of wireless. *Communications News, 39,* 6.

Gorlenko, L., & Merrick, R. (2003). No wires attached: Usability challenges in the connected mobile world. *IBM Systems Journal, 42*(4), 639-651.

Krull-Naraj, K. (2004). *Information flows in patient-centred healthcare.* Barrie, Ontario.

Lenz, R., & Kuhn, K. A. (2004). Towards a continuous evolution and adaptation of information systems in healthcare. *International Journal of Medical Informatics, 73*(1), 75-89.

Maglaveras, N., Koutkias, V., Chouvarda, I., Goulis, D. G., Avramides, A., Adamidis, D., et al. (2002). Home care delivery through the mobile telecommunications platform: The Citizen Health Citizen (CHS) perspective. *International Journal of Medical Informatics, 68*, 99-111.

Mendonca, E. A., Chen, E. S., Stetson, P. D., McKnight, L. K., Lei, J., & Cimino, J. J. (2004). Approach to mobile information and communication for health care. *International Journal of Medical Informatics, 73*, 631-638.

Mikkelsen, G., & Aasly, J. (2001). Concordance of information in parallel electronic and paper based patient records. *International Journal of Medical Informatics, 63*, 123-131.

Olla, P., & Atkinson, C. (2004). Developing a wireless reference model for interpreting complexity in wireless projects. *Industrial Management and Data Systems, 104*(3), 262-272.

Rivard, S., Aubert, B. A., Patry, M., Pare, G., & Smith, H. A. (2004). *Information technology and organizational transformation*. Amsterdam, Netherlands: Elsevier.

Rosson, M. B., & Carroll, J. M. (2002). *Usability engineering: Scenario-based development of human-computer interaction*. San Francisco, CA: Academic Press.

Sabat, H. K. (2002). The evolving mobile wireless value chain and market structure. *Telecommunications Policy, 26*, 505-535.

Scalise, D. (2005). One generation to the next. *Hospitals and Health Networks*(Winter), 10-15.

Schoenberg, R., Safran, C., & Sands, D. Z. (2000). *Studying clinician-computer interaction in Web-based systems.* Paper presented at the Annual AMIA Symposium, Los Angeles, CA, November 4-8.

Tarasewich, P. (2003). Wireless devices for mobile commerce: User interface design and usability. In B. E. M. a. T. J. Strader (Ed.), *Mobile commerce: Technology, theory, and applications* (pp. 26-50). Hershey, PA: IRM Press.

Walker, J., Pan, E., Johnston, D., Adler-Milstein, J., Bates, D. W., & Middleton, B. (2005, January 19). The value of health care information exchange and interoperability. *Health Affairs*, w5-10–w15-18.

Wang, B., & Paper, D. (2005). A case of an IT-enabled organizational change intervention: The missing pieces. *Journal of Cases on Information Technology, 7*(1), 34-52.

Wheelwright, G. (2002, Dec. 3). The business benefits of mobility. *Financial Times of London*, p. 11.

Wiberg, M., & Ljungberg, F. (2001). Exploring the vision of "Anytime, Anywhere" in the context of mobile work. In Y. Malhotra (Ed.), *Knowledge management and business model innovation* (pp. 153-165). Hershey, Pennsylvania: Idea Group Publishing.

Worthen, B. (2002, December 1). When wireless works. *CIO, 16*, 1.

Zhu, W., Nah, F. F.-H., & Zhao, F. (2003). Factors influencing user adoption of mobile computing. In J. Mariga (Ed.), *Managing e-commerce and mobile computing technologies* (pp. 260-271). Hershey, PA: IRM Press.

ENDNOTES

1. This research was supported by a grant from the Social Sciences and Humanities Research Council of Canada.
2. http://www.hl7.org/library/implement/implementation.htm
3. Trademark of iNTERFACEWARE Inc. http://www.interfaceware.com/
4. Venus County is a pseudonym, and Venus County CCAC, Mars Home Health, and Jupiter Hospital are pseudonyms for the health care organizations involved in the project. Aquarius Research Centre and Zodiac Wireless Inc. are pseudonyms for the research and business organizations involved.

This work was previously published in Mobile Government: An Emerging Direction in E-Government, edited by I. Kushchu, pp. 155-170, copyright 2007 by IGI Publishing (an imprint of IGI Global).

Chapter 28
The Internet, Health Information, and Managing Health:
An Examination of Boomers and Seniors

Christopher G. Reddick
The University of Texas at San Antonio, USA

ABSTRACT

This article examines the use of the Internet for gathering health information by boomers and seniors. This study attempts to determine whether online health seekers (individuals that have Internet access and have searched for health information online) have changed their behaviors from the information they found online. Essentially, has online health information helped them to manage their health more effectively? This research analyzes the Kaiser Family Foundation e-Health and the Elderly public opinion dataset of access by boomers and seniors to online health information. The major results indicate that boomers marginally use online health information more than seniors for the management of their health. The most significant results indicated that boomers and seniors who are more aware and have positive feelings toward online health information would use it more to manage their health.

INTRODUCTION AND BACKGROUND

For baby boomers, the Internet has become the most important source of health information other than consultation with their family doctor (Kaiser Family Foundation, 2005). The focus of this article is on both baby boomers, those in the age range of 50 to 64, and seniors, or those 65 and older.[1] This study examines the use of online health information by baby boomers and seniors and how they use the information for managing their health. The primary objectives of this article are to examine the differences in behavior between boomers and seniors and to test for the presence of a variety of associations among their characteristics and a number of management of health variables.

This study explores five specific questions. First, are there any differences between boomers and seniors and their access to health information for managing health? Second, will healthier boomers and seniors rely less on online health information in order to manage their health because they would have less need? Third, will the presence of boomers and seniors that have more experience and familiarity with the Internet lead to greater use of online health information to manage health? Fourth, will individuals who are in a lower sociodemographic status rely less on online health information because of lack of resources to access this information? Finally, will avid Internet users use online health information more often to manage their health because they would have greater access to and familiarity with the Internet?

The American health care system is different from many Western countries, since it is administered primarily by the private marketplace. The majority of the United States population contracts with a private provider for his or her health insurance coverage. Medicare is a federal health insurance program for people age 65 and older. In addition, Medicaid, a program sponsored by the federal government and administered by states, is intended to provide health care and health-related services to low-income individuals. However, there are millions of Americans who do not fit into either the Medicare or Medicaid plans and, essentially, remain uninsured. Online health information is especially important, given the millions of uninsured Americans trying to get information on their health situation. Individuals can use this online health information to make informed choices on their health care needs. They potentially can use information on the Internet to better manage their health.

Essentially, has online health information influenced the behaviors of boomers and seniors with respect to their health care needs? This influence could be as extensive as visiting a doctor or simply talking to family or friends about health information that a boomer or senior found online.

Access to timely and reliable information on health and health care long has been a goal for seniors, who face a greater number of health conditions and use prescription drugs and health care services at a higher rate than younger adults (Kaiser Family Foundation, 2005). However, the online behavior of seniors has not been studied as closely as that of health information searches of adolescents (Gray, Klein, Noyce, Sesselberg, & Cantrill, 2005), women (Pandey, Hart, & Tiwary, 2003), cancer patients (Eysenbach, 2003; Ziebland, 2004), those affected by the digital divide (Skinner, Biscope, & Poland, 2003), and those that compare online and off-line behavior (Cotton & Gupta, 2004). There is little empirical research that examines whether online health searches affect the management of health (Lueg, Moore, & Warkentin, 2003; Nicholas, Huntington, Williams, & Blackburn, 2001), one of the two objectives of this study. This study measures whether Internet health information changed the self-reporting behavior of boomers and seniors and does not specifically address change in health outcomes.

There are two reasons why this study does a comparison of both boomers and seniors. First, baby boomers represent future seniors, and by examining this age group, this study can provide some indication about what the future holds for the Internet and health information. Second, both boomers and seniors are in the greatest need of health information, since they are more prone to have health problems than other age groups.

This study is different from existing works of Nicholas et al. (2001), Lueg et al. (2003), and Huntington et al. (2004), since it focuses on the use of online health information in the management of health. This study focuses especially on comparing two groups, boomers and seniors, while the existing empirical work examines the entire Internet population. This study is different from studies that conduct a meta-analysis, which combine published results from different sources (Eysenbach, 2003). This research performs a statistical analysis that leads to conclusions that

Figure 1. Conceptual framework of access to online health information by boomers and seniors

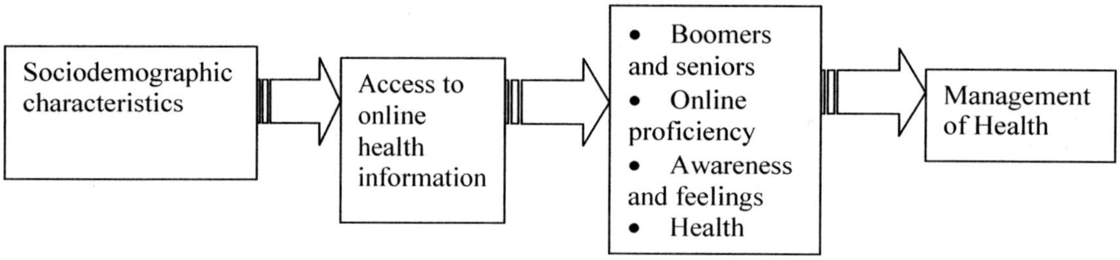

are different from the original dataset (Kaiser Family Foundation, 2005). The aim of this study is not just to learn about the differences between boomers and seniors and access to online health information; it is to discern the magnitude of differences between these groups and the impact of factors such as awareness and feelings on health management.

In order to accomplish the goal of examining online health information and the management of boomers' and seniors' health, this article is divided into several sections. First, this research examines the literature on the use of the Internet as a health information source. Second, this article outlines how the literature can be summarized into hypotheses that model the most probable impacts on management of boomers' and seniors' health. Third, this research provides details of the Kaiser Family Foundation's e-Health and the Elderly dataset that is used to model public opinion data of online health information (Kaiser Family Foundation, 2005). The fourth and fifth sections discuss the models and results of tests on the use of online health information for health care management. The sixth section provides a discussion that outlines how the test results confirm or deny the specified hypotheses and shows the broader significance of this work. The last section provides avenues for future research and presents limitations of this study.

LITERATURE REVIEW

The following section outlines the common themes found in the literature on the Internet and health information and the management of health. They can be divided into the factors of differences between age groups, the health of the individual, online proficiency, sociodemographic characteristics, and awareness and feelings about online health information. Existing research shows that little is known about how Internet usage, health status, and sociodemographic characteristics affect health information seeking (Cotton & Gupta, 2004).

Eysenbach (2003) provides a conceptual framework of the possible link between Internet use and cancer. Some of the important factors, according to that author's meta-analysis, indicate that Internet use is related to communication, community, and content, leading to an impact on cancer outcomes. In a similar line of inquiry, a study by Lueg et al. (2003) provided a conceptual framework of Internet searches for online health information. These authors examine the situations with which individuals find themselves confronted in terms of health needs and frequency of use, predicting access to health information. Eysenbach's (2003) conceptual framework is different from Lueg et al. (2003), in that the former examines the social aspects of Internet use and health information, while the latter study focuses on the situation involvement and the frequency of Internet use. The conceptual framework of this study is similar to Eysenbach (2003) and Lueg et al. (2003) but differs, in that it examines boomers and seniors and factors such as frequency and satisfaction having an influence on the management of health (Figure 1).

Online Health Information and Managing Boomers' and Seniors' Health

If the Internet can be used to change the behavior of individuals, this is one assessment of the long-term utility of this information resource. If individuals just look at information online and do not use it in any substantial way, it does not make much sense to invest in Internet health resources. The Internet suggests a remarkable change from the traditional doctor-knows-best approach (Eysenbach & Jadad, 2001). The Internet can be seen as challenging hierarchical models of information sharing, in which the provider of the information decides how the information should be delivered (Ziebland, 2004).

For example, existing research in a 2001 survey showed that 44% of online health information seekers said that the information they found online affected a decision about how to treat an illness or to cope with a medical condition (Fox & Rainie, 2002). A majority of respondents to a survey of adolescents and use of Internet health information reported that it helped them to start a conversation with a lay or professional medical person (Gray et al., 2005). Online health information seekers mostly are going online to look for specific answers to targeted questions (Fox & Rainie, 2000). In addition, four out of 10 young people say that they have changed their personal behaviors because of health information that they obtained online (Rideout, 2002). In an Internet survey, more than one-third of the respondents said that their conditions had improved after having visited a Web site, and more than one in four said that the Web information had resulted in a deferred visit or had actually replaced a visit to the doctor (Nicholas et al., 2001). Therefore, the existing research has examined adolescents' and all age groups' behavioral changes but has not focused on seniors and their use of the Internet for managing health. There are five factors outlined in the literature, which are differences between boomers and seniors, the health of boomers and seniors, their online proficiency, their sociodemographic characteristics, and awareness and feelings toward online health information that are predicted to have an impact on whether online health information is used.

Boomers' and Seniors' Differences

Existing empirical evidence shows that health seekers are proportionately more middle-aged than very young or old, with the highest proportion of usage witnessed in those between the ages of 30 and 64 (Fox & Rainie, 2000). A more recent survey indicates that 70% of baby boomers has gone online in 2004, while only 31% of seniors has gone online (Kaiser Family Foundation, 2005). Boomers will retire shortly, and the amount of online health information for which they will search should increase dramatically compared to what seniors are currently consuming. In order to explore both the present and what the future will hold for online health information and seniors, it is important to compare both age groups. In addition, individuals over the age of 50 may have a greater need for more information on health care than someone much younger because of the greater chance of facing health problems (Brodie et al., 2000).

Health of Boomers and Seniors

The literature also mentions that individuals who are in worse health will want to search more for online health information. The Internet becomes an additional tool in order for them to search for health information. Empirical evidence shows that there is a link between an individual's health and his or her need for online health information. Less healthy individuals are more likely to explore different aspects of a Web site and to use more health-related interactive features and, in doing so, improve their well being (Lueg et al., 2003). Individuals who were suffering with an illness were two and half times as likely, compared to respondents without a standing illness, to say that they had used information from the Internet as an alternative to seeing their general practitioner (Nicholas et al., 2001). In many cases, information seekers were acting on behalf of others, such as family and friends. However, access to online health information also should be related to the consumer's ability to use the Internet, not just on whether they are healthy.

Online Proficiency

The ability to use the Internet also should have an impact on whether boomers and seniors use online health information to manage their health. Individuals who use Internet information more to manage their health have broadband Internet access, are frequently online, spend many hours online, and search for information on many different topics. Research shows that individuals using a Web site regularly were more likely to have said that the information was helpful (Nicholas et al., 2001). A survey of adolescents shows that there are issues of the disparity of Internet access and quality of Internet access such as dial-up vs. broadband connection (Skinner et al., 2003).

Sociodemographic Characteristics of Online Health Seekers

Another factor explored in the literature that should have an impact on access to online health information is the sociodemographic characteristics of the individual. There is research on the digital divide, between the haves and the have-nots of Internet access. This research predicts that those who have greater access to the Internet would have more resources in society. For instance, those groups of individuals who are more disadvantaged economically in the United States would have less access to the Internet and online health resources. Hispanics, the largest minority group in the United States, traditionally have had less Internet access (Fox & Rainie, 2000). Those with medium to high family incomes should be able to access the Internet more for health information because of greater resources.

Existing research shows that individuals who are older, have lower incomes, are minorities, are less educated, and are males will be less likely to use the Internet for health information seeking (Cotton & Gupta, 2004; Anderson, 2004). In contrast, women increasingly rely on the Internet to supplement health information received from traditional sources (Pandey et al., 2003) and are more likely than men to seek online health information (Fox & Rainie, 2000; Nicholas et al., 2001). Awareness and feelings toward online health information also should have an impact on using this information to manage consumers' health.

Awareness and Feelings Toward Online Health Resources

A final factor that should explain access to Internet health information is the awareness and feelings of the individual toward online health information. If boomers and seniors have more positive feelings about the Internet as a health information resource, they will utilize it more often than someone who harbors more negative feelings toward the Internet. In addition, individuals who go online for health information frequently should use it more to manage their health. If a boomer's or senior's doctor or medical professional recommends or uses the Internet as a communication device, the patient is more likely to use it to manage his or her health. In summary, the prediction is that boomers and seniors who are more aware of online health resources should use these resources more to manage their health. In addition, boomers and seniors who have positive feelings about the benefits of online health information will use this resource more to manage their health.

Empirical evidence shows that there is a relationship between using the Internet more often and accessing health information (Lueg et al., 2003). Those using the Web once a day were twice as likely to report that it helped a lot in terms of being better informed from health information found on the Web (Nicholas et al., 2001). E-mail is still a new medium for obtaining access to consumer health information and also is explored in the research as a way to manage a consumer's health (Huntington et al., 2004). The literature just outlined can be formally specified with the following hypotheses that demonstrate the relationship between boomers and seniors, the Internet, and the management of health.

HYPOTHESES

In order to examine whether online health information has affected the choices that individuals make in managing their health and the differences between boomers and seniors, several hypotheses are tested in this article. These hypotheses are derived from the literature mentioned in the previous section and are divided into five areas:

Boomers' and Seniors' Differences

Hypothesis 1: Online health seekers who are baby boomers are more likely to believe that online health information has helped them to manage their health better compared with seniors.

Health of Boomers and Seniors

Hypothesis 2: Online health seekers who are healthy or who have family and friends that are healthy will rely less on online health information because of lack of need.

Online Proficiency

Hypothesis 3: Online health seekers who have broadband Internet access will go online more for health information to manage their health.

Hypothesis 4: Online health seekers who go online more often and conduct many online activities will use Internet health information more to manage their health.

Sociodemographic Status

Hypothesis 5: Boomers and seniors who are females will rely more on online health information.

Hypothesis 6: Boomers and seniors who are college educated will rely more on online health information.

Hypothesis 7: Boomers and seniors who are Hispanics will go online less for health information.

Hypothesis 8: Boomers and seniors who have family income above $75,000 will go online more for health information.

Awareness and Feelings Toward Online Health Resources

Hypothesis 9: Online health seekers who most of the time and always look to see who provides medical information on the Internet will use online health information more to manage their health.

Hypothesis 10: Online health seekers who access health information online once or twice a month will have a greater likelihood of using online health information to manage their health.

Hypothesis 11: If a doctor has recommended a Web site to an online health seeker, he or she is more likely to use health information to manage his or her health.

Hypothesis 12: If an online health seeker has communicated with his or her doctor via e-mail, he or she is more likely to use online health information to manage his or her health.

Hypothesis 13: Online health seekers that have more positive feelings about looking for health information on the Internet are more likely to use this information to manage their health.

These hypotheses are examined with a dataset that surveyed public opinion of both baby boomers and seniors on their use and acceptance of online health information.

DATASET AND METHODS

The e-Health and the Elderly dataset is a nationally representative random digit dial telephone survey of 1,450 adults age 50 and older.[2] Included in this sample were 583 respondents age 65 and older. The survey was designed by Kaiser Family Foundation (KFF) (2005) in consultation with Princeton Survey Research Associates (PSRA), and the survey was administered in the field by PSRA. The survey interviews were conducted between March 5 and April 8, 2004. The entire dataset of 1,450 respondents was first examined to determine the characteristics of boomers and seniors and access to online health information.

Out of the 1,450 responses to the survey, this study also has taken a subsample of 628 respondents, of which there were 464 boomers and 164 seniors surveyed. Therefore, the original dataset was split, and the sample sizes differ for both age groups. The 628 boomers and seniors represent those individuals who are called online health seekers. They both have Internet access and have looked for online health information. This group is of interest, since in this study, there is a comparison of the characteristics of those that actually look up online health information.

Table 1. Boomers and seniors who go online for health information

Go online for health information (Yes or No)	Age group	Frequency	Percent
No	50-64	335	42.5
	65+	454	57.5
	Total	789	100
Yes	50-64	464	78.2
	65+	129	21.8
	Total	593	100

In this study, we use a consumer survey to explore the differences between boomers and seniors and their use of online health information to manage health. This research uses both descriptive statistics and logistic regression to explore differences in access to online health information between boomers and seniors.[3]

DESCRIPTIVE STATISTICS OF BOOMERS AND SENIORS AND ONLINE HEALTH INFORMATION

In order to model the relationship between seniors and boomers, online health information, and its impact on managing health care needs, this study has specified the following variables that will comprise the models tested.

Table 1 provides information on boomers and seniors who go online for health information. Boomers that go online for health information represent 78.2%, while seniors that go online for health information represent just over 21% of those surveyed in this category. This table generally supports the notion that boomers tend to go online more for health information than seniors. Boomers that do not go online for health information represent 43%, and seniors that do not go online represent 58% of those surveyed in this category.

Table 2. Demographic information of boomers and seniors and going online for health information

Go online for health information (Yes or No)		N	Mean	Standard Deviations
No	College educated	822	0.15	0.36
	Gender is female	822	0.65	0.48
	Race is Hispanic	822	0.03	0.18
	Family income 2003 above $75,000	822	0.07	0.25
	Age	822	68.79	12.41
Yes	College educated	628	0.43	0.50
	Gender is female	628	0.61	0.49
	Race is Hispanic	628	0.03	0.17
	Family income 2003 above $75,000	628	0.27	0.45

Table 2 outlines demographic information of boomers and seniors that go online and do not go online for health information. The digital divide is very evident with the data presented in this table. For instance, 43% of college-educated individuals go online for health information compared with only 15% who are college-educated that do not go online for health information. Among females and Hispanics, there is not much of a difference in the percentage who go online and do not go online for health information. However, boomers and seniors that have a family income above $75,000 in 2003 were more likely to go online for health information. Finally, age seems to have an impact on accessing online health information. The mean age was 61 years for individuals that go online and 69 years for consumers who do not go online for health information. Higher income implies greater use of online health information, and having a college education means a greater likelihood of going online for health information. This finding also indicates that boomers are more likely to go online for health information, since the average age range was just over 61 years old.

Logistic regression is used to test whether sociodemographic variables predict whether boomers or seniors go online for health information. Logistic regression was used, since this study models dependent variables that are binary, represented by either a 1 or 0 (Nicholas et al., 2001; Lueg et al., 2003). The odds ratio can be used to interpret the relative impact of the observance of a 1 in the dependent variable. Table 3 shows that almost all of the sociodemographic variables help to explain whether someone goes online for health information, with the only exception being Hispanic. For instance, having a college education means that a boomer or senior is four times more likely to go online for health information. Having a higher income indicates that boomers and seniors are two times more likely to go online for health information. However, as the age of the respondent increases, this marginally decreases the likelihood of someone going online for health information.

Dependent Variables

Table 4 provides a list of the dependent and predictor variables and also demonstrates whether there were differences between boomers and seniors in these variables. Perhaps the most important dependent variable is whether "somewhat" or "a lot" of information on the Internet has helped to take care of a senior's or a boomer's health. The mean score indicates that 59% of boomers and 46% of

Table 3. Logistic regression results of sociodemographic variables predicting going online for health information

Dependent Variable	Go Online for Health Information		
Predictor Variables	Odds Ratio	Wald Statistic	Prob. Sig.
Age	0.95	(301.47)***	0.00
College educated	4.05	(300.72)***	0.00
Gender is female	1.25	(11.49)***	0.00
Race is Hispanic	1.06	0.26	0.61
Family income 2003 above $75,000	2.25	(63.38)***	0.00
Constant	11.34	(139.67)***	0.00
Nagelkerke R-Square	0.25		

Note: significant at the 0.01 level

seniors believed that the Internet has helped them to take care of their health, demonstrating some impact on the management of their health.

The second dependent variable measures whether online health seekers had a conversation with family or friends about health information that they found online (Table 4). Family and friends who go online for health information may guide someone else as to whether they should see a doctor because of this information (Eysenbach, 2003). The results indicate that 66% of boomers said that they had a conversation with family members or friends, and only 48% of seniors said that they had this conversation about the information they saw online. There were statistically significant differences between seniors and boomers for this question with the reported F-statistic being significant at the 0.01 level, meaning that boomers were more likely to have a conversation with family and friends about health information that they found online.

The third dependent variable measures whether online health information changed the behavior of boomers and seniors (Table 4). Thirty-six percent of boomers' behaviors changed as a result of online health information, compared with 25% of seniors. This result also was shown to have a statistically significant difference between boomers and seniors at the 0.01 level. Around one-third of boomers changed their behaviors, which is a good indication that the information that they are finding is affecting their health.

A fourth management of health issue was whether boomers or seniors made a decision on treatment of an illness as a result of the information they found online (Table 4). The results showed that 34% of boomers believed that they made a decision about how to treat an illness because of information they found online, while only 26% of seniors made a decision on treatment. This result also showed a statistically significant difference between the two age groups at the 0.01 level.

Another dependent variable was visiting a doctor as a result of the health information found online (Table 4). Only 16% of boomers visited a doctor as a result of health information they found online, while 13% of seniors visited a doctor. Visiting a doctor was the least utilized change in behavior as a result of online health information.

Referring back to Hypothesis 1 on whether online health information has been used to manage a boomer's or a senior's health, this study has found that overall, there were differences between both groups of online health seekers (Table 4). The mean values for all five dependent variables were higher for boomers compared with seniors. In addition, three out of the five dependent

Table 4. Difference of means tests of dependent and predictor variables for online health seekers; boomers are significantly different from seniors

Variable Name	Mean of Boomers	Standard Deviations Boomers	Mean of Seniors	Standard Deviations Seniors	Probability Significantly Different Boomers and Seniors
Dependent Variables					
Somewhat and a lot of information on Internet helped take care health	0.59	0.49	0.46	0.50	0.07
Had a conversation family or friend about online health information	0.66	0.47	0.48	0.50	0.00
Online health information changed behavior	0.36	0.48	0.25	0.43	0.00
Made a decision about how to treat an illness because of online health information	0.34	0.48	0.26	0.44	0.00
Visited a doctor because of information found online	0.16	0.37	0.13	0.34	0.07
Predictor Variables: Health					
Excellent or very good health	0.58	0.49	0.52	0.50	0.07
Health problems index	3.95	2.45	3.80	2.41	0.48
Predictor Variables: Online Proficiency					
Broadband Internet access	0.43	0.50	0.29	0.45	0.00
Online more than 10 hrs week	0.28	0.45	0.23	0.42	0.00
Online every day	0.57	0.50	0.51	0.50	0.08
Online activities index	2.86	0.97	2.45	1.14	0.00
Predictor Variables: Online Health Information					
Most of the time and always look to see who provides medical information on Internet	0.40	0.49	0.24	0.43	0.00
Access health information online once or twice a month or greater	0.38	0.49	0.34	0.48	0.04
Doctor recommended a health or medical Website	0.06	0.23	0.04	0.20	0.13
Communicated with doctor or other health care provider through email	0.12	0.32	0.11	0.31	0.55
Positive feelings about looking for health information on the Internet Index	2.59	0.73	2.23	0.94	0.00
Negative feelings about looking for health information on the Internet	0.68	0.78	0.71	0.81	0.25

Notes: The number of observations are 464 for boomers and 164 for seniors.

variables showed statistically significant differences between boomers and seniors at the 0.01 level. With these dependent variables outlined, this research also should describe the predictor variables and their characteristics.

Predictor Variables

The predictor variables used to explain how the Internet has managed the health care of boomers and seniors also are presented in Table 4. Many of the predictor variables are represented in terms of binary numbers in order to capture the specific impacts on the dependent variables. As previously noted, this study has divided the hypotheses into the differences between boomers and seniors, the relative health of the individual, his or her online proficiency, and how active he or she is at seeking online health information. This study discerns the impact that these factors have on the management of the health care of boomers and seniors.

To see all of the predictor variables, refer to Table 4. We will only mention a few of them in this section. For instance, an index was created of the health problems that boomers and seniors or someone they know have faced in the past year. An individual who has more health problems or is concerned with someone else's health problems would score higher on the index. The health problems index indicates less than four issues that they or someone they know faced, indicated by online health seekers (out of nine possible health problems). The nine possible health problems listed were cancer, heart disease, obesity and weight loss, arthritis, diabetes, Alzheimer's, high cholesterol, osteoporosis, and mental health.

The online activities index measures the amount of activities that boomers and seniors conduct online, and the average is around two activities (Table 4). The prediction is that health seekers who conduct more online activities have a greater likelihood of using health information to manage their health because of their familiarity and comfort with the Internet. The four online activities that comprised the index were using instant messaging, reading news, buying a product, and checking the weather.

The online health information predictor variables also show the capacity of the individual to look up health information on the Internet (Table 4). Seniors are more trusting of the health information that they read online, with only 24% of seniors "most of the time" and "always" looking to see who provides medical information on the Internet. On the other hand, 40% of boomers are looking to see who provides the online health information. This difference was also statistically significant at the 0.01 level. In addition, boomers are more frequent consumers of online health information, using it at least once or twice a month, as represented by 38% of the sample. Seniors consume online health information marginally less frequently with 34% doing so.

With regard to overall positive feelings toward the Internet, there was an average score of two on an index scaled from zero to three, indicating that boomers and seniors have overall positive feelings toward the Internet as a source of health information. The index was calculated by adding up the specific responses to whether the online health seeker agreed that online health information gave them information quickly, whether it helped them feel more informed when they go to the doctor, and whether it allows them to get information from a lot of different sources.

On an index of zero being the lowest and two being the highest, less than one was found, indicating that very few online health seekers harbor negative feelings toward the Internet as a source of health information. Having positive feelings about online health information also showed a statistically significant difference between boomers and seniors at the 0.01 significance level. Similarly, this negative feelings index was calculated by adding the individual responses, if they agreed that online health information was frustrating because it is hard to find what they were searching for and if it is confusing because there is too much information. The following section tests the relationship between accessing online health information and managing a boomer's and a senior's health.

RESULTS OF LOGISTIC REGRESSION MODELS OF ONLINE HEALTH INFORMATION MANAGING HEALTH

This study uses logistic regression with five separate management-of-health dependent vari-

Table 5. Logistic regression of factors predicting whether online health information has managed a boomer's or a senior's health

Dependent Variables	Somewhat and a lot of information on Internet helped take care health		Had a conversation family or friend about online health information		Online health information changed behavior		Made a decision about how to treat an illness because of online health information		Visited a doctor because of information found online	
Independent Variables	Odds Ratio	Wald Statistic	Odds Ratio	Wald Statistic	Odds Ratio	Wald Statistic	Odds Ratio	Wald Statistic	Odds Ratio	Wald Statistic
Boomers = 1 (age between 50 to 64)	1.31	(4.49)**	1.49	(10.67)***	1.71	(14.99)***	1.66	(12.63)***	0.90	(0.36)
Health										
Excellent or very good health	1.11	(0.88)	1.64	(21.39)***	1.21	(3.06)	1.36	(7.09)***	1.10	(0.41)
Health problems index	0.99	(0.36)	1.14	(34.51)***	1.04	(3.40)	1.00	(0.00)	1.04	(1.35)
Online Proficiency										
Broadband Internet access	0.82	(2.79)	0.63	(15.51)***	0.90	(0.80)	0.68	(9.37)***	0.89	(0.51)
Online every day	1.55	(13.13)***	1.31	(5.01)**	1.82	(22.22)***	1.43	(7.15)***	1.41	(3.99)**
Online more than 10 hrs week	0.65	(9.62)***	0.89	(0.71)	0.97	(0.05)	1.46	(7.26)***	0.81	(1.39)
Online activities index	1.01	(0.01)	0.93	(1.50)	0.95	(0.55)	0.92	(1.83)	0.80	(7.75)***
Online Health Information										
Access health information online once or twice a month or greater	3.51	(115.95)***	1.59	(17.35)***	2.29	(54.99)***	3.11	(95.83)***	1.82	(16.15)***
Communicated with doctor or other health care provider through email	0.91	(0.28)	1.95	(12.45)***	1.58	(7.28)***	2.83	(35.37)***	1.86	(9.94)***
Doctor recommended a health or medical Website	0.76	(0.97)	0.91	(0.10)	1.17	(0.31)	2.13	(7.10)***	3.68	(22.13)***
Positive feelings about looking for health information on the Internet Index	2.46	(119.44)***	1.63	(46.32)***	1.85	(42.97)***	1.70	(31.68)***	1.84	(19.73)***
Most of the time and always look to see who provides medical information on Internet	1.31	(4.86)**	2.80	(63.13)***	1.61	(15.80)***	1.57	(13.23)***	1.69	(11.21)***
Negative feelings about looking for health information on the Internet	0.75	(16.82)***	0.81	(10.16)***	0.71	(21.06)***	0.70	(20.83)***	0.77	(6.21)***
Constant	0.08	(89.93)***	0.13	(65.14)***	0.03	(122.43)***	0.04	(103.03)***	0.03	(66.25)***
Nagelkerke R-Square		0.27		0.22		0.22		0.26		0.13

*Notes: ** significant at the 0.05 level and *** significant at the 0.01 level.*

ables. A "1" was recorded for each of the five dependent variables if (1) the online health seeker said "somewhat" or "a lot" of information on the Internet helped them to take care of their health; (2) they had a conversation with family or friend about online health information; (3) online health information changed their behavior; (4) they made a decision about how to treat an illness because of online health information; and (5) they visited a doctor because of information found online. A "0" was recorded for each of the five dependent variables if this was not the case.

The results in Table 5 indicate that for four of the five dependent variables, boomers were slightly more likely to use the Internet to manage their health. For instance, an odds ratio of 1.31 for the dependent variable of "somewhat" or "a lot" of information on the Internet has helped to take care of the online health seekers' problems implies that consumers are around one and one-third times more likely to say that this is the case, if they are a boomer rather than a senior.

Changing behavior for boomers because of information found online registered an odds ratio of 1.71, having a conversation with family or friend about online health information had an odds ratio of 1.49, and making a decision about how to treat an illness had an odds ratio of 1.66 (Table 5). Overall, the results showed that boomers are around one and one-half times more likely than seniors to change their behavior and to use online health information to manage their health, which is not that high, given the attention placed on the differences between these age groups (Kaiser Family Foundation, 2005).

In terms of online proficiency, those who had broadband Internet access were less likely to have a conversation with a family member or a friend about what they saw online and less likely to make a decision about how to treat an illness. However, for those online health seekers who are online every day, this had a consistent impact across all five dependent variables, if they used online health information to manage their health. For instance, there was a 1.82 times greater chance that daily online users changed their behavior because of online health information. In addition, individuals who go online every day were 1.41 times more likely to visit a doctor because of information that they found online. In terms of being online more than 10 hours a week, this had a negative likelihood for the dependent variables "somewhat" or "a lot" of information on the Internet helped to take care of their health, but had a positive impact with an odds ratio of 1.46 for making a decision on how to treat an illness. Overall, there was no overwhelming support that being more proficient with the Internet had a substantial impact on using health information to manage an online health seeker's health. The only consistently significant variable that had an impact on managing health was being online every day.

Boomers and seniors who had excellent or very good health were 1.64 times more likely to have a conversation with a family member or a friend about online health information. In addition, the boomer or senior who had more health problems or who knew someone who was experiencing health problems was 1.14 times more likely to have a conversation with family or friends about online health information. Individuals who were in excellent and very good health were 1.36 times more likely to use online health information to make a decision about how to treat an illness because of online health information. Generally, the health of the individual was not a strong predictor of using health information to manage a boomers' or seniors' health.

The strongest predictors of using health information to manage health were for the online health information awareness and feelings variables. Frequent consumers of online health information were 3.51 times more likely to use the Internet to take care of their health. It has become a valuable tool for their health care management needs. There was also a 3.11 greater likelihood of someone making a decision about treating an illness to use the Internet more than once a month for health information. In fact, frequently accessing health information registered an impact for all of the dependent variables.

Individuals who had positive feelings about online health information were more likely to use online health information to manage their health. Boomers and seniors who had more negative feelings toward online health information were less likely to use it for health management. This finding was consistently found across all five of the dependent variables. Online health seekers who usually looked to see who provided the health information were more likely to use this to manage their health. For instance, individuals who looked to see who provided the health information were 2.80 times more likely to have a conversation with family or friends about the information that they saw online. If a doctor recommended a health or medical Web site, online health seekers were 2.13 times more likely to make a decision about how to treat an illness because of online health information, and they were 3.68 times more likely to visit a doctor because of information they found online. In addition, individuals who communicated with a doctor or a health care provider via e-mail were 1.95 times more likely to have a conversation with a family member or a friend about health information that they found online. Overall, the logistic regression results indicate the most consistent and highest support for increased awareness and positive feelings toward online health information as a driver for helping to manage boomers' and seniors' health.

CLASSIFICATION TREES ANALYSIS OF TAKING CARE OF BOOMERS' AND SENIORS' HEALTH

Another way to examine the relationship between boomers and seniors and online health information is a classification tree analysis. Classification trees are used to predict membership of cases or objects in the classes of a categorical dependent variable from their measurements on one or more predictor variables. Classification tree analysis is a common data mining technique. Figure 2 shows that the taking care of health variable is related to boomers and seniors having positive feelings toward looking for online health information. In addition, having positive feelings about online health information is related to accessing health information online once or twice a month or more. These findings reinforce the logistic regression results that awareness and feeling toward online health information helps in the management of a boomer's or a senior's health. How do these findings relate to the hypotheses outlined in the beginning of this article?

DISCUSSION OF RESULTS AND HYPOTHESES

This section will discuss how the empirical results of this study confirm or deny the hypotheses (see Table 6). First, the evidence shows through the difference of means tests that boomers and seniors are different in terms of their use of online health information in the management of their health. The mean values scored higher for boomers in using online health information to take care of their health, having a conversation with a family or a friend about the health information found online, changing their behavior because of online health information, and making a decision about treating an illness because of online health information. There is some evidence that boomers will use more online health information to manage their health, supporting Hypothesis 1. However, there is no overwhelming support for differences between boomers and seniors and using health information to manage their health, with boomers only utilizing this information one and one-half times more than seniors.

The health of the individual, or Hypotheses 2, only predicted the use of online health information to manage a boomer's and a senior's health when

Figure 2. Classification tree of impact of online health information taking care of a boomer's and a senior's health

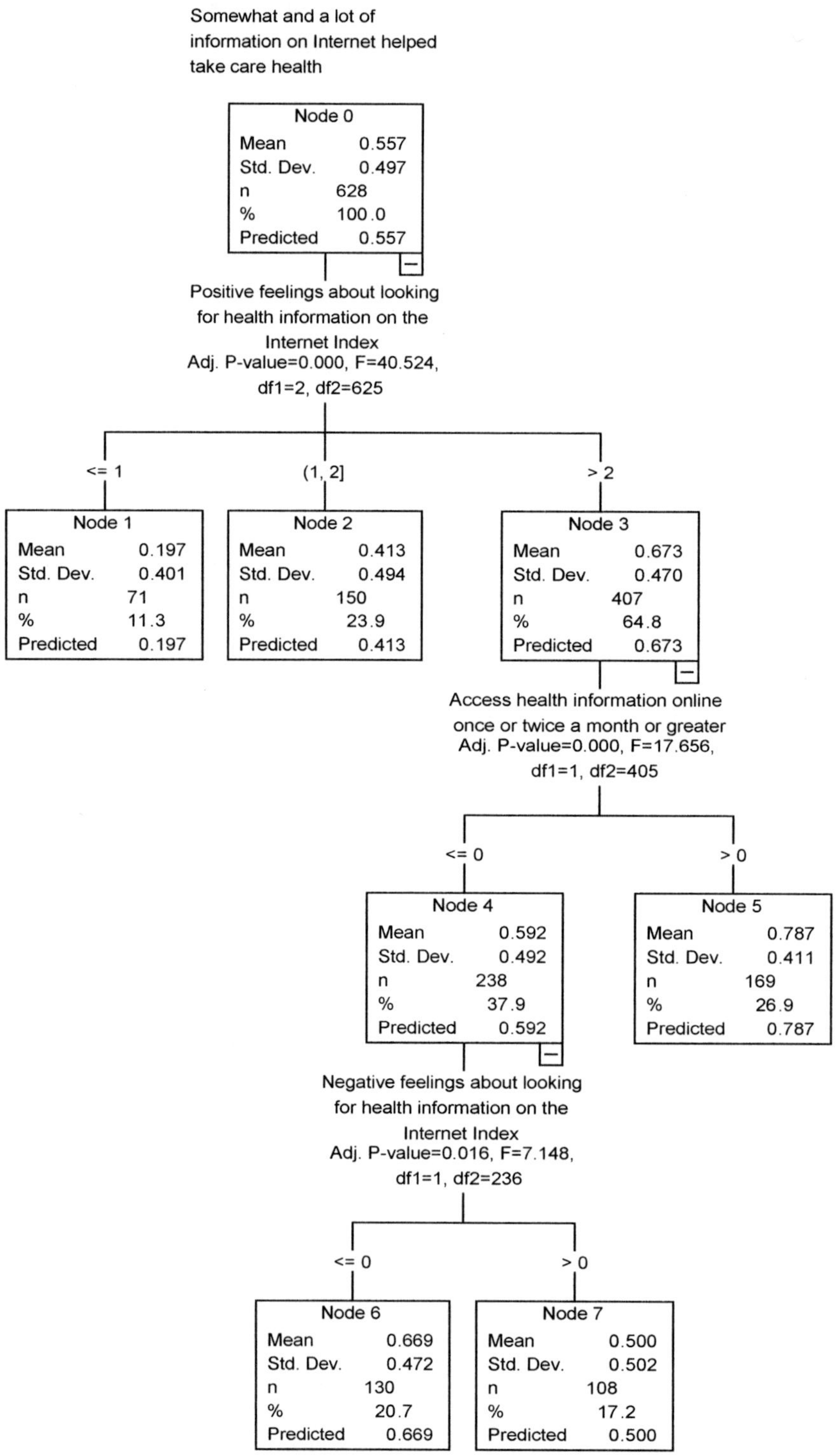

Table 6. Support for hypotheses of boomers and seniors and online health information

Hypotheses	Supported? (Yes, No, or Partially)	Major Test(s) Performed
Hypothesis 1: Online health seekers who are baby boomers are more likely to believe that online health information has helped them manage their health better compared with seniors.	Yes	Descriptive statistics, difference of means tests, and logistic regression
Hypothesis 2: Online health seekers who are healthy or who have family and friends that are healthy will rely less on online health information because of lack of need.	Partially	Logistic regression
Hypothesis 3: Online health seekers who have broadband Internet access will go online more for health information to manage their health	No	Logistic regression - Evidence found in the opposite direction
Hypothesis 4: Online health seekers who go online more often and conduct many online activities will use Internet health information more to manage their health.	Yes	Logistic regression
Hypothesis 5: Boomers and seniors who are females will rely more on online health information.	Yes	Logistic regression
Hypothesis 6: Boomers and seniors who are college educated will rely more on online health information.	Yes	Logistic regression
Hypothesis 7: Boomers and seniors who are Hispanics will go online less for health information.	No	Logistic regression -No support found in logistic regression
Hypothesis 8: Boomers and seniors who have family income above $75,000 will go online more for health information.	Yes	Logistic regression
Hypothesis 9: Online health seekers who most of the time and always look to see who provides medical information on the Internet would use online health information more to manage their health.	Yes	Logistic regression
Hypothesis 10: Online health seekers who access health information online once or twice a month would have a greater likelihood of using online health information to manage their health.	Yes	Logistic regression
Hypothesis 11: If a doctor has recommended a Website to an online health seeker he or she is more likely to use health information to manage their health.	Partially	Logistic regression
Hypothesis 12: If an online health seeker has communicated with his or her doctor via email he or she is more likely to use online health information to manage their health.	Yes	Logistic regression
Hypothesis 13: Online health seekers that have more positive feelings about looking for health information on the Internet are more likely to use this information to manage their health.	Yes	Logistic regression

they had a conversation with a family member or a friend about online health information and when they made a decision about how to treat an illness. In addition, the health variable predicted a boomer's and a senior's behavior when he or she talked to his or her doctor about information that he or she found online. Overall, there was not overwhelming support that the health of the boomer or senior had an impact on use of online health information to manage his or her health.

Hypotheses 3 and 4 examine whether being more proficient online means that the online health seeker will use the Internet more to manage his or her health. The results consistently showed that those who go online every day were more likely to use the Internet to manage their health. There was not much support that being more proficient with the Internet meant that boomers and seniors would use it more often for health information, since many of the other independent variables in this category were not statistically significant. This is most likely explained by what these online health seekers are doing on the Internet; they are looking for information, which does not require, for instance, broadband Internet access, since a standard dial-up connection will suffice. Therefore, this research cannot confirm that being more proficient with the Internet means that online health seekers will use this communication media to manage their health more than those who are not as proficient. However, this could change with greater availability of streaming video health information, which is much more suited to a broadband Internet connection.

Boomers and seniors of higher sociodemographic status use the Internet for health information much more than lower sociodemographic status individuals (Hypotheses 5-8). Therefore, this research confirms that there is a digital divide in access to online health information, and public policy should attempt to address this issue. It should be noted that one-third of the United States adult population has not gone online and, therefore, would not be able to benefit from online health information (Pew Internet & American Life, 2005).

Hypothesis 10 was confirmed in the logistic regression results that those who are frequent patrons of online health information actually will use it more often to manage their health. The results showed that health seekers who are accessing health information online once or twice a month or more will be more likely to actually use this information to manage their health. Therefore, these individuals are not just searching for information; they actually are using some of what they find online. Individuals who have positive feelings about online health information also will use it more often to manage their health, and individuals that harbor more negative feelings will use it less often (Hypothesis 13). Online health seekers who are very aware of who provides the medical information on the Internet are more likely to use this information to manage their health (Hypothesis 9). Finally, where there is communication with their doctor via e-mail or at the doctor's office about online health information, boomers and seniors are more likely to use online health information to manage their health (Hypothesis 12). Awareness and feelings toward online health information generally were well-supported predictor variables (Hypotheses 9-13), having an impact on a boomer's or a senior's use of this information to manage his or her health care needs.

RECOMMENDATIONS, LIMITATIONS, AND FUTURE RESEARCH

This article examined the use of the Internet for accessing health information by boomers (age 50 to 64) and seniors (age 65 and over). Boomers generally use Internet health information to manage their health more than seniors. However, there was no overwhelming differences between boomers and seniors, which is the main difference in the finding from another study (Kaiser Family Foundation, 2005). For instance, boomers are much more likely to talk to a doctor about health information that they saw online. Boomers are around one and one-half times more likely than seniors to use online health information to manage their health. This study found that awareness and feelings toward online health information provided the best explanation of health information for management of boomers' and seniors' health.

Since boomers were found to use online health information marginally more than seniors, what are the implications of this observation? Will seniors of tomorrow be similar to seniors of today? Perhaps boomers will continue to seek online health information as they get older. The implication that boomers and seniors may be in the greatest need of health information may not be true in the future with the growing obesity epidemic in the United States, which affects all age groups.

Some policy recommendations should be noted in order to bring more seniors online and to enhance the quality of Internet health resources. Health care professionals should recommend Web sites, promote more effective search and evaluation techniques, and be more involved in developing and promoting uniform standards for health Web sites (Morahan-Martin, 2004). Since only a minority of seniors has ever gone online, this represents a significant digital divide. These findings confirm that for the foreseeable future, the Internet is less likely to be a primary source of information for most seniors, which suggests a need to invest more heavily in education and outreach strategies. This is especially the case for seniors with low or modest incomes, who are least likely to go online for this information. These recommendations could make seniors more aware and could create a positive experience when going online for health information.

In the near future, the Internet will become a decision-making tool for seniors, who will need to make choices about the Medicare prescription drug benefits. They will need to decide which plan has the most attractive premium and to determine whether it will cover the medications they take and will work with the pharmacy they use. Seniors also will need to manage the Internet to make these important decisions. Web site design is part of the solution, since seniors have problems scrolling on Web sites and remembering Web pages (Voelker, 2005).

There are some limitations of this research. With any type of public opinion data, especially when asking subjective questions about sensitive topics of consumers' health, respondents may not be as forthcoming with information. Another limitation is that of the general applicability of the results, given that the proportion of the sample is different for seniors and boomers. In addition, there is no question that specifically addressed whether there was an improvement in the health outcome, just that people felt better informed. Future research could do a longitudinal follow up of this dataset, which might reveal shifts in the use of Internet health information for managing health with boomers and seniors, looking at other measures to see if there is an impact on change in the person's health.

REFERENCES

Anderson, J. G. (2004). Consumers of e-health: patterns of use and barriers. *Social Science Computer Review, 22*(2), 242-248.

Brodie, M., Flournoy, R. E., Altman, D. E., Blendon, R. J., Benson, J. M., & Rosenbaum, M. D. (2000). Health information, the Internet, and the digital divide. *Health Affairs, 19*(6), 255-265.

Cotton, S. R., & Gupta, S. S. (2004). Characteristics of online and offline health information seekers and factors that discriminate between them. *Social Science & Medicine, 59*(9), 1795-1806.

Eysenbach, G. (2003). The impact of the Internet on cancer outcomes. *CA A Cancer Journal for Clinicians, 53*(6), 356-371.

Eysenbach, G., & Jadad, A. R. (2001). Evidence-based patient choice and consumer health informatics in the Internet age. *Journal of Medical Internet Research, 3*(2), e35.

Fox, S., & Rainie, L. (2000). *The online health care revolution: How the Web helps Americans take better care of themselves*. Washington, DC: Pew Internet & American Life.

Fox, S., & Rainie, L. (2002). *Vital decisions: How Internet users decide what information to trust when they or their loved ones are sick*. Washington, DC: Pew Internet & American Life.

Gray, N. J., Klein, J. D., Noyce, P. R., Sesselberg, T. S., & Cantrill, J. A. (2005). Health information-seeking behavior in adolescence: The place of the Internet. *Social Science & Medicine, 60*(7), 1467-1478.

Huntington, P., Nicholas, D., Homewood, J., Polydoratou, P., Gunter, B., Russell, C., et al. (2004). The general public's use of (and attitudes towards) interactive, personal digital health information and advisory services. *Journal of Documentation, 60*(3), 245-265.

Kaiser Family Foundation. (2005). *E-health and the elderly: How seniors use the Internet for health information*. Washington, DC: Kaiser Family Foundation.

Lueg, J. E., Moore, R. S., & Warkentin, M. (2003). Patient health information search: An explanatory model of Web-based search behavior. *Journal of End User Computing, 15*(4), 49-61.

Morahah-Martin, J. M. (2004). How Internet users find, evaluate, and use online health information: A cross-cultural review. *CyberPsychology & Behavior, 7*(5), 497-510.

Nicholas, D., Huntington, P., Williams, P., & Blackburn, P. (2001). Digital health information provision and health outcomes. *Journal of Information Science, 27*(4), 265-276.

Pandey, S. K., Hart, J. J., & Tiwary, S. (2003). Women's health and the Internet: Understanding emerging trends and implications. *Social Science & Medicine, 56*(1), 179-191.

Pew Internet & American Life. (2005). *January 2005 Internet tracking survey*. Retrieved May 10, 2005, from http://www.pewinternet.org

Rideout, V. (2002). Generation Rx.com: What are young people really doing online? *Marketing Health Services, 22*(1), 27-30.

Skinner, H., Biscope, S., & Poland, B. (2003). Quality of Internet access: Barrier behind Internet use statistics. *Social Science & Medicine, 57*(5), 875-880.

Voelker, R. (2005). Seniors seeking health information need help crossing the "digital divide." *JAMA, 293*(11), 1310-1312.

Ziebland, S. (2004). The importance of being expert: The quest for cancer information on the Internet. *Social Science & Medicine, 59*(9), 1783-1793.

ENDNOTES

1 In this study, for simplicity, baby boomers are classified as those individuals between the ages of 50 and 64, and seniors are classified as 65 and older.

2 This author would like to thank Victoria Rideout, M.A., Vice President and Director, Program for the Study of Entertainment Media and Health, Kaiser Family Foundation (KFF), for the dataset and documentation used in the statistical analysis of this study. I would also like to thank Virginia Rodgers for her editorial assistance.

3 For the data analysis, the software package used was SPSS version 13.0.

This work was previously published in International Journal of Healthcare Information Systems and Informatics, Vol. 1, Issue 2, edited by J. Tan , pp. 20-38, copyright 2006 by IGI Publishing, formerly known as Idea Group Publishing (an imprint of IGI Global).

Chapter 29
Evaluation of Health Information Systems: Challenges and Approaches

Elske Ammenwerth
University for Health Sciences, Medical Informatics & Technology, Austria

Stefan Gräber
University Hospital of Saarland, Germany

Thomas Bürkle
University of Erlangen, Germany

Carola Iller
University of Heidelberg, Germany

ABSTRACT

This chapter summarizes the problems and challenges that occur when health information systems are evaluated. The main problem areas presented are the complexity of the evaluation object, the complexity of an evaluation project, and the motivation for evaluation. Based on the analysis of those problem areas, the chapter then presents recommendations of how to address them. In particular, it discusses in more detail what benefits can be obtained from applying triangulation in evaluation studies. Based on the example of the evaluation of a nursing documentation system, it shows how both the validation of results and the completeness of results can be supported by triangulation. The authors hope to contribute to a better understanding of the peculiarities of evaluation in healthcare, and to provide information how to overcome them.

INTRODUCTION

It is hard to imagine healthcare without modern information and communication technology (ICT). It is evident that the use of modern information technology (IT) offers tremendous opportunities to reduce clinical errors, to support healthcare professionals, and to increase the efficiency of care, and even to improve the quality of patient care (Institute of Medicine, 2001).

However, there are also hazards associated with ICT in healthcare: Modern information systems (ISs) are costly, their failures may cause negative effects on patients and staff, and possibly, when inappropriately designed, they may result in healthcare professional's spending more time with the computer than with the patient. This all could have a negative impact on the efficiency of patient care. Therefore, a rigorous evaluation of IT in healthcare is recommended (Rigby, 2001) and is of great importance for decision makers and users (Kaplan & Shaw, 2002). Evaluation can be defined as the decisive assessment of defined objects, based on a set of criteria, to solve a given problem (Ammenwerth et al., 2004).

The term ICT refers to technologies as such. Whether the use of these technologies is successful depends not only on the quality of the technological artifacts but also on the actors (i.e., the people involved in information processing and the organizational environment in which they are employed). ICT embedded in the environment, including the actors, is often referred to as an IS in a sociotechnical sense (Berg, Aarts, & van der Lei, 2003; Winter et al., 2001).

Many different questions can lead the evaluation of IT. Within evaluation research, two main (and often rather distinct) traditions can be found: The objectivist (positivistic) and the subjectivistic tradition (Friedman & Wyatt, 1997), which are related to the dominant use of either quantitative or qualitative methods (for details, see Chapter XII).

Despite a large amount of published evaluation studies (e.g., van der Loo, 1995) found over 1,500 citations on evaluation of healthcare IT between 1967 and 1995, and Ammenwerth and de Keizer (2004) found 1,035 studies between 1982 and 2002; many authors report problems during evaluation. One of the main problems frequently discussed is the adequate choice of evaluation methods. While objectivistic researchers tend to concentrate on quantitative methods, subjectivistic researchers mainly rely on qualitative methods. Sometimes, a mixture of methods is applied. For example, qualitative methods are used to prepare quantitative studies, or quantitative measurements are used to support qualitative argumentation. However, there is still usually one tradition which dominates typical evaluation studies, leading to a focus either on quantitative or qualitative methods.

Many researchers point to the fact that this domination of one method or tradition may not be useful, but that a real integration of various methods from both traditions can be much more helpful to get comprehensive answers to given research questions. The integration of the complementary methods (and even beyond this, of data sources, theories and investigators), is discussed under the term triangulation.

In this chapter, we first want to review some of the underlying reasons that make evaluation of healthcare IT so difficult. We will structure the problems into three main problem areas: the complexity of the object of evaluation, the complexity of the evaluation project, and the motivation to perform evaluation. We will discuss means how to overcome the discussed problems.

As one more detailed example, we then discuss what benefits can be obtained from applying triangulation in an evaluation study. Based on the example of the evaluation of a nursing documentation system, we show how both the validation of results and the completeness of results can be supported by triangulation.

TYPICAL PROBLEMS IN EVALUATION OF IT IN HEALTHCARE

First Problem Area: Complexity of the Evaluation Object

When understanding IT as part of the IS of an organization, it is clear that evaluation requires not only an understanding of computer technology, but also of the social and behavioral processes that affect and are affected by the technology. This complexity of the evaluation objects has some important consequences. First, the introduction of IT takes time. It is not enough to implement the technology and then to immediately measure the effects. Users and workflow need a lot of time to get used to new tools and to completely exploit the new possibilities (Palvia, Sharma, & Conrath, 2001). Thus, evaluation results can develop and change during this first period of use. Then, even after an introduction period, the evaluation object may steadily change (Moehr, 2002; moving evaluation target). For example, the use of IT may be affected by changes in work organization, or in staff. It is nearly impossible to reach a stable situation in a flexible healthcare environment which makes evaluation results dependant of the point in time where the evaluation took place. In addition, each IS in our definition is quite unique. While the IT may be similar in various departments, workflow, users and used functionality may be different. In addition, the organization of its introduction as well as the overall user motivation may differ. Thus, even when the same IT is introduced, its effects may be varying (Kaplan & Shaw, 2002). The influence of such factors on the results of an evaluation study is often hard to disentangle (Wyatt, 1994), posing the problem of external validity (Moehr, 2002): Many evaluation studies may be valid only for the particular institutions with their specific IS.

The complexity of the evaluation object is an inherent attribute in healthcare IT evaluation and cannot be reduced. However, there are some ways to handle this problem in evaluation studies. To address the problem of external validity, the IT and its environment that is going to be evaluated should be defined in detail before the beginning of the study. Not only the software and hardware used should be described, but also the number of users and their experience and motivation, the way IT is introduced and used, the general technical infrastructure (e.g., networks) and any further aspects that may influence the usage of IT and its effects. The functionality and the way it is really used should also be of importance. Only this information may allow interpretation of the study results and comparison of different locations. Then, to address the problem of the moving evaluation target, all changes in the IT and its interaction with the users should be carefully documented during the study. For example, changes in workflow, in staffing, or in hardware or software should be documented with reference to the ongoing evaluation. This permits the explanation of changes and differences in effects measured during the study period. Another approach to address the problem of the moving evaluation target may be to define smaller evaluation modules. This would allow the evaluation design or evaluation questions to be adapted to changes in the environment. Each module answered a question related to a defined phase of the introduction of the IT. In addition, an evaluation must be planned in a long-term perspective in order to allow the users and the environment to integrate the new IT. Hence enough resources for long-term evaluation (e.g., over several months or even years) should be available.

Second Problem Area: Complexity of the Evaluation Project

Evaluation of IT is performed in the real and complex healthcare environment, with its different professional groups, and its high dependency on external influences such as legislation, economic constraints, or patient clientele. This poses problems to the evaluation projects, meaning the planning, executing and analyzing of an IT evaluation study. For example, the different stakeholders often have different conceptions and views of successful IT (Palvia et al., 2001). The different stakeholder requirements can serve as a frame of reference for evaluation during the early phases of the IT life cycle, but also guide evaluations during later phases. In each case, multiple-stakeholder views may lead to a multitude of (possibly conflicting) evaluation questions (Heathfield et al., 1999).

Depending on the point of view adopted, the evaluation will require different study designs and evaluation methods. The evaluation researcher must decide, for example, on the evaluation approach, on the adequate evaluation methods (e.g., quantitative vs. qualitative), and on the study design (e.g., RCT vs. observational study). Each has its own advantages and drawbacks (Frechtling, 1997; Moehr, 2002), making their selection a rather challenging endeavor. This multitude of possible evaluation questions and available evaluation methods makes the planning of an evaluation study quite complex.

The complexity of the evaluation project has several consequences. First, the overall success of IT is elusive to define (Palvia et al., 2001), and it is therefore often difficult to establish clear-cut evaluation criteria to be addressed in a study (Wyatt, 1994). Each stakeholder group may have individual questions, and a universal evaluation in terms of absolute or relative benefits is usually not feasible (or, from a more subjectivistic point of view, not even possible). It is also unrealistic to expect that the IT itself will have a direct and easy to measure effect on the outcome quality of patient care, like in a drug trial (Wyatt, 1994). Thus, indirect measures are often used such as user satisfaction or changes of clinical processes, which, however, do not give a really complete picture of the benefits of IT. Often, changes in the evaluation questions may occur during the study (e.g., based on intermediate evaluation results, new insights, changes in stakeholders' opinions, or changes of the IT [scope creep]; Dewan & Lorenzi, 2000). Changes in study questions, however, may be difficult to balance with study resources. Finally, the selection of adequate evaluation designs and evaluation methods is often regarded as a problem during evaluation studies. Evaluators may not be sufficiently aware of the broadness of available approaches, or be too deeply embedded in either the qualitative or the quantitative paradigm, neglecting the possible contributions of the complementary approach. Thus, inadequate methods or study designs may be chosen which may not be able to answer the original study questions.

The following suggestions may be useful in order to deal with the complexity of the evaluation project. First, it is recommended that the general intention of the evaluation and the starting point should be agreed early on. In principle, evaluation should start before the new IT is implemented, in order to allow for early gathering of comparative data, and then continue during all phases of its life cycle (VATAM, 2000). Then, the areas of evaluation should be restricted to aspects which are of most importance to the involved stakeholders, and which can be measured with the available resources. A complete evaluation of all aspects of a system (such as economics, effectiveness, and acceptance) is usually not feasible. A balance between the resources of a study and the inclusion of the most relevant aspects has to be found. In addition, sufficient time should be invested into the definition of relevant study questions. All involved stakeholder groups should discuss and agree on the goals of evaluation (VATAM, 2000). The selected study questions should be relevant for decision-making with regard to introduction, operation or justification of IT (Ammenwerth et al., 2004). Conflicting goals should be discussed and solved, as they are not only problematic for an evaluation, but for the overall management of new IT. Fourth, when new evaluation questions emerge during the study, they should only be included in the study design when it is possible without creating problems. Otherwise, they should be tackled in consecutive studies. Each shift in evaluation questions must thoroughly be documented. For each study question, adequate methods must be chosen. A triangulation of methods may be useful to best answer the study questions (Heathfield, Pitty, & Hanka, 1998). For example, to address the effects of a nursing documentation system, both quantitative methods (time measurement, user acceptance scales, documentation quality measurement) as well as qualitative methods (focus group interviews) were used. We will discuss this example later on in more detail.

Third Problem Area: Motivation for Evaluation

An evaluation study can normally only be conducted when there is sufficient funding, and a sufficient number of participants (e.g., staff members, wards). Both these variables depend on the motivation of stakeholders (e.g., hospital management) to perform an evaluation. Sometimes, this motivation is not very high, because, for example, of fear for negative outcome, or of fear for revealing deficiencies of already implemented technology (Rigby, Forsström, Roberts, & Wyatt, 2001). In addition, the introduction of IT in an organization is a deep intervention that may have large consequences. It is thus often very difficult to organize IT evaluation in the form of an experiment, and to easily remove the system again at the end of the study in case the evaluation was too negative.

Even with a motivated management, it may be difficult to find suitable participants. Participating in a study usually requires some effort from the involved staff. In addition, while the users have to make large efforts to learn and use a new, innovative system, the benefit of joining a pilot study is usually not obvious (the study is conducted in order to investigate possible effects), but participation may even include some risks for the involved staff such as disturbances in workflow. In summary, due to the given reasons, the hospital management as well as involved staff members is often reluctant to participate in IT evaluation studies.

The described problem has consequences for the study. Without the support and motivation of the stakeholders to conduct an evaluation study, it will be difficult to get sufficient resources for an evaluation and sufficient participants willing to participate. Second, due to the given problems, the study organizer tends to recruit any participant who volunteers to participate. However, those participants may be more motivated to participate than the "normal" user. This leads to the well-known volunteer effect, where results are better when participants are motivated. In addition, evaluation results are not only important for the involved units, but also for the overall organization or for similar units in other organizations. To allow transfer of results, the pilot wards or pilot users must be sufficiently representative for other wards or users. But, as each IT within its environment is quite unique (see Problem Area 1); it is difficult to find comparable or representative participants.

To increase the number of participants, two approaches should be combined. First, the responsible management should be informed and motivated to support the study. The result of an evaluation study may be important to decide on new IT, and to support its continuous improvement. Then, the possible participants could be directly addressed. It should be made clear that the study provides the opportunity to influence not only the future development of IT in healthcare but also the own working environment. User feedback of study results may act as an important driving force for users to participate in the study. Offering financial compensation or additional staff for the study period may help to gain support from participants and from management. As in clinical trials, multicentric studies should be considered (Wyatt & Spiegelhalter, 1992). This would largely increase the number of available participants. This means however, that study management requires much more effort. A multicentric study design is difficult when the environment is completely different. In addition, the variation between study participants will be bigger in multicentric trials than in single-center ones. This may render interpretation and comparison of results even more difficult (cp. discussion in Problem Area 1).

Summary of General Recommendations

The above discussed problems and approaches will now be summarized in a list of 12 general recommendations for IT evaluation in healthcare:

1. Evaluation takes time; thus, take your time for thorough planning and execution.
2. Document all of your decisions and steps in a detailed study protocol. Adhere to this protocol; it is your main tool for a systematic evaluation.
3. Strive for management support, and try to organize long-term financial support.
4. Clarify the goals of the evaluation. Take into account the different stakeholder groups. Dissolve conflicting goals.
5. Reduce your evaluation questions to an appropriate number of the most important questions that you can handle within the available time and budget. If new questions emerge during the study, which cannot easily be integrated, postpone them for a new evaluation study.
6. Clarify and thoroughly describe the IT object of your evaluation and the environment. Take note of any changes of the IT and its environment during the study that may affect results.
7. Select an adequate study design. Think of a stepwise study design.
8. Select adequate methods to answer your study questions. Neither objectivist nor subjectivist approaches can answer all questions. Take into account the available methods. Consider being multimethodic and multidisciplinary, and consider triangulation of methods, data sources, investigators, and theories. Strive for methodical (e.g., biometrics) advice.
9. Motivate a sufficient number of users to participate. Consider multicentric trials and financial or other compensation.
10. Use validated evaluation instruments wherever possible.
11. Be open to unwanted and unexpected effects.
12. Publish your results and what you learned to allow others to learn from your work.

One of the most discussed aspects is the selection of adequate methods and tools (Point 6) and, here especially, the adequate application of multimethodic and multidisciplinary approaches (Ammenwerth et al., 2004). The interdisciplinary nature of evaluation research in medical informatics includes that a broad choice of evaluation methods is available for various purposes. In Sections II and III of this book, several distinct quantitative and qualitative evaluation methods have been presented and discussed in detail. All of them have their particular application area. However, in many situations, the evaluator may want to combine the methods to best answer the evaluation questions at hand. Especially in more formative (constructive) studies, a combination of methods may seem necessary to get a more complete picture of a situation. To support this, the method of triangulation has been developed and will now be presented in more detail.

THE THEORY OF TRIANGULATION

The term triangulation comes from navigation and means a technique to find the exact location of a ship base on the use of various reference points. Based on this idea, triangulation in evaluation means the multiple employments of data sources, observers, methods, or theories, in investigations of the same phenomenon (Greene & McClintock, 1985). This approach has two main objectives: First, to support a finding with the help of the others (validation); second, to complement the data with new results, to find new information, to get additional pieces to the overall puzzle (completeness; Knafl & Breitmayer, 1991).

Triangulation is, based on work by Denzin (1970), usually divided into the following four types, which can be applied at the same time:

- **Data triangulation:** Various data sources are used with regard to time, space, or persons. For example, nurses from different sites are interviewed, or questionnaires are applied at different times.
- **Investigator triangulation:** Various observers or interviewers with their own specific professional methodological background take part in the study, gathering and analyzing the data together. For example, a computer scientist and a social scientist analyze and interpret results from focus group interviews together.
- **Theory triangulation:** Data is analyzed based on various perspectives, hypotheses or theories. For example, organizational changes are analyzed using two different change theories.
- **Methods triangulation:** Various methods for data collection and analysis are applied. Here, two types are distinguished: within-method triangulation (combining approaches from the same research tradition), and between-method triangulation (combining approaches from both quantitative and qualitative research traditions, also called across-method triangulation). For example, two different quantitative questionnaires may be applied to access user attitudes, or group interviews as well as questionnaires may be applied in parallel.

It should be noticed that the term triangulation is only used when one phenomenon is investigated with regard to one research question.

The term triangulation is often seen strongly related to the term multimethod evaluation; because methods triangulation is seen as the most often used triangulation approach. However, as we want to stress, it is not limited on the combination of methods, but also describes combination of data sources, investigators, or theories.

Example: Triangulation during the Evaluation of a Nursing Documentation System

Background of the Study

Nursing documentation is an important part of clinical documentation. There have been some attempts and discussions on how to support the nursing documentation using computer-based documentation systems.

In 1997, Heidelberg University Medical Center started to introduce a computer-based nursing documentation system in order to systematically evaluate preconditions and consequences. Four different (psychiatric and somatic) wards were chosen for this study.

In the following paragraphs, we will concentrate on those parts of the study that are relevant for the triangulation aspects of the study. Please refer to other publications for more details on methods and results, such as (Ammenwerth, Mansmann, Iller, & Eichstädter, 2003; Ammenwerth et al., 2001).

Three of the four study wards had been selected by the nursing management for the study. On all three wards, the majority of nurses agreed to participate. Ward B volunteered to participate. The four study wards belonged to different departments. Wards A and B were psychiatric wards, with 21 resp. 28 beds; Ward C was a pediatric ward for children under two years of age, with

15 beds; Ward D was a dermatological ward, with 20 beds.

Our study wards were quite different with regard to nursing documentation. In Wards A and B, a complete nursing documentation based on the principles of the nursing process–for details on nursing process, see, for example, Lindsey and Hartrick (1996)–had been established for several years. In contrast, in Wards C and D, only a reduced care plan was documented; documentation was mostly conducted in the ward office. Only in Ward C, major parts of documentation were also conducted in the patients' rooms. The youngest staff member could be found in Ward D; the staff least experienced in computer use was in Ward C.

Study Design

The software PIK (Pflegeinformations-und Kommunikationssystem, a German acronym for "nursing information and communication system") was introduced on those four wards. The functionality covered the six phases of the nursing care process. The study period was between August 1998 and October 2001. Wards A and B started in 1998 with the introduction of the documentation system; Wards C and D joined in 2000.

The study consisted of two main parts: The objective of the more quantitative study was to analyze the changes in the nurses' attitudes with regard to nursing process, computers in nursing, and nursing documentation system, after the introduction of the computer-based system. Standardized, validated questionnaires were applied based on Bowman, Thompson, and Sutton (1983), for nurses' attitudes on the nursing process; on Nickell and Pinto (1986), for computer attitudes; on Lowry (1994), for nurses' attitudes on computers in nursing; and on Chin (1988) and Ohmann, Boy, and Yang (1997), for nurses' satisfaction with the computer-based nursing documentation system. We carefully translated those questionnaires into German and checked the understandability in a prestudy. We used a prospective intervention study with three time measurements: approximately three months before introduction ("before"); approximately three months after introduction ("during"); and approximately nine months after introduction ("after").

The second part of the study was a more qualitative study. Here, the objective was to further analyze the reasons for the different attitudes on the wards. The quantitative study exactly described these attitudes, and the qualitative study was now intended to further explain those quantitative results. The qualitative study was conducted in February 2002, after the analysis of the quantitative study was finished. In this qualitative study, open-ended focus group interviews were conducted with up to four staff members from each ward (most of them already have taken part in the quantitative study), with the three project managers from each department, and with the four ward managers from the wards. Open-ended means that the interviews were not guided by predefined questions. We used two general questions that started the interviews (e.g., "How are you doing with PIK?" "How was the introduction period")? The rest of the interview was mostly guided by the participants themselves, with relatively little control exerted by the interviewers.

All interviews were conducted by a team of two researchers. They took about one hour each. The interviews were audio taped and analyzed using inductive, iterative content analysis based on Mayring (1993). This means that the transcripts were carefully and stepwise analyzed, using the software WinMaxProf98.

In the following paragraphs, only those results of the quantitative and qualitative study relevant for the triangulation aspects of the study will be presented. Please refer to the already mentioned study publications for more details.

Results of Quantitative Analysis of User Attitudes

All in all, 119 questionnaires were returned: 23 nurses answered all three questionnaires, 17 nurses answered two, and 16 nurses answered one questionnaire. The return rates were 82% for the first questionnaire, 86.5% for the second questionnaire, and 90.2% for the third questionnaire. A quantitative analysis of the individual items of the questionnaires revealed unfavorable attitudes, especially in Ward C. In both Wards C and D, the nurses stated that the documentation system does not "save time" and does not "lead to a better overview on the course of patient care." In addition, in Ward C, the nurses stated that they "felt burdened in their work" by the computer-based system and that the documentation system does not "make documentation easier." In Wards A and B, the opinions with regard to those items were more positive.

The self reported daily usage of the computer-based documentation system was quite similar among all wards: about 1 to 2 hours a day during the second and third questionnaires, with highest values in Ward B and lowest values in Ward A. The self-confidence with the system, as stated by the nurses, was rather high on all wards during both the second and third questionnaire. The mean values were between 3 and 3.7 during the second questionnaire and between 3.4 and 3.8 during the third questionnaire (1=minimum, 4=maximum).

Statistical analysis revealed that the overall attitude on the documentation system during the third questionnaire was positively correlated to the initial attitude on the nursing process, to the attitude on computers in general and to the attitude on computers in nursing. Both computer attitude scores were in turn positively correlated to the years of computer experience. For details, see (Ammenwerth, Mansmann, et al., 2003).

Overall, the results of quantitative analysis pointed to a positive attitude on the computer-based nursing documentation already shortly after its introduction, which significant increase on three of the four wards later on. However, on ward C, the quantitative results revealed negative reactions, showing a heavy decline in the attitude scores during the second questionnaire. On ward C, the overall attitude of the computer-based system remained rather negative, even during the third questionnaire. What could be the reasons? In order to answer this question, a subsequent qualitative study was conducted.

Results of Qualitative Analysis of User Attitudes

This part of the study was conducted as planned. Overall, about 100 pages of interview transcript were analyzed. Details of the interviews are published elsewhere (Ammenwerth, Iller, et al., 2003); we will summarize only the main points.

In Ward C, some distinct features came up in the interviews that seem to have lead to low attitude scores at the beginning. For example, the nursing process had not been completely implemented before, thus the documentation efforts now were much higher. Documentation of nursing tasks covered a 24 hour day, due to the very young patients and their high need for care. Thus, the overall amount of documentation on Ward C was higher. Patient fluctuation was also highest in ward C. Nurses found it time-consuming to create a complete nursing anamnesis and nursing-care plan for each patient. The previous computer experience and number and availability of motivated key users was seen as rather low in Ward C. Then, during the introduction of the nursing documentation system, the workload was rather high in Ward C due to staff shortage, which increased pressure on the nurses. Finally, and most important, nursing documentation had previously at least partly been carried out in the patients' rooms. However, during our study, computers were installed only in the ward office. No mobile computers were available, which, according to the nurses, lead to time-consuming and inefficient double documentation.

Interesting differences were found between the nurses and the project management. For example, the nurses stated in the interviews that they were not sufficiently informed on the new documentation system, while the project management stated to have offered information that had not been used. Another example is that the nurses felt that training was insufficient. In the opinion of the project management, sufficient opportunities had been offered. We will later see how this divergent information helps to complete the overall picture.

In Ward D, the attitude on the documentation system was high in the interviews. The nurses saw benefits, especially in a more professional documentation, which would lead to a greater acknowledgment of nursing. Standardized care planning was seen to make care planning much easier, without reducing the individuality of the patient. Overall, the ward felt at ease while working with the new documentation system.

In Wards A and B, the attitudes were also positive. The nurses stressed the better legibility of nursing documentation in the interviews. They said that time effort for nursing care planning was lower, but overall, time effort for nursing documentation was much higher than before. The interviews showed that the introduction period had been filled with anxiety and fear about new requirements for the nurses. Now, after some time, the nurses felt self-confident with computers. An interesting discussion arose on the topic of standardization. Most nurses felt that standardized care plans reduced the individuality of the care plans, and that they did not really reflect what is going on with the patient. Finally, those wards, too, mentioned insufficient teaching and support in the first weeks.

These rather short summaries, from the interviews, should highlight some distinct features of the wards, showing similarities (e.g., on insufficient teaching and fears at the beginning), but also differences (e.g., on the question on standardized care plans or time effort).

APPLICATION OF TRIANGULATION IN THIS STUDY

After analysis of the quantitative study and the qualitative study, we now want to see how the different results can be put together to get a broader picture of the effects and preconditions of a nursing documentation system. We thus applied all four types of triangulation as described by Denzin (1970):

- **Data triangulation:** Various data sources were used: Within the quantitative study, data triangulation with regard to time was used as the questionnaires were submitted three times to the same users (data triangulation with regard to time). In addition, in the interviews, not only nurses but also project management and ward management were interviewed (data triangulation with regard to persons).
- **Investigator triangulation:** Within the qualitative study, the two interviewers had different backgrounds (one more quantitative coming from medical informatics, the other, more qualitative, coming from social science). Both acted together as interviewers, analyzed the transcript together, and discussed and agreed on results and conclusions.
- **Theory triangulation:** We learned from various complementing theories to better understand the results of our studies. For example, to explain the implementation phases, we took ideas both from the book of Lorenzi and Riley (1995; first-, middle-, and second-order change) as well as from the change theory of (Lewin, 1947; unfreezing, moving, refreezing phase). With regard to user evaluation, we used the technology

acceptance model (TAM) of Davis (1993), and the task-technology-fit model (TTF) of Goodhue (1995).
- **Methods triangulation:** We applied between-methods triangulation by applying both quantitative questionnaires and qualitative focus-group interviews to investigate user's attitudes.

As stated in the introduction, triangulation has two main objectives: To confirm results with data from other sources (validation of results) and to find new data to get a more complete picture (completeness of results). We will now briefly discuss whether triangulation helped to achieve those goals.

Validation of Results

Validation of results is obtained when results from one part of the study are confirmed by congruent (not necessarily equal) results from other parts of the study. In our example, some parts of the study showed congruent results:

First, both the questionnaire and the interviews focused on attitudes issues. In this area, both approaches lead to congruent results, showing, for example, favorable attitudes in three wards. In addition, both the questionnaires and the interviews showed problems with regard to the user satisfaction with the nursing documentation system in Ward C. However, as the interviews were conducted later, they could better show the long-term development in the wards. Hence, both data sources thus showed congruent results.

Second, we found congruent results of the two scales attitudes on nursing process and attitude on the computer-based nursing documentation system within the standardized questionnaires. Both focus on different attitude items, both showed comparable low results in Ward C and higher results on the other wards, pointing to congruent measurements.

Those two selected examples show how results of some parts of the study could be validated by congruent results from other parts of the studies.

Completeness of Results

Besides validation, triangulation can increase completeness when one part of the study presents results which have not been found in other parts of the study. By this new information, the completeness of results is increased. The new information may be complementary to other results, or it may present divergent information.

In our study, both questionnaires and interviews presented partly complementary results, which led to new insights. For example, impact of the computer-based documentation system on documentation processes and communication processes had not been detected by the questionnaire (this aspect had not been included in the questions). However, the documentation system seems to have influenced the way different healthcare professionals exchanged patient-related information. This led to some discussion on this topic on all wards in the interviews and seems to have had an impact on the overall attitude. Those effects only emerged in the group interviews (and not in the questionnaires); enlarging the picture of the effects of the nursing documentation system and helping to better understand the reactions of the different wards.

Another example is the complementarity of the results in the interviews and questionnaires in Ward C. The interviews were done some time after the questionnaires. Thus, during this time, changes may have occurred. The change theory of Lewin (1947) stated that organizational changes occur in three phases: unfreezing (old patterns must be released, combined with insecurity and problems), moving (new patterns are tested), and refreezing (new patterns are internalized and seen as normal). The low attitude scores in Ward C, even at the last measurement point, indicate that the ward was in the moving phase during this time. During the interviews, the stress articulated by the nurses seems to be less severe. This can be interpreted as Ward C's slowly changing from the moving into the refreezing phase.

Triangulation can thus help to get a more complete picture of the object under investigation. Often, especially when applying various methods during the investigation, the results will not be congruent, but they may be divergent (e.g., contradictory). This is an important aspect of triangulation, as divergent results can especially highlight some points, present new information, and lead to further investigation.

In our study, we found some divergent results. For example, during the group interviews, nurses from one ward stressed that they do not see a reduction in effort needed for documentation by the computer-based system. However, in the questionnaires, this ward indicated strong time reductions. This differences can lead to the questions of whether time efforts are judged with regard to the situation without the nursing documentation system (where the amount of documentation was much lower, and so was the time effort), or with regard to the tasks that have to be performed (the same amount of documentation can be done much quicker with the computer-based system). This discussion can help one better understand the answers. Interesting differences of point of view could also be found between the staff and the project management of one ward in the group interviews. While the nurses of this ward claimed in the interviews that training was suboptimal, the project management stated that sufficient offers had been made. Those apparent contradictions may point to different perceptions of the need for training by the different stakeholders. Those insights may help to better organize the teaching on other wards.

As those (selected) examples show, triangulation helped us to obtain a better picture of the reaction of the four wards. The evaluation results also led to some decision on how to improve the technical infrastructure as well as how to better organize the teaching and support in some wards. All wards are still working with the computer-based nursing documentation system.

DISCUSSION

Medical informatics is an academic discipline and, thus, evaluation is an important part of any system development and implementation activity (Shahar, 2002; Talmon & Hasmann, 2002). However, many problems with regard to healthcare IT evaluation have been reported. Wyatt and Spiegelhalter (1992) as well as Grémy and Degoulet (1993) already discussed the complexity of the field, the motivation issue, and methodological barriers to evaluation. Examples of meta-analysis of IT evaluation studies confirm those barriers (e.g. Brender, 2002; Johnston, Langton, Haynes, & Mathieu, 1994; Kaplan, 2001).

In this chapter, we elaborated on a number of important problems and categorized them into three areas: the complexity of the evaluation object, the complexity of the evaluation project with its multitude of stakeholders, and the motivation for evaluation.

A kind of framework to support evaluation studies of ISs may be useful to address the problem areas discussed in this chapter. In fact, many authors have formulated the necessity for such a framework (e.g., Grant, Plante, & Leblanc, 2002; Shaw, 2002). Chapter XIV will present a framework for evaluation in more detail. One important part of such a framework is the call for a multimethod evaluation. While triangulation has long been discussed and applied in research (one of the first being Campbell & Fiske, 1959), the idea of the possible advantages of multimethod approaches or triangulation in more general terms is not really reflected in medical informatics literature.

The background of multimethod approaches has been more deeply discussed in Chapter XII.

In general, both quantitative and qualitative methods have their areas and research questions where they can be successfully applied. By triangulating both approaches, their advantages can be combined. We found that both complementary and divergent results from the different sources gave important new information and stimulation of further discussion.

In the past, there has been a more basic discussion about whether intermethods triangulation is possible at all. It is discussed that the epistemological underpinnings between quantitative and qualitative research paradigms may be so different that a real combination may not be possible (Greene & McClintock, 1985; Sim & Sharp, 1998). However, this argumentation is not taking into account that a tradition of research has formed beyond subjectivistic and objectivistic paradigms. Evaluation methods are chosen accordingly to research questions and the research topic. Thus, the question of which methods to apply and how to combine them only can be answered with respect to the research topic and the research question and not on a general basis. Thus, as important as this discussion might be in the light of progress in research methods, evaluation researchers in medical informatics may be advised to start to select and combine methods based on their distinctive research question. This gives evaluation researchers a broad range of possibilities to increase both completeness and validity of results, independent of his or her research tradition.

CONCLUSIONS

Evaluation studies in healthcare IT take a lot of time, resources, and know-how. Clearly defined methodological guidelines that take the difficulties of IS evaluation in healthcare into account may help to conduct better evaluation studies. This chapter has classified some of the problems encountered in healthcare IT evaluation under the three main problem areas of a) complexity of the evaluation object, b) complexity of the evaluation project, and c) limited motivation for evaluation. We suggested a list of 12 essential recommendations to support the evaluation of ISs. A broadly accepted framework for IT evaluation in healthcare that is more detailed seems desirable, supporting the evaluator during planning and executing of an evaluation study.

Focusing on methodological aspects, we have presented some basics on triangulation and illustrated them in a case study. The correct application of triangulation requires–as other evaluation methods–training and methodological experience. Medical informatics evaluation research may profit from this well-established theory.

ACKNOWLEDGMENT

This chapter is based on two earlier publications, published by Elsevier (Ammenwerth, Gräber, Herrmann, Bürkle, & König, 2003; Ammenwerth, Mansmann, & Iller, 2003).

REFERENCES

Ammenwerth, E., Brender, J., Nykänen, P., Prokosch, U., Rigby, M., & Talmon, J. (2004). Visions and strategies to improve evaluations of health information systems-Reflections and lessons based on the HIS-EVAL workshop in Innsbruck. International Journal of Medical Informatics, 73(6), 479-91.

Ammenwerth, E., & de Keizer, N. (2004). An inventory of evaluation studies of information technology in healthcare: Trends in evaluation research 1982-2002. Methods of Information in Medicine, 44, 44-51.

Ammenwerth, E., Eichstädter, R., Haux, R., Pohl, U., Rebel, S., & Ziegler, S. (2001). A randomized evaluation of a computer-based nursing documentation system. Methods of Information in Medicine, 40(2), 61-8.

Ammenwerth, E., Gräber, S., Herrmann, G., Bürkle, T., & König, J. (2003). Evaluation of health ISs-Problems and challenges. International Journal of Medical Informatics, 71(2/3), 125-135.

Ammenwerth, E., Iller, C., Mahler, C., Kandert, M., Luther, G., Hoppe, B., et al. (2003). Einflussfaktoren auf die Akzeptanz und Adoption eines Pflegedokumentationssystems-Studienbericht (2/2003). Innsbruck: Private Universität für Medizinische Informatik und Technik Tirol.

Ammenwerth, E., Mansmann, U., & Iller, C. (2003). Can evaluation studies benefit from a triangulation of quantitative and qualitative methods? A case study. International Journal of Medical Informatics, 70(2/3), 237-248.

Ammenwerth, E., Mansmann, U., Iller, C., & Eichstädter, R. (2003). Factors affecting and affected by user acceptance of computer-based nursing documentation: Results of a two-year study. Journal of the American Medical Informatics Association. 10(1), 69-84.

Berg, M., Aarts, J., & van der Lei, J. (2003). ICT in healthcare: Sociotechnical approaches. Methods of Information in Medicine, 42, 297-301.

Bowman, G., Thompson, D., & Sutton, T. (1983). Nurses attitudes towards the nursing process. Journal of Advanced Nursing, 8(2), 125-129.

Brender, J. (2002). Methodological and methodical perils and pitfalls within assessment studies performed on IT-based solutions in healthcare. Aalborg: Virtual Centre for Health Informatics.

Campbell, D., & Fiske, D. (1959). Convergent and discriminant validity by the muli-trait, multi-method matrix. Psychological Bulletin, 56, 81-105.

Chin, J. (1988). Development of a tool measuring user satisfaction of the human-computer interface. Proceedings: Human factors in Computing, Chi'88 Conf (pp. 213-218). New York: Association for Computing Machinery.

Davis, F. (1993). User acceptance of information technology: System characteristics, user perceptions and behavioral impacts. International Journal of Man-Machine Studies, 38, 475-487.

Denzin, N. (1970). Strategies of multiple triangulation. In N. Denzin (Ed.), The research act (3rd ed., pp. 297-331). Chicago: Aldine.

Dewan, N., & Lorenzi, N. (2000). Behavioral health information systems: evaluating readiness and user acceptance. MD Computing, 17(4), 50-52.

Frechtling, J. (1997). User-friendly handbook for mixed method evaluation [Ausdruck im Eval-Ordner]. Retrieved May 2005, from http://www.ehr.nsf.gov/EHR/REC/pubs/NSF97-153/start.htm

Friedman, C., & Wyatt, J. C. (1997). Evaluation methods in medical informatics. New York: Springer.

Goodhue, D. (1995). Understanding user evaluations of information systems. Management Science, 41(12), 1827-44.

Grant, A., Plante, I., & Leblanc, F. (2002). The TEAM methodology for the evaluation of information systems in biomedicine. Computers in Biology and Medicine, 32(3), 195-207.

Greene, J., & McClintock, C. (1985). Triangulation in evaluation: Design and analysis issues. Evaluation Review, 9(5), 523-545.

Grémy, F., & Degoulet, P. (1993). Assessment of health information technology: Which questions for which systems? Proposal for a taxonomy. Medical Informatics, 18(3), 185-193.

Heathfield, H., Hudson, P., Kay, S., Mackay, L., Marley, T., Nicholson, L., et al. (1999). Issues in the multi-disciplinary assessment of healthcare information systems. Assessment of Healthcare Information Technology & People, 12(3), 253-275.

Heathfield, H., Pitty, D., & Hanka, R. (1998). Evaluating information technology in health care: Barriers and challenges. British Medical Journal, 316, 1959-1961.

Institute of Medicine. (2001). Crossing the quality chasm: A new health system for the 21st century. Washington: National Academy Press.

Johnston, M., Langton, K., Haynes, R., & Mathieu, A. (1994). Effects of computer-based clinical decision support systems on clinician performance and patient outcome: A critical appraisal of research. Annuals of Internal Medicine, 120, 135-142.

Kaplan, B. (2001). Evaluating informatics applications: Clinical decision support systems literature review. International Journal of Medical Informatics, 64, 15-37.

Kaplan, B., & Shaw, N. (2002). People, organizational and social issues: Evaluation as an exemplar. In R. Haux & C. Kulikowski (Eds.), Yearbook of medical informatics 2002 (pp. 91-102). Stuttgart, Germany: Schattauer.

Knafl, K., & Breitmayer, B. (1991). Triangulation in qualitative research: Issues of conceptual clarity and purpose. In J. Morse (Ed.), A contemporary dialogue (pp. 226-239). Newbury Park, CA: Sage.

Lewin, K. (1947). Frontiers in group dynamics: Concepts, methods, and reality of social sciences: Social equalization and social change. Human Relations, 1, 5-14.

Lindsey, E., & Hartrick, G. (1996). Health-promoting nursing practice: The demise of the nursing process? Journal of Advanced Nursing, 23(1), 106-112.

Lorenzi, N., & Riley, R. (1995). Organizational aspects of health informatics - Managing technological change. New York: Springer.

Lowry, C. (1994). Nurses' attitudes toward computerised care plans in intensive care. Part 2. Intensive and Critical Care Nursing, 10, 2-11.

Mayring, M. (1993). Einführung in die qualitative Sozialforschung. Weinheim: Psychologie-Verlag-Union.

Moehr, J. R. (2002). Evaluation: Salvation or nemesis of medical informatics? Computers in Biology and Medicine, 32(3), 113-125.

Nickell, G., & Pinto, J. (1986). The computer attitude scale. Computers in Human Behaviour, 2, 301-306.

Ohmann, C., Boy, O., & Yang, Q. (1997). A systematic approach to the assessment of user satisfaction with healthcare systems: Constructs, models and instruments. In C. Pappas (Ed.), Medical Informatics Europe '97. Conference proceedings (Vol. 43, Pt. B, pp. 781-5). Amsterdam: IOS Press.

Palvia, S., Sharma, R., & Conrath, D. (2001). A socio-technical framework for quality assessment of computer information systems. Industrial Management & Data Systems, 101(5), 237-251.

Rigby, M. (2001). Evaluation: 16 powerful reasons why not to do it-And 6 over-riding imperatives. In V. Patel, R. Rogers, & R. Haux (Eds.), Proceedings of the 10th World Congress on Medical Informatics (Medinfo 2001,Vol. 84, pp. 1198-1202). Amsterdam: IOS Press.

Rigby, M., Forsström, J., Roberts, R., & Wyatt, W. (2001, September 8). Verifying quality and safety in health informatics services. British Medical Journal, 323, 552-556.

Shahar, Y. (2002). Medical informatics: Between science and engineering, between academia and industry. Methods of Information in Medicine, 41, 8-11.

Shaw, N. (2002). CHEATS: a generic information communication technology (ICT) evaluation framework. Computers in Biology and Medicine, 32, 209-200.

Sim, J., & Sharp, K. (1998). A critical appraisal of the role of triangulation in nursing research. International Journal of Nursing Studies, 35(1/2), 23-31.

Talmon, J., & Hasmann, A. (2002). Medical informatics as a discipline at the beginning of the 21st century. Methods of Information and Medicine, 41, 4-7.

van der Loo, R. (1995). Overview of published assessment and evaluation studies. In E. M. S. J. van Gennip & J. S. Talmon (Eds.), Assessment and evaluation of information technologies (pp. 261-82). Amsterdam: IOS Press.

VATAM. (2000). The VATAM Websites. Validation of health telematics applications (VATAM). Retrieved May 2005, from http://www-vatam.unimaas.nl

Winter, A., Ammenwerth, E., Bott, O., Brigl, B., Buchauer, A., Gräber, S., et al. (2001). Strategic information management plans: The basis for systematic information management in hospitals. International Journal of Medical Informatics, 64(2/3), 99-109.

Wyatt, J. (1994). Clinical data systems, part 3: Development and evaluation. The Lancet, 344, 1682-1688.

Wyatt, J., & Spiegelhalter, D. (1992). Field trials of medical decision-aids: Potential problems and solutions. In P. Clayton (Ed.), 15th Annual Symposium on Computer Applications in Medical Care (pp. 3-7). New York: McGraw-Hill.

Chapter 30
Mobile Information Systems in a Hospital Organization Setting

Agustinus Borgy Waluyo
Monash University, Australia

David Taniar
Monash University, Australia

Bala Srinivasan
Monash University, Australia

ABSTRACT

The emerging of wireless computing motivates radical changes of how information is obtained. Our paper discusses a practical realisation of an application using push and pull based mechanism in a wireless ad-hoc environment. We use a hospital information system as a case study scenario for our proposed application. The pull mechanism is initiated from doctors as mobile client to retrieve and update patient records in the central database server. The push mechanism is initiated from the server without a specific request from the doctors. The application of push mechanism includes sending a message from central server to a specific doctor, and multicasting a global message to all doctors connected to the server application. The global message can be disabled by each doctor to perform selective recipients.

INTRODUCTION

Recent advances in wireless technology have led to mobile computing, a new dimension in data communication and processing. Many predict a new emerging, gigantic market with millions of mobile users carrying a small, battery-powered terminal equipped with wireless connection (Acharya, Alonso, Franklin, & Zdonik, 1995; Barbara, 1999; Imielinski & Viswanathan, 1994). The main properties of mobile computing include mobility, severe power and storage restriction, frequency of disconnection is much greater than in a traditional network, bandwidth capacity, and asymmetric communications costs. Radio wireless transmission usually requires approximately 10 times more power as compared to the reception operation (Zaslavsky & Tari, 1998).

There are two ways of data delivery in wireless environment. One is called *pull* mechanism, and the other is *push* mechanism (Aksoy et al., 1999). In this paper, we apply these two mechanisms in a wireless ad-hoc environment. We use hospital information system as a case study scenario to show the effective uses of the mechanisms. The hospital information system relates to doctors as the principal clients to a server application. Pull mechanism refers to data delivery on a demand basis. In the hospital information system, we apply this mechanism for doctors to retrieve his/her patients. Once the patient has been diagnosed, doctors can update the record in the database. In push mechanism, the server initiates the delivery of data without a specific request from the client. We apply this mechanism to send a direct message to a specific doctor, and to distribute information to all or selective doctors such as news bulletin. The information or message is sent from central server.

Push mechanism can be categorized into 1-1 (unicast) and 1-N (multicast/broadcast) communication type. Unicast communication involves a server and a client, and the data is sent from the server to the client. 1-N communication can be either multicast or broadcast mode. In multicast mode, the recipients are known and the data are delivered only to those recipients, for example; the information is delivered to doctors and nurses that are registered in a specific domain. On the contrary, the broadcast mode simply sent the data without knowing the number of clients who might receive the data. This paper concerns with 1-N (multicast mode) communication type.

Push-based data dissemination approaches can be performed in aperiodic or periodic manner (Franklin & Zdonik, 1997). Aperiodic data dissemination is event-driven; whereas, periodic data dissemination adheres to a pre-defined schedule. An example of aperiodic push-based event is when the central administrator sends an urgent message to a specific doctor in the hospital. In contrast, periodic push-based transmission is managed by an automated server program transmitting data (or information) according to a pre-defined schedule such as, distribution of news bulletin to doctors in every hour or so.

The advantage of push mechanism over pull mechanism is that query performance is not overwhelmed by multiple client requests. Push mechanism avoid the possibility of congested channel bandwidth and server queue causes by increase of number of clients, request arrival rate, and overlap in user"s requests. The congested channel and server queue may severely affect the power consumption of mobile clients. Figure 1 illustrates the push and pull mechanism.

This application will demonstrate the usability of wireless networks, and improve the mobility of doctors through wireless data dissemination. The subsequent sections in this paper are organized as follows. The following section provides the infrastructure of push and pull wireless information system. The next section describes the client and server processes in the system. It is then followed by the development of push and pull wireless information system in a hospital environment. Finally, the last section concludes the paper.

PUSH AND PULL MOBILE INFORMATION SYSTEMS: INFRASTRUCTURE

In this section, we describe the infrastructure of a push and pull wireless information system. We use the hospital information system scenario for implementation purposes. This section includes design overview, technology aspect, database aspect, server, and client model. The model is designed to realize and to demonstrate pull-based

Figure 1. The pull and push mechanism

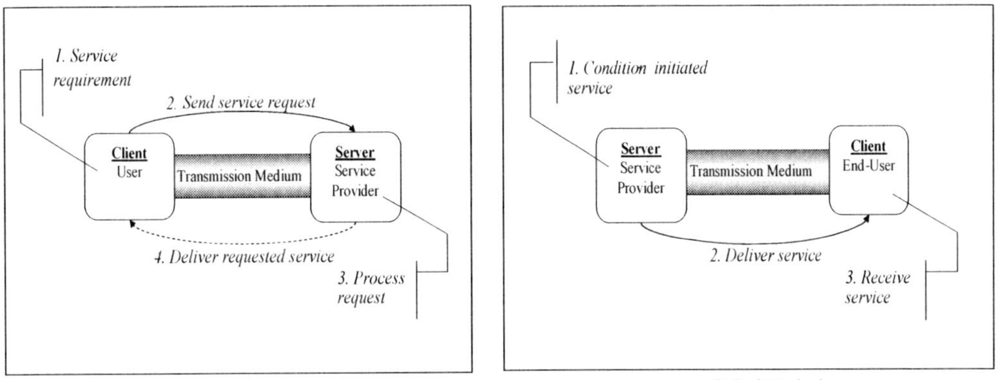

(a) Pull Mechanism

(b) Push Mechanism

and push-based approaches for data dissemination.

Design Overview

The proposed model comprises of three specific components. The three components are: (1) a data source, (2) a server application, and (3) a client application. The data source component is a simple Microsoft Access® database. The proposed model intends to retrieve information from the database for pull-based and push-based communications. All pull-based and push-based communications are routed through a server component. The data source and server components are located on the same server device. The server component is an application that functions as a mediator between the data source and client application. The client application accepts push-based information from the server; or the client can create requests for processing (by the server application). The client component does not access the data source directly. The diagram shown in Figure 2 illustrates the three components of the test application.

The client application is required to connect to the server application. This is a necessary requirement for two-way communication between the server and the client. Without an initial connection, communication between the server and client is impossible. The connection over the TCP/IP network is created via the Winsock controls on both the server and client application. The Winsock control allows for both pull-based and push-based communications. A dummy client application is located within the server application.

The dummy client application mimics the client component of the proposed model. The purpose of the dummy client is to enable multi-client experimentation. Since the client application is located on a Personal Digital Assistant, the dummy client application enables multi-client experimentation without the exorbitant cost of procuring multiple PDAs.

The database utilized by the application comprises of three related tables. The three tables are titled *Doctors*, *Patients*, and *Remote*. The Doctors table stores records of doctors employed by the hospital. The Patients table stores records of patient details; including the doctor assigned to care for the patient. Finally, the Remote table stores a list of IP addresses. Each IP address stored in the Remote table is assigned to a doctor. The diagram shown in Figure 3 depicts the relationship between the three tables.

It indicates that there is a one-to-many relationship between the records in the Doctors table and the records in the Patients table. This relationship implies that each record in the Patients table can have one associated doctor; but each record in the Doctors table can be assigned to several patient

Figure 2. Proposed model

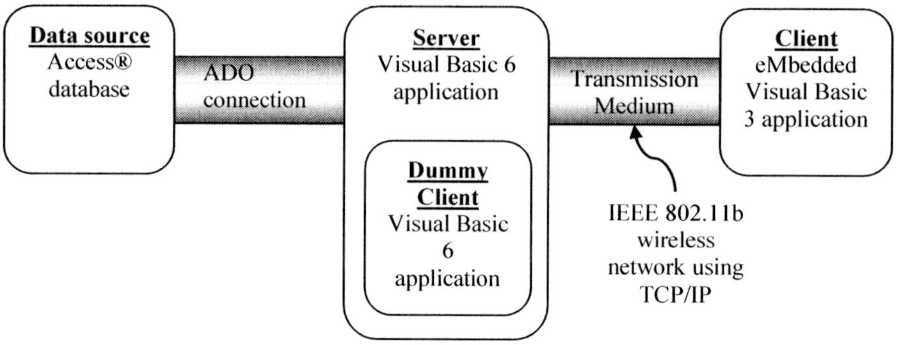

Figure 3. Table relationships for hospital database

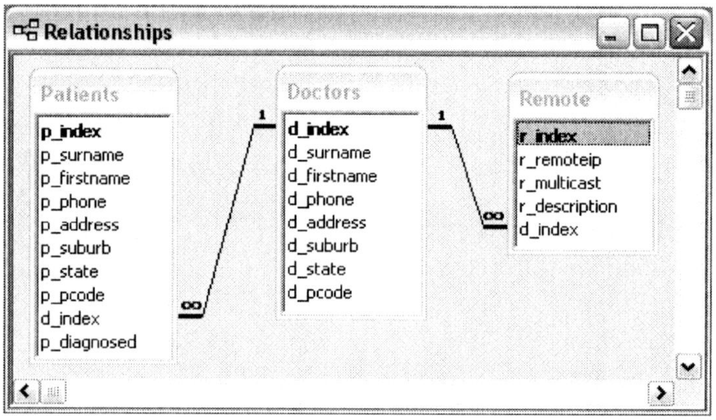

records. Basically, a patient can be cared by one doctor only; but a doctor can care for several patients.

Furthermore, it also indicates that there is a one-to-many relationship between the records in the Doctors table and the records in the Remote table. This relationship implies that each record in the Remote table can have one associated doctor; but each record in the Doctors table can be assigned to several records in the Remote table. However, assigning a doctor to multiple records in the Remote table is ill-advised. The purpose of the Remote table is to separate network-related information from the Doctors table. The desired relationship between the Doctors and Remote table is a one-to-one relationship. Hence, each doctor in the Doctors table is assigned one (and only one) IP address from the Remote table. Furthermore, the Remote table acts as a quasi-subscription table to track all remote client devices.

Technology

The hardware technology we use is a computer as the server side, and pocket PC-based personal digital assistant (PDA) as the client device. Hewlett Packard iPAQ™ H5450 Pocket PC is the type of PDA that we use. The PDA communicates with the server device over a wireless LAN. Since the transmission medium is wireless, the nominated wireless transmission standard is 802.11b. Figure 4 illustrates the communication architecture of client and server model.

As for the software technology, we utilize Microsoft® WindowsTM 2000 for operating system software for the server device, and Microsoft®

Figure 4. Communication architecture

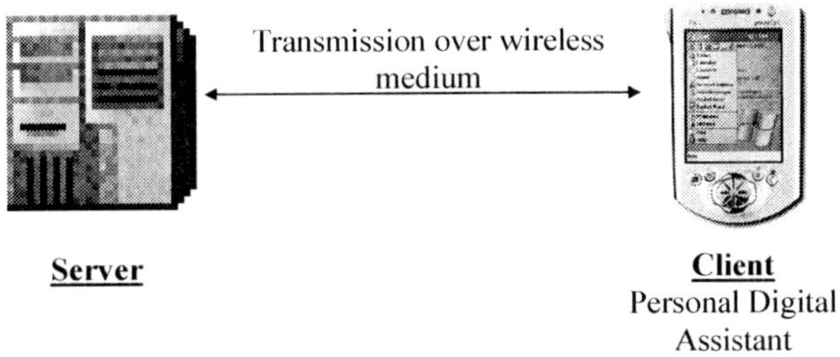

Pocket PC 2002 for the client system software. Furthermore, Microsoft® Pocket PC 2002 also features a set of network-related services required by the proposed model. Two software development products that we employee are Microsoft® Visual Basic® 6.0 and Microsoft® eMbedded Visual Basic® 3.0.Microsoft® eMbedded Visual Basic® 3.0 is an object-oriented/event-driven high-level programming language. It is similar to Microsoft® Visual Basic® 6.0; except, it is a software component that enables Visual Basic® 6.0 applications to connect to various data sources such as a Microsoft® Access®2002 database to perform search and update functions.

The service device and the PDA both use 802.11b to create a wireless ad-hoc network (Blake, 2002). The TCP/IP protocols are used to manage the transmission of messages between the server device and client device over the 802.11b wireless network. TCP/IP is a necessity on the server device and client device because the two software development programs use a control called Winsock (Zak, 1999). The Winsock control is added to both the server application and client application at design time. This enables the server application and client application to communicate messages over a TCP/IP network.

Server

The server is designed to perform push-based mechanism. We classify the application into two categories, one is sending a message from server to client, and second is multicasting information from server to client(s).

In Figure 5, we assume a database is attached in the central server. Figure 5 (a) illustrates a situation when a message is sent from server to a specific doctor in the network but first the central server needs to connect to the database and check the available doctors. Figure 5 (b) depicts a scenario when the message are multicast to all doctors in the network periodically. In this case, the server not only checks the doctors in the network but also checks whether the doctor is interested in receiving the global message, and selectively send the message to the interested recipient in the list.

Client

Mobile client application is expected to perform pull-based mechanism. In this paper we designed the doctors as mobile client to be able to conduct conventional patient information retrieval via wireless channel as illustrated in Figure 6, as well as updating the content of the database.

SERVER AND CLIENT PROCESSES IN PUSH AND PULL MOBILE INFORMATION SYSTEMS

In this section, we describe the underlying concept of server and client processes in the wireless hospital information system. These processes explain the main functions for both server and client application in the system.

Figure 5. Push-based application: (a) Sending a message from server to client; (b) multicasting information from server to client(s)

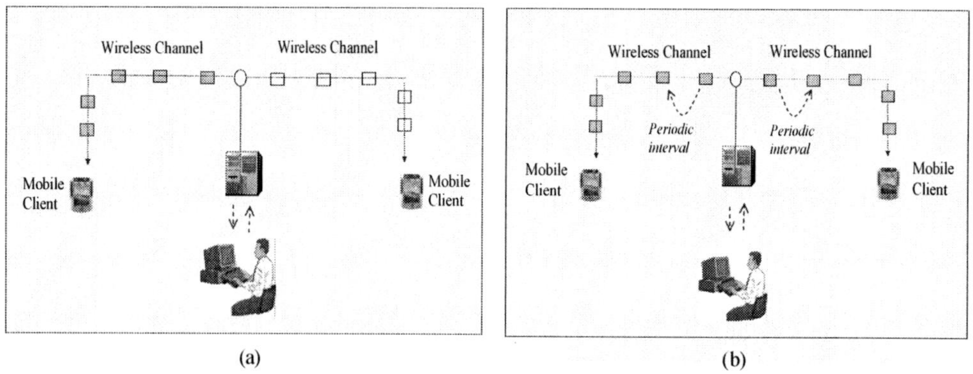

Figure 6. Pull-based application

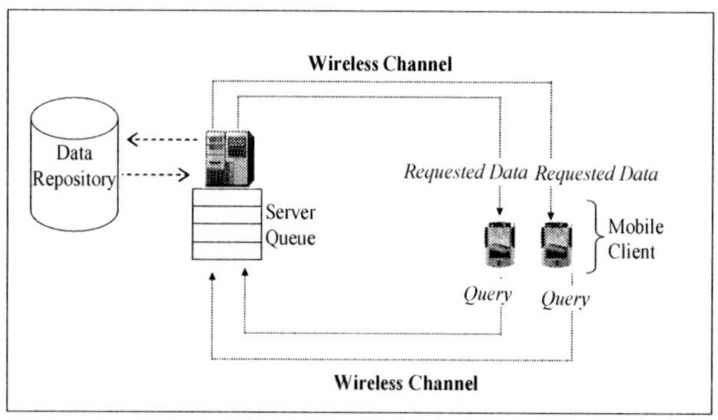

Server Processes

There are four important functions of the server application. The four functions cover: (1) how the server accept and close connection from client; (2) how the server processes messages sent by the client; (3) how the server retrieves information from the database; and (4) how the server handles client messages or requests.

Accepting and Closing Connections

Whenever a remote client requests a connection, the connection request event procedure of the Winsock control is executed. Firstly, the event procedure checks if the connection request resulted from the Winsock listener control wskTCP(0). The event procedure then uses the form-level variables (declared in general declarations) to label the connection and to track the number of connections. With each incoming connection request, the counter lngCounter and connection identifier lngConnection are both incremented by the value of one. The new value of the connection identifier lngConnection is assigned to each new connection. A new Winsock control is created and loaded according to the connection identifier lngConnection. The following diagram shown in Figure 7 illustrates how the connection identifier is used to identify each new connection.

The connection request event procedure also resizes the arrays strRetrieveBuffer(), strData(), and strRemoteHostIP() to provide storage spaces for new connections. The first two arrays are used

Figure 7. Connection identifier lngConnection

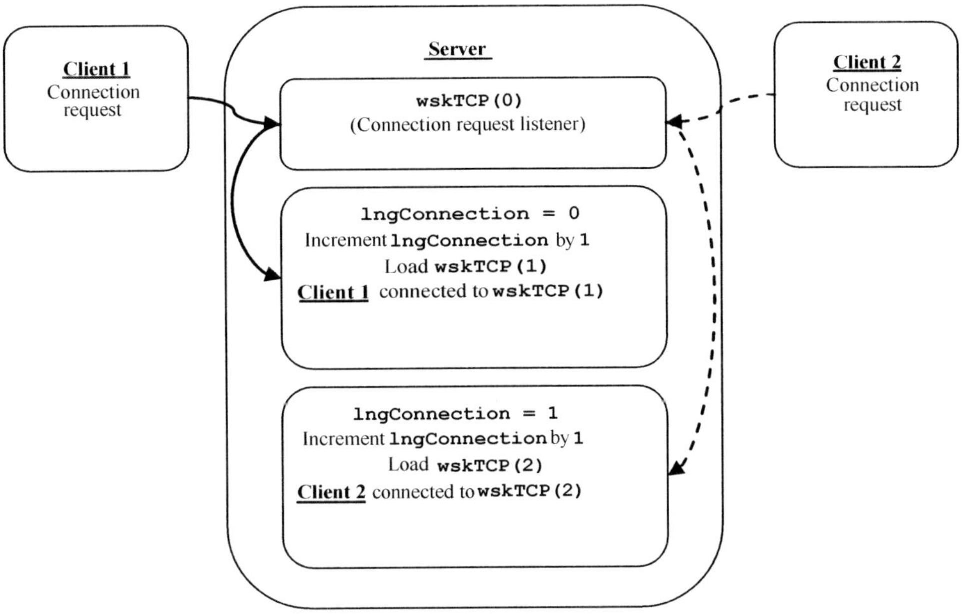

Figure 8. Re-sizing arrays strRetrieveBuffer(), strData(), and strRemoteHostIP()

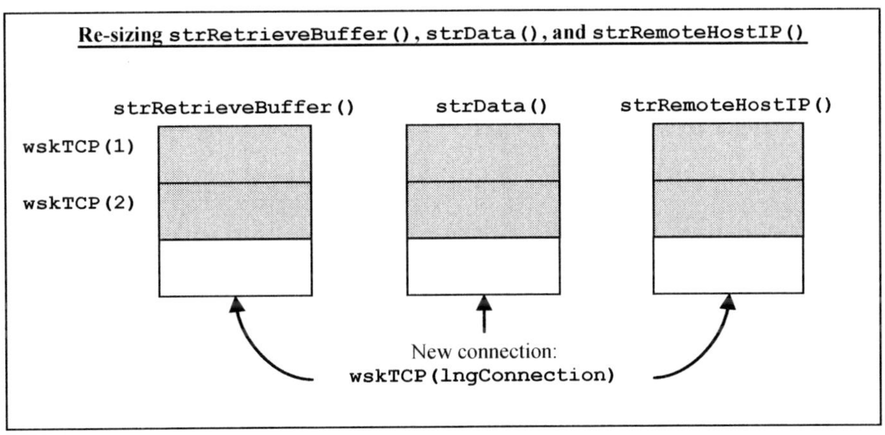

as storage spaces for incoming data received from pull-based interactions, whereas the last array is used to store the IP address of the remote client device. The size of the three arrays is determined by the value of lngConnection, which acts as a maxima value for the number of connections and hence the size of each array needs to be the sized (or resized). The following diagram shown in Figure 8 depicts the resizing of the three arrays.

Finally, the connection request event procedure checks if the value of lngCounter is greater than zero. If it is greater than zero, then the button that executes a Push-based data transmission is enabled.

When a remote client attempts to disconnect from the server application, the Winsock close event procedure is executed. The event procedure receives an Index value, which is the same as the

Figure 9. Message array processing

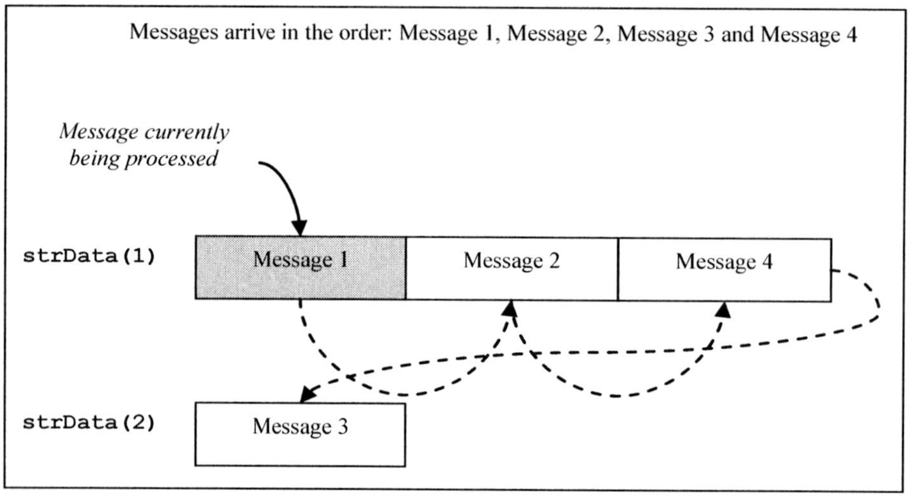

Figure 10. Example data processing subroutine

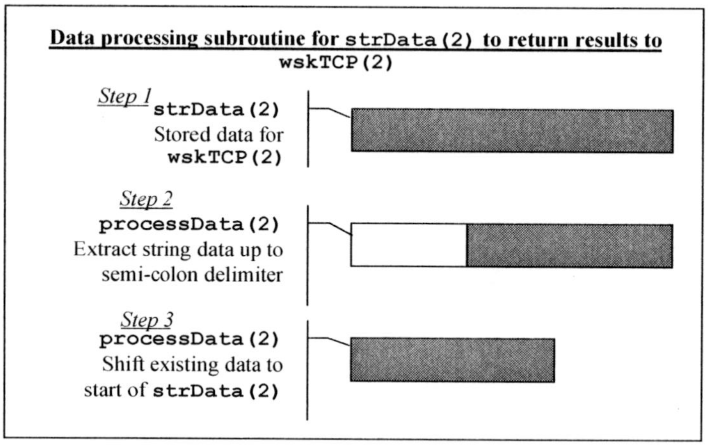

connection identifier. By passing the connection identifier through the parameter Index, the event procedure is able to discern which connection is being closed. When the connection is closed, the Winsock control is also unloaded.

The event procedure also checks the value of the form-level variable lngCounter to determine if there are any remaining connections. If lng-Counter is zero, then the button that executes a push-based data transmission is disabled.

Processing a Message

A timer event periodically checks the strData() array for any unprocessed data. If the array is not empty, then the event procedure calls the processData() subroutine to process the array. A loop is employed to cycle through all clients connected to the server application. A second (nested) loop is used to process the contents of the array. Figure 9 depicts the logic used to determine whether the array is empty; or if any further processing is required.

The processData() subroutine processes the data in the array strData() based on the value passed by its parameter Index, which accepts a value from the connection identifier lngConnection. The subroutine uses the Index value to perform a search on the array.

The data extracted by the subroutine can be a SQL query string or a special keyword. Given that the extracted data is a SQL query string, the subroutine passes the data to another subroutine for further processing. The subroutine retrieveRecord() accepts a SQL query string. This subroutine uses the SQL query string to connect to the database, search the database to obtain relevant results, and to return the results to the client.

Finally, the extracted data is removed from the array and any remaining data is shifted to the start of the array. The unprocessed data in is left for future processing. Figure 10 illustrates the processData() subroutine as it processes data in strData()array.

Retrieves Information from Database

The retrieval of records from the database is performed by the generic subroutine retrieveRecord(), which is executed by numerous event procedures in the server application. The subroutine accepts two parameters: SQLString and Index. The parameter SQLString passes a SQL query string that is used to search the database. The subroutine also creates a Recordset object by using the form-level connection string and the parameter SQLString to create a local copy of the records returned by the query in SQLString.

The subroutine first checks if the Recordset object returns any records. If no records are returned, the subroutine is terminated. Otherwise, the subroutine sends the message to the appropriate client based on the value of Index. Before the subroutine ends, a timer event is started for a brief period delay. This is a necessary step to allow the SendData method of the Winsock control to execute correctly. A peculiarity in the Winsock control necessitates a delay prior to the end of the subroutine.

Handles a Message or Request

The server application accommodates traditional pull-based interactions by accepting messages from remote client devices via the Winsock data

Figure 11. Data buffering process

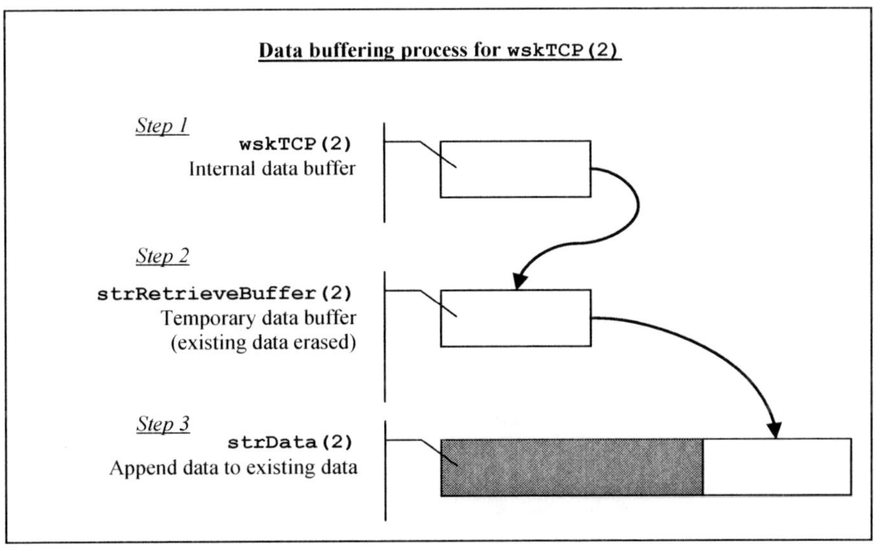

arrival event procedure. The data arrival event procedure is only triggered when the data buffer is not empty. This condition is met when data arrives from any remote client. To determine which Winsock control triggered the data arrival event procedure, an Index value, which is representative of the connection identifier lngConnection is passed as a parameter in the wskTCP_DataArrival() event procedure. For example, an Index value of two refers to the connection assigned by lngConnection; and is the Winsock control wskTCP(2).

To retrieve the buffered data, the GetData method for the corresponding Winsock control is used to retrieve the buffered data. The buffered data is a string value, and is placed into temporary storage in the strRetrieveBuffer() array. The data is then immediately appended into the strData() array. This step is necessary because the GetData method does not append data, it instead overwrites the data in strRetrieveBuffer(). If the GetData method is executed for wskTCP(2), the buffered data is then placed into the array strRetrieveBuffer(2) in position 2. The data in strRetrieveBuffer(2) is subsequently appended into strData(2). Figure 11 illustrates the steps taken to transfer buffered data into strData().

The retrieval of the buffered data into the strData() essentially queues the data for processing. The queue size is finite at approximately two billion characters (the maximum allowable string length in the Microsoft® Visual Basic 6.0) (Zak, 1999). The size of the strData() array is determined by the highest value of connection identifier lngConnection. The wskTCP_DataArrival() event procedure is triggered for any client sending a message to the server. To individualise each message for each connection, the two string arrays strRetrieveBufer() and strData() are used to store the messages received by the server. This ensures that a message sent by wskTCP(1) does not overwrite a message sent by wskTCP(2).

Client Processes

The tasks performed by client application include a situation when: (1) the client attempts to connect or disconnect from the server application; (2) the client attempts to send a message to the server application; and (3) the client application receives a message from the server. It is followed by brief description of using keywords and delimiters for data processing

Creating and Closing Connections

To connect to the server application, the client application provides a command button cmdConnect. The event procedure connects the Winsock CE control wskTCP. The Connect method uses the initialized Winsock properties in the form load event procedure (namely Protocol, RemoteHost and RemotePort) to connect to the server application.

Upon connection, the command button cmdConnect is disabled. This step is necessary

Figure 12. Message construct

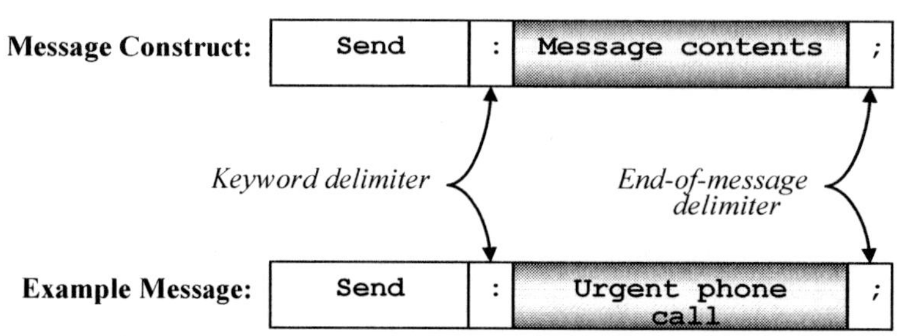

to prevent the client from performing a second connection attempt while the first attempt is in progress. If the server application is terminated, then the connection to the client is also terminated. The Winsock CE control closes the connection when the server application closed. The client application uses the cmdDisconnect command button to close the connection, and to enable and disable appropriate buttons and controls.

Sending a Message

When the client application is connected to the server application, the client application can send data by using the SendData method of the Winsock CE control wskTCP. A command button is provided to generate a pull-based interaction with the server. A SQL query string is stored in a local variable strQuery. The contents of strQuery are sent to the server application by calling the SendData method of wskTCP. The server accepts the string for processing and returns relevant results.

Alternatively, the client can communicate with the server application by sending keywords to prompt the server to perform some form of maintenance action to the database. There is another event procedure prompts the server application to enable or disable the multicasting of data from the server.

Receiving a Message

When the client application receives data from the server, the Data Arrival event procedure of the Winsock CE control wskTCP is triggered. This may be the result of a pull-based or push-based interaction between the client and the server. The data received from the server is retrieved using the GetData method of the Winsock CE control wskTCP. The data is immediately assigned to the text box txtOutput for display on the client screen.

Using Keywords and Delimiters for Data Processing

Keywords are special words used to distinguish different messages sent between the server and client application. Keywords are amended to the beginning of every message. This is true for messages sent by the server application; and for messages sent by the client application. Therefore, the message construct is as follows: (1) the keyword is placed at the beginning of the message; followed by; (2) a colon delimiter value; then (3) the message contents; and finally (4) a semi-colon as the end-of-message delimiter. The following diagram shown in Figure 12 graphically demonstrates the message construct.

The algorithm employed by the data processing subroutines in both the server application and client application are identical. Each data processing subroutine retrieves and parses the message. The first step is to determine the nature of the message. This is achieved by inspecting the value of the keyword. By inspecting the value of the keyword, each data processing subroutine is then able to act appropriately on the message contents.

PUSH AND PULL MOBILE INFORMATION SYSTEM IN A HOSPITAL ENVIRONMENT

In this section, the infrastructure and processes will be put to use in a wireless hospital information system. The system focuses on doctors as the principal clients to a server application. In terms of data dissemination, the application aims to demonstrate two uses of pull-based communications and two uses of push-based communications. The four techniques for demonstrating the dissemination of data are as follows: (1) a pull-based event to retrieve information from a database; (2) a pull-based event to update information in the database; (3) a push-based event to send a simple

Figure 13. Server form at design time

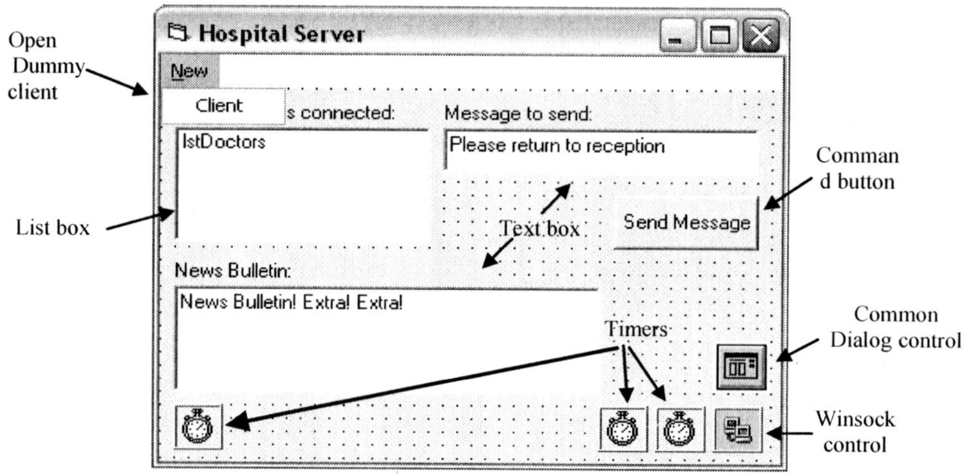

Figure 14. Server form at runtime

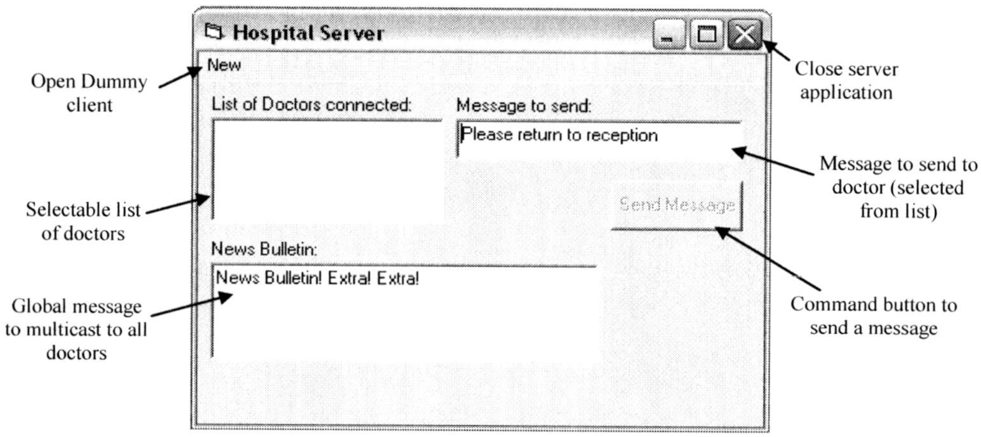

message to a client; and (4) a push-based event to multicast information to all clients, as well as to multicast information to selective clients.

Server

The server application form comprises of: a command button entitled "*Send Message*"; two text boxes; one list box; three timers; a Winsock control; a Common Dialog control; and a menu item "*New → Client*." The image shown in Figure 13 depicts the server form during design time. When the server application is executed, the image in Figure 14 is displayed.

The server application responds to four human-generated events: opening a dummy client, sending a message to a specific doctor, multicasting a global message to all doctors connected to the server application, and closing the server application. The command button "*Send Message*" is used to send a message to a specific doctor selected from the list box. The list box is populated when a doctor (or doctors) connects to server application.

The "*Send Message*" command button is only enabled when at least one doctor is connected to the server application. Finally, the text box labeled "*News Bulletin*" is used to multicast a global message to all doctors connected to the server application.

Although the server application form is visually sparse, the server application also performs several additional functions. Some functions require human intervention; while other functions do not require human intervention.

Sending a Message from Server to Client

Whenever a doctor connects to the server, a list of all doctors currently connected is displayed on the server application. This is shown in Figure 15. The list is created or updated whenever a doctor connects or disconnects from the server application. When a doctor attempts to connect the server, a connection request is sent via Winsock Connection Request. It will then create a connection for each connection request; and adds the details of the doctor to the list.

To send a message to the client, the server operator simply: selects the desired client from the list; types the desired message into the "*Message to send*" text box; and clicks "*Send Message*." This is shown in Figure 16.

When the server operator clicks the "*Send Message*" button, the event procedure cmdSendMessage_Click() is triggered. The code segment for the cmdSendMessage_Click() event procedure is

Figure 15. One client connected to the server

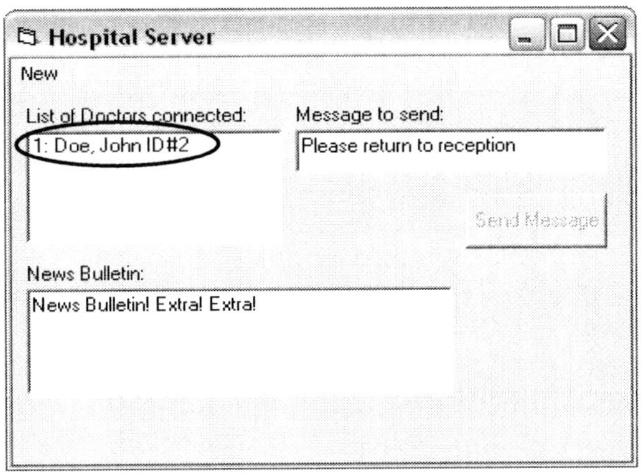

Figure 16. Sending a message from server to client

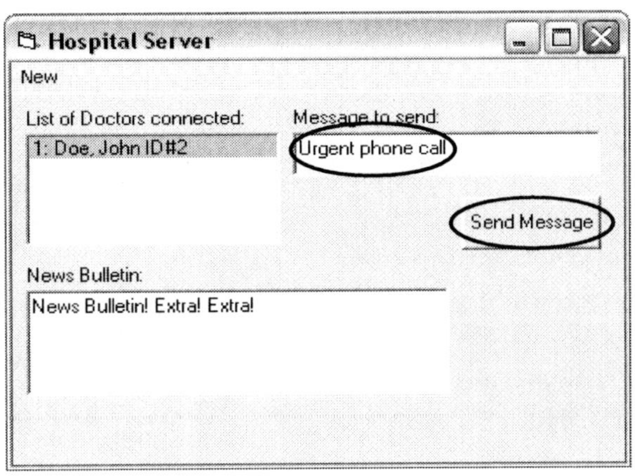

Figure 17. The "Send Message" button event procedure

```
Private Sub cmdSendMessage_Click()

  '** Notes:
  '** - This buttons sends the contents of txtMessage to selected Doctor.
  '** - The message is appended to the keyword "Send:".
  '** - A semi-colon is used to mark the end of the message.

    'Declare local string variable for storing the Connection Identifier.
    Dim strIndex As String

    'Determine the Connection Identifier from the list.
    'The Connection Identifier is the numeric value preceding the colon.
    strIndex = Mid(lstDoctors.List(lstDoctors.ListIndex), 1, _
    InStr(lstDoctors.List(lstDoctors.ListIndex), ":") - 1)

    'Send the contents of txtMessage to the selected client.
    wskTCP(strIndex).SendData "Send:" & txtMessage.Text & ";"

End Sub
```

shown in Figure 17. The selected doctor in the list box is evaluated to determine the necessary connection identifier value required by the Winsock control wskTCP. The event procedure searches for a specific value—the delimiter value ":". The number preceding the delimiter is the connection identifier value required by the Winsock control wskTCP. Using Figure 16, the event procedure extracts the value of 1 from the selected doctor.

The Winsock control wskTCP uses the connection identifier value and the SendData method to send a message to the correct doctor. The cmdSendMessage_Click() event procedure retrieves the text message in the "*Message to send*" text box and amends prefix "Send:" keyword and an end-of-message delimiter ";".The complete message as shown in Figure 16 is: Send:Urgent phone call;. Therefore, the complete command to send a message to the selected doctor is: wskTCP(1).SendData "Send:Urgent phone call;". Since the message originates from the server application, the transmission is push-based.

When the client application receives a message, the entire message is processed to determine the nature of the message. The keyword Send is utilised by the client application to identify the nature of the message. The processData() subroutine in the client application searches for a keyword

Figure 18.Result of sending message at client side

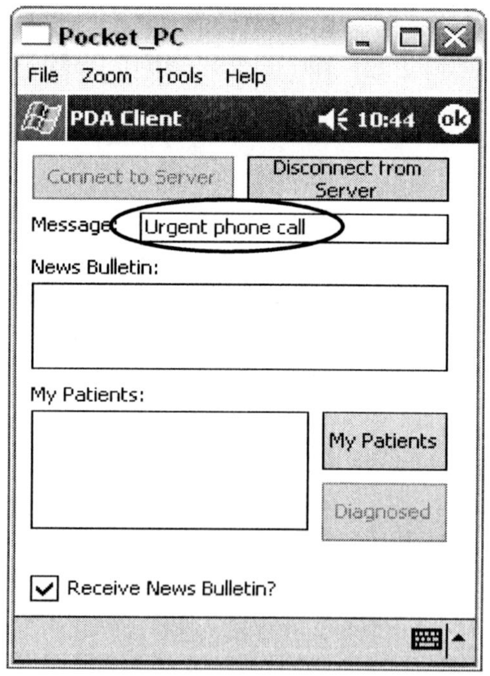

in the message and determines that Send is the keyword. The processData() subroutine extracts the message and displays it to the "*Message*" text box on the client application. The image shown in Figure 18 demonstrates the result of the server application sending a message to the client application.

Multicasting Information from Server to Client(s)

The server application automatically sends a news bulletin to each doctor connected to the server. The server application uses a timer to periodically send the news bulletin to each doctor every 25 seconds. Whenever a client connects to the server application, the IP address of the client is stored in a form-level string array on the server application. The server application determines which clients are the recipients of the news bulletin by comparing the values stored in strRemoteHostIP() to the r_remoteip field in the *Remote* table. Furthermore, the server application also determines if the doctor wishes to receive a copy of the news bulletin.

This is determined by the r_multicast field in the *Remote* table. If the checkbox field in r_multicast is checked, then the doctor requires a copy of the news bulletin. The image shown in Figure 19 depicts the table and fields used by the server application.

When the timer interval expires, the timer event procedure tmrSendBulletin_Timer() is triggered. Figure 20 depicts the event procedure that is executed every 25 seconds. The event procedure performs a check to determine which doctors require a copy of the news bulletin.

If a match is determined, the event procedure retrieves the text message in the "*News Bulletin*" text box. The text message is then amended with the prefix "NewsBulletin:" keyword and an end-of-message delimiter ";". Figure 21 shows an image when the server sends a news bulletin to doctors, complete message is: NewsBulletin:News Bulletin! Extra! Extra!;. The news bulletin is then sent to each client that requires a copy of the news bulletin.

To modify the contents of the news bulletin, the server operator simply changes the text in the "*News Bulletin*" text box. When the 25 second

Figure 19. Remote table and the fields used for multicasting the news bulletin

Remote : Table

	r_index	r_remoteip	r_multicast	r_description	d_index
▶	1	192.168.0.2	☑	HP iPaq	2
	2	10.0.0.50	☑	PC	1
	3	10.0.0.100	☑	Laptop	3
*	(AutoNumber)				0

Record: 1 of 3

Figure 20. The "Send Bulletin" timer event procedure

```
Private Sub tmrSendBulletin_Timer()
On Error Resume Next

  '** Notes:
  '** - This timer event auto-sends the news bulletin to all clients
  '**   that have 'r_multicast' field set to True in Remote table.
  '** - The news bulletin is the contents of txtNewsBulletin.
  '** - The message is appended to the keyword "NewsBulletin:".
  '** - A semi-colon is used to mark the end of the message.
  '** - The 'r_multicast' field from 'Remote' table is matched to a
  '**   string array strRemoteHostIP()
  '** - The string array strRemoteHostIP() stores the IP address of
  '**   currently-connected clients.
  '** - This is an automatic 'Push' event that triggers depending
  '**   on the time interval set.
```

Figure 20. continued

```
'** - Interval currently set to 25 seconds.

 'Declare local rst object for ADO Recordset and local variables.
 Dim rst As ADODB.Recordset
 Dim strQuery As String
 Dim i As Integer

 i = 0

 'Set rst object variable as ADO.Recordset object
 Set rst = New ADODB.Recordset

 'Retrieve records from the remote table.
 strQuery = "SELECT * FROM remote;"

 'Open the Recordset based on strQuery using global Connection
 'String cnn.
 rst.Open strQuery, cnn, adOpenStatic, adLockReadOnly

 'Check to see if the RecordCount is 0.
 If rst.RecordCount = 0 Then
     'If it is 0, exit this subroutine.
     Exit Sub

 Else

     'Otherwise, move to the first record.
     rst.MoveFirst

     'Move through the Recordset rst from first record to last record.
     Do While Not rst.EOF

         'Send to all clients connected and when lngCounter > 0.
         For i = 1 To lngConnection And lngCounter > 0

             'On Error Resume Next used to avoid situations where
             'i for Connection Identifier is a non-existent valuc.
             'This may occur when a client manually disconnects.

             'Call retrieveRecord if the value of 'r_multicast'
             'matches the strRemoteHostIP for the value i.
             If rst!r_multicast = True And _
             rst!r_remoteip = strRemoteHostIP(i) Then

                 'Send the contents of txtNewsBulletin to the
                 'clients that require the News Bulletin.
                 wskTCP(i).SendData "NewsBulletin:" _
                 & txtNewsBulletin.Text & ";"

             End If
```

interval expires, the new contents of the "*News Bulletin*" text box are sent to each doctor who requires a copy of the news bulletin. When the client application receives a message, the entire message is processed to determine the nature of the message. The keyword NewsBulletin is utilised by the client application to identify the nature of the message. The processData() subroutine in the client application searches for a keyword in the message and determines that NewsBulletin is the keyword. The processData() subroutine extracts the message and displays it to the "*News Bulletin*" box on the client application. The image shown in Figure 22 demonstrates the result of the server application sending a message to the client application.

Figure 21. Sending a news bulletin to doctors connected to the server application

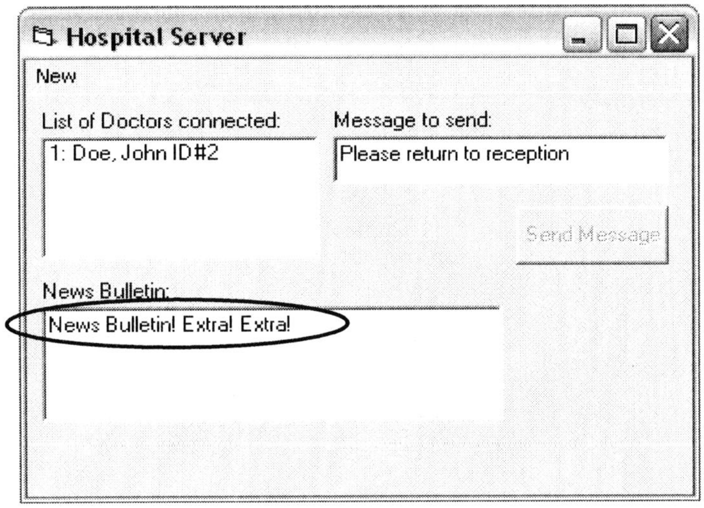

Figure 22. Result of sending the news bulletin

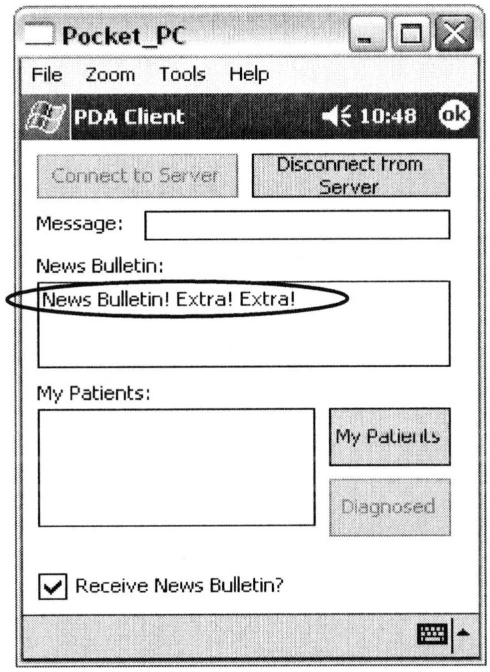

The client can enable or disable the automatic sending of the news bulletin by selecting or deselecting the check box marked "*Receive News Bulletin?*" Figure 23 illustrates this feature. Once the record is located, the value is set to True or False for BulletinYes and BulletinNo respectively. The image shown in Figure 24 highlights the fields that is updated as a result of select or deselect the bulletin check box

Clicking the "*Receive News Bulletin*" check box triggers the chkSelectiveMulticast_Click() event procedure to send a message to the server application. The message contains a keyword. The keyword is either BulletinYes or BulletinNo. The

Figure 23. Check box for receiving news bulletin

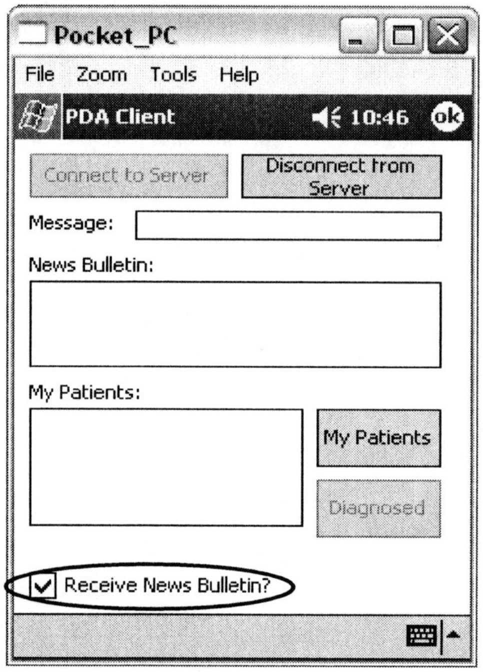

Figure 24. Remote table and the field affected by bulletin check box

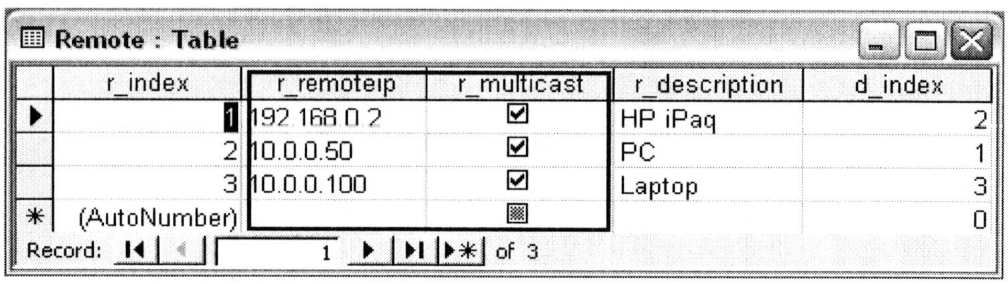

Figure 25. The "Receive News Bulletin" check box event procedure

```
Private Sub chkSelectiveMulticast_Click()
   '** Notes:
   '** - Once connected to the server application, the user can elect
   '**   to enable or disable selective multicasting.
   '** - Sending the keyword 'BulletinYes' prompts the server
   '**   application to enable selective multicasting to this client.
   '** - Sending the keyword 'BulletinNo' turns off selective multicasting.

    'Check if the checkbox is checked.
    If Me.chkSelectiveMulticast.Value = 1 Then

        'If it is, send 'BulletinYes'
        wskTCP.SendData "BulletinYes:;"

    Else
        'Otherwise, send 'BulletinNo;'
        wskTCP.SendData "BulletinNo:;"
```

Figure 26. The sendBulletin() subroutine

```
Private Sub sendBulletin(Index As Integer, Multicast As String)
    '** Notes:
    '** - Modify the Remote table in the database to determine which
    '**   IP addresses (and hence, doctors) require the auto-sending
    '**   of the news bulletin.

    'Declare local rst object for ADO Recordset
    'and local string variable for SQL query.
    Dim rst As ADODB.Recordset
    Dim strQuery As String

    'Set rst object variable as ADO.Recordset object.
    Set rst = New ADODB.Recordset

    'Retrieve records from the remote table.
    strQuery = "SELECT * FROM remote;"

    'Open Recordset based on strQuery using global Connection String cnn.
    rst.Open strQuery, cnn, adOpenDynamic, adLockOptimistic

    'Check to see if the RecordCount is 0.
    If rst.RecordCount = 0 Then
        'If it is 0, exit this subroutine.
        Exit Sub
    Else
        'Otherwise, explicitly move to the first record.
        rst.MoveFirst

        'Find the record for r_remoteip equalled to
        'strRemoteHostIP(Index), e.g. r_remoteip = '192.168.0.2'.
        'The r_remoteip field in Remote table doesn't allow
        'duplicate values.
        rst.Find "r_remoteip = '" & strRemoteHostIP(Index) & "'"

        'If a match is found, change the value of r_multicast field
        'to True/False depending on the value of the Multicast parameter.
        If rst!r_remoteip = strRemoteHostIP(Index) Then

            'Multicast parameter is either 'BulletinYes' or 'BulletinNo'
            Select Case Multicast
                'BulletinYes: set r_multicast to True
                Case "BulletinYes"
                    rst.Fields("r_multicast") = True
                    rst.Update
                'BulletinNo: set r_multicast to False
                Case "BulletinNo"
                    rst.Fields("r_multicast") = False
                    rst.Update
            End Select
        End If
    End If

    'Close the Recordset object rst and set it to Nothing.
    rst.Close
    Set rst = Nothing
End Sub
```

keyword is amended with suffix ":;". The colon delimiter is used by the processData() subroutine on the server application to determine the nature of the message. The semi-colon delimiter is used to mark the end of the message. Figure 25 depicts the code segment of the client application used to send the keyword to enable or disable the sending of the news bulletin.

The server application receives the message from the client application. The processData() subroutine transfers the keyword to the sendBulletin() subroutine for additional processing. The code segment for sendBulletin() is shown in Figure 26 The sendBulletin() subroutine uses the connection identifier value associated with the (connected) client application and strRemoteHostIP() to locate the appropriate record in the *Remote* table. Once the record is located, the value of r_multicast is set to True or False for BulletinYes and BulletinNo respectively.

Since this function involves more than one client, dummy clients are used to represent multi users. The code segment in Figure 27 depicts the creation of a dummy client, which is the server-side version of the client application.

Client

Client application form comprises of: four command buttons; two text boxes; one list box; one check box; one timer; and a Winsock CE control. The image shown in Figure 28 depicts the client form at design time. When the client application is executed on the Personal Digital Assistant, the image in Figure 29 is displayed to the client. The client application responds to six human-generated events. The six events are as follows: clicking any of four command buttons, clicking the check box; and closing the client application.

When the doctor clicks the command button "*Connect to Server*," the application attempts to connect to the server. Once connected, the doctor can choose to retrieve relevant information about patients from the database (via the server application). This is achieved by clicking the "*My Patients*." Once a list of patients is returned to the list box labeled "*My Patients*," the doctor can choose to diagnose a patient. The doctor can diagnose a patient by: selecting the desired patient; and then clicking the "*Diagnosed*" button.

The client can also enable or disable the multicasting of a global news bulletin (sent by the server application). The doctor simply enables or disables the multicasting feature by selecting or deselecting the check box labeled "*Receive News Bulletin?*" The doctor can choose to disconnect from the server application by clicking the "*Disconnect from Server*" command button. Finally, clicking the "*OK*" button situated to the

Figure 27. Create a dummy client event procedure

```
Private Sub Client_Click(Index As Integer)
    '** Notes:
    '** - Create 'Dummy' clients by creating newClient objects.
    '** - Connect to this application via Winsock to mimic behaviour of PDA.

    'Explicitly create newClient objects based on Form frmClient.
    Dim newClient As Form
    Set newClient = New frmClient

    'Use lngCounter form-level variable to display the Form based on
    'connection order.
    newClient.Caption = "Client " & Str(lngCounter + 1)

    'Load the newClient object and display it.
    Load newClient
    newClient.Show
```

Figure 28. Client form at design time

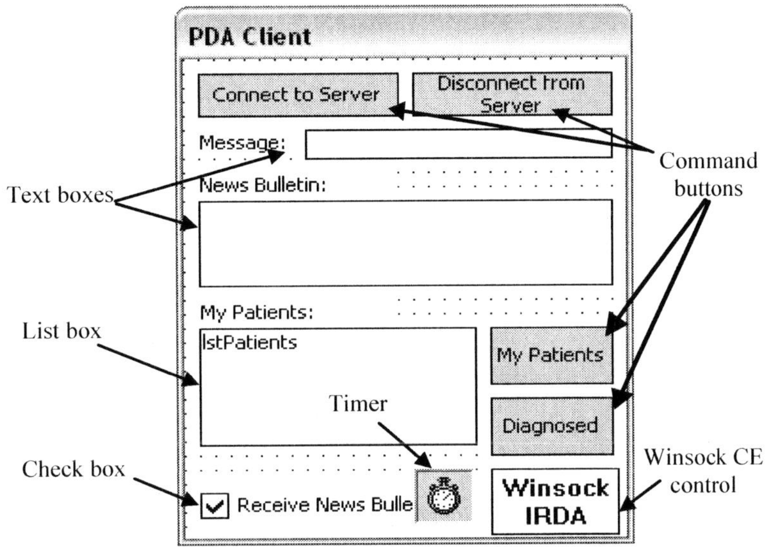

Figure 29. Client form at runtime

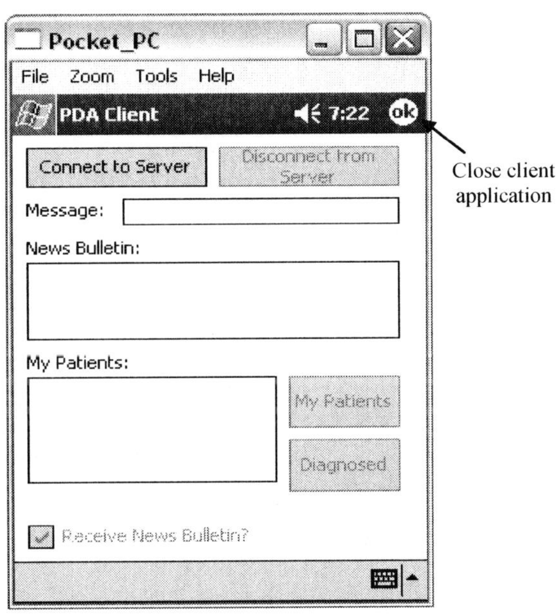

Figure 30. Doctors table and the identity field

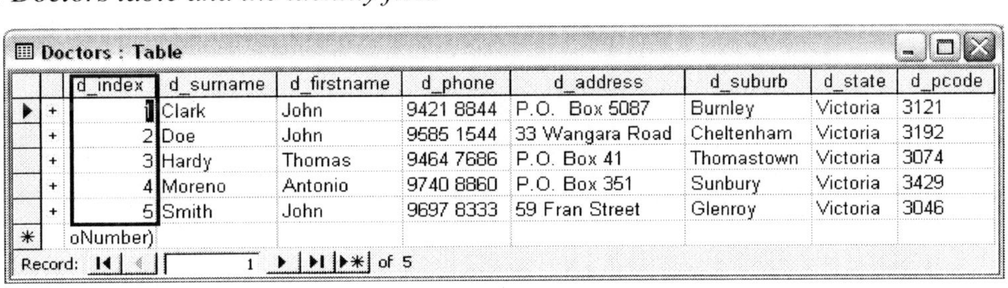
Doctors : Table

d_index	d_surname	d_firstname	d_phone	d_address	d_suburb	d_state	d_pcode
1	Clark	John	9421 8844	P.O. Box 5087	Burnley	Victoria	3121
2	Doe	John	9585 1544	33 Wangara Road	Cheltenham	Victoria	3192
3	Hardy	Thomas	9464 7686	P.O. Box 41	Thomastown	Victoria	3074
4	Moreno	Antonio	9740 8860	P.O. Box 351	Sunbury	Victoria	3429
5	Smith	John	9697 8333	59 Fran Street	Glenroy	Victoria	3046
oNumber)							

Record: 1 of 5

top right of the application window causes the client application to close.

The objective of client application is to display the results client-specific messages such as a global news bulletin, retrieving patient records, and diagnosing patients. The client-specific messages and the global news bulletin result from push-based communications. Retrieving patient records and diagnosing patients result from pull-based communications with the server application. Additionally, the client application also performs several additional functions. Some functions require human intervention; while other functions do not require human intervention.

Client Retrieving Data from the Database

When a doctor connects to the server application, the doctor may retrieve a list of patients from the database. The list of patients is displayed in the list box entitled "*My Patients*." When a doctor creates a connection with the server application, a specific identity value is automatically sent by the server application to the client application. The specific identity value sent by the server application is the primary key value assigned to the doctor in the *Doctors* table.

The field in the *Doctors* table representing the primary key is the d_index field. The image shown in Figure 30 highlights the primary key field of the *Doctors* table. Using the specific identity value stored in the d_index field enables a doctor to return information from the database that is relevant (or related) to the doctor. However, the *Doctors* table does not supply enough information to determine which identity value needs to be implicitly sent to the client application. Therefore, the server application uses the *Doctors* table in conjunction with the *Remote* table to determine the necessary identity value required by the client program. Figure 31 highlights the foreign key of the *Remote* table that relates to the *Doctors* table.

One of the event procedures uses the relationship between the *Doctors* and *Remote* table, in conjunction with the IP addresses stored in the r_remoteip field of the *Remote* table, to determine the correct identity value to send to the client device. If a doctor wishes to retrieve a list of patients, the doctor simply clicks the "*My Patients*" button on the client application. The image shown in Figure 32 highlights the "My Patients" button on the client program.

The cmdMyPatients_Click() event procedure sends the identity value (supplied as a result of the initial connection request) to the server application. The code segment shown Figure 33 depicts the cmdMyPatients_Click() subroutine that is sent to the server.

The identity value is stored in form-level variable entitled strMyID. This value is available for use after the client application successfully connects to the server application. The cmdMyPatients_Click() event procedure utilizes the value stored in strMyID by amending the prefix "MyPatients:" keyword and an end-of-message

Figure 31. Remote table showing the identity field for doctors

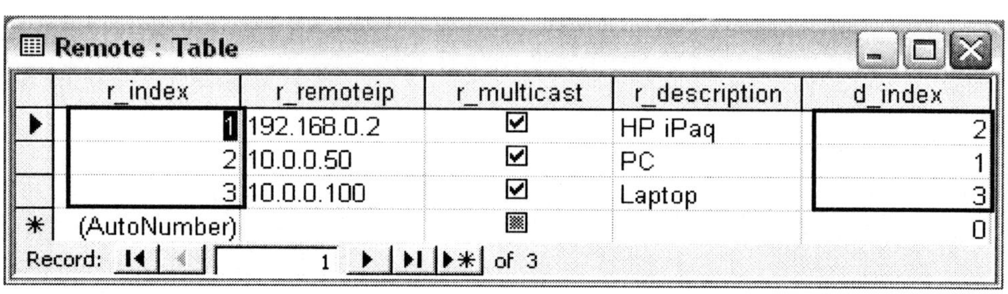

Figure 32. The "My Patients" button

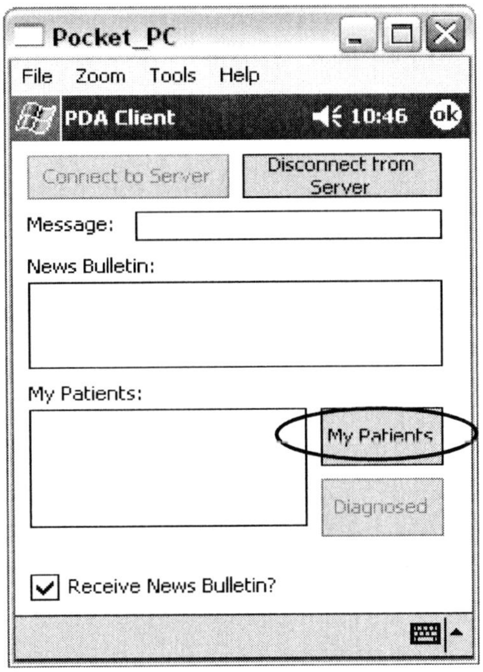

Figure 33. The "My Patients" button event procedure

```
Private Sub cmdMyPatients_Click()
    '** Notes:
    '** - When the doctor connects to the server, the doctor's ID
    '**   d_index is automatically sent to the client device.
    '** - When the doctor wishes to retrieve the list of patients under
    '**   his/her care, the doctor clicks on the 'My Patients' button.
    '** - The button sends the keyword 'MyPatients' followed by the
    '**   doctor's ID to the server application.
    '** - The message is sent using the keyword followed by a colon
    '**   delimiter (to mark the end of the keyword), the ID of the doctor,
    '**    and a semi-colon delimiter to mark the end of the message.

    'Clear the list of patients if it is not already blank.
    lstPatients.Clear

    'Send request for service using keyword 'MyPatients' and strMyID.
    wskTCP.SendData "MyPatients:" & strMyID & ";"
End Sub
```

delimiter ";" to create a complete message. Given that the value of strMyID is 2, then the complete message is: MyPatients:2;. The complete message is subsequently sent to the server application for processing. When the server application receives the complete message, a local subroutine processData() parses the complete message. The keyword MyPatients is utilised by the processData() subroutine to determine the nature of the message. The processData() subroutine determines the keyword by searching for the keyword delimiter ":". After determining the nature of the message from the keyword, the server application extracts

Figure 34. The myPatients() subroutine

```
Private Sub myPatients(myID As String, Index As Integer)

    '** Notes:
    '** - This subroutine is called when the client (doctor) requests
    '**   a list patients under his/her care.
    '** - It is called from two places:
    '**   1. processData() - The data processor; when requested by the
    '**      client.
    '**   2. patientDiagnosed - When a patient is diagnosed; the client
    '**      list is refreshed.
    '** - This subroutine expects the parameters myID and Index.
    '** - myID represents the ID of the doctor d_index.
    '** - Index represents the connection identifier of the doctor's
    '**   device.

    'Declare local string variable.
    Dim strQuery As String

    'Query string to be used to perform a search.
    'The Query string is built using the string value list lstDoctors.
    strQuery = "SELECT p_index, p_firstname, p_surname FROM patients " _
    & "WHERE p_diagnosed = False AND d_index = " & myID & ";"

    'Pass strQuery to retrieveRecord subroutine and send
    Call retrieveRecord(strQuery, Index)

End Sub
```

the identity value from the message. The identity value is then transferred to a myPatients() subroutine on the server application. The code segment for the myPatients() subroutine is shown in Figure 34.

The myPatients() subroutine creates a query string which searches the *Patients* table for undiagnosed patients. Furthermore, the query string returns patient records relevant to the doctor. The query string is then utilized by another local subroutine on the server application entitled retrieveRecord(). The code segment for the retrieveRecord() subroutine is shown in Figure 35.

The query string utilised by retrieveRecord() is to search the *Patients* table and to return any patient records related to the identity value supplied by the doctor. The subroutine retrieves: the surname from p_surname; the first name from p_firstname; and patient identity value from p_index.

Figure 35. The retrieveRecord() subroutine

```
Private Sub retrieveRecord(ByVal SQLString As String, ByVal Index As Integer)
    '** Notes:
    '** - Generic procedure to return records from the database based
    '**   on SQLString parameter for the wskTCP control in question
    '**   (based on the Index).
    '** - This procedure is used extensively for all 'Pull' and 'Push'
    '**   events.
    'Declare local rst object for ADO Recordset.
    Dim rst As ADODB.Recordset

    'Set rst object variable as ADO.Recordset object
    Set rst = New ADODB.Recordset

    'Open the Recordset based on SQLString using global Connection
    'String cnn.
    rst.Open SQLString, cnn, adOpenStatic, adLockReadOnly
```

Figure 35. continued

```
    'Check to see if the RecordCount is 0.
    If Not rst.RecordCount = 0 Then

        'Otherwise, move to the first record in the Recordset
        rst.MoveFirst

        'SQLString returns only 1 record, but this is necessary
        'for correctness.
        Do While Not rst.EOF
            'Send requested data from nominated field (m_surname) to
            'client wskTCP of paramater Index.
            'This is somewhat less than ideal.
            'However, since the SQLString always contains a 'WHERE'
            'clause for the Identity (Primary) Key field of the table,
            'only 1 result is ever returned.

            Dim strSend As String

            strSend = "Results:" & rst!p_surname & ", " &
                       rst!p_firstname _& ", ID#" & rst!p_index & ";"
                       wskTCP(Index).SendData strSend

            'Use a delay timer tmrWait to send record(s) to all clients.
            'For some peculiar reason only the last connected client
            'receives any data. This deliberate pause ensures that all
            'clients receives data.
            'Even though this procedure is often called in a loop, the
            'error described still occurs.
            'It is assumed that the loop runs too fast...
            'Turn on the timer object tmrWait.
            tmrWait.Enabled = True

            'Force a loop while tmrWait is true (to delay the
            'processing). This avoids the error described above.
            Do While tmrWait.Enabled = True

            'While forcing a delay (pause), let other events run their
            'course.
                DoEvents
            Loop
            'Move to the next record in rst.

            rst.MoveNext
        Loop
    End If
    'Close the Recordset object rst and set it to Nothing.
    rst.Close
    Set rst = Nothing
End Sub
```

The image shown in Figure 37 highlights the targeted fields in the table. Given that p_index as 1 is the first record retrieved, then the complete message is: Results:Hsieh, Raymond, ID#1.The complete message is sent by the server application to the client application. The client application parses the complete message and processes the complete message for display. The client application updates the list box entitled "*My Patients*" by displaying the surname, first name and identity value of each patient. The following image shown in Figure 36 illustrates the client application displaying patient details.

Client Updating the Database

As an extension to retrieving patient information from the database, the client application also enables the doctor to diagnose a patient. Once a list of patients is retrieved from the server application, the doctor may click the "*Diagnosed*" button to remove a selected patient from the list of patients.

Figure 36. Client details returned for display

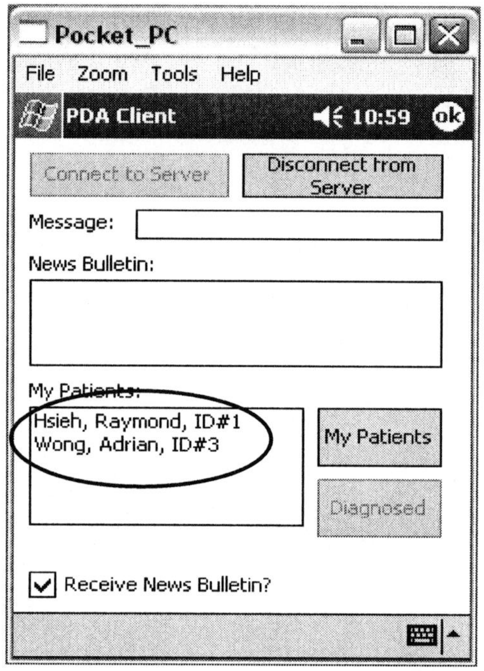

Figure 37. Patients table showing the identity value, surname and first name of each patient

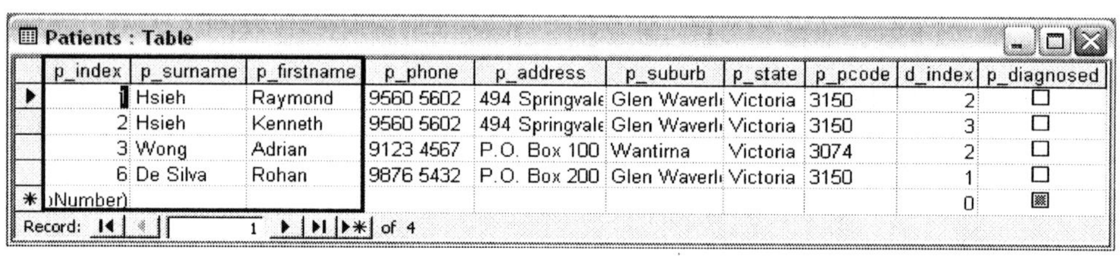

Patients : Table

p_index	p_surname	p_firstname	p_phone	p_address	p_suburb	p_state	p_pcode	d_index	p_diagnosed
1	Hsieh	Raymond	9560 5602	494 Springvale	Glen Waverl	Victoria	3150	2	☐
2	Hsieh	Kenneth	9560 5602	494 Springvale	Glen Waverl	Victoria	3150	3	☐
3	Wong	Adrian	9123 4567	P.O. Box 100	Wantirna	Victoria	3074	2	☐
6	De Silva	Rohan	9876 5432	P.O. Box 200	Glen Waverl	Victoria	3150	1	☐
(Number)								0	▣

Record: 1 of 4

The image shown in Figure 38 illustrates a selected patient and the relevant "*Diagnosed*" button.

The cmdDiagnosed_Click() event procedure creates a message by amending the prefix "Diagnosed:" keyword to the patient identity value. The patient identity value is succeeded by a special separator keyword "&" and the doctor identity value. The end-of-message delimiter ";" is then appended to the end of the message. The code segment shown Figure 39 depicts how cmdDiagnosed_Click() event procedure creates the complete message. Given that the extracted patient identity value is 1 and the doctor identity value is 2, then the complete message is: Diagnosed:1&2;.

The complete message created by the cmdDiagnosed_Click() event procedure is sent by the client application to the server application. The server application receives the message and the message is parsed by the processData() subroutine. The keyword Diagnosed is utilised by the processData() subroutine to determine

Figure 38. Selected patient and "Diagnosed" button

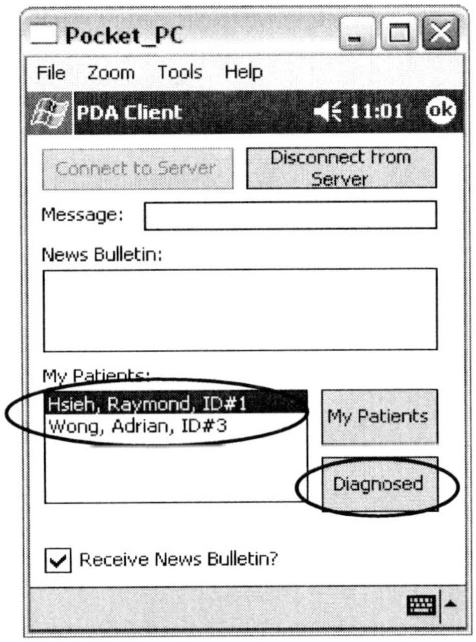

Figure 39. The "Diagnosed" button event procedure

```
Private Sub cmdDiagnosed_Click()

    '** Notes:
    '** - When the doctor completes a diagnosis on a patient, the
    '**   doctor selects the patient from the list and clicks the
    '**   Diagnosed button.
    '** - The button sends the keyword 'Diagnosed' followed by the
    '**   patients's ID to the server application.
    '** - The message is sent using the keyword followed by a colon
    '**   delimiter (to mark the end of the keyword), the ID of the
    '**   patient, and a semi-colon delimiter to mark the end of the
    '**   message.

    'Declare local variable to store the ID of the patient.
    Dim strPatientID As String

    'Strip out the ID of the patient from lstPatients as a string value.
    strPatientID = Right(lstPatients.List(lstPatients.ListIndex), _
    Len(lstPatients.List(lstPatients.ListIndex)) - _
    InStr(lstPatients.List(lstPatients.ListIndex), "#"))

    'Send request for service using keyword 'Diagnosed' and strPatientID.
    wskTCP.SendData "Diagnosed:" & strPatientID & "&" & strMyID & ";"

    'Clear the patients list (this will be filled after the list is
    'refreshed).
    lstPatients.Clear
```

Figure 40. The patientsDiagnosed() subroutine

```
Private Sub patientDiagnosed(PatientID As String, myID as String, Index As
Integer)
    '** Notes:
    '** - This subroutine is called when the client (doctor) has
    '**   completed diagnosing a patient.
    '** - It is called from processData() when requested by the
    '**   client.
    '** - This subroutine expects the parameters PatientID and Index.
    '** - PatientID represents the ID of the patient p_index.
    '** - myID represents the ID of the doctor d_index.
    '** - Index represents the connection identifier of the doctor's
    '**   device.
    '** - When the patient table is update, a call to myPatients()
    '**   subroutine is made to update the list of patients on the
    '**   client device.

    'Declare local rst object for ADO Recordset and local variables.
    Dim rst As ADODB.Recordset
    Dim strQuery As String

    'Set rst object variable as ADO.Recordset object
    Set rst = New ADODB.Recordset

    'Source string for Recordset rst.
    strQuery = "SELECT p_diagnosed FROM patients WHERE p_index = " _
    & PatientID & ";"

    'Open the Recordset based on strQuery using global Connection
    'String cnn.
    rst.Open strQuery, cnn, adOpenStatic, adLockOptimistic

    'Check if the query string returns any records.
    If rst.RecordCount = 0 Then

        'If it does not, exit this subroutine.
        Exit Sub

    Else

        'The query should return only 1 record.
        'Move to the first record.
        rst.MoveFirst

        'Update the record for field p_diagnosed
        rst.Fields("p_diagnosed") = True
        rst.Update

    End If

    'Close the Recordset object rst and set it to Nothing.
    rst.Close
    Set rst = Nothing

    'Update patient list on client device.
```

the nature of the message. The processData() subroutine determines the keyword by searching for the keyword delimiter ":". After determining the nature of the message from the keyword, the server application extracts the patient and doctor identity values from the message. The identity values are then transferred to a patientsDiagnosed() subroutine on the server application. The code segment for the patientsDiagnosed() subroutine is shown in Figure 40.

Figure 41. Patient removed from client display

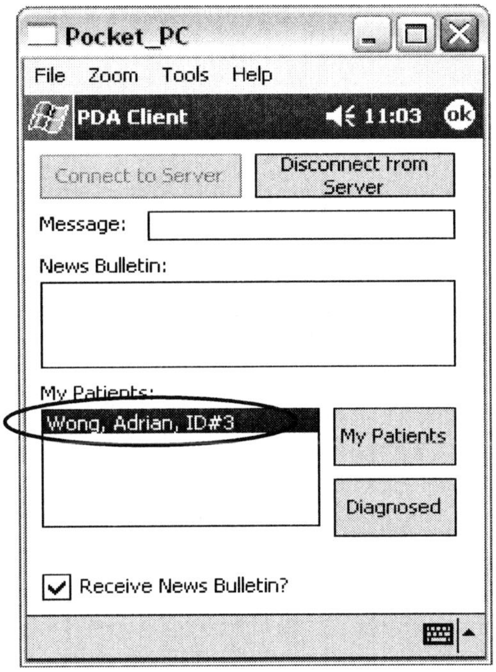

Figure 42. Patients table and the "Diagnosed" field for each patient

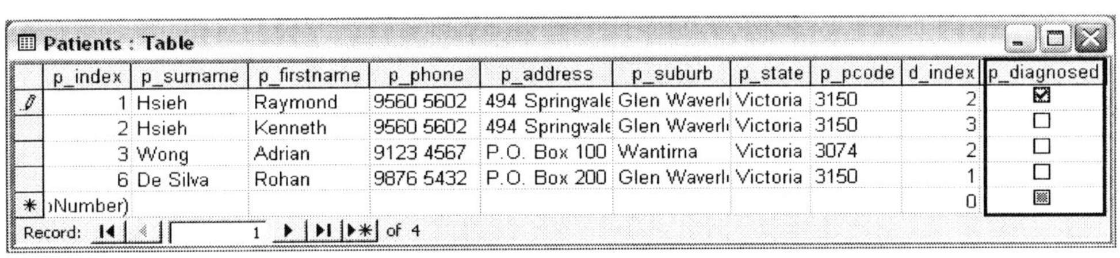

Patients : Table

	p_index	p_surname	p_firstname	p_phone	p_address	p_suburb	p_state	p_pcode	d_index	p_diagnosed
	1	Hsieh	Raymond	9560 5602	494 Springvale	Glen Waverl	Victoria	3150	2	☑
	2	Hsieh	Kenneth	9560 5602	494 Springvale	Glen Waverl	Victoria	3150	3	☐
	3	Wong	Adrian	9123 4567	P.O. Box 100	Wantirna	Victoria	3074	2	☐
	6	De Silva	Rohan	9876 5432	P.O. Box 200	Glen Waverl	Victoria	3150	1	☐
*	Number)								0	

Record: 1 of 4

The patientDiagnosed() subroutine uses the patient identity value to update the relevant record in the *Patients* table. The patientDiagnosed() subroutine targets a specific field in the *Patients* table – namely the p_diagnosed field. The patientDiagnosed() subroutine updates the value of the p_diagnosed field from unchecked to checked. The image shown in Figure 42 highlights the p_diagnosed field and the status of the patient.

Once a patient is diagnosed, the list of patients on the client application is updated to reflect the changes made to the *Patients* table. The patientDiagnosed() subroutine ends by calling the myPatients() subroutine and passing the doctor identity value into the parameter myID. The myPatients() subroutine updates the client display accordingly. The image shown in Figure 41 illustrates the updated client display.

CONCLUSION AND FUTURE WORK

A wireless network environment enables mobility. Personal Digital Assistants enable portability. Together, they provide a potentially useful tool for highly mobile users. However, traditional methods to data dissemination often involve the client requesting data or information from a server.

This is practical if the client requires something specific from the server. However, this pull-based method does not cater to all scenarios.

In this paper, we present pull-based and push-based wireless information system. In order to demonstrate the effective uses of the application, we use hospital information system information system scenario. The hospital information system relates to doctors as the principal clients to a server application. The system demonstrates the use of the pull-based mechanism to retrieve specific information from the database. Furthermore, the information retrieved from the database can be acted upon by the client. In doing so, the database is updated by the client. This is demonstrated via the retrieval and updating of patient records by doctors.

The server application is also able to push information to the client application. The server application utilizes push-based mechanisms to send messages to specific doctor in the hospital. Furthermore, the server application is able to multicast a global message to all doctors connected to the server application. The global message can be disabled by each doctor; demonstrating a pull-based interaction with the server application.

For future work, we plan to incorporate a sensor positioning device e.g. global positioning system (GPS) used to detect the location of mobile users. This way enables us to push information based on the location of the user. With regard to hospital context, location based services will support doctors in diagnosing patients by disseminate relevant data whenever the doctor is about to diagnose a patient. This will enhance the flexibility and efficiency of the activity.

REFERENCES

Acharya, S., Alonso, R., Franklin, M., & Zdonik, S. (1995). Broadcast disks: Data management for asymmetric communication environments. In *Proceedings of the ACM Sigmod* (pp. 199-210).

Aksoy, D., Altinel, M., Bose, R., Cetintemel, U., Franklin, M., Wang, J., & Zdonik, S. (1999). Research in data broadcast and dissemination. In *Proceedings of the AMCP* (LNCS 1554, pp. 194-207).

Barbara, D. (1999). Mobile computing and databases: A survey. *IEEE TKDE, 11*(1), 108-117.

Blake, R. (2002). *Electronic communication systems* (2nd ed.). New York: Thomson Learning.

Franklin, M., & Zdonik, S. (1997). A framework for scalable dissemination-based systems. In *Proceedings of the 12th ACM OOPSLA, 32* (pp. 94-105).

Housel, B. C., Samaras, G., & Lindquist, D.B. (1998). WebExpress: A client/intercept based system for optmising Web browsing in a wireless environment. *ACM/Baltzer MONET, 3*(4), 419- 431.

Imielinski, T., & Viswanathan, S. (1994). Adaptive wireless information systems. In *Proceedings of the SIGDBS* (pp. 19-41).

Imielinski, T., Viswanathan, S., & Badrinath, B. R. (1994). Energy efficient indexing on air. In *Proceedings of the ACM Sigmod* (pp. 25-36).

Kistler, J.J., & Satyanarayanan, M. (1992). Disconnected operation in the code file system. *ACM Trans. on Computer Systems, 10*(1), 213-225.

Leong, H. V., & Si, A. (1997). Database caching over the air-storage. *The Computer Journal, 40*(7), 401-415.

Satyanarayanan, M., Kistler, J.J., Kumar, P., Okasaki, M.E., Siegel, E.H., & Steere, D.C. (1990). Coda: A highly available file system for a distributed workstation environment. *IEEE Trans. on Computers, 39(*4), 447-459.

Si, A., & Leong, H. V. (1999). Query optimization for broadcast database. *DKE, 29*(3), 351-380.

Terry, D., Demers, A. J., Peterson, K., Spreitzer, M.J., Theimer, M.M., & Welch, B. (1994). Session guarantees for weakly consistent replicated data. In *Proceedings PDIS* (pp. 140-149).

Terry, D., Theimer, M.M., Peterson, K., Demers, A. J., Spreitzer, M.J., & Hauser, C.H. (1995). Managing update conflicts in Bayou: A weakly connected replicated storage system. In *Proceedings of the ACM Symposium on OS* (pp. 172-183).

Zak, D. (1999). *Programming with Microsoft Visual Basic 6.0.* Thomson Publishing.

Zaslavsky, A., & Tari, S. (1998). Mobile computing: Overview and current status. *Australian Computer Journal, 30*(2), 42-52.

This work was previously published in Business Data Communications and Networking: A Research Perspective, edited by J. Gutiérrez, pp.151-186, copyright 2007 by IGI Publishing (an imprint of IGI Global).

Compilation of References

Aarts, J., Ash, J., & Berg, M. (2007). Extending the understanding of computerized physician order entry: Implications for professional collaboration, workflow, and quality of care. *International Journal of Medical Informatics, 76*(Suppl 1), 4–13. doi:10.1016/j.ijmedinf.2006.05.009

Aarts, J., Doorewaard, H., & Berg, M. (2004). Understanding implementation: The case of a computerized physician order entry system in a large Dutch university medical center. *Journal of the American Medical Informatics Association, 11*(3), 207–216. doi:10.1197/jamia.M1372

Acharya, S., Alonso, R., Franklin, M., & Zdonik, S. (1995). Broadcast disks: Data management for asymmetric communication environments. In *Proceedings of the ACM Sigmod* (pp. 199-210).

Adamides, E. D., & Karacapilidis, N. (2006). A knowledge centred framework for collaborative business process modeling. *Business Process Management Journal, 12*(5), 557–575.doi:doi:10.1108/14637150610690993

Adams, C., & Fitch, T. (2006). Social Inclusion and the Shifting Role of Technology: Is Age the New Gender in Mobile Access? In *Social Inclusion: Societal and Organizational Implications for Information Systems* (pp. 203-215).

Adams, J. S. (1965). Inequity in social exchange. In L. Berkowitz (Ed.), *Advances in experimental social psychology*. New York: Academic Press.

Adams, S., de Bont, A., & Berg, M. (2006). Looking for answers, constructing reliability: An exploration into how Dutch patients check web-based medical information. *International Journal of Medical Informatics, 75*(1), 66–72. doi:10.1016/j.ijmedinf.2005.07.036

Adler, A. (2000). *A Cost-Effective Portable Telemedicine Kit for Use in Developing Countries*", Unpublished masters thesis, Massachusetts Institute of Technology, Cambridge.

Agency for Healthcare Research and Quality. (2001). Reducing and preventing adverse drug events to decrease hospital costs. *Research in Action, 1*. Rockville, MD: AHRQ Publication Number 01-0020.

Aggouram, H., & Ingham, J. (2003). In K. Kangas, (Ed.) National culture and the meaning of information systems success: a framework for research and its implications for IS standardization in multinational organizations, *Business Strategies for Information Technology Man-*

agement. Hershey, PA: IGI Global.

Aichholzer, G. (2003). Scenarios of e-government in 2010 and implications for strategy design. *Electronic Journal of E-government.* Retrieved from http://www.ejeg.com

Aitken, C. J. (2007). Design integrity and EA governance. In P. Saha (Ed.) *Advances in Government Enterprise Architecture.* Hershey, PA: Idea Group

Ajzen, I. (1991). The theory of planned behaviour. *Organizational Behavior and Human Decision Processes, 50*, 179–211. doi:10.1016/0749-5978(91)90020-T

Ajzen, I., & Fishbein, M. (1980). *Understanding Attitudes and Predicting Social Behaviour.* Englewood Cliffs, NJ: Prentice-Hall.

Aksoy, D., Altinel, M., Bose, R., Cetintemel, U., Franklin, M., Wang, J., & Zdonik, S. (1999). Research in data broadcast and dissemination. In *Proceedings of the AMCP* (LNCS 1554, pp. 194-207).

Al-adawi, Z., Yousafzai, S., & Pallister, J. (2005). Conceptual model of citizen adoption of e-government. *The Second International Conference on Innovations in Information Technology, IIT'05.*

Alexander, C., Ishikawa, S., & Silverstein, M. (1977). *A Pattern Language: Towns, Buildings, Construction.* New York: Oxford University Press.

Alexander, J., & Ziebland, S. (2006). The web – bringing support and health information into the home: the communicative power of qualitative research. *International Journal of Nursing Studies, 43*(4), 389–391. doi:10.1016/j.ijnurstu.2005.10.012

Alexopoulos, P., Benetou, X., Tagaris, T., Georgolios, P., & Kafentzis, K. (2007). An ontological approach for fraud detection in the healthcare domain. *In Proceedings of the International Conference on Information Technologies (InfoTech - 2007)*, Vol. 1, Bulgaria.

Aloisio, G., Cafaro, M., Fiore, S., & Mirto, M. (2005). ProGenGrid: a grid-enabled platform for bioinformatics. *Studies in Health Technology and Informatics, 112*, 113–126.

Aloisio, G., Cafaro, M., Fiore, S., & Mirto, M. (2005). ProGenGrid: a workflow service infrastructure for composing and executing bioinformatics grid services. In *Proceedings of the 18th IEEE symposium on computer-based medical systems*, (pp. 555-560). Washington, DC: IEEE Computer Society.

Alonso, J. M., Hernandez, V., & Molto, G. (2005). Experiences on a large scale grid deployment with a computationally intensive biomedical application. In *Proceedings of the 18th IEEE symposium on computer-based medical systems*, (pp. 567-569). Washington, DC: IEEE Computer Society.

Alvarado, C. (2007). The physical environment in health-care. In P. Carayon (Ed.), *Handbook of human factors and ergonomics in health care and patient safety* (pp. 287-307). Mahwah, NJ: Erlbaum.

Ambler, S. (2000). Reuse patterns and antipatterns. *Software development.*

American Cancer Society (2008). Retrieved July 12, 2008, from http://www.cancer.org.

American Medical Association. (2008). *Patient confidentiality.* Retrieved from http://www.ama-assn.org/ama/pub/category/4610.html

Ammenwerth, E., & de Keizer, N. (2005). An inventory of evaluation studies of information technology in healthcare-trends in evaluation research 1982-2002. *Methods of Information in Medicine, 44*(1), 44–56.

Ammenwerth, E., Brender, J., Nykanen, P., Prokosch, H. U., Rigby, M., & Talmon, J. (2004). Visions and strategies to improve evaluation of health information systems - Reflections and lessons based on the HIS-EVAL workshop in Innsbruck. *International Journal of Medical Informatics, 73*, 479–491. doi:10.1016/j.ijmedinf.2004.04.004

Ammenwerth, E., Ehlers, F., Hirsch, B., & Gratl, G. (2007). HIS-Monitor: An approach to assess the quality of information processing in hospitals. *International Journal of Medical Informatics, 76*(2-3), 216–225. doi:10.1016/j.ijmedinf.2006.05.004

Ammenwerth, E., Eichstadter, R., Haux, R., Pohl, U., Rebel, S., & Ziegler, S. (2001). A randomized evaluation of a computer-based nursing documentation system. *Methods of Information in Medicine*, *40*, 61–68.

Ammenwerth, E., Graber, S., Herrmann, G., Burkle, T., & Konig, J. (2003). Evaluation of health information systems-problems and challenges. *International Journal of Medical Informatics*, *71*, 125–135. doi:10.1016/S1386-5056(03)00131-X

Ammenwerth, E., Iller, C., Mahler, C., Kandert, M., Luther, G., Hoppe, B., et al. (2003). Einflussfaktoren auf die Akzeptanz und Adoption eines Pflegedokumentationssystems-Studienbericht (2/2003). Innsbruck: Private Universität für Medizinische Informatik und Technik Tirol.

Ammenwerth, E., Mansmann, U., & Iller, C. (2003). Can evaluation studies benefit from a triangulation of quantitative and qualitative methods? A case study. International Journal of Medical Informatics, 70(2/3), 237-248.

Ammenwerth, E., Mansmann, U., Iller, C., & Eichstädter, R. (2003). Factors affecting and affected by user acceptance of computer-based nursing documentation: Results of a two-year study. Journal of the American Medical Informatics Association. 10(1), 69-84.

Amoroso, D. L. (1998). *Developing a model to understand Reengineering project success*. Washington, DC: IEEE.

Andersen, J. G. (1997). Clearing the way for physicians' use of clinical information systems. *Communications of the ACM*, *40*(8), 83–90. doi:10.1145/257874.257895

Anderson, G. F., Frogner, B. K., Johns, R. A., & Reinhardt, U. E. (2006). Health care spending and use of information technology in OECD countries. *Health Affairs (Project Hope)*, *25*(3), 819-831.

Anderson, J. G. (2003). A systems approach to preventing adverse drug events. In S. Krishna, E.A. Balas, & S.A. Boren (Eds.), *Information technology business models for quality health care: An EU/US dialogue* (pp. 95-102). Amsterdam: IOS Press.

Anderson, J. G. (2004). Consumers of e-health: patterns of use and barriers. *Social Science Computer Review*, *22*(2), 242-248.

Anderson, J. G. (2004). Information technology for detecting medication errors and adverse drug events. *Expert Opinion on Drug Safety*, *3*(5), 1–7. doi:10.1517/14740338.3.5.449

Anderson, J. G. (2008). Regional patient safety initiatives: the missing element of organizational change., In A. Kushniruk and E.M. Borycki (Eds.), *The human and social Side of health information systems*. Hershey, PA: Idea Group Publishing.

Anderson, J. G., & Bales, E. A. (2006). Computerization of primary care in the United States. *International Journal of Healthcare Information Systems and Informatics*, *1*(3), 1–23.

Anderson, J. G., Jay, S. J., Anderson, M. M., & Hunt, T. J. (2002). Evaluating the capability of information technology to prevent adverse drug events: A computer simulation approach. *Journal of the American Medical Informatics Association*, *9*, 479–490. doi:10.1197/jamia.M1099

Anderson, J. G., Ramanujam, R., Hensel, D., & Siro, C. A. (In Press). Reporting trends in a regional medication error data-sharing system. *Health Care Management Science*.

Anderson, J. G., Ramanujam, R., Hensel, D., Anderson, M., & Siro, C. A. (2006). The need for organizational change in patient safety initiatives. *International Journal of Medical Informatics*, *75*(12), 809–817. doi:10.1016/j.ijmedinf.2006.05.043

Anderson, J.G. (1999). Increasing the acceptance of clinical information systems. *MD Computing, 16*, 62–65.

Anderson, J.G. (2004). Using IT for medication safety: systems available. *Hospital Pharmacy Europe, July/August, 1-2*.

Archer, N. (2004). *The business case for employee mobility support* (Working Paper No. 9). Hamilton, ON: DeGroote School of Business, McMaster University.

Argyris, C., & Schon, D. (1996). *Organizational learning II: Theory, method, and practice*. Reading, MA: Addison-Wesley.

Ash, J. S., & Bates, D. W. (2005). Factors and forces affecting EHR system adoption: Report of a 2004 ACMI discussion. *Journal of the American Medical Informatics Association*, *12*(1), 8–12. doi:10.1197/jamia.M1684

Ash, J. S., Berg, M., & Coiera, E. (2004). Some unintended consequences of information technology in healthcare: The nature of patient care information system-related errors. *Journal of the American Medical Informatics Association*, *11*(2), 104–112. doi:10.1197/jamia.M1471

Ash, J. S., Gorman, P. N., & Hersh, W. R. (1998). Physician order entry in U.S. hospitals. *Proceedings of the AMIA Symposium* (pp. 236-239).

Ash, J. S., Gorman, P. N., Lavelle, M., Payne, T. H., Massaro, T. A., Frantz, G. L., & Lyman, J. A. (2003). A cross-site qualitative study of physician order entry. *Journal of the American Medical Informatics Association*, *10*(2), 188–200. doi:10.1197/jamia.M770

Ash, J. S., Sittig, D. F., Dykstra, R. H., Guappone, K., Carpenter, J. D., & Seshadri, V. (2007). Categorizing the unintended sociotechnical consequences of computerized provider order entry. *International Journal of Medical Informatics*, *76*(Suppl 1), 21–27. doi:10.1016/j.ijmedinf.2006.05.017

Ash, J. S., Sittig, D. F., Poon, E. G., Guappone, K., Campbell, E., & Dykstra, R. H. (2007). The extent and importance of unintended consequences related to computerized provider order entry. *Journal of the American Medical Informatics Association*, *14*(4), 415–423. doi:10.1197/jamia.M2373

Aspden, P., Corrigan, J. M., Wolcott, J., & Erickson, S. M. (Eds.). (2004). *Patient safety: Achieving a new standard for care*. Washington, DC: The National Academies Press.

Aspden, P., Julie, W., Bootman, J. L., & Cronenwett, L. R. (Eds.). (2006). *Preventing medication errors*. Washington, D.C.: National Academies Press.

Athey, S., & Stern, S. (2002). The impact of information technology on emergency health care outcomes. *The Rand Journal of Economics*, *33*(3), 399–388. doi:10.2307/3087465

Avison, D., & Young, T. (2007). Time to Rethink Health Care and ICT? *Communications of the ACM*, *50*(6), 69–74. doi:10.1145/1247001.1247008

Axelrod, R. (1984). *The Evolution of Cooperation*, New York: Basic Books.

Axisa, F., Gehin, C., Delhomme, G., Collet, C., Robin, O., & Dittmar, A. (2004). Wrist Ambulatory Monitoring System and Smart Glove for Real Time Emotional, Sensorial and Physiological Analysis. In *Proc. of the 26th Annual Int. Conf. of the IEEE EMBS*, (pp. 2161-2164). San Francisco, CA.

Baezner, D., Lomow, G., & Unger, B. W. (1990). Sim++: The transition to distributed simulation. In D. Nicol (Ed)., *Proceedings of the 1990 SCS Western Multiconference on Simulation: Distributed Simulation*, January 17-19 (pp. 211-218). San Diego, CA: Society for Computer Simulation.

Bagni, R., Berchi, R., & Cariello, P. (2002). A comparison of simulation models applied to epidemics. *Journal of Artificial Societies and Social Simulation*, *5*(3).

Ballantine, J. A., Galliers, R. D., & Stray, S. J. (1999). Information systems technology evaluation practices: Evidence from UK organizations. In L. P. Willcocks & S. Lester (Eds.), *Beyond the IT productivity paradox* (pp. 123-149). Chichester, UK: John Wiley & Sons.

Bandara, W., Gable, G. G., & Rosemann, M. (2005). Factors and measures of business process modeling: Model building through a multiple case study. *European Journal of Information Systems*, *14*, 347–360. doi:10.1057/palgrave.ejis.3000546

Bång, M., Larsson, A., & Eriksson, H. (2003). NOSTOS: A paper-based ubiquitous computing healthcare environment to support data capture and collaboration. *American Medical Informatics Association Annual Symposium Proceedings* (pp. 46-50). Washington DC.

Banks, J. (2001). *Discrete-event system simulation* (3rd Ed.). Upper Saddle River, NJ: Prentice Hall.

Bar Lev, S., & Harrison, M. (2005). Localization of health IT: How users "repair" electronic medical record systems. *Best Paper Proceedings of the 2005 Academy of Management Meeting*, Honolulu, Hawaii.

Bar Lev, S., & Harrison, M. I. (2006). Negotiating time scripts during implementation of an electronic medical record. *Health Care Management Review, 31*(1), 11–17.

Barbara, D. (1999). Mobile computing and databases: A survey. *IEEE TKDE, 11*(1), 108-117.

Bardram, J. E. (2004). Applications of context-aware computing in hospital work: Examples and design principles. In *Proceedings of the 2004 ACM Symposium on Applied Computing* (pp. 1574-1579). Nicosia, Cyprus: ACM.

Bardram, J. E., & Bossen, C. (2005). Mobility work: The spatial dimension of collaboration at a hospital. [CSCW]. *Computer Supported Cooperative Work, 14*(2), 131–160. doi:10.1007/s10606-005-0989-y

Barker, K. N., & Allan, E. L. (1995). Research on drug-use-system errors. *American Journal of Health-System Pharmacy, 52*, 400–403.

Barker, K. N., Flynn, E. A., Pepper, G. A., Bates, D. W., & Mikeal, R. L. (2002). Medication errors observed in 36 health care facilities. *Archives of Internal Medicine, 162*, 1897–1903. doi:10.1001/archinte.162.16.1897

Barnett, G. A., & Hwang, J. M. (2006). The Use of the Internet for Health Information and Social Support: A Content Analysis of Online Breast Cancer Discussion Groups. In M. Murero and R. E. Rice (Eds.), *The Internet and Healthcare: Theory, Research, and Practice* (pp. 233-253). Mahwah, NJ: Lawrence Erlbaum Associates.

Barton, P., Bryan, S., & Robinson, S. (2004). Modelling in the economic evaluation of health care: selecting the appropriate approach. *Journal of Health Services Research & Policy, 9*(2), 110–118. doi:10.1258/135581904322987535

Bates, D. (2005). Computerized physician order entry and medication errors: Finding a balance. *Journal of Biomedical Informatics, 38*(4), 259–261. doi:10.1016/j.jbi.2005.05.003

Bates, D. W. (1996). Medication errors: How common are they and what can be done to prevent them? *Drug Safety, 5*, 303–310. doi:10.2165/00002018-199615050-00001

Bates, D. W. (2000). Using information technology to reduce rates of medication errors in hospitals. *British Medical Journal, 320*, 788–791. doi:10.1136/bmj.320.7237.788

Bates, D. W., & Gawande, A. A. (2003). Improving safety with information technology. *The New England Journal of Medicine, 348*(25), 2526–2534. doi:10.1056/NEJMsa020847

Bates, D. W., Cohen, M., Leape, L. L., Overhage, M., Shabot, M. M., & Sheridan, T. (2001). Reducing the frequency of errors in medicine using information technology. *Journal of the American Medical Informatics Association, 8*(4), 299–308.

Bates, D. W., Cullen, D., & Laird, N. (1995). Incidence of adverse drug events and potential adverse drug events: implications for prevention. *Journal of the American Medical Association, 274*, 29–34. doi:10.1001/jama.274.1.29

Bates, D. W., Evans, R. S., Murff, H., Stetson, P. D., Pizziferri, L., & Hripcsak, G. (2003). Detecting Adverse Events using information technology. *Journal of the American Medical Informatics Association, 10*, 115–128. doi:10.1197/jamia.M1074

Bates, D. W., Evans, R. S., Murff, H., Stetson, P. D., Pizziperri, L., & Hripcsak, G. (2003). Policy and the future of adverse drug event detection using information technology. *Journal of the American Medical Informatics Association, 10*, 226–228. doi:10.1197/jamia.M1268

Bates, D. W., Leape, L. L., & Cullen, D. J. (1998). Effect of computerized physician order entry and a team intervention on prevention of serious medication errors. *Journal of the American Medical Association, 280*, 1311–1316. doi:10.1001/jama.280.15.1311

Bates, D. W., O'Neil, A. C., Boyle, D., Teich, J., Chertow, G. M., Komaroff, A. L., & Brennan, T. A. (1994). Potential identifiability and preventability of adverse events using information systems. *Journal of the American Medical Informatics Association, 1*, 404–411.

Bates, D. W., Spell, N. S., & Cullen, D. J. (1997). The costs of adverse drug events in hospitalized patients. *Journal of the American Medical Association, 277*, 307–311. doi:10.1001/jama.277.4.307

Bates, D. W., Teich, J. M., & Lee, J. (1999). The impact of computerized physician order entry on medication error prevention. *Journal of the American Medical Informatics Association, 6*, 313–321.

Bates, D.W., Ebell, M., Gotlier, E. Zapp, J., & Mullins, H.C. (2003). A proposal for electronic medical records in U.S. primary care. *Journal of the American Medical Informatics Association, 10*, 1–10.

Bates, D.W., Leape, L.L., Cullen, D.J., Laird, N., Petersen, L.A., Teich, J.M., et al. (1998). Effect of computerized physician order entry and a team intervention on prevention of serious medication errors. *Journal of the American Medical Association, 280*, 1311–1316.

Becker, J., Kugeler, M., & Rosemann, M. (2003). Process Managament - a guide for the design of business processes. Berlin, Germany: Springer.

Benaroia, M., Elinson, R., & Zarnke, K. (2007). Patient-directed intelligent and interactive computer medical history-gathering systems: a utility and feasibility study in the emergency department. *International Journal of Medical Informatics, 76*(4), 283–288. doi:10.1016/j.ijmedinf.2006.01.006

Benjamin, R. I., & Levinson, E. (1993). A framework for managing IT-enabled change. *Sloan Management Review*, ▪▪▪, 23–33.

Benkner, S., Berti, G., Engelbrecht, G., Fingberg, J., Kohring, G., Middleton, S. E., & Schmidt, R. (2005). GEMSS: Grid-infrastructure for medical service provision. *Methods of Information in Medicine, 44*(2), 177–181.

Berg, M. (1997). Problems and promises of the protocol. *Social Science & Medicine, 44*, 1081–1088. doi:10.1016/S0277-9536(96)00235-3

Berg, M. (1997). *Rationalizing medical work: Decision support techniques and medical practices*. Cambridge, MA: MIT Press.

Berg, M. (1999). Patient care information systems and healthcare work: A sociotechnical approach. *International Journal of Medical Informatics, 55*(2), 87–101. doi:10.1016/S1386-5056(99)00011-8

Berg, M., Aarts, J., & van der Lei, J. (2003). ICT in healthcare: Sociotechnical approaches. Methods of Information in Medicine, 42, 297-301.

Bergmann, J., Bott, O. J., Pretschner, D. P., & Haux, R. (2007). An e-consent-based shared EHR system architecture for integrated healthcare networks. *International Journal of Medical Informatics, 76*(2-3), 130–136. doi:10.1016/j.ijmedinf.2006.07.013

Berkowitz, L. L. (2002). Clinical informatics tools in physician practice. *Healthcare Informatics, 19*(4), 41–44.

Berman, F., Chien, A., Cooper, K., Dongarra, J., Foster, I., & Gannon, D. (2001). The GrADS project: Software support for high-level grid application development. *International Journal of High Performance Computing Applications, 15*(4), 327–344. doi:10.1177/109434200101500401

Berner, E. S., Detmer, D. E., & Simborg, D. (2005). Will the wave finally break? A brief view of the adoption of electronic medical records in the United States. *Journal of the American Medical Informatics Association, 12*(1), 3-7.

Bertelsen, O. W., & Bødker, S. (2002). Discontinuities. In Y. Dittrich, C. Floyd, & R. Klischewski (Eds.), *Social thinking - software practice* (pp. 409-424). Cambridge, MA: The MIT Press.

Bertelsen, O. W., & Bødker, S. (2002). Interaction through multi-artifacts. In S. Bagnara, S. Pozzi, A. Rizzo, & P. Wright (Eds.), *ECCE 11 - Cognition, Culture and Design Eleventh European Conference on Cognitive Ergonomics* (pp. 103-111). Rome: Instituto di scienze e technologie della cognizione consiglio nazionale delle ricerche.

Berti, G., Benker, S., Fenner, J. W., Fingberg, J., Lonsdale, G., Middleton, S. E., et al. (2003). Medical simulation services via the Grid. In *Proceedings of HealthGrid Workshop 2003.* Retrieved February 1st, 2008 from http://www.ccrl-nece.de/gemss/Presentations/healthgrid.pdf

Berwick, D. (2005). 'A deficiency of will and ambition': A conversation with donald berwick. interview by robert galvin. *Health Affairs (Project Hope), Suppl Web Exclusives,* W5-1-W5-9.

Berwick, D. M. (2003). Disseminating innovations in health care. *JAMA : The Journal of the American Medical Association, 289*(15), 1969-1975.

Bevan, N., & Macleod, M. (1993). Usability assessment and measurement. In M. Kelly (Ed.), *The management and measurement of software quality.* Ashgate Technical/Gower Press.

Bevan, N., Petrie, H., & Claridge, N. (2007). Strategies for providing guidance on usability and accessibility. In *Proceedings HCI International 2007.* Springer.

Beynon-Davies, P. (1999). Human error and information systems failure: The case of the London ambulance service computer-aided dispatch system project. *Interacting with Computers, 11,* 699-720.

Bhutan Department of Information Technology. (2007). *Bhutan's journey towards open source.* Paper presented at the DebConf7, Edinburgh, Scotland. https://penta.debconf.org/~joerg/events/25.en.html.

Bilykh, I., Bychkov, Y., Dahlem, D., Jahnke, J. H., McCallum, G., et al. (2003). Can grid services provide answers to the challenges of national health information sharing? In *Proceedings of the 2003 conference of the Centre for Advanced Studies on Collaborative research (CASCON '03),* (pp. 39-53). IBM Press.

Blake, J. A., & Bult, C. J. (2006). Beyond the data deluge: Data integration and bio-ontologies. *Journal of Biomedical Informatics, 39*(3), 314–320. doi:10.1016/j.jbi.2006.01.003

Blake, R. (2002). *Electronic communication systems* (2nd ed.). New York: Thomson Learning.

Blomberg, J., Suchman, L., & Trigg, R. H. (1996). Reflections on a work-oriented design project. *Human-Computer Interaction, 11*(3), 237–265. doi:10.1207/s15327051hci1103_3

Blumenthal, D. (1994). The variation phenomenon in 1994. *The New England Journal of Medicine, 331*(15), 1017–1018. doi:10.1056/NEJM199410133311511

Blumenthal, D., & Glaser, J. (2007). Information technology comes to medicine. *The New England Journal of Medicine, 356*(24), 2527–2534. doi:10.1056/NEJMhpr066212

Boccia, V., Guarracino, M. R., D'Amore, L., & Laccetti, G. (2005). A grid enabled PSE for medical imaging: experiences on MedIGrid. In *Proceedings of the 18th IEEE Symposium on computer-based medical systems,* (pp. 529-536). Washington, DC: IEEE Computer Society.

Bodenheimer, T. (1999). The American health care system: The movement for improved quality in health care. *The New England Journal of Medicine, 340,* 488–492. doi:10.1056/NEJM199902113400621

Boer, C. A. (2005). *Distributed simulation in industry.* PhD thesis, Erasmus Research Institute of Management (ERIM), Erasmus University Rotterdam, The Netherlands. Retrieved February 4th, 2008 from https://ep.eur.nl/handle/1765/6925.

Boiano, S., Borda, A., Bowen, J. P., Faulkner, X., Gaia, G., & McDaid, S. (2007). Gender Issues in HCI Design for Web Access. In S. Kurniawan & P. Zaphiris (Eds.), *Advances in Universal Web Design and Evaluation: Research, Trends and Opportunities* (pp. 116-153). Hershey, PA: IGI Global.

Bolaños, M., Nazeran, H., Gonzalez, I., Parra, R., & Martinez, C. C. (2004). A PDA-based Electrocardiogram/Blood Pressure Telemonitor for Telemedicine. In *Proc. of the 26th Annual Int. Conf. of the IEEE EMBS* (pp. 2169-2172). San Francisco, CA.

Booch, G. (1994). *Object-Oriented Analysis and Design with Applications*. (2nd Ed.). Redwood City, CA: The Benjamin/Cummings Publishing Company, Inc.

Boon, S. D., & Holmes, J. G. (1991). The dynamics of interpersonal trust: resolving uncertainty in the face of risk. In: Hinde, R.A., & Groebel, J. (eds.), *Cooperation and Prosocial Behaviour*, (pp. 190-211). Cambridge, UK: Cambridge University Press.

Borshchev, A., Karpov, Y., & Kharitonov, V. (2002). Distributed simulation of hybrid systems with AnyLogic and HLA. *Future Generation Computer Systems*, *18*(6), 829–839. doi:10.1016/S0167-739X(02)00055-9

Borum, F., & Christiansen, J. K. (2006). Actors and structure in IS projects: What makes implementation happen? *Scandinavian Journal of Management*, *22*(3), 213–237. doi:10.1016/j.scaman.2006.10.006

Bosch (1991). CAN specification Ver 2.0, Robert Bosch GmbH, Stuttgart, Germany.

Bostrom, R. P., & Heinen, J. S. (1977). MIS problems and failures: A sociotechnical perspective part I: The causes. *MIS Quarterly*, *1*(3), 17–32. doi:10.2307/248710

Bostrom, R. P., & Heinen, J. S. (1977). MIS problems and failures: A sociotechnical perspective part II: The application of sociotechnical theory. *MIS Quarterly*, *1*(December), 11–28. doi:10.2307/249019

Botha, R. A., & Eloff, J. H. P. (2001). Separation of duties for access control enforcement in workflow environments. *IBM Systems Journal*, *40*(3), 666–682.

Bower, A. G. (2005). *The diffusion and value of healthcare information technology*. Santa-Monica, CA: RAND Publishing.

Bowman, G., Thompson, D., & Sutton, T. (1983). Nurses attitudes towards the nursing process. Journal of Advanced Nursing, 8(2), 125-129.

Boxwala, A. A., Peleg, M., Tu, S., Ogunyemi, O., Zeng, Q. T., & Wang, D. (2004). GLIF3: a representation format for sharable computer-interpretable clinical practice guidelines. *Journal of Biomedical Informatics*, *37*(3), 147–161. doi:10.1016/j.jbi.2004.04.002

Boxwala, A. A., Tu, S., Peleg, M., Zeng, Q., Ogunyemi, O., & Greenes, R. A. (2001). Toward a representation format for sharable clinical guidelines. *Journal of Biomedical Informatics*, *34*(3), 157–169. doi:10.1006/jbin.2001.1019

Boyd, C., & Mathuria, A. (2003). *Protocols for Authentication and Key Establishment*. Berlin, Germany: Springer-Verlag.

Braa, K., & Ogrim, L. (1995). Critical view of the application of the Iso standard for quality assurance. *Information Systems Journal*, *5*(4), 253–269. doi:10.1111/j.1365-2575.1995.tb00098.x

Brady, J. M., Gavaghan, D. J., Simpson, A. C., Parada, M. M., & Highnam, R. P. (2003). eDiaMoND: A grid-enabled federated database of annotated mammograms. In Berman, F., Fox, G. C. and Hey, A. J. C. (eds.), *Grid computing: making the global infrastructure a reality*, (3rd Ed., pp. 923-943). Hoboken, NJ: Wiley.

Brailer, D. J. (2005, January 19). Interoperability: The key to the future health care system. *Health Affairs*, W5-19–W15-21.

Brailer, D.J., & Terasawa, E.L. (2003). *Use and adoption of computer-based patient records*. Oakland, CA: California Health Care Foundation.

Brailsford S. C., Churilov L. & Liew S-K., (2003). *Treating ailing emergency departments with simulation: an integrated perspective*.

Brailsford, S. C., Lattimer, V. A., Tarnaras, P., & Turnbull, J. C. (2004). Emergency and on-demand health care: modelling a large complex system. *The Journal of the Operational Research Society*, *55*(1), 34–42. doi:10.1057/palgrave.jors.2601667

Braithwaite, D., Emery, J., de Lusignan, S., & Sutton, S. (2003). Using the Internet to conduct surveys of health professionals: A valid alternative? *Family Practice*, *19*, 587–590.

Braithwaite, D., Sutton, S., Smithson, W.H., & Emery, J. (2002). Internet-based risk assessment and decision support for the management of familial cancer in primary care: Survey of GP's attitudes and intentions. *Family Practice*, *20*(5), 545–551.

Brender, J. (2002). Methodological and methodical perils and pitfalls within assessment studies performed on IT-based solutions in healthcare. Aalborg: Virtual Centre for Health Informatics.

Brender, J. (2006). *Handbook of evaluation methods for health informatics.* USA: Elsevier Academic Press Publications.

Breton, V., Dean, K., & Solomonides, T. (2005). The healthgrid white paper. *Studies in Health Technology and Informatics, 112*, 249–321.

Briggs, A., Claxton, K., & Sculpher, M. J. (2006). *Decision modelling methods for health economic evaluation.* Oxford: Oxford University Press.

Brodie, M., Flournoy, R. E., Altman, D. E., Blendon, R. J., Benson, J. M., & Rosenbaum, M. D. (2000). Health information, the Internet, and the digital divide. *Health Affairs, 19*(6), 255-265.

Brooks, R. G., & Menachemi, N. (2006). Physicians' use of email with patients: Factors influencing electronic communication and adherence to best practices. *Journal of Medical Internet Research, 8*(1), e2.

Brush, J. E., Balakrishnan, S. A., Brough, J., Hartman, C., Hines, G., & Liverman, D. P. (2006). Implementation of a continuous quality improvement program for percutaneous coronary intervention and cardiac surgery at a large community hospital. *American Heart Journal, 152*, 379–385. doi:10.1016/j.ahj.2005.12.014

Budnitz, D. S., Pollock, D. A., Weidenbach, K. N., Mendelsohn, A. B., Schroeder, T. J., & Annest, J. L. (2006). National surveillance of emergency department visits for outpatient adverse drug events. *Journal of the American Medical Association, 296*(15), 1858–1866. doi:10.1001/jama.296.15.1858

Buetow, S. (2005). Why the need to reduce medical errors is not obvious. *Journal of Evaluation in Clinical Practice, 11*, 53–57. doi:10.1111/j.1365-2753.2004.00497.x

Burgess, L. (2004, October 13-15). A conceptual framework for understanding and measuring perceived service quality in net-based customer support systems. *CollECTeR LatAm Conference*, Santiago, Chile.

Burke, D. E., & Menachemi, N. (2004). Opening the black box: Measuring hospital information technology capability. *Health Care Management Review, 29*(3), 207–217.

Burkow, T., Vognild, L., Krogstad, T., Borch, N., Østengen, G., Bratvold, A., & Risberg, M. (2008). An Easy to Use and Affordable Home-Based Personal eHealth System for Chronic Disease Management Based on Free Open Source Software. *Studies in Health Technology and Informatics, 136*, 83–88.

Burns, R. B. (1994). *Introduction to Research Methods,* (2nd Ed.). London: Longman Cheshire Pty Ltd.

Burt, C. W., & Sisk, J. E. (2005). Which physicians and practices are using electronic medical records? *Health Affairs (Project Hope), 24*(5), 1334-1343.

Burt, C.W., & Hing, E. (2005). *Use of computerized clinical support systems in medical settings: United States 2001-03. Advanced data from vital and health statistics, No. 353.* Hyattsville, MD: National Center for Health Statistics.

Cadili, S., & Whitley, E. A. (2005). On the interpretative flexibility of hosted ERP systems. *The Journal of Strategic Information Systems, 14*, 167–195. doi:10.1016/j.jsis.2005.04.006

Cain, M. & Mittman, M. (2002). Diffusion of Innovation in Health Care. *iHealth Reports*, May, 1-20. California HealthCare Foundation.

Caldwell, B., Cooper, M., Reid, L., & Vanderheiden, G. (2007, December 11). *Web content accessibility guidelines 2.0, W3C working draft.*

California Health Care Foundation. (2003, October). *Electronic medical records: Lessons from small physician practices. ihealthreports.*

California Healthcare Foundation. (2008). *Snapshot: The state of healthcare information technology in California.* Retrieved on January 24, 2008, from http://www.chcf.org/documents/chronicdisease/HITSnapshot08.pdf

California Senate Bill 1875 (2000). Chapter 816, 1393.63.

Campbell, D., & Fiske, D. (1959). Convergent and discriminant validity by the muli-trait, multi-method matrix. Psychological Bulletin, 56, 81-105.

Campbell, E., Sittig, D., Ash, J., Guappone, K., & Dykstra, R. (2006). Types of unintended consequences related to computerized provider order entry. *Journal of the American Medical Informatics Association, 13*(5), 547–556. doi:10.1197/jamia.M2042

Campbell, E., Sittig, D., Ash, J., Guappone, K., & Dykstra, R. (2007). In reply to "e-Iatrogenisis: the most critical consequence of CPOE and other HIT." *Journal of the American Medical Informatics Association, 14*(3), 389–390. doi:10.1197/jamia.M2385

Campbell, P. (2005). Prehospital triage of acute myocardial infarction: wireless transmission of electrocardiograms to the on-call cardiologist via a handheld computer. *Journal of Electrocardiology, 38*(4), 300–309. doi:10.1016/j.jelectrocard.2005.05.003

Canero, C., Thomos, N., Triantafyllidis, G. A., Litos, G. C., & Strintzis, M. G. (2005). Mobile tele-echography: user interface design. *IEEE Transactions on Information Technology in Biomedicine, 9*(1), 44–49. doi:10.1109/TITB.2004.840064

Cannataro, M., Comito, C., Congiusta, A., & Veltri, P. (2004). PROTEUS: a bioinformatics problem solving environment on grids. *Parallel Processing Letters, 14*(2), 217–237. doi:10.1142/S0129626404001842

Cannataro, M., Guzzi, P. H., Mazza, T., Tradigo, G., & Veltri, P. (2005). Preprocessing of mass spectrometry proteomics data on the grid. In *Proceedings of the 18th international symposium on computer-based medical systems*, (pp.549-554). Washington, DC: IEEE Computer Society.

Carayon, P. (2006). Human factors and ergonomics in healthcare and patient safety. In P. Carayon (Ed.), *Handbook of human factors and ergonomics in healthcare and patient safety.* Mahwah, NJ: Lawrence Erlbaum Associates.

Carayon, P., & Smith, M. (2000). Work organization and ergonomics. *Applied Ergonomics, 31*, 649–662. doi:10.1016/S0003-6870(00)00040-5

Carter, L., & Belanger, F. (2004). Citizen adoption of electronic government initiatives. IN *Proceedings of 37th Annual Hawaii International Conference on System Sciences*, Big Island, Hawaii.

Castelfranchi, C., & Falcone, R. (1999). *Social Trust: A Cognitive Approach.*Presentation at the International Workshop on Agent-Oriented Information Systems, CAiSE 1999, Heidelberg. Retrieved from http://www.aois.org/99/ castelfranchi-Social-Trust-paper.doc

Castelfranchi, C., & Falcone, R. (2001). Social Trust: A Cognitive Approach. In Castelfranchi, C., & Tan, Y.-H. (Eds.), *Trust and Deception in Virtual Societies* (pp. 55-90). Norwell, MA; Kluwer Academic Publisher.

Chandy, K.M. & Misra, J. (1979). *Distributed Simulation: A Case Study in Design and Verification of Distributed Programs, 5*(5), 440-452.

Chang, J. C. J., & King, W. R. (2005). Measuring the performance of information systems: A functional scorecard. *Journal of Management Information Systems, 22*(1), 85–115.

Chatterjee, S., & Wernerfelt, B. (1991). The Link between Resources and Type of Diversification: Theory and Evidence. *Strategic Management Journal, 12*, 33–48. doi:10.1002/smj.4250120104

Chau, P. Y. K., & Hu, P. J. (2002). Examining a model of information technology acceptance by individual professionals: An exploratory study. *Management Information Systems, 18*(4), 191–229.

Chau, P. Y. K., & Hu, P. J.-H. (2002). Investigating healthcare professionals' decision to accept telemedicine technology: An empirical test of competing theories. *Information & Management, 39*, 297–311. doi:10.1016/S0378-7206(01)00098-2

Chau, P., & Hu, P. (2001). Information technology acceptance by individual professionals: A model comparison approach. *Decision Sciences, 32*(4). doi:10.1111/j.1540-5915.2001.tb00978.x

Chaudhry, B., Wang, J., Wu, S., Maglione, M., Mojica, W., & Roth, E. (2006). Systematic review: Impact of health information technology on quality, efficiency, and costs of medical care. *Annals of Internal Medicine*, *144*(10), 742–752.

Chein, I., Cook, S. W., & Harding, J. (1948). The field of action research. *The American Psychologist*, *3*, 43–50. doi:doi:10.1037/h0053515

Chen, E., Mendoca, E. A., McKnight, L. K., Stetson, P. D., Lei, J., & Cimino, J. J. (2003). PalmCIS: A Wireless Handheld Application for Satisfying Clinician Information Needs. *Journal of the American Medical Informatics Association*, *11*(1), 19–28. doi:10.1197/jamia.M1387

Chen, M.-J. (1996). Competitor Analysis and Interfirm Rivalry: Toward a Theoretical Integration. *Academy of Management Review*, *21*(1), 100–134. doi:10.2307/258631

Cheng, C. G. M. K., Geller, E., & Levitt, R. E. (2003). The effects of CPOE on ICU workflow: An observational study. In *Proceedings of the Medical Informatics Symposium*, Palo Alto, CA.

Chetty, K. S. (2007). Equity Promoting Health Care Policies in South Africa. *Report to the Health Systems Knowledge Network*. Retrieved Jan 10, 2008 from http://www.wits.ac.za/chp/kn/Chetty%202007%20Equity.pdf

Chiasson, M., Davidson, E., Kaplan, B., Lau, F., & Reddy, M. (2004, September). *Interdisciplinary windows for studying information systems in healthcare: Challenges and opportunities*. Paper presented at IT in healthcare: Socio-technical Approaches Second International Conference, Oregon, USA.

Chin, J. (1988). Development of a tool measuring user satisfaction of the human-computer interface. Proceedings: Human factors in Computing, Chi'88 Conf (pp. 213-218). New York: Association for Computing Machinery.

Chisholm, R. F., & Ziegenfuss, J. T. (1986). A review of applications of the sociotechnical systems approach to healthcare organizations. *The Journal of Applied Behavioral Science*, *22*(3), 315–327. doi:10.1177/002188638602200310

Chismar, W. G., & Patton, S. W. (2003). *Does the extended technology acceptance model apply to physicians?* 36th Hawaii International Conference on System Sciences, Hawaii.

Chismar, W. R., & Wiley-Patton, S. (2006). Predicting Internet Use: Applying the Extended Technology Acceptance Model to the Healthcare Environment. In T.A.M. Spil & R.W. Schuring (Eds.), *E-Health Systems Diffusion and Use: The Innovation, the User and the USE IT Model*. Hershey, PA: Idea Group Publishing.

Chu, Y., & Ganz, A. (2004). A mobile teletrauma system using 3G networks. *IEEE Transactions on Information Technology in Biomedicine*, *8*(4), 456–462. doi:10.1109/TITB.2004.837893

Chung, S., Singh, H., & Lee, K. (2000). Complementarity, Status Similarity and Social Capital as Drivers of Alliance Formation. *Strategic Management Journal*, *21*, 1–22. doi:10.1002/(SICI)1097-0266(200001)21:1<1::AID-SMJ63>3.0.CO;2-P

Clarke III, I., & Flaherty, T. B. (2003). Mobile portals: The development of m-commerce gateways. In B. E. M. a. T. J. Strader (Ed.), *Mobile commerce: Technology, theory, and applications* (pp. 185-201). Hershey, PA: IRM Press.

Classen, D. C., Pestotnik, S. L., Evans, R. S., & Burke, J. P. (1991). Computerized surveillance of adverse drug events in hospital patients. *Journal of the American Medical Association*, *266*, 2847–2851. doi:10.1001/jama.266.20.2847

Classen, D. C., Pestotnik, S. L., Evans, R. S., Lloyd, J. F., & Burke, J. P. (1997). Adverse drug events in hospitalized patients: excess length of stay, extra costs, and attributable mortality. *Journal of the American Medical Association*, *277*, 301–306. doi:10.1001/jama.277.4.301

Cleland, J. (2006). An investigation of the effect of telemedicine on outcomes in Europe: The trans-European network–home care management system study. *Dis Manage Health Outcomes*.

Coiera, E. (1997). *Guide to medical informatics, the internet, and telemedicine.* New York: Chapman & Hall.

Coiera, E. (2003). *Guide to health informatics, second ed.* London: Hodder Arnold.

Coiera, E. (2004). Four rules for the reinvention of healthcare. *BMJ (Clinical Research Ed.), 328*, 1197–1199. doi:10.1136/bmj.328.7449.1197

Coiera, E., & Clarké, R. (2003). e-Consent: The Design and Implementation of Consumer Consent Mechanisms in an Electronic Environment. *Journal of the American Medical Informatics Association, 11*(2), 129–140. doi:10.1197/jamia.M1480

Coleman, J. S. (1990). *Foundations of Social Theory.* Cambridge MA: Harvard University Press.

Comden, S. C., & Rosenthal, J. (2002). *Statewide Patient Safety Coalitions: A Status Report.* Portland. ME: National Academy for State Health Policy.

Conn, J. (2007). A long-term solution. *Modern Healthcare, 37*(45), 52–54.

Conn, J. C. (2007, October 30). Failure, deinstallation of EHRs abound: Study. *Modern Healthcare.* Retrieved on November 2, 2007, from http://www.modernhealthcare.com/apps/pbcs.dll/article?AID=/20071030/FREE/310300002/0/FRONTPAGE

Connell, N., & Young, T. (2007). Evaluating healthcare information systems through an "enterprise" perspective. *Information & Management, 44*(4), 433–440. doi:10.1016/j.im.2007.04.002

Conrick, M., Dunne, A. & Skinner, J., (1999). *Learning together: Using Simulation to foster the integration of theory and practice.*

Contractor, F. J., & Lorange, P. (1988). *Cooperative Strategies in International Business.* Lexington, MA: Lexington Books.

Cook, C., Heath, F., & Thompson, R.L. (2000). A meta-analysis of response rates in Web- and Internet-based surveys. *Educational and Psychological Measurement, 60*(6), 821–836.

Cooper, K., Brailsford, S. C., & Davies, R. (2007). Choice of modelling technique for evaluating health care interventions. *The Journal of the Operational Research Society, 58*(2), 168–176.

Cooper, K., Davies, R., & Brailsford, S. (2007). Choice of modelling technique for evaluating health care interventions. *The Journal of the Operational Research Society, 58*, 168–176.

Cornford, T. (2003). Information systems and new technologies: Taking shape in use. In C. Avgerou & R. La Rovere (Eds.), *Information systems and the economics of innovation* (pp. 1-16). London: Edward Elgar.

Cotton, S. R., & Gupta, S. S. (2004). Characteristics of online and offline health information seekers and factors that discriminate between them. *Social Science & Medicine, 59*(9), 1795-1806.

Creswell, J. W. (2003). *Research design. Qualitative, quantitative, and mixed methods approaches.* Thousand Oaks, CA: SAGE Publications.

Cronholm, S., & Goldkuhl, G. (2003, September 25-26). Six generic types of information systems evaluation. *The 10th European Conference on Information Technology Evaluation (ECITE-2003)*, Madrid.

CrossGrid.org. (2008). *CrossGrid project homepage.* Retrieved February 1st, 2008 from http://www.crossgrid.org/main.html

Crosson, J. C., Ohman-Strickland, P. A., Hahn, K. A., DiCicco-Bloom, B., Shaw, E., & Orzano, A. J. (2007). Electronic medical records and diabetes quality of care: Results from a sample of family medicine practices. *Annals of Family Medicine, 5*(3), 209–215. doi:10.1370/afm.696

Cullen, D. J., Bates, D. W., & Small, S. D. (1995). The incident reporting system does not detect adverse drug events: A problem for quality improvement. *Journal of Quality Improvement, 21*, 541–548.

Cullen, J. B., Johnson, J. L., & Sakano, T. (1995). Japanese and Local Partner Commitment to IJVs: Psychological Consequences of Outcomes and Investments in the IJV

Relationship. *Journal of International Business Studies*, *26*(1), 91–115. doi:10.1057/palgrave.jibs.8490167

Curtis, B., Krasner, H., & Iscoe, N. (1988). A field study of the software design process for large systems. *Communications of the ACM*, *31*(11). doi:10.1145/50087.50089

Dahl, Y. (2007). *Ubiquitous computing at point of care in hospitals: A user-centered approach.* Doctoral Thesis. Norwegian University of Science and Technology 2007:147.

Dahl, Y. Svanaes, D. & Nytro, Ø. (2006). Designing pervasive computing for hospitals: learning from the media affordances of paper-based medication charts. *Pervasive Health Conference and Workshops* (pp. 1-10). Washington, DC: IEEE.

Dahl, Y., & Svanæs, D. (2008). A comparison of location and token-based interaction techniques for point-of-care access to medical information. *Personal and Ubiquitous Computing*, *12*(6), 459–478. doi:10.1007/s00779-007-0141-8

Dangerfield, B. C. (1999). System dynamics applications to European health care issues. *The Journal of the Operational Research Society*, *50*(4), 345–353.

Darmstadt, G., Bhutta, Z., Cousens, S., Adam, T., Walker, N., & Berni, L. (2005). Evidence-based, cost-effective interventions: How many newborn babies can we save?. *The Lancet*, *365*(9463), 977-988.

Das, T. K., & Teng, B. S. (2000). A Resource Based Theory of Strategic Alliances . *Journal of Management*, *26*(1), 31–61. doi:10.1016/S0149-2063(99)00037-9

Das, T. K., & Teng, B.-S. (2000). Instabilities of Strategic Alliances: An Internal Tensions Perspective. *Organization Science*, *11*, 77–101. doi:10.1287/orsc.11.1.77.12570

Das, T. K., & Teng, B.-S. (2002). The Dynamics of Alliance Conditions in the Alliance Development Process. *Journal of Management Studies*, *39*(5), 725–746. doi:10.1111/1467-6486.00006

Das, T. K., & Teng, B.-S. (2003). Partner Analysis and Alliance Performance. *Scandinavian Journal of Management*, *19*, 279–308. doi:10.1016/S0956-5221(03)00003-4

Davenport, T. (1993). *Process innovation: Reengineering work through information technology.* Cambridge, MA: Harvard Business School press.

Davidson, E., & Heslinga, D. (2007). Bridging the IT Adoption Gap for Small Physician Practices: An Action Research Study on Electronic Health Records. *Information Systems Management*, *24*(1), 15–28. doi:10.1080/10580530601036786

Davidson, S. M., & Heineke, J. (2007). Toward an Effective Strategy for the Diffusion and Use of Clinical Information Systems. *Journal of the American Medical Informatics Association*, *14*(3), 361–367. doi:10.1197/jamia.M2254

Davies, F. D., Bagozzi, R. P., & Warshaw, P. R. (1989). User acceptance of computer technology: A comparison of two theoretical models. *Communications of the ACM*, *35*(8), 982–1003.

Davies, R., & Bensley, D. (2005). Editorial. *The Journal of the Operational Research Society*, *56*(2), 123. doi:10.1057/palgrave.jors.2601930

Davis, F. (1989). Perceived usefulness, perceived ease of use, and user acceptance of information technology. *MIS Quarterly*, *13*(3), 319–340. doi:10.2307/249008

Davis, F. (1993). User acceptance of information technology: System characteristics, user perceptions and behavioral impacts. International Journal of Man-Machine Studies, 38, 475-487.

Davis, L., Domm, J., Konikoff, M., & Miller, R. (1999). Attitudes of first-year medical students toward the confidentiality of computerized patient records. *Journal of the American Medical Informatics Association*, *6*(1).

Davis, R. (2002). Pursue front end solutions to revenue problems. *Healthcare Financial Management*, *56*(8), 30–36.

Davis, R. (2006). British Telecom - Six-Level Process Hierarchy. In *Proceedings of the Process days conference*, Sydney Australia, August 22-24.

Davis, R., & Bradander, E. (2007). *Aris Design Platform: Getting Started with BPM.* Berlin, Germany: Springer-Verlag.

Davis, S., & Bostrom, R. (1993). Training end users: An experimental investigation of the roles of the computer interface and training methods. *MIS Quarterly*, (1): 61–85. doi:10.2307/249510

De Giacomo, G., Lespérance, Y., & Levesque, H. J. (2000). ConGolog, a concurrent programming language based on the situation calculus. *Artificial Intelligence*, *121*(1-2), 109–169. doi:10.1016/S0004-3702(00)00031-X

de Keizer, N., & Ammenwerth, E. (2005). Trends in evaluation research 1982-2002: A study on how the quality of IT evaluation studies develop. *Studies in Health Technology and Informatics*, *116*, 581–586.

DeLone, W. H., & McLean, E. R. (2003). The DeLone and McLean model of information systems success: A ten-year update. *Journal of Management Information Systems*, *19*(4), 9–30.

Deming, W. E. (1990). *Out of the Crisis*. Cambridge, UK: Cambridge University Press.

Demiris, G. (2006). The Diffusion of Virtual Communities in Health Care: Concepts and Challenges. *Patient Education and Counseling*, *62*, 178–188. doi:10.1016/j.pec.2005.10.003

Denzin, N. (1970). Strategies of multiple triangulation. In N. Denzin (Ed.), The research act (3rd ed., pp. 297-331). Chicago: Aldine.

Deodhar, J. (2002). Telemedicine by e-mail—experience in neonatal care at a primary care facility in rural India. *Journal of Telemedicine and Telecare*, *8*(Suppl 2), 20-21.

Department of Health and Ageing. (2007). *2003-08 Australian Health Care Agreements- Information sheet number 1 - April 2007*. Retrieved July, 2008, from http://www.health.gov.au/internet/main/publishing.nsf/Content/ahca0308-infosheet1.htm

Department of Health and Ageing. (2007). *Budget statements for 2008-09*. Retrieved July 7th 2008, from http://www.health.gov.au/internet/budget/publishing.nsf/Content/2008-2009_Health_PBS/$File/Department_Overview.pdf

Department of Health. (2002). *Delivering 21st century IT support for the NHS: National specification for integrated care records service*. Retrieved on July 26, 2004, from http://www.dh.gov.uk/assetRoot/04/07/16/76/04071676.pdf

Department of Health. (2004). *National HIV and Syphillis Antenatal Seroprevalence Survey in South Africa 2003*. Retrieved January 10, 2008, from http://www.doh.gov.za/docs/2003hiv-f.html.

Desmedt, Y. G., & Frankel, Y. (1989). *Threshold cryptosystems*. Paper presented at the Advances in Cryptology.

Dewan, N., & Lorenzi, N. (2000). Behavioral health information systems: evaluating readiness and user acceptance. MD Computing, 17(4), 50-52.

Dick, R.S., & Steen, E.B. (1997). *The computer-based patient record: An essential technology for health care*. Washington, DC: National Academy Press, Institute of Medicine.

Diffie, W., & Hellman, M. (1976). New directions in cryptography. *IEEE Transactions on Information Theory*, *22*(6), 644–654. doi:10.1109/TIT.1976.1055638

Dingwall, R. (1997). Accounts, interviews, and observations. In G. Miller & R. Dingwall (Eds.), *Context and method in qualitative research*. London: Sage Publications.

DITIS: Virtual Collaborative Teams for Home Healthcare. (n.d.). Retrieved July 2005 from http://www.ditis.ucy.ac.cy

Doherty, N. F., Coombs, C. R., & Loan-Clarke, J. (2006). A re-conceptualization of the interpretive flexibility of information technologies: redressing the balance between the social and the technical. *European Journal of Information Systems*, *15*, 569–582. doi:10.1057/palgrave.ejis.3000653

Donahue, K. T., & Vanostenberg, P. (2000). Joint commission international accreditation: Relationship to four models of evaluation. *International Journal for Quality in Health Care*, *12*(3), 243–246. doi:10.1093/intqhc/12.3.243

Dormann, H., Muth-Selbach, U., Krebs, S., & Criegee-Rieck, M. (2000). Incidence and costs of adverse drug reactions during hospitalization: Computerized monitoring versus stimulated spontaneous reporting. *Drug Safety*, *22*(2), 161–168. doi:10.2165/00002018-200022020-00007

Dorr, D., Bonner, L. M., Cohen, A. N., Shoai, R. S., Perrin, R., & Chaney, E. (2007). Informatics systems to promote improved care for chronic illness: A literature review. *Journal of the American Medical Informatics Association*, *14*, 156–163. doi:10.1197/jamia.M2255

Dourish, P., & Bellotti, V. (1992). Awareness and Coordination in Shared Workspaces. *ACM Conference on Computer Supported Cooperative Work*, New York, NY, (pp. 107-114).

Dyer, O. (2003). Patients will be reminded of appointments by text messages. *British Medical Journal*, *326*(402), 281.

Dyer, W. G., & Wilkins, A. L. (1991). Better Stories, Not Better Constructs, To Generate Better Theory: A Rejoinder To Eisenhardt. *Academy of Management Review*, *16*(3), 613–619. doi:10.2307/258920

Dymsza, W. A. (1988). Success and Failures of Joint Ventures in Developing Countries: Lessons from Experience. In F. J. Contractor, P. Lorange (Eds.) *Cooperative Strategies in International Business* (pp. 403-424). Lexington, MA: Lexington Books.

Eccles, R. G. (1991). The performance-measurement manifesto. *Harvard Business Review*, *69*(1), 131–137.

Eddy, D. M. (2005). Evidence-based medicine: A unified approach. *Health Affairs*, *24*(1), 9–17. doi:10.1377/hlthaff.24.1.9

EFQM. (2006). *The EFQM excellence award.* Retrieved on October 10, 2007, from http://www.efqm.org/2006

EGEE. (2008). *Enabling grids for e-science project.* Retrieved February 1st, 2008 from http://www.eu-egee.org/

E-Health Insider. (2006). *Virgin to upgrade telemedicine across fleet.* Retrieved January 23, 2008, from http://www.e-health-insider.com/News/1925/virgin_to_upgrade_telemedicine_across_fleet.html

Ehn, P. (1988). Work oriented design of computer artifacts. *Arbetslivscentrum (Swedish Center for Working Life).*

Eisenhardt, K. M. (1989). Building Theories from Case Study Research. *Academy of Management Review*, *14*(4), 532–550. doi:10.2307/258557

Eldabi, T., Paul, R. J., & Taylor, S. J. E. (2000). Simulating economic factors in adjuvant breast cancer treatment. *The Journal of the Operational Research Society*, *51*(4), 465–475.

Eldabi, T., Paul, R. J., & Young, T. (2007). modelling in healthcare: reviewing legacies and investigating futures. *The Journal of the Operational Research Society*, *58*(2), 262–270.

ElGamal, T. (1985). A public key cryptosystem and a signature scheme based on discrete logarithms. *Information Theory . IEEE Transactions on*, *31*(4), 469–472.

Ellisman, M., & Peltier, S. (2004). Medical data federation: the biomedical informatics research network. In I. Foster, and C. Kesselman, (Eds.), *The Grid: Blueprint for a New Computing Infrastructure* (2nd Ed.). San Francisco, CA: Morgan Kaufmann.

Ellisman, M., Brady, M., Hart, D., Lin, F., Muller, M., & Smarr, L. (2004). The emerging role of biogrids. *Communications of the ACM*, *47*(11), 52–57. doi:10.1145/1029496.1029526

Eng, T. R. (2002). E-Health research and evaluation: Challenges and opportunities. *Journal of Health Communication*, *7*(4), 267–272. doi:10.1080/10810730290001747

Engeström, Y. (1993). Developmental studies of work as a test bench of activity theory: the case of primary care medical practice. In S. Chaiklin & J. Lave (Eds.), *Understanding practice: perspectives on activity and context* (pp. 64-103). Cambridge, MA: Cambridge University Press.

Eskeland, S., & Oleshchuk, V. (2006). *Anonymity authorization granting in medical information networks* Paper presented at the European Conference on eHealth 2006, Fribourg, Switzerland.

Eskeland, S., & Oleshchuk, V. (2007). *Collusion-resistant threshold decryption.* Paper presented at the Communication, Network, and Information Security CNIS 2007, Berkeley, California, USA.

Eskeland, S., & Oleshchuk, V. (2007). *Hierarchical Multi-Party Key Agreement for Wireless Networks.*

Eskeland, S., & Oleshchuk, V. (2007). *EPR Access Authorization of Medical Team Based on Patient Consent.* Paper presented at the Conference on eHealth 2007, Oldenburg, Germany

Eskeland, S., & Oleshchuk, V. (2008). Secure Team-Based EPR Access Acquisition in Wireless Networks. *Availability, Reliability and Security, 2008. ARES 08. Third International Conference on*, 943-949.

Eskeland, S., & Prasad, N. (2006, July 17, 2006,). *A Novel Decentralized Hierarchical Access Control Scheme for the Medical Scenario.* Paper presented at the International Workshop on Ubiquitous Access Control, San Jose, CA, USA.

Estrella, F., Hauer, T., McClatchey, R., Odeh, M., Rogulin, D., & Solomonides, T. (2007). Experiences of engineering Grid-based medical software. *International Journal of Medical Informatics*, *76*(8), 621–632. doi:10.1016/j.ijmedinf.2006.05.005

Evans, R. S., Classen, D. C., Pestotnik, S. L., Lundsgaarde, H. P., & Burke, J. P. (1994). Improving empiric antibiotic selection using computer decision support. *Archives of Internal Medicine*, *154*, 878–884. doi:10.1001/archinte.154.8.878

Evans, R. S., Pestotnik, S. L., Classen, D. C., & Horn, S. D. (1994). Preventing adverse drug events in hospitalized patients. *The Annals of Pharmacotherapy*, *28*, 523–527.

Evans, R.S., Pestotnik, S., Classen, D., Clemmer, T., Weaver, L., Orme, J., et al. (1998). A computer-assisted management program for antibiotics and other anti-infective agents. *New England Journal of Medicine*, *338*, 232–238.

Eysenbach, G. (2001). What is e-health?. *J Med Internet Res*, *3*(2), e20.

Eysenbach, G. (2003). The impact of the Internet on cancer outcomes. *CA A Cancer Journal for Clinicians*, *53*(6), 356-371.

Eysenbach, G. (2005). Using the Internet for surveys and research. In J.G. Anderson, & C.E. Aydin (Eds.), *Evaluating the organizational impact of healthcare information systems* (2nd ed.) (pp. 129–143). New York: Springer.

Eysenbach, G., & Jadad, A. R. (2001). Evidence-based patient choice and consumer health informatics in the Internet age. *Journal of Medical Internet Research*, *3*(2), e35.

Fan, Y. (2000). A classification of Chinese culture. *Cross Cultural Management–An International Journal*, *7*(2), 3–10. doi:10.1108/13527600010797057

Farbey, B., Land, F., & Targett, D. (1995). A taxonomy of information systems applications: The benefits evaluation ladder. *European Journal of Information Systems*, *4*, 41–50. doi:10.1057/ejis.1995.5

Farbey, B., Land, F., & Targett, D. (1999). Evaluating investments in IT: Findings and a framework. In L. P. Willcocks & S. Lester (Eds.), *Beyond the IT productivity paradox* (pp. 183-215). Chichester, UK: John Wiley & Sons.

Feagin, J., Orum, A., & Sjoberg, G. (Eds.). (1991). *A case for case study.* Chapel Hill, NC: University of North Carolina Press.

Feenberg, A. (1991). *Critical theory of technology.* New York: Oxford University Press.

Feenberg, A. (1999). *Questioning technology.* London: Routledge.

Fiscella, K., & Geiger, H. J. (2006). Health information technology and quality improvement for community health centers. *Health Affairs*, *25*(2), 405–412. doi:10.1377/hlthaff.25.2.405

Fischer, M. C., Adams, A., & Miller, G. (1994). Aggregate level simulation protocol (ALSP) - training for the future. In *Proceedings of the 1994 Military Operations Research Symposium*. Military Operations Research Society (MORS), USA. Retrieved February 15th, 2008 from http://ms.ie.org/alsp/biblio/mors_94_fischer/mors_94_fischer.html

Fischer, S., Stewart, T. E., Mehta, S., Wax, R., & Lapinsky, R. (2003). Handheld Computing in Medicine. *Journal of the American Medical Informatics Association*, *10*(2), 139–149. doi:10.1197/jamia.M1180

Fitzgerald, B., & Howcroft, D. (1998, December). *Competing dichotomies in IS research and possible strategies for resolution.* AIS International Conference on Information Systems, Helsinki, Finland.

Fitzhenry, F., Peterson, J. F., Arrieta, M., Waitman, L. R., Schildcrout, J. S., & Miller, R. A. (2007). Medication administration discrepancies persist despite electronic ordering. *Journal of the American Medical Informatics Association*, *14*(6), 756–764. doi:10.1197/jamia.M2359

Fleiss, J. L. (1981). *Statistical Methods for Rates and Proportions* (2nd Ed., pp. 38-46). New York: John Wiley.

Flint, A., & Milligan, S. (1999, 10 December). Your Tragedy Is Ours: President Joins Thousands in Saluting Fallen Firefighters. *Boston Globe*.

Flowers, L., & Riley, T. (2001). *State-based Mandatory Reporting of Medical Errors: An Analysis of the Legal and Policy Issues*. Portland, ME: National Academy for State Health Policy.

Fone, D., Hollinghurst, S., Temple, M., Round, A., Lester, N., & Weightman, A. (2003). Systematic review of the use and value of computer simulation modelling in population health and health care delivery. *Journal of Public Health*, *25*(4), 325–335. doi:10.1093/pubmed/fdg075

Fontelo, P., Ackerman, M., Kim, G., & Locatis, C. (2003). The PDA as a portal to knowledge sources in a wireless setting. *Telemedicine Journal and e-Health*, *9*(2), 141–147. doi:10.1089/153056203766437480

Forrester, J. W. (1961). *Industrial dynamics*. Cambridge MA: M.I.T. Press.

Forster, F. (2006). The idea Behind Business Process Improvement: Towards a Business Process Improvement Pattern Framework. *Business Process Trend Advisor*, 04-06.

Foster, I., Kesselman, C., Nick, J. M., & Tuecke, S. (2003). The physiology of the grid. In F. Berman, G. Fox, and T. Hey, (eds.), *Grid Computing: Making the Global Infrastructure a Reality* (pp. 217-249). New York: John Wiley & Sons.

Fowler, M. (1997). *Analysis Patterns: Reusable Object Models*, (Vol. Reading). Reading MA: Addison- Wesley.

Fox, J., & Bury, J. (2000). A quality and safety framework for point-of-care clinical guidelines. *Proc AMIA Symp*, 245-249.

Fox, J., Johns, N., & Rahmanzadeh, A. (1998). Disseminating medical knowledge: the PROforma approach. *Artificial Intelligence in Medicine*, *14*(1-2), 157–181. doi:10.1016/S0933-3657(98)00021-9

Fox, J., Johns, N., Lyons, C., Rahmanzadeh, A., Thomson, R., & Wilson, P. (1997). PROforma: a general technology for clinical decision support systems. *Computer Methods and Programs in Biomedicine*, *54*(1-2), 59–67. doi:10.1016/S0169-2607(97)00034-5

Fox, S., & Rainie, L. (2000). *The online health care revolution: How the Web helps Americans take better care of themselves*. Washington, DC: Pew Internet & American Life.

Fox, S., & Rainie, L. (2002). *Vital decisions: How Internet users decide what information to trust when they or their loved ones are sick*. Washington, DC: Pew Internet & American Life.

Fox, W. (1995). Sociotechnical system principles and guidelines: Past and present. *The Journal of Applied Behavioral Science*, *31*(1), 91–105. doi:10.1177/0021886395311009

Framinan, J. M., Parra, C. L., Perez, P., & Montes, M. (2005). Guidelines for conducting Business Process Modelling as support to healthcare process management. In *Int. Conf. on Industrial Engineering and Systems Management (ISEM)*.

Franklin, M., & Zdonik, S. (1997). A framework for scalable dissemination-based systems. In *Proceedings of the 12th ACM OOPSLA*, *32* (pp. 94-105).

Frechtling, J. (1997). User-friendly handbook for mixed method evaluation [Ausdruck im Eval-Ordner]. Retrieved May 2005, from http://www.ehr.nsf.gov/EHR/REC/pubs/NSF97-153/start.htm

Freeman, R. E. (1984). *Strategic management: A stakeholder approach*. Cambridge, MA: Ballinger Publishing Co.

Frenzel, C. W., & Frenzel, J. C. (2004). *Management of Information Technology*, (4th ed.). Boston: Thomson.

Friedman, C., & Wyatt, J. C. (1997). Evaluation methods in medical informatics. New York: Springer.

Fruhling, A., & Lee, S. (2004, September). Designing trustworthy e-health services for rural consumers. [*American Medical Informatics Association Proceedings*.]. *Medinfo*, 2004.

Frykberg, E., & Tepas, J. J. III. (1988). Terrorist Bombings: Lessons Learned from Belfast to Beirut. *Annals of Surgery*, *208*(5), 569–576. doi:10.1097/00000658-198811000-00005

Fujimoto, R. M. (1990). Parallel discrete event simulation. *Communications of the ACM*, *33*(10), 30–53. doi:10.1145/84537.84545

Fujimoto, R. M. (1999). Parallel and distributed simulation. In P. A. Farrington, H. B. Nembhard, D. T. Sturrock, & G. W. Evans, (Eds.), *Proceedings of the 31st Winter Simulation Conference*, (pp. 122– 131). New York: ACM Press.

Fujimoto, R. M. (1999). *Parallel and distributed simulation systems*. New York: John Wiley & Sons.

Fujimoto, R. M. (2001). Parallel and distributed simulation systems. In B. A. Peters, J. S. Smith, D. J. Medeiros, & M. W. Rohrer (eds.), *Proceedings of the 33rd Winter Simulation Conference*, (pp. 147-157). Washington, DC: IEEE Computer Society.

Fujimoto, R. M. (2003). Distributed simulation systems. In S. Chick, P. J. Sánchez, D. Ferrin, & D. J. Morrice (Eds.) *Proceedings of the 35th Winter Simulation Conference*, (pp. 124-134). Winter Simulation Conference, USA.

Fujimoto, R. M., & Weatherly, R. M. (1996). Time management in the DoD high level architecture. In *Proceedings of the 10th Workshop on Parallel and Distributed Simulation Workshop* (pp. 60-67). Washington, DC: IEEE Computer Society.

Galanter, W.L., Didomenico, R.J., & Polikaitis, A. (2005). A trial of automated decision support alerts for contraindicated medications using computerized physician order entry. *Journal of the American Medical Informatics Association, 12*(3), 269–274.

Galpottage, P. A. B., & Norris, A. C. (2005). Patient consent principles and guidelines for e-consent: a New Zealand perspective. *Health Informatics Journal, 11*(1), 5–18. doi:10.1177/1460458205050681

Gambetta, D. (Ed.). (1988). *Trust: making and breaking cooperative relations*. Oxford, UK: Department of Sociology, University of Oxford.

Gamma, E., Helm, R., Johnson, R., & Vlissides, J. (1995). *Design Patterns: Elements of Re-usable Object-Oriented Software*. Reading, MA: Addison – Wesley.

Gan, B. P., Lendermann, P., Low, M. Y. H., Turner, S. J., Wang, X., & Taylor, S. J. E. (2005). Interoperating Autosched AP using the high level architecture. In M. E. Kuhl, N. M. Steiger, F. B. Armstrong, & J. A. Joines (Eds.) *Proceedings of the 37th Winter Simulation Conference*, (pp. 394-401). Winter Simulation Conference, USA.

Gans, D., Kralewski, J., Hammons, T., & Dowd, B. (2005). Medical groups' adoption of electronic health records and information systems. *Health Affairs (Project Hope), 24*(5), 1323-1333.

Gans, G. (n.d.). *An Agent-Based Modeling- and Simulation-Methodology for Strategic Inter-Organizational Networks*. Ph.D. Thesis, RWTH Aachen University, Germany.

Gans, G., Jarke, M., Kethers, S., & Lakemeyer, G. (2003). Continuous requirements management for organisation networks: a (dis)trust-based approach. *Requirements Engineering*, *8*(1), 4–22. doi:10.1007/s00766-002-0163-8

Gao, Tia, Logan K. Hauenstein, Alex Alm Daivid Crawford, Cassius K. Sims, Azmat Hussain & Daivid M. White (2006). Vital Signs Monitoring and Patient Tracking Over a Wireless Network. *Johns Hopkins APL technological Digest, 27*(1), 66–74.

Garawi, S., Istepanian, R. S. H., & Abu-Rgheff, M. A. (2006). 3G wireless communications for mobile robotic tele-ultrasonography systems. *IEEE Communications Magazine*, *44*(4), 91–96. doi:10.1109/MCOM.2006.1632654

Garritty, C., & Emam, K. E. (2006). Who's Using PDAs? Estimates of PDA Use by Health Care Providers: A Systematic Review of Surveys. *Journal of Medical Internet Research*, *8*(2), e7. doi:10.2196/jmir.8.2.e7

Gawande, A. A., Thomas, E. J., & Zinner, M. J. (1999). The incidence and nature of surgical adverse events in Colorado and Utah in 1992. *Surgery*, *126*(1), 66–75. doi:10.1067/msy.1999.98664

Geddes, J., Lloyd, S., Simpson, A., Rossor, M., Fox, N., Hill, D., et al. (2005). NeuroGrid: using grid technology to advance neuroscience. In *Proceedings of the 18th IEEE symposium on computer-based medical systems*, (pp. 570-572). Washington, DC: IEEE Computer Society.

Gehl, J. (2001). *Life between buildings*. Copenhagen, Denmark: Arkitektens Forlag.

Geringer, J. M., & Hebert, L. (1991). Measuring Performance of International Joint Ventures. *Journal of International Business Studies*, *22*(2), 249–263. doi:10.1057/palgrave.jibs.8490302

Giddens, A. (1984). *The constitutions of society: Outline of the theory of structuration*. Berkeley University of California Press.

Gill, P. J. (1999). Application Development: Business Snapshot -Business Modeling Tools Help Companies Align Their Business and Technology Goals. *Information Week*.

Gillott, I. (2002, April). The ROI benefits of wireless. *Communications News, 39,* 6.

Giovas, P., Thomakos, D., Papazachou, O., & Papadoyannis, D. (2006). Medical aspects of prehospital cardiac telecare. In R.H. Istepanian, S. Laxminarayan,C.S. Pattichis, (Eds.), *M-Health: Emerging Mobile Health Systems*, (pp. 389-400)New York: Springer.

Gipps, P. J. (1986). The role of computer graphics in validating simulation models. *Mathematics and Computers in Simulation*, *28*, 285–289. doi:10.1016/0378-4754(86)90049-2

Glasgow, R. E. (2007). E-Health evaluation and dissemination research. *American Journal of Preventive Medicine*, *32*(5Suppl), S119–S126. doi:10.1016/j.amepre.2007.01.023

Glasser, J. P. (2002). *The strategic application of information technology in health care organizations*, (2nd ed.). San Francisco, CA: Jossey-Bass.

Glatard, T., Montagnat, J., & Pennec, X. (2005). Grid-enabled workflows for data intensive medical applications, pp. 537-542. In *Proceedings of the 18th IEEE symposium on computer-based medical systems*, (pp. 570-572). Washington, DC: IEEE Computer Society.

Goldsmith, J., Blumenthal, D., & Rishel, W. (2003). Federal health information policy: A case of arrested development. *Health Affairs, 22*(4), 44–55.

Gonzalez-Velez, V., & Gonzalez-Velez, H. (2005). A grid-based stochastic simulation of unitary and membrane Ca/sup 2+/ currents in spherical cells. In *Proceedings of the 18th IEEE symposium on computer-based medical systems*, (pp. 171-176). Washington, DC: IEEE Computer Society.

Goodhue, D. (1995). Understanding user evaluations of information systems. Management Science, 41(12), 1827-44.

Gorlenko, L., & Merrick, R. (2003). No wires attached: Usability challenges in the connected mobile world. *IBM Systems Journal, 42*(4), 639-651.

Goyal, S., & Giri, B. (2001). Recent trends in modeling of deteriorating inventory. *European Journal of Operational Research*, *134*(1), 1–16. doi:10.1016/S0377-2217(00)00248-4

Grant, A., Plante, I., & Leblanc, F. (2002). The TEAM methodology for the evaluation of information systems in biomedicine. Computers in Biology and Medicine, 32(3), 195-207.

Grant, M., Preece, S. B., & Baetz, M. C. (1999). Dangers of Dependence: The Impact of Strategic Alliance Use by Small Technology-based Firms. *Journal of Small Business Management*, *37*(2), 20–29.

Gray, N. J., Klein, J. D., Noyce, P. R., Sesselberg, T. S., & Cantrill, J. A. (2005). Health information-seeking behavior in adolescence: The place of the Internet. *Social Science & Medicine, 60*(7), 1467-1478.

Green, S., & Ould, M. (2006). *The primacy of process architecture*. Retrieved Nov 22nd from http://www.csm.uwe.ac.uk/~sjgreen/paper2.pdf

Greenbaum, J., & Kyng, M. E. (1991). *Design at work: Cooperative design of computer systems*. Hillsdale, NJ: Lawrence Erlbaum.

Greene, J., & McClintock, C. (1985). Triangulation in evaluation: Design and analysis issues. Evaluation Review, 9(5), 523-545.

Greenfield, S., & Kaplan, S. H. (2004). Creating a culture of quality: The remarkable transformation of the department of veterans affairs health care system. *Annals of Internal Medicine, 141*(4), 316-318.

Grémy, F., & Degoulet, P. (1993). Assessment of health information technology: Which questions for which systems? Proposal for a taxonomy. Medical Informatics, 18(3), 185-193.

Grover, V., Jeong, S. R., & Segars, A. H. (1996). Information systems effectiveness: The construct space and patterns of applications. *Information & Management*, *31*(4). doi:10.1016/S0378-7206(96)01079-8

Gruber, T. R. (1993). A translation approach to portable ontology specifications. *Knowledge Acquisition*, *5*(2), 199–220. doi:10.1006/knac.1993.1008

Guerlain, S., Hayes, C., Pritchett, A., & Smith, P. (2001). Exercises/techniques for teaching cognitive systems engineering. In *Proceedings of the Human Factors and Ergonomics Society 45th Annual Meeting.*

Gulati, R. (1998). Alliances and networks. *Strategic Management Journal*, *19*(4), 293–317. doi:10.1002/(SICI)1097-0266(199804)19:4<293::AID-SMJ982>3.0.CO;2-M

Gulla, V. (2005). *Telemedicine potential business models*. Retrieved from http://www.aditechsrl.com/doc/WP_Telemedicine_potential_Business.pdf

Gulla, V. (2005, November 19-21). *The telemedicine market a fast growing technology.* Paper presented at the E-Merging/E-Learning conference, Dubai.

Gulla, V. (2006). *Broadband in Europe markets and trends*. Paper presented at the *WCIT 2004, Information Technology Conference,* Athens, May 19-21, 2004.

Gulla, V. (2006, November). *Understanding DSL developments*. DSL Forum Market Committee Chairman–Carriers World CEE Conference Acts, Budapest.

Gulla, V. (2007, June). *Telemedicine is a driver for quality of life improving broadband application*. Paper presented at the 3rd Croatian & International Congress on Telemedicine and e-Health. Retrieved from http://www.aditechsrl.com/doc/WP_Absstract_proposal_handbook%20.pdf

Gururajan, R., et al. (2005). *Drivers and Barriers to adoption of wireless handheld system in WA healthcare: Selected views*. Paper presented at the HIC 2005, Melbourne, Australia.

Gururajan, R., Moloney, C., & Kerr, D. (2005). *Drivers for wireless handheld technology: views from Queensland nurses*. Paper presented at the Australian Business & Behavioural Sciences Association (ABBSA) Conference, Cairns, Australia.

Gururajan, R., Quaddus, M., Fink, D., Vuori, T., & Soar, J. (2005). *Drivers and Barriers to adoption of wireless handheld system in WA healthcare: Selected views*. Paper presented at the HIC 2005, Melbourne, Australia.

Gururajan, R., Toleman, M., & Soar, J. (2004). *Necessity for a new technology acceptance model to predict adoption of wireless technology in healthcare*. Paper presented at the Let's Make a Difference with Health ICT, HIC Conference, July 25-27.

Gurwitz, J. H., Field, T. S., Avorn, J., McCormick, D., Jain, S., & Eckler, M. (2000). Incidence and preventability of adverse drug events in nursing homes. *The American Journal of Medicine*, *109*(2), 87–94. doi:10.1016/S0002-9343(00)00451-4

Gurwitz, J. H., Field, T. S., Harrold, I. R., Rotthschild, J., Debellis, K., & Seger, A. C. (2003). Incidence and preventability of adverse drug events in among older persons in the ambulatory setting. *Journal of the American Medical Association*, *289*(9), 1107–1116. doi:10.1001/jama.289.9.1107

Gustafson, D., & Wyatt, J. (2004). Evaluation of e-health systems and services. *British Medical Journal*, *328*, 1150. doi:10.1136/bmj.328.7449.1150

Gustafson, D., Hawkins, R., Pingree, S., McTavish, F., Arora, N., & Salner, J. (2001). Effect of computer support on younger women with breast cancer. *Journal of General Internal Medicine*, *16*, 435–445. doi:10.1046/j.1525-1497.2001.016007435.x

Hall, E., Vawdrey, D. K., Knutson, C. D., & Archibald, J. K. (2003). Enabling remote access to personal electronic medical records. *IEEE Engineering in Medicine and Biology Magazine*, *22*(3), 133–139. doi:10.1109/MEMB.2003.1213636

Hameed, K. (2003). The application of mobile computing and technology to health care services. *Telematics and Informatics*, *20*, 99–106. doi:10.1016/S0736-5853(02)00018-7

Hammer, M., & Champy, J. M. (1993). *Reengineering the corporation: a manifesto for business revolution*. London: Nicholas Brealey Publishing, Allen and Urwin.

Hammersley, M., & Atkinson, P. (1983). *Ethnography: Principles in Practice*. London: Tavistock.

Hammersley, M., & Atkinson, P. (1995). *Ethnography. Principles in practice* (2nd Ed.). London, Routledge.

Han, Y. Y., Carcillo, J. A., Venkataraman, S. T., Robert, S. B., Clark, R., & Watson, S. (2005). Unexpected increased mortality after implementation of a commercially sold computerized physician order entry system. *Pediatrics*, *116*(6), 1506–1512. doi:10.1542/peds.2005-1287

Hanlon, G., Strangleman, T., Goode, J., Luff, D., O'Cathain, A., & Greatbatch, D. (2005). Knowledge, technology and nursing: The case of NHS direct. *Human Relations*, *58*, 147–171. doi:10.1177/0018726705052179

Hans, O., Rizo, C., Enkin, M., & Jadad, A. (2005, February 24). What is e-health? A systematic review of published definitions. *Journal of Medical Internet Research*.

Hansen, D. L., Derry, H. A., Resnick, P. J., & Richardson, C. R. (2003). Adolescents Searching for Health Information on the Internet: An Observational Study. *Journal of Medical Internet Research*, *5*(4), e25. doi:10.2196/jmir.5.4.e25

Harkke, V. (2005). *Physicians' usage experiences of a mobile information system*. 38th Hawaii International Conference on System Sciences, Hawaii.

Harmon, P. (2003). "Business Process Change: A Manager's guide to improving redesigning, and automating processes". Amsterdam, Boston: Morgan Kaufmann.

Harn, L. (1994). Group-oriented (t, n) threshold digital signature scheme and digital multisignature. *IEE Proceedings. Computers and Digital Techniques*, *141*(5), 307–313. doi:10.1049/ip-cdt:19941293

Harris Interactive. (2001). The increasing impact of eHealth on physician behavior. *HarrisInteractive Health Care News*, *1*(31), 1–14.

Harris Interactive. (2001). U.S. trails other English speaking countries in use of electronic medical records and electronic prescribing. *HarrisInteractive Health Care News*, *1*(28), 1–3.

Harris Interactive. (2002). European physicians especially in Sweden, Netherlands and Denmark lead U.S. in use of electronic medical records. *HarrisInteractive Health Care News, 2*(16), 1–3.

Harris Interactive. (2002). The future use of the Internet in 4 countries in relation to prescriptions, physician communication and health information. *HarrisInteractive Health Care News, 2*(13), 1–4.

Harris Interactive. (2003). eHealth influence continues to grow as usage of the Internet by physicians and patients increases. *HarrisInteractive Health Care News, 3*(6), 1–7.

Harris Interactive. (2005). Many nationwide believe in the potential benefits of electronic medical records and are interested in online communications with physicians. *The Wall Street Journal Online Health Care Poll, 4*(4), 1–5.

Harrison, M. I., & Shirom, A. (1999). *Organizational diagnosis and assessment: Bridging theory and practice*. Thousand Oaks, CA: Sage.

Harrison, M., Koppel, R., & Bar-Lev, S. (2007). Reducing unintended consequences of health information technology through interactive sociotechnical analysis. *Journal of the American Medical Informatics Association, 14*(5), 542–549. doi:10.1197/jamia.M2384

Hartzband, P., & Groopman, J. (2008). Off the record--avoiding the pitfalls of going electronic. *The New England Journal of Medicine, 358*(16), 1656-1658.

Health Care Financing Administration. (1997). Medicare and Medicaid Programs; hospital conditions of participation; provider agreements and supplier approval. *Federal Register, 62*(244), 66726–66757.

Healthcare Information and Management Systems Society. (2006). *A desire for change: Strong leadership required in the EMR-EHR Revolution*. Retrieved on May 23, 2007, from http://www.himss.org/content/files/davies/Davies_WP_Leadership.pdf

Heathfield, H., Hudson, P., Kay, S., Mackay, L., Marley, T., Nicholson, L., et al. (1999). Issues in the multi-disciplinary assessment of healthcare information systems. Assessment of Healthcare Information Technology & People, 12(3), 253-275.

Heathfield, H., Pitty, D., & Hanka, R. (1998). Evaluating information technology in health care: Barriers and challenges. British Medical Journal, 316, 1959-1961.

Hendrich, A., Chow, M. P., Skierczynski, B. A., & Lu, Z. (2008). A 36-hospital time and motion study: how do medical-surgical nurses spend their time? *The Permanente Journal, 12*(3), 25–34.

Henwood, F., Wyatt, S., Hart, A., & Smith, J. (2003). Ignorance is bliss sometimes: constraints on the emergence of the "informed patient" in the changing landscape of health information. *Sociology of Health & Illness, 25*(6), 589–607. doi:10.1111/1467-9566.00360

Herbst, K., Littlejohns, P., Rawlinson, J., Collinson, M., & Wyatt, J. C. (1999). Evaluating computerized health information systems: hardware, software and human ware: experiences from the Northern Province, South Africa. *Journal of Public Health Medicine, 21*, 305–310. doi:10.1093/pubmed/21.3.305

Herxheimer, A., McPherson, A., Miller, R., Shepperd, S., Yaphe, J., & Ziebland, S. (2000). Database of patients' experiences (DIPEx): a multi-media approach to sharing experiences and information. *Lancet, 355*(9214), 1540–1543. doi:10.1016/S0140-6736(00)02174-7

Heymann, D., & Rodier, G. (2004). Global surveillance, national surveillance, and SARS. *Emerging Infectious Diseases Journal, 10*(2). Retrieved December 1, 2006, from http://origin.cdc.gov/ncidod/EID/vol10no2/03-1038.htm.

Hill, R. C., & Hellriegel, D. (1994). Critical Contingencies in Joint Venture Management: Some Lessons from Managers. *Organization Science, 5*(4), 594–607. doi:10.1287/orsc.5.4.594

Hillestad, R., Bigelow, J., Bower, A., Girosi, F., Meili, R, Scoville, R., et al. (2005). Can electronic medical record systems transform health care? Potential health benefits, savings, and costs. *Health Affairs, 24*(5), 1103–1117.

HIMSS 13th annual HIMSS leadership survey. (2002). Retrieved from http://www.himss.org/2002survey

Hing, E. S., Burt, C. W., & Woodwell, D. A. (2007). Electronic medical record use by office-based physicians and their practices: United states, 2006. *Advance Data, (393)*(393), 1-7.

Hippel, E. (2001). Innovation by user communities: Learning from open source software. *MIT Sloan Management Review, 42*(4), 82.

Hisham, S., & Edwards, A. D. N. (2007). Aging and its Implications for Elderly Web Experience. In S. Kurniawan & P. Zaphiris (Eds.) *Advances in Universal Web Design and Evaluation: Research, Trends and Opportunities* (pp. 97-114). Hershey, PA: IGI Global.

Hofstede, G. (1980). Culture's Consequences: International Differences in Work-Related Values. Beverly Hills, CA: Sage.

Hollocks, B. W. (2006). Forty years of discrete-event simulation - a personal reflection. *The Journal of the Operational Research Society, 57*(12), 1383–1399. doi:10.1057/palgrave.jors.2602128

Holt, D. H., & Wigginton, K. W. (2002). *International Management* (2nd Ed.). Mason, OH: Thomson Southwestern.

Homer, C. J., Forbes, P., Horvitz, L., Peterson, L. E., Wypij, D., & Heinrich, P. (2005). Impact of a quality improvement program on care and outcomes for children with asthma. *Archives of Pediatrics & Adolescent Medicine, 159*, 464–469. doi:10.1001/archpedi.159.5.464

Honigman, B., Lee, J., & Rothschild, J. (2001). Using computerized data to identify adverse drug events in outpatients. *Journal of the American Medical Informatics Association, 8*, 254–266.

Horan, T. A., Tule, B., & Hilton, B. N. (2006). Understanding physician use of online systems: An empirical assessment of an electronic disability evaluation system. In T.A.M. Spil & R.W.Schuring (Eds.), *E-Health Systems Diffusion and Use: The Innovation, the User and the USE IT Model.* London: Idea Group Publishing.

Horan, T. A., Tulu, B., Hilton, B., & Burton, J. (2004). *Use of online systems in clinical medical assessments: An analysis of physician acceptance of online disability evaluation systems.* 37th Hawaii International Conference on System Sciences, Hawaii.

Horan, T., Abhichandani, T., & Rayalu, R. (2006). Assessing user satisfaction of e-government services: Development and testing of quality-in-use satisfaction with advanced traveler information systems (ATIS). *In Proceedings of the 39th Hawaii International Conference on System Sciences.*

Houghton, J. (2002). Information Technology and the Revolution in Healthcare. Working paper 4, Centre for Strategic Economic Studies, Victoria University of Technology, Australia. Retrieved February 1, 2008 from http://www.cfses.com/documents/pharma/04-IT_and_Healthcare.pdfHuang, X., Huang, L. & Li, M. (2006). Grid-enabled medical image processing application system based on OGSA-DAI techniques. In *Proceedings of the International workshops on advanced Web, network technologies and Applications*, (pp. 460-464). In Shen, H. T., Li, J., Li, M., Ni, J. & Wang, W. (eds.). (LNCS, Vol. 3842). Berlin, Germany: Springer-Verlag.

Housel, B. C., Samaras, G., & Lindquist, D.B. (1998). WebExpress: A client/intercept based system for optmising Web browsing in a wireless environment. *ACM/Baltzer MONET, 3*(4), 419- 431.

Howard, A., Gururajan, R., Hafeez-Baig, A., & Howard, S. (2006). *Clinical Usefulness of Wireless Technology in Healthcare: An Indian Study.* Paper presented at the Australasian Conference on Information Systems, University of South Australia, Australia.

Howard, M., Vidgen, R., & Powell, P. (2003). Overcoming stakeholder barriers in the automotive industry: Building to order with extra-organizational systems. *Journal of Information Technology, 18*, 27-43.

Howcroft, D., & Trauth, E. M. (2005). *Handbook of critical information systems research theory and application.* Cheltenham, UK: Edward Elgar Publishing.

Hu, P. J., Chau, P. Y. K., & Liu Sheng, O. R. (2002). Adoption of telemedicine technology by health care organisations: An exploratory study. *Journal of Organizational Computing and Electronic Commerce*, *12*(3), 197–222. doi:10.1207/S15327744JOCE1203_01

Hu, P. J., Chau, P. Y. K., & Tam, K. Y. (1999). Examining the technology acceptance model using physician acceptance of telemedicine technology. *Journal of Management Information Systems*, *16*(2), 91–112.

Hufnagel, E. M., & Conca, C. (1994). Use response data: The potential for errors and biases. *Information Systems Research*, *5*, 48–73. doi:10.1287/isre.5.1.48

Huntington, P., Nicholas, D., Homewood, J., Polydoratou, P., Gunter, B., Russell, C., et al. (2004). The general public's use of (and attitudes towards) interactive, personal digital health information and advisory services. *Journal of Documentation, 60*(3), 245-265.

Hyder, A. S., & Abraha, D. (2004). Product and Skills Development in Small-and Medium-sized High-tech Firms through International Strategic Alliances. *Singapore Management Review*, *26*(2), 1–24.

IEEE. 1516 (2000). *IEEE standard for modelling and simulation (M&S) high level architecture (HLA)*. New York: Institute of Electrical and Electronics Engineers.

Iluyemi, A., Fitch, C., Parry, D., & Briggs, J. (2007). *Health information system for community-based health workers: A case for mobile and wireless technologies.* Paper presented at the IST-Africa, Maputo Mozambique.

Imielinski, T., & Viswanathan, S. (1994). Adaptive wireless information systems. In *Proceedings of the SIGDBS* (pp. 19-41).

Imielinski, T., Viswanathan, S., & Badrinath, B. R. (1994). Energy efficient indexing on air. In *Proceedings of the ACM Sigmod* (pp. 25-36).

Indulska, M., Chong, S., Bandara, W., & Sadiq, S. (2006). *Major Issues in Business Process Management: An Australian Perspective*. Paper presented at the Australian Conference on Information Systems (ACIS 2006).

Institute for Safe Medication Practices. Over-reliance on computer systems may place patients at great risk. *ISMP Medication Safety Alert, Feb. 12, 1999.* Huntingdon Valley, PA: ISMP.

Institute of Medicine. (2001). *Crossing the quality chasm: A new health system for the 21st century.* Washington, D.C.: National Academy Press.

International Ergonomics Association. (2006). *The discipline of ergonomics*. Retrieved on August 8, 2006, from http://www.iea.cc/ergonomics/

International Telecommunications Union. (2006). *Bhutan to be testbed for ITU's e-post venture with universal postal union.* Retrieved April 20, 2006, from http://www.itu.int/newsarchive/press_releases/2002/10.html.

ISACA. (2007). *COBIT: Control objectives for information and related technology.* Retrieved on November 11, 2007, from www.isaca.org/cobit/

Islam MT, H. Y., Waxman R, Bhuiyan AB. (2006). Implementation of emergency obstetric care training in Bangladesh: Lessons learned. *Reproductive Health Matters, 14*(27), 61-72.

ISO-20000. (2007). *ISO 20000.* Retrieved on August 13, 2007, from http://en.wikipedia.org/wiki/ISO/IEC_20000

ISO-9126. (2007). *The ISO 9126 standard.* Retrieved on August 13, 2007, from http://en.wikipedia.org/wiki/ISO_9126

Issa, O., Grégoire, J.-C., Belala, Y., & Wong, J. (2008). 3G Embedded Communication System for Medical Applications. In *IEEE International Systems Conference (SysCon 2008*(pp. 1–8). 7–10 April 2008

Ivers, B., & Gururajan, R. (2006). *Management issues in telecommunications: videoconferencing & telehealth.* Paper presented at the International Conference on Recent Trends in Information Systems Proceedings, India.

Jakobovits, R., Rosse, C., & Brinkley, J. (2002). WIRM an open source toolkit for building biomedical Web applications. *J Am Med Inform Assoc, 9*(6), 557-570.

Jarke, M., Klamma, R., Lakemeyer, G., & Schmitz, D. (2008). Continuous, Requirements-Driven Support for Organizations, Networks, and Communities. In *3rd Int. i* Workshop*, CEUR Workshop Proceedings (Vol. 322, pp. 47-50).

Jarvinen, O. (2005). *Privacy management of e-health. Content analysis of 39 U.S. health providers' privacy policies*. Turku School of Economics and Business Administration, Series A.

Jaspers, M. W. M., Knaup, P., & Schmidt, D. (2006). The computerized patient record: Where do we stand? *Methods of Information in Medicine*, *45*, 29–39.

Jayasuriya, R. (1997). Evaluating health information systems: An assessment of frameworks. *Australian Health Review*, *20*(3), 68–85.

Jayasuriya, R. (1998). Determinants of microcomputer technology use: Implications for education and training of health staff. *International Journal of Medical Informatics*, *50*, 187–194. doi:10.1016/S1386-5056(98)00067-7

Jefferson, D. R. (1985). Virtual Time. *ACM Transactions on Programming Languages and Systems*, *7*(3), 404–425. doi:10.1145/3916.3988

Jensen, K. (1997). A brief introduction to coloured Petri Nets, pp. 203-208. (LNCS Vol. 1217).Berlin, Germany: Springer-Verlag.

Jensen, T. B., & Aanestad, M. (2007). Hospitality and Hostility in Hospitals: A Case Study of an ERP Adoption Among Surgeons. *European Journal of Information Systems*, *16*(6), 672–680. doi:10.1057/palgrave.ejis.3000713

Jerant, A., Schlachta, L., Epperly, T. D., & Barnes Camp, J. (1998). Back to the Future: The Telemedicine House Call. *Family Practice Management*, *5*(1) Retrieved Jan 23, 2008, from http://www.aafp.org/fpm/980100fm/lead.html

Jha, A. K., Ferris, T. G., Donelan, K., DesRoches, C., Shields, A., & Rosenbaum, S. (2006). How common are electronic health records in the United States? A summary of the evidence. *Health Affairs*, *25*, w496–w507. doi:10.1377/hlthaff.25.w496

Jha, A. K., Kuperman, G. J., Teich, J. M., & Leape, L. L. (1998). Identifying adverse drug events: Development of a computer-based monitor and comparison with chart review and stimulated voluntary report. *Journal of the American Medical Informatics Association*, *5*, 305–314.

Jha, A. K., Perlin, J. B., Kizer, K. W., & Dudley, R. A. (2003). Effect of the transformation of the veterans affairs health care system on the quality of care. *The New England Journal of Medicine*, *348*(22), 2218-2227.

Jithesh, P. V., Kelly, N., Donachy, P., Harmer, T., Perrott, R., McCurley, M., et al. (2005). GeneGrid: grid based solution for bioinformatics application integration and experiment execution. In *Proceedings of the 18th IEEE symposium on computer-based medical systems*, pp. 523-528. Washington, DC: IEEE Computer Society.

Johnson, G. J., & Ambrose, P. J. (2006). Neo-Tribes: The Power and Potential of Online Communities in Health Care. *Communications of the ACM*, *49*(1), 107–113. doi:10.1145/1107458.1107463

Johnson, J. A., & Bootman, J. L. (1995). Drug-related morbidity and mortality: A cost of illness model. *Archives of Internal Medicine*, *155*, 1949–1956. doi:10.1001/archinte.155.18.1949

Johnson, J. L., Cullen, J. B., Sakano, T., & Takenouchi, H. (1996). Setting the Stage for Trust, and Strategic Integration in Japanese-U.S. Cooperative Alliances. *Journal of International Business Studies*, *27*(4), 981–1004. doi:10.1057/palgrave.jibs.8490160

Johnson, K. B. (2001). Barriers That Impede the Adoption of Pediatric Information Technology. *Archives of Pediatrics & Adolescent Medicine*, *155*, 1374–1379.

Johnston, D., Pan, E., Walker, J., Bates, D. W., & Middleton, B. (2004). *Center for Information Technology Leadership: Patient Safety in the Physician's Office: Assessing the Value of Ambulatory CPOE.* Oakland, CA: California HealthCare Foundation.

Johnston, G., Crombie, I. K., Alder, E. M., Davies, H. T. O., & Millard, A. (2000). Reviewing audit: barriers and facilitating factors for effective clinical audit. *Quality & Safety in Health Care*, *9*, 23–36.

Johnston, M., Langton, K., Haynes, R., & Mathieu, A. (1994). Effects of computer-based clinical decision support systems on clinician performance and patient outcome: A critical appraisal of research. Annuals of Internal Medicine, 120, 135-142.

Jonassen, D. H. *Technology as cognitive tools: Learners as designers*. Retrieved in 2007, from http://itech1.coe.uga.edu/itforum/paper1/paper1.html

Jones, D. M., Fenner, J. W., Berti, G., Kruggel, F., Mehrem, R. A., Backfrieder, W., et al. (2004). The GEMSS Grid: An evolving HPC environment for medical applications. In *Proceedings of HealthGrid 2004*. Retrieved February 1, 2008 from http://www.ccrl-nece.de/gemss/Reports/Jones-healthgrid2004.pdf

Josefsson, U. (2006). Patients' Online Information Seeking Behavior. In M. Murero and R. E. Rice (Eds.), *The Internet and Healthcare: Theory, Research, and Practice* (pp. 127-147). Mahwah, NJ: Lawrence Erlbaum Associates.

Joy, S., & Benrubi, G. (2004). Personal digital assistant use in Florida in obstetrics and gynaecology residency programs. *Southern Medical Journal*, *97*(5), 430–433. doi:10.1097/00007611-200405000-00002

Jun, J. B., Jacobson, S. H., & Swisher, J. R. (1999). Application of discrete-event simulation in health care clinics: A survey. *The Journal of the Operational Research Society*, *50*(2), 109–123.

Kaiser Family Foundation. (2005). *E-health and the elderly: How seniors use the Internet for health information*. Washington, DC: Kaiser Family Foundation.

Kanagarajah, A. K., Lindsey, P., Miller, A., & Parker, D. (2006). An explorarion into the uses of Agent-Based modeling to Improve Quality of Health Care. In Minai, A., Braha, D. and Bar-Yam, Y., *Proceedings of the 6th International Conference on Complex Systems. 6th International Conference on Complex Systems*, Boston, MA, (1-10). 25-30 June, 2006. Cambridge, MA: The New England Complex Systems Institute.

Kantor, G., Wilson, W., & Midgley, A. (2003). Open source software and the primary care EMR. *Journal of the American Medical Informatics Association*, *10*(6), 616.

Kaplan, B. (2001). Evaluating informatics applications: Clinical decision support systems literature review. International Journal of Medical Informatics, 64, 15-37.

Kaplan, B., & Shaw, N. (2002). People, organizational and social issues: Evaluation as an exemplar. In R. Haux & C. Kulikowski (Eds.), Yearbook of medical informatics 2002 (pp. 91-102). Stuttgart, Germany: Schattauer.

Karahanna, E., Straub, D. W., & Chervany, N. L. (1999). Information technology adoption across time: A cross-sectional comparison of pre-adoption and post-adoption beliefs . *MIS Quarterly*, *23*(2), 183–213. doi:10.2307/249751

Karlsson, M., & Olsson, L. (2001). pRTI 1516 - rationale and design. In *Proceedings of the 2001 Fall Simulation Interoperability Workshop* (01F-SIW-038). Orlando, FL: Simulation Interoperability Standards Organization.

Karnon, J. (2003). Alternative decision modelling techniques for the evaluation of health care technologies: Markov processes versus discrete event simulation. *Health Economics*, *12*(10), 837–848. doi:10.1002/hec.770

Karsh, B.-T., Holden, R. J., Alper, S. J., & Or, C. K. L. (2006). A human factors engineering paradigm for patient safety: Designing to support the performance of the healthcare professional. *Quality and safety in health care*, *15*(suppl_1), i59-i65.

Katsaliaki, K. (2008). Cost effective practices in the blood service sector. *Health Policy*.

Katsaliaki, K., & Brailsford, S. B. (2007). Using Simulation to Improve the U.K. Blood Supply Chain. *The Journal of the Operational Research Society*, *58*, 219–227.

Katsaliaki, K., Mustafee, N., Taylor, S.J.E., Brailsford, S. (2007). Comparing Conventional and Distributed Approaches to Simulation in a Complex Supply-Chain Health System. *Journal of the Operation Research Society*.

Kaushal, R., Barker, K. N., & Bates, D. W. (2001). How can information technology improve patient safety and reduce medication errors in children's healthcare? *Archives of Pediatrics & Adolescent Medicine*, *155*(9), 1002–1007.

Kaushal, R., Blumenthal, D., Poon, E. G., Jha, A. K., & Franz, C. (2005). The costs of a national health information network. *Annals of Internal Medicine, 143*, 165–173.

Kaushal, R., Shojania, K. G., & Bates, D. W. (2003). Effects of computerized physician order entry and clinical decision support systems on medication safety. *Archives of Internal Medicine, 163*, 1409–1416. doi:10.1001/archinte.163.12.1409

Kayango, M., Esquiche, E., Luna, M., Frias, G., Vega-Centeno, L., & Bailey, P. (2006). Strengthening emergency obstetric care in Ayacucho, Peru. *International Journal of Gynecology and Obstetrics, 92,* 299-307.

Kempf, G., M. Eckrich & O. Rumf (n.d.). Data Reduction in Automotive Multiplexing Systems., (SAE No. 940135, pp. 45-50).

Kethers, S. (2000). *Multi-Perspective Modeling and Analysis of Cooperation Processes*. Ph.D. Thesis, RWTH Aachen University, Germany.

Kethers, S. (2002). Capturing, Formalising, and Analysing Cooperation Processes: a Case Study. *10th European Conf. on Information Systems (ECIS)*, Gdańsk, Poland, (pp. 1113-1123).

Kethers, S., Gans, G., Schmitz, D., & Sier, D. (2005). Modelling Trust Relationships in a Healthcare Network: Experiences with the TCD Framework. *13th European Conf. on Information Systems (ECIS)*, Regensburg, Germany, (pp. 1321-1328).

Khoumbati, K., & Themistocleous, M. (2006). Integrating the IT Infrastructures in Healthcare Organisations: a Proposition of Influential Factors. *The Electronic . Journal of E-Government, 4*(1), 27–36.

Kidd, M.R. (2000). Clinical practice guidelines and the computer on your desk. *Medical Journal of Australia, 173*, 373–375.

Kistler, J.J., & Satyanarayanan, M. (1992). Disconnected operation in the code file system. *ACM Trans. on Computer Systems, 10*(1), 213-225.

Kivits, J. (2006). Informed Patients and the Internet. *Journal of Health Psychology, 11*(2), 269–282. doi:10.1177/1359105306061186

Kjeldskov, J., & Skov, M. B. (2007). Studying usability in sitro: Simulating real world phenomena in controlled environments. *International Journal of Human-Computer Interaction, 22*(1-2), 7–37. doi:10.1207/s15327590ijhc2201-02_2

Klamma, R., Spaniol, M., Cao, Y., & Jarke, M. (2006). Pattern-based cross media social network analysis for technology enhanced learning in Europe. *Innovative Approaches for Learning and Knowledge Sharing, First European Conference on Technology Enhanced Learning (EC-TEL)*, Crete, Greece, Springer, LNCS 4227, (pp. 242–256).

Klapan, I. (2005). *Telemedicine*. Telemedicine Association Zagreb.

Klecun, E., & Cornford, T. (2005). A critical approach to evaluation. *European Journal of Information Systems, 14*, 229–243. doi:10.1057/palgrave.ejis.3000540

Klein, H. K., & Myers, M. D. (1999). A set of principles for conducting and evaluating interpretive field studies in information systems. *MIS Quarterly, 23*(1), 67–94. doi:10.2307/249410

Kleinke, J. D. (2005). Dot-gov: Market failure and the creation of a national health information technology system. *Health Affairs (Project Hope), 24*(5), 1246-1262.

Kling, R. (2000). Learning about information technologies and social change: The contribution of social informatics. *The Information Society, 16*(3), 217–232. doi:10.1080/01972240050133661

Kling, R., McKim, G., & King, A. (2003). A bit more to it: Scholarly communication forums as sociotechnical interaction networks. *Journal of the American Society for Information Science and Technology, 54*(1), 47–67. doi:10.1002/asi.10154

Knafl, K., & Breitmayer, B. (1991). Triangulation in qualitative research: Issues of conceptual clarity and purpose. In J. Morse (Ed.), A contemporary dialogue (pp. 226-239). Newbury Park, CA: Sage.

Knox, G. E., & Simpson, K. R. (2004). Teamwork: The fundamental building block of high reliability organizations and patient safety. In B. Youngberg & J. Hatlie (Eds.), *The patient safety handbook* (pp. 379-414). Boston: Jones and Bartleett.

Kohli, R., & Kettinger, W. J. (2004). Informating the Clan: Controlling Physicians' Costs and Outcomes. *MIS Quarterly, 27*(2), 197–235.

Kohn, L. T., Corrigan, J. M., & Donaldson, M. S. (Eds.). (1999). *To Err is Human: Building a Safer Health System*. Washington, DC: National Academy Press.

Koppel, R., Davidson, S. M., Wears, R. L., & Sinsky, C. (in press). Healthcare information technology to the rescue: Panacea, golden calf, and fat cows. In R. F. J. Waring & E. Rowley, (Eds.), *Patient safety: Critical perspectives*. Ithaca, NY: ILR Press Cornell University Press.

Koppel, R., Metlay, J. P., Cohen, A., Abaluck, B., Localio, A. R., & Kimmel, S. E. (2005). Role of computerized physician order entry systems in facilitating medication errors. *Journal of the American Medical Association, 293*(10), 1197–1203. doi:10.1001/jama.293.10.1197

Koppel, R., Wetternick, T., Telles, J. L., & Karsh, B.-T. (in press). Workarounds to barcode medication administration systems: Their occurrences, causes, and threats to patient safety. *Journal of the American Medical Informatics Association, 15(4), 408-423.*

Krippendorff, K. (2006). *The semantic turn. A new foundation for design*. New York: Taylor & Francis Group.

Krull-Naraj, K. (2004). *Information flows in patient-centred healthcare.* Barrie, Ontario.

Kuhn, R. A., & Reider, R. S. (1994). A C++ framework for developing Medical Logic Modules and an Arden Syntax compiler. *Computers in Biology and Medicine, 24*(5), 365–370. doi:10.1016/0010-4825(94)90003-5

Kuhn, T. (1962). *The structure of scientific revolutions.* Chicago: University of Chicago Press.

Kuo, F., Shen, V., Chen, T., & Lai, F. (1999). Cryptographic key assignment scheme for dynamic access control in auser hierarchy. *IEE Proceedings - Computers and Digital Techniques (Now: let Computers and Digital Techniques), 146*(5), 235-240.

Kuutti, K., Iacucci, G., & Iacucci, C. (2002). *Acting to know: Improving creativity in the design of mobile services by using performances.* Paper presented at The Fourth Conference on Creativity & Cognition, Loughborough, UK.

Kyhlbäck, H., & Persson, H. (2003). Wound care documentation project at municipal elder care. In A. Moreno & J.L. Nealon (Eds.), *Application of software agent technology in the health care domain* (pp. 125-141). Basel, Switzerland: Whitestein series in software agent technologies, Birkhäuser.

Kyng, M. (1994). Scandinavian design: Users in product development. In *Proceedings of the SIGCHI conference on Human Factors in Computing Systems: Celebrating interdependence* (pp. 3-9). New York & Boston: ACM Press.

Kyriacou, E., Pattichis, M. S., Pattichis, C. S., Panayides, A., & Pitsillides, A. (2007, February). m-Health e-Emergency Systems: Current Status and Future Directions. *IEEE Antennas and Propagation Magazine, 49*(1), 216–231. doi:10.1109/MAP.2007.371030

Kyriacou, E., Pavlopoulos, S., Berler, A., Neophytou, M., Bourka, A., Georgoulas, A., et al. (2003). Multi-purpose HealthCare Telemedicine Systems with mobile communication link support. *BioMedical Engineering OnLine, 2*(7). Retrieved 22 August, 2008 from http://www.biomedical-engineering-online.com

Lambe, C. J., Spekman, R. E., & Hunt, S. D. (2002). Alliance Competence, Resources, and Alliance Success: Conceptualization, Measurement, and Initial Test. *Journal of the Academy of Marketing Science, 30*(2), 141–158. doi:10.1177/03079459994399

Lane, D. C., Monefeldt, C., & Rosenhead, J. V. (2000). Looking in the wrong place for healthcare improvements: A system dynamics study of an accident and emergency department. *The Journal of the Operational Research Society, 51*(5), 518–531.

Lane, P. J., & Lubatkin, M. (1998). Relative Absorptive Capacity and Interorganizational Learning. *Strategic Management Journal, 19*, 461–477. doi:10.1002/(SICI)1097-0266(199805)19:5<461::AID-SMJ953>3.0.CO;2-L

Lapointe, L., Lamothe, L., & Fortin, J. (2006). The dynamics of IT adoption in a major change process in healthcare delivery. In T.A.M. Spil & R.W. Schuring (Eds.), *E-Health Systems Diffusion and Use: The Innovation, the User and the USE IT Model*. London: The Idea Group Publishing. Mingers, J. (2001). Combining IS research methods: Towards a pluralist methodology. Information Systems Research, 12(3), 240-259.

Lapointe, L., Lamothe, L., & Fortin, J. P. (2002). The dynamics of IT adoption in a major change process in healthcare delivery. In *Proceedings of the 35th HICSS Conference*, Big Island, Hawaii.

LaRosa, & Koppel, R. (2007). Evaluation of antimicrobal therapy. *Infection Control and Hospital Epidemiology, 28*(5), 551–556. doi:10.1086/513535

Larsen, M. A., & Myers, M. D. (1998). BPR Success or failure? A business Process reengineering project in the financial services industry. *Communications of the ACM*, 367–381.

Larson, P., & Janower, M. (2005). The nighthawk: Bird of paradise or albatross?. *Journal of the American College of Radiology, 2*(12), 967-970.

Latour, B. (1987). *Science in action*. Cambridge, MA: Harvard University Press.

Latour, B. (1990). Drawing things together. In M. Lynch & S. Woolgar (Eds.), *Representation in scientific practice* (pp. 19-68). Cambridge, MA: The MIT Press.

Lauer, T., Joshi, K., & Browdy, T. (2000). Use of the equity implementation model to review clinical system implementation efforts. *Journal of the American Medical Informatics Association, 7*(1).

Law, A. M. (2007). *Simulation Modelling & Analysis*. New York: McGraw-Hill International Edition.

Law, A. M., & Kelton, W. D. (2000). *Simulation Modelling and Analysis*. New York: McGraw Hill Higher Education.

Lazar, J., & Preece, J. (1999). Designing and implementing Web-based surveys. *Journal of Computer Information Systems, 39*(4), 63–67.

Lazarou, J., Pomeranz, B. H., & Corey, P. N. (1998). Incidence of adverse drug reactions in hospitalized patients: a meta-analysis of prospective studies. *Journal of the American Medical Association, 279*, 1200–1205. doi:10.1001/jama.279.15.1200

Leaning, M. (1993). The new information management and technology strategy of the NHS. *British Medical Journal, 307*(6898), 217.

Leape, L. L., & Berwick, D. M. (2005). Five years after To Err is Human: What have we learned. *Journal of the American Medical Association, 293*, 2384–2390. doi:10.1001/jama.293.19.2384

Leape, L. L., Bates, D. W., & Cullen, D. J. (1995). Systems analysis of adverse drug events. *Journal of the American Medical Association, 274*, 35–43. doi:10.1001/jama.274.1.35

Leape, L. L., Cullen, D. J., & Clapp, M. D. (1999). Pharmacist participation on physician rounds and adverse drug events in the intensive care unit. *Journal of the American Medical Association, 272*, 267–270. doi:10.1001/jama.282.3.267

Lee, K. S., Lim, G. H., & Tan, S. J. (1999). Dealing with Resource Disadvantage: Generic Strategies for SMEs. *Small Business Economics, 12*(4), 299–311. doi:10.1023/A:1008085310245

Lee, M.-C., & Jones, A. M. (2004). How Did Dentists Respond to the Introduction of Global Budgets in Taiwan? An Evaluation Using Individual Panel Data. *International Journal of Health Care Finance and Economics, 4*(4), 307–326. doi:10.1023/B:IHFE.0000043760.57999.36

Leimeister, J. M., & Krcmar, H. (2006). Designing and Implementing Virtual Patient Support Communities: A German Case Study. In M. Murero and R. E. Rice (Eds.), *The Internet and Healthcare: Theory, Research, and Practice* (pp. 255-276). Mahwah, NJ: Lawrence Erlbaum Associates.

Lenhart, A., Horrigan, J., Rainie, L., Allen, K., Boyce, A., Madden, M., et al. (2003). *The ever-shifting Internet population. A new look at Internet access and the digital divide.* Washington, D.C.: Pew Internet & American Life Project.

Lenz, R., & Kuhn, K. A. (2004). Towards a continuous evolution and adaptation of information systems in healthcare. *International Journal of Medical Informatics, 73*(1), 75-89.

Leong, H. V., & Si, A. (1997). Database caching over the air-storage. *The Computer Journal, 40*(7), 401-415.

LeRouge, C., Mantzana, V., & Wilson, E. V. (2007b). Healthcare Information Systems Research, Revelations and Visions. *European Journal of Information Systems, 16*(6), 669–671. doi:10.1057/palgrave.ejis.3000712

Leung, G.M., Johnston, J.M., Ho, L.M., Wong, F.K., & Cameo, S.C. (2001). Computerization of clinical practice in Hong Kong. *International Journal of Medical Informatics, 62*, 143–154.

Lewicki, R. J., McAllister, D. J., & Bies, R. J. (1998). Trust and distrust: New relationships and realities. *Academy of Management Review, 23*(3), 438–458. doi:10.2307/259288

Lewin, K. (1947). Frontiers in group dynamics: Concepts, methods, and reality of social sciences: Social equalization and social change. Human Relations, 1, 5-14.

Lewin, S. A., Skea, Z. C., Entwistle, V., Zwarenstein, M., & Dick, J. (2001). Interventions for providers to promote a patient-centered approach in clinical consultations [Review]. *Cochrane Database of Systematic Reviews (Online : Update Software)*, 4.

Li, C.-H., & Pieprzyk, J. (1999). *Conference Key Agreement from Secret Sharing.* Paper presented at the Proceedings of the 4th Australasian Conference on Information Security and Privacy.

Li, M. F., & Ye, L. R. (1999). Information technology and firm performance: Linking with environmental, strategic, and managerial contexts. *Information & Management, 35*(1), 43–51. doi:10.1016/S0378-7206(98)00075-5

Li, Y. C., Chang, I. C., Hung, W. F., & Fu, H. K. (2005). *The critical factors affecting hospital adoption of mobile nursing technologies in Taiwan.* Proceedings of the 38th Hawaii International Conference on System Sciences, Hawaii, USA.

Lin. (1997). Dynamic key management schemes for access control in a hierarchy. *Computer Communications, 20*(15), 1381.

Linden Research. (2007). *Second Life.* Retrieved February 9th, 2008 from http://secondlife.com/.

Linder, J. A., Ma, J., Bates, D. W., Middleton, B., & Stafford, R. S. (2007). Electronic health record use and the quality of ambulatory care in the United States. *Archives of Internal Medicine, 167*(13), 1400–1405. doi:10.1001/archinte.167.13.1400

Lindsey, E., & Hartrick, G. (1996). Health-promoting nursing practice: The demise of the nursing process? Journal of Advanced Nursing, 23(1), 106-112.

Littlejohns, P., Wyatt, J., & Garvican, L. (2003). Evaluating computerised health information systems: Hard lessons still to be learnt. *British Medical Journal, 326*(7394), 860-863.

Lofstedt, U. (2005). E-Government–assessment of current research and some proposals for future directions. *International Journal of Public Information Systems, 2005*(1).

Loiacono, E. T., Watson, R. T., & Goodhue, D. L. (2002, Winter). Webqual: A Web site quality instrument. In *Proceedings of the AMA Winter Marketing Educators' Conference*, Austin, TX.

Lorenz, T. & Jost, A., (2006). *Towards an orientation framework in multi-paradigm modeling.*

Lorenzi, N. M., & Riley, R. T. (2000). Managing change: An overview. *Journal of the American Medical Informatics Association, 7*(2), 116–124.

Lorenzi, N. M., & Riley, R. T. (2003). Organizational issues = change. *International Journal of Medical Informatics, 69*(2/3), 197–203. doi:10.1016/S1386-5056(02)00105-3

Lorenzi, N., & Riley, R. (1995). Organizational aspects of health informatics - Managing technological change. New York: Springer.

Lorincz, K., Malan, D. J., Fulford-Jones, T. R. F., Nawoj, A., Clavel, A., & Shnayder, V. (2004, October-December). Sensor networks for emergency response: challenges and opportunities. *IEEE Pervasive Computing / IEEE Computer Society [and] IEEE Communications Society, 3*(4), 16–23. doi:10.1109/MPRV.2004.18

Lowry, C. (1994). Nurses' attitudes toward computerised care plans in intensive care. Part 2. Intensive and Critical Care Nursing, 10, 2-11.

Lu, Y. C., Xiao, Y., Sears, A., & Jacko, J. A. (2005). A review and a framework of handheld computer adoption in healthcare. *International Journal of Medical Informatics, 74*(5), 409–422. doi:10.1016/j.ijmedinf.2005.03.001

Lueg, J. E., Moore, R. S., & Warkentin, M. (2003). Patient health information search: An explanatory model of Web-based search behavior. *Journal of End User Computing, 15*(4), 49-61.

Luhmann, N. (1988). Familiarity, confidence, trust: problems and alternatives. In Gambetta, D. (Ed.), *Trust: Making and Breaking Cooperative Relations*, (pp. 94-107). Oxford.

Luo, W., & Najdawi, M. (2004). Trust-building measures: a review of consumer health portals. *Communications of the ACM, 47*(1), 108–113. doi:10.1145/962081.962089

Maes, S., Leventhal, H., & de Ridder, D. T. D. (1996). Coping with Chronic Diseases. In M. Zeidner and S. E. Norman (Eds.), *Handbook of Coping. Theory, Research, Applications* (pp. 221-251). New York: John Wiley & Sons, Inc.

Maglaveras, N., Koutkias, V., Chouvarda, I., Goulis, D. G., Avramides, A., Adamidis, D., et al. (2002). Home care delivery through the mobile telecommunications platform: The Citizen Health Citizen (CHS) perspective. *International Journal of Medical Informatics, 68*, 99-111.

Maines, D., & Charlton, J. (1985). The negotiated order approach to the analysis of social organization. In H. Farberman & R. Perinbanayagam (Eds.), *Studies in symbolic interaction (foundations of interpretive sociology: original essays in symbolic interaction)* (Vol. Suppl. 1, pp. 263-270). Greenwich, CT: JAI.

MammoGrid. (2008). European federated mammogram database implemented on a grid structure. Retrieved February 1st, 2008 from http://mammogrid.vitamib.com

Mantzana, V., & Themistocleous, M. (2006). A method for the identification of actors involved in the adoption of innovations in healthcare organizations. In *Proceedings of the 39th Hawaii International Conference on System Sciences.*

Mantzana, V., Themistocleous, M., Irani, Z., & Morabito, V. (2007). Identifying Healthcare Actors Involved in the Adoption of Information Systems. *European Journal of Information Systems, 16*(1), 91–102. doi:10.1057/palgrave.ejis.3000660

Marsh, S. (1994). Trust in Distributed Artificial Intelligence. In Castelfranchi, C. & Werner, E. (Eds.), *Artificial Social Systems*, (pp. 94-112). Berlin: Springer.

Martin, S. (2003). More than half of MDs under age 35 now using PDAs. *Canadian Medical Association Journal, 16*(2), 952–952.

Mascarenhas, L., Eliot, B., & MacKenzie, I. (1992). A comparison of perinatal outcome, antenatal and intrapartum care between England and Wales, and France. *Br.J.Obstet.Gynaecol., 99*(12), 955-958.

Mass, M., & Eriksson, O. (2006). Challenges in the adoption of medical information systems. *Proceedings of the 39th Annual Hawaii International Conference on System Sciences* (HICSS '06), *5*, 95.

Mayer, R. C., Davis, J. H., & Schoorman, F. D. (1995). An integrative model of organizational trust. *Academy of Management Review, 20*(3), 709–734. doi:10.2307/258792

Mayring, M. (1993). Einführung in die qualitative Sozialforschung. Weinheim: Psychologie-Verlag-Union.

McAlearney, A. S., Vrontos, J., Schneider, P. J., Curran, C. R., Czerwinski, B. S., & Pedersen, C. A. (2007). Strategic work-arounds to accommodate new technology: The case of smart pumps in hospital care. *Journal of Patient Safety, 3*(2), 75–81. doi:10.1097/01.jps.0000242987.93789.63

McCarthy, J., Riaz, K., & Nolan, Y. (2007). An Interactive Outpatient Reminder System. *The Internet Journal of Medical Informatics*, 3(1). Retrieved June 18, 2008, from http://www.ispub.com/ostia/index.php?xmlFilePath=journals/ijmi/vol3n1/outpatient.xml

McDonald, C., Schadow, G., Barnes, M., Dexter, P., Overhage, J., Mamlin, B., et al. (2003). Open source software in medical informatics—why, how and what. *International Journal of Medical Informatics, 69*(2-3), 175-184.

McDonald, K., & Metzger, J. (2002, September). Achieving tangible IT benefits in small physician practices. *California HealthCare Foundation, ihealth Report.*

Meadows, D. H., & Robinson, J. (1985). *The electronic oracle: computer models and social decisions.* Chichester, UK: Wiley.

Medical Group Management Association. (2001). *Medical group management association survey 2001.*

Medical Records Institute. (2002). *4th annual Medical Records Institute's survey of electronic health record trends and usage, 2002.*

Medicare Payment Advisory Commission. (1999). *Report to the Congress: Selected Medicare Issues.* Washington, DC: Medicare Payment Advisory Commission.

Medication Errors Reduction Act of 2001 (2001). S 824, 107th congress. 1st Session.

Melander-Wikman, A., Jansson, M., & Gard, G. (2005). The mobihealth usability evaluation questionnaire. *E-health International Journal.*

Melby, L. (2007). *Talk, pen, and paper: A sociological analysis of the use of medical information and communication practices among hospital physicians (in Norwegian).* Doctoral Thesis. Norwegian University of Science and Technology, 2007:80.

Melone, N. P. (1990). A theoretical assessment of the user satisfaction construct in information systems research. *Management Science, 36*, 76–91. doi:10.1287/mnsc.36.1.76

Menachemi, N., Matthews, M. C., Ford, E. W., & Brooks, R. G. (2007). The influence of payer mix on electronic health record adoption by physicians. *Health Care Management Review, 32*(2), 111-118.

Mendonca, E. A., Chen, E. S., Stetson, P. D., McKnight, L. K., Lei, J., & Cimino, J. J. (2004). Approach to mobile information and communication for health care. *International Journal of Medical Informatics, 73*, 631-638.

Mikkelsen, G., & Aasly, J. (2001). Concordance of information in parallel electronic and paper based patient records. *International Journal of Medical Informatics, 63*, 123-131.

Miles, M. B., & Huberman, A. M. (1994). *Qualitative Data Analysis: An Expanded Sourcebook.* Beverly Hills, CA: Sage.

Miller, D. C., & Thorpe, J. A. (1995). SIMNET: the advent of simulator networking. *Proceedings of the IEEE, 83*(8), 1114–1123. doi:10.1109/5.400452

Miller, R. H., & West, C. E. (2007). The value of electronic health records in community health centers: Policy implications. *Health Affairs, 26*(1), 206–214. doi:10.1377/hlthaff.26.1.206

Miller, R. H., West, C., Brown, T. M., Sim, I., & Ganchoff, C. (2005). The value of electronic health records in solo or small group practices. *Health Affairs (Project Hope), 24*(5), 1127-1137.

Miller, R.A., Gardner, R.M., Johnson, K.B., & Hripcsak, G. (2005). Clinical decision support and electronic prescribing systems: A time for responsible thought and action. *Journal of the American Medical Association, 12*(4), 403–409.

Miller, R.H., & Sims, I. (2004). Physicians' use of electronic medical records: Barriers and solutions. *Health Affairs, 23*(2), 116–126.

Mingers, J., & Stowell, F. (1997). *Information systems: An emerging discipline? Information systems series* (pp. 239-266). London: McGraw-Hill.

Minister of Ageing. (2008, June 12th). *Historic meeting of ministers for ageing/seniors – responding to Australia's changing demographics*. Retrieved July 7th 2008, from http://www.health.gov.au/internet/ministers/publishing.nsf/Content/A58A5B08571D0BDDCA2574650024A4C1/$File/JE082.pdf

Misbahuddin, S., & Al-Holou, N. (2003, July 14–18). Efficient communication techniques for Controller Area Network (CAN) protocol. In *Proceedings of ACS/IEEE International conference on computer and their applications*, Tunis.

MIT-BIH. (2008). *Database Distribution Series, Heart Rate Time Series*. Retrieved on Jan 23rd 2008, from http://ecg.mit.edu/

Mitchell, J. (2000). Increasing the cost-effectiveness of telemedicine by embracing e-health. *Journal of Telemedicine and Telecare*, *6*(Suppl 1), 16–19. doi:10.1258/1357633001934500

Mitchell, R., Agle, B., & Wood, D. (1997). Towards a theory of stakeholder identification and salience. *Academy of Management Review, 22*(4), 853-887.

Mockus, A., Fielding, R., & Herbsleb, J. (2000). *A case study of open source software development: The Apache server.* Paper presented at the Software Engineering, 2000.

Moehr, J. R. (2002). Evaluation: Salvation or nemesis of medical informatics? Computers in Biology and Medicine, 32(3), 113-125.

Moehr, J. R., Anglin, C., Schaafsma, J., Pantazi, S., & Grimm, N. (2006). Lest formalisms impede insight and success: Evaluation in health informatics - A case study. *Methods of Information in Medicine*, *45*, 67–72.

Mol, A. (1999). Ontological politics: a word and some questions. In J.Law & J. Hassard (Eds.), *Actor network theory and after* (pp. 74-89). Oxford, UK; Malden, MA: Blackwell/Sociological Review.

Mont, D. (2007). *Measuring disability prevalence* (SP Discussion Paper No. 0706). Retrieved from http://siteresources.worldbank.org/DISABILITY/Resources/Data/MontPrevalence.pdf

Moor, J. H. (1997). Towards a theory of privacy in the information age. *Computers & Society*, *27*(3), 27–32. doi:10.1145/270858.270866

Morahan-Martin, J. M. (2004). How Internet users find, evaluate, and use online health information: A cross-cultural review. *Cyberpsychology & Behavior*, *7*(5), 497–510.

Morecroft, J. & Robinson, S., (2005). *Explaining puzzling dynamics: Comparing the use of system dynamics and discrete event simulation.*

Morris, S., Devlin, N. J., & Parkin, D. 2007. *Economic analysis in health care.* Hoboken, NJ: J. Wiley & Sons.

Mount, C.D., Kelman, C.W., Smith, L.R., & Douglas, R.M. (2000). An integrated electronic health record and information system for Australia. *Medical Journal of Australia, 172*, 25–27.

Mumford, E. (1983). *Designing human systems for new technology: The ETHICS method.* Retrieved on May 7, 2007, from http://www.enid.u-net.com/C1book1.htm

Mumford, E. (2003). *Redesigning human systems*. Hershey, PA: Information Science Reference.

Mumford, E., & Banks, O. (1967). *The computer and the clerk.* London: Routledge & Kegan Paul.

Murero, M., & Rice, E. R. (Eds.). (2006). *The Internet and Healthcare: Theory, Research, and Practice*. Mahwah, NJ: Lawrence Erlbaum Associates.

Murphy, F., & Staples, S. (1998). Reengineering in Australia: Factors affecting success. In *Proceedings of the Australasian Conference of Information systems*, Sydney, Australia.

Musen, M. A., Tu, S. W., Das, A. K., & Shahar, Y. (1996). EON: a component-based approach to automation of protocol-directed therapy. *Journal of the American Medical Informatics Association*, *3*(6), 367–388.

Mustafee, N. (2004). *Performance evaluation of interoperability methods for distributed simulation.* MSc. thesis, Department of Information Systems, Computing and Mathematics, Brunel University, UK.

Mustafee, N., & Taylor, S. J. E. (2006). Investigating distributed simulation with COTS simulation packages: experiences with Simul8 and the HLA. In J. Garnett, S. Brailsford, S. Robinson, & S. Taylor, (Eds.) *Proceedings of the 2006 Operational Research Society Simulation Workshop (SW06),* (pp. 33-42). Birmingham, UK: Operational Research Society.

Myers, M. D. (1997). Qualitative research in Information Systems. *MIS Quarterly, 21*(2), 241–242. doi:10.2307/249422

Nakamura, M., Yang, Y., Kubota, S., Shimizu, H., Miura, Y., & Wasaki, K. (2003). Network system for alpine ambulance using long distance wireless LAN and CATV LAN. *Igaku Butsuri, 23*(1), 30–39.

Nambisan, S., & Wang, Y. M. (1999). Roadblocks to web technology adoption? *Communications of the ACM, 42*(1), 98–101. doi:10.1145/291469.291482

Nardonne, D. (1990). Collecting and Analysing Data: Doing and Thinking. In H.K.Walker, W. D. Hall, & J. W. Hurst (Eds.), *Clinical Methods.* Stoneham, MA.: Butterworth Publishers.

Naseer, A., & Stergioulas, L. K. (2006). Discovering healthgrid services. In *Proceedings of the IEEE International Conference on Services Computing (SCC '06)*, (pp. 301-306). Washington, DC: IEEE Computer Society

Naseer, A., & Stergioulas, L. K. (2006). Resource discovery in grids and other distributed environments: States of the art. *Multiagent and Grid Systems - . International Journal (Toronto, Ont.), 2*(2), 163–182.

Naseer, A., & Stergioulas, L. K. (2007). Combining web services and grid services: practical approaches and implications to resource discovery. In Periorellis, P. (Ed.), *Securing Web Services: Practical Usage of Standards and Specifications* (pp. 298-317). Hershey, PA: IGI Global.

National Digital Mammography Archive. (2008). Retrieved February 1, 2008 from http://www.hoise.com/primeur/05/articles/monthly/AE-PR-02-05-1.html

National Multiple Sclerosis Society (2007). Retrieved November 20, 2007, from http://www.nmss.org

National Tourette Syndrome Association (2007). Retrieved November 20, 2007, from http://www.tsa-usa.org

Needham, R. M., & Schroeder, M. D. (1978). Using encryption for authentication in large networks of computers. *Communications of the ACM, 21*(12), 993–999. doi:10.1145/359657.359659

Neilson, J. (1998). Ultrasound for fetal assessment in early pregnancy. *Cochrane Database of Systematic Reviews* (4).

Nemeth, C. P., Cook, R. I., & Woods, D. D. (2004). The messy details: Insights from the study of technical work in healthcare. *IEEE Transactions on Systems, Man, and Cybernetics, 34*, 689–692. doi:10.1109/TSMCA.2004.836802

Nemeth, C., & Cook, R. (2005). Hiding in plain sight: What Koppel et al. tell us about healthcare IT. *Journal of Biomedical Informatics, 38*, 262-263. doi:10.1016/j.jbi.2005.05.010

Nicholas, D., Huntington, P., Williams, P., & Blackburn, P. (2001). Digital health information provision and health outcomes. *Journal of Information Science, 27*(4), 265-276.

Nickell, G., & Pinto, J. (1986). The computer attitude scale. Computers in Human Behaviour, 2, 301-306.

Nicol, D., & Heidelberger, P. (1996). Parallel Execution for Serial Simulators. *ACM Transactions on Modeling and Computer Simulation, 6*(3), 210–242. doi:10.1145/235025.235031

Nielsen, J. (1993). Usability engineering (interactive technologies). New York: Academic Press, Orlando.

Nøhr, C., Andersen, S. K., Vingtoft, S., Bernstein, K., & Bruun-Rasmussen, M. (2005). Development, implementation and diffusion of EHR systems in Denmark. *International Journal of Medical Informatics*, *74*(2–4), 229–234. doi:10.1016/j.ijmedinf.2004.04.025

Nohria, N., & Garcia-Pont, C. (1991). Global Strategic Linkages and Industry Structure. *Strategic Management Journal, 12*(Summer Special Issue), 105-124.

Nonaka, I., & Takeuchi, H. (1995). *The Knowledge-creating Company.* New York: Oxford University Press.

Norman, D. (1988). *The psychology of everyday things.* New York: Basic Books.

Norman, D. A. (1993). *Things that make us smart.* Cambridge, MA: Perseus Books.

Norman, D., & Draper, S. W. (1986). *User centered system design: New perspectives on human-computer interaction.* Lawrence Erlbaum Associates Inc.

Nozaki, K., Akiyama, T., Shimojo, S., Maeda, S., & Tamagawa, H. (2005). Integration of computational fluid dynamics and computational aero acoustics on grid for dental applications. In *Proceedings of the 18th IEEE Symposium on Computer-Based Medical Systems*, (pp. 517-522). Washington, DC: IEEE Computer Society.

O'Neill, L., & Klepack, W. (2007). Electronic medical records for a rural family practice: A case study in systems development. *Journal of Medical Systems, 31*(1), 25-33.

Office of Government Commerce. (2007). *IT infrastructure library (ITIL), Office of government commerce.* Retrieved on August 13, 2007, from http://www.ogc.gov.uk/guidance_itil_4672.asp

Ohmann, C., Boy, O., & Yang, Q. (1997). A systematic approach to the assessment of user satisfaction with healthcare systems: Constructs, models and instruments. In C. Pappas (Ed.), Medical Informatics Europe '97. Conference proceedings (Vol. 43, Pt. B, pp. 781-5). Amsterdam: IOS Press.

Ohno-Machado, L., Gennari, J. H., Murphy, S. N., Jain, N. L., Tu, S. W., & Oliver, D. E. (1998). The guideline interchange format: a model for representing guidelines. *Journal of the American Medical Informatics Association*, *5*(4), 357–372.

Öien, R. F. (2002). *Leg ulcer management in primary care with special reference to pinch grafting.* Doctoral thesis Malmö University Hospital, Lund University, Lund, Sweden.

Öien, R. F., & Ragnarson Tennvall, G. (2006). Accurate diagnosis and effective treatment of leg ulcers reduce prevalence, care time and costs. *Journal of Wound Care*, *15*(6), 259–262.

Olk, P. (1997). The Effect of Partner Differences on the Performance of R&D Consortia. In P. W. Beamish, & J. P. Killing (Eds.), *Cooperative Strategies: North American Perspectives* (pp. 133-159). San Francisco, CA: New Lexington Press.

Olla, P., & Atkinson, C. (2004). Developing a wireless reference model for interpreting complexity in wireless projects. *Industrial Management and Data Systems, 104*(3), 262-272.

OLPC. (2006). *One laptop per child.* Retrieved December 1, 2006, from http://laptop.org/.

Oram, A. (Ed.). (2001). *Peer-to-peer: harnessing the benefits of a disruptive technology.* Sebastopol, CA: O'Reilly.

Orlikowski, W. (2000). Using technology and constituting structures: A practice lens for studying technology in organizations. *Organization Science*, *11*(4), 404–428. doi:10.1287/orsc.11.4.404.14600

Orlikowski, W. J., & Baroudi, J. J. (1991). Studying information technology in organizations: Research approaches and assumptions. *Information Systems Research, 2*(1), 1-28.

Ozkan, S. (2004) Information systems quality vs. software quality: A process based assessment model within the context of organisation. In *Proceedings of the 9th Association of Information Management Conference, AIM2004*, Paris, France.

Ozkan, S. (2005). All together now: Merging information technology quality and other business performance management frameworks. *Cutter IT Journal The Journal of Information Technology Management*, *18*(3), 16–20.

Ozkan, S. (2006) *PB-ISAM: A process-based framework for information systems effectiveness assessment in organisational contexts*. Unpublished doctoral dissertation, Middle East Technical University, Turkey.

Ozkan, S., & Bilgen, S. (2003). Notes towards IS assessment: A comparison of two models within the context of the Internet. In *Proceedings of the IADIS International Conference WWW/Internet 2003* (Vol. 2, pp.1215-1219), Faro, Portugal.

Ozkan, S., Hackney, R., & Bilgen, S. (2007). Process based information systems for international business evaluation. *Journal of Enterprise Information Management, 20*(6), 700–725. doi:10.1108/17410390710830736

Padarath, A., Chamberlain, C., McCoy, D., Ntuli, A., Rowson, M., & Loewenson, R. (2003). *Health personnel in Southern Africa: Confronting maldistribution and brain drain*. Equinet discussion paper no. 4, Health Systems Trust, South Africa.

Page, E. H., & Nance, R. E. (1994). Parallel discrete event simulation: a modeling methodological perspective. In *Proceedings of the 8th Workshop on Parallel and Distributed Simulation*, (pp. 88-93). New York: ACM Press.

Pagliari, C., Sloan, D., Gregor, P., Sullivan, F., Detmer, D., Kahan, P., et al. (2005). What is e-health (4): A scoping exercise to map the field. *J Med Internet Res, 7*(1), e9.

Pal, A., Mbarika, V., Cobb-Payton, F., Datta, P., & McCoy, S. (2005). Telemedicine diffusion in a developing Country: The case of India. *Information Technology in Biomedicine, IEEE Transactions on, 9*(1), 59-65.

Palfrey, C., Thomas, P., & Phillips, C. (2004). Mulitple Perspectives and Decision Making. In *Effective Health Care Management: An Evaluative Approach* (1st Ed., pp. 55-60). Oxford, UK: Blackwell Publishing.

Palfrey, C., Thomas, P., & Phillips, C. (2004). Performance management: Concepts and approaches. In *Effective Health Care Management: An Evaluative Approach* (1st Ed., pp. 93-99). Oxford, UK: Blackwell Publishing.

Palvia, S., Sharma, R., & Conrath, D. (2001). A socio-technical framework for quality assessment of computer information systems. Industrial Management & Data Systems, 101(5), 237-251.

Pan American Health Organization. (1999). *Setting up healthcare services information systems: A guide for requirement analysis, application specification, and procurement*. Washington, D.C.: Essential Drugs and Technology Program, Division of Health Systems and Services Development, PAHO/WHO.

Pandey, S. K., Hart, J. J., & Tiwary, S. (2003). Women's health and the Internet: Understanding emerging trends and implications. *Social Science & Medicine, 56*(1), 179-191.

Panella, M., Marchisio, S., & Di Stanislao, F. (2003). Reducing clinical variations with clinical pathways: do pathways work? *International Journal for Quality in Health Care, 15*, 509–521. doi:10.1093/intqhc/mzg057

Parati., G. (2006). *Roberto Antonicelli "manuale di telemedicina."* Pavia: EDVIES.

Pare, G. (2004). Investigating information systems with positivist case study research. *Communications of the Association for Information Systems, 13*, 233–264.

Pare', G. & Trudel, M. (2007). Knowledge barriers to PACS adoption and implementation in hospitals. *International Journal of Medical Informatics*, 22 33.

Parry, E., Sood, R., & Parry, D. (2006). Investigation of optimization techniques to prepare ultrasound images for electronic transfer [abstract]. *Ultrasound in Obstetrics and Gynecology, 28*(4), 487-488.

Patel, V. L., Branch, T., Wang, D., Peleg, M., & Boxwala, A. (2002). Analysis of the process of encoding guidelines: a comparison of GLIF2 and GLIF3. *Methods of Information in Medicine, 41*(2), 105–113.

Patel, V. L., Cytryn, K. N., Shortliffe, E. H., & Safran, C. (2000): The Collaborative Health Care Team: The Role of Individual and Group Expertise. *Stanford Medical Informatics Report* (No SMI-1999-0768). Retrieved from http://smi-web.stanford.edu/pubs/SMI_Abstracts/SMI-1999-0768.html

Patterson, E., Cook, R., & Render, M. (2002). Improving patient safety by identifying side effects from introducing bar coding in medication administration. *Journal of the American Medical Informatics Association, 9*(5), 540–553. doi:10.1197/jamia.M1061

Pattichis, C., Kyriacou, E., Voskarides, S., Pattichis, M. S., Istepanian, R., & Schizas, C. N. (2002). Wireless Telemedicine Systems: An Overview. *IEEE Antennas & Propagation Magazine, 44*(2), 143–153. doi:10.1109/MAP.2002.1003651

Patton, M. Q. (1990). *Qualitative evaluation and research methods, second ed.* London: Sage Publications.

Paul, L., John, I., & Pierre, C. (2003, January). Why do people use information technology? A critical review of the technology acceptance model. *Association for Information Systems, 40*(3), 191.

Paul, R. J., & Balmer, D. W. (1993). *Simulation modelling.* Bromley, UK: Chartwell-Bratt.

Pavlopoulos, S., Kyriacou, E., Berler, A., Dembeyiotis, S., & Koutsouris, D. (1998). A novel emergency telemedicine system based on wireless communication technology – AMBULANCE. *IEEE Trans. Inform. Tech. Biomed., –. Special Issue on Emerging Health Telematics Applications in Europe, 2*(4), 261–267.

Pech, E. (2004). *Making innovation happen* (Tech. Rep.). Detecon, Inc.

Pedersen, T. (1991). A Threshold Cryptosystem without a Trusted Party. In *Advances in Cryptology — EUROCRYPT '91* (pp. 522-526).

Pederson, C. A., Schneider, P. J., & Santell, J. P. (2001). ASHP national survey of pharmacy practice in hospital settings: prescribing and transcribing – 2001. *American Journal of Health-System Pharmacy, 58*, 2251–2266.

Peffers, K., & Saarinen, T. (2002). Measuring the business value of IT investments: Inferences from a study of senior bank executives. *Journal of Organizational Computing and Electronic Commerce, 12*(1), 17–38. doi:10.1207/S15327744JOCE1201_03

Pekkola, S. (2003). Designed for unanticipated use: common artefacts as design principle for CSCW applications. *ACM SIGGROUP conference on Supporting group work table of contents* (pp. 359-368). Sanibel Island, FL: ACM.

Peleg, M., Boxwala, A. A., Bernstam, E., Tu, S., Greenes, R. A., & Shortliffe, E. H. (2001). Sharable representation of clinical guidelines in GLIF: relationship to the Arden Syntax. *Journal of Biomedical Informatics, 34*(3), 170–181. doi:10.1006/jbin.2001.1016

Peleg, M., Boxwala, A. A., Ogunyemi, O., Zeng, Q., Tu, S., Lacson, R., et al. (2000). GLIF3: the evolution of a guideline representation format. *Proc AMIA Symp*, 645-649.

Peleg, M., Tu, S., Bury, J., Ciccarese, P., Fox, J., & Greenes, R. A. (2003). Comparing computer-interpretable guideline models: a case-study approach. *Journal of the American Medical Informatics Association, 10*(1), 52–68. doi:10.1197/jamia.M1135

Pelissero, G., & Velo, D. (2004). *Competition in health systems.* European Union, AIOP.

Perera, R., Dowell, T., Crampton, P., & Kearns, R. (2007). Panning for gold: An evidence-based tool for assessment of performance indicators in primary healthcare. *Health Policy (Amsterdam), 80*(2), 314–327. doi:10.1016/j.healthpol.2006.03.011

Peterson, R. R., Smits, M., & Spanjers, R. (2000). Exploring IT-Enabled Networked Organisations in Health Care: Emerging Practices and Phases of Development. *8th European Conf. on Information Systems (ECIS)*, Vienna, Austria, (pp. 1253-1260).

Pew Internet & American Life. (2005). *January 2005 Internet tracking survey.* Retrieved May 10, 2005, from http://www.pewinternet.org

Pidd, M. (2004). *Computer simulation in management science* (5th Ed.). Chichester, UK: John Wiley & Sons.

Pidd, M. (2004). Simulation worldviews: so what? In R. G. Ingalls, M. D. Rossetti, J. S. Smith, & B. A. Peters, (eds.) *Proceedings of the 36th Winter Simulation Conference*, (pp. 288-292). Winter Simulation Conference, USA.

Pidd, M., & Cassel, R. A. (2000). Using Java to develop discrete event simulations. *The Journal of the Operational Research Society, 51*, 405–412.

Piggott, D., Teljeur, C., & Kelly, A. (2004). Exploring the potential for using the grid to support health impact assessment modelling. *Parallel Computing, 30*(9-10), 1073–1091. doi:10.1016/j.parco.2004.07.012

Pinch, T., & Biker, W. (1987). The social construction of facts and artifacts: Or how the sociology of science and the sociology of technology might benefit each other. In W. E. Biker, T. Hughes & T. Pinch (Eds.), *The social construction of technology systems: New directions in the sociology and history of technology*. Cambridge, MA: MIT Press.

Pitsillides, A., Pitsillides, B., Samaras, G., Dikaiakos, M., Christodoulou, E., Andreou, P., et al. (2005). DITIS: A collaborative virtual medical team for the home healthcare of cancer patients. In *M-health: Emerging mobile health* (pp. 247-266). Kluwer Academic/Plenum Publishers. Springer: New York.

Pitsillides, B., Pitsillides, A., Samaras, G., Christodoulou, E., Panteli, N., Andreou, P., et al. (2004). *User perspective of DITIS: Virtual collaborative teams for home-healthcare: Vol. 100. Current situation and examples of implemented and beneficial e-health applications* (pp. 205-216). IOS Press: The Netherlands.

Plsek, P. (2001). Redesigning healthcare with insights from the science of complex adaptive systems. In Institute of Medicine, *Crossing the quality chasm: A new health system for the 21st century* (pp. 309-322). Washington, D.C.: National Academy of Sciences.

Pollack, M. R. P., & Disler, P. B. (2002). Rehabilitation of patients after stroke. *The Medical Journal of Australia, 177*(8), 452–456.

Porn, L. N., & Patrick, K. (2002). Mobile computing acceptance grows as applications evolve. *Healthcare Financial Management, 56*, 66–70.

Pouloudi, A., & Whitley, E. A. (1997). Stakeholders identification in inter-organizational systems: Gaining insights for drug use management systems. *European Journal of Information Systems, 6*, 1-14.

Powell, P. L. (1999). Evaluation of information technology investments: Business as usual. In L. P. Willcocks & S. Lester (Eds.), *Beyond the IT productivity paradox* (pp. 151-182). Chichester, UK: John Wiley & Sonspp.

Powell, W. (1990). Neither Market Nor Hierarchy: Network Forms of Organization. *Research in Organizational Behavior, 12*, 295–336.

Power, D., Politou, E., Slaymaker, M., Harris, S., & Simpson, A. (2004). A relational approach to the capture of DICOM files for Grid-enabled medical imaging databases. In *Proceedings of the 2004 ACM symposium on applied computing*, (pp.272-279). New York: ACM Press.

Power, D., Slaymaker, M., Politou, E., & Simpson, A. (2005). Protecting sensitive patient data via query modification. In *Proceedings of the 2005 ACM symposium on applied computing*, pp.224-230. New York: ACM Press.

Prater, E., & Ghosh, S. (2005). Current Operational Practices of U.S. Small and Medium-Sized Enterprises in Europe. *Journal of Small Business Management, 43*(2), 155–169.

President's Information Technology Advisory Committee, Health Care Delivery and Information Technology (HIT) Subcommittee. (2004, April 13). *Draft Recommendations.*, Retrieved from www.nitrd.gov/pitac

President's Information Technology Advisory Committee. (2004). *Revolutionizing health care through information technology*. Arlington, VA: National Coordination Office for Information Technology Research and Development.

Presti, S., Butler, M., Leuschel, M., & Booth, C. (2006). Holistic trust design of e-services. In R. Song, L. Korba & G. Yee (Eds.), *Trust in e-services: Technologies, practices, and challenges* (pp. 113-139). Hershey, PA: Idea Group Publishing.

Purves, I.N., Sugden, B., Booth, N., & Sowerby, M. (1999). The PRODIGY project—The iterative development of the release one model. In *Proceedings of the AMIA Annual Symposium* (pp. 359–363).

Q-rec European Quality Labelling and Certification of Electronic Health Record Systems (EHRs). Retrieved on August 13, 2007, from: http://www.eurorec.org/projects/qrec.cfm

Raento, M., Oulasvirta, A., Petit, R., & Toivonen, H. (2005). ContextPhone: A prototyping platform for context-aware mobile applications, *4*, 51-59.

Rafaeli, S., & Hutchison, D. (2003). A survey of key management for secure group communication. *ACM Computing Surveys*, *35*(3), 309–329. doi:10.1145/937503.937506

Ragam, M. R. (2007). Information technology in healthcare creating a stronger healthcare system. *Asian Hospital & Healthcare Management*, *12*, 60–63.

Rahimi, B., & Vimarlund, V. (2007). Methods to evaluate health information systems in healthcare settings: A literature review. *Journal of Medical Systems*, *31*, 397–432. doi:10.1007/s10916-007-9082-z

Rahimpour, M., Lovella, N. H., Branko, G. C., & McCormick, J. (2008). Patients' perceptions of a home telecare system. *International Journal of Medical Informatics*, *77*(7), 486–498. doi:10.1016/j.ijmedinf.2007.10.006

Ramakrishnan, M., Sier, D., & Taylor, P. G. (2005). A two-time-scale model for hospital patient flow. *IMA Journal of Management Mathematics*, *16*, 197–215. doi:10.1093/imaman/dpi014

Randall, D., Harper, R., & Rouncefield, M. (2007). *Fieldwork for design. Theory and practice*. London: Springer.

Ranerup, A. (2008). In What Ways does Web Technology Support the Individual in Choice Reforms in Healthcare? *International Journal of Healthcare Information Systems and Informatics*, *3*(2), 48–68.

Rapoport, R. N. (1970). Three dilemas of action research. *Human Relations*, *23*, 499–513. doi:10.1177/001872677002300601

Reardon, J. L., & Davidson, E. (2007). An organizational learning perspective on the assimilation of electronic medical records among small physician practices. *European Journal of Information Systems*, *16*, 681–694. doi:10.1057/palgrave.ejis.3000714

Reason, J. (1990). *Human error*. Cambridge, UK: Cambridge University Press.

Reihle, D., & Zullighoven, H. (1995). A pattern Language for tool construction and integration based on the tools and materials metaphor. In J.O Coplian & D.C Schmindt (Eds.), *Pattern Languages of Program Design*. Reading, MA: Addison Wesley Professional.

Reinecke, I. (2004) *Managing Information in Health*. Melbourne National Health Information Summit.

Reponen, J., Ilkko, E., Jyrkinen, L., Tervonen, O., Niinimaki, J., Karhula, V., & Koivula, A. (2000). Initial experience with a wireless personal digital assistant as a teleradiology terminal for reporting emergency computerized tomography scans. *Journal of Telemedicine and Telecare*, *6*(1), 45–49. doi:10.1258/1357633001933943

Resar, R., Rozich, J., & Classen, D. (2003). Methodology and rationale for the measurement of harm with trigger tools. *Quality & Safety in Health Care*, *12*(6), 39–45.

Reynolds, P. F. (1988). A spectrum of options for parallel simulation. In M. Abrams, P. Haigh, and J. Comfort (Eds.), *Proceedings of the 20th Winter Simulation Conference*, (pp. 325 –332). New York: ACM Press.

Rideout, V. (2002). Generation Rx.com: What are young people really doing online? *Marketing Health Services*, *22*(1), 27-30.

Ridge, D., Ziebland, S., Anderson, J., Williams, I., & Elford, J. (2007). Positive prevention: Contemporary issues facing HIV positive people negotiating sex in the UK. *Social Science & Medicine*, *65*, 755–770. doi:doi:10.1016/j.socscimed.2007.03.049

Rigby, M. (2001). Evaluation: 16 powerful reasons why not to do it-And 6 over-riding imperatives. In V. Patel, R. Rogers, & R. Haux (Eds.), Proceedings of the 10th World Congress on Medical Informatics (Medinfo 2001, Vol. 84, pp. 1198-1202). Amsterdam: IOS Press.

Rigby, M., Forsström, J., Roberts, R., & Wyatt, W. (2001, September 8). Verifying quality and safety in health informatics services. British Medical Journal, 323, 552-556.

Rindfleisch, T. C. (1997). Privacy, information technology, and health care. *Communications of the ACM, 40*(8), 92–100. doi:10.1145/257874.257896

Ritchie, J., & Lewis, J. (2003). *Qualitative Research Practice: A Guide for Social Science Students and Researchers.* London: Sage Publications.

Rivard, S., Aubert, B. A., Patry, M., Pare, G., & Smith, H. A. (2004). *Information technology and organizational transformation.* Amsterdam, Netherlands: Elsevier.

Rivest, R. L., Shamir, A., & Adleman, L. (1978). A method for obtaining digital signatures and public-key cryptosystems. *Communications of the ACM, 21*(2), 120–126. doi:10.1145/359340.359342

Robbins, S. P., & De Cenzo, D. A. (1996). *Fundamentals of Management* (6th ed.). New York: Prentice Hall.

Robertson, B., Elliot, L., & Washington, D. (2007, October 3). Cognitive tools. *Emerging perspectives on learning, teaching, and technology.* Retrieved on December 3, 2007, from http://projects.coe.uga.edu/epltt/index.php?title=Cognitive_Tools

Robinson, M. (1993). Design for unanticipated use.... In G. de Michelis, C. Simone, & K. Schmidt (Eds.), *Third European Conference on Computer Supported Cooperative Work (ECSCW'93)* (pp.187-202). Amsterdam, the Netherlands: Kluwer Academic Publishers.

Robinson, S. (1994). *Successful Simulation: A Practical Approach to Simulation Projects*, Maidenhead, UK: McGraw-Hill.

Robinson, S. (2005). Discrete-event simulation: from the pioneers to the present, what next? *The Journal of the Operational Research Society, 56*(6), 619–629. doi:10.1057/palgrave.jors.2601864

Rodrigues, R. (2003). Deploying e-health solutions in Latin America and the Caribbean: Development and policy issues. *Forum PL11: Workshop on Telemedicine,* Geneva.

Rogers, E. M. (1995). *Diffusion of innovations* (4th ed.). New York: Free Press.

Rogerson, S. (2000), Ethicol: Electronic Patient Records, *IMIS Journal, 10*(5), retrieved from: http://www.ccsr.cse.dmu.ac.uk/resources/general/ethicol/Ecv10no5.html

Rogoski, R. (2005). Wireless by Design. *Health Management Technology*, (January): 1–7.

Rohleder, T. R., Bischak, D. P., & Baskin, L. B. (2007). Modeling patient service centers with simulation and system dynamics. *Health Care Management Science, 10*(1), 1–12. doi:10.1007/s10729-006-9001-8

Rohleder, T., & Klassen, K. (2002). Rolling Hori zon Appointment Scheduling: A Simulation Study. *Health Care Management Science, 5*(3), 201–209. doi:10.1023/A:1019748703353

Romano, J., Lam, D., Moses, G., Gilbert, G., & Marchessault, R. (2006). The future of military medicine has not arrived yet, but we can see it from here. *Telemedicine and e-Health, 12*(4), 417-425.

Rosemann, M. (2006). *Understanding Context-awareness in buisness process design.* Paper presented at the Australasian Conference on Information Systems, Dec 6-8, Adelaide.

Rosenbloom, S. T., Harrell, F., Lehman, C., Schneider, J., Spooner, S., & Johnson, K. (2006). Perceived increase in mortality after process and policy changes implemented with computerized physician order entry [letter]. *Pediatrics, 117*(4), 1452–1455. doi:10.1542/peds.2005-3163

Rosenthal, D. A., & Layman, E. J. (2008). Utilization of information technology in eastern north carolina physician practices: Determining the existence of a digital divide. *Perspectives in Health Information Management / AHIMA, American Health Information Management Association, 5*, 3.

Rosenthal, J. & Booth, M. (2004, October). *State Patient Safety Centers: A new approach to promote patient safety.* Portland, ME: National Academy for State Health Policy.

Rosenthal, M. B., Landon, B. E., Howitt, K., Song, H. R., & Epstein, A. M. (2007). Climbing up the pay-for-performance learning curve: Where are the early adopters now? *Health Affairs (Project Hope), 26*(6), 1674-1682.

Rosson, M. B., & Carroll, J. M. (2002). *Usability engineering: Scenario-based development of human-computer interaction*. San Francisco, CA: Academic Press.

Rouse, A., & Dick, M. (1994). The Use of Computerized Tools in Qualitative Information Systems Studies. *Proceedings of the 5th Australasian Conference on Information Systems (ACIS 1994),* (Vol. I, pp. 209-220), Monash University, Melbourne, Australia.

Royston, G. (1999). Commentary: trials versus models in appraising screening programmes. *British Medical Journal, 318*, 360–361.

Rubenstein, L. V., Meredith, L. S., Parker, L. E., Gordon, N. P., Hickey, S. C., & Oken, C. (2006). Impacts of evidence-based quality improvement on depression in primary care: A randomized experiment. *Journal of General Internal Medicine, 21*, 1027–1035. doi:10.1111/j.1525-1497.2006.00549.x

Rubinstein, R. Y. (1981). *Simulation and the Monte Carlo Method.* New York: John Wiley & Sons.

Russell, S. (2004). The economic burden of illness for households in developing countries: A review of studies focusing on malaria, tuberculosis, and human immunodeficiency virus/acquired immunodeficiency syndrome. *Am J Trop Med Hyg, 71*(2_suppl), 147-155.

Sabat, H. K. (2002). The evolving mobile wireless value chain and market structure. *Telecommunications Policy, 26*, 505-535.

Saboor, S., Chimiak-Opoka, J., & Ammenwerth, E. (2007). Supporting the Systematic Assessment of Clinical Processes: the MedFlow Method. *Methods of Information in Medicine, 46*(5), 586–594.

Sackett, D. L., Rosenberg, W. M., Gray, J. A., Haynes, R. B., & Richardson, W. S. (1996). Evidence based medicine: what it is and what it isn't. *BMJ (Clinical Research Ed.), 312*(7023), 71–72.

Saeednia, S., & Ghodosi, H. (1999). A Self-Certified Group-Oriented Cryptosystem without a Combiner. In *Information Security and Privacy* (pp. 192-201).

Salmon, S., Brnt, G., Marshall, D., & Bradley, A. (2000). Telemedicine use in two-nurse-led injuries units. *Journal of Telemedicine and Telecare, 6*(Suppl. 1), 43-45.

Salvador, C., Pascual Carrasco, M., Gonzalez de Mingo, M. A., Munoz Carrero, A., Marquez Montes, J., & Sosa Martin, L. (2005). Airmed-cardio: a GSM and Internet services-based system for out-of-hospital follow-up of cardiac patients. *IEEE Transactions on Information Technology in Biomedicine, 9*(1), 73–85. doi:10.1109/TITB.2004.840067

Sarkar, M. B., Echambadi, R., Cavusgil, S. T., Preet, S., & Aulakh, . (2001). The Influence of Complementarity, Compatibility, and Relationship Capital on Alliance Performance. *Journal of the Academy of Marketing Science, 29*(4), 358–373. doi:10.1177/03079450094216

Sarker, S., & Wells, J. D. (2003). Understanding mobile handheld device use and adoption. *Communications of the ACM, 46*(12), 35–40. doi:10.1145/953460.953484

Satyanarayanan, M., Kistler, J.J., Kumar, P., Okasaki, M.E., Siegel, E.H., & Steere, D.C. (1990). Coda: A highly available file system for a distributed workstation environment. *IEEE Trans. on Computers, 39(*4), 447-459.

Sauer, C. (1993). *Why information systems fail: A case study approach.* Henley on Thames, UK: Alfred Waller.

Sausser, G. D. (2003). Thin is in: web-based systems enhance security, clinical quality. *Healthcare Financial Management, 57*(7), 86–88.

Sax, U., Kohane, I., & Mandl, K. D. (2005). Wireless Technology Infrastructures for Authentication of Patients: PKI that Rings. *Journal of the American Medical Informatics Association, 12*(3), 263–268. doi:10.1197/jamia.M1681

Scalise, D. (2005). One generation to the next. *Hospitals and Health Networks*(Winter), 10-15.

Schabetsberger, T., Ammenwerth, E., Breu, R., Hoerbst, A., Goebel, G., & Penz, R. (2006). E-health approach to link-up actors in the health care system of Austria. *Studies in Health Technology and Informatics, 124*, 415–420.

Schäl, T. (1996). *Workflow Management Systems for Process Organisations,* (2nd Ed.) (LNCS 1096). Berlin: Springer Verlag.

Scheepers, R., Scheepers, H., & Ngwenyama, O. K. (2006). Contextual Influences on User Satisfaction with Mobile Computing: Findings from Two Healthcare Organizations. *European Journal of Information Systems, 15*, 261–268. doi:10.1057/palgrave.ejis.3000615

Scheer, A.-W. (1994). *Business Process Engineering – Reference Models for Industrial Companies* (2nd Ed.). Berlin: Springer Verlag.

Schein, E. H. (1992). *Organizational Culture and Leadership*, (3rd ed.). San Francisco, CA: Jossey-Bass

Scheres, S. H. W., Merino, A. J., Sorzano, C. O. S., & Carazo, J. M. (2005). Grid computing in 3D-EM image processing using Xmipp. In *Proceedings of the 18th symposium on computer-based medical system*, (pp. 561-563). Washington, DC: IEEE Computer Society.

Schieritz, N. & Milling, P.M., (2003). *Modeling the Forest of Modeling the Trees: A comparison of System Dynamics and Agent-Based Simulation*, July 20-24.

Schiff, G.D., & Rucker, D. (1998). Computerized prescribing: Building the electronic infrastructure for better medication usage. *Journal of the American Medical Association, 280*, 516–517.

Schneider, J. E., & Schneider, K. H. (2006). *Report on electronic health record-associated errors and near miss reporting systems*. Rockville, MD: Agency for Healthcare Research and Quality.

Schneier, B. (2006). *Applied Cryptography*. Hoboken, NJ: Wiley.

Schoenberg, R., Safran, C., & Sands, D. Z. (2000). *Studying clinician-computer interaction in Web-based systems*. Paper presented at the Annual AMIA Symposium, Los Angeles, CA, November 4-8.

Schön, D. (1983). *The reflective practitioner – how professional think in action*. New York: Basic Books.

Schroeder, R. G., Linderman, K., Liedtke, C., & Choo, A. S. (2007). Six sigma: Definition and underlying theory. *Journal of Operations Management*.

Schulman, J. (2004). *Evaluating the processes of neonatal intensive care*. London: BMJ Books.

Schulman, J. (2006). *Managing your patients' data in the neonatal and pediatric ICU: An introduction to databases and statistical analysis*. Oxford, UK: Blackwell.

Schulman, J., Kuperman, G. J., Kharbanda, A., & Kaushal, R. (2007). Discovering how to think about a hospital patient information system by struggling to evaluate it: A committee's journal. *Journal of the American Medical Informatics Association, 14*(5), 537–541. doi:10.1197/jamia.M2436

Schulman, J., Kuperman, G. J., Kharbanda, A., & Kaushal, R. (2007). Discovering how to think about a hospital patient information system by struggling to evaluate it: A committee's journal. *Journal of the American Medical Informatics Association, 14*(5), 537–541. doi:10.1197/jamia.M2436

Seland, G. (2006). System designer assessments of role play as a design method: A qualitative study. In *Proceedings of the 4th Nordic Conference on Human-Computer Interaction: Changing roles* (pp. 222-231). New York: ACM Press.

Semantic grid project. (2008). Retrieved February 1, 2008 from http://www.semanticgrid.org/

Serafeimidis, V., & Smithson, S. (2000). Information systems evaluation in practice: A case study of organizational change. *Journal of Information Technology, 15*(2), 93–105. doi:10.1080/026839600344294

Serour, G. I. (2006). Confidentiality, privacy and security of patients' health care information: FIGO Committee for the Ethical Aspects of Human Reproduction and Women's Health. *International Journal of Gynaecology and Obstetrics: the Official Organ of the International Federation of Gynaecology and Obstetrics, 93*(2), 184–186. doi:10.1016/j.ijgo.2006.03.011

Shahar, Y. (2002). Medical informatics: Between science and engineering, between academia and industry. Methods of Information in Medicine, 41, 8-11.

Shahar, Y., Miksch, S., & Johnson, P. (1998). The Asgaard project: a task-specific framework for the application and critiquing of time-oriented clinical guidelines. *Artificial Intelligence in Medicine*, *14*(1-2), 29–51. doi:10.1016/S0933-3657(98)00015-3

Shamir, A. (1979). How to share a secret. *Communications of the ACM*, *22*(11), 612–613. doi:10.1145/359168.359176

Shamliyan, T., & Kane, R. (2007, June 26). Just what the doctor ordered. Review of the evidence of the impact of computerized physician order entry system on medication errors. *Health Services Research, Online Early Articles.*

Shaw, M. C., Wolfe, C. D., Devaja, O., & Raju, K. S. (2003). Development of an evidence-based algorithm for the management of ovarian cancer. *European Journal of Gynaecological Oncology*, *24*, 117–125.

Shaw, N. (2002). CHEATS: a generic information communication technology (ICT) evaluation framework. Computers in Biology and Medicine, 32, 209-200.

Sheaff, R., & Peel, V. J. (1995). *Managing health service information systems: an introduction.* Buckingham, UK: Open University Press.

Shekelle, P. G., Morton, S. C., & Keeler, E. B. (2006). *Costs and Benefits of Health Information Technology. (Prepared by the Southern California Evidence-based Practice Center under Contract No. 290-02-0003.)* (Rep. No. 132). Rockville, MD: Agency for Healthcare Research and Quality.

Shiffman, R. N. (1997). Representation of clinical practice guidelines in conventional and augmented decision tables. *Journal of the American Medical Informatics Association*, *4*(5), 382–393.

Short, J. C., Palmer, T. B., & Ketchen, D. J. Jr. (2002). Resources-Based and Strategic Group Influences on Hospital Performance. *Health Care Management Review*, *27*(4), 7–17.

Shortliffe, E. H. (2005). Strategic action in health information technology: Why the obvious has taken so long. *Health Affairs*, *24*(5), 1222–1233. doi:10.1377/hlthaff.24.5.1222

Shortliffe, E. H., & Cimino, J. J. (Eds.). (2006). *Biomedical informatics computer applications in healthcare and biomedicine*. Springer-Verlag.

Si, A., & Leong, H. V. (1999). Query optimization for broadcast database. *DKE*, *29*(3), 351-380.

Sidorov, J. (2006). It ain't necessarily so: The electronic health record and the unlikely prospect of reducing health-care costs. *Health Affairs*, *25*(4), 1079–1085. doi:10.1377/hlthaff.25.4.1079

Sillesen, M., Ripa, M. S., Strange, S., Nielsen, S. L., Jorgensen, E., Lippert, F. K., & Clemmensen, P. M. (2006). Telemedicine in the transmission of pre-hospitalization EKGs of patients with suspected acute myocardial infarction. *Ugeskrift for Laeger*, *68*(11), 1133–1136.

Silva, J. S., & Ball, M. J. (2002). Prognosis for year 2013. *International Journal of Medical Informatics*, *66*(1-3), 45–49. doi:10.1016/S1386-5056(02)00035-7

Silverman, D. (2001). *Interpreting qualitative data.* London: Sage Publications.

Silverman, D. (2005). *Doing Qualitative Research*, (2nd Ed.). London: Sage Publications.

Silverstein, S. (2006). Sociotechnologic issues in clinical computing: Common examples of healthcare IT failure. Retrieved on April 21, 2006, from http://www.ischool.drexel.edu.faculty/ssilverstein/failurecases/

Sim, J., & Sharp, K. (1998). A critical appraisal of the role of triangulation in nursing research. International Journal of Nursing Studies, 35(1/2), 23-31.

Simon, H. A. (1996). *The sciences of the artificial.* Cambridge, MA: The MIT Press.

Simpson, A., Power, D., Slaymaker, M., & Politou, E. (2005). GIMI: generic infrastructure for medical informatics. In *Proceedings of the 18th symposium on computer-based medical system*, (pp. 564-566). Washington, DC: IEEE Computer Society.

Simpson, R. L. (2003). The patient's point of view—IT matters. *Nursing Administration Quarterly, 27*(3), 254–256.

Siro, C. A., Segel, K. T., Keyser, D. J., Harrison, E. I., & Lloyd, J. C. (2003). Pittsburgh regional healthcare initiative: a systems approach for achieving perfect patient care. *Health Affairs, 22*(5), 157–165. doi:10.1377/hlthaff.22.5.157

Skinner, H., Biscope, S., & Poland, B. (2003). Quality of Internet access: Barrier behind Internet use statistics. *Social Science & Medicine, 57*(5), 875-880.

Slaymaker, M., Politou, E., Power, D., & Lloyd, S. (2004). E-Health security issues: The eDiaMoND perspective. In *Proceedings of the 2004 UK e-Science All Hands Meeting.*

Smaglik, P., Hawkins, R., Pingree, S., & Gustafson, D. (1998). The quality of interactive computer use among HIV infected individuals. *Journal of Health Communication, 3*, 53–68. doi:10.1080/108107398127508

Smit, M., McAllister, M., & Slonim, J. (2005). Public Trust and Electronic Health Records. *Conf. on Privacy, Security and Trust (PST).*

Smith, C. (2004). New Technology Continues to Invade Healthcare: What are the Strategic Implications/Outcomes? *Nursing Administration Quarterly, 28*(2), 92–98.

Smith, D. E. (2005). *Institutional ethnography. A sociology for people.* Lanham, MD: Altamira Press.

Smith, H., & Fingar, P. (2003). Business Process Management. *The Third Wave.* Tampa, FL: Meghan-Kiffer Press.

Smith, P. C., & Van Ackere, A. (2002). A note on the integration of system dynamics and economic models. *Journal of Economic Dynamics & Control, 26*(1), 1–10. doi:10.1016/S0165-1889(00)00025-7

Smith, R. (2007). *Business Process Management and the Balanced Scorecard: Using Processes as Strategic Drivers.* Hoboken, NJ: John-Wiley and Sons.

Snyder, C. R. (Ed.). (1999). *Coping – The psychology of what works.* New York: Oxford University Press.

Software Engineering Institute. *CMMI: Capability maturity model integrated.* Retrieved on November 1, 2007, from www.sei.cmu.edu/cmmi/

Software Quality Institute GU. *SPICE software process improvement and capability determination.* Retrieved on August 13, 2007, from: http://www.sqi.gu.edu.au/spice/

Song, J., & Zahedi, F. (2007). Trust in health infomediaries. *Decision Support Systems, 43*(2), 390–407. doi:10.1016/j.dss.2006.11.011

Sørby, I. D. (2007). *Observing and analyzing clinicians' information and communication behaviour: An approach to requirements engineering for mobile health information systems.* Doctoral Thesis. Norwegian University of Science and Technology, 2007:220.

Sørby, I. D., & Nytrø, Ø. (2007). Analysis of communicative behaviour: Profiling roles and activities. *Studies in Health Technology and Informatics, 130*, 111–120.

Sørby, I. D., Melby, L., & Nytrø, Ø. (2006). Characterizing cooperation in the ward: Framework for producing requirements to mobile electronic healthcare records. *International Journal of Healthcare Technology and Management, 7*(6), 506–521.

Sørby, I. D., Melby, L., & Seland, G. (2005). Using scenarios and drama improvisation for identifying and analysing requirements for mobile electronic patient records. In J. L. Maté & A. Silva (Eds.), *Requirements engineering for sociotechnical systems* (pp. 266-283). Hershey, PA: Information Science Publishing.

Sorzano, C. O. S., Marabini, R., Velázquez-Muriel, J., Bilbao-Castro, J. R., Scheres, S. H. W., Carazo, J. M., & Pascual-Montano, A. (2004). XMIPP: A new generation of an open-source image processing package for electron microscopy. *Journal of Structural Biology, 148*(2), 194–204. doi:10.1016/j.jsb.2004.06.006

Spil, T. A. M., & Schuring, R. W. (2006). E-Health system Diffusion and Use. Hershey, PA: Idea Group Publishing.

Srinivasan, R., Rangaswamy, A., & Lilien, G. L. (2005). Turning Adversity into Advantage: Does Proactive Marketing during a Recession Pay Off? *International Journal of Research in Marketing*.

Stahl, B. C. (2008). The ethical nature of critical research in information systems. *Information Systems Journal, 18*, 137–163. doi:10.1111/j.1365-2575.2007.00283.x

Star, S. L., & Griesemer, J. R. (1989). Institutional ecology, translations, and boundary objects: Amateurs and professionals in Berkley's Museum of Vertebrate Zoology 1907-39. *Social Studies of Science, 19*, 387–420. doi:10.1177/030631289019003001

Steiner, J. G., Neuman, B. C., & Schiller, J. I. (1988, February). *Kerberos: An Authentication Service for Open Network Systems.* Paper presented at the Winter 1988 Usenix Conference.

Steinfeld, E., & Danford, G. S. (1999). *Enabling environments. Measuring the impact of environment on disability and rehabilitation.* New York: Kluwer Academic.

Sterman, J. (2000). *Business dynamics: systems thinking and modeling for a complex world.* London: Irwin/McGraw-Hill.

Stevens, R., McEntire, R., Goble, C., Greenwood, M., Zhao, J., Wipat, A., & Li, P. (2004). myGrid and the drug discovery process. *Drug Discovery Today: BIOSILICO, 2*(4), 140–148. doi:10.1016/S1741-8364(04)02412-6

Stewart, C. A. (2004). Introduction to the edition. *Communications of the ACM, 47*(11), 30–33. doi:10.1145/1029496.1029522

Stoop, A., Heathfield, H., de Mul, M., & Berg, M. (2004). Evaluation of patient care information systems: theory and practice. In M. Berg, E. Coiera, H. Heathfield, et al. (Eds.), *Health information management* (pp. 206-229). London: Routledge.

Strauss, A. L., Fagerhaug, S., Suczek, B., & Wiener, C. (1997). *Social organization of medical work.* New Brunswick: Transaction Publishers.

Stroetmann, K., Jones, T., & Dobrev, A. (2006, May 10-12). Evaluating the economic impact of e-health applications approach and method. *E-Health Conference 2006*, Malaga, Spain.

Stuart, D., & Bawany, K. (2001). *Wireless Services: United Kingdom* (Operational Management Report No. DPRO-90741). Gartner.

Suchman, L. (1987). *Plans and situated actions: the problem of human-machine communication.* Cambridge, UK: Cambridge University Press.

Suchman, L. (1995). Making work visible. *Communications of the ACM, 38*(9), 56–65. doi:10.1145/223248.223263

Suchman, M. C. (1995). Managing legitimacy: Strategic and institutional approaches. *Academy of Management Review, 20*, 571-610.

Suomi, R. (2006). Introducing electronic patient records to hospitals: Innovation adoption paths. In T.A.M. Spil & R.W.Schuring (Eds.), *E-Health Systems Diffusion and Use: The Innovation, the User and the USE IT Model.* Hershey, PA: IGI Global.

Susman, G., & Evered, R. (1978). *An assessment of scientific merits of action research* (Vol. 25, pp. 582-603).

Sutton, D. R., & Fox, J. (2003). The syntax and semantics of the PROforma guideline modeling language. *Journal of the American Medical Informatics Association, 10*(5), 433–443. doi:10.1197/jamia.M1264

Svanæs, D. (2001). Context-aware technology: A phenomenological perspective. *Human-Computer Interaction, 16*(2), 379–400. doi:10.1207/S15327051HCI16234_17

Svanæs, D., & Seland, G. (2004). Putting the users center stage: Role playing and low-fi prototyping enable end users to design mobile systems. In *Proceedings of the SIGCHI Conference on Human Factors in Computing Systems (CHI 2004)* (pp. 479-486). New York: ACM Press.

Swedish Cancer Society (2008). Retrieved July 12, 2008, from http://www.cancerfonden.se.

Sweeney, L. (1997). Guaranteeing anonymity when sharing medical data, the Datafly System. *Proceedings/AMIA Annual Fall Symposium*, (pp. 51-55).

Swinfen, P., Swinfen, R., Youngberry, K., & Wootton, R. (2005). Low-cost telemedicine in Iraq: An analysis of referrals in the first 15 months. *Telemedicine and Telecare, 11*(Suppl 2), 113.

Systems Engineering Initiative for Patient Safety. (2003). *SEIPS model.* Retrieved on May 12, 2006, from http://www2.fpm.wisc.edu/seips/SEIPS

Talmon, J., & Hasmann, A. (2002). Medical informatics as a discipline at the beginning of the 21st century. Methods of Information and Medicine, 41, 4-7.

Tanriverdi, H., & Iacono, C. N. (1999). Knowledge barriers to diffusion of telemedicine. In *Proceedings of the 20th International Conference on Information Systems*, Charlotte, NC, (pp. 39–50).

Tao, W. (2005). *IP broadband access network construction–network marketing department* (Tech. Rep.). Huawei Technologies Co., Ltd.

Tarasewich, P. (2003). Wireless devices for mobile commerce: User interface design and usability. In B. E. M. a. T. J. Strader (Ed.), *Mobile commerce: Technology, theory, and applications* (pp. 26-50). Hershey, PA: IRM Press.

Taylor, C. (2003). *Reference Models for IT service Provision.* Masters dissertation, Queensland University of Technology, Brisbane, Australia.

Taylor, K., & Lane, D. (1998). Simulation applied to health services: opportunities for applying the system dynamics approach. *Journal of Health Services Research & Policy, 3*, 226–232.

Taylor, S. J. E., Sharpe, J., & Ladbrook, J. (2003). Time management issues in COTS distributed simulation: a case study. In S. Chick, P. J. Sánchez, D. Ferrin, & D. J. Morrice, (Eds.) *Proceedings of the 35th Winter Simulation Conference*, (pp. 838-846). Winter Simulation Conference, USA.

Taylor, S. J. E., Sudra, R., Janahan, T., Tan, G., & Ladbrook, J. (2002). GRIDS-SCF: An infrastructure for distributed supply chain simulation. *Simulation, 78*(5), 312–320. doi:10.1177/0037549702078005553

Taylor, S. J. E., Wang, X., Turner, S. J., & Low, M. Y. H. (2006). Integrating heterogeneous distributed COTS discrete-event simulation packages: an emerging standards-based approach. *IEEE Transactions on Systems . Man and Cybernetics: Part A, 36*(1), 109–122. doi:10.1109/TSMCA.2005.859167

Taylor, W. F. (1911). *Modern History Sourcebook: The Principles of Scientific Management.* Retrieved November 22nd, 2006 from http://www.fordham.edu/halsall/mod/1911taylor.html

Terry Ma, H., & Zaphiris, P. (2003). The usability and content accessibility of the e-government in the UK. London: Centre for Human-Computer Interaction Design, City University. Retrieved from http://www.soi.city.ac.uk/~zaphiri/Papers/HCII2003/HCII2003-Accessibility.pdf

Terry, D., Demers, A. J., Peterson, K., Spreitzer, M.J., Theimer, M.M., & Welch, B. (1994). Session guarantees for weakly consistent replicated data. In *Proceedings PDIS* (pp. 140-149).

Terry, D., Theimer, M.M., Peterson, K., Demers, A. J., Spreitzer, M.J., & Hauser, C.H. (1995). Managing update conflicts in Bayou: A weakly connected replicated storage system. In *Proceedings of the ACM Symposium on OS* (pp. 172-183).

Thakurdas, P., Coster, G, Guirr, E., & Arroll, B. (1996). New Zealand general practice computerisation: Attitudes and reported behavior. *New Zealand Medical Journal, 109*, 419–422.

The Center for the Evaluative Clinical Sciences. D. M. S. (1998). *The Dartmouth atlas of healthcare 1998.* Chicago: American Hospital Publishing.

The Open Group. (2007). The Open Group Architecture Framework (TOGAF 8.1.1). Retrieved July 14th 2008 from http://www.opengroup.org/bookstore/catalog/g063v.htm

The Royal Society, (2006). *Digital healthcare: the impact of information and communication technologies on health and healthcare.*

The Simputer Trust. (2000). *Simputer(TM) - Welcome.* Retrieved December 1, 2006, from http://www.simputer.org/.

Thomas, R., Robinson, J., Waring, T., Wainwright, D., & Maguire, S. (1995). Information Management and Technology in England's Large Acute NHS Hospitals. *Journal of Management in Medicine, 9*(1), 40–49. doi:10.1108/02689239510080476

Thompson, T. G., & Brailer, D. J. (2004). *The decade of health information technology: Delivering consumer-centric and information-rich healthcare.* Retrieved on July 23, 2004, from http://www.hhs.gov/onchit/framework/hitframework.pdf

Timmermans, S., & Berg, M. (2003). *The gold standard. The challenge of evidence-based medicine and standardization in healthcare.* Philadelphia: Temple University Press.

Timmermans, S., & Berg, M. (2003). The practice of medical technology. *Sociology of Health & Illness, 25*(3), 97–114.

Tirado-Ramos, A., Groen, D., & Sloot, P. (2005). On-line application performance monitoring of blood flow simulation in computational grid architectures. In *Proceedings of the 18th symposium on computer-based medical system*, (pp. 511-516). Washington, DC: IEEE Computer Society.

Tita, A., Stringer, J., Goldenberg, R., & Rouse, D. (2007). Two decades of the safe motherhood initiative: Time for another wooden spoon award?. *Obstet Gynecol, 110*(5), 972-976.

Tohsato, Y., Kosaka, T., Date, S., Shimojo, S., & Matsuda, H. (2005). *Heterogeneous database federation using grid technology for drug discovery process*, (pp. 43-52). (LNCS Vol. 3370). Berlin, Germany: Springer-Verlag.

Tomasi, E., Augusto, L., & Maria de Fatima Santos, M. (2004). Health information technology in primary healthcare in developing countries: A literature review. *Bull World Health Organ, 82*(11), 867-874.

Tornatzky, L., & Klein, K. (1982). Innovation characteristics and innovation adoption-implementation: A meta-analysis of findings. *IEEE Transactions on Engineering Management, 29*(1), 28–45.

Torp, S., Hanson, E., Hauge, S., & Magnusson, L. (2008). A pilot study of how information and communication technology may contribute to health promotion among elderly spousal carers in Norway. *Health & Social Care in the Community, 16*(1), 75–85.

Tu, S. W., Campbell, J. R., Glasgow, J., Nyman, M. A., McClure, R., & McClay, J. (2007). The SAGE Guideline Model: achievements and overview. *Journal of the American Medical Informatics Association, 14*(5), 589–598. doi:10.1197/jamia.M2399

Turisco, F. (2000). Mobile computing is next technology frontier for health providers. *Healthcare Financial Management, 54*(11), 78–82.

Turisco, F., & Case, J. (2001). Wireless and Mobile Computing. *Health Reports.* California Healthcare Foundation.

Vadhiyar, S. S., & Dongarra, J. J. (2005). Self adaptivity in grid computing. *Concurrency and Computation, 17*(2-4), 235–257. doi:10.1002/cpe.927

Van Bemmel, J. H., Musen, M. A., & Helder, J. C. (1997). *Handbook of medical informatics.* Heidelberg, Germany: Bohn Stafleu Van Loghum; Springer Verlag.

van der Aalst, W. M. P., & van Hee, K. M. (1996). Business process redesign: A Petri-net-based approach. *Computers in Industry, 29*(1–2), 15–26. doi:10.1016/0166-3615(95)00051-8

Van der Aalst, W. M. P., ter Hofstede, A. H. M., & Weske, M. (2003). Business Process Management: A Survey. In *Proceedings of the International conference of Business Process Management*, Eidhoven, The Netherlands, June 26-27.

van der Loo, R. (1995). Overview of published assessment and evaluation studies. In E. M. S. J. van Gennip & J. S. Talmon (Eds.), Assessment and evaluation of information technologies (pp. 261-82). Amsterdam: IOS Press.

Van Der Meijden, M. J., Tange, H. J., Troost, J., & Hasman, A. (2003). Determinents of success of inpatient clinical information systems: A literature review. *Journal of the American Medical Informatics Association, 10*(3), 235–243. doi:10.1197/jamia.M1094

van der Sijs, H., Aarts, J., Vulto, A., & Berg, M. (2006). Overriding of drug safety alerts in computerized physician order entry. *Journal of the American Medical Informatics Association, 13*(2), 138–147. doi:10.1197/jamia.M1809

van Donselaar, K. H., van Woensel, T., Broekmeulen, R. A. C. M., & Fransoo, J. C. (2006). Inventory control of perishables in supermarkets. *International Journal of Production Economics, 104*(2), 462–472. doi:10.1016/j.ijpe.2004.10.019

van't Riet, A., Berg, M., Hiddema, F., & Sol, K. (2001). Meeting patients' needs with patient information systems: potential benefits of qualitative research methods. *International Journal of Medical Informatics, 64*, 1–14. doi:10.1016/S1386-5056(01)00185-X

Vanier, F. (2008). *World broadband statistics Q1*. Point Topic Ltd.

Varley, P. (2007). *World broadband statistics Q2*. Point Topic Ltd.

Varshney, U. (2006). Using wireless technologies in healthcare. *International Journal of Mobile Communications, 4*(3), 354–368.

VATAM. (2000). The VATAM Websites. Validation of health telematics applications (VATAM). Retrieved May 2005, from http://www-vatam.unimaas.nl

Venkatesh, V., & Davis, F. D. (2000). A theoretical extension of the technology acceptance model: Four longitudinal field studies. *Management Science, 46*(2), 186–204. doi:10.1287/mnsc.46.2.186.11926

Venkatesh, V., Morris, M. G., Davis, G. B., & Davis, F. (2003). User Acceptance of Information Technology: Toward A Unified View. *MIS Quarterly, 27*(3), 425–478.

Vera, A., & Kuntz, L. (2007). Process-based organization design and hospital efficiency. *Health Care Management Review, 32*(1), 55–65.

Vermaas, K., & Wijngaert, L. (2005). Seeking Health Information on the Internet. Different genders, different uses, different risks. In *Proceedings of 13th European Conference on Information Systems*, May 26-28, 2005, Regensburg, Germany.

Voelker, R. (2005). Seniors seeking health information need help crossing the "digital divide." *JAMA, 293*(11), 1310-1312.

Voskarides, S., Pattichis, C. S., Istepanian, R., Michaelides, C., & Schizas, C. N. (2003). Practical evaluation of GPRS use in a telemedicine system in Cyprus. In *CD-ROM Proceedings of the 4th Int. IEEE EMBS Special Topic Conference on Information Technology Applications in Biomedicine,* Birmingham.

Wachter, R. (2004). The end of the beginning: Patient safety five years after 'to err is human'. *Health Affairs, 23*(Suppl. 2), W4-534–W545.

Wachter, R. (2006). Expected and unanticipated consequences of the quality and information technology revolutions. *Journal of the American Medical Association, 295*(23), 2780–2783. doi:10.1001/jama.295.23.2780

Wachter, R. M., & Shojania, K. (2004). Handoffs and Fumbles. In Wachter, R. & Shojania, K. (Eds.), *Internal Bleeding: The Truth Behind America's Terrifying Epidemic of Medical Mistakes*. New York: Rugged Land, LLC.

Walker, J., Pan, E., Johnston, D., Adler-Milstein, J., Bates, D. W., & Middleton, B. (2005, January 19). The value of health care information exchange and interoperability. *Health Affairs,* w5-10–w15-18.

Walshe, K., & Freeman, T. (2002). Effectiveness of quality improvement: learning from evaluations. *Quality & Safety in Health Care, 11*, 85–87. doi:10.1136/qhc.11.1.85

Wang, B., & Paper, D. (2005). A case of an IT-enabled organizational change intervention: The missing pieces. *Journal of Cases on Information Technology, 7*(1), 34-52.

Wang, D., Peleg, M., Tu, S. W., Boxwala, A. A., Greenes, R. A., & Patel, V. L. (2002). Representation primitives, process models and patient data in computer-interpretable clinical practice guidelines: a literature review of guideline representation models. *International Journal of Medical Informatics, 68*(1-3), 59–70. doi:10.1016/S1386-5056(02)00065-5

Wang, D., Peleg, M., Tu, S. W., Boxwala, A. A., Ogunyemi, O., & Zeng, Q. (2004). Design and implementation of the GLIF3 guideline execution engine. *Journal of Biomedical Informatics, 37*(5), 305–318. doi:10.1016/j.jbi.2004.06.002

Wang, L., Bretschneider, S., & Gant, J. (2005). Evaluating Web-based e-government services with a citizen-centric approach. In *Proceedings of 38th Annual Hawaii International Conference on Systems Sciences*, Big Island, Hawaii.

Wang, S. J., Middleton, B., Prosser, L. A., Bardon, C. G., Spurr, C. D., Carchidi, P. J., et al. (2003). A cost-benefit analysis of electronic medical records in primary care. *The American Journal of Medicine, 114*(5), 397-403.

Wang, Y., Gräther, W., & Prinz, W. (2007). *Suitable notification intensity: the dynamic awareness system.* ACM SIGGROUP Conference on Supporting Group Work (GROUP), Sanibel Island, Florida, USA, November 4-7, pp. 99-106.

Wears, R., & Berg, M. (2005). Computer technology and clinical work: Still waiting for Godot. *Journal of the American Medical Association, 293*(10), 1261–1263. doi:10.1001/jama.293.10.1261

Weick, K. (1979). *The social psychology of organizing, second ed.* New York: McGraw-Hill.

Weick, K. (1990). Technology as equivoque: Sensemaking in new technologies. In P. Goodman & L. Sproull (Eds.), *Technology and organizations* (pp. 1-44). San Francisco: Jossey Bass.

Weiner, J., Kfuri, T., Chan, K., & Fowles, J. (2007). "e-Iatrogensis": The most critical unintended consequence of CPOE and HIT. *Journal of the American Medical Informatics Association, 14*(3), 387–388. doi:10.1197/jamia.M2338

Weinrauch, D. J., Mann, O. K., Robinson, P. A., & Pharr, J. (1991). Dealing with Limited Financial Resources: A Marketing Challenge for Small Business. *Journal of Small Business Management, 29*(4), 44–54.

Weiser, M. (1991). The computer for the 21st century. *Scientific American, 265*(3), 66–75.

Welch, S. J., & Allen, T. L. (2006). Data-driven quality improvement in the emergency department at a level one trauma and tertiary care hospital. *The Journal of Emergency Medicine, 30*, 269–276. doi:10.1016/j.jemermed.2005.07.007

West, D. (2000). *Assessing e-government: The Internet, democracy, and service delivery by state and federal governments.* Brown University. Retrieved from www.insidepolitics.org/policyreports.html

Westbrook, J. I., & Gosling, A. S. (2002). *The impact of point of care clinical systems on healthcare: A review of the evidence and a framework for evaluation.* Sydney, Australia: Centre for Health Informatics, University of New South Wales.

Westbrook, J. I., Braithwaite, J., Georgiou, A., Ampt, A., Creswick, N., Coiera, E., & Iedema, R. (2007). Multimethod Evaluation of Information and Communication Technologies in Health in the Context of Wicked Problems and Sociotechnical Theory. *Journal of the American Medical Informatics Association, 14*(6), 746–755. doi:10.1197/jamia.M2462

Westerberg, K. (2000). *The important activity - work, tools and tensions of municipal middle managers in elder care.* Doctoral thesis: Department of Applied Psychology, Umeå Universitet, Umeå, Sweden.

Weyer, J. (Ed.). (2000). *Soziale Netzwerke. Konzepte und Methoden der sozialwissenschaftlichen Netzwerkforschung.* München/Wien, Germany: Oldenbourg.

Wheelwright, G. (2002, Dec. 3). The business benefits of mobility. *Financial Times of London,* p. 11.

Whittle, R., & Myrick, C. (2005). Enterprise Business Architecture: The formal results between strategy and results. Boca Raton, FL: Auerbach Publications.

WHO. (2004). *eHealth for Health-care Delivery: Strategy 2004-2007*. Geneva, Switzerland: WHO. Retrieved from www.who.int/eht/en/EHT_strategy_2004-2007.pdf.

Wiberg, M., & Ljungberg, F. (2001). Exploring the vision of "Anytime, Anywhere" in the context of mobile work. In Y. Malhotra (Ed.), *Knowledge management and business model innovation* (pp. 153-165). Hershey, Pennsylvania: Idea Group Publishing.

Wickramasinghe, N., & Goldberg, S. (2004). How M=EC2 in healthcare. *International Journal of Mobile Commerce*.

Wickramasinghe, N., & Misra, S. (2004). A wireless trust model for healthcare. *International Journal e-Health*.

Wiki (2008). *Wireless Sensor Networks*. Retrieved on Jan 23, 2008, from http://en.wikipedia.org/wiki/Category:Wireless_sensor_network

Willcocks, L., & Lester, S. (1993, May 17-19). How do organizations evaluate and control information-systems investments-recent UK survey evidence. In D. Avison, et al. (Eds.), *Human, organizational, and social dimensions of IS development. Proceedings of the IFIP WG8.2 Working Group Conference,* Noordwijkerhout, Netherlands. Amsterdam: Elsevier North Holland.

Wilson, M., & Howcroft, D. (2002). Re-conceptualising failure: social shaping meets IS research. *European Journal of Information Systems, 11*, 236–250. doi:10.1057/palgrave.ejis.3000437

Wilson, P., Leitner, C., & Moussalli, A. (2004). Mapping the Potential of eHealth: Empowering the Citizen through eHealth Tools and Services. Paper presented at the eHealth Conference, Cork, Ireland, 5-6 May, 2004, European Institute of Public Administration, Maastricht, the Netherlands.

Winter, A., Ammenwerth, E., Bott, O., Brigl, B., Buchauer, A., Gräber, S., et al. (2001). Strategic information management plans: The basis for systematic information management in hospitals. International Journal of Medical Informatics, 64(2/3), 99-109.

Winter, R., & Munn-Giddings, C. (2001). *A handbook for action research in health and social care*. New York: Routledge.

Wisnicki, H. J. (2002). Wireless networking transforms healthcare: physician's practices better able to handle workflow, increase productivity (The human connection). *Ophthalmology Times, 27*(21), 38–41.

Witkowski, M., Artikis, A., & Pitt, J. (2000). Trust and Cooperation in a Trading Society of Objective-Trust Based Agents. In Falcone, R., Singh, M., & Tan, Y.H. (Eds.), *Autonomous Agents Workshop on Deception, Fraud and Trust in Agent Societies.* Barcelona, Spain.

Woods, D. D. (1998). Designs are hypotheses about how artifacts shape cognition and collaboration. *Ergonomics, 41*(2), 168–173. doi:10.1080/001401398187215

Wooton, R. (2001). Telemedicine and developing countries—successful implementation will require a shared approach. *Telemedicine and Telecare, 7*(Suppl 1), 1-6.

World Bank. (2006). *Connecting People, Improving Health: the Role of ICTs in the Health Sector of Developing Countries*, (pp.5-6).

World Health Organization. (2006). *Estimates of child and adult mortality and life expectancy at birth by country.* Retrieved January 17, 2007, from http://www.who.int/healthinfo/statistics/mortlifeexpectancy/en/index.html.

World Health Organization. (2006). *Introduction to the 'Making Pregnancy Safer' initiative*. Retrieved October 1, 2007, from http://w3.whosea.org/pregnancy/introf.htm.

World Markets Research Centre & Brown University. (2001). *Global e-government survey 2001.* Retrieved from http://www.worldmarketsanalysis.com/pdf/e-govreport.pdf

Worthen, B. (2002, December 1). When wireless works. *CIO, 16,* 1.

Wright, K. B., & Bell, S. B. (2003). Health-related Support Groups on the Internet: Linking Empirical Findings to Social Support and Computer-mediated Communication Theory. *Journal of Health Psychology, 8*(1), 39–54. doi:10.1177/1359105303008001429

Wu, B., Dovey, M., Ng, M. H., Tai, K., Murdock, S., Jeffreys, P., et al. (2004). A web / grid portal implementation of BioSimGrid: A biomolecular simulation database. In *Proceedings of the Information Technology: Coding and Computing*, (pp. 50-54).

Wu, J. H., Wang, S. C., & Lin, L. M. (2005). *What drives mobile healthcare? An empirical evaluation of technology acceptance.* 38th Hawaii International Conference on System Sciences, Hawaii.

Wu, J. H., Wang, S. C., & Lin, L. M. (2007). Mobile computing acceptance factors in the healthcare industry: A structural equation model. *International Journal of Medical Informatics, 76*(1), 66–77. doi:10.1016/j.ijmedinf.2006.06.006

Wyatt, J. (1994). Clinical data systems, part 3: Development and evaluation. The Lancet, 344, 1682-1688.

Wyatt, J. (2000). When to use Web-based surveys. *Journal of the American Medical Informatics Association, 7*(4), 426–430.

Wyatt, J. C. (1995). Hospital information management: the need for clinical leadership. *BMJ (Clinical Research Ed.), 311*, 175–178.

Wyatt, J. C., & Wyatt, S. M. (2003). When and how to evaluate health information systems? *International Journal of Medical Informatics, 69*, 251–259. doi:10.1016/S1386-5056(02)00108-9

Wyatt, J., & Spiegelhalter, D. (1992). Field trials of medical decision-aids: Potential problems and solutions. In P. Clayton (Ed.), 15th Annual Symposium on Computer Applications in Medical Care (pp. 3-7). New York: McGraw-Hill.

Xing, L., Wang, J., & Zhou, B. (2006). Integration and access of data resources in simulation grid system. *Journal of System Simulation, 18*(2), 369–372.

Yin, R. K. (2003). *Case Study Research Design and Methods: Applied Social Research Methods.* Thousand Oaks, CA: Sage.

Young, T., Brailsford, S., Connell, C., Davies, R., Harper, P., & Klein, J. H. (2004). Using industrial processes to improve patient care. *British Medical Journal, 328*(7432), 162–164. doi:10.1136/bmj.328.7432.162

Zak, D. (1999). *Programming with Microsoft Visual Basic 6.0.* Thomson Publishing.

Zakaria, N., & Mohd Yusof, S. (2001). The role of human and organizational culture in the context of technological change. In *Proceedings of IEMC--Change Management and the New Industrial Revolution.*

Zamboulis, L., Fan, H., Belhajjame, K., Siepen, J., Jones, A., Martin, N., et al. *Data access and integration in the ISPIDER proteomics Grid.* Retrieved February 1, 2008 from http://www.cs.man.ac.uk/~norm/papers/dils06.pdf

Zaslavsky, A., & Tari, S. (1998). Mobile computing: Overview and current status. *Australian Computer Journal, 30*(2), 42-52.

Zeithaml, V. A., Parasuraman, A., & Malhotra, A. (2000). A conceptual framework for understanding e-service quality: Implications for future research and managerial practice. *Marketing Sciences Institute: Working Paper Series, 00*(115), 2000.

Zeng, X., & Parmanto, B. (2004). Web content accessibility of consumer health information. Web sites for people with disabilities: A cross sectional evaluation. *Journal of Medical Internet Research, 6*(2), e19. doi:10.2196/jmir.6.2.e19

Zhu, W., Nah, F. F.-H., & Zhao, F. (2003). Factors influencing user adoption of mobile computing. In J. Mariga (Ed.), *Managing e-commerce and mobile computing technologies* (pp. 260-271). Hershey, PA: IRM Press.

Zhuchkov, A., Tverdokhlebov, N., & Kravchenko, A. (2006). Advancing of Russian ChemBioGrid by bringing data management tools into collaborative environment. *Studies in Health Technology and Informatics, 120*, 179–186.

Ziebland, S. (2004). The importance of being expert: the quest for cancer information on the Internet. *Social Science & Medicine, 59*(9), 1783–1793. doi:10.1016/j.socscimed.2004.02.019

Zielstorff, R. D. (1998). Online practice guidelines: issues, obstacles, and future prospects. *Journal of the American Medical Informatics Association, 5*(3), 227–236.

Zikmund, W. (1994). *Business research methods* (International Ed.), Orlando, FL: The Dryden Press.

Zineldin, M. A. (1998). Towards an Ecological Collaborative Relationship Management. *European Journal of Management*, *32*(11/12), 1138–1164.

Zonabend, F. (1992). The monograph in European ethnology. *Current Sociology*, *40*(1), 49–60. doi:10.1177/001139292040001005

Zou, X., Ramamurthy, B., & Magliveras, S. (2001). Chinese Remainder Theorem Based Hierarchical Access Control for Secure Group Communication. In *Information and Communications Security* (pp. 381-385).

Zuboff, S. (1988). *In the age of the smart machine the future of work and power*. New York: Basic Books.

About the Contributors

Khalil Khoumbati is a Professor in the Institute of Information and Communication Technology University of Sindh, Jamshoro, Sindh, Pakistan. He gets hold of his PhD in "*Evaluation the Adoption of Enterprise Application Integration in Healthcare Organizations*" from the School of Information Systems, Computing and Mathematics, Brunel University, UK. MSc in Computer Technology and BSc in Electronics from Institute of Information and Communication Technology, University of Sindh, Jamshoro, Pakistan. His current research focus is on the adoption of enterprise application integration health informatics and e-government applications. He is on the editorial board of several international journals such as *Transforming Government: People, Process and Policy*. He has published 25 research papers in internationally refereed journals such as *Journal of Management Information Systems* and *Journal of Computer and Information Systems*. He has presented 16 papers in international conferences such as HICSS, AMCIS, ECIS and EMCIS. He can be reached at khalil.khoumbati@gmail.com

Yogesh K. Dwivedi is a Lecturer in the School of Business and Economics at Swansea University in the UK. He was awarded his MSc and PhD by Brunel University in the UK, receiving a Highly Commended award for his doctoral work by the European Foundation for Management and Development. His research focuses on the adoption and diffusion of ICT in organisations and in addition to authoring a book and numerous conference papers, has co-authored papers accepted for publication by journals such as *Communications of the ACM*, the *Information Systems Journal*, the *European Journal of Information Systems*, and the *Journal of the Operational Research Society*. He is Senior Editor of *DATABASE for Advances in Information Systems*, Assistant Editor of *Transforming Government: People, Process and Policy* and a member of the editorial board/review board of a number of other journals, and is a member of the Association of Information Systems, IFIP WG8.6 and the Global Institute of Flexible Systems Management, New Delhi. He can be reached at ykdwivedi@gmail.com

Aradhana Srivastava is a geographer with a keen research interest in the geography of health. She holds a PhD in Geography of Health from Centre for the Study of Regional Development, Jawaharlal Nehru University, New Delhi, one of the premier national universities in India. She has to her credit several publications in health and social development on issues in health status, morbidity analysis, ageing and health care, social morbidity, nutrition, maternal and child health, and information and communication technologies in health sector. She is currently working with Urban Health Resource Centre (UHRC), a premier national Non-Governmental Organization, on issues of urban poverty and access to healthcare among the poor in India's cities. She can be reached at ara.sriv@gmail.com

Banita Lal is a lecturer in the Nottingham Business School, Nottingham Trent University, UK. She obtained her Ph.D. and M.Sc. in Information Systems from the School of Information Systems, Computing and Mathematics, Brunel University. Her research interests involve examining the individual and organizational adoption and usage of ICTs and technology-enabled alternative forms of working. She has published several research papers in internationally refereed journals such as *Industrial Management and Data Systems, Information Systems Frontiers, Electronic Government, International Journal of Mobile Communications*, and *Transforming Government: People, Process and Policy*, and has presented several papers at several international conferences. She can be reached at banita.la.@ntu.ac.uk

***

James G. Anderson Ph.D. earned a B.E.S. in Chemical Engineering, M.S.E. in Operations Research and Industrial Engineering, M.A.T. in Chemistry and Mathematics, and a Ph.D. in Education and Sociology from the Johns Hopkins University. He is a Fellow of the American College of Medical Informatics. Dr. Anderson is the former Director of the Division of Engineering of the Evening College at Johns Hopkins University. He is currently professor of medical sociology and health communication at Purdue University. While at Purdue, he has served as Assistant Dean for Analytical Studies of the School of Humanities, Social Sciences and Education (1975-1978, Director of the Social Research Institute (1995-1998), and Co-Director of the Rural Center for AIDS/STD Prevention (1994-2006). He is the author/co-author of five books including *Evaluating the Organizational Impact of Health Care Information Systems*, (Springer, 2005); *Ethics and Information Technology: A Case-Based Approach to a Health Care System in Transition*, (Springer, 2002); *Evaluating Health Care Information Systems: Methods and Applications*, (Sage, 1994); and *Use and Impact of Computers in Clinical Medicine*, (Springer-Verlag, 1987).

Wasana Bandara has worked for 8 years as an academic in Information Systems (IS), She currently holds a Senior Lecturer position at the Faculty of Science and Technology, Queensland University of Technology (QUT). Wasana is an internationally recognized researcher in the areas of Business Process Management and Process Modelling. She has published in leading academic and practitioner outlets and has been an invited speaker in a number of business process management conferences and events. Wasana Completed her PhD on '*Business Process Modelling Success Factors and Measures*' in 2007, and received the Australian Council of Professors and Heads of Information Systems (ACPHIS) medal (awarded for the best IS PhD Study in Australia).

Nesaar Banderker was born and bred in Cape Town, South Africa. I obtained a Bachelor of Commerce degree specializing in Information Systems and Auditing in 1997. Post that degree I obtained a BCom (Hons) in 2005 and I am currently completing my MCom degree. I am currently a project manager working for a large international financial services company. I am married to a health professional hence my interest in health information systems. And I have two exceptionally lively boys. The 8 year old is wise in the ways of the world and is starting to ask very awkward questions. The 4 year old is wise in ways of being exceptionally entertaining, playful and naughty.

Nazife Baykal is the director of the Informatics Institute and a member of Senate at Middle East Technical University (METU), Ankara, Turkey. She also acts as the director of the METU E-Government Centre which was established in 2006 to provide academic support to e-transformation Turkey projects. She has been involved with many e-Government projects in Turkey both as a consultant and project manager.

Sally Brailsford is Professor of Management Science at the University of Southampton, UK. She received a BSc in Mathematics from the University of London, and an MSc and PhD in Operational Research from the University of Southampton. Her research interests include simulation modeling methodologies, system dynamics, health service research and disease modeling, and the modeling of human behavior in healthcare systems. She is on the editorial boards of *Health Care Management Science*, the *Journal of Modeling in Management* and the *Journal of Simulation*. She is currently Vice President of the UK OR Society and co-chair of its 50th Annual Conference.

Kirandeep Chahal is a research student at the Centre for Applied Simulation Modeling (CASM) in the School of Information Systems, Computing and Mathematics, Brunel University, Uxbridge, United Kingdom. Her research interests are in modeling information systems, decision making in Organizations and modeling Biological systems. Her email address is kirandeep.chahal@brunel.ac.uk.

Yngve Dahl is a research scientist at Telenor Research and Innovation (R&I) in Trondheim, Norway. His research interests are pervasive and ubiquitous computing systems, computer supported cooperative work (CSCW), and human-computer interaction (HCI). The primary application area of this research is within clinical care and domestic environments. Dahl has previously been a research fellow at the Norwegian University of Science and Technology (NTNU), Department of Computer and Information Science. Here he investigated usability and interaction modelling issues related to ubiquitous computing designs for point-of-care usage in hospitals. Dahl received his PhD in computer science from NTNU in 2008.

Herbert Daly is a professional simulation modeller and researcher at the School of Information Systems Computing and Mathematics, Brunel University where he is a member of the Centre for Applied Simulation Modeling. His research interests are in multi method modeling, and software engineering. Contact him at School of Information Systems Computing and Mathematics, Brunel University, Uxbridge Middlesex, UB8 3PH, United Kingdom UB8 3PH; herbert.daly@brunel.ac.uk.

Tillal Eldabi is a senior lecturer at Brunel Business School, Brunel University, UK. He received a B.Sc. in Econometrics and Social Statistics from the University of Khartoum. He received his M.Sc. in Simulation Modeling and his Ph.D. from Brunel University. His research is in aspects of healthcare management and the intervention of simulation and his main research also concentrates on the economy of healthcare delivery. He is looking to exploit the means of simulation on the wider information systems management area to assist in problem understanding. Dr. Eldabi's email address is tillal.eldabi@brunel.ac.uk.

Sigurd Eskeland is currently working with the Norwegian Patent Office. He received his PhD in information security in 2008 from Aalborg University, Denmark. He received a master degree in information technology in 2000 and a bachelor degree in electronics engineering in 1997, both from University of Agder, Norway. He has published 15 papers in journals and peer-reviewed conferences and workshops in the fields of information security and group-oriented cryptographic protocols.

Arild Faxvaag is associate professor in rheumatology at Faculty of medicine, Norwegian University of Science and Technology (NTNU), Trondheim, Norway, and practicing Rheumatologist at St. Olavs Hospital (Trondheim University Hospital). Since 2000 Arild Faxvaag has been involved in numerous healthcare IT projects at NTNU and St. Olavs Hospital and he is now a senior researcher at The Norwegian Centre for electronic patient records research (NSEP). His research interests are development of high quality clinical databases for collection of data from patient cohorts with the purpose of clinical decision support, systems for quality development, evaluation of Electronic Health Record systems from the perspective of the health care worker and research on development and evaluation of clinical decision support systems. Arild Faxvaag has broad teaching experience as associate professor in Rheumatology at NTNU. He has been a lecturer at numerous courses in medicine, rheumatology and medical informatics.

Günter Gans received his Diploma in Computer Science from RWTH Aachen University, Germany, in 2000. He then joined the Knowledge-Based Systems Group also at RWTH Aachen University to work on an interdisciplinary project together with social scientists. His research concerns an agent-based modeling and simulation methodology for strategic inter-organizational networks. Günter has published about 9 scientific papers and has reviewed papers for several international conferences and workshops. Currently, he is finishing his doctoral thesis.

Vincenzo Gullà has over 20 years of experience in the global telecommunications industry. Graduated in Electronic Engineering at the University of Rome, he worked in several technology areas such as Satellite communications, Mobile, Wireless, GPS, High Definition video, Broadband , telecommunication services and markets. In the 1980's he was appointed as delegate of the Italian PTT for the ITU organisation. During his carrier he worked with a wide variety of manufacturing and services providers including Alenia Spazio, Telespazio and Telecom Italia. Joined Aethra in 2001, taking responsibility of the Telecoms Marketing Department and latter Vertical Applications Market Director, focused on vertical markets videocommunication applications. In the last years he has been very active in the broadband and telemedicine market. He covered the roles of Chairman of the European Market Focus Group, Chairman of the DSL-Forum Marketing Committee, member of the Scientific Committee of the e-magazine Telemeditalia, of EMIT and SIT (Italian Scientific Telemedicine Society) and executive manager of the International Telemedicine Club . In 2006 he founded ADiTech a new start up company based in Italy, focused on broadband solutions addressing telemedicine applications. In 2007 Dr.V.Gullà has been appointed as associated professor for teaching "Telemedicine devices" in the "Master in Oil and Gas telemedicine and telepharmacy "of the University of Camerino-Italy. He holds two patents (e.i US Patent 6169877 - High density TV motion picture distribution network) for High definition broadband applications and has developed a significant number of projects and scientific publications in telecommunication, broadband, video and telemedicine.

Raj Gururajan is an Associate Professor of Information Systems. Currently, also working as Associate Dean of Research, Faculty of Business. His research interests include technology adoption in health care, technology diffusion and mobile learning. He is currently supervising 7 PhD students and 2 Masters Students in the above areas. He has over 100 publications and attracted over $1,000,000 in research grants.

Alalwany Hamid has more than 17 years industrial experience gained in the areas of systems design and control, project management and quality assurance. During this period, he has held positions as information systems adviser, senior control systems engineer, team leader and project manager. Mr. Alalwany main research interest area is information systems evaluation, specifically within the context of healthcare and education. He is currently working on a research project that aims to develop and assess a holistic evaluation framework for e-services in public sector. He is also working on content modeling for e-learning and the evaluation of e-learning applications.

Michael I. Harrison is a Senior Research Scientist at AHRQ. He leads Agency activities in Health System Redesign; manages and contributes to research in delivery systems across the United States; and conducts research on organizational improvement and health information technology implementation. He holds a Ph.D. in Sociology from the University of Michigan. He was previously a faculty member at SUNY (Stony Brook) and at Bar Ilan University in Israel; a visiting professor at Boston College and Haifa University; and a visiting scholar at Brandeis, Georgetown, Harvard, and the Nordic School of Public Health. His recent publications include papers in leading health services research journals, *Diagnosing Organizations: Methods, Models, and Processes* (Sage, 2005), and *Implementing Change in Health Systems: Market Reforms in the United Kingdom, Sweden, and the Netherlands* (Sage, 2004).

Sharique Hasan is Doctoral Candidate in Management Science and Organizations in the H. John Heinz III School of Public Policy and Management at Carnegie Mellon University. His research interests include social network analysis, careers, diversity, statistical and machine learning methods for network analysis and decision making (e.g. medical), and decision support systems. His current areas of consulting and research are in supply chain optimisation with a focus on collaborative and adaptive strategies for improving efficiency in supply chains with multiple, and often competing, players.

Yu-An Huang is an Assistant Professor in the Department of International Business Studies, National Chi Nan University. He received a Ph.D. in technology management from National Cheng Chi University. He was a visiting scholar at Curtin University of Technology in Perth, Australia. He has published papers in *European Journal of Information Systems*, *International Journal of Electronic Business*, *Journal of Marketing Channels*, *Technovation*, and numerous other journals.

Michael P. Johnson is Associate Professor in the John W. McCormack Graduate School of Policy Studies Department of Public Policy and Public Affairs at the University of Massachusetts Boston. Professor Johnson's primary application areas are public sector facility location and service delivery, particularly subsidized and affordable housing and elderly services design.

Ulrika Josefsson work as a researcher at the IT-university of Göteborg in Sweden. She has previously worked in the public sector administration and in the healthcare. In 2007 she defended her doctoral thesis in informatics titled "*Coping Online - Patients' use of the Internet*". Her research interests concern IT/ Internet use in the relationship between patients and healthcare providers. In particular her research focuses the patient perspective and how IT can support the development of patient centred care. At the IT-university she is affiliated to the Medical Informatics research group. She is currently working in two research projects focusing on the patient's subjective view of health and illness (patient narrative) as a part of the development of patient centred care and how technology can support this.

Korina Katsaliaki is a Lecturer in the Business School at the University of Middlesex. She completed her PhD at the University of Southampton. Her research has been largely in the area of health care modelling (examples include resource allocation, business process reengineering, system improvement, hospital capacities and workforce planning). She has worked with a number of organisations such as the National Blood Service, County Council Social Services, Care homes, NHS Trusts, Primary Care Trusts and private and public hospitals. Her expertise is on supply chains of perishable products, with emphasis on inventory and transportation management, resource utilisation and cost benefit analysis. She has also thoroughly worked at care pathway analysis. The main modelling tools she uses are discrete-event simulation and statistical analysis. In addition to these, she uses programming and distributed simulation to facilitate modelling.

Stefanie Kethers received her Dr. (ph.D.) from RWTH Aachen University, Germany, in 2000 with a thesis on modelling and analysing cooperative processes. She then joined CSIRO in Melbourne, Australia, to continue her work on cooperative processes. In 2006, she worked for Monash University in Melbourne, Australia, as a senior research fellow. After taking time off to look after her baby son, Stefanie rejoined Monash University as a casual research assistant in 2008. Stefanie has published more than 20 scientific papers and has reviewed papers for several international conferences and workshops. Her research interests include supporting group work, modelling cooperative processes, and investigating trust relationships in diverse settings.

Ross, Koppel Ph.D., is on the faculty of the University of Pennsylvania's Sociology Department and a principal investigator at the Center for Clinical Epidemiology and Biostatistics (School of Medicine) where he directs Penn's study on hospital workplace culture and medication errors. Professor Koppel has written about workplace stress, medical sociology, the impact of technology on jobs and skills, evaluation methods, policy analysis, educational policy, disease costs, management-union cooperation, and ethics in social research. Much of Koppel's work focuses on the use of healthcare information technology (HIT). His articles in *JAMA* on the *Role of Computerized Physician Order Entry Systems in Facilitating Medication Errors* and in *JAMIA* on *Barcoded Medication Administration* are part of his studies on hospital as workplaces. In the past 3 years, Ross Koppel has authored almost two dozen articles and chapters on failures of HIT—focusing on ways of understanding and correcting its difficulties.

Hans Kyhlbäck is engaged in teaching and research at Blekinge Institute of Technology (BTH), Sweden. His main interest is interdisciplinary in the fields of computer and work science. Since the 70's he has a background working as an industrial electrician, but in the late 80's he changed direction towards the academia. Human computer interaction and design of user interfaces is at the core of his competence. Field studies with an ethnographic approach adds to his experience and knowlegde of work "at the shop floor". He has a research focus in projects within both health care and metal manufacturing. Developmental work research and the cultural-historical activity theory (CHAT) provides his perspective on the everyday practice of nurses and blue collar workers.

Chad Lin is a Research Fellow at Curtin University of Technology, Australia. Dr Lin has conducted extensive research in the areas of: e-commerce, e-health, health communication, health informatics, IS/IT investment evaluation and benefits realization, IS/IT outsourcing, IT adoption and diffusion, RFID, social marketing, strategic alliance in healthcare, and virtual teams. He has authored more than 30 internationally refereed journal papers (e.g. *Decision Support Systems*, *European Journal of Information Systems*, *Information and Management*, *International Journal of Electronic Commerce*, *Information Technology and People*, *Techonovation*, and *Medical Journal of Australia*) in the last five years. He has also served as a member of editorial review board for several prestigious international journals.

Line Melby holds a PhD in sociology from the Norwegian University of Science and Technology (NTNU) in Trondheim, Norway. Her PhD work was an ethnographic study of physicians' information and communication practices in mobile settings in a hospital. She currently works as a researcher at the Norwegian Research Centre for Electronic Patient Records (NSEP), NTNU, and is particularly studying the implementation of electronic interaction across organisational borders in health care and organisational effects of such systems. Melby has been working within the area of health informatics since 2000, and her research interests include health informatics, medical sociology, and science and technology studies (STS).

Syed Misbahuddin received the BE degree in Electronics from Dawood College of Engineering & Technology, Karachi Pakistan in 1983, MS in Electrical Engineering and Computer Engineering from King Fahd University of Petroleum and Minerals, Dhahran, Saudi Arabia in 1988 and doctor of Engineering in Electrical and Computer Engineering from the University of Detroit Mercy, Detroit, MI, USA in 1998. From 1988-1992, he was an Assistant Professor in Computer Systems department, NED University of Engineering and Technology, Karachi, Pakistan, where he was engaged in variety of computer engineering research. From 2000 to 2005, he was serving as Faculty member in Computer Systems Department in King Fahd University of Petroleum and Minerals, Hail, Saudi Arabia. Presently, Dr Syed Misbahuddin is working as Assistant Professor in department of Computer Science and Software engineering, University of Hail., Saudi Arabia. His research interests are in embedded systems, parallel and distributed computing and data reduction algorithms.

Navonil Mustafee completed PhD in Information Systems and Computing from Brunel University in June 2007. He hold a Masters degree "with Distinction" in Distributed Systems from Brunel, a BA degree from Calcutta University and a Post Graduate Certificate in Applied Computer Science from CMC Ltd - Education & Training. I come from Calcutta (now "Kolkata"), the capital of the state of West Bengal, in India. Presently working as a Research Fellow in the EU-funded FP7 project on e-Infrastructure called BELIEF. He is based in the School of Information Systems, Computing and Mathematics in Brunel University. Prior to this, He worked as a Reserch Fellow in Healthcare Modelling and Simulation at Warwick Business School, University of Warwick. His research interests include Grid Computing, Parallel and Distributed Simulation and Healthcare Simulation. I am also doing research in Commercial-Off-The-Shelves (COTS) simulation package interoperability using middleware for distributed simulation.

Aisha Naseer is a Research Fellow working on an EPSRC-funded project RIGHT (Research into Global Healthcare Tools) at the School of Information Systems, Computing and Mathematics, Brunel University, UK. She received her Ph.D. (2007) in Computer Science from Brunel University, UK, specialising in Grid-Based Semantic Integration of Heterogeneous Data Resources on HealthGrids. She has taught various Computer Science and Information Systems courses at both the undergraduate and postgraduate level. She has published several papers in journals and international conferences and also has chapters published in several books. She has chaired various conference sessions and reviewed many papers and book chapters. Her research interests include HealthGrids, semantic interoperability, intelligent data management, HealthGrid applications, health informatics, Grid computing, artificial intelligence and simulation & modelling of healthcare systems.

Øystein Nytrø has a PhD in computer science from the Norwegian University of Science and Technology (NTNU) in Trondheim, Norway, and is currently associate professor and leader of the program for healthcare informatics at NTNU. His research interests include information systems for coordinated care, context- and guideline-aware intelligent interfaces to the computerized patient record system, mining and analysis of patient histories, and information architectures for distributed, healthservicewide records.

Vladimir Oleshchuk is Professor of Computer Science in Department of Information and Telecommunication Technology, University of Agder, Norway. He received his MSc in Applied Mathematics (1981) and PhD in Computer Science (1988), and MSc in Innovations and Entrepreneurship (2007). He was visiting research fellow at University of Oslo, University of Pittsburgh, USA and University of Aizu, Japan. His current research interests include formal methods and information security. He has published more than 80 papers in journals and peer-reviewed conferences and workshops in the fields of information security and privacy, theoretical computer science and information retrieval. He holds 4 patents. He is a member of advisory boards and associate editor for several international journals. He is a senior member of ACM, member of IEEE Computer and Communication Society and Elected Member of Agder Academy of Sciences and Letters.

Sevgi Ozkan is a lecturer at Brunel University Business School, UK. She is a member of Information Systems Evaluation and Integration Research Group (ISEing) and has a PhD in the area of Information Systems Evaluation, with a particular focus on assessing success and effectiveness of information systems. She received her BA and her MA in Engineering – Electrical and Information Sciences from the University of Cambridge; her MSc in Business Information Systems from the University of London, and her PhD from Middle East Technical University. She has published her work in well acclaimed journals as well as in international conferences. She is on the Executive Board of the European and Mediterranean Conference on Information Systems (EMCIS). She has worked for IBM UK and Motorola UK prior to her doctorate studies and she was an IT Governance consultant for Hewlett-Packard Turkey. Her research interests are information and communication technology management in the public sector, information technology governance, evaluation of e-Government systems. Dr. Ozkan is a fellow of the UK Higher Education Academy.

Rema Padman is Professor of Management Science and Healthcare Informatics in the H. John Heinz III College of Public Policy and Management at Carnegie Mellon University. Professor Padman' research interests include healthcare information systems, operational planning and management, and data mining and decision support methods.

Ray J. Paul is a Professor of Simulation Modeling, Director of the Centre for Applied Simulation Modeling, creator of the Centre for Living Information Systems Thinking, all at Brunel University, UK. He is the editor of the Springer-Verlag *Practitioner* book series. His research interests are in methods of automating the process of modeling, and the general applicability of such methods and their extensions to the wider arena of information systems. He is editor of the *European Journal of Information Systems* and Guiding Editor of the *Journal of Simulation*. Contact him at the School of Information Systems Computing and Mathematics, Brunel University, Uxbridge Middlesex, UB8 3PH; ray.paul@brunel.ac.uk

Alshawi Sarmad has more than 15 years of academic experience and currently lectures Aviation Management and Business Intelligence at the Business School, Brunel University, UK. Dr Alshawi is an active member of research groups at Brunel, with research in Business Intelligence, Data Management, Data Warehousing, CRM and E-government. Dr Alshawi has written in internationally refereed journals, spoken at conferences word-wide, and has guest-edited special issue journals. He has participated in many research projects, and currently is a co-investigator on the EPSRC funded MATCH healthcare project

Dominik Schmitz received his Diploma in Computer Science from RWTH Aachen University, Germany, in 2003. He then joined the Graduate School 643 "Software for Mobile Communication Systems" also at RWTH Aachen University and worked on agent technology, requirements engineering, and simulations in inter-organizational networks. Since 2006 he is with the Fraunhofer Institute for Applied Information Technology to work on an interdisciplinary project that aims at integrating the model-based approaches within software and automatic control engineering. Dominik has published about 10 scientific papers.

Joseph Schulman is Associate Professor of Pediatrics/Newborn Medicine, and Public Health/Outcomes and Effectiveness, at Weill Cornell Medical College; and an attending physician at the New York Presbyterian Hospital in New York City. He received his MD from the University of Pennsylvania, and MS degree in the evaluative clinical sciences from Dartmouth College. He also was a National Library of Medicine Medical Informatics Fellow at the Marine Biological Laboratory, Woods Hole, Massachusetts. He has a leadership role in promoting data collection and reporting for benchmarking and quality improvement among all regional perinatal centers in New York State. His publications include articles and textbooks about analyzing and interpreting clinical performance data and about using database technology and statistical software to advance front line clinical care. His IT evaluative perspective benefits from experience as a software developer: he created a database application that has been in use for many years, for managing patient information in neonatal intensive care units.

Gry Seland is currently a researcher in the POCMAP (Point-of-Care Multi-Aware Clinical Pilot) project at the Norwegian University of Science and Technology (NTNU). At the same time she is pursuing a PhD degree at NTNU concerning role play as a method to develop requirements for mobile IT systems. Seland has a master's degree in psychology from NTNU in 2001. Her main research interest is exploration and evaluation of methods for user-centred development of IT systems in health care organizations. She is particularly interested in how to engage users and help users contribute in exploring needs and requirements in early system development phases.

Mark C. Shaw is a Visiting Academic in Health Informatics in the Centre for Computing and Social Responsibility at De Montfort University, Leicester, UK. He is a medical doctor who is a member of the England's Faculty of Public Health. He obtained a second degree in Mathematics and Computing and his interests are in developing an object model for the long term representation of health data and in creating expert systems to support users during their use of health care software.

David Sier is a principal scientist at CSIRO Mathematical and Information Sciences. He has 16 years experience in industrial optimisation and simulation and has carried out consulting work for a wide range of companies and government organisations.

Murat Sincan is a medical doctor and a PhD student at Informatics Institute, Middle East Technical University, Ankara, Turkey. His research interests are health informatics, health information systems, information technology in the healthcare.

Inger Dybdahl Sørby holds a PhD in computer science from the Norwegian University of Science and Technology (NTNU) in Trondheim, Norway. She currently works as a researcher in the POCMAP (Point-of-Care Multi-Aware Clinical Pilot) project at Department of Computer and Information Science at NTNU. Her research interests include health informatics, requirements engineering, and human-computer interaction. In particular, she focuses on empirical based requirements engineering for point of care clinical systems. Sørby has been working in the field of health informatics since 2001 and is also affiliated with the Norwegian Research Centre for Electronic Patient Records (NSEP) in Trondheim.

Bernd Carsten Stahl is a Reader in Critical Research in Technology in the Centre for Computing and Social Responsibility at De Montfort University, Leicester, UK. His interests cover philosophical issues arising from the intersections of business, technology, and information. This includes the ethics of computing and critical approaches to information systems. He is the Editor-in-Chief of the *International Journal of Technology and Human Interaction*. More information can be found under: http://www.cse.dmu.ac.uk/~bstahl/

Christine Stephenson has worked for the Queensland State Government as an Enterprise Architect specialising in Business Architecture and ICT Strategic Planning. She currently works for a Leading Airline Company as the Manager of Enterprise Architecture. In amongst her skills sets, she is a leading expert in Business Analysis, Business Process Modelling and Business Process Management. She is passionate about perpetuating a structured approach to managing process information in organisations through the use of well defined and simple methodologies. Christine is currently undertaking a Professional Doctorate in IT Management specialling in Enterprise Architecture, Business and ICT Strategy and Business Process Management.

Lampros K. Stergioulas is a Reader and Director of Undergraduate Studies in the Department of Information Systems and Computing at Brunel University, UK. He is a qualified Chartered Engineer. He has published over 150 papers in journals and international conferences. He has supervised and examined numerous PhD dissertations in the areas of information systems, information processing, and computer science in general. He has held many National and European Grants in educational computing, human-centred communications and computing, information processing, modelling and simulation, and intelligent systems. He has chaired several International Conferences and has been the coordinator of interdisciplinary, international projects. His research interests include human-centred information systems, educational computing, intelligent data processing, information management, modelling and simulation of business processes, and healthcare information systems.

Berthel Sutter is a senior lecturer at Blekinge Institute of Technology (BTH), and has been working with the perspective of the cultural-historical activity theory (CHAT) since the 70's. Before he moved to BTH he lectured at the educational program for psychologists at the Department of Psychology at Umeå University. At BTH he did research within the field of human work science, and lectured at the educational program People-Computers-Work. His main focus of research is learning and its relation to development. In particular he is interested in development of activities of diverse kinds. It encompasses the role of artefacts in learning, the relation between instruction and learning, co-coaching as mutual instruction among participants in collaborative work, "productive learning" or learning the societal new in addition to learning what is culturally given. It also includes the special form of action research that has been developed within activity theory, "developmental work research", and its basic idea of learning by expanding.

Simon J.E. Taylor is the Founder and Chair of the COTS Simulation Package Interoperability Product Development Group (CSPI-PDG). He has served as the Chair of ACM's Special Interest Group on Simulation (SIGSIM) 2005 to 2008. He is a Reader in the School of Information Systems, Computing and Mathematics at Brunel.

Imran Tasadduq obtained PhD from the Department of Electrical and Computer Engineering, University of Western Ontario, Canada, MS in Systems Engineering from King Fahd University, Saudi Arabia and B.E. in Electrical Engineering from N.E.D. University, Pakistan. He has worked with University of Ottawa, Research Institute of King Fahd University, Sir Syed University and Siemens. At present, he is Professor and Head of Electrical Engineering Department at FAST–National University of Computer & Emerging Sciences, Pakistan. He has produced thirty research publications in international journals and conferences, and has served on the technical committees of various international conferences. His research interests include performance of OFDM, cognitive radio, multicarrier CDMA, digital signal processing and applications of artificial neural networks and network applications in medicine.

Pieter Toussaint holds a PhD in informatics from the University of Leiden in the Netherlands. He has a background in informatics and linguistics. Since 1993 he has been involved in national and international medical informatics projects. These projects included research into the development of electronic patient records and public websites. His main research areas of interest are requirements engineering and evaluation of information systems. He has published in several peer reviewed journals within health informatics and has initiated and led a number of research projects in this field. In the summer of 2007 he moved to Trondheim, where he is employed as an associate professor in Health Informatics at Department of Computer and Information Science at the Norwegian University of Science and Technology (NTNU).

Jean-Paul Van Belle is an associate professor in Information Systems at the University of Cape Town. Before joining UCT, he set up the Information Systems department at the University of the Western Cape. He obtained his MBA in the field of financial modelling and his doctorate in the field of enterprise modelling. Currently he is researching the adoption of technologies (including mobile technologies) in South Africa, ICTs for development and the e-readiness of SMEs and NGOs. He supervises a number of doctoral and masters students in this area. He is a family man with 3 children and a keen outdoors person.

Shafiz Affendi Mohd Yusof working as a Senior Lecturer at the Graduate Department of Information Systems, College of Arts and Sciences at Universiti Utara Malaysia, Shafiz received his graduate degrees from School of Information Studies at Syracuse University. His Ph.D. degree is awarded in Information Science & Technology, while his Master's degree is in Telecommunications and Network Management. Shafiz's research passion lies in understanding the emergence of virtual communities, particularly on building social relationships in online gaming, cultural impact on designing human computer interface for web, and use of online gaming in education and business sectors. Shafiz is currently working on a research grant which explores the effect of social capital on virtual communities. He has also been participating in many international conferences, and has published several book chapters, encyclopedia, and journals published by IGI Global in his area of expertise.

Nasriah Zakaria is a lecturer at the School of Computer Sciences, University Sains Malaysia (USM). She received her Ph.D degree in Information Science and Technology in 2006 from Syracuse University, New York. She gained her Masters and Bachelors degree in Biomedical Engineering from Rensselaer Polytechnic Institute, Troy, New York. She also has experience working at Motorola Technology, Penang as a R&D software engineer for eighteen months. Her main research interest is in sociotechnical aspect of ICT specifically in ICT health communication. Up till now she has (co)written several journal articles, conference papers and posters. She also became the reviewers for the following conferences: MEDINFO 2007, i-Conference 2008 and ROVISP 2007(International Conferences on Robotics, Visions and Signal Processing) and book chapters' reviewer (Handbook of Research on Advances in Health Informatics and Electronic Healthcare Applications: Global Adoption and Impact of Information Communication Technologies and Qualitative Research: Theory, Method, and Practice).

Norhayati Zakaria is a Senior Lecturer at College of Business, Universiti Utara Malaysia. She received her Ph.D. in Information Science & Technology at Syracuse University, USA, and MSc. in Management of Technology at Rensselaer Polytechnic Institute, USA. Her expertise combines two interdisciplinary fields which are cross-cultural management and computer-mediated communication (CMC) technology, looking at impacts of cultural values and intercultural communication on the effectiveness on online cross-cultural training for global virtual teams, and building culturally sensitive cyberinfrastructure collaboratories. She has written over 40 conference papers, actively participating in numerous international conferences, and published in journals and book chapters. At current, she is also an affiliated researcher (2005-present) in the Collaboratory on Technology Enhanced Learning Communities (Cotelco), a social research laboratory located in School of Information Studies, Syracuse University, USA.

Kai Zheng is Assistant Professor of Health Management and Policy in the School of Public Health and Assistant Professor of Information in the School of Information at the University of Michigan. Professor Zheng's research and teaching are in the area of information systems, particularly focusing on health informatics, which studies the use of information, communication, and decision technologies in healthcare delivery and management.

Junaid Ahmed Zubairi received his BE (Electrical Engineering) from NED University of Engineering, Pakistan and MS and Ph.D. (Computer Engineering) from Syracuse University, USA. He worked in Sir Syed University Pakistan and Intl' Islamic University Malaysia before joining State University of New York at Fredonia where currently he is an Associate Professor in the Department of Computer Science. Dr. Zubairi is a recipient of many awards including Malaysian Government IRPA award, National Science Foundation MACS grant and SUNY Scholarly Incentive award. He has authored several chapters and scholarly articles in books, international journals and conference proceedings. His research interests include network traffic engineering, performance evaluation of networks and network applications in medicine. He can be reached at zubairi@fredonia.edu.

Index

A

B

C

D

E

F

G

H

Q

R

S

T

U

V

W

Z